December 5–8, 2017
Austin, Texas, USA

**Association for
Computing Machinery**

Advancing Computing as a Science & Profession

UCC'17

Proceedings of the10th International Conference on
Utility and Cloud Computing

Sponsored by:

ACM SIGARCH & IEEE TCSC

**Association for
Computing Machinery**

Advancing Computing as a Science & Profession

ISBN: 978-1-4503-5149-2 (Digital)

ISBN: 978-1-4503-5689-3 (Print)

IEEE/ACM UCC/BDCAT 2017
Message from the General Chairs

We would like to welcome everyone to the 10th International Conference on Utility and Cloud Computing (UCC 2017) and 4th International Conference on Big Data Computing, Applications and Technologies (BDCAT 2017), sponsored by the IEEE Computer Society and the Association for Computing Machinery (ACM). The sustained interest in UCC and BDCAT reflects the significant focus on advanced methods to apply distributed utility and cloud computing to solve important large-scale problems in data analytics in academia, industry and government. These paradigms continue to influence research and development in computer science and their results have significant impacts and implications for society.

It is a pleasure to host the combined UCC/BDCAT event 2017 in Austin – a multi-cultural city boasting some of the leading international universities, financial and scientific institutions and a diverse and rich history. It is also useful to see the good quality of submissions received this year in the main tracks as well as in the workshops. Previous events were held in Shanghai, China (Cloud 2009), Melbourne, Australia (Cloud 2010 and UCC 2011), Chennai, India (UCC 2010), Chicago, USA (UCC 2012), Dresden, Germany (UCC 2013), London, UK (UCC 2014 and BDCAT 2014), Cyprus (UCC 2015 and BDCAT 2015), Shanghai China (UCC 2016 and BDCAT 2016) and this year in Austin, Texas (UCC 2017 and BDCAT 2017). The next conference is expected to be held in Zurich, Switzerland (UCC 2018 and BDCAT 2018). This continuous record of high-quality results truly demonstrates the vibrancy of this community and the potential for it to grow in subsequent years.

The continued increase in the size, availability, and capabilities of data centres around the world and their use in processing large datasets continue to change the way that computation and data are being provisioned and processed. Dramatic changes have taken place both for individuals (through crowd sourcing and personalised analytics) and for organisations and businesses (through efficient data centre provision, system and application intelligence and high-performance analytics). New methods for efficient management of such data centres have enabled reduction in prices, improved energy efficiency, and more recently, significant improvements in tools for data analysis. Many of these methods and improvements are explored in this conference, including ways in which user demand and market forces will continue to influence how such data centres operate in the future, and the types of services that will be made available through them.

The main UCC and BDCAT conference tracks together provide a dedicated forum for enabling participants from academia and industry to come together to discuss recent advances and potential future directions in these two areas. Participating researchers, developers, service providers, users and solutions architects/engineers can use these to obtain insight into new research and industry products, and also to carry out discussion and collaboration to share their cutting-edge work. A panel session focusing on research directions and potential for "Next-Generation Infrastructures for Large-Scale Data Analytics" is also contained within the event, and includes forefront participants from both academia and industry.

The event feature keynotes in areas that range from data centre and infrastructure management to novel data analytics methods for big data being delivered by leading industry and academic experts. These cover novel cloud applications and systems (Towards an Experimental Instrument for Computer Science Research by Kate Keahey and Cloud Trek - The Next

Generation by Richard Sinnott), topics on Big Data (NIST Big Data Reference Architecture for Analytics and Beyond by Wo Chang and Components and Rationale of a Big Data Toolkit Spanning HPC, Grid, Edge and Cloud Computing by Geoffrey Fox), and high performance computing scenarios supporting cloud and big data paradigms (Modern Large Scale HPC Infrastructures by Dan Stanzione and Jetstream - Early Operations Performance, Adoption, and Impacts by David Hancock).

Practical deployment of cloud systems remains an important area – demonstrating how research carried out translates into practice. This year we have several major components of the conference focusing on this aspect, including the first "International Workshop on Data-center Automation, Analytics, and Control" (DAAC 2017) and number of good tutorials (in collaboration with research partners), both part of the UCC/BDCAT 2017 programme. We also have a number of other high-quality workshops and tutorials on topics ranging from cloud applications to forefront Big Data analysis methods. Ensuring that this event continues to represent the views of and to train the next generation of researchers in Cloud and Utility computing and Big Data, we also have the Doctoral Symposium at UCC 2017 – bringing together students actively engaged in research in this area. All of these activities have undergone a review process to ensure the best of all submissions received have been selected for inclusion in the programme.

The conference programme offers a high-quality selection of talks as regular and short papers, as well as a poster session coordinated by Dong Dai (Texas Tech University) and Mai Zheng (New Mexico State University, USA). We also have a number of tutorials delivered by presenters from both industry and academia. The credit for soliciting and selecting very high quality tutorials goes to Omer Rana (Cardiff University, UK). Our programme chairs, Geoffrey Fox (Indiana University), Xinghui Zhao (Washington State University) and Yong Chen (Texas Tech University) have selected around 20% of the submissions received in both conferences. We have an additional 5 workshops and 7 tutorials co-located with UCC/BDCAT 2017 (each workshop and the tutorial also carried out a rigorous peer review process to ensure that the best submissions made it into the conference programme).

We would like to thank the UCC steering committee for continuing to engage and provide support for the conference, the previous conference organisers for raising the quality bar on which we are now acting, the local organising team for their invaluable assistance in system setup and on-site help (especially staff at the Texas Tech University, such as Jerry Perez, Ravi Vadapalli, Zhangxi Lin and many others). We would also like to thank the publicity chairs for disseminating the call and ensuring that we continued to get engagement with the community. We would like to thank the industry chair, Ravi Vadapalli, for supporting promotion of this event to industry. We are grateful to our supporters at IEEE and ACM, in particular Lisa Tolles for the production of the proceedings at ACM (whose professionalism and patience – two rare attributes not often mentioned together, have been essential to produce a high quality proceedings).

We hope that you will enjoy UCC/BDCAT 2017 by actively participating, learning, exchanging, interacting and debating the relevant topics with other researchers. It will be rewarding for us if you can fully utilise the conference and the co-located workshops to improve yourself and your understanding of this area. We have created a Facebook page for UCC/BDCAT 2017 (https://www.facebook.com/UCC-2017-and-BDCAT-2017-260161371174448/) and a twitter feed (@UCC_BDCAT) for distributing and sharing activities at the event. Please continue to engage through these channels with the event.

Most importantly, we would like to thank the local organising chair – Tim Cockerill – and members of this committee, who played an essential role in hosting this event. Their dedication, hard work, and significant contribution is evident through the variety of activities taking place at UCC/BDCAT 2017. This event would not be possible without their dedication and continuous active engagement throughout most of last year.

Alan Sill
UCC/BDCAT General Co-Chair
Texas Tech University
Lubbock, Texas, USA

Ashiq Anjum
UCC/BDCAT General Co-Chair
University of Derby
Derby, UK

Message from the UCC 2017 Technical Program Committee Co-Chairs

On behalf of the UCC 2017 program committee, it is our great pleasure to welcome you to the 10th IEEE/ACM International Conference on Utility and Cloud Computing (UCC 2017), held in Austin, TX, USA.

UCC is a premier IEEE/ACM conference covering all areas related to cloud and utility computing and provides an international forum for leading researchers and practitioners in this important and growing field. We are delighted to see UCC 2017 travels to Austin, Texas, and with the previous successful instances of this conference series, UCC 2017 brings academics and industrial researchers together to discuss leading innovations in cloud computing, utility computing, and other forms of advanced distributed computing, as well as numerous multidisciplinary research areas.

UCC 2017 received a total of 63 complete submissions. Each paper was reviewed by at least three reviewers, and many papers received four or five reviews. Overall we have 270 reviews, with 4.3 reviews per paper on average. The paper selection and decision were made with considering both reviews and online discussions. We accepted 17 out of the 63 total submissions into the main conference program, with an acceptance rate of 27%. In addition to these 17 submissions accepted as conference papers, we recommended 13 submissions as a workshop paper or a conference poster. Out of these 13 papers, the authors of 7 papers accepted our recommendation and will present their studies at a workshop of their choice, and one paper chose to present as a poster. We also recommended another 12 submissions directly as conference poster presentation, and several authors accepted this offer.

UCC 2017 truly represents an international forum for leading researchers and practitioners. The authors of submissions are from 31 countries, with United States (51 authors), Brazil (19 authors), United Kingdom (14 authors), and Canada (14 authors) rank among top four countries in terms of the number of authors. The program committee well represents an international community too, with a total of 72 members from 24 countries. We have an additional 37 external reviewers who contributed 48 reviews.

A successful conference will not be possible without excellent leadership and all program committee members and external reviewers' hard work. We would like to take this opportunity to express our sincere gratitude to conference general chairs, Dr. Alan Sill of Texas Tech University and Dr. Ashiq Anjum of University of Derby, UK, and all committee members and external reviewers.

We hope that you will find the UCC 2017 technical program interesting and that it can stimulate ideas and discussions among researchers and practitioners from academia and industry around the world. We also hope you enjoy the conference with all of its tracks and have a wonderful time at UCC 2017 conference and the city of Austin.

Geoffrey Fox, *Indiana University, USA*
Yong Chen, *Texas Tech University, USA*
UCC 2017 Technical Program Committee Co-Chairs

Table of Contents

Components and Rationale of a Big Data Toolkit Spanning HPC, Grid, Edge and Cloud Computing

Geoffrey Fox
Indiana University, Department of Intelligent Systems Engineering
Bloomington, Indiana, USA
gcf@iu.edu

ABSTRACT

We look again at Big Data Programming environments such as Hadoop, Spark, Flink, Heron, Pregel; HPC concepts such as MPI and Asynchronous Many-Task runtimes and Cloud/Grid/Edge ideas such as event-driven computing, serverless computing, workflow, and Services. These cross many research communities including distributed systems, databases, cyberphysical systems and parallel computing which sometimes have inconsistent worldviews. There are many common capabilities across these systems which are often implemented differently in each packaged environment. For example, communication can be bulk synchronous processing or data flow; scheduling can be dynamic or static; state and fault-tolerance can have different models; execution and data can be streaming or batch, distributed or local. We suggest that one can usefully build a toolkit (called Twister2 by us) that supports these different choices and allows fruitful customization for each application area. We illustrate the design of Twister2 by several point studies. We stress the many open questions in very traditional areas including scheduling, messaging and checkpointing.

CCS Concepts/ACM Classifiers

• **Computer systems organization~Cloud computing**
• *Computer systems organization~Grid computing* • *Computer systems organization~Sensor networks* • **Software and its engineering~Data flow architectures** • **Software and its engineering~Publish-subscribe / event-based architectures**
• Software and its engineering~Message oriented middleware

Author Keywords

Cloud Computing; MapReduce; MPI; HPC; Dataflow; Edge Computing; Global Machine Learning

BIOGRAPHY

Fox received a Ph.D. in Theoretical Physics from Cambridge University where he was Senior Wrangler. He is now a distinguished professor of Engineering, Computing, and Physics at Indiana University where he is director of the Digital Science Center, and both Department Chair and Interim Associate Dean for Intelligent Systems Engineering at the School of Informatics, Computing, and Engineering. He previously held positions at

Caltech, Syracuse University, and Florida State University after being a postdoc at the Institute for Advanced Study at Princeton, Lawrence Berkeley Laboratory, and Peterhouse College Cambridge. He has supervised the Ph.D. of 70 students and published around 1300 papers (over 450 with at least 10 citations) in physics and computing with an hindex of 76 and over 31000 citations. He is a Fellow of APS (Physics) and ACM (Computing) and works on the interdisciplinary interface between computing and applications.

REFERENCES

[1] Supun Kamburugamuve, Kannan Govindarajan, Pulasthi Wickramasinghe, Vibhatha Abeykoon, Geoffrey Fox, "Twister2: Design of a Big Data Toolkit" Technical Report, October 7 2017 http://dsc.soic.indiana.edu/publications/twister2_design_big_data_toolkit.pdf

[2] Geoffrey Fox, Judy Qiu, Shantenu Jha, Saliya Ekanayake, and Supun Kamburugamuve, "Big Data, Simulations and HPC Convergence" Workshop on Big Data Benchmarking, New Delhi India, December 14, 2015. Springer Lecture Notes in Computer Science LNCS 10044. http://dx.doi.org/10.1007/978-3-319-49748-8_1

[3] Geoffrey C. Fox, Vatche Ishakian, Vinod Muthusamy, Aleksander Slominski, "Status of Serverless Computing and Function-as-a-Service(FaaS) in Industry and Research", Workshop on Serverless Computing (WoSC) Atlanta, June 5 2017 https://arxiv.org/abs/1708.08028

[4] Supun Kamburugamuve, Pulasthi Wickramasinghe, Saliya Ekanayake, Geoffrey C Fox, "Anatomy of machine learning algorithm implementations in MPI, Spark, and Flink", The International Journal of High Performance Computing Applications, July 2, 2017 https://doi.org/10.1177/1094342017712976

[5] http://www.spidal.org/ Middleware and High-Performance Analytics Libraries for Scalable Data Science SPIDAL project

[6] High Performance Computing Enhanced Apache Big Data Stack http://hpc-abds.org/kaleidoscope/

NIST Big Data Reference Architecture for Analytics and Beyond

Wo Chang
National Institute of Standards and Technology
Gaithersburg, Maryland, USA
wchang@nist.gov

ABSTRACT

Big Data is the term used to describe the deluge of data in our networked, digitized, sensor-laden, information driven world. There is a broad agreement among commercial, academic, and government leaders about the remarkable potential of "Big Data" to spark innovation, fuel commerce, and drive progress. The availability of vast data resources carries the potential to answer questions previously out of reach. However, there is also broad agreement on the ability of Big Data to overwhelm traditional approaches.

Big Data architectures come in many shapes and forms ranging from academic research settings to product-oriented workflows. With massive-scale dynamic data being generate from social media, Internet of Things, Smart Cities, and others, it is critical to analyze these data in real-time and provide proactive decision. With the advancement of computer architecture in multi-cores and GPUs, and fast communication between CPUs and GPUs, parallel processing utilizes these platforms could optimize resources at a reduced time.

This presentation will provide the past, current, and future activities of the NIST Big Data Public Working Group (NBD-PWG) and how the NIST Reference Architecture may address the rate at which data volumes, speeds, and complexity are growing requires new forms of computing infrastructure to enable Big Data analytics interoperability such that analytics tools can be re-usable, deployable, and operational.

The focus of NBD-PWG is to form a community of interest from industry, academia, and government, with the goal of developing consensus definitions, taxonomies, secure reference architectures, and standards roadmap which would create vendor-neutral, technology and infrastructure agnostic framework. The aim is to enable Big Data stakeholders to pick-and-choose best analytics tools for their processing under the most suitable computing platforms and clusters while allowing value-additions from Big Data service providers and flow of data between the stakeholders in a cohesive and secure manner.

CCS Concepts/ACM Classifiers

General and reference ~ Computer systems organization ~ Distributed architectures

Author Keywords

Big Data Reference Architecture; Big Data Analytics; high-performance computing; Many CPUs/Cores/GPUs

BIOGRAPHY

Mr. Wo Chang is of Digital Data Advisor for the National Institute of Standards and Technology (NIST) Information Technology Laboratory (ITL). His responsibilities include working with data interoperability; promoting a vital and growing Big Data community at NIST and with external stakeholders in the commercial, academic, and government sectors. Mr. Chang currently the Convener of the ISO/IEC JTC 1/WG9 Working Group on Big Data, co-chairs the NIST Big Data Public Working Group, and chairs the IEEE Big Data Governance and Metadata Management.

In the past, Mr. Chang was manager of the Digital Media Group in ITL and his duties included oversees several key projects including digital data archival and preservation, management of electronic health records, motion image quality, and multimedia standards. Chang was the Deputy Chair for the US INCITS L3.1, chaired other key projects for MPEG, participated with HL7 and ISO/IEC TC215 for health informatics, IETF for the protocols development, and was one of the original members of the W3C's SMIL and developed one of the SMIL reference software. Mr. Chang's research interests include many CPUs/Cores/GPUs high performance analytics and computing, scalable real-time graph mining algorithms and visual analytics for massive audiovisual content, digital data mashup, cloud computing, content metadata description, multimedia synchronization, and Internet protocols.

REFERENCES

1. https://bigdatawg.nist.gov

Cloud Trek – The Next Generation

Prof. Richard O. Sinnott
University of Melbourne,
Melbourne, Australia
rsinnott@unimelb.edu.au

ABSTRACT

Educating the next generation of software engineers is essential with the increased move to an Internet-based society. The need to support big data and data analytics are challenging many of the typical scenarios and paradigms associated with software engineering. In the digital age, data is often messy, distributed and growing exponentially. In this context there are swathes of technologies that are shaping the landscape for dealing with these phenomenon. Cluster and high performance computing has been a core approach for processing larger scale data sets, but Cloud computing has now gained increasing prominence and acceptance. In this context, training and educating the next generation of software engineers to be savvy Cloud application developers is essential. Prof Sinnott has taught Cluster (HPC) and Cloud Computing at the University of Melbourne for 5 years and exposed students to the latest technologies for big data analytics. Many of these efforts are shaped by the portfolio of major projects utilising numerous big data technologies within the Melbourne eResearch Group (www.eresearch.unimelb.edu.au). This presentation covers the pedagogy of the course and describes the way in which it utilizes national cloud and storage resources made available across Australia. Examples of the shaping eResearch projects and the solutions developed by the students are illustrated to demonstrate the practical experiences in developing Cloud-based solutions that focus especially on 'big data' challenges.

CCS Concepts/ACM Classifiers

Computer systems organization → Cloud computing; Applied computing → Education.

Author Keywords

Cloud computing; pedagogy; big data.

BIOGRAPHY

Professor Richard O. Sinnott is the Director of eResearch at the University of Melbourne and Professor of Applied Computing Systems. In these roles he is responsible for all aspects of eResearch (research-oriented IT development) at the University. He has been lead software engineer/architect on an extensive portfolio of national and international projects, with specific focus on those research domains requiring finer-grained access control (security). Prior to coming to Melbourne, Richard was the Technical Director of the UK National e-Science Centre; Director of e-Science at the University of Glasgow; Deputy Director (Technical) for the Bioinformatics Research Centre also at the University of Glasgow, and for a while the Technical Director of the National Centre for e-Social Science. He has a PhD in Computing Science, an MSc in Software Engineering and a BSc in Theoretical Physics (Hons). He has over 300 peer-reviewed publications across a range of computing and application-specific domains. He teaches High Performance Computing and Cloud Computing at the University of Melbourne.

UCC'17, December 5-8, 2017, Austin, Texas, USA.
© 2017 Copyright is held by the owner/author(s).
ACM ISBN 978-1-4503-5149-2/17/12.
DOI: https://doi.org/10.1145/3147213.3155014

Jetstream - Early Operations Performance, Adoption, and Impacts

David Hancock
Indiana University
Bloomington, IN
dyhancoc@iu.edu

ABSTRACT

Jetstream[1], built with OpenStack, is the first production cloud funded by the NSF for conducting general-purpose science and engineering research as well as an easy-to-use platform for education activities. Unlike many high-performance computing systems, Jetstream uses the interactive Atmosphere graphical user interface developed as part of the iPlant (now CyVerse) project and focuses on interactive use on uniprocessor or multiprocessor. This interface provides for a lower barrier of entry for use by educators, students, practicing scientists, and engineers. A key part of Jetstream's mission is to extend the reach of the NSF's eXtreme Digital (XD) program to a community of users who have not previously utilized NSF XD program resources, including those communities and institutions that traditionally lack significant cyberinfrastructure resources. OpenStack deployments all have the same five basic services: identity, images, block storage, networking, and compute. There are additional services offered; however, by and large, they are underutilized. The use of these services will be discussed as well as highlights from the first year of production operations, and future plans for the project.

CCS Concepts/ACM Classifiers

• Computer systems organization, distributed computing, cloud computing, applied computing

Author Keywords

cloud; openstack; digital; education; outreach; training; research; Jetstream; architecture; storage; identity; Globus; Atmosphere; cyberinfrastructure

BIOGRAPHY

David Hancock is the program director for advanced cyberinfrastructure within the Indiana University Pervasive Technology Institute's Research Technologies[2] division. Hancock is responsible for directing IU's local and national high-performance computing (HPC) systems and cloud resources for research. Hancock is a senior investigator and acting primary investigator for the Jetstream project funded by the National Science Foundation (NSF). He is also responsible for directing IU system administrators who participate in the NSF XSEDE project as well as being senior personnel on a number of other completed NSF projects.

Hancock is also an active participant in a number of national and international HPC organizations and is currently serving as the president of the Cray User Group and a representative in the XSEDE Service Provider (SP) Forum. Previously he served as the vice president for the IBM HPC User Group, vice president and program chair for the Cray User Group, and vice chair of the XSEDE SP Forum.

REFERENCES

1. Jetstream Project, http://jetstream-cloud.org

2. IU Pervasive Technology Institute http://www.pti.iu.edu

UCC'17, December 5-8, 2017, Austin, Texas, USA.
© 2017 Copyright is held by the owner/author(s).
ACM ISBN 978-1-4503-5149-2/17/12.
DOI: https://doi.org/10.1145/3147213.3155104

Scheduling Scientific Workloads in Private Cloud: Problems and Approaches

Dalibor Klusáček
CESNET a.l.e.
Brno, Czech Republic
klusacek@cesnet.cz

Boris Parák
CESNET a.l.e.
Brno, Czech Republic
parak@cesnet.cz

Gabriela Podolníková
Faculty of Informatics, Masaryk University
Brno, Czech Republic
xpodoln@fi.muni.cz

András Ürge
Faculty of Informatics, Masaryk University
Brno, Czech Republic
andris@mail.muni.cz

ABSTRACT

Public cloud providers are using the "pay-per-use" model when providing their resources to customers. Among other advantages, it allows the provider to react to changing demands, e.g., by modifying prices or by extending its physical capacities using the profit obtained. In this paper we deal with a completely different model. We describe a private scientific cloud where resources are provided to researchers for free. As we demonstrate, the "absence of money" means that the system must employ other mechanisms to guarantee reasonable performance and utilization. Especially, the problem of guaranteeing user-to-user fairness represents a major issue. Moreover, since there is no financial burden related to the use of cloud infrastructure, many resources can be wasted by long running idle virtual machines (VM) that their users no longer need. This leads to underutilization and resource fragmentation. This paper discusses these problems using real-life data from the CERIT Scientific Cloud and proposes several techniques to guarantee fair and efficient use of system resources. Furthermore, we present a prototype of a new experimental OpenNebula-compatible VM scheduler which was designed as a replacement for the default scheduler provided in OpenNebula distribution. Unlike the default scheduler, our new scheduler provides complex fair-sharing mechanisms as well as modular and easy-to-extend architecture to enable further development of advanced VM scheduling policies.

CCS CONCEPTS

• **Computing methodologies → Planning and scheduling;** • **Computer systems organization → Cloud computing; Grid computing;**

KEYWORDS

Private Cloud; Fairness; Fair-Sharing; Scheduling; OpenNebula

UCC'17, December 5–8, 2017, Austin, TX, USA.
© 2017 Association for Computing Machinery.
ACM ISBN 978-1-4503-5149-2/17/12. . . $15.00
https://doi.org/10.1145/3147213.3147223

1 INTRODUCTION

The increasing popularity of resource virtualization introduces new scheduling problems. For example, different types of applications/frameworks can now be hosted simultaneously in a shared physical infrastructure. This was not a usual scenario 15 years ago. Today, applications and services can be relatively easily encapsulated as, e.g., VMs or containers and run in an isolated fashion within a data-center [7]. Therefore, users now have many ways how to actually use the underlying infrastructure. Although this flexibility is surely beneficial, it also puts extra requirements on the overall resource management.

The aim of this paper is to discuss some of these challenges, especially focusing on the practical problems related to providing cloud resources to a scientific/research community. For this purpose, we use our experience and research conducted within the Czech national distributed infrastructure *MetaCentrum*. MetaCentrum provides computational and storage capacities for scientific purposes [12], such that every researcher affiliated with a university or a research institution in the Czech Republic can obtain a free access to MetaCentrum's resources. MetaCentrum offers a variety of computing environments, including classic grid-like clusters for batch jobs, virtualized clusters for cloud computations as well as a dedicated cluster for Hadoop-like computations.

The major difference to commonly analyzed and studied scenarios from the public "pay-per-use" cloud domain is that in this case the resources are provided in a "free of charge" fashion. Using real data from the CERIT Scientific Cloud (CERIT-SC) — which is the largest resource provider in MetaCentrum — we will demonstrate that the absence of monetary cost leads to several serious problems that must be carefully addressed by the resource manager/scheduler. For example, in our cloud environment the lifetime of a VM is not explicitly bounded. Since there is no money involved, users often forget to switch off their VMs, leaving a lot of unused VMs in the system which negatively impacts the utilization. At the same time, the relatively naive VM scheduler provided in OpenNebula causes that VMs are scheduled statically in a suboptimal fashion, further decreasing performance and increasing resource fragmentation. Also, unlike the grid partition, the cloud framework currently does not employ any fair-sharing policies, therefore the allocations of resources may not be fair with respect to different users of the system.

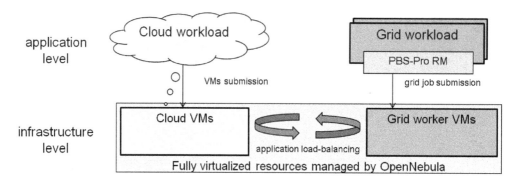

Figure 1: The scheme of the shared virtualized infrastructure in CERIT-SC.

This paper provides several contributions to the field. First of all, Section 2 provides an insight into the production infrastructure of CERIT-SC that hosts two different types of computations: a HPC-like batch job computations and an OpenNebula-driven cloud computing framework. In Section 3 we use the data from this production system and provide a detailed analysis of the utilization patterns of these two different computing paradigms (grid and cloud) that share the same set of hardware resources. Using this real-life workloads, we describe the major problems and challenges related to the model used in our system, i.e., the "free of charge" approach where users do not pay for their computations. We show that although this "compute for free" model is efficiently handled by the grid batch scheduling system, it introduces many fundamental problems in the cloud framework, including poor utilization, resource fragmentation and fairness-related issues. Therefore, in Section 4 we present a set of proposed and/or adopted scheduling and management policies that aim at reducing the adverse effects that were observed in the production deployment of the cloud framework. Furthermore, we present a newly developed experimental VM scheduler for OpenNebula that provides advanced fair-sharing mechanisms as well as modular and easy-to-extend architecture, enabling development of advanced VM scheduling policies. Finally, we conclude the paper and present the considered future work.

2 SYSTEM DESCRIPTION

The problems described in this paper are based on our observations from the *CERIT-SC* site, which is the largest partition of the Czech national distributed computing infrastructure MetaCentrum. MetaCentrum has some 13,374 CPU cores out of which 5,512 belong to the CERIT-SC partition. Within CERIT-SC, 3,912 CPU cores (71%) are fully virtualized using OpenNebula framework [13] and can be used by various applications (mostly by grid jobs and cloud VMs), while the remaining 1,600 CPU cores are not virtualized and are exclusively used for "bare metal" grid computations[1]. This paper only focuses on the fully virtualized partition.

---

[1]These "bare metal" nodes represent more "exotic" hardware architectures such as Intel's Xeon Phi or SGI's UV 2000 machines.

2.1 Shared Infrastructure

This virtualized partition is managed by OpenNebula [13] and allows for simultaneous execution of two major classes of application workloads. The first type is represented by classic *cloud virtual machines (VM)* that are submitted by the users of the system and serve for various purposes, e.g., they host a database or a web server, or they encapsulate some "exotic" software or operating system (OS) which cannot be executed on the "bare metal" nodes that all use the Debian 8 OS. Second, there is a special type of VM which we call a *"grid worker" VM*. Once deployed and started, this VM behaves as a "normal" node of the grid infrastructure, i.e., it can execute computational jobs from the CERIT-SC's batch resource manager (RM). The biggest advantage of this mechanism is that the actual amount of resources available either to the grid or to the cloud can be easily and dynamically adapted, simply by changing the number of running grid worker VMs. This allows for greater flexibility and better distribution of resources compared to the standard situation where resources are statically allocated either to the cloud or to the grid and cannot be easily reallocated. The exact amount of physical resources that are delegated to the grid-like computations using "grid worker" VMs is selected by the system administrator, i.e., there is no automatic load-balancing feature applied in the system. Originally, the grid-to-cloud resource ratio was approximately 7:1, however in the past 18 months the cloud component was steadily growing so the current resource ratio is roughly 2:1 (grid:cloud). The scheme of the current system configuration is shown in Fig. 1.

2.2 Resource Managers

CERIT-SC is using two independent resource managers within its shared infrastructure. First, it is the OpenNebula software stack [13] which is responsible for virtualization and VM life-cycle management. Using OpenNebula, both regular users' VMs are deployed as well as those special "grid worker" VMs that serve for running computational batch jobs from the grid batch system, which uses the PBS-Pro resource manager [16]. While every user of our system can run a regular VM, only the system administrator can manipulate with those "grid worker" VMs.

2.3 Operational Constraints and Policies

In our system, most operational constraints are related to the batch scheduling system, i.e., the PBS-Pro resource manager. This system is heavily optimized using a complex set of system policies and usage constraints. For example, jobs are automatically assigned into system queues, the amount of resources available to a given queue or user is carefully selected, and the backfilling [14] scheduling policy is used in order to efficiently use the available infrastructure. Importantly, job scheduling is subject to a fair-sharing mechanism that guarantees that resources are used in a fair fashion with respect to system users, i.e., the system automatically balances the amount of resources consumed by each active user. More details about the system configuration and applied constraints can be found in [9].

In contrast to the batch system, the cloud-operating OpenNebula framework represents a rather simple environment. We use the default VM scheduler in OpenNebula (mm_sched), which uses a simple VM-matching approach. No advanced methods like VM prioritization, fair-sharing or automatic VM migrations/re-scheduling are applied because they are not currently supported.

2.4 System Goals and Objectives

Before we proceed to the description of the actual system performance (Section 3), we have to describe the operational goals and optimization criteria used in the CERIT-SC infrastructure. Based on their knowledge we can later analyze how the existing as well as proposed solutions influence the performance of the system. Before we start, we would like to stress that all goals and optimization criteria are only enforced in a "best-effort" manner, i.e., no formal Service Level Agreements are established, although there are various Service Level Indicators/Objectives [4] that are optimized/targeted.

Concerning the whole physical infrastructure, there is only one global optimization criterion — to maximize the overall CPU utilization (number of allocated CPUs throughout the time). The grid and cloud partition then each use different sets of optimization objectives (and their indicators, i.e., metrics) which we describe now.

2.4.1 Grid Optimization Criteria. In the grid partition, the primary goal is to maximize *resource utilization*, i.e., to minimize the number of idle CPUs throughout the time. The second goal is to guarantee *user-to-user fairness*. For this purpose, waiting jobs are dynamically re-ordered in the queues following a (dynamic) priority, which is calculated using the fair-sharing algorithm of PBS-Pro's scheduler. Simply put, a user's priority is changing in time based on the amount of resources he or she has used so far. It follows the well-known *max-min* strategy, i.e., a user with lower resource usage gets higher priority over more active users and vice versa [2]. In other words, the goal of the fair-share algorithm is to minimize the *wait time* of the least active user. In order to achieve these two goals, the scheduler is using job queues ordered by fair-share in conjunction with the backfilling algorithm [14].

2.4.2 Cloud Optimization Criteria. The cloud partition (currently) uses only two simple objectives but further criteria are likely to be included/developed in the future. First, the goal is to minimize the *wait time* of (newly submitted) pending VMs, while maximizing the number of *concurrently running* VMs. In other words, the goal is to minimize the number of VMs that have to wait for their deployment due to insufficient capacity, plus reduce

such wait time if waiting is inevitable. This two criteria (number of waiting VMs and their wait time) are currently used by the system administrators when (de)allocating physical nodes for the cloud partition. The "algorithm" is to keep a decent part of the cloud nodes free (~5-10%) for newly arriving VMs. The utilization criterion is used as an auxiliary indicator when deciding whether to allocate or deallocate resources to/from the cloud from/to the grid. In this case a low utilization implies that some nodes should be returned to the grid and vice versa. No further indicators/objectives are currently (actively) measured and optimized/enforced. A notable difference with respect to the grid partition is the (current) absence of any fairness-related objective and/or technique to enforce fair use of resources. This situation is currently causing problems because the system is used "free of charge", not using the "pay-per-use" model (or some other equivalent of money/credit), so the resulting distribution of resources among users is neither fair nor justifiable. We will demonstrate these issues closely in Section 3.

2.4.3 Users Expectations. Beside the aforementioned criteria, there are also some "general expectations" concerning the behavior of the two systems. In the grid, the users favor but do not expect immediate access to the resources. They understand the nature of batch computations where jobs in the queues may have to wait until required resources are available. In that case, what the users are really expecting is fairness. The situation is different in the cloud. The service is provided/designed as "interactive", i.e., it is expected that a user's VM should start (almost) immediately (in a best effort manner, i.e., with no guarantees). Of course, this is not always possible, but the expectations are virtually the same as would be in, e.g., Amazon's or Google's public cloud. Again, we will demonstrate closely in the following Section 3 how these expectations complicate the management of our infrastructure.

3 SYSTEM PERFORMANCE ANALYSIS

Although the CERIT-SC system is production-grade and currently operates without any major problems, we can identify several unresolved (scheduling) problems that must be addressed in the (near) future. This section discusses these problems and their origins and provides several real-life examples of their impact on the system. We focus primarily on the cloud partition, because the grid is stable and well-tuned environment with proper policies in place to guarantee good performance.

3.1 "Free of charge" Computing and Resource-Reclaiming

As discussed in Section 2, the major benefit of resource virtualization in CERIT-SC is that the actual amount of resources available either to the grid or to the cloud can be easily and dynamically adapted, simply by changing the number of running "grid worker" VMs. In practice however, this mechanism does not work that easily due to the nature of our cloud workload. In fact, it works flawlessly when more resources are required for the cloud VMs. In that case, several "grid worker" nodes are first drained, i.e., all grid jobs running inside the worker are completed and new jobs are not allowed to start there. Then the given "grid worker" VM is terminated and its host becomes available for the classic cloud VMs. The problem is that the same mechanism does not work so easily in the opposite

11

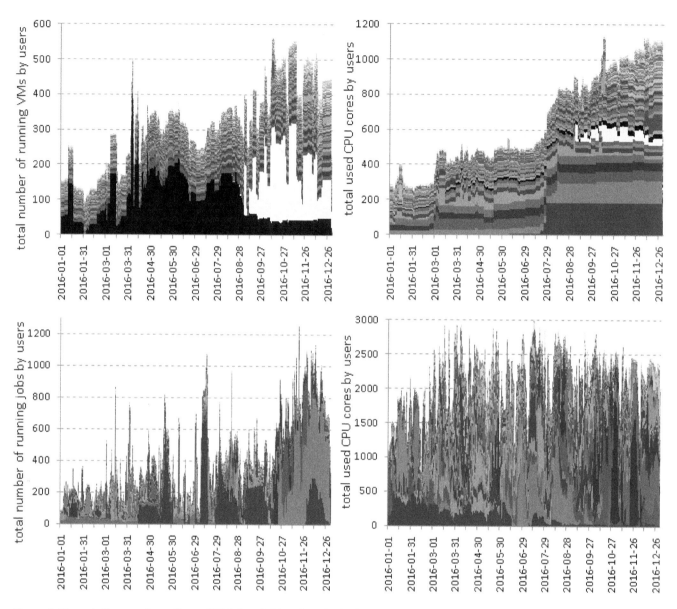

Figure 2: Cumulative number of users' VMs (top left) and grid jobs (bottom left) running in the system. Cumulative users' CPU usage over the time for cloud VMs (top right) and grid jobs (bottom right).

direction, i.e., it is not always easy to drain a host that is hosting running VMs. In CERIT-SC, the runtime of a cloud VM is unbounded and unknown, in general. Therefore it is impossible to drain a node by the same mechanism that works in the grid, where each job has a maximum allowed walltime limit.

Theoretically, VMs that execute on a node can be migrated, but this may not be always possible, e.g., when the infrastructure is already saturated by running VMs. Another problem is that CERIT-SC *provides its resources for free* to anyone who is affiliated with the scientific/academia community in the Czech Republic (university students/teachers, academic researchers, etc.). Thus, it does not use some form of the "pay-per-use" model which is otherwise very suitable to motivate users to stop their VMs once they are not

needed anymore. At the same time, CERIT-SC's budget is fixed, i.e., we cannot buy another cluster whenever the demand approaches the available capacity.

This is currently our major threat, since the cloud allocations in our system are increasing very quickly, yet we do not have any "automated" resource-reclaiming mechanism. For example, during the year 2016 the amount of allocated CPUs for the cloud partition has increased four times (~300 vs. ~1200). To illustrate the difficulties observed in the cloud partition, we provide Fig. 2, which shows two major characteristics of the 2016 workload. First, it is the cumulative number of users' VMs (top left) and grid jobs (bottom left) running in the system. Second, it is the cumulative CPU core allocation (per user) both for the cloud VMs (top right) and grid

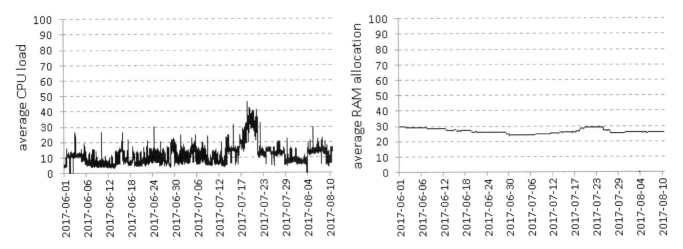

Figure 3: The average CPU load of running VMs (left) and the corresponding average RAM allocation percentage (right).

jobs (bottom right). Fig. 2 reveals that the number of running VMs per user is not the best indicator of user's impact on utilization. For example, there are two users (denoted in black and white) that together have ~50% of all VMs (see Fig. 2 top left). However, all those "black and white" VMs only consume a small fraction of the overall capacity, as shown in the top right chart in Fig. 2. The same chart also reveals, that the majority of CPU cores (~2/3) in the cloud partition is consumed by ~20 users with long running (continuous) and often growing workloads[2]. In the grid, the situation is rather opposite. Although there are few very active users that have dozens of simultaneously running jobs (Fig. 2 bottom left), most CPU cores are still consumed by many different users that execute rather time-constrained workloads (every grid job has a firm runtime limit). This strict limitation combined with typical day-to-day and weekly cycles makes the overall utilization curve of the grid workload much more "noisy".

To conclude, the observed situation in the cloud partition is problematic because users often consume more and more resources (as those are "free") and are not forced to return them back by some effective resource-reclaiming mechanism.

3.2 VM-to-Host Packing and Adaptive Re-scheduling

In the cloud environment, we would like to improve the quality of VM scheduling. Especially, we want to investigate whether VMs can be efficiently "packed" on the physical nodes, such that their combined resource requests (e.g., CPU, RAM, disk space, disk I/O and network I/O) are reasonably balanced *throughout the time*. Here we are facing the limits of the current VM scheduler used in the OpenNebula framework which does not provide any intelligent VM (re)scheduling heuristic that would adapt VMs allocations over the time. By default, it only schedules VMs upon their deployment based on their predefined resource requests. No further optimization — based on an actual performance of a running VM — is done during a VM's lifetime.

Clearly, this leaves an open space for improvements as currently some nodes may be occupied by idle VMs (resource wasting) while other nodes may be overloaded with VMs competing for resources such as CPUs, I/O, etc. To illustrate this situation, we provide Fig. 3 that shows the actual CPU load of running VMs (left) and the corresponding percentage of RAM being allocated to those VMs (right). Clearly, there seem to be many opportunities how to improve the utilization of the system, because the figure reveals that many nodes are actually underutilized (although they are fully allocated to running VMs by means of their initial resource requests). A suitable solution to improve this situation is to use the VM scheduler to dynamically reschedule idle VMs. Such VMs then may be migrated to already overbooked nodes, thus freeing their original hosts for more demanding or new (pending) VMs. Similarly, when a node becomes overloaded by its VMs, some of them should be rescheduled/migrated to decrease host's contention.

In order to actually enable such functionality one must however not only develop a new advanced scheduler but also invest in the underlying infrastructure to allow such live VM migrations. Further details on these issues are discussed in Section 4.

3.3 Fair-Sharing in Cloud

The absence of the "pay-per-use" model and the rather poor resource-reclaiming in our cloud bring another problem — the resources are allocated to the users without considering some overall user-to-user fairness. This is in great contrast with the grid installation, where fairness is one of the major optimization goals and is managed by the *fair-sharing* job-prioritization approach [6].

As was shown in Fig. 2 (top right), the majority of cloud resources is consumed by few users over a long time period, yet there is no automated mechanism that would force them to decrease their allocations, letting other users to use the system in a fair fashion. Apparently, we should adopt some analogy of the fair-sharing approach in our cloud installation [5]. Perhaps a good starting point would be to prioritize users (based on their resource usage) and automatically decrease allocations for long running VMs of low priority users (i.e., increase overcommitment factor of such VMs).

---

[2]In total, there were 130 active users in the cloud and 279 users in the grid during 2016.

Solving this problem will however require major changes in the current rather naive approach applied in the OpenNebula's default scheduler.

3.4 Inter Application Load-Balancing

Upon solving the problems mentioned in Sections 3.1–3.3 we also focus on the global scheduling problems such as load-balancing among the various applications and frameworks that use the infrastructure. Certainly, our workloads indicate that there are many opportunities to use temporarily idle resources (see Fig. 3). For example, short jobs from the grid can probably "steal cycles" when cloud VMs are idle, because the average load of allocated CPU cores and RAM memory in the cloud is currently bellow 30% in most cases. For this purpose a "sleeping grid worker" VM could be launched on every cloud host with a huge overcommitment factor during its idle phase. Then, upon the request of the batch system, a sleeping grid worker VM can be woken up by increasing its resource allocations and used to execute (short) grid jobs. In this way, many "short and small" grid jobs can use even very time-limited opportunities, e.g., when cloud VMs are idle during the night.

The question is how to actually implement such an inter-application scheduling? One way is to try to build upon existing frameworks like Apache Mesos [1], or use some form of a load-balancing module in the existing underlying virtualization platform – in this case inside the OpenNebula SW stack. The decision process is further complicated by the fact that new frameworks like OpenStack [3], Singularity [10], and Docker [11] are currently tested and will be offered as a service to our users in the near future. Therefore, the complexity and the amount of work needed to solve this issue will rise, rather than cease. Thus, we must not only focus on the "optimal result" but also keep in mind that our development team has a strictly limited capacity, where every new framework and/or functionality then inevitably brings not only opportunities but problems as well.

4 PROPOSED POLICIES AND THE NEW VM SCHEDULER

This section discusses the approaches intended to solve at least some of the current shortcomings observed in our infrastructure. As was shown in previous Section 3, the problems are mostly related to the cloud system, while the grid partition is operating satisfactory. Also, we have shown that there is not a single origin of these problems, but multiple factors mutually contribute to the situation. Those include the lack of *advanced VM (re)scheduling* capabilities, the absence of *fair-sharing mechanism* as well as the *"free of charge" computing approach* that together contribute to several undesired issues like the poor resource utilization or unsatisfactory resource reclaiming. In the following text we describe the methods that have been developed to address some of these issues. We start with the description of policies and approaches that have already been put into practice, following with the description of our new OpenNebula-compatible scheduler called *ONEScheduler*.

4.1 Production Policies and Approaches

The steadily increasing allocations of cloud VMs together with their rather low CPU loads and the apparent reluctance of our users to

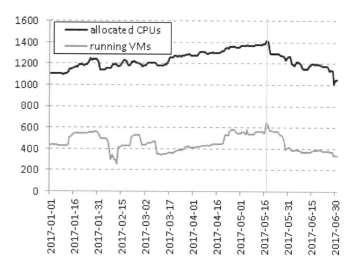

Figure 4: Impact of VM lifetime limit introduced in May 2017 (starting point shown by vertical line).

switch off old/unused VMs was causing a lot of trouble recently. By the end of 2016 it was decided, that the current policy concerning maximum VM lifetime must be changed. Instead of a theoretically unlimited lifetime, each VM now has a predefined maximum lifetime limit being 3 months. Once a VM passes this time frame, it is automatically terminated unless a user requests further prolongation. Using this mechanism which has been deployed since the mid of May 2017, we were able to remove some old "zombie" VMs, that were blocking our resources for a very long time. Figure 4 illustrates the impact of this new policy showing significant reduction in the number of running VMs and the corresponding allocated CPUs.

Moreover, additional preparations to improve the scheduling in the cloud are done in parallel. Beside the new experimental scheduler (see Section 4.2) we are also currently testing additional mechanisms that are needed to enable our planned advanced VM scheduling features. For example, many of the considered scheduling techniques rely on the (theoretical) ability of the cloud environment to "live migrate" running VMs. Truly safe live migrations however require a robust underlying infrastructure, based on a dedicated distributed storage facility (e.g., using a GPFS-like parallel file system [19] or a remote object storage like *Ceph* [21]). Such a robust infrastructure has not been fully operational in CERIT-SC so far, but we have recently started testing of the Ceph-based solution.

4.2 ONEScheduler

The default scheduler provided with OpenNebula is a stand-alone module (mm_sched). Sadly, it is not very well documented and it does not allow for an easy extensions due to its complicated and undocumented code structure. Beside that, it also lacks any support for automatic VM prioritization (VMs are only processed in the FIFO fashion), which in turn means that it would be quite complicated to develop any fairness-oriented scheduling mechanisms. Furthermore, the scheduler does not support any advanced features such as the ability to dynamically reschedule VMs based on some criteria. Hence some of the resources might get overloaded during

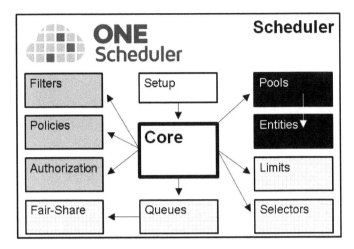

Figure 5: Main modules within the *Scheduler* package of ONEScheduler.

the time whilst others become/remain underloaded. Therefore, several projects have tried to develop a new scheduler for OpenNebula in the past, such as Haizea [22] or Green Cloud Scheduler [20]. Sadly, both these projects are now obsolete and no longer active.

4.2.1 Overall Structure. In order to address our goals, we have decided to develop a new, modular and easy to extend scheduler, which represents one of the main contributions of this paper. This new experimental OpenNebula-compatible VM scheduler is written in Java and is freely available at GitHub [18]. ONEScheduler has been designed in order to allow for easy configuration, extensions and/or modifications. For this purpose, a great deal of work was dedicated to the development of an efficient way for representing the data and logical parts of the scheduler. We use logically organized packages with well-defined and documented classes and interfaces allowing for transparent communication among scheduler's entities which simplifies further development. Detailed package and class description of ONEScheduler is beyond the scope of this paper but it can be found in the master's thesis [17]. For the sake of clarity, we only provide the most essential description of the scheduler's package structure and functionality in the following text. In ONEScheduler, a module represents one separated package that groups classes with similar goals, like fair-sharing, resource filtering or authorization. The most important modules (packages) that represent the functionality of the Scheduler package are shown in Figure 5.

Black-colored packages represent the data structures (pools of entities such as VMs, hosts, users, etc.) while the gray-colored packages correspond to features that are used when mapping VMs to hosts by the scheduling policy. Packages *Queues, Fair-Share, Selectors, Limits* and *Core* represent newly developed mechanisms that ONEScheduler has introduced in order to enable more complex queue-based VM scheduling. First, the *Fair-Share* package allows to choose a fair-sharing prioritization policy for pending VMs (see Section 4.2.3). The *Queues* package allows to model one or more queues for pending VMs. If fair-sharing is enabled, each user or group of users will have its own queue, and the queue priority will

be dynamically adapted with respect to the selected fair-sharing policy. All VMs within a queue are then ordered by their arrival time (default) or by their priority (fair-share). The *Selector* package provides ways to implement a specific policy defining in what order VMs will be selected from queues. Currently, we support basic "queue-by-queue" policy and "round robin". Finally, the *Limits* package allows to specify various resource-usage limits for users or groups. These limits can, for example, control the overall resource usage or number of simultaneously running VMs. All limits are enforced before a pending VM is considered for scheduling. Finally, the *Core* package contains the main class which manages the scheduling process which we describe in the following section.

4.2.2 VM Scheduling. The scheduler can operate in two distinct modes — it either communicates directly with the OpenNebula using its Java OCA interface or it can be executed in a standalone fashion (e.g., for simulations and testing purposes), where it uses a set of pre-generated XML files that "emulate" the normal kind of messages provided by the OpenNebula core. The current operation mode as well as many additional features (e.g., scheduling policy, fair-share, etc.) can be dynamically configured by the configuration file.

Using the provided data, the scheduler then repeatedly performs a full scheduling loop (with a given time interval). In each such loop, the current configuration is updated and the scheduler obtains up-to-date information about the current state of the infrastructure. That means that it creates a representation of all important entities in the cloud such as VMs, datastores, users, hosts and corresponding clusters. Then it constructs the queue(s) for pending VMs, using the priorities and additional setup as defined in the configuration. Finally, the queues are checked one-by-one and the corresponding VMs are selected based on their priorities and/or the configured VM selection mechanism (e.g., round robin). For a selected VM the scheduler then tries to find suitable host(s), following the selected scheduling policies and user's authorization to use such node(s) (using ACL). Currently, we use a slightly optimized set of scheduling policies as provided in the OpenNebula's match-making scheduling algorithm. If suitable host(s) and datastore(s) are found for a given VM the best match is identified [17]. If a group/user's resource usage limit is not exceeded then this VM is scheduled to be deployed on the selected host and datastore. The loop then continues with remaining VMs and queues respectively.

4.2.3 Fair-Sharing. Fair-sharing capability is the integral part of the newly developed scheduler. As discussed in Section 4.2.1, the scheduler uses fair-sharing mechanism to compute dynamic priorities for pending VMs, in order to fairly prioritize which user will deploy his or her VM first. It uses similar baseline approach as many mainstream batch scheduling systems like PBS Pro, SLURM or Maui [2]. The mechanism is following so called "max-min" strategy where a user with lower resource usage gets higher priority for his or her VMs than more active users and vice versa [2]. For this purpose, *fairshare algorithm* keeps track of past (finished) and currently running VMs of all users in the system. Using this data, it then calculates so called "fairshare usage" F_u for each user u. The user with the smallest fairshare usage then gets the highest priority. In its simplest form (see Formula 1), F_u is the sum of all user's VMs

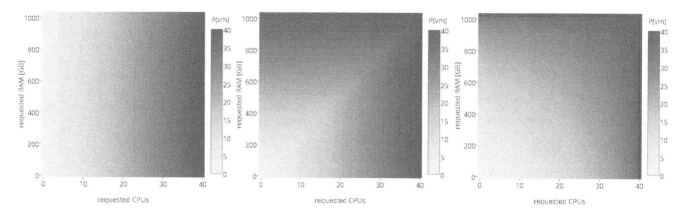

Figure 6: Heatmaps showing the values and differences among different implementations of the penalty function $P(vm)$. CPU-based penalty (left), Max-based penalty (middle) and the Root-based penalty (right).

"usages", where the "usage" of a given VM vm can be defined as the product of VM's runtime and the so called "VM penalty" $P(vm)$.

$$F_u = \sum_{vm \in VM_u} runtime_{vm} \cdot P(vm) \qquad (1)$$

There are many approaches how to define the VM penalty. In the simplest scenario — when users are prioritized based on their previously consumed CPU hours — the "VM penalty" $P(vm)$ is equal to the number of allocated CPUs for that particular machine vm. Our scheduler supports both this basic form as well as more complex penalties that beside the CPU also consider other consumed resources such as RAM and disk storage. In such cases, the $P(vm)$ is more complicated since it has to somehow aggregate different resources into a single scalar. Various techniques can be used [8], in our case we support both Max-based and Root-based penalties [23]. Here the penalty $P(vm)$ is computed using either a maximum of relative resource consumptions on a host (dominant resource) or by using a root-based function that also takes into account the non-dominant resources. To illustrate the difference between the basic CPU-oriented penalty and the more advanced multi-resource aware penalties we provide Figure 6 that shows how different penalties behave subject to various VM's CPU and RAM demands[3]. The figure uses heatmaps to show the value of $P(vm)$, where CPU demands are shown on the x-axis while y-axis depicts the amount of requested RAM for a VM. Starting from the left, Figure 6 shows heatmaps for the CPU-based, Max-based and Root-based penalty, respectively.

Concerning the CPU-based penalty function (Figure 6 left), every column has the same value as the penalty is only based on CPU requirements while the used RAM is completely ignored. In case of Max-based penalty, $P(vm)$ values are assigned on the basis of the virtual machine's dominant resource. Unlike in the previous case, now the VMs requiring a higher amount of RAM are assigned with a much higher penalties. Due to the "binary" nature of the Max function, the heatmap is symmetrical. Root-based penalty considers every resource requirement in the formula, not just the dominant

one. Therefore, its "surface" is smoothly curved, producing smaller penalties than the Max-based penalty for virtual machines with highly asymmetric requirements. Both the Max- and Root-based penalties assign maximum penalty as soon as any resource on a host is completely occupied by a VM. Further details and examples can be found in the related master's thesis [23].

4.2.4 Runtime. ONEScheduler has been also tested with respect to its speed. Since our long term goal is to develop rather complex (re)scheduling techniques that will require fast and frequent schedule modifications (e.g., VM migrations and load balancing) it was necessary to analyze how long does it take to perform one scheduling loop. For this purpose, we have constructed a synthetic experiment, which measured the scheduling time (runtime of one loop) with the goal to analyze how long does it take to schedule a given number of VMs on a given number of hosts. Except for the general analysis whether the scheduler is "fast enough", we have also analyzed what is the most important factor that influences the speed of the scheduler, i.e., how fast/slow are different scheduling policies and/or whether the runtime is more influenced by the number of scheduled VMs or by the number of available hosts (that must be filtered by the scheduler). The second goal was to analyze whether and how the sizes of both VMs and hosts being scheduled influence the resulting runtime.

To fulfill these goals we have designed a series of experiments where the sizes and the numbers of VMs and hosts were varying. We have used 4 sizes of VMs: tiny (0.25 CPU, 1 GB RAM), small (0.5 CPU, 4 GB RAM), medium (1 CPU, 6 GB RAM) and big (4 CPUs, 32 GB RAM). Similarly, 4 sizes of host have been used: tiny (8 CPUs, 128 GB RAM), small (12 CPUs, 90 GB RAM), medium (16 CPUs, 128 GB RAM) and big (40 CPUs, 256 GB RAM)[4]. This setup leads to 4×4 VM-to-host combinations. For each such combination we have measured the average time needed to schedule n VMs on m hosts, where $n = \{2, 8, 32, 128, 512, 1024\}$ and $m = \{1, 4, 16, 64, 256, 512\}$, respectively. This created 6×6 combinations for a given VM and host type. Finally, three different scheduling policies have been used. First, two basic OpenNebula-inspired techniques called *Packing* and

---

[3]Disk storage as the third resource is omitted in this case for simplicity. The axis ranges are based on the real ranges observed in CERIT-SC, where all VMs require at most 40 CPUs and at most ~1 TB of RAM.

[4]The sizes of VMs and hosts are based on the most frequent sizes of hosts and VMs observed in the CERIT-SC's cloud workloads.

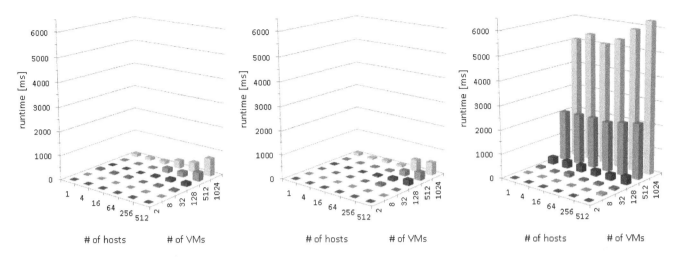

Figure 7: The runtime in milliseconds needed to perform one scheduling loop with respect to different policies and numbers of VMs and hosts. From left to right: Packing, Striping and Fair-sharing policies.

Striping, that tries to pack as much VMs on one host as possible or spreads VMs evenly on the suitable nodes, respectively [15]. The third policy included was the newly developed *fair-sharing* policy, that prioritizes VMs based on their owners' resource usage in order to fairly distribute resources among users (see Section 4.2.3). To sum up, the experiment measuring runtime comprised of 1728 different setups, each one of them was then used 10 times in order to obtain more stable average runtime results.

The experiments were conducted on an ordinary PC with Intel Core i5-2400 CPU running on 3.1 GHz, having 8 GB of RAM. Results of all those 1728 experiments, including ONEScheduler's sources and experimental data-sets, can be found at GitHub [18]. Here, due to the lack of space, we limit our presentation only to the most interesting findings. Of those 16 VM-to-host combinations we have chosen those that exhibited the largest maximum runtime under the given VM-to-host combination. Figure 7 presents these runtime-related results for the three considered scheduling policies — from left to right: *Packing*, *Striping* and *Fair-sharing* policies, respectively. For Packing policy, the most demanding VM-to-host combination (which is shown in the figure) was to schedule medium VMs on large hosts. For Striping policy the most time-consuming combination was to schedule medium VMs on tiny nodes, while in case of Fair-sharing the "slowest" runtime was observed for tiny VMs scheduled on small nodes. Each figure shows the average runtime needed to schedule n VMs on m nodes (36 combinations per figure).

As can be seen in Figure 7 (left and middle), the basic OpenNebula-inspired policies are very fast, capable of scheduling hundreds of VMs well within one second. Also, it is easily visible that the runtime grows rather linearly with the growing size of n and m (more VMs scheduled over more hosts). In general, the Packing policy is slightly more time consuming, because it takes a little more time to find the "best match", while the Striping policy just needs to find a host with the least number of running VMs. The situation is different when Fair-sharing policy is applied (Figure 7 right). As we can see, for larger numbers of VMs, the time needed to schedule these VMs grows significantly, being roughly 10× higher than for those

simpler policies. This is not surprising, because Fair-sharing policy must constantly recalculate VMs' priorities in order to guarantee fair allocations of resources among users. This fact also explains why the runtime is dominantly influenced by the growing number of VMs, while the growing number of hosts plays a little role. Still, the time needed to perform a scheduling loop is acceptable, at least for systems like CERIT-SC, where the average number of simultaneously running VMs is typically well below 600 (see Figure 4).

5 CONCLUSION AND FUTURE WORK

In this paper we have provided detailed insight into the private production virtualized system that executes mixed workloads coming from two different domains — the cloud and the grid. We have discussed the pros and cons of the current solution, especially focusing on the weaknesses related to the cloud partition. We have studied the characteristics of both the cloud and the grid workload to demonstrate how the two systems co-exist together. Based on this analysis, we have identified several weak spots that should be addressed in the future. In order to solve them, we have proposed and implemented the prototype of an advanced cloud scheduler for OpenNebula framework called *ONEScheduler*. This experimental scheduler has been evaluated by means of its runtime requirements, in order to demonstrate its capability to fluently schedule VMs on the underlying infrastructure.

Clearly, a lot of work is ahead of us as the current implementation still needs further development. For example, we need to develop and evaluate new scheduling policies that would perform dynamic VM (re)scheduling, given a set of criteria (e.g., a fair-share based criterion). For this purpose, the presented scheduler is very suitable, since it is well-documented, modular and capable of running in a simulation mode. All sources and data sets used in this paper as well as the complete experimental results can be found in our GitHub repository [18].

ACKNOWLEDGMENTS

We kindly acknowledge the support of CESNET LM2015042 and the CERIT Scientific Cloud LM2015085 provided under the programme "Projects of Large Research, Development, and Innovations Infrastructures" and the project Reg. No. CZ.02.1.01/0.0/0.0/16_013/0001797 co-funded by the Ministry of Education, Youth and Sports of the Czech Republic. We also highly appreciate the access to CERIT Scientific Cloud workload traces.

REFERENCES

[1] Benjamin Hindman, Andy Konwinski, Matei Zaharia, Ali Ghodsi, Anthony D. Joseph, Randy Katz, Scott Shenker, and Ion Stoica. 2011. Mesos: A Platform for Fine-grained Resource Sharing in the Data Center. In *Proceedings of the 8th USENIX Conference on Networked Systems Design and Implementation (NSDI'11)*. USENIX Association, Berkeley, CA, USA, 295–308.

[2] David Jackson, Quinn Snell, and Mark Clement. 2001. Core Algorithms of the Maui Scheduler. In *Job Sched. Strategies for Paral. Proc.*, Dror G. Feitelson and Larry Rudolph (Eds.). LNCS, Vol. 2221. Springer, 87–102.

[3] Kevin Jackson. 2012. *OpenStack Cloud Computing Cookbook*. Packt Publishing.

[4] Chris Jones, John Wilkes, Niall Murphy, Cody Smith, and Betsy Beyer. 2016. Service Level Objectives. In *Site Reliability Engineering: How Google Runs Production Systems*, Betsy Beyer, Chris Jones, Jennifer Petoff, and Niall Murphy (Eds.). O'Reilly Media, Chapter 4. https://landing.google.com/sre/book.html.

[5] Dalibor Klusáček. 2014. Experience with Multi-Resource Aware Fair Sharing in Highly Heterogeneous Private Clouds. In *Proceedings of the 2014 IEEE/ACM 7th International Conference on Utility and Cloud Computing (UCC'14)*. IEEE, 487–488.

[6] Dalibor Klusáček and Václav Chlumský. 2017. Planning and Metaheuristic Optimization in Production Job Scheduler. In *Job Scheduling Strategies for Parallel Processing (LNCS)*, Vol. 10353. Springer, 198–216.

[7] Dalibor Klusáček and Boris Parák. 2017. Analysis of Mixed Workloads from Shared Cloud Infrastructure. In *Job Scheduling Strategies for Parallel Processing (LNCS)*. Springer, 1–18. To appear.

[8] Dalibor Klusáček and Hana Rudová. 2015. Multi-Resource Aware Fairsharing for Heterogeneous Systems. In *Job Scheduling Strategies for Parallel Processing*

[9] Dalibor Klusáček, Šimon Tóth, and Gabriela Podolníková. 2017. Real-life Experience with Major Reconfiguration of Job Scheduling System. In *Job Scheduling Strategies for Parallel Processing (LNCS)*, Vol. 10353. Springer, 83–101.

[10] Gregory M. Kurtzer, Vanessa Sochat, and Michael W. Bauer. 2017. Singularity: Scientific containers for mobility of compute. *PLoS ONE* 12, 5 (May 2017).

[11] Dirk Merkel. 2014. Docker: Lightweight Linux Containers for Consistent Development and Deployment. *Linux Journal* 2014, 239, Article 2 (March 2014).

[12] meta 2017. MetaCentrum. (February 2017). http://www.metacentrum.cz/.

[13] Ruben S. Montero, Ignacio M. Llorente, and Dejan Milojièiæ. 2011. OpenNebula: A Cloud Management Tool. *IEEE Internet Computing* 15, 2 (2011), 11–14.

[14] Ahuva W. Mu'alem and Dror G. Feitelson. 2001. Utilization, Predictability, Workloads, and User Runtime Estimates in Scheduling the IBM SP2 with Backfilling. *IEEE Transactions on Parallel and Distributed Systems* 12, 6 (2001), 529–543.

[15] ones 2017. OpenNebula Scheduler. (August 2017). http://docs.opennebula.org/5.4/operation/host_cluster_management/scheduler.html.

[16] PBS Works 2017. *PBS Professional 14.2 Administrator's Guide*. PBS Works. http://www.pbsworks.com.

[17] Gabriela Podolníková. 2017. Cloud Scheduler for OpenNebula Middleware. (2017). Masaryk University, master's thesis. https://is.muni.cz/th/396214/fi_m/thesis.pdf.

[18] Gabriela Podolníková, András Ürge, and Dalibor Klusáček. 2017. ONEScheduler: a custom open source cloud scheduler for OpenNebula. (August 2017). https://github.com/CESNET/ONEScheduler.

[19] Dino Quintero, Matteo Barzaghi, Randy Brewster, Wan Hee Kim, Steve Normann, Paulo Queiroz, Robert Simon, and Andrei Vlad. 2011. *Implementing the IBM General Parallel File System (GPFS) in a Cross-Platform Environment* (1 ed.). IBM.

[20] Ioan Salomie. 2017. Green Cloud Scheduler. (July 2017). http://coned.utcluj.ro/GreenCloudScheduler.

[21] Karan Singh. 2016. *Ceph Cookbook*. Packt Publishing.

[22] Borja Sotomayor, Rubén S. Montero, Ignacio M. Llorente, and Ian Foster. 2009. Virtual Infrastructure Management in Private and Hybrid Clouds. *IEEE Internet Computing* 13, 5 (September 2009), 14–22.

[23] András Ürge. 2017. Managing user fair-sharing in cloud computing systems. (2017). Masaryk University, master's thesis. https://is.muni.cz/th/373859/fi_m/thesis.pdf.

Adaptive Service Performance Control using Cooperative Fuzzy Reinforcement Learning in Virtualized Environments

Olumuyiwa Ibidunmoye
Umeå University
Department of Computing Science
SE-901 87
Umeå, Sweden
muyi@cs.umu.se

Mahshid Helali Moghadam
University of Kashan
Department of Computer Engineering
Kashan, Iran
mhelali@grad.kashanu.ac.ir

Ewnetu Bayuh Lakew,
Erik Elmroth
Umeå University
Department of Computing Science
SE-901 87
Umeå, Sweden
{ewnetu,elmroth}@cs.umu.se

ABSTRACT

Designing efficient control mechanisms to meet strict performance requirements with respect to changing workload demands without sacrificing resource efficiency remains a challenge in cloud infrastructures. A popular approach is fine-grained resource provisioning via auto-scaling mechanisms that rely on either threshold-based adaptation rules or sophisticated queuing/control-theoretic models. While it is difficult at design time to specify optimal threshold rules, it is even more challenging inferring precise performance models for the multitude of services. Recently, reinforcement learning have been applied to address this challenge. However, such approaches require many learning trials to stabilize at the beginning and when operational conditions vary thereby limiting their application under dynamic workloads. To this end, we extend the standard reinforcement learning approach in two ways: a) we formulate the system state as a fuzzy space and b) exploit a set of cooperative agents to explore multiple fuzzy states in parallel to speed up learning. Through multiple experiments on a real virtualized testbed, we demonstrate that our approach converges quickly, meets performance targets at high efficiency without explicit service models.

CCS CONCEPTS

• **Computer systems organization** → **Cloud computing**; • **Networks** → *Network performance evaluation*; • **Computing methodologies** → *Machine learning*;

KEYWORDS

Performance control; Resource allocation; Quality of service; Reinforcement learning; Autoscaling; Autonomic computing.

1 INTRODUCTION

One of the main attractiveness of cloud computing is the ability to provision computing resources (e.g. compute, memory, storage, etc.) on demand on a pay-as-you-go basis. Thanks to advancements in virtualization technologies, cloud infrastructures enable applications to achieve rapid elasticity by dynamically acquiring and releasing resources on the fly according to changing workload levels. However, determining the right amount of resource capacity to increase or decrease automatically remains a challenge given the dynamic nature of workloads, plurality of services and quality of service (QoS) requirements.

Autoscaling [17, 19] is a technique that have been employed to address the aforementioned challenge on different fronts. It involves automatically adjusting the amount of resources available to an application in response to changing workload demand in order to meet QoS requirements (e.g. performance and resource efficiency). Autoscaling techniques typically scale applications in two ways–horizontally and vertically. Vertical scaling modifies the amount of resources allocated to a service's virtual machine (VM) such as CPU cores or memory. Horizontal scaling adjusts the number of VMs available to a service often with a higher configuration latency. The later is more widely available in commercial clouds (e.g. Amazon, Google, Windows Azure, Rackspace, etc.) as it requires no extra support from the hypervisor unlike the former which may require rebooting and has to be supported by both the hypervisor and guest operating system's kernel [15]. While only a few providers such as CenturiLink[1] and ProfitBricks[2] offer some form of vertical scaling, most modern hypervisors such as Xen, KVM and VMware provides built in support such as CPU hot-plugging, capping and memory ballooning [19]. We focus on vertical scaling in this paper since it is less explored than the horizontal case. In addition, since fractional resource capacity (e.g. CPU core) can be allocated with configuration latency of less than 0.5s [21], it can compliment horizontal scaling towards truly actualizing the *pay-as-use* pricing model.

Autoscaling solutions rely on a variety of strategies for decision making. The most basic strategy is based on a set of predefined IF..THEN rules consisting of logical conditions (e.g. CPU%>70) and corresponding actions (e.g. adding 1 more CPU core) [4, 9, 10]. In order to cope with the limitation of rule-based techniques under dynamic workloads, sophisticated approaches build analytical models of execution environments using techniques from a variety of mathematical disciplines [1, 6–8, 11, 15, 21, 23]. However, accurate estimation of scaling models often require detail knowledge of service and workload characteristics thereby limiting their applicability to handle heterogeneous service mix. Recently, reinforcement

---

[1]https://www.ctl.io/autoscale/#VerticalAutoscale
[2]https://www.profitbricks.com/help/Live_Vertical_Scaling

learning (RL) has been applied to achieve a more generic approach to the autoscaling problem without precise model of service workloads and its execution context [5, 12, 13, 16]. However, the bad initial performance–requiring many learning trials to stabilize at the beginning and when conditions change required by such approaches limits their application in real-time deployments [17].

In this paper, we present the design and evaluation of an adaptive mechanisms for meeting QoS requirements (such as performance SLA and resource efficiency) using cooperative fuzzy reinforcement learning (CoFReL). Specifically, CoFReL extends the standard RL (Q-learning) approach in two ways to speed up learning: a) we formulate the system state as a fuzzy space and b) exploit a set of cooperative agents to explore multiple fuzzy states in parallel. The hypothesis is that a set of cooperating agents sharing a collective experience explore the state space faster than a single agent. We demonstrate the efficacy of our approach through multiple experiments on a real virtualized testbed. In particular, our technique converges, on average, within the first 11 learning cycles with an overall average convergence rate of 6.7 learning cycles. In addition to meeting performance SLA even for response time targets as low as 0.5s, it consistently achieve a resource efficiency of at least 96% across workloads.

The rest of the paper is organized as follows; Section 2 discusses background and motivation while Section 3 summarizes the proposed approach while technical details of its main components discussed in Section 4 and Section 5. Experimental evaluation and results are presented in Section 6. The paper concludes with a review of Related Work in Section 7 and Conclusion in Section 8.

2 MOTIVATION AND BACKGROUND
2.1 Motivation
Though virtualization technologies allows cloud service providers to scale services and optimize server utilization in a cost-effective way, balancing the trade-off between efficient utilization of allocated resources and meeting performance service-level agreements (SLA) remains a major objective. On one hand, allocating resources in excess of actual demand–*overprovisioning*–results in wastage due to under-utilization and extra monetary cost, while on the other hand, insufficient resource allocations–*underprovisioning*–causes performance degradation and SLA violations.

Model-driven autoscaling solutions targeting this trade-off belong to one of two groups: a) white-box techniques based on queuing models [7, 23], fuzzy control [11], b) black-box techniques based on control theory [1, 6, 15],time-series and predictive analysis [8]. While the white-box techniques may demand precise system model based on knowledge of service composition, propagation of service requests and workload characteristics, the black-box may require different models for individual different QoS metrics (e.g. response time, throughput) and scenarios (e.g. average vs tail latency or scale-up vs scale-down).

Nevertheless, major barriers to achieving adaptive performance control in cloud environments include a) the complexity and heterogeneity of infrastructures and services making it hard to craft precise models of the execution environment and b) the dynamism of workloads making workload predictions and consequent scaling decisions unreliable. These characteristics suggest the need for a more generic framework for performance control in heterogeneous environments which does not require precise model of services nor their workloads.

2.2 Reinforcement Learning for Adaptive Performance Control
Adaptive performance control is an interactive decision-making problem involving a *controller* which continuously monitors one or more QoS indicators (e.g. performance, utilization) of a *controlled system* and dynamically decreases or increases resource capacity to maintain the QoS at a desired target level. The controlled system in this paper is a virtualized application deployed in a VM hosted in an Infrastructure as a Service (IaaS) cloud.

Reinforcement Learning (RL) [22] is a mechanism that can be used for handling such interactive scenarios. This interaction involves an *agent* (the controller) which continually senses the *state* (e.g. latency, CPU usage) of the *environment* (system or application). The agent uses its experiences to select an *action* (e.g. add/remove CPU cores) to be applied to the environment which affects the state and in return receives a reinforcement signal in the form of a scalar *reward* (e.g. -1 for a bad action and +1 for a good action in a specific state). In order to meet a given learning *goal* (e.g. meeting latency targets), the agent follows a *policy* that takes actions in a way that maximizes the long-term cumulative reward. The agent autonomously learns this policy via a systematic *trial-and-error* scheme of selecting high-value actions (*exploitation*) and trying out a variety of actions to discover good ones (*exploration*). In general, it is supposed that the environment is non-deterministic, so that applying the same action to the environment on two occasions may lead to two different next states and/or reinforcement signal values. However, it is also supposed that the environment is stationary, so that the probabilities of states transitions or receiving specific values of reinforcement signal is fixed over the time.

To find the optimal policy, the agent must sequentially estimate the utility the long-term cumulative reward of taking each action in the each state. Q-learning [22] is an RL algorithm for learning such functions in an online manner. It is an off-policy technique as the value function is learned independently of the policy being followed by the agent. Once the optimal policy is learned, the agent will replay it while occasionally trying out unexplored actions.

3 SYSTEM OVERVIEW
In this section we briefly present an overview of our framework for adaptive performance control using a model-free technique which we call Cooperative Fuzzy Reinforcement Learning (CoFReL). As shown in Fig. 1, CoFReL consists of two main components namely:

1) The *State Detector* is responsible for observing the current state of the controlled system and computing associated rewards. It receives the values of the QoS metrics at time t; the Response Time, RT_t, and CPU utilization, CPU_t of the controlled service via a sensor.[3] The metrics are combined using fuzzy rules to classify the system into one or more fuzzy states. The reward, R_t, is derived using continuous function that quantifies the utility of the system in terms of compliance with given SLA target and

---
[3]Note that time-indexed variables will be written in the form X_t rather than the standard functional form $X(t)$ throughout this paper.

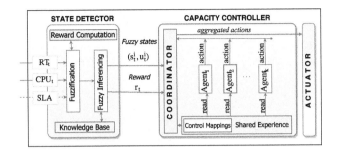

Figure 1: System Overview

achieved resource efficiency. In this paper, we consider performance SLA characterized by a target value, τ, and a tolerance band, $tol = [\tau^-, \tau^+]$ where $\tau^- = \tau - \varepsilon$, $\tau^+ = \tau + \varepsilon$, and ε is a small tolerance value.

2) The *Capacity Controller* employs semi-supervised learning to autonomously adjust the amount of compute capacity available to the service VM in order to adapt to incoming workload. Inputs to the capacity controller includes the set of observed fuzzy states and the reward of the action taken in the previous step. The major building block of the controller is a coordinator which manages a set of cooperative learning agents to explore multiple fuzzy states in parallel. Based on the current states and the memory of shared experience, each agent recommends a scaling action (e.g. add or remove a fractional capacity). To make capacity actuation atomic as much as possible, the coordinator aggregates actions by taking the arithmetic sum of recommended actions each scaled by the degree of membership in the corresponding state. Finally, the coordinator updates the shared experience. The aggregated action is applied to the service VM using VM management API of the hypervisor. Capacity actuations are applied in an incremental fashion, so that total capacity after an action is an accumulation of past actuations. To improve control stability and speed up state-action exploration, the administrator can define control mappings which are high-level rules to guide the agents on what category of actions not to explore when in a specific state.

We discuss further the technical details of two components in sections 4 and 5 respectively.

4 STATE DETECTION

Sensing and recognizing states of the controlled system is a major task in a reinforcement learning problem. According to Fig. 2, the system state is represented as a two dimensional space of the two QoS indicators to be optimized namely performance (Response Time) and resource usage (CPU utilization). Whereas the former acts like a proxy for end-user performance, the later indirectly captures the service workload. Also, due to the imprecise nature of state boundaries the state formulation is such that the system can be in one or more state(s) at varying degrees. To address the uncertainty in the state space, we apply fuzzy membership functions and fuzzy rules [2], in Section 4.1, to characterize system state at any given time. In addition, the computation of rewards is performed externally from the controller, as part of state detection, so that

the agents do not have control over how rewards are estimated thereby preventing overcompensation. In Section 4.2 we describe a continuous utility function for computing rewards.

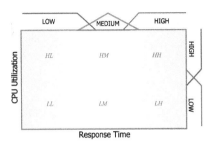

Figure 2: 2-dimensional fuzzy state representation.

4.1 Fuzzy State Classification

The standard state detection in RL problems typically assumes that states are mutually exclusive. For example, in Fig. 2, it would be supposed that the system can be in only a distinct state HL, for example, when the CPU utilization is High and Response Time is Low. The challenge of such crisp representation includes knowing what is high enough to be a good threshold for each attribute's category, how to treat boundary values, as well as how to recognize vague expert concepts of the environment such as Very Low or Medium. Fuzzy logic facilitates the formalization of these kind of uncertainties using interpretable fuzzy rules based informal domain knowledge and simple fuzzy operators.

Fuzzy state classification [14] is a form of soft labelling operation in which an QoS measurement, (RT_t, CPU_t), of the controlled system is assigned to one or more states with varying degrees using fuzzy sets and rules (soft labeling). While *CPU* metric is bounded between $[0\%, 100\%]$, the *RT* metric is not so bounded, so the domain of *RT* is normalized to interval $[a, b]$ using an inverse tangent function as follows:

$$RT_t = b \cdot \frac{2}{\pi} \tan^{-1}\left(\frac{RT'_t}{\tau} - a\right) \qquad (1)$$

where RT'_t is the measured response time at time t, τ is the target value (SLA), while a and b are the lower and upper response time limits set to 0 and 100 similar to the *CPU* metric. The implication of this function is such that when $RT'_t = \tau$, the normalized value is 50 and $RT'_t > \tau$ are normalized to values towards 100 while $RT'_t < \tau$ are normalized towards 0. The normalization is necessary to ensure that the 2D state-space is bounded which simplifies reasoning and exploration of the state space.

Fuzzification involves defining category membership functions over the domain of each QoS metric [2]. A category membership function is identified by a linguistic term such as Low, or High mapped to a fuzzy set and the set of all membership functions of a given metric is an overlapping ranges of values over its domain. A fuzzy set A in a continuous domain $X:\mathbb{R}$ is defined as $A = \{(x, \mu_A(x)) | x \in X\}$ and characterized by a membership function $\mu_A : x \rightarrow [0, 1]$. For all $x \in X$, $\mu_A(x)$ describes the degree to which x belongs in A. Though the membership function, $\mu_A(x)$, can take one of several shapes [2], we have used trapezoidal for

Low and High categories and triangular for Medium as shown in Fig. 2. In our case, ranges of membership functions are estimated empirically and can be automatically updated to reflect prevailing workload behaviour.

Fuzzy Inferencing allows us to reason about all possible states the system can assume using fuzzy rules constructed from domain knowledge [2]. A rule, as shown in Eq.(2), is made up of two parts namely the *antecedent*–logical combination of the linguistic terms of one or more variables using appropriate fuzzy operators, and the *consequent* which determines the extent of being in the associate state.

$$f_1 : \text{IF } \underbrace{\text{CPU\% is Low AND RT is High}}_{\text{rule antecedent}}$$
$$\text{THEN } \underbrace{\text{STATE is LH}}_{\text{rule consequent}} \qquad (2)$$

The output variable of a rule is realised using a singleton membership function so that the output of each rule is the support for being in the associated state. Given an input vector, $\vec{x}$, the degree of activating rule f_i or support for the associated state, is derived as $\tau(\vec{x}) = \prod_{j=1}^{n} \mu_{A_j}(x_j)$ where n is the number of linguistic terms in the rule. In our case, we have a total of six rules in total, so the output of the inference engine is a set of remaining state-degree pairs, $\{s_t^i, \mu_t^i\}$, after filtering those pairs where $\mu_t^i = 0$.

4.2 Reward Computation

To compute the reward signal, we derive a utility of the system as a weighted combination of performance and efficiency as follows:

$$U_t = \omega H_t + (1 - \omega)E_t \qquad (3)$$

where H_t is the degree of compliance with performance SLA and E_t is the resource efficiency, and ω, $0 \leq \omega \leq 1$, is a multiplier to allow administrator prioritize either performance or efficiency. The SLA compliance, H_t, is estimated using a triangular function:

$$H_t = \begin{cases} 0, & RT_t \leq \tau^- \\ \frac{RT_t - \tau^-}{\tau - \tau^-}, & \tau^- < RT_t \leq \tau \\ \frac{\tau^+ - RT_t}{\tau^+ - \tau}, & \tau < RT_t \leq \tau^+ \\ 0, & RT_t \geq \tau^+ \end{cases}$$

while resource efficiency, E_t, is the ratio between current CPU utilization and maximum utilization value possible, that is, $E_t = CPU_t/CPU_{max}$. Note that τ^- and τ^+ are the lower and upper limit of the tolerance region respectively. Finally, the reward value is computed as an inverse function of the hyperbolic tangent of the utility function:

$$r_t = \frac{1}{1 - \tanh(U_t)} \qquad (4)$$

A major property of Eq.(4) is that it ensures the continuity and proportionality of reward values, so that the lower the utility the lower the reward and vice versa. Also, the hyperbolic tangent acts like an activation function with finite output in the range $(-1, 1)$. Since the hyperbolic tangent of boundary utility values 0 and 1 are defined, the reward function is stable with defined output.

The set of state-degree pairs, $\{s_t^i, \mu_t^i\}$, and corresponding scalar reward, r_t, form the input to the controller introduced in the next section.

5 RESOURCE CONTROL USING COOPERATIVE FUZZY Q-LEARNING

In this section, we describe the detail of the cooperative fuzzy Q-learning based capacity controller, introduced in Section 3.

The goal of the controller is to automatically learn auto-scaling policies to drive the system to desired state via incremental capacity adjustments. The learning task involves the coordination of k parallel reinforcement learning agents each exploring the state-action space of a given state over all possible actions in that state. The controller interacts with the environment at discrete time steps, $t = 0, 1, 2, 3, ...,$. At each time t, the controller receives a set of state-degree pairs, $\{s_t^i, \mu_t^i\}_{i=1}^{k}$ from the state detector, and $s_t^i \in S$ is the ith fuzzy state and μ_t^i is the extent of the system in that state. The controller then activates the associated agent for each fuzzy state s_t^i. Based on past experience maintained in a lookup table, the q-table, of state-action values, each agent recommends an action $a_t^i \in A(s_t^i)$ where $A(s_t^i)$ is the set of actions available in state s_t^i and A is the set of all possible actions. Actions involve increasing (scale-up) or decreasing (scale-down) the cumulative CPU capacity by a fractional factor in the set $\{0, 2/5, 3/5, 4/5, 1, 3/2, 2\}$.

To make actuations atomic, the coordinator aggregates recommendations by taking the arithmetic sum of recommended actions each scaled by the associated degree $\mu_i(t)$:

$$a_t = \sum_{i=1}^{k} \mu_t^i \cdot a_t^i \qquad (5)$$

The coordinator sends the aggregated action a_t to the actuator which adjusts cumulative capacity of the system accordingly. After one time step, $t + 1$, the agent receives a numerical signal $r_{t+1} \in \mathbb{R}$, the immediate reward, as well as a new set of fuzzy state-degree pairs $\{s_t^i, \mu_t^i\}_{i=1}^{\ell}$ and the procedure is repeated.

The learning goal is to find a policy $\pi : S \rightarrow A$ mapping every state, s, with the best action, a, which maximizes the expected discounted rewards over the future as follows [22]:

$$R_t = r_{t+1} + \gamma r_{t+2} + \gamma^2 r_{t+3} + \cdots = \sum_{k=0}^{\infty} \gamma^k r_{t+k+1} \qquad (6)$$

where γ, $0 \leq \gamma \leq 1$, is a discount factor which determines the importance given to future rewards compared to immediate rewards as well as to avoid infinite rewards. Furthermore, the policy $\pi(s, a)$, the probability of taking action a in state s, is associated with an expected utility value $Q^\pi(s, a)$ defined as [22]:

$$Q^\pi(s, a) = E \left\{ \sum_{k=0}^{\infty} \gamma^k r_{t+k+1} | s_t = s, a_t = a \right\} \qquad (7)$$

Each agent, at each control interval, relies on $Q^\pi(s, a)$ to make action recommendations, which captures the desirability of taking action a while in state s under the policy π.

Due to the infinite nature of Eq. 7, the quantity $Q^\pi(s, a)$ is typically evaluated in an online manner via temporal differencing. This involves maintaining an in-memory lookup table, the q-table, to keep track of the expected value of each state for all possible actions, and applying incremental updates to each state-action entry.

Given the fuzzy nature of our scenario, the update is based on two heuristics a) that the q-value of the state-action associated with each agent is updated individually according to their contribution to the aggregate action, and b) that the cooperation between the k agents at time t moved the system from states $\{s_t^i\}_{i=1}^k$ to $\{s_t^i\}_{i=1}^\ell$. Hence, the reward r_{t+1} obtained as a result of having taken aggregated action a_t in the previous time step should be shared among the agents. The one-step cooperative fuzzy Q-learning update rule for each agent is defined as:

$$Q(s_t^i, a_t^i) = \left[(1-\alpha)Q(s_t^i, a_t^i) + \alpha(\mu_t^i \cdot r_{t+1} + \gamma V_{t+1})\right]\mu_t^i \quad (8)$$

$$V_{t+1} = \max\left(\{\mu_t^i \cdot \max_{a' \in A} Q(s_{t+1}^i, a')\}_{i=1}^\ell\right) \quad (9)$$

Whereas the first term of Eq. 8 is the value of s_t^i before action a_t^i was taken, the second term is sum of shared reward and the best discounted return or utility value across all the resulting states (Eq. 9). Parameter α, $0 \leq \alpha \leq 1$, controls the rate of learning in terms of the impact of new utility value on the q-value.

Eventually, each agent will find the optimal policy π^* which selects the action that maximizes the q-value of a given state s:

$$a(s) = \arg\max_{a' \in A} Q(s, a') \quad (10)$$

Adaptation. Following only Eq. 10, the agents will greedily select high-value actions, without trying out other actions that may yield even better value. The action selection procedure employs the ϵ-greedy strategy to prevent this situation. With probability $1 - \epsilon$, the best action according to Eq. 10 will be selected and with probability ϵ a random action will be chosen to explore a variety of actions thereby gaining more experience.

Improving learning performance. RL approaches generally suffer slow convergence rate due to unfeasibly long training time required to explore the state space using a single agent. This concern informed our fuzzy state detection and the use of cooperative agents to explore multiple fuzzy states in parallel. In addition, large action space may introduce undesirable fluctuations in controller behaviour which may introduce arbitrary spikes in end-user service performance. To attenuate this effect, we define control mappings based on high-level domain knowledge to guide the agents on what category of actions not to explore when in a specific state. For example, when in state LL of Fig. 2, agents can be discouraged from making high fractional increments since allocated resource is currently underutilized. The control mappings is implemented according to the following initialization:

$$Q(s_i, a_j) = \begin{cases} -1, & (s_i, a_j) \in \psi \\ 0, & otherwise \end{cases} \quad (11)$$

where $i = 1, 2, ..., |S|$, $j = 1, 2, ..., |A|$ and ψ is a set of invalid state action pair.

The entire control procedure is described in Algorithm 1. The state representation in Fig. 2 yields a finite state space of dimension 2×3 making a total of 6 states. Also, there are a total of 13 possible actions to choose from. Hence, storing the q-table in memory is computationally feasible. Finally, the control methodology introduced in this section is general and can easily be extended for different use-cases.

Algorithm 1 Cooperative Fuzzy Q-Learning
___
Require: $S, A, \alpha, \gamma, \epsilon, \psi$
1: Initialize q-values:
   $Q(s_i, a_j) = -1$ **if** $(s_i, a_j) \in \psi$ **else** 0, $\forall i \leq |S|, j \leq |A|$
2: Observe k fuzzy state-degree pairs $\{s_t^i, \mu_t^i\}_{i=1}^k$
3: Select an action for each fuzzy state s_t^i
   $a_t^i = \arg\max_{a \in A} Q(s_t^i, a)$ with probability $1 - \epsilon$ or $a_t^i = $ random$\{a_j, j = 1, 2, ..., |A|\}$ with probability ϵ
4: Compute aggregate control action
   $a_t = \sum_{i=1}^k \mu_t^i \cdot a_t^i$
5: Take action and let system go to the next set of fuzzy states
6: In the next control interval $t + 1$, observe the new fuzzy state-degree pairs $\{s_{t+1}^i, \mu_t^i\}_{i=1}^\ell$ and the reinforcement signal r_{t+1}
7: Compute the best utility value from the next states $V_{t+1} = \max\left(\{\mu_t^i \cdot \max_{a' \in A} Q(s_{t+1}^i, a')\}_{i=1}^\ell\right)$
8: Compute the residual error between the values of the new and previous states
   $\Delta Q = [\mu_t^i \cdot r_{t+1} + \gamma V_{t+1} - Q(s_t^i, a_t^i)]$
9: Update the q-value of each previous state s_t^i with respect to the recommended action a_t^i
   $Q(s_t^i, a_t^i) = \mu_t^i \cdot [Q(s_t^i, a_t^i) + \alpha \Delta Q]$
10: Repeat for every newly observed fuzzy states and reward signal until end of episode
___

6 EVALUATION

In this section, we describe the experimental evaluation of the proposed adaptive performance control framework, CoFReL. The goal is to assess the efficacy and applicability of CoFReL for controlling the QoS of a real application benchmark running on a realistic virtualized testbed.

6.1 Setup

The experimental testbed is composed of an HP ProLiant Physical Machine (PM) equiped with a total of 32 CPU cores and 56 GB of memory. The server runs a Xen hypervisor[3] to emulate a typical virtualized environment and to enable vertical auto-scaling. The service under test is the RUBiS[4] web application benchmark, an eBay-like e-commerce application that provides selling, browsing and bidding functionalities. The service is deployed as a monolithic package in a single VM hosting an Apache 2.0 web server and MySQL 5.0 server. Since the focus is on compute capacity allocation, we configured the VM with 10 GB of memory to prevent unnecessary disk activity.

To generate realistic workload for the test, we emulated virtual web users concurrently interacting with the applications using an open source HTTP load generator, httpmon[5]. The tool dynamically generates realistic user behaviour by issuing HTTP GET or POST requests at varying intensities with exponential inter-arrival times. Requests are generated in a closed loop fashion according to three workload patterns as shown in Fig 3 a) *STEP*: abrupt increase or decrease in the number of concurrent users to emulate dynamic

---
[4]http://rubis.ow2.org/index.html
[5]https://github.com/cloud-control/httpmon

changes in workload levels b) *RAMP*: continuous increase in the number of concurrent users to emulate traffic phenomena such as flash-crowds, c) *TRI* phase: a hybrid of the step and ramp patterns composed of three phases where the service experiences rapid increase in users, followed by a short period of constant number of users, and a downward ramp.

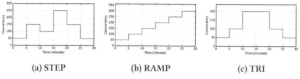

| (a) STEP | (b) RAMP | (c) TRI |

Figure 3: Workload pattern

To monitor service performance, the Response Time, and resource usage, CPU utilization, we deployed a lightweight sensor to collect and send measurements to the controller running on the PM via UDP communication. The sampling rate was maintained at a 10s interval in all experiments. Capacity allocations and deallocation are actuated directly via the Xen hypervisor CPU hot-plugging API[6].

6.2 Performance Metrics

The analysis of the proposed system is described in terms of 5 attributes namely

1) *Achieved QoS*: a summarized value of the observed performance (response time) aggregated over the entire experiment period.

2) *Adjusted Integral of Absolute Error (AIAE)*: the Integral of Absolute Error aggregates the total errors (deviations) observed over an experiment given a control target. We adjust for controlling within a tolerance band by computing the deviation according to the following function:

$$e_t = \begin{cases} RT_t - \tau^+, & RT_t \geq \tau^+ \\ RT_t - \tau^-, & RT_t \leq \tau^- \\ RT_t - \tau, & \tau^- \leq RT_t \leq \tau^+ \end{cases}$$

where τ is the target service performance and τ^- and τ^+ are the lower and upper limit of the tolerance region around the target respectively. The adjusted quantity is then computed as:

$$AIAE = \sum |e_t| \tag{12}$$

3) *Allocation*: the average resource capacity allocated to the service VM over an experiment in terms of the number of CPUs.

4) *Efficiency*: the ratio between the normalized average resource allocation and resource utilization

5) *Adaptivity*: the average number of monitoring epochs required to converge to the tolerance band after an overshoot or undershoot. We also report the average number of monitoring epochs required to converge after an abrupt increase (UP) and decrease (DOWN) in workload level, as well as the initial convergence rate (START).

[6]https://wiki.xen.org/wiki/Credit_Scheduler

6.3 A RL-based Baseline Controller

For the purpose of comparison we designed a baseline controller to determine if we are better off without the fuzzy state representation and parallel state exploration. Unlike the technique described in Section 4, the state detection mechanism is non-fuzzy and contains 3 discrete states. When the service performance is within the tolerance band, the system is said to be in a NORMAL state, VIOLATION if above the upper tolerance band, and LOW if below the lower tolerance band. The reward computation remains the same as in Section 4.2. The learning mechanism is based on the standard Q-learning algorithm involving only a single agent. A detail description of the basic Q-learning technique can be found in Sutton et al [22]. The action space and selection strategy are the same as described for CoFReL.

6.4 Experiments and Results

In this section, we describe and present the results of a number of experiments aimed at addressing some research questions. The objective is to examine how the proposed framework performs under different conditions.

All experiments were staged for a total length of 30 minutes, with workload intensity changing every 5 minutes. Unless otherwise stated, most of the experiments were run with a baseline configuration of target $\tau = 1s$, action selection strategy, $\epsilon = 0.1$, learning rate, $\alpha = 0.1$, and discount rate, $\gamma = 0.5$. Since end-user experience is crucial, we prioritize SLA compliance over resource efficiency by setting $\omega = 0.6$ in the utility function of Eq.(3). Also, for each experiment, the nominal compute capacity of the test VM was initialized to 1 CPU.

6.4.1 Time Series Analysis (RQ1). In order to characterize controller behaviour, we performed a total of nine experiments under varying load conditions and performance targets. Fig. 4 shows the time series plots of observed service performance, the allocated capacity as well as utilized capacity over time for the experiments. Each plot contains a control chart of service response time at the top and a line chart of allocated and utilized capacity at the bottom. The shaded region in the bottom chart represent unused capacity.

Clearly, the plots show that CoFReL adapt well with workload patterns while meeting performance requirements by scaling up and down in response to changes in workload levels. The plots also demonstrate the consistency of capacity allocations since roughly the same amount of capacity is allocated for a given workload level regardless of workload patterns. For the case of 1s target, about 3 CPUs are allocated to handle 100 concurrent users in all three workload patterns. The controller also exhibit correct replay of learned scaling policies. For example, under the RAMP load, the amount of capacity allocated for 200 users remain the same for 250 and even 300 users since performance requirement continued to be met. Note that spikes and dips in the control charts are change points indicating sudden increase and decrease in service workload respectively.

6.4.2 Aggregate Analysis (RQ2). Here, we present aggregate analysis of controller behaviour for the experiments in Section 6.4.1. The results are summarized in Table 1 under 5 performance measures.

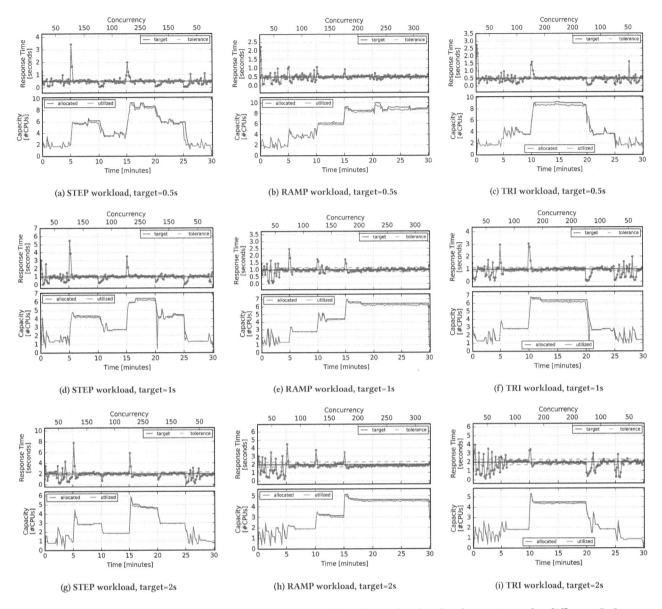

Figure 4: Time series plots of service performance (average RT), allocated and utilized capacity under different QoS targets and workload patterns. Parameters: ($\epsilon = 0.1$, $\alpha = 0.1$, $\gamma = 0.5$)

According to Table 1, CoFReL more easily meets performance requirement at a lower target of 0.5s and 1s than at higher target of 2s, but at a cost of lower resource efficiency. This observation remain consistent regardless of workload pattern. It is thus intuitive that it consumes more compute capacity at low targets (5.4 and 4 CPUs) than at the higher target (2.8 CPUs). The in ability to meet performance requirements at the 2s targets can be explained by high performance variability (AIAE) and not under provisioning since 2% of allocated capacity is unused.

6.4.3 Adaptation (RQ3). The last column of Table 1 shows that CoFReL adapts faster in most cases when controlling for the 1s target with an average of 6.7 epochs (i.e. 1.11mins at 10s control interval). However, a break down of this value presented in Table 2 shows that CoFReL converge to the tolerance band within the first 11.3 epochs (1.88mins) on average. Furthermore, CoFReL takes 6.3 epochs (approximately 1mins) to stabilize after an increase in workload level (scale up) and 12.6 epochs (2.1mins) after a decrease in workload level (scale down). Overall, the TRI load pattern has the fastest initial and scale-up adaptivity but also the slowest scale-down adaptivity.

Table 1: Control performance of proposed controller under different targets and workloads

Target	Workload	Achieved QoS	AIAE	Allocation	Efficiency	Adaptivity
0.5s	STEP	0.5s	23	4.8	96%	7.9
	RAMP	0.5s	15	6.5	96%	7.7
	TRI	0.5s	22	5.0	96%	7.9
	Mean	**0.5s**	**20**	**5.4**	**96%**	**7.8**
1s	STEP	1.01s	37	3.5	97%	6.2
	RAMP	0.99s	19	4.7	97%	7.0
	TRI	0.91s	36	3.7	97%	7.0
	Mean	**0.97s**	**31**	**4.0**	**97%**	**6.7**
2s	STEP	1.88s	62	2.5	99%	5.6
	RAMP	1.81s	49	3.4	97%	7.8
	TRI	1.83s	54	2.6	98%	16.3
	Mean	**1.84s**	**55**	**2.8**	**98%**	**9.9**

Table 2: Convergence rates under different workload

Workload	START	UP	DOWN	Mean
STEP	11.0	6.5	8.6	6.2
RAMP	16.0	8.5	–	7.0
TRI	7.0	4.0	16.5	7.0
Mean	11.3	6.3	12.6	6.7

6.4.4 Comparative Analysis (RQ4). We perform two sets of experiments which involve deploying CoFReL and the baseline controller of Section 6.3 independently to control a *mean* RT target of 1s with the baseline configuration. Results in Table 3 show that using multiple agents to explore the fuzzy state space in parallel as implemented in CoFReL is more efficient than using only one single agent as in the case of the baseline. CoFReL meets the performance requirement with only 4 CPU which is much lower than capacity allocated by the baseline controller. While the baseline controller never converges, CoFReL converges after 6.7 epochs on average.

Table 3: Performance comparison with a baseline controller

	Achieved QoS	AIAE	Allocation	Efficiency	Adaptivity
Baseline	0.21s	127	23	50%	NA
CoFReL	0.97s	31	4.0	97%	6.7

6.4.5 Sensitivity Analysis (RQ5). Controller behaviour can be influenced in various ways such as by varying parameter settings. Also, disturbances from the service execution context, such as the influence of noisy tenants, can impact capacity allocations. Hence, we staged two sets of experiments to characterize these effects.

The first set of experiments involves systematically varying the value of each learning parameters while keeping others constant. Table 4 summarizes results from all experiments where the emboldened columns correspond to baseline parameter settings. For example, to obtain the results of varying the learning rate (α), we set the action selection strategy (ϵ) and discounting rate (γ) to 0.1 and 0.5 respectively. The same methodology applied to the other

two parameters. All experiments were performed with a target average RT of 1s under the STEP workload.

The baseline configuration offers the best control performance in terms of meeting the target (1.01s) by efficiently utilizing (97%) the least amount of capacity allocations (3.5 CPUs) while offering the fastest adaptation rate (6.2 epochs) in most cases. Varying the learning rate does not seem to affect capacity allocations, resource efficiency, and controller adaptivity as much as the achieved QoS. The controller violates performance requirement and shows poor adaptivity when $\alpha = 0.5$ with only 6% of allocated capacity unused. Increasing the probability of random action selection seems to over-provision in order to maintain performance stability except when $\epsilon = 0.5$. The controller is only able to meet QoS requirement when there is a balance between future and immediate rewards (i.e. $\gamma = 0.5$), otherwise it introduces oscillations that inhibits convergence to the tolerance region.

Lastly, we examine the effect of resource interference on capacity allocations by emulating a situation where the controlled service is colocated with another VM hosting a compute intensive service. A compute contention event is injected after the first 7 minutes of the experiment lasting for roughly 10 minutes by using the stress[7] utility to spawn a set of workers spinning on sqrt(). The experiment is performed with an average RT target of 1s under the TRI workload while using the baseline learning parameter settings. Fig. 5 is the resulting time series plot of observed service RT, capacity allocation and utilization. This plot is complementary

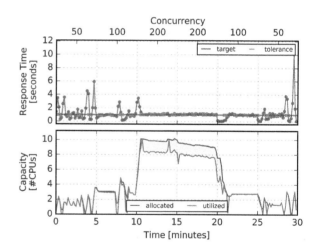

Figure 5: Impact of resource contention

to Fig. 4f, an instance of the same experiment where there is no contention. The impact of the event is immediate, causing undesirable variation at the start of the event. The immediate impact of the contention event is the observed anomalous variation in performance as well as capacity allocation and utilization around the 7th minute mark. The event also causes CoFReL to over-provision compute capacity in order to meet performance requirement. The obtained control performance is summarized in Table 5. Notice that

[7]https://people.seas.harvard.edu/~apw/stress/

Table 4: Effects of varying learning parameters

	Action Selection Strategy (ϵ)					Learning Rate (α)					Discounting Rate (γ)				
	0.1	0.3	0.5	0.7	0.9	**0.1**	0.3	0.5	0.7	0.9	0.1	0.3	**0.5**	0.7	0.9
Achieved QoS	**1.01s**	0.91s	0.85s	0.93s	0.90s	**1.01s**	1.10s	1.26s	1.04s	1.16s	1.11s	1.56s	**1.01s**	1.34s	1.41s
AIAE	**37**	70.0	50.0	44.0	51.0	**37**	56.0	101.0	55.0	63.0	69.0	154.0	**37**	128.0	133.0
Allocation	**3.5**	8.0	6.2	6.1	6.1	**3.5**	3.5	3.5	3.6	3.5	3.8	3.7	**3.5**	3.8	3.8
Efficiency	**97%**	84%	92%	94%	94%	**97%**	96%	94%	95%	94%	94%	93%	**97%**	93%	90%
Adaptivity	**6.2**	8.3	10.4	13.4	27	**6.2**	6.7	8.3	5.3	3.9	10.6	10.8	**6.2**	8.1	11.2

there is a high performance variation under the colocated scenario leading to performance violations. Aggregate resource efficiency is also hindered by the resource contention. Considering Fig. 4f, the unused capacity between the 10th and 20th time period has two indications; over-provisioning–because more capacity are allocated for the same workload level of 200 users as in Fig. 4f, approximately 6.5 CPUs compared to about 9 CPUs, and capacity deprivation– since the VM is only able to use about 8 CPUs of that perhaps due to stolen CPU cycles by the antagonist tenant.

Table 5: Control performance under difference execution contexts

Context	Achieved QoS	AIAE	Allocation	Efficiency	Adaptivity
Isolated	0.91s	36	3.7	97%	7
Colocated	1.17s	76	4.7	86%	11

7 RELATED WORK

There is a large body of research contributions addressing the autoscaling of distributed and/or virtualized services [17, 19]. In this section, we classify the most relevant works into three categories namely ruled-based, model-driven and model-free approaches.

Rule-based approaches employ the use of threshold-based rules to specify autoscaling policies that determine when and how much to scale. For instance, Chieu et al [4] provision additional VM instances when the scaling indicators (e.g. CPU utilization) of all indicators are above a certain threshold and turn off idle instances otherwise. A similar approach is employed in [10] to scale up the number of VM instances when CPU utilization is high. Hasan et al [9] developed sophisticated threshold strategies based on correlation between resources to achieve integrated autoscaling. More sophisticated rule-based controllers such as RobustT2Scale [11] rely on fuzzy rules for horizontal scaling. Such fuzzy rules have also been applied in [6] to coordinate the scaling decision of both a CPU and memory controllers. Rules, however, rely on detail knowledge of services or workloads while associated thresholds may easily become obsoletes. Though the design of the proposed approach involves the use of fuzzy rules, this is only used for state recognition and not for learning optimal control actions.

Model-based approaches rely on different types of models of services and workloads to allocate resources correctly. Such models typically capture the propagation of transactions across distributed components or estimate the relationship between workload and performance or resource consumption. Queueing theory is very

popular in the design of controllers. The horizontal scaling mechanism in [23] estimates capacity demands of multi-tier web applications using queueing networks with a different model for each time-scale. A queueing based analytical model is presented in [1] for horizontal scaling but evaluated in a simulated environment. To meet performance requirement, Lakew et al [15] introduced a fine-grained vertical scaling technique based on the inverse relationship between service latency and allocated capacity. A layered approach for vertical scaling is presented in [21] which uses both a queueing-theoretic model and a feedback controller. The goal is to meet SLA requirements via fine-grained vertical autoscaling. ApRM, a hierarchical control mechanism is introduced in [18]. The technique used a feedback controller to adjusts capacity allocations for each application and a cluster-wide controller to account for potential contentions within a pool of application. Wahajat et al [25] presents MLScale, a technique for preventing SLA violations via blackbox horizontal scaling. MLScale builds a performance model capturing the relationship between SLA violation and low level resource metrics using neural networks and statistical regression. Similarly, Rameshan et al [20] used a binary SVM classifier to capture the relationship between resource consumption and state of SLO compliance. The main objective is to investigate impact of resource interference on controller behaviour and finding a means to factor in such interference. Unlike most of the aforementioned techniques, the proposed technique is easily amenable to varying workload, objectives and scaling scenario (e.g. tail or mean targets, scale-up or scale-down) since it does not require precise service models. *Model-free* approaches typically apply reinforcement learning (RL) algorithms for autonomously learning optimal autoscaling policies. Dutreilh et al [5] employed a single decision agent to learn the number of VMs to be allocated via Q-learning. However, the state representation requires knowledge of service workloads. A RL-based mechanism is introduced in [16] to achieve distributed resource provisioning and placement in cloud environments. Distribution is achieved via explicit knowledge sharing where controllers publish their Q-values to peers in the network. The design of FQL4KE [12] is similar to our proposed mechanism in that the goal is towards achieving QoS control using fuzzy Q-learning. However, the difference is that while FQL4KE focused on horizontal scaling, CoFReL instead deals with the vertical scaling problem. In addition, unlike CoFReL, FQL4KE's state representation requires knowledge of service workloads while the system can only assume a single state. Finally, FQL4KE involves a single learning agent to adapt its fixed set of control rules. Kontarinis et al [13] formulated horizontal scaling as an MDP problem and applied Q-learning to learn optimal scaling policies. However, it is not suitable under dynamic workloads as states are formulated as a function of workload and capacity allocation. The closest technique to the proposed mechanism is Auto-scale [24], an RL-based technique for adaptive QoS control via vertical scaling using Neuro-Fuzzy function approximations. However, the focus is only on meeting performance target without regards for efficiency. Besides relying on workload behaviour in its state representation, the convergence rate of the controller was not investigated. CoFReL is designed to strike a balance between meeting desired performance SLA and resource efficiency without explicit service or workload model. The technique strives for fast online adaptation by using multiple RL agents to explore the state space in parallel. Also, the fuzzy state formulation not only aids adaptation, it also enhances the effect of actions via fine-grained actuations.

8 CONCLUSION

Dynamic resource provisioning towards meeting end-user performance SLA while ensuring efficient utilization of allocated capacity remains a challenge in virtualized environments. While most commercial solutions rely on thresholding rules that adapt poorly with workloads researchers have investigated sophisticated models that are often too cumbersome to adapt to different scaling scenarios and sometimes require knowledge of service or workload characteristics. In this paper, we present a generic approach for adaptive performance control in virtualized environments using cooperative fuzzy reinforcement learning. In particular, we focus on minimizing the long training and adaptation time that inhibit applicability of RL techniques by formulating the state space as a two-dimensional fuzzy space and deploying multiple goal-seeking agents to explore the state space while actively sharing their experience. Using a real experimental testbed and application benchmark, we evaluated the efficacy of proposed mechanism in meeting performance SLA targets under varying conditions as well as assessing the impact of resource interference on its behaviour. Future work will focus on comparison with a variety of model-based techniques, integrate both vertical and horizontal scaling, and addressing interference-aware autoscaling.

ACKNOWLEDGMENT

This work is supported by the Swedish Research Council (VR) under contract C0590801 for the Cloud Control project and the Swedish Strategic Research Program (eSSENCE).

REFERENCES

[1] Ahmed Ali-Eldin, Johan Tordsson, and Erik Elmroth. 2012. An Adaptive Hybrid Elasticity Controller for Cloud Infrastructures. In *Network Operations and Management Symposium (NOMS), 2012 IEEE*. IEEE, 204–212.
[2] Ying Bai and Dali Wang. 2006. Fundamentals of Fuzzy Logic Control–Fuzzy Sets, Fuzzy Rules and Defuzzifications. In *Advanced Fuzzy Logic Technologies in Industrial Applications*. Springer, 17–36.
[3] Paul Barham, Boris Dragovic, Keir Fraser, Steven Hand, Tim Harris, Alex Ho, Rolf Neugebauer, Ian Pratt, and Andrew Warfield. 2003. Xen and the Art of Virtualization. *ACM SIGOPS Operating Systems Review* 37, 5 (2003), 164–177.
[4] Trieu C Chieu, Ajay Mohindra, and Alexei A Karve. 2011. Scalability and Performance of Web Applications in a Compute Cloud. In *8th International Conference on e-Business Engineering (ICEBE)*. IEEE, 317–323.
[5] Xavier Dutreilh, Sergey Kirgizov, Olga Melekhova, Jacques Malenfant, Nicolas Rivierre, and Isis Truck. 2011. Using Reinforcement Learning for Autonomic Resource Allocation in Clouds: Towards a Fully Automated Workflow. In *ICAS 2011, The Seventh International Conference on Autonomic and Autonomous Systems*. 67–74.
[6] Soodeh Farokhi, Ewnetu Bayuh Lakew, Cristian Klein, Ivona Brandic, and Erik Elmroth. 2015. Coordinating CPU and Memory Elasticity Controllers to Meet Service Response Time Constraints. In *International Conference on Cloud and Autonomic Computing (ICCAC)*. IEEE, 69–80.
[7] Anshul Gandhi, Parijat Dube, Alexei Karve, Andrzej Kochut, and Li Zhang. 2014. Adaptive, Model-driven Autoscaling for Cloud Applications.. In *ICAC*, Vol. 14. 57–64.
[8] Anshul Gandhi, Mor Harchol-Balter, Ram Raghunathan, and Michael A Kozuch. 2012. Autoscale: Dynamic, Robust Capacity Management for Multi-tier Data Centers. *ACM Transactions on Computer Systems (TOCS)* 30, 4 (2012), 14.
[9] Masum Z Hasan, Edgar Magana, Alexander Clemm, Lew Tucker, and Sree Lakshmi D Gudreddi. 2012. Integrated and Autonomic Cloud Resource Scaling. In *Network Operations and Management Symposium (NOMS), 2012*. IEEE, 1327–1334.
[10] Waheed Iqbal, Matthew N Dailey, David Carrera, and Paul Janecek. 2011. Adaptive Resource Provisioning for Read Intensive Multi-tier Applications in the Cloud. *Future Generation Computer Systems* 27, 6 (2011), 871–879.
[11] Pooyan Jamshidi, Aakash Ahmad, and Claus Pahl. 2014. Autonomic Resource Provisioning for Cloud-based Software. In *Proceedings of the 9th International Symposium on Software Engineering for Adaptive and Self-Managing Systems*. ACM, 95–104.
[12] Pooyan Jamshidi, Amir Sharifloo, Claus Pahl, Hamid Arabnejad, Andreas Metzger, and Giovani Estrada. 2016. Fuzzy Self-learning Controllers for Elasticity Management in Dynamic Cloud Architectures. In *12th International ACM SIGSOFT Conference on Quality of Software Architectures (QoSA), 2016*. IEEE, 70–79.
[13] Alexandros Kontarinis, Verena Kantere, and Nectarios Koziris. 2016. Cloud Resource Allocation from the User Perspective: A Bare-Bones Reinforcement Learning Approach. In *International Conference on Web Information Systems Engineering*. Springer, 457–469.
[14] L. I. Kuncheva. 2008. Fuzzy Classifiers. *Scholarpedia* 3, 1 (2008), 2925. Revision 133818.
[15] Ewnetu Bayuh Lakew, Cristian Klein, Francisco Hernandez-Rodriguez, and Erik Elmroth. 2014. Towards Faster Response Time Models for Vertical Elasticity. In *Proceedings of the 2014 IEEE/ACM 7th International Conference on Utility and Cloud Computing*. IEEE Computer Society, 560–565.
[16] Han Li and Srikumar Venugopal. 2011. Using Reinforcement Learning for Controlling an Elastic Web Application Hosting Platform. In *Proceedings of the 8th ACM international Conference on Autonomic Computing*. ACM, 205–208.
[17] Tania Lorido-Botran, Jose Miguel-Alonso, and Jose Antonio Lozano. 2014. A Review of Auto-scaling Techniques for Elastic Applications in Cloud Environments. *J. Grid Comput.* 12, 4 (2014), 559–592.
[18] Lei Lu, Xiaoyun Zhu, Rean Griffith, Pradeep Padala, Aashish Parikh, Parth Shah, and Evgenia Smirni. 2014. Application-driven Dynamic Vertical Scaling of Virtual Machines in Resource Pools. In *Network Operations and Management Symposium (NOMS), 2014 IEEE*. IEEE, 1–9.
[19] Chenhao Qu, Rodrigo N Calheiros, and Rajkumar Buyya. 2016. Auto-scaling Web Applications in Clouds: a Taxonomy and Survey. *arXiv preprint arXiv:1609.09224* (2016).
[20] Navaneeth Rameshan, Ying Liu, Leandro Navarro, and Vladimir Vlassov. 2016. Elastic Scaling in the Cloud: A Multi-Tenant Perspective. In *IEEE 36th International Conference on Distributed Computing Systems Workshops (ICDCSW), 2016*. IEEE, 25–30.
[21] Simon Spinner, Samuel Kounev, Xiaoyun Zhu, Lei Lu, Mustafa Uysal, Anne Holler, and Rean Griffith. 2014. Runtime Vertical Scaling of Virtualized Applications via Online Model Estimation. In *IEEE Eighth International Conference on Self-Adaptive and Self-Organizing Systems (SASO)*. IEEE, 157–166.
[22] Richard S Sutton and Andrew G Barto. 1998. *Reinforcement learning: An Introduction*. Vol. 1. MIT press Cambridge.
[23] Bhuvan Urgaonkar, Prashant Shenoy, Abhishek Chandra, Pawan Goyal, and Timothy Wood. 2008. Agile Dynamic Provisioning of Multi-tier Internet Applications. *ACM Transactions on Autonomous and Adaptive Systems (TAAS)* 3, 1 (2008), 1.
[24] T Veni and S Mary Saira Bhanu. 2016. Auto-scale: Automatic Scaling of Virtualised Resources Using Neuro-Fuzzy Reinforcement Learning Approach. *International Journal of Big Data Intelligence* 3, 3 (2016), 145–153.
[25] Muhammad Wajahat, Anshul Gandhi, Alexei Karve, and Andrzej Kochut. 2016. Using Machine Learning for Black-box Autoscaling. In *Seventh International Conference on Green and Sustainable Computing Conference (IGSC0)*. IEEE, 1–8.

Dynamic Network Scheduler
for Cloud Data Centres with SDN

Christopher B. Hauser
Institute of Information
Resource Management
University of Ulm
Germany
christopher.hauser@uni-ulm.de

Santhosh Ramapuram Palanivel
Institute of Information
Resource Management
University of Ulm
Germany
ramapurampalanivel@gmail.com

ABSTRACT

The presented dynamic network scheduler improves the fairness and efficiency of network utilization in a Cloud data centre. The proposed design utilizes a directed graph which represents the network comprising routers, switches, physical hypervisors, and virtual machines (VMs) as graph nodes, and represents the physical network connections as weighted edges. The edges have a guaranteed transmission rate derived from the number of devices sharing an outgoing link with a defined bandwidth. Moreover, to maximize utilization of the resources, each node gets a deserved rate dynamically depending on the measured utilization metrics. A VM throttles up or down its traffic up to its deserved rate. The conceptual design of a dynamic network scheduler is further prototypically implemented and evaluated. The implementation uses Software Defined Networking (SDN) with OpenFlow, Ryu SDN controller, and Open vSwitch as software switch on the hypervisor level. The presented dynamic network scheduler uses OpenFlow for monitoring and applying flows to control the link bandwidth. The evaluation shows that the dynamic network scheduler maximizes fairness in resource sharing while minimizing the unutilized resources.

KEYWORDS

Cloud Computing; Network Scheduling; Software Defined Networking; Data Centre Network

1 INTRODUCTION

One of the essential characteristics of Cloud computing according to the NIST definition[10] is resource pooling, which allows to dynamically allocate the virtual resources such as virtual machines (VMs) when needed. The dynamic resource allocation is powered by sharing the physical resources in a data centre among multiple customers. Another significant characteristic is broad network access, which describes the extensive availability of network bandwidth. Inside a Cloud computing data centre, the physical infrastructure

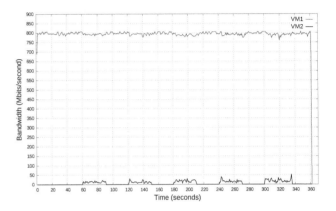

Figure 1: Unfair, best effort network bandwidth sharing

such as CPU, memory, network, or storage is shared as virtual resources among VMs. The network resources in a data centre are offered by a hierarchical set of multiple distributed physical devices, where it is harder to gain control over the bandwidth, e.g. compared to local and rather slowly changing memory allocation.

In our work, we assume an Infrastructure-as-a-Service (IaaS)[10] Cloud with full control over the physical infrastructure, and unknown black box VMs of competing customers. Since the VMs are, from the network perspective, randomly placed in a data centre cluster by the IaaS Cloud scheduler, the resulting network traffic pattern is certainly unpredictable. Without having any network bandwidth scheduling or limitation policies, one VM from customer A can influence the resource utilization of another VM from customer B, while sharing a common network link. Figure 1 shows that VM1 has the throughput measured at 800 Mbit/s while sending continuous data to a shared network link, whereas VM2 has a rate of approx. 25 Mbit/s while sending periodic data to the same link. In this simple artificial experiment, we simulated the Cloud data centre using a Linux server, which hosts two VMs (VM1 and VM2) with KVM as a hypervisor and Open vSwitch as a software switch. The server had a physical network link with a theoretical total capacity of 1 Gbit/s (cf. section 7). The network load requested by VM2 is up to 150 Mbit/s, while the shared network link is unfairly dominated by traffic from VM1.

In a Cloud data centre, e.g. controlled by software like OpenStack, the bandwidth distribution between virtual resources and customers takes place either based on best effort approaches or by limiting the maximum bandwidth per VM or per customer (cf.

section 4). Statically limiting the bandwidth is a popular approach, since it requires only a local and stateless configuration close to the VMs, which is relatively simple to implement. Yet, on one hand, the best effort approach does not guarantee a specified throughput, while on the other hand, limiting the bandwidth can lead to inefficient utilization of available resources. In this paper, we present a *Dynamic Network Scheduler for Cloud Data Centres*. We assume that all the available network devices have an interface to query statistics and to set network flow actions to control the network utilisation for each network device like VMs on the physical data link layer. With these two powerful functionalities at hand, a global view of the data centre network capacity and traffic pattern can be captured to schedule the resources in a fair and an optimal manner to the customers. Due to the increased adoption of SDN in modern data centres, the dynamic network scheduler uses the OpenFlow protocol, which is supported by many switches. The OpenFlow protocol allows to query statistics from both hardware and software switches in a Cloud data centre, and offers to define switching rules.

This paper is structured as follows. Section 2 will first clarify the problem statement in addition to the motivation given in this introduction. To provide sufficient background on used software and technology, we introduce SDN, OpenFlow, Open vSwitch, and the hierarchical token bucket scheduler in section 3. The related work is presented in section 4. The paper's contribution is described conceptually with our design approach in section 5, and then, we present our prototypical implementation in section 6. The evaluation of the prototype in section 7 shows how the proposed dynamic network scheduler improves fairness in resource allocation, immunity to unexpected network loads, and the efficiency in overall network utilization. The paper concludes finally in section 8.

2 PROBLEM STATEMENT

The problem statement will first clarify the assumptions we have to develop a dynamic network scheduler. The most important assumption is regarding the scope of the network scheduler, which is only within a Cloud data centre with full control of its physical resources. This work deals with physical servers, VMs, and virtualization provided by hypervisors. Moreover, we consider a physical server farm with a Linux-based operating system and black-box VMs which are placed on any of the physical servers by the scheduling algorithm of the Cloud middleware. The physical servers, hosting the hypervisor and hence the VMs, have a software switch with OpenFlow support to share its physical network and provide virtual networks to the customers. We also assume an architecture in which multiple physical servers are located in a rack, where a top-of-rack (ToR) switch provides an uplink network for all the servers in the rack, which may have a larger bandwidth towards the outside than towards the servers inside. This setup hence defines a tree-based network topology (cf. figure 2): a data centre cluster has one outbound switch, which is connected to multiple ToR switches, which in turn is connected to physical servers in a rack. The physical network in the server level are then further extended by the software switch inside a server, which provides network access to available VMs. Other tree-based topologies than ToR are similarly supported. It is note worthy, that Cloud data centres usually overbook their physical

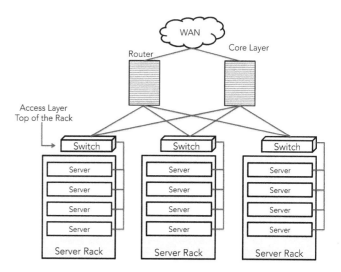

Figure 2: Cloud data centre setup

resources. Guided by the assumption that customers often don't utilize their virtual resources fully, the physical resource capacity is offered multiple times as "the same" virtual resource to different customers [12]. For overbooking the network resources, at least a fair share of physical resources to demanding customers must be guaranteed.

With the introduced data centre topology in mind, the communication and the network load of VMs can be manifold. When VMs within a data centre communicate with each other, the resulting network traffic stays inside the data centre cluster, or may stay even inside the rack, or on the same physical server. Since typical Cloud middleware schedulers like the OpenStack Nova Scheduler[4] do not consider communication patterns when placing VMs on the physical servers, the resulting network traffic for inter-VM communication is arbitrary and random. On the other hand, communication from VMs to the outside world and back will always use a central outbound link of the data centre.

An example for the problem statement addressed by the dynamic network scheduler is shown in figure 1. In principle, VM2 is expected to transmit its data at 50 Mbit/s in the first and last peak, at 100 Mbit/s in the second and fourth peak, and at 150 Mbit/s in the third peak. However, the achieved throughput is far lesser from expected. It is, nevertheless, reasonable as VM1 uses UDP and VM2 uses TCP as their transport protocols. The congestion control of the TCP, which eventually should help to achieve equality in sharing bandwidth, has surrendered to the dominating UDP traffic, thus resulting in unfairness in sharing the resources. This behaviour in resource sharing is not suitable for hosting network sensitive services on the virtualized servers. Even when all the VMs generate only TCP traffic, from a Cloud provider's perspective, the network bandwidth sharing should be under the control of the Cloud provider. As the TCP/UDP traffic is generated by the customers' applications, the provider cannot rely on the congestion control mechanisms of the transport layer. Moreover, having black box VMs also means to have no control over the customers network layer and above.

Since IaaS also provides virtual networking, the Cloud data centres use overlay networks to enable virtual private networks for customers on top of the physical network infrastructure. These virtualized networks may use VLAN tagging or encapsulation techniques like GRE or VXLAN. To be flexible and to not harm the black box restriction, a network traffic control should be applied at the physical level, which is under the Cloud provider's control. We, therefore, assume that the network traffic is controlled on the *Ethernet layer* in the following.

Concluding the problem statement, the presented work in upcoming sections addresses a hierarchically organized network architecture in a Cloud data centre with multiple customers sharing the physical network. The research questions a dynamic network scheduler has to answer are as follows:

(1) How to read statistics from which devices to detect unfair or unutilized bandwidth sharing with multiple VMs?

(2) How is a fair share achievable in a hierarchical network architecture, with OpenFlow and the network statistics as the basis?

(3) Can a centralized dynamic network scheduler guarantee a fair share of network resources for VMs without affecting the total utilization of the network bandwidth?

3 BACKGROUND

The dynamic network scheduler for Cloud data centres, presented in this paper, is built on the Software Defined Networking (SDN) technology with the OpenFlow protocol, Ryu Controller and Open vSwitch. The Ryu controller acts as the SDN controller whereas the Open vSwitch works as the software switch on physical servers. Further, we make use of the Hierarchical Token Bucket Scheduler, which is part of the Linux kernel to schedule network packets.

3.1 Software Defined Networking & OpenFlow

Traditional networks are comparably statically administrated and do not effectively support dynamic needs in modern computing environments such as Cloud data centres. To overcome this problem, programmable networks with programmable routers and switches have evolved as a new network architecture for distributed networks[9]. In a traditional router or switch, the packet forwarding and the high-level routing decisions take place on the same device. In contrast, in a programmable Software Defined Network (SDN), the control plane which makes routing and switching decisions is decoupled from the data plane that does packet forwarding. A remote controller acts as the control plane for the device and installs the forwarding decisions in the data plane. The remote controller, also referred as SDN controller, is a software platform that provides essential resources and abstractions to facilitate the programming of forwarding devices. The controller can be either centralized to the whole network or be distributed across the network.

The network between controllers and forwarding devices is built on top of open and standard interfaces such as OpenFlow. OpenFlow is an open source API that provides a standard interface to program and query a switch or router from the SDN controller. OpenFlow ensures interoperability in configuration and communication between a variety of proprietary data plane and control plane devices. There are multiple open source OpenFlow controllers available in the market such as NOX/POX, Ryu, Floodlight, OpenDayLight and more.

3.2 Open vSwitch

The fast-growing virtualized deployment environments in data centres impose requirements on networking infrastructure where traditional networking models have shown limitations. In a virtualized environment, with multiple VMs hosted on a single server, a virtual switch enables network virtualization with in-host switching. Open vSwitch is one such open source virtual switch implemented by software that provides network connectivity for VMs hosted on a server. It can run on a hypervisor as a software switch and also as the control stack for dedicated switching hardware.

In a typical virtualized environment, a hypervisor should bridge the traffic between multiple VMs hosted on it and the physical network interface of the server. On Linux based hypervisors, Linux bridge provides this feature with good performance and reliability, but it lacks support for multi-server virtualized deployments and OpenFlow. Open vSwitch on the other hand, along with these functions, provides a broad range of features such as visibility into inter-VM communication via NetFlow or sFlow, Link Aggregation Control Protocol (LACP) support, multicast snooping, per VM interface traffic policing, kernel and user-space forwarding engine options amongst others[1].

3.3 Hierarchical Token Bucket Scheduler

A network scheduler (or a network packet scheduler) in Linux is a resource management program that manages the flow of packets in a Network Interface Controller (NIC). The packets arriving from different flows are temporarily queued in a buffer until they are transmitted. The buffer can have multiple queues, with each queue holding the packets from a particular flow, for example, packets with two different destination IP addresses can be stored in two separate queues. The network scheduler decides which packet has to be transmitted from the list of multiple queues. Network schedulers attempt to manage the resources either by dropping the packets that arrive beyond the buffer limits or by reordering the packets that are already present in the buffer for reducing the latency for Quality of Service (QoS) measures[11].

Network scheduling algorithms (or queueing disciplines) have been developed over a period where each algorithm has its unique way of reordering or dropping of network packets from its buffers. Some of the notable queueing disciplines (qdisc) that were implemented in Linux kernel modules over time are Token Bucket Filter (TBF), First In First Out (FIFO), Hierarchical Token Bucket (HTB), and Hierarchical Fair Service Curve (HFSC).

The HTB scheduler, utilized in the dynamic network scheduler, uses a hierarchical approach that is well suited for setups where there is a fixed amount of bandwidth which has to be divided for different purposes. It is a class based algorithm where multiple classes are created for different requirements. Each such class is assigned a queue. A queue has different characteristics such as minimum guaranteed rate, maximum allowed rate, burst rate, and priority. The packets from different services are directed to one of these queues using packet filtering techniques. After the packets are directed to the queues, the HTB scheduling algorithm decides on the next packet to be transmitted from these queues. The HTB scheduler guarantees minimum rate for each of these queues while maximizing total utilization of available bandwidth[8].

4 RELATED WORK

The related work for the problem statement in section 2 is either a) limiting the resources to $\frac{1}{n}$th of the total available bandwidth with n VMs, and adjusting or planning the physical infrastructure accordingly, or b) controlling the resources by applying limitations on a single server instead of a multi server data centre, leading to a fair share of the network bandwidth among VMs on a single hypervisor only.

In the recent years, there has been an increasing interest in providing bandwidth guarantees for customers with time-sensitive applications in IaaS Clouds. The work by Gaetano F. Anastasi et al. in [2] to provide QoS guarantees for network bandwidth in private Clouds leverages the Linux Traffic Control (TC) techniques and Service Level Agreements (SLA). Another method which uses an SDN controller and Open vSwitch to allocate the available bandwidth based on a VM's priority is presented in [5]. Both of these work are a static allocation of network resources using the QoS feature provided by the Hierarchical Token Bucket (HTB) scheduling technique in Linux with a min-max approach. The techniques presented in their work focuses on QoS guarantee only for VMs hosted on the same server. Besides TC and HTB, cgroups can be used manually to limit bandwidth locally within a Linux-based server.

The authors of [6] proposed an OpenFlow-assisted Quality of Experience (QoE) Fairness Framework (QFF) that aims to fairly improve the QoE of multiple competing clients in a network environment for video streaming applications. By leveraging the Software Defined Networking using OpenFlow, the authors provide a control plane that orchestrates this functionality. QFF guarantees QoS in the network to provide users suitable and more stable bandwidth. However, their work only considers effects on the video application with TCP traffic, while our work dynamically schedules the network resources for VMs hosted on multiple servers.

The authors of [14] evaluate the impact of dynamic resource allocation on a per-flow basis for an access network with two applications competing for limited network resources. They show the potential to increase the QoE of the involved applications and highlight possible side-effects affecting the end-to-end performance. The authors emphasize that the impact of dynamic resource allocation has to be analyzed and well understood before it can be applied in an SDN environment. VMPatrol presented in [7] employs a framework that creates queues in each of the servers in a data centre network to provide QoS requirements for VM migration. VMPatrol decreases the adverse impact of VM migrations on other network flows using its QoS mechanisms. Raphael Durner et al. in [3] have studied the performance of dynamic QoS Management for OpenFlow-enabled SDN switches. Their measurement results show a noticeable diversity for different OpenFlow switches in the performance of QoS management.

More complex approaches monitor the resource consumption of VMs to compile behaviour models, which in turn are used to simulate and optimise the overall data centre utilisation [13]. Since our approach is to enable a lightweight network scheduling at run

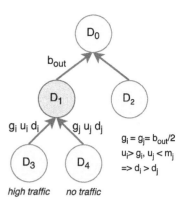

Figure 3: Data Centre Network as Directed Graph

time, building complex statistical models is out of scope for this work, but will be considered for future work.

5 DESIGNING A DYNAMIC NETWORK SCHEDULER

Controlling the traffic originating from the outside towards a Cloud data centre is comparably challenging since the sender is not under the control of the Cloud provider. In contrast, by monitoring the network traffic statistics per network port, controlling outgoing traffic originating from the VMs in a Cloud data centre is possible by limiting the bandwidth for each VM at runtime. The bandwidth limitations help to prevent network congestion and unfair bandwidth utilization.

With a global idea of the recent traffic in the data centre network, a dynamic network scheduler can make decisions and enforce limitations at the source of the traffic generators: the senders, which are the VMs.

5.1 Conceptual Considerations

We assume a tree based network structure (cf. section 2) and consider the controllable outgoing network traffic of a Cloud data centre. This setup can be represented as a directed graph G, where nodes are network devices D and the directed edges E are network paths between them (cf. figure 3). A network device can be a router, a (software) switch, a physical server or a VM. VMs are represented as leaf nodes, without incoming edges (or D_i with $deg_G^-(D_i) = 0$), and the outside network is represented as root node, without an outgoing edge (or D_0 with $deg_G^+(D_0) = 0$). Besides the root and leaf nodes, the network devices D can have zero or more incoming edges ($deg_G^-(D_i) > 0 \ \forall \ D_i \neq leaf \ node$), and exactly one outgoing edge ($deg_G^+(D) = 1 \ \forall \ D \neq D_0$). From the leaf nodes towards the root, the outgoing traffic of incoming edges share commonly used outgoing edges. Looking at a single network device, all incoming edges share one outgoing edge. For multipath setups where two or more links are bound together to improve bandwidth capacities, we consider the bunch of links as one edge with the capacities summed up.

Each edge in this directed graph has multiple weights, or properties: the *bandwidth* b_i capacity limited by e.g. hardware resources, and the monitored current bandwidth *utilization* u_i of the link with $u_i <= b_i$. Considering a single network device in a fair share setup, one outgoing edge with bandwidth b_{out} has to be shared among n incoming edges, leading to the *guaranteed* utilization g_i for each incoming edge as an equal share of outgoing bandwidth $g_i = \frac{1}{n} \cdot b_{out}$. However, with this approach, the total outgoing bandwidth will not be utilized efficiently if one of the incoming edges is not utilizing its guaranteed rate while another would need more bandwidth (e.g. example in figure 3).

To solve this shortcoming, we introduce two more edge properties: the *deserved* rate d_i and the *minimum* rate m_i. Both edge properties on incoming edges represent the incoming edge's share on the outgoing edge. The minimum rate is a static or percentual value to always reserve a minimum amount of bandwidth for an incoming edge on the outgoing edge's bandwidth. The deserved rate with $m_i <= d_i < b_{out}$ changes dynamically, depending on the utilization values u_i of all other incoming edges. If all the incoming edges are fully utilizing the outgoing edge, the deserved rates are equal to the guaranteed rates. If an incoming edge is not demanding any bandwidth of b_{out}, the deserved rate will go down to m_i to lend its unused bandwidth on the outgoing edge temporarily to other incoming edges. Yet, the sum of all deserved rates cannot exceed the bandwidth of the outgoing edge, minus the minimum rates for each incoming edge: $\sum_i d_i <= b_{out} - \sum_j m_j$.

The guaranteed rate $g_i = \frac{1}{n} \cdot b_{out}$ changes when *i)* the amount of incoming edges changes (e.g. by adding more physical or VMs) and hence n changes, or *ii)* when the outgoing bandwidth changes (e.g. when the deserved rate for the outgoing edge changes from a higher level device). Since the minimum rate may relate to the guaranteed rate, it has to be recalculated. The deserved rate depends on the actual utilization and can go up to b_{out}, hence has to be recalculated when b_{out} changes to avoid overbooking like $\sum_i d_i > b_{out} - \sum_j m_j$. A change in utilization impacts the deserved rates, and influences the attached child nodes in the graph, downwards to the leaf nodes where bandwidth limitations are applied.

A node with edge $u_i < d_i$ is defined as the *donor port* and it can donate its guaranteed bandwidth temporarily to a *receiver port*. A *receiver port* is a node which requires additional bandwidth (a higher deserved rate). For the donor port, the deserved rate should be immediately its guaranteed rate when needed, to not decrease the performance. The receiver port has at least the guaranteed rate, but may have more bandwidth than its guaranteed rate for an undefined time until the donor port seeks its resources back. With this concept of donor/receiver port and the deserved rate, the available bandwidth can be fully utilized optimally, while the fair share is still guaranteed for all devices at any time.

5.2 Integration in Cloud Data Centres

The directed graph with the edge weights bandwidth, deserved rate, guaranteed rate, minimum rate and utilization has to be compiled out of monitoring data in a Cloud data centre. Further, the deserved rate has to be computed dynamically at runtime, depending on the utilization metrics. While different approaches for monitoring and resource restrictions can be considered, our approach is based on the hard- and software independent OpenFlow specifications. This SDN driven approach has the benefit of having the required global

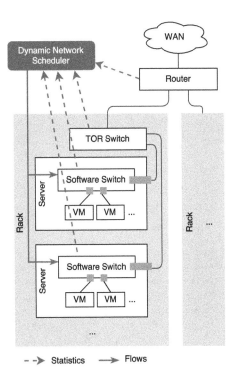

Figure 4: Dynamic Network Scheduler in a Cloud data centre

view of the data centre network as part of the conceptual basics. OpenFlow supports both the querying of network port and queue statistics to calculate used bandwidth, and the definition of flow rules to control the deserved rates.

The dynamic network scheduler for a Cloud data centre connects to all available network devices, starting with the software switches inside the physical servers, the ToR switch and all other hierarchically allocated network devices (cf. figure 4). The OpenFlow protocol is then used to collect statistics about available ports, the queue length for each port, and the traffic utilization in number of transmitted Ethernet packets and bytes.

We assign each VM a queue on the server using the software switch, where the maximum transmission rate of the queue can be modified at runtime, e.g. by configuring the HTB scheduler. A queue has to be monitored in detail to detect the necessity for a change in the deserved rate, namely when the queue length increases or the utilization is getting close to the deserved rate.

The collected statistics from all network devices are then internally analyzed and processed to feed a global network view in the form of a directed graph with weighted edges and the introduced properties into a scheduling algorithm to define an optimal resource share dynamically at runtime.

5.3 Architecture: Components & Tasks

The main tasks of the dynamic network scheduler are to query monitoring statistics and apply deserved rates in the network devices. From this requirement, we derived three main components (cf. figure 5): device manager, throughput estimator, and scheduler.

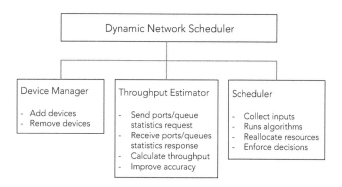

Figure 5: Dynamic Network Scheduler: Components and Tasks

The *device manager* is triggered whenever device-level changes occur in the network: when VMs are added or removed, or when compute nodes are powered on or off. The *throughput estimator* queries the connected network devices for statistics, aggregates and smooths single statistic values to compute a reliable and stable throughput value. The *scheduler* component finally is triggered with input from the device manager and the throughput estimator, to calculate the deserved rates and apply them on the network devices.

The device manager is triggered based on events. The throughput estimator runs periodically to query the network devices. The scheduler runs periodically, but gets triggered either by the device manager when a device is added or removed or by the throughput estimator when bottlenecks are detected and the scheduler has to react.

6 PROTOTYPICAL IMPLEMENTATION

The conceptually described design for a dynamic network scheduler in section 5 has been prototypically implemented and evaluated in the presented work at hand. Before the prototypical implementation can be described, we limit the previously described field of usage for the prototype. Then, we describe the used software components for the implementation and explain the implemented scheduling algorithm.

6.1 Limitations and Assumptions

To evaluate the conceptual design, the prototypical implementation reduces complexity to allow a proof of concept. We assume a data centre network with a hierarchical depth of three levels: virtual machines, software switches and one physical router as an outbound gateway. Further we assumed that the virtual machines are under control instead of inaccessible black boxes as in the real world environment. This assumption is relevant to run and control artificial network workloads for evaluations.

A technical limitation occurred at the development time: the Open vSwitch currently offers APIs only to create and delete queues; not to modify the existing queues using the OpenFlow protocol. To overcome this shortcoming in the prototype, we create queues with different network bandwidth characteristics beforehand and assign VMs dynamically at runtime to these existing queues. The technical

limitation can, however, be solved by using a REST API in Open vSwitch, which requires additional development effort and was out of focus for the prototypical implementation and evaluation to prove the functioning of our dynamic network scheduler.

For the prototypical implementation, due to restrictions from the testing hardware, a Gigabit Ethernet network is used throughout the small-scale data centre setup.

6.2 Selected Software

The prototype is implemented using the Open vSwitch as software switch with HTB for limiting the bandwidth for outgoing traffic at each VM in a fine-grained manner. The Open vSwitch supports latest versions of the OpenFlow standard, and therefore, is integrated as intended by our proposed design into the dynamic network scheduler. Further, Open vSwitch is available in a major stable version 2.7, and is continuously improved by its strong community. Deciding on Open vSwitch makes an integration in typical OpenStack Cloud data centres possible, where it is wide spread on the host hypervisor already.

From the list of OpenFlow SDN controllers available, the open source Ryu controller has gained particular attention for its extendible Python-based framework. The Ryu controller specifies well-defined application programming interfaces (APIs) on the so called north bound to create network management applications on top of Ryu, while it supports the OpenFlow protocol from version 1.0 to 1.5 on the south bound to communicate with connected network devices. The implemented dynamic network scheduler is built on top of Ryu as SDN controller, due to it's component based approach and extendibility.

Since Cloud data centres are often powered by a Linux operating system, we used the open source enterprise distribution Centos 7 in our prototype. Further we assume a KVM hypervisor, which hosts VMs with Centos 7 as guest operating system. To control and create the VMs we used the libvirt software to abstract the communication with the KVM hypervisor.

6.3 Scheduling Algorithm

While the conceptual considerations for developing a dynamic network scheduler are described in section 5, we developed a scheduling algorithm for the prototypical implementation.

The scheduler looks at five important questions iteratively while updating the deserved rate for VMs in the system. The scheduler, in each execution, iterates these questions and recalculates the deserved rate as long as there is a recipient port and a donor port. If there is no recipient port or donor port, the scheduler, using the OpenFlow protocol, updates the flow table for all the affected VMs with a queue for its corresponding (and new) deserved rate. The scheduler, then waits for a configurable update interval until the next execution. The flow diagram for the functioning of the scheduler is shown in figure 6 and described in detail in the following:

1. Is there a recipient port? For every iteration in the execution, the scheduler chooses the best possible recipient port. A recipient port is defined when the $d_i - u_i <= threshold$, namely when the measured utilization is close to the deserved rate. If more than

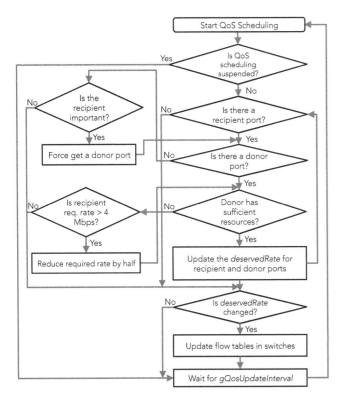

Figure 6: Dynamic Network Scheduler: Scheduling Algorithm

one recipient ports are identified, the importance of the ports is considered.

2. How important is the recipient port? A recipient port whose deserved rate is smaller than the guaranteed rate ($d_i < g_i$) is considered to be more important. Such a recipient port must get a donor port, which perhaps is over utilizing the resources. In contrast, a recipient port whose deserved rate is larger than the guaranteed rate ($d_i > g_i$) is not as important and the scheduler doesn't force a donor to donate in this case. If still more than one port is found, the one with measured utilization closer to the deserved rate ($min(d_i − u_i)\ \forall i$) is chosen.

3. How much bandwidth the recipient port needs? The additional required rate of a recipient port increases in an exponential manner every time the recipient is chosen, starting with the exponent value as four (2^4 Mbps). When the recipient cannot get its required rate from a donor, the required rate of a recipient is reduced down in an exponential manner and checks if a donor can donate the reduced amount of resources. The required rate of the recipient, however, cannot go lower than the exponent value as two (2^2 Mbps).

4. Is there a donor port? For a recipient port, the scheduler checks for a donor port. At every execution of the scheduler, a port can be chosen as a donor only once, so that a recipient port cannot drain all of the donor resources at one point of time. However, a port can be a recipient more than once in the same execution of the scheduler. Donor ports are defined as ports, which can serve parts of their bandwidth, while ports with $d_i > g_i$ are prioritised

over ports with $d_i < g_i$. If multiple donor ports are found, the one with the largest deserved rate d_i is selected.

5. How much bandwidth does the donor port has in excess? As the chosen recipient is the best possible recipient and the chosen donor is the best possible donor, if the recipient needs more bandwidth than what a donor can offer, the donor can donate only what it has in excess. If the donor has fewer resources than what the recipient needs at the least, then the scheduler exits the iteration.

When multiple ports are overusing the resources from their guaranteed rate and the scheduler has to handle an increase in deserved rate for a port with $d_i < g_i$, the scheduler equally divides the required bandwidth over multiple and forced donors.

7 EVALUATION

The dynamic network scheduler, in principle, identifies the network bandwidth requirements of individual VMs hosted on different servers in a Cloud data centre and dynamically assigns the bandwidth limitation for each VM. In doing that, it should provide *fairness* in allocating the resources among multiple VMs, and fully utilize the network capacity to improve the *efficiency* provided VMs generate sufficient traffic. The evaluation considers two and four VMs on two physical servers, and varies the traffic characteristics with TCP and UDP packets. Three different workload types are evaluated with and without the prototypical implementation of the dynamic network scheduler.

7.1 Evaluation Setup

The testing hardware for the evaluation of our implementation consists of a hardware switch with OpenFlow support, and two physical servers: Host1 and Host2 (HP Proliant Microserver Gen8) with Linux and KVM as a hypervisor. Each of these two servers hosted two VMs: VM1 and VM2 on Host1, VM3 and VM4 on Host2 respectively. The hardware switch was connected to a third server which hosted the SDN controller (in turn the dynamic network scheduler) and worked as the outbound gateway to an external network. All hardware devices were using a Gigabit Ethernet connection for networking.

Our evaluation method uses iperf3 tool to produce the artificial workload and measure the throughput achieved by the VMs. When an experiment is performed with only two VMs, the iperf3 client in VM1 and VM2 generate traffic, while the iperf3 server in VM3 and VM4 receive the traffic respectively. When the throughput behaviour is measured for four VMs, all the VMs from both the servers generate traffic using the iperf3 client, while iperf3 servers running in parallel on the third server is used to measure the throughput. Figure 7 depicts the evaluation setup.

7.2 Test Cases

The test cases are designed to elaborate on artificially generated but realistic scenarios. Since TCP with its congestion control falsifies the results for the bandwidth control, the test cases often use UDP as the transport protocol. However, UDP and TCP are used in parallel in one test case to elaborate on the scenario introduced in the problem statement (sec. 2). In a real world scenario, a VM may generate adequate traffic to fully utilize the available bandwidth,

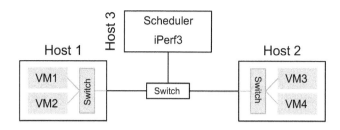

Figure 7: Evaluation Setup

Table 1: Evaluation Test Cases

	VMs	Protocols	Network Load [Mbit/s]
TC1	2	UDP	both unlimited
TC2	4	UDP	all four unlimited
TC3	2	UDP	one unltd; one 100, 200, unltd.
TC4	2	UDP/TCP	UDP unltd.; TCP 50, 100, 150

or it doesn't which leads to partial utilization. Therefore, the test cases evaluate both these scenarios.

Table 1 lists four test cases used for the evaluation. TC1 and TC2 use two and four VMs, where each VM generates as much UDP traffic as required to flood the network during the test execution. While these two test cases are meant to describe circumstances with very highly utilized network links, TC3 and TC4 describe the scenario where some VMs only partially utilize its available bandwidth. TC3 elaborates on UDP traffic only, where one VM floods traffic to fully utilize the bandwidth, and a second VM attempts to transmit data at 100 MBit/s, 200 MBit/s, or floods traffic from time to time with shorter or longer time frames. On the other hand, in TC4, while one VM floods traffic to fully utilize the bandwidth, a second VM tries to send TCP traffic at 50 MBit/s, 100 MBit/s and 150MBit/s periodically.

All four test cases were executed with and without the dynamic network scheduler. From the network throughput measured using iperf3, the results of test cases with and without the dynamic network scheduler can be compared to evaluate on its success in guaranteeing fairness while efficiently utilising available network bandwidth.

7.3 Evaluation Results

The described test cases were executed on the evaluation setup. The results are represented in figures 1, 8, 9, and 10 and are analysed for fairness and efficiency.

7.3.1 Fairness. The *TC1* is represented in figure 8a without any mechanisms for network scheduling or QoS control, while in figure 8b TC1 shows a very accurate and an equal share of network bandwidth over the two VMs. The fairness in this test case with the dynamic network scheduler is hence guaranteed, while without the scheduler a previously existing VM receives slightly more bandwidth than the newly starting VM (cf. seconds 120 to 240, and 360 to 480).

The same effect appears when changing from two VMs to four VMs in TC2, as shown in figure 8c without and in figure 8d with the dynamic network scheduler. With more VMs, the unfairness becomes even worse, like for VM3 from second 360 on until the end. The unfairness for VMs randomly changes over different evaluation runs, consequently leading to neither fair nor deterministic behaviour in resource sharing. The dynamic network scheduler clearly schedules the available resources fairly to demanding VMs (e.g. VM3 gets from second 600 to 720 approx. 400 MBit/s instead of arbitrary 150 MBit/s).

The results of *TC3* with the dynamic network scheduler is represented in figure 9, while the result for fairness is identical to the result from TC1. The workload is changing more often in time, which is supported by the dynamic network scheduler due to its change driven activation.

Finally *TC4* with TCP involved, is shown in figure 1 from the problem statement in sec. 2 without any mechanism for fairness, and shown in figure 10 with the dynamic network scheduler for comparison. The unfairness for VM2, which barely transmits data due to the massive network load from VM1 is solved with the dynamic network scheduler. The sudden peaks at the beginning of each transmission block is due to TCP slow start and the design of the dynamic network scheduler that a VM taking its guaranteed resources back from another VM, does it in an exponential manner. The dynamic network scheduler initially does not know how much resources VM2 actually needs. It allocates VM2 more resources as long as its rate is within the guaranteed rate, and then takes back the unutilised resources to provide it to VM1. The VM1 which is already using more resources than its guaranteed value, takes the unutilised resources from VM2 rather slowly. This ensures that VM2 gets its resources instantly in case there is a further increase in its traffic rate. VM1 during this phase gets less network bandwidth than the capacity could provide, but still more than its actual fair share of 400 MBit/s.

In all four test cases, the dynamic network scheduler provides at least the fair share of the total network capacity to the demanding VMs. Therefore, the evaluation towards fairness is successfully demonstrated.

7.3.2 Efficiency. Deriving efficiency by rate-limiting the bandwidth for each VM is not part of this evaluation, since the results would show inefficient use of resources by definition, and is not useful for comparison. The evaluation of efficiency is done by analysing if the dynamic network scheduler can assign the unutilised resources to the VMs in need, in addition to ensuring fairness as shown before.

Figure 9 shows the average of the summed up network utilisation, for each time interval with changing demands. While in TC3, as VM1 floods the network with UDP traffic, the most efficient use of the network would be 100% utilisation. Due to the careful assignment of bandwidth from a donor VM to a recipient VM, this utilisation cannot be fully achieved with rapidly changing load patterns (cf. seconds 720 to 840).

The efficiency is also represented in any other figure, for example, in figure 8b. Both VMs in this test case TC1 receive the full network capacity and hence twice their fair share whenever only one VM transmits data. The efficiency in comparison to mechanisms that

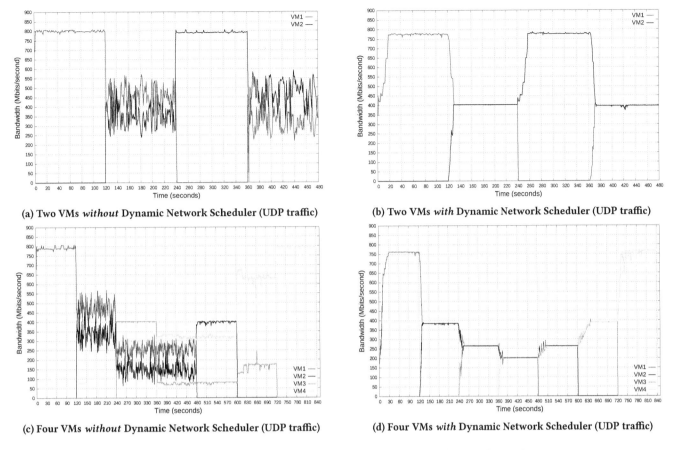

(a) Two VMs *without* Dynamic Network Scheduler (UDP traffic)

(b) Two VMs *with* Dynamic Network Scheduler (UDP traffic)

(c) Four VMs *without* Dynamic Network Scheduler (UDP traffic)

(d) Four VMs *with* Dynamic Network Scheduler (UDP traffic)

Figure 8: Network Fairness with and without Dynamic Network Scheduler

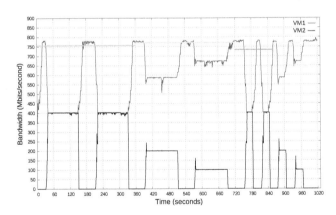

Figure 9: Overall bandwidth utilization with Dynamic Network Scheduler when VM1 and VM2 generate UDP traffic

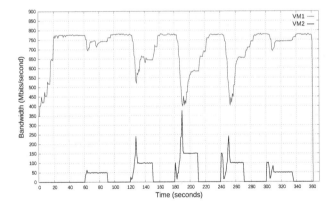

Figure 10: Unequal loads *with* Dynamic Network Scheduler (VM1 UDP, VM2 TCP), cf. Figure 1 without the scheduler

limit VMs to their fair share is hence reasonable better with the dynamic network scheduler, which borrows unused bandwidth temporarily.

7.3.3 Behaviour Analysis. From the evaluation results, the scheduling algorithm of the dynamic network scheduler can be evaluated

as well. While the algorithm provides unused bandwidth from a donor port to a recipient port rather slowly (cf. figure 8b seconds 0 to 20), it gives back the bandwidth immediately to a donor port when needed (cf. figure 8b seconds 120 to 125). From these scheduling decisions, we can clearly see that the activation of the dynamic network scheduler functions as intended, and that the scheduling algorithm works.

7.4 Concluding Evaluation

Based on the presented experiments, the dynamic network scheduler, has its performance better than the best-effort basis in ensuring fairness in resource allocation. However, its performance is not commendable in utilizing the total available bandwidth efficiently, and it is majorly due to its proximity from the VMs. It is important to recall that the dynamic network scheduler runs outside the server, and should enforce the decisions on the server using OpenFlow protocol. However, the efficiency is still higher compared to rate-limiting the bandwidth for each VM. The trade off between efficiency and fair share is hence in an acceptable ratio.

8 CONCLUSION

Concluding the presented dynamic network scheduler for cloud data centres, we first described how we think the fair share of network resources can be solved while fully utilizing bandwidth resources. From the conceptual design we derived a prototypical implementation and evaluated that the approach improves the fairness while still guaranteeing bandwidth to users without adhering to strict static bandwidth limits.

While the concept for the dynamic network scheduler works for cloud data centres, the prototype was limited to a rather flat scenario. Nevertheless, we believe that this proof of concept can be scaled up to a full data centre. The central approach following the SDN design pattern could be a limiting factor. However, SDN has solved these limitations by scaling the controlling part horizontally. In our case, the dynamic network scheduler could even be split in multiple sub graphs, which can be scheduled in parallel to avoid bottlenecks.

The next steps for our work is an integration of the dynamic network scheduler into an OpenStack cluster, to extend the prototype towards a stable component of a Cloud data centre. Further planned extensions are continuous monitoring and profiling of the network traces for VMs in a cluster. With a better understanding of typical network usage patterns, the dynamic network scheduler can be extended to a) include predictions, and b) give feedback to the Cloud middleware to increase the set of optimisation actions.

ACKNOWLEDGMENT

The research leading to these results has received funding from the federal state of Baden-Württemberg (Germany), under the Project "ViCE - Virtual Open Science Collaboration Environment".

REFERENCES

[1] [n. d.]. Open vSwitch 2.5.0 Documentation. http://openvswitch.github.io/support/dist-docs-2.5/. ([n. d.]). Accessed: 2016-10-20.

[2] Martin A. Brown, Klaus Rechert, and Patrick McHardy. [n. d.]. HFSC Scheduling with Linux. linux-ip.net/articles/hfsc.en/. ([n. d.]). Accessed: 2016-11-14.

[3] Raphael Durner, Andreas Blenk, and Wolfgang Kellerer. 2015. Performance study of dynamic QoS management for OpenFlow-enabled SDN switches. In *Quality of Service (IWQoS), 2015 IEEE 23rd International Symposium on*. IEEE, 177–182.

[4] OpenStack Foundation. 2017. Scheduling - OpenStack Configuration Reference. (June 2017). https://docs.openstack.org/kilo/config-reference/content/section_compute-scheduler.html

[5] Q. Fu, L. Qing, A. Yingzhu, and F. Yamei. 2015. A priority based virtual network bandwidth guarantee method in software defined network. In *2015 6th IEEE International Conference on Software Engineering and Service Science (ICSESS)*. 153–156. https://doi.org/10.1109/ICSESS.2015.7339026

[6] Panagiotis Georgopoulos, Yehia Elkhatib, Matthew Broadbent, Mu Mu, and Nicholas Race. 2013. Towards network-wide QoE fairness using openflow-assisted adaptive video streaming. In *Proceedings of the 2013 ACM SIGCOMM workshop on Future human-centric multimedia networking*. ACM, 15–20.

[7] Vijay Mann, Anilkumar Vishnoi, Aakash Iyer, and Parantapa Bhattacharya. 2012. Vmpatrol: Dynamic and automated qos for virtual machine migrations. In *Proceedings of the 8th International Conference on Network and Service Management*. International Federation for Information Processing, 174–178.

[8] Devera Martin. [n. d.]. Hierachical Token Bucket Theory. luxik.cdi.cz/~devik/qos/. ([n. d.]). Accessed: 2016-11-10.

[9] Nick McKeown, Tom Anderson, Hari Balakrishnan, Guru Parulkar, Larry Peterson, Jennifer Rexford, Scott Shenker, and Jonathan Turner. 2008. OpenFlow: Enabling Innovation in Campus Networks. *ACM SIGCOMM Computer Communication Review* 38, 2 (2008), 69–74.

[10] Peter Mell, Tim Grance, et al. 2011. The NIST definition of cloud computing. (2011).

[11] Saravanan Radhakrishnan. [n. d.]. QoS Support in Linux: Queuing Disciplines. qos.ittc.ku.edu. ([n. d.]). Accessed: 2016-11-10.

[12] Athanasios Tsitsipas, Christopher B Hauser, Jörg Domaschka, and Stefan Wesner. 2016. Towards Usage-Based Dynamic Overbooking in IaaS Clouds. In *International Conference on the Economics of Grids, Clouds, Systems, and Services*. Springer, 263–274.

[13] Stefan Wesner, Henning Groenda, James Byrne, Sergej Svorobej, Christopher Hauser, and Jörg Domaschka. 2014. Optimised Cloud data centre operation supported by simulation. In *eChallenges e-2014, 2014 Conference*. IEEE, 1–9.

[14] Thomas Zinner, Michael Jarschel, Andreas Blenk, Florian Wamser, and Wolfgang Kellerer. 2014. Dynamic application-aware resource management using Software-Defined Networking: Implementation prospects and challenges. In *Network Operations and Management Symposium (NOMS), 2014 IEEE*. IEEE, 1–6.

LambdaLink: an Operation Management Platform for Multi-Cloud Environments

Kate Keahey
Argonne National Laboratory
Argonne, Illinois, USA
keahey@mcs.anl.gov

Pierre Riteau
University of Chicago
Chicago, Illinois, USA
priteau@uchicago.edu

Nicholas P. Timkovich
University of Chicago
Chicago, Illinois, USA
npt@uchicago.edu

ABSTRACT

The last several years have seen an unprecedented growth in data availability, with dynamic data streams from sources ranging from social networks to small, inexpensive sensing devices. This new data availability creates an opportunity, especially in geospatial data science where this new, dynamic, data allows novel insight into phenomena ranging from environmental to social sciences. Much work has focused on creating venues or portals for publishing and accessing such dynamic datasets. However access to data in itself is not sufficient—to turn data into information the data needs to be filtered, correlated, and otherwise analyzed using methods that are dynamically developed and constantly improved by a distributed community of experts. Further, these methods are increasingly required to deliver results with specific qualities of service, e.g., providing results by a certain deadline or ensuring a certain accuracy of the results. Delivering such qualities of service requires generic but often sophisticated tools managing the execution of operations and ensuring their correctness. This paper presents LambdaLink, an operation management platform for multi-cloud environments, and explains how it supports the structured contribution and repeatable, time-controlled execution of operations. We describe the architecture and implementation of LambdaLink, its approach to appliance management in a multi-cloud context, and compare it with related systems.

CCS CONCEPTS

• **Computer systems organization** → **Cloud computing**;

KEYWORDS

Operation Management Platform; Cloud computing; Lambda; Repeatable Execution

1 INTRODUCTION

The last several years have seen an unprecedented growth in data availability with dynamic data streams from sources ranging from social networks to small, inexpensive sensing devices. The latter in particular is increasingly creating new sources of information: the proliferation of energy-efficient, cheap, and robust sensors,

Publication rights licensed to ACM. ACM acknowledges that this contribution was authored or co-authored by an employee, contractor or affiliate of the United States government. As such, the Government retains a nonexclusive, royalty-free right to publish or reproduce this article, or to allow others to do so, for Government purposes only.

UCC '17, December 5–8, 2017, Austin, TX, USA

© 2017 Copyright held by the owner/author(s). Publication rights licensed to Association for Computing Machinery.
ACM ISBN 978-1-4503-5149-2/17/12...$15.00
https://doi.org/10.1145/3147213.3147224

sometimes referred to as *second Moore's law*, is now creating new opportunities for measuring various physical, chemical, and biological characteristics of the environment. As small, specialized sensor devices, capable of both reporting on environmental factors and interacting with the environment, become more ubiquitous, reliable, and cheap, increasingly more domain sciences are creating instruments, composed of dynamic groups of sensors whose outputs are capable of being aggregated and correlated to answer new questions. This new data availability creates an opportunity, especially in geospatial data science where this new, dynamic, data allows unprecedented insight into phenomena ranging from environmental to social sciences.

Much work has focused on creating venues or portals for publishing and accessing such dynamic datasets. However access to data in itself is not sufficient—to turn data into information the data needs to be filtered, correlated, and otherwise analyzed using methods that are dynamically developed and constantly improved by a distributed community of experts. Further, the methods are often used to generate results with specific qualities of service, e.g., providing results by a certain deadline or ensuring a certain accuracy of the results. Delivering such qualities of service requires generic but often sophisticated tools managing the execution of such methods and ensuring their correctness.

Thus we propose to extend the concept of a dynamic data portal to a portal supporting the structured contribution and repeatable, time-controlled execution of operations (sometimes referred to as *lambdas*) as well as access to data. In particular, the proposed platform should support the following capabilities:

- *Operation Publishing.* It allows contributing users to easily publish new operations in such a way that they can be automatically executed by others without the need to understand any of their implementation dependencies or other details. Such operations should become referencable objects, i.e., they should be capable of being published via a Digital Object Identifier (DOI) and easily reenacted by others.
- *Versioning and Repeatability.* The platform should support users in repeating the execution of operations under the same condition as the original, i.e., should manage operation versions and record and provide sufficient information about the condition of the original execution for the user to recreate those conditions.
- *Time-Controlled Execution.* The architecture should support mechanisms for demand-based integration of resources to trade-off quality of service considerations such as response time, accuracy of results, and cost.
- *Variety of Platforms.* The solution should integrate support for multiple commercial and academic platforms including

academic clouds such as Jetstream [42] and Chameleon [44], commercial platforms such as Amazon Web Services [3] or Azure [29], as well as Grid resources such as XSEDE [46] or OSG [33].

In this paper we present LambdaLink, an operation management platform and demonstrate how it fulfills the objectives stated above. Our focus is on developing the abstractions as well as design and interfaces for the system and demonstrating how existing technologies can be integrated to implement it. Since the questions of dynamic scaling by integrating on-demand resources [25, 38] as well as job execution management on remote resources [10] have been investigated in the context of other research, here we focus on mechanisms to bring those results together in a platform that supports repeatable execution.

Our paper is organized as follows. In Section 2, we demonstrate that the concept of appliance underlying our approach can be consistently and cost-effectively implemented across different types of platforms. In Section 3, we build on this concept to present the LambdaLink architecture, discuss the operation publication process it supports as well as its implementation. In Section 4, we discuss the architecture in the context of our goals stated above. We present related work in Section 5 and conclude in Section 6.

2 APPLIANCE AS ABSTRACTION

Our approach relies on the concept of an appliance [39]]: a complete and actionable representation of a user's environment. An appliance is capable of packaging all the software dependencies of a user's program—from operating system, through libraries and tools, to environment variables—in such a way that it is easy for the user to manipulate. In this section, we seek to explain how the concept of an appliance fulfilling our requirements above—whether representing an individual deployment or a cluster with complex relationships—can be supported by integrating existing tools.

Popular implementations of appliances include virtual machines such as KVM [23] and Xen [7], containers such as Docker [28], Shifter [8], or Singularity [24], or bare metal images such as those supported by Chameleon [44]. Most of those implementations consist of disk images that can be deployed to create an instance, i.e., an interactive environment based on a given appliance deployed onto a specific resource allocation. Once an appliance is deployed, a user can log into the instance interactively, modify it, and snapshot it (i.e., save the new disk image), thus creating a new appliance.

Most targeted cloud platforms, such as Amazon EC2 [3], Jetstream [42], or Chameleon [44] have specific requirements for the format of a disk image (e.g., raw or QCOW2 [35]), its disk layout (e.g., whole disk image or partition image), or the environment included in the image (e.g., cloud-init required to be installed and run on boot for injecting SSH keys, a DHCP client configured on specific interfaces, etc.) making images incompatible between various providers. Cloud users typically address this problem by deploying, manually customizing, and then snapshotting images for each platform. However, this approach is not sustainable: it is not only hard to automate (and thus costly) but also prone to errors that may result in an environment that is not consistent between platforms. This poses further questions in the light of our objectives to create an appliance compatible across a range of academic and commercial platforms: how can we generate appliance disk images for all those platforms in such a way that they are consistent, i.e., reflect the same properties for each platform? Will it be possible to maintain (i.e., update or upgrade) such appliances cost-effectively in practice without impacting consistency?

We investigated and compared two approaches in this space: (1) offline creation of images compatible with the requirements of the cloud platform, and (2) online customization and snapshotting. Each method starts with a base image (e.g., a bare-bones operating system installation, sometimes called JeOS for *Just Enough Operating System*), which can be created from scratch by populating its content using an operating system installation procedure, or are produced by some Linux distributions.

The first approach is exemplified by diskimage-builder [12], a tool for automatically building customized operating system images for use in OpenStack [32] clouds (both KVM and bare metal). It takes as input a set of elements, describing which disk image to use as base image, which image format to use, and which customizations to apply to this image (each customization element is a script, usually written in shell). It extracts the file system hierarchy from the base image, applies customizations to it using chroot, and from it creates a disk image in the intended format. Diskimage-builder can be run on any machine that has the required dependencies (libguestfs, QEMU image tools, etc.). The resulting disk image must then be uploaded to the target cloud platform(s).

The second approach relies on snapshotting capabilities of cloud platforms and is an automation of the *deploy, customize, and snapshot* approach described above. Its implementation is exemplified by the Packer [19] tool. Packer takes as input a configuration describing which cloud platform to use and how to access it (including credentials), which disk image to run, and how to customize it. Packer then performs all the steps required to generate the image which include: generating a dedicated SSH key, launching an instance on the cloud platform such that it is accessible with the generated SSH key, and applying customization steps defined by the user (e.g., via shell scripts or configuration management systems such as Puppet [34], Chef [9], or Ansible [5]). When all steps are successfully applied, Packer snapshots the instance on the cloud platform. The tool is supported for a wide range of platforms, in particular AWS [3], virtualized OpenStack clouds including Rackspace Cloud Servers [37], Google Compute Engine [17], and Azure [29].

To compare, the offline approach offers more control over the exact type of image being generated (e.g. whole disk image vs partition image, raw vs QCOW2), but requires knowledge of the format supported by the targeted cloud platforms. For example, while diskimage-builder may be able to create images for any OpenStack cloud based on KVM or bare metal, it does not provide out of the box support for other commercial clouds such as Amazon EC2. The online approach is directly compatible with each cloud platform, but it requires support for a call to the cloud platform's snapshotting API method which is not always available (e.g., OpenStack does not support snapshotting for bare metal deployments out of the box). In addition, the online approach requires credentials and credits for each target cloud platform so that an image can be uploaded, deployed, and later stored there—the offline method does not require uploading the image to the platform until it is actually needed. Thus the two methods represent different trade-offs and provide coverage for different types of platforms.

To achieve the most complete coverage of platforms we have combined both approaches by first establishing a library of base images for a range of targeted platforms (i.e., a family of OS images, such as CentOS 7, or more specific, e.g. Ubuntu 16.04.3) that can be used as base for either method. For each image we then define what customizations should be applied (in our case usually Bash shell scripts, though other methods can also be used). The system works by selecting a base image for the right method and delegating to tools implementing either the online or offline approach as appropriate. Further, some appliances may use a modification of the *deploy, customize, and snapshot* method that omits the *snapshot* step. In this case, configuration is always redone when the image is deployed. This leads to long deployment times and is often unreliable as the installation process may access remote repositories that are not always available. For this reason, we decided agains using this process in our reference implementation.

An additional challenge is defined by the need to represent within the system platforms that are not appliance-based, i.e., do not let users deploy environments and instead rely primarily on fixed environments pre-configured on various sites, such as XSEDE [46]. While we cannot influence the configuration of those sites, we can represent their configurations as an appliance giving users the option to run at scale on one of the XSEDE sites—but also use appliance-based platforms as needed, e.g., when XSEDE resources are not available or—using an XSEDE appliance with slight modifications—to implement and debug their applications within an environment that allows for a hightened level of privilege such as e.g., superuser access.

Finally, the last challenge consists of deploying what we call *complex appliances*—appliances typically deployed as multiple instances implementing complex relationships—such as a virtual cluster (e.g., a Torque [1] cluster with potentially multiple specialized management nodes and a set of worker nodes) or a cloud deployment (such as e.g., OpenStack or Hadoop [6] deployments). In addition to the disk image, such deployments require integrating on deployment additional information e.g., exchanging security information (based on keys generated at deployment time) or configuration information (IP addresses generated at deployment time)—a process called contextualization [22]—and potentially recontextualizing [27] dynamically as new nodes are added to a virtual cluster or a cloud. These capabilities are supported by orchestration services that typically use an image and a template defining how the images are deployed and the information is exchanged among them. These services are implemented by Heat [20] for OpenStack, Cloud Formation [2] for AWS, Google Cloud Deployment Manager [16] for Google Compute Engine, etc., giving us a coverage of the platforms of interest.

3 LAMBDALINK ARCHITECTURE

In the previous section, we demonstrated the properties of appliances in LambdaLink. This section describes the architecture of the system.

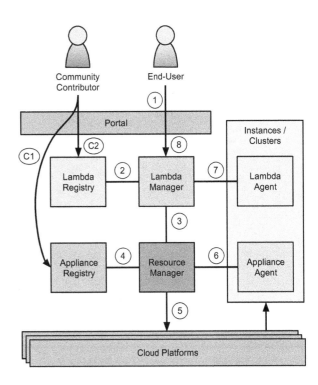

Figure 1: Diagram of the LambdaLink architecture

3.1 Critical Components

Figure 1 shows an outline of the LambdaLink architecture. The architecture is composed of the following components:

- A **Portal**, or another means for users to communicate with the system, which allows users to request the execution of specific operations on specific data. It also manages information relevant to users (e.g., credential information for multiple cloud services).

- The **Appliance Registry**, which stores appliances as well as the corresponding appliance implementations required to deploy them on different cloud platforms. To support repeatability at the level of environments, updates to appliances as well as appliance implementations are tracked using version numbers.

- The **Resource Manager** manages appliance deployments. It is in charge of choosing the best option between using an existing appliance instance (if available), expanding the resource allocation for one, or creating a new one on a new resource allocation, as needed to manage the overall response time. The Resource Manager uses the information about appliances in the Appliance Registry to deploy appliances on allocated resources. It then uses interfaces to multiple clouds to deploy the appliance, leveraging or integrating with orchestration mechanisms to create complex appliances as needed.

- The **Appliance Agent** carries out functions within the appliance, such as credential management or monitoring, on behalf of the Resource Manager.

register_appliance()
add/remove_implementation()
add_version() / delete_version()
get_appliance(site)

Appliance Registry

Appliance

- Name
- Owner
- Version

Site

- Name
- API type
- API endpoint

Appliance Implementation

- Name
- Author
- Deployment Template / Scripts
- Version

Figure 2: Appliance Registry interfaces

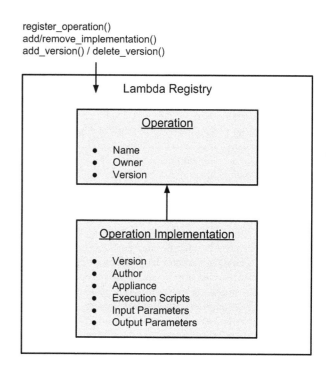

register_operation()
add/remove_implementation()
add_version() / delete_version()

Lambda Registry

Operation

- Name
- Owner
- Version

Operation Implementation

- Version
- Author
- Appliance
- Execution Scripts
- Input Parameters
- Output Parameters

Figure 3: Lambda Registry interfaces

- The **Lambda Registry**, which stores information about operations in the form of scripts or execution recipes (e.g., how to execute them, what appliance they need, pre- and post-execution actions, etc.) that allow the Lambda Manager to execute them automatically. The operations are also tracked at the level of version numbers as multiple operation versions can map to the same appliance version.
- The **Lambda Manager**, which takes user requests for the execution of specific operations and executes them based on information provided by Lambda Registry. The Lambda Manager also works with the Resource Manager to ensure the availability of the required environment on the right amount of resources, possibly triggering the deployment of a new appliance.
- The **Lambda Agent** carries out functions within the appliance, such as starting a job locally and monitoring and reporting on its progress, on behalf of the Lambda Manager.

The system operates on virtual data, i.e., data that can be globally identified and efficiently managed based on global identifier, creating local copies as needed, such as implemented by Chimera [14].

3.2 User Workflows

The system assumes two types of users: (a) a community contributor, who contributes operations/lambdas to the system via the portal, and (b) an end-user, who uses those operations. Below we describe only the interfaces opened to community contributors and end users.

Community Contributor Workflow. To contribute an operation to the system, the user takes the following steps:

- The user conceptualizes a new appliance for the contributed operation and uses methods described in Section 2 to configure one or more implementation of this appliance for a set of resource providers. The user then tests these images to verify that they support the execution of the required operation across appliance implementations, and support other properties of the appliance.
- Once the appliance configuration step is complete, the user first adds an appliance entry/record to the Appliance Registry (Figure 1, step C1) as well as implementation records for each cloud provider using interfaces shown in Figure 2.
- After the appliance entry is created, the user proceeds to define a lambda/operation entry in the Lambda Registry (Figure 1, step C2) using interfaces shown in Figure 3.
- The user then defines a new operation implementation entry for a specific operation. The operation implementation record references the appliance required for its execution, and may consist of the command to execute the process, any pre- and post- processing commands, as well as links to virtual data representing input and output parameters.

End-User Workflow. The execution of operations/lambdas is triggered by the end-user and unfolds in the steps described below. We assume that the end-user has an account with the portal and that the account is associated with a set of credentials associated with resources that the user wants to use; these can be either provided by the portal administrator or constitute (potentially partially delegated) user's credentials.

Invoking an operation triggers the following steps:

- The user logs into the portal and browses through a list of contributed operations, their versions and descriptions, and requests the application of a specific operation to specific data (Figure 1, step 1).
- After the user's request is conveyed to the Lambda Manager, the latter takes the following actions: a Lambda Instance record providing information about the executing operation is created (it will be updated with relevant information throughout operation execution); the Lambda Manager retrieves the information about how to run the operation from the Lambda Registry (Figure 1, step 2), and asks the Resource Manager to select a suitable appliance for its execution (Figure 1, step 3).
- The Resource Manager first checks if the appliance has been deployed within the system and takes the following actions:
  - If no appliance available to the user (via such mechanisms as e.g., membership in the same project) has been deployed in the system, the Resource Manager first selects a platform consistent with the user's credentials as present in the system. Users may provide hints on resource preferences, though the actual decision takes into account factors such as resource availability, the availability of an appliance implementation for the specific resource, and cost. Once a platform is selected, the Resource Manager uses information about the appliance implementation retrieved from the Appliance Registry (Figure 1, step 4) and deploys it on the platform (Figure 1, step 5), also creating an Appliance Instance record with relevant information. The Resource Manager then authenticates and interacts with the Appliance Agent to create an account associated with the requesting user (Figure 1, step 6).
  - If an appliance has been deployed in the system, but needs to be modified in some way, e.g., the user's account does not exist, or the resource allocation is insufficient to accommodate the user's request, the Resource Manager takes the appropriate action. In the former case, it asks the Appliance Agent to create an account for the user; the agent then securely returns the authentication token for it. If the appliance lacks resources to provide the desired response time, has been deployed but the resource allocation associated with the instance is insufficient to accommodate the user's request, the Resource Manager scales the instance up or out, following scaling strategies such as described in [38]. The allocations are monitored and scaled down as needed.
  - If the appliance has been deployed and fulfills the requirements, it is a no-op and the Resource Manager simply returns the resource record.

  In all cases, the Resource Manager returns a resource record containing the IP address of the appliance instance and the user's authentication token for this appliance deployment.

- Once the appliance is available, the Lambda Manager prepares for deployment, based on the requirements described in the operation record retrieved from the Lambda Registry, and launches the execution of the operation by interacting with the Lambda Agent running on the node (or the master node of a cluster) (Figure 1, step 7).
- Once the execution of the operation is finished, the Lambda Agent notifies the Lambda Manager. The Lambda Manager then orchestrates post-processing as per the operation record retrieved from the Lambda Registry and ultimately notifies the user (Figure 1, step 8).

3.3 Implementation

We have prototyped the LambdaLink architecture in the following reference implementation. Components of LambdaLink are implemented independently as microservices with HTTP REST APIs. Each service is written in Python, using Django for HTTP, object-relational mapping, and authentication, then Django REST Framework to provide the API. Persistent data is stored in a MySQL database.

Requests made to services are authenticated by custom Django middleware that validates a token. For external requests by a user, the token is provided by an authentication service, and for inter-service requests, a generated token is signed with a shared key. After authentication, authorization is validated, then the request is handled.

Endpoints that do not represent instantiated resources, for example, the appliance definition and implementation, have a simple CRUD API to modify properties of the objects. For endpoints reliant on external resources accessed in an asynchronous manner, the two Managers use additional processes running a Celery task queue [40] to make requests and poll for expected changes. For example, when the Resource Manager determines that it needs to launch an appliance on a cloud provider, it creates an object and immediately returns it to the user marked in a *pending* state. A task is created to command the provider to start creation, then to check for provisioning to finish, and finally to check if the Appliance Agent is contactable.

Our refernce implementation supports OpenStack clouds, such the ROGER OpenStack cloud at NCSA [31] or the Chameleon [44] KVM and bare-metal OpenStack deployments, with Heat [20] for deploying complex appliances. It has been used to deploy operations of UrbanFlow [41], a geospatial data analysis platform from the CyberGIS center [47] for synthesizing social media fine-resolution data with authoritative urban dataset.

Our deployment model assumes that LambdaLink will be operated as a service, where the service provider provides cycles and storage to manage and store the operations information, appliances, and their implementations (though some implementations may be cached at suitable cloud providers).

4 DISCUSSION AND ANALYSIS

We have defined the LambdaLink architecture, developed a reference implementation, and applied it in the context of CyberGIS computations [47]. The main innovation of our approach is a design separation of the function of resource provisioning/configuring and job/operation management united in traditional schedulers—and then demonstrating how they can be used together to provide an architecture fulfilling our requirements, in particular generating information for repeatable execution and response time management.

We note that the operation/lambda management in our architecture is similar to mechanisms used in grid computing [10, 48]. The main differences consist in the ability of the Lambda Manager to (1) negotiate with the Resource Manager to provide specific types or amounts of resources and (2) the ability to provide a structured, persistent, and versioned definition of operations in the Lambda Registry. The existing mechanisms could thus be adapted to fit into this architecture with relatively little effort. The former could be implemented by extending them to provide the appliance selection operation (see Figure 1, step 3); the latter by providing an implementation of the Lambda Registry (a relatively lightweight elaboration on already existing mechanisms). For this reason, our reference implementation focuses on the appliance and resource management parts of the architecture, as well as articulating interfaces for better integration of existing methods.

We now turn to analysis of our system in the context of its stated objectives. We have provided a platform that supports contributing/publishing operations (lambdas) as well as their automated execution allowing for implementation of qualities of service. Section 3.2 outlines a contributor's workflow and showed how, based on specific and well-defined artifacts provided by the contributor, we can automate both the automatic execution of the operations and manage quality of service by automatically integrating resources. The ability to package, version, and publish operations in this way makes them not only shareable but also referencable entities that can be easily re-applied by others to different data sets or different problems. Execution based on appliances ensures a smoother experience which assures that the dependencies of a specific applications are met.

The ability to faithfully repeat an execution of a specific program operating on a specific dataset usually depends on two factors: the ability to execute on the exact same hardware, and the ability to recreate on this hardware the exact same environment used in the original execution. Though the first repeatability factor is sometimes downplayed—as not all changes to hardware will affect all executions—changes in hardware configuration and firmware upgrades can have a noticeable effect on the results injecting nontrivial inconsistencies into the results that only repeating an experiment in the exact same conditions can resolve. Two factors need to be present to resolve it: a record of the exact resources used, and versioning of those resources to describe changes that happened to them in the intervening time between executions. Having this information means that even if it is not economically possible to roll back the changes or restore decommissioned hardware based on those records, differences can still be reasoned about. The availabililty of this information is currently dependent on the provider; while commercial platforms provide little information in this space, both record of used resources and resource versioning are currently supported by the Chameleon platform [45] and the developed methods are published and shareable by other platforms. Versioning of appliances in the LambdaLink architecture allows us to point to the exact environment used for a specific execution. Since associating operations with environments is performed by the system we can manage and export exact records of how specific data was produced. Combining these two factors allows for exact reenactment of a specific run (currently not automated in the architecture though the relevant information is available).

Many applications and science portals have successfully managed to leverage on-demand cloud resources to adapt to a varying number of users/requests with varying workloads in order to provide a predictable response time for all requests [26, 36, 38]. Although integrating resources dynamically into an ongoing computation has proven effective in the case of e.g., high throughput computing (HTC) workloads [30], it is significantly more challenging for applications that have to manage a dynamic configuration, such as data distribution targeting a fixed number of nodes. Specifically, in the case of dynamically scaling Hadoop applications—used in many geospatial computations—the overhead of making the application aware of additional resources can incur more cost than it brings benefit if not done carefully. Thus, while we have proved that our approach will work for certain types of applications [41], we are currently investigating the boundaries of dynamic scaling of Hadoop and strategies for management of Hadoop workloads. Recognizing which applications are capable of consuming the additional resources and thus will benefit by their inclusion will ultimately form a part of the negotiation process with the user as described in [4].

The ability to support a range of platforms, commercial and academic alike, is dependent on two factors. The first one is implementing the appliance abstraction, i.e., developing models for generating and cost-effectively maintaining a set of appliance implementations (i.e., images) that is consistent across a set of those platforms; their advantages and limitations were described in Section 2. While we of course cannot deploy appliances on platforms that do not support this functionality (such as e.g., platforms providing an interface to batch-scheduled workloads), we can provide a one-way bridge allowing the users of those platforms to move to LambdaLink by configuring appliances with corresponding configuration. The increased interest in adopting container solutions such as Singularity [24] or Docker [28] in scientific platforms is likely to improve the situation on this front in the future. The second factor is the ability to adapt the Resource Manager to interface with and leverage a set of platform-specific tools to implement basic functions such as monitoring or deployment of complex appliances; this is currently well supported by tools [11] such as Apache Libcloud and Apache jclouds, and likely to develop in the future as more systems are interested in reaching out to multiple platforms.

5 RELATED WORK

Science gateways [21, 49] are a popular way to share catalogs of applications and services among a large scientific community. However, these gateways are generally linked to specific execution platforms, with their use in multi-cloud environments only explored recently. Farkas et al. [13] and Gugnani et al. [18] extend the WS-PGRADE/gUSE workflow-oriented science gateway with the CloudBroker Platform to support execution on multiple cloud platforms. However, neither of these systems deal with repeatable execution of operations, which LambdaLink handles by integrating versioning into its registries.

Scientific workflow management tools [50] is another type of systems that can include comparable capabilities to LambdaLink. The main difference is that they focus on executing workflows of inter-dependent tasks, while LambdaLink operations are not tied to this concept: for example, an operation could be the deployment of a virtual cluster based on a complex appliance, providing a long-lived service to a community. Among these workflow management tools, the AWE/Shock ecosystem for bioinformatic workflow applications [43] is extended by Skyport [15] to use Linux container virtualization technologies (namely, Docker [28]) to handle software deployment across various cloud platforms. In comparison, the implementation of LambdaLink natively supports image-based deployments (either virtual machines or bare metal), but could also support Docker containers.

6 CONCLUSIONS AND SUMMARY

The unprecedented growth in data availability—with dynamic data streams from sources ranging from social networks to small, inexpensive sensing devices—creates an opportunity, especially in geospatial data science where this new, dynamic, data allows new insight into phenomena ranging from environmental to social sciences. While much work has focused on creating venues or portals for publishing and accessing such dynamic datasets, access to data in itself is not sufficient: data needs to be filtered, correlated, and otherwise analyzed using methods that are dynamically developed and constantly improved by a distributed community of experts.

In this paper, we have presented LambdaLink, an operation management platform for multi-cloud environments. Its architecture separates the management of appliances and operations/lambdas and fulfills the needs of two categories of users: community contributors, who create and share appliances and operations, and end-users, who run these operations on a variety of cloud platforms. We discussed the two main approaches available for appliance management in cloud systems and how they can both be leveraged by LambdaLink.

In future works, we plan to explore more deeply the integration of data management systems and protocols with LambdaLink, as well as advanced policies for dynamic scaling. In particular, we are currently investigating the boundaries of dynamic scaling of Hadoop and strategies for management of Hadoop workloads, with the aim of integrating the resulting algorithms and policies in LambdaLink.

7 ACKNOWLEDGEMENTS

This material was supported by the National Science Foudation grant 1443080, and, in part, by the U.S. Department of Energy, Office of Science, under contract DE-AC02-06CH11357. Work presented in this paper was obtained using the Chameleon testbed supported by the National Science Foundation.

REFERENCES

[1] Adaptive Computing. 2017. TORQUE Resource Manager. http://www.adaptivecomputing.com/products/open-source/torque/. (2017). [Online; accessed 15-Aug-2017].
[2] Amazon Web Services. 2017. AWS CloudFormation. https://aws.amazon.com/cloudformation/. (2017). [Online; accessed 15-Aug-2017].
[3] Amazon Web Services. 2017. Elastic Compute Cloud (EC2). https://aws.amazon.com/ec2/. (2017). [Online; accessed 15-Aug-2017].
[4] Alain Andrieux, Karl Czajkowski, Asit Dan, Kate Keahey, Heiko Ludwig, Toshiyuki Nakata, Jim Pruyne, John Rofrano, Steve Tuecke, and Ming Xu. 2007. Web services agreement specification (WS-Agreement). In Open Grid Forum, Vol. 128. 216.
[5] Ansible HQ. 2017. Ansible. https://www.ansible.com. (2017). [Online; accessed 15-Aug-2017].
[6] Apache Hadoop contributors. 2017. Apache Hadoop. http://hadoop.apache.org. (2017). [Online; accessed 15-Aug-2017].
[7] Paul Barham, Boris Dragovic, Keir Fraser, Steven Hand, Tim Harris, Alex Ho, Rolf Neugebauer, Ian Pratt, and Andrew Warfield. 2003. Xen and the art of virtualization. In ACM SIGOPS operating systems review, Vol. 37. 164–177.
[8] Richard Shane Canon and Doug Jacobsen. 2016. Shifter: Containers for HPC. In Cray Users Group Conference (CUG'16).
[9] Chef. 2017. Chef. https://www.chef.io/chef/. (2017). [Online; accessed 15-Aug-2017].
[10] Karl Czajkowski, Ian Foster, Nicholas Karonis, Carl Kesselman, Stuart Martin, Warren Smith, and Steven Tuecke. 1998. A Resource Management Architecture for Metacomputing Systems. In Workshop on Job Scheduling Strategies for Parallel Processing. 62–82.
[11] Beniamino Di Martino, Giuseppina Cretella, and Antonio Esposito. 2015. Cross-platform cloud APIs. In Cloud Portability and Interoperability. 45–57.
[12] Diskimage-builder contributors. 2017. Diskimage-builder Documentation. https://docs.openstack.org/developer/diskimage-builder/. (2017). [Online; accessed 15-Aug-2017].
[13] Zoltán Farkas, Péter Kacsuk, and Ákos Hajnal. 2016. Enabling Workflow-Oriented Science Gateways to Access Multi-Cloud Systems. Journal of Grid Computing 14, 4 (2016), 619–640.
[14] Ian Foster, Jens Vöckler, Michael Wilde, and Yong Zhao. 2002. Chimera: A Virtual Data System for Representing, Querying, and Automating Data Derivation. In Proceedings of the 14th International Conference on Scientific and Statistical Database Management. 37–46.
[15] Wolfgang Gerlach, Wei Tang, Kevin Keegan, Travis Harrison, Andreas Wilke, Jared Bischof, Mark D'Souza, Scott Devoid, Daniel Murphy-Olson, Narayan Desai, et al. 2014. Skyport: container-based execution environment management for multi-cloud scientific workflows. In Proceedings of the 5th International Workshop on Data-Intensive Computing in the Clouds. 25–32.
[16] Google Cloud Platform. 2017. Google Cloud Deployment Manager. https://cloud.google.com/deployment-manager/. (2017). [Online; accessed 15-Aug-2017].
[17] Google Cloud Platform. 2017. Google Compute Engine - IaaS. https://cloud.google.com/compute/. (2017). [Online; accessed 15-Aug-2017].
[18] Shashank Gugnani, Carlos Blanco, Tamas Kiss, and Gabor Terstyanszky. 2016. Extending Science Gateway Frameworks to Support Big Data Applications in the Cloud. Journal of Grid Computing 14, 4 (2016), 589–601.
[19] HashiCorp. 2017. Packer. https://www.packer.io. (2017). [Online; accessed 15-Aug-2017].
[20] Heat contributors. 2017. Welcome to the Heat documentation! — heat documentation. https://docs.openstack.org/heat/. (2017). [Online; accessed 15-Aug-2017].
[21] Péter Kacsuk. 2014. Science Gateways for Distributed Computing Infrastructures: Development framework and exploitation by scientific user communities. Springer.
[22] Kate Keahey and Tim Freeman. 2008. Contextualization: Providing One-Click Virtual Clusters. In 2008 IEEE Fourth International Conference on eScience. 301–308.
[23] Avi Kivity, Yaniv Kamay, Dor Laor, Uri Lublin, and Anthony Liguori. 2007. kvm: the Linux Virtual Machine Monitor. In Proceedings of the 2007 Linux Symposium. 225–230.
[24] Gregory M. Kurtzer, Vanessa Sochat, and Michael W. Bauer. 2017. Singularity: Scientific containers for mobility of compute. PLOS ONE 12, 5 (05 2017), 1–20.
[25] Ming Mao, Jie Li, and Marty Humphrey. 2010. Cloud auto-scaling with deadline and budget constraints. In 11th IEEE/ACM International Conference on Grid Computing (GRID 2010). 41–48.
[26] Paul Marshall, Kate Keahey, and Tim Freeman. 2010. Elastic site: Using clouds to elastically extend site resources. In 10th IEEE/ACM International Conference on Cluster, Cloud and Grid Computing (CCGrid 2010). 43–52.
[27] Paul Marshall, Henry M Tufo, Kate Keahey, David LaBissoniere, and Matthew Woitaszek. 2012. Architecting a Large-scale Elastic Environment: Recontextualization and Adaptive Cloud Services for Scientific Computing.. In ICSOFT. 409–418.
[28] Dirk Merkel. 2014. Docker: Lightweight Linux Containers for Consistent Development and Deployment. Linux Journal 2014, 239 (2014), 2.
[29] Microsoft Azure. 2017. Virtual machines – Linux and Azure virtual machines. https://azure.microsoft.com/services/virtual-machines/. (2017). [Online; accessed 15-Aug-2017].
[30] Ruben S Montero, Rafael Moreno-Vozmediano, and Ignacio M Llorente. 2011. An elasticity model for high throughput computing clusters. J. Parallel and Distrib. Comput. 71, 6 (2011), 750–757.

[31] NCSA. 2017. ROGER: The CyberGIS Supercomputer. https://wiki.ncsa.illinois.edu/display/ROGER. (2017). [Online; accessed 15-Aug-2017].

[32] OpenStack contributors. 2017. OpenStack Open Source Cloud Computing Software. https://www.openstack.org. (2017). [Online; accessed 15-Aug-2017].

[33] Ruth Pordes, Don Petravick, Bill Kramer, Doug Olson, Miron Livny, Alain Roy, Paul Avery, Kent Blackburn, Torre Wenaus, Frank Würthwein, et al. 2007. The Open Science Grid. In *Journal of Physics: Conference Series*, Vol. 78. IOP Publishing.

[34] Puppet. 2017. Puppet. https://puppet.com. (2017). [Online; accessed 15-Aug-2017].

[35] QEMU contributors. 2017. QCOW2. http://bit.ly/qcow2. (2017). [Online; accessed 15-Aug-2017].

[36] Andres Quiroz, Hyunjoo Kim, Manish Parashar, Nathan Gnanasambandam, and Naveen Sharma. 2009. Towards autonomic workload provisioning for enterprise grids and clouds. In *10th IEEE/ACM International Conference on Grid Computing (GRID 2009)*. 50–57.

[37] Rackspace. 2017. Virtual Cloud Servers Powered by OpenStack. https://www.rackspace.com/cloud/servers. (2017). [Online; accessed 15-Aug-2017].

[38] Pierre Riteau, Myunghwa Hwang, Anand Padmanabhan, Yizhao Gao, Yan Liu, Kate Keahey, and Shaowen Wang. 2014. A Cloud Computing Approach to On-demand and Scalable Cybergis Analytics. In *Proceedings of the 5th ACM Workshop on Scientific Cloud Computing (ScienceCloud '14)*. 17–24.

[39] Constantine Sapuntzakis, David Brumley, Ramesh Chandra, Nickolai Zeldovich, Jim Chow, Monica S. Lam, and Mendel Rosenblum. 2003. Virtual Appliances for Deploying and Maintaining Software. In *Proceedings of the 17th USENIX Conference on System Administration (LISA '03)*. 181–194.

[40] Ask Solem et al. 2017. Celery: Distributed Task Queue. http://www.celeryproject.org. (2017). [Online; accessed 15-Aug-2017].

[41] Kiumars Soltani, Aiman Soliman, Anand Padmanabhan, and Shaowen Wang. 2016. UrbanFlow: Large-scale Framework to Integrate Social Media and Authoritative Landuse Maps. In *Proceedings of the XSEDE16 Conference on Diversity, Big Data,*

and Science at Scale. 2.

[42] Craig A. Stewart, Timothy M. Cockerill, Ian Foster, David Hancock, Nirav Merchant, Edwin Skidmore, Daniel Stanzione, James Taylor, Steven Tuecke, George Turner, et al. 2015. Jetstream: A self-provisioned, scalable science and engineering cloud environment. In *Proceedings of the 2015 XSEDE Conference: Scientific Advancements Enabled by Enhanced Cyberinfrastructure*. Article 29.

[43] Wei Tang, Jared Wilkening, Narayan Desai, Wolfgang Gerlach, Andreas Wilke, and Folker Meyer. 2013. A scalable data analysis platform for metagenomics. In *Big Data, 2013 IEEE International Conference on*. 21–26.

[44] The Chameleon project. 2017. Chameleon Cloud Homepage. https://www.chameleoncloud.org. (2017). [Online; accessed 15-Aug-2017].

[45] The Chameleon project. 2017. Chameleon Hardware Discovery page. https://www.chameleoncloud.org/hardware/. (2017). [Online; accessed 15-Aug-2017].

[46] John Towns, Timothy Cockerill, Maytal Dahan, Ian Foster, Kelly Gaither, Andrew Grimshaw, Victor Hazlewood, Scott Lathrop, Dave Lifka, Gregory D. Peterson, et al. 2014. XSEDE: Accelerating Scientific Discovery. *Computing in Science & Engineering* 16, 5 (2014), 62–74.

[47] Shaowen Wang. 2010. A CyberGIS Framework for the Synthesis of Cyberinfrastructure, GIS, and Spatial Analysis. *Annals of the Association of American Geographers* 100, 3 (2010), 535–557.

[48] Shaowen Wang, Marc P. Armstrong, Jun Ni, and Yan Liu. 2005. GISolve: A grid-based problem solving environment for computationally intensive geographic information analysis. In *Challenges of Large Applications in Distributed Environments (CLADE 2005)*. 3–12.

[49] Nancy Wilkins-Diehr, Dennis Gannon, Gerhard Klimeck, Scott Oster, and Sudhakar Pamidighantam. 2008. TeraGrid science gateways and their impact on science. *Computer* 41, 11 (2008).

[50] Jia Yu and Rajkumar Buyya. 2005. A taxonomy of workflow management systems for grid computing. *Journal of Grid Computing* 3, 3-4 (2005), 171–200.

Secure and Privacy-Aware Data Dissemination for Cloud-Based Applications

Lilia Sampaio
Universidade Federal de Campina Grande
Campina Grande, Brasil
liliars@lsd.ufcg.edu.br

Fábio Silva
Universidade Federal de Campina Grande
Campina Grande, Brasil
fabiosilva@lsd.ufcg.edu.br

Amanda Souza
Universidade Federal de Campina Grande
Campina Grande, Brasil
amandasouza@lsd.ufcg.edu.br

Andrey Brito
Universidade Federal de Campina Grande
Campina Grande, Brasil
andrey@lsd.ufcg.edu.br

Pascal Felber
Université de Neuchâtel
Neuchâtel, Switzerland
pascal.felber@unine.ch

ABSTRACT

In this paper we propose a data dissemination platform that supports data security and different privacy levels even when the platform and the data are hosted by untrusted infrastructures. The proposed system aims at enabling an application ecosystem that uses off-the-shelf trusted platforms (in this case, Intel SGX), so that users may allow or disallow third parties to access the live data stream with a specific sensitivity-level. Moreover, this approach does not require users to manage the encryption keys directly. Our experiments show that such an approach is indeed practical for medium scale systems, where participants disseminate small volumes of data at a time, such as in smart grids and IoT environments.

CCS CONCEPTS

• **Security and privacy** → **Privacy-preserving protocols**; **Hardware security implementation**; **Data anonymization and sanitization**; **Privacy protections**;

KEYWORDS

smart grids, privacy, Intel SGX, publish/subscribe

ACM Reference format:
Lilia Sampaio, Fábio Silva, Amanda Souza, Andrey Brito, and Pascal Felber. 2017. Secure and Privacy-Aware Data Dissemination for Cloud-Based Applications. In *Proceedings of 10th International Conference on Utility and Cloud Computing, Austin, Texas USA, December 5–8, 2017 (UCC'17)*, 10 pages.
https://doi.org/10.1145/3147213.3147230

1 INTRODUCTION

The "digital transformation" enables an increase in productivity and quality of life through the usage of information technologies. The growing number of data sources combined with analytics techniques that generate actionable information from a large volume of raw data have a strong impact in all aspects of our daily lives. Nevertheless, these opportunities are also coupled with several challenges, especially the need for affordable and scalable infrastructures to hosts data and applications, as well as the mitigation of risks related to the leakage of private data.

On the one hand, the challenge of providing scalable infrastructures has been addressed by the advances in cloud computing. In contrast to the situation in the last couple of decades, where developers of novel applications would have to consider the risk of investing in hardware infrastructures, new applications start today in the cloud, where the cost is proportional to the resources actually used (at the granularity of cents) and the infrastructure can be scaled within minutes. In addition, there are hundreds of cloud providers that offer more than simple computing and storage resources paid by the hour. These providers offer higher level platform services to ease the development of applications. This combination of simplicity and cost efficiency has promoted the cloud as the *de facto* environment where applications are hosted.

On the other hand, cloud providers are an obvious and attractive target for attacks that aim to steal data or compromise applications. There are many reasons that increase the risk of data leakage when using cloud infrastructures [7], for example: *(i)* vulnerabilities in the infrastructure may allow attackers to access data outside their VMs or tenants; *(ii)* employers may have access to raw data and use these access to steal data; or *(iii)* cyber-espionage may compromise the confidential data of companies and even governments. At the same time, cloud platform services store increasingly more sensitive information, such as voice snippets, like in AWS Lex[1], and face images, as in AWS Rekognition[2].

While there are many guidelines for building cloud native applications, if the infrastructure cannot be trusted as are the cases listed above protecting data becomes challenging. Encrypting data at rest,

---

[1]https://aws.amazon.com/lex/?nc2=h_a1
[2]https://aws.amazon.com/rekognition/?nc1=h_ls

using good encryption keys, and limiting the scope and permissions of the users cannot protect from insider attacks or remote attacks in which the attacker has manage to compromise the physical host. In such scenarios, some approaches, such as homomorphic encryption, are effective even in such cases as the data can be kept encrypted at all times, even during processing. Nevertheless, it is very hard to compile generic functions into an application that uses homomorphic encryption. Finally, the usage of secure co-processors have been considered for decades, but required specialized hardware that was typically not widespread.

More recently, the idea of having secure coprocessors have gained additional traction. It started on the domain of embedded devices with ARM Trustzone, but with SGX has reached common workstations and servers[3]. Intel SGX enables code to be executed in a secure enclave in a way that its data is protected even from the operating system. In addition, it supports attestation, where the code running in such secure enclave has its signature validated. After SGX, other mainstream processor manufacturers, such as AMD, have then also proposed similar approaches and with the amount of sensitive data being kept in our machines, the trend is that these hardware technologies will become ubiquitous.

In this paper, we address this problem by exploiting tools that enable the usage of SGX to host communication and processing systems. We than propose a system that combines and extend tools such as Intel SGX, SCONE [3], and SCBR [22] in a way that enables data producers to be aware of the entities that are going to consume its data (through remote attestation) and even restrict the level of granularity that these entities can consume. Through this combination of features, it is viable to produce an ecosystem of applications in which a data source produces very sensitive data that is repeatedly anonymized or aggregated by trusted entities. Less sensitive versions of the data can then be consumed by less trustworthy (or even untrusted) applications.

The rest of the paper is organized as follows. Section 2 discusses tools and concepts that are fundamental for the approach presented and a running example that will help illustrate the approach described is Section 3. After that, Section 4 presents experiments of the proof-on-concept implementation. The paper is concluded with related work in Section 5 and some final remarks in Section 6.

2 BACKGROUND

In this section, we provide a brief description of the key concepts to aid the understanding of the context and the components that will be used in our proposed architecture.

2.1 Intel SGX: Software Guard eXtensions

Securing data in order to guarantee its privacy and integrity is highly desired by end users aiming to protect sensitive information from malicious attacks. Some approaches that attempt to provide this security, specially on cloud environments, lack the ability to protect the application data from software with higher privilege levels such as hypervisors [25, 26]. In this context, Intel's Software Guard eXtensions (SGX) [10, 11] has emerged, a hardware-based

technology that ensures privacy and data integrity, protecting application code even if components such as the OS, hypervisor, etc. are untrusted.

In order to achieve this goal, Intel SGX provides a set of instructions to allow changes in memory access, creating protected areas named enclaves [19]. The enclave page cache (EPC) is where application code and data reside, managed by CPU access control policies, which prevent attacks against its content. Code outside an enclave cannot access enclave memory. However, enclave code can access untrusted memory outside the EPC, being responsible for verifying the integrity of this data.

Intel SGX also offers local and remote attestation features [1], which can be performed by a third-party to guarantee that an expected piece of software is securely running inside an enclave, on a known SGX-capable platform. Remote attestation, used in this paper, requires asymmetric cryptography, since the verification comes from outside the platform, and a special component, the quoting enclave. This enclave is responsible for creating the Intel Enhanced Privacy ID (EPID) key used for signing attestations to be certified by an EPID backend infrastructure. Only the quoting enclave knows this EPID key, which is connected to the version of the processor's firmware.

Possible usage of Intel SGX [5, 15] includes authentication technologies, online financial transactions, logging of user activities and personal information, video conferencing, and many others. Besides these examples on client machines, it is also possible to use SGX to protect backend applications. For instance, VC3 [23] runs distributed MapReduce computations in the cloud guaranteeing data privacy and ensuring the correctness and completeness of results. VC3 uses SGX to isolate memory regions, and to deploy new protocols that secure distributed MapReduce computations.

2.2 SCONE: Secure Linux Containers

With the advent of SGX and the growing use of containers for hosting applications, new approaches to handle security and privacy aspects of such structures have emerged. Here, we use SCONE [3], a Secure CONtainer Environment for Docker that uses SGX to protect given container processes, using SGX protected enclaves. This mechanism offers secure containers together with insecure operational systems, and does that in a transparent way to already existent Docker environments. For this to happen, it is only required that the host machine has a SGX-capable Intel CPU and a Linux SGX kernel driver[4] installed.

Amongst the features offered by SCONE, there are (*i*) an asynchronous system call interface to the host OS provided to container processes, allowing them to perform system calls without having to exit threads inside enclaves; (*ii*) support for transparent encryption and authentication of data through a mechanism called *shielding*, ensuring data integrity and confidentiality; (*iii*) no changes to the application code being deployed, since SCONE's special compiler automatically prepares the code to be SGX-compatible; (*iv*) simple Docker integration relying on a secure container image specially built for this purpose.

---

[3]Currently, processors with Intel SGX support are the sixth and newer generations processors of the Intel Core family and some recent Intel Xeon processors, such as the E3-1200 family, fifth generation and newer.

[4]https://01.org/intel-softwareguard-eXtensions (visited: June 05, 2017).

Besides that, providing a secure container requires a SCONE client extension to enable the creation of configuration files, spawning of such containers and for secure communication with them. During container startup, a configuration file is necessary containing keys for encryption, application arguments and environment variables. Also, the application code must be statically compiled with its library dependencies and the SCONE library.

In general lines, SCONE provides secure containers maintaining a small Trusted Computing Base (TCB) size, and reducing overheads naturally imposed by SGX enclave transitions, thanks to its asynchronous system calls mechanism and custom kernel module.

2.3 Secure Content-Based Routing

Content-based routing (CBR) is a known paradigm for communication between distributed processes that routes messages based on their content rather than by a specified destination. This allows for more scalability, dynamicity and flexibility, besides removing from the sender application the knowledge of where sent messages will end up. Such publish/subscribe communication mechanism [12, 20] can be improved by adding an extra security layer to the process, since in this scenario, the router has access to the content of the messages and subscriptions, representing a threat to the data confidentiality and integrity which might be compromised.

Considering this, here we use a Secure Content-Based Routing mechanism [22] that relies on the SGX technology previously described to provide a routing engine in an enclave. We add to SCBR features a protocol for exchanging cryptographic keys between both ends of the communication chain, producers and consumers of smart metering data, and the routing engine. As a consequence, because publications and subscriptions are encrypted and signed, the system raises protection levels against malicious attacks that could compromise the data being exchanged.

2.4 Python-SGX interpreter

The Intel SGX SDK is a development toolkit available only for C and C++ languages. This means only applications written in these languages can be adapted to run and communicate with enclaves. This presents itself as a limitation for the Intel SGX technology as porting code is an obstacle and may lead to additional bugs.

Among popular programming languages, Python deserves special attention. This year, Python was considered the Top 1 programming language in the 2017 Programming Languages ranking promoted by IEEE[5]. Very popular softwares are written in Python as well, such as OpenStack, YouTube, DropBox, Instagram and many others.

Using Intel SDK to implement SGX applications might require extra effort to port existing code, or even creating new pieces of software. For this purpose, SCONE provides a modified C compiler, based on the *libmusl*[6] library. This compiler, named *sgxmusl-gcc*[7], automatically generates the object code to be executed inside SGX enclaves, making it easier to have hardware protected applications ready to run. However, the *sgxmusl-gcc* compiler is obviously restricted to C code, and possibly with GCC supported languages, such as Fortran, through the *libgfortran* library[8].

In the light of this, and the increasing use of the Python language mentioned before, enabling Python code to run in SGX becomes attractive. We then leverage the *sgxmusl-gcc* to produce a modified Python interpreter. Our Python interpreter is compiled with the *sgxmusl-gcc* and extended to interpret and attest Python code inside SGX enclaves. All things considered, this approach increases the range of applications that can be executed using SGX as well as the number of developers capable of leveraging the technology.

However, the *sgxmusl-gcc* compiler has a few limitations. One of the major limitations is the fact that dynamic linking of libraries is not allowed. All the system libraries, such as *openssl*[9] and *ncurses*[10], together with the native Python modules required by the user's application, should be statically linked upon Python-SGX building.

Unfortunately, it is not possible to include all native Python modules at once. Static linking requires the code from all the libraries to be included in the binary file, causing a large memory overhead upon execution. Adding extra code also introduces the risk for bugs in the generated code. In practice, limiting imports is not necessarily critical as most applications, even highly complex ones, are unlikely to use too many libraries. This observation is specially true when considering the microservice approach, where functionally is well divided into a large number of services.

When it comes to external libraries, there is a level of complexity added when they are not pure Python. By default, it is not possible to interpret application code that requires such modules. However, we managed to support some important ones as the PyCrypto[11] library. This Python cryptography toolkit provides a stable and trustworthy base for writing Python code that requires cryptographic functions, such as the AES-CTR encryption mode used in this paper. To make the link possible, we had to introduce PyCrypto as a native Python module. To do this, the PyCrypto library had to be modified to be included in the Python-SGX source tree, and then able to be linked as the rest of the native libraries.

In addition, we also use Python-SGX to interpret the code for some of the components explained in Section 3.1, and we attest them in a way that guarantees the code is the one expected by the developer. We do this by introducing in the interpreter code checks for the SHA-256 hash of the application code. The hash of the code to be executed is calculated before the start of the interpretation and checked against the hash provided during the SCONE attestation process of the Python binary itself. In the big picture, Python-SGX is considered trusted because it is previously attested by SCONE and this trust is extended to the Python code executed over it.

In a summary, considering the above limitations, we managed to make possible for complex applications written in Python to be interpreted by our Python-SGX, and therefore, securely executed inside SGX enclaves in a transparent way.

---

[5]http://spectrum.ieee.org/computing/software/the-2017-top-programming-languages
[6]https://www.musl-libc.org/
[7]https://sconedocs.github.io

[8]https://gcc.gnu.org/wiki/GFortran
[9]https://www.openssl.org/
[10]https://en.wikipedia.org/wiki/Ncurses
[11]https://pypi.python.org/pypi/pycrypto

2.5 Application example: a smart metering infrastructure

For detailing the approach proposed in this paper we consider a smart metering use case. The motivation for such an application scenario is that the availability of detailed power consumption information enables analytics that can reduce power consumption by detecting anomalies and undesired configurations, recommending actions that will result in more efficient usage of the electricity.

As an example, collecting measurements at each second may enable the identification of individual appliances running in a consumer's unit. This is known as Non-Intrusive Load Monitoring (NIALM) [6]. With this information, customized recommendations can lead consumers to save considerable amounts of power [2]. Nevertheless, even without disaggregation, the usage of detailed metering for home energy management systems [4] has proved its value in practice.

On the negative side, providing detailed power consumption information reveals much more than it may seem at the first glance. Previous research has shown that even details on the multimedia content in users' TVs may be detected through detailed data [14]. It then becomes clear that even less information can reveal much about the habits of individuals of a residence.

In a summary, having detailed power consumption is clearly useful. Power utilities can use the data to better plan power generation and to understand and, therefore, influence consumers. Consumers may benefit from analytics approaches being executed over its data. However, even with clear benefits, the data should not be trusted to any application. In addition, not every customer will want to share his data. Consequently, a system that enables users to have better control over who access the data and reduces the risks of leakage can be a seed for sophisticated privacy-aware applications not only in smart grid infrastructures, but also in other smart cities and IoT application domains.

3 PRIVACY-AWARE DATA DISSEMINATION

This section describes our data dissemination platform. It begins by describing the basic components and then continues to describe a simple publication workflow. The description ends by detailing how the example introduced in Section 2 can be improved based on the platform.

3.1 Components

3.1.1 Smart Meter. Smart meters are a key component for smart grids. Such devices are responsible for collecting energy data of households, buildings, and other environments, enabling customers to reduce electricity costs by wisely monitoring their energy consumption. A smart meter can read these fine-grained measurements at specified time intervals, and communicate this information to a utility provider. For future generations smart energy systems, it is expected that not only the utility will consume this data, but also third parties will offer applications that monitor consumption and recommend efficiency actions, as discussed in Section 2.

In our scenario, we consider the Smart Meter component a device that is able to directly or indirectly send data to a remote server. In practice, because of regulatory or cost constraints this is typically done indirectly, meters send data to gateways and these send the

data to a processing system at the utility. Nevertheless, because of this indirect communication, there is much flexibility in the implementation of the communication. In our proof-of-concept we consider different meters that can be accessed through a wireless or cabled network. We then consider that energy consumption data is collected by a Metering Data Collector (MDC) component that may be specific to an equipment model or brand and then the measurements are forwarded to other systems.

3.1.2 Metering Data Collector. This component is responsible for collecting energy consumption data from the smart meter device. The MDC application connects to the device via a TCP/IP network and retrieves new data every second. The communication protocol may be specific to that device. Because the next component, named *Dispatcher*, is untrusted, encryption is needed to guarantee some security. In our use case, this untrusted component is the Dispatcher, detailed below. This encryption is currently implemented using the AES-CTR encryption mode (possibly a rotating key).

In addition, because the sole purpose of the key is to protect from the untrusted dispatcher, there are two ways this key can be created and managed: (*i*) the key is negotiated with the SCBR during the attestation process (described below); (*ii*) the key will be generated by the data source and shared with all trusted participants in the system. As we will detail later, the first approach introduces higher load to the SCBR, reducing its scalability. In contrast, the second approach requires some periodic rotation of keys.

Because the MDC sees raw data it needs to be trusted. This trust can be gained through certification and sealing (as the meters typically are) or through the usage of a trusted execution environment. In our case we consider the second. Therefore, the MDC is executed in a special Python interpreter that was generated with SCONE (as detailed in Sections 2.2 and 2.4). By executing the MDC inside an SGX enclave, we are able to validate this code before execution, ensuring that only versions with the expected signatures will be executed.

3.1.3 Dispatcher. In our scenario, the Dispatcher works as a gateway, passing along the measurements received from the MDC application to the message bus. Because the MDC may be limited in functionality, the usage of the Dispatcher enables further flexibility in the setup of the rest of the system. Furthermore, because the Dispatcher does not need to be trusted, it has many more implementation and deployment options. As an example, with an untrusted dispatcher, it is trivial to change the message bus if SCBR guarantees are not needed.

In our specific implementation, the communication with the bus requires ZeroMQ[12] connections and the Python-SGX interpreter has limited support for importing Python modules. As it is likely to occur in practice, by using an indirection level we decouple a trusted component, the MDC, from the communication protocol used by the data infrastructure running in the cloud. This decoupling eliminates the need of reimplementing the bus's communication protocol, which would possibly add more complexity to the proposed platform and its usage.

Thus, the Dispatcher simply implements a layer of communication with the bus via ZeroMQ and communicates with the MDC

---

[12]http://zeromq.org/

through simple sockets. Finally, the received encrypted measurements are sent to the Secure Content-Based Routing (SCBR) component.

3.1.4 Secure Content-Based Routing. The Secure Content-Based Routing component follows the publish–subscribe paradigm [12], in which senders of messages, named publishers, do not address messages explicitly, but rather categorize such messages regardless of which receivers, the subscribers, will be receiving them. From the subscribers' perspective, subscribers express interest in one or more type of messages and receive the ones they are interested in, regardless of their publishers.

Differently to other regular publish-subscribe middleware, SCBR has a mode in which only the publisher can submit subscriptions to its publications. We use this mode so that subscribers have to communicate with the publishers at the beginning. During this initial communication, the publisher will attest the candidate consumer, and if passed, it can handle encryption keys.

The SCBR bus securely routes messages between publishers and subscribers, as detailed in Section 2.3. Its security and privacy-awareness are consequence of the fact that the routing decisions are taken inside SGX. In our use case, we consider that sensitive information will carry its sensitivity level (in the Pub/Sub topic).

Depending on the choice on the encryption approach in the MDC, as discussed above, there are two choices: (*i*) if the MDC encryption key was negotiated with the SCBR, SCBR would decrypt the data and this data would be disseminated unencrypted; (*ii*) if the encryption key is negotiated with the trusted parties, the sensitive information (e.g., the measurements is kept encrypted even within the SCBR enclave), this could be useful for connecting systems that store information, even if the systems themselves cannot read it.

Sent messages follow a specific header format, containing the message type, or privacy level, and its encryption mode which can also be *plain-text*. SCBR allows for configuring the security level of its core, which can be set to use SGX or not. The bus uses the Intel SDK tool in its implementation and, by enabling SGX, executes the routing engine inside an enclave. From the client side, if the SGX mode is required, it can be checked as the attestation process only works if the SGX enclaves are in use.

3.1.5 Attestor. In the proposed platform, in order for consumers to receive data from SCBR, besides being registered in the bus, they need to be considered trusted and therefore, attested. With this approach, the consumer knows how to decrypt the encrypted measurements, and can have access to the published information.

The attestation process here follows the remote attestation protocol specified by SGX, as explained in Section 2.1, and uses the Intel Attestation Service (IAS). The Attestor is then responsible for mediating the attestation process of the consumers by the IAS, and then, the encryption/decryption key exchange during attestation. The process is further discussed in Section 3.2.

3.1.6 Aggregator. Aggregating individual measurements to produce full energy consumption reports and its respective billing is an important feature desired by utility providers in a smart metering scenario. Here, the Aggregator component serves this purpose and aggregates measurements generating new aggregated energy data. Time intervals may vary between minutes, hours, or months, but

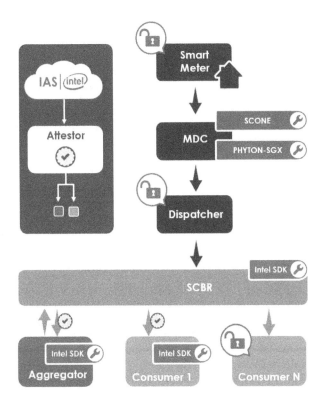

Figure 1: Architecture of data dissemination platform for smart metering infrastructures.

every message received by the Aggregator is an individual raw measurement as previously published by the Smart Meters.

During initialization, the Aggregator is attested by the IAS through the Attestor, and is then able to decrypt the received messages. After the key exchange, this component is also able to encrypt the aggregated data to be published again into the SCBR bus and later consumed by final consumers. In our implementation, this piece of code was written using the Intel SDK.

3.1.7 Final Consumers. There can be many final consumers, which are able to register to the SCBR bus and express interest in a certain type of messages. For the registration, they need to contact publishers and then will be attested by the IAS through the Attestor. As a consequence, they will receive the key to decrypt published messages. This piece of code is also developed using the Intel SDK tool. An alternative is that the consumer requests public data. In this case, the publisher would simply register it without actual attestation.

3.2 Architecture Workflow

As seen in Figure 1, the flow starts with measurements being recorded by Smart Meters. These data is then sent to the MDC application, which is interpreted by the Python-SGX interpreter. Python-SGX is attested by SCONE, and afterwards, can attest the MDC component and guarantee that the SHA-256 hash of the application code matches the hash provided during the SCONE attestation process.

The MDC then collects measurements every second from the Smart Meter, via a secure HTTPS channel, and encrypts them using the AES-CTR encryption mode. The key used for encryption is generated from an Initialization Vector (IV) and the respective decryption key is handed in during the consumer's attestation process. The MDC then sends the encrypted measurements to the Dispatcher via TCP sockets. To complete the publication flow, the Dispatcher communicates via a ZeroMQ connection with the SCBR bus, and publishes the encrypted measurement according to its privacy level.

From the same figure we can also see that the bottom half of the SCBR component represents the consumers interested in the messages published by the Dispatcher. The figure illustrates two types of consumers, Aggregators and Final Consumers, as described in Section 3.1. In our scenario, we have one aggregator and a number of final consumers. All of them should first register to the bus through the producers, and declare which type of messages they are interested in. Upon registration, such consumers are attested by the IAS through the Attestor component. This process is indicated in Figure 1 by the yellow ticks over the arrows connecting the consumers to the bus. When the attestation process is completed, the consumers will receive the key able to decrypt the published encrypted messages. This shared key is sent encrypted by a symmetric key also negotiated during the attestation.

From this point on, consumers are able to decrypt the messages received from the SCBR bus. By definition, the aggregator receives the encrypted raw measurements and aggregates them according to specific time frames previously defined. These frames may vary between seconds, hours, months, and so on. After the data is aggregated, it can be encrypted or not, and published again to the SCBR bus by the aggregator itself, which in this scenario also works as a publisher. Upon publication, the privacy level of the information is defined, and the final consumers receive them accordingly.

3.3 Securely aggregating measurements

As discussed in Section 2, we envisage a scenario where a meter will collect detailed information that is valuable for many uses. For example, a user may be interested in receiving customized recommendations on how to reduce consumption. For that, it opts in to an application that request access to its second-level data. Another user, concerned about privacy, does not take part in such application and allows only aggregated measurements (e.g., daily) to be accessible.

For our running example, we classify the impact level about criticality and sensitivity of aggregate data. We adjusted the FIPS 199 [21] model as an assessment criteria in the current example. The security model for data aggregation classifies potential impact in three levels: Low, Moderate or High. These levels can be interpreted as follows:

(1) High impact characterizes private data (e.g., an individual data collection from a particular smart meter), and the information must only be available to an aggregation system, protected by enclaves, or to applications explicitly trusted by producers (the smart meter owners). The risk of exposure or data violation would be unacceptable, resulting in

severe or catastrophic impact or noncompliance with legal requirements and loss of customer confidence.

(2) Moderated impact defines protected data (e.g., as a set of local data aggregation from a collection of smart meters), and the measurements should only be available to power supplies. The risk of exposure or data violation would be marginally acceptable, causing certain impact or reputation losses on normal activity, with adverse effects on organizational operations, assets or individuals.

(3) Low impact identifies public data (e.g., as a set of aggregated data from regional smart meters), and the information may be available freely. The risk of exposure or data violation would be acceptable for the energy company, resulting in minimal impact on normal activity.

Thus, in our example we consider that meters high-frequency measurements are published by the meters as *high impact*. These data are subscribed to by the Aggregator and by the Consumer 1, both have been explicitly trusted by the Smart Meter owner. The Aggregator computes hourly averages from the consumer measurements (e.g., for billing purposes, compatible with hour-of-the-day tariffs) and regional hourly averages (e.g., for public viewing). These two aggregations are published as *moderate* and *low-impact*, respectively. Consumer N subscribes to low-impact measurements and receives these publications even though it cannot be attested, as it is not running in an enclave.

4 EVALUATION

In this section we discuss the experiments that validate the proposed architecture. All experiments were executed in workstations with an Intel Core SGX-enabled *i7-6700* processor and 8 *GB* of RAM running Ubuntu Linux 16.04 Xenial.

In the first set of experiments, we compare a simple aggregation implemented with homomorphic encryption, which would also enable trusted data processing in untrusted infrastructures, with SGX (but without any other components of the proposed architecture), and in pure C, without SGX. The implementation used in the homomorphic encryption aggregation is based on the scheme proposed by Busom et al [8]. The goal is to illustrate how the raw SGX performance compares to a traditional approach that would enable comparable benefits for running protected data analysis in cloud environments, and to an approach that offers no security, but also no overhead.

Because of the huge discrepancies in the overhead two sets of tests were executed. The first compares homomorphic encryption and Intel SGX and the second compares Intel SGX with the pure C implementation. The results of the first tests are depicted in Figure 2. Each point in the figure is calculated from 10 experiment runs. The tests are split into two parts: on the left-hand side, it considered that 10, 50, 100 and 200 meters (or measurements) would be aggregated together to mask individual reads; on the right-hand side, the experiments consider 200, 400, 800, and 1000 measurements.

The remaining experiments consider the proposed platform. The smart meters were simulated from regular processes that would connect to the MDC component (see Section 3.1 for details). The experiments process up to 1 million measurements. Typically, two curves or box plots are shown: one, described as *SGX*, illustrates

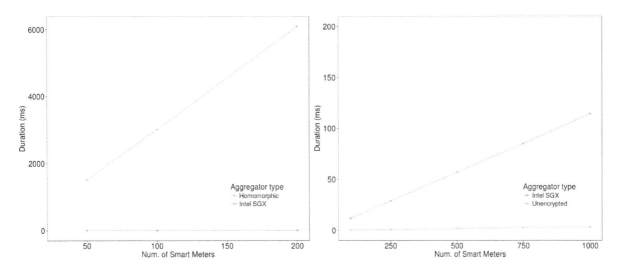

Figure 2: Example of HE vs. SGX.

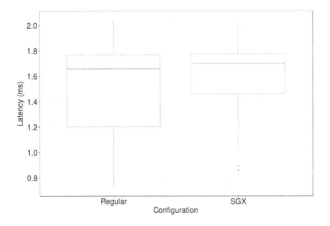

Figure 3: Latency for an isolated publication.

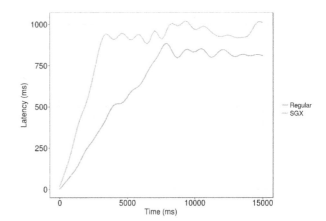

Figure 4: Latency for a burst of 1 million publications.

executions where Intel SGX usage was enabled; the other, described as *regular* considered executions in which SGX is disabled in the trusted components. In both executions, SGX and regular, the components use AES-CTR encryption for the measurement data sent through the bus. For each scenario that considers a specific data rate, the configurations were repeated 60 times. The CPU measurements consider the usage of the SCBR processes.

In the experiment depicted in Figure 3 the system was under very light load. A single measurement was published each second. In this scenario, it is possible to see that the latency for publishing a single measurement, passing through a message bus in the same physical host is not statistically different between the two configurations. We can also see that the higher latency value is similar for both configurations, meaning the worst case scenario when using SGX also happens without it.

Next, because experiments considering one isolated measurement might not be representative for more complex execution scenarios, we analyzed the system's behavior under a heavier load, processing a burst of 1 million publications from a single producer.

Figure 4 depicts the first 15 seconds of execution. The latency for publishing the measurement passing through SCBR shows an increasing behavior in the beginning of the execution, which means the message bus receives as many measurements as possible until its internal queues are full. From that moment on, we see only a small variance in latency, between 900 and 1000 milliseconds. This can be explained as a type of back-pressure mechanism, which in our case means the bus causes the transmitting device to hold off on sending data packets until the bus's bottleneck has been eliminated. We can see that such condition happens in both configurations, only in different moments, happening a slightly earlier when using SGX. After the bus' saturation occurs, the latency for both cases is similar.

Considering the same heavy load scenario of processing a burst of 1 million publications, Figure 5 shows that the CPU usage maintains the mean identified for the higher power consumption publication rate, which is around 20000 *measurements/s*, for both configurations (as will be detailed shortly). We can also see that in a regular scenario, the time to process all the publications is around

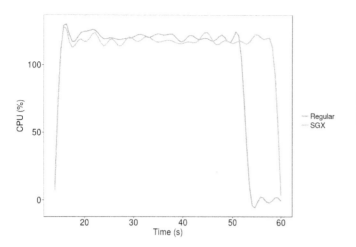

Figure 5: CPU usage for a burst of 1 million publications.

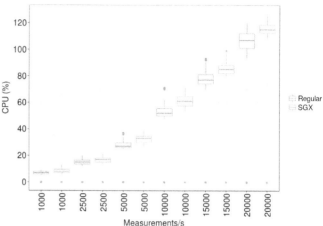

Figure 7: CPU usage for specific measurements rates.

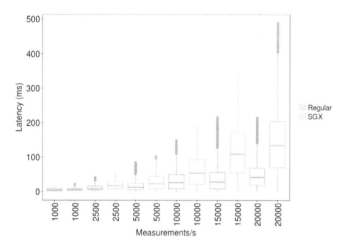

Figure 6: Latency for specific measurements rates.

53 seconds, which is smaller then when SGX is being used. Seven seconds later, in case SGX is enabled, the processes are finished.

Experiments considering a variation of publication rates can be seen in Figures 6 and 7. Considered rates were 1000, 2500, 5000, 10000, 15000 and 20000 measurements per second, being the last one the guaranteed number of publications processed in a second without accumulated delays. In Figure 6, we see that only from 15000 *measurements/s* the mean latency for both configurations starts to differ considerably. For smaller rates, differences are barely noticeable.

Figure 7 then depicts CPU consumption of the message bus. For both configurations, the usage increases as the publication rates increase. From the results we can see that there is no significantly difference between regular scenarios and when using SGX.

Our last experiment depicts the behavior of the system in the presence of periodic intense bursts of events. Each sub-figure of Figure 8 depicts one step in the progression from executing experiments with 1000 measurements/s up to 20000 measurements/s, in each step we can see how the actual delay deviates from the

ideal delay. For example, the ideal curve is depicted in red and is a straight line with an 45 degree angle. For some publications rates, the actual latency deviates from this perfect behavior.

Figure 8 depicts the executions in a 2-second time frame. This value was chosen because it depicts two cycles, hinting the recurring behavior, while not making the figure unreadable. We can see that for rates up to 5000 *measurements/s*, there is no significant visible latency deviation, the lines almost overlap each other. From 10000 *measurements/s*, we can identify a small latency when using SGX, and more clearly for both configurations when considering 20000 *measurements/s*.

5 RELATED WORK

There is a number of prior works focusing on privacy-protecting data dissemination in untrusted environments [9, 17, 28]. We further reviewed secure data dissemination solutions to understand its contributions in the context of cloud computing, focused into two fronts: privacy-preserving data and privacy-assured models for smart metering.

In order to find a solution to address the weaknesses on data exchange between cloud users and providers, the paper by Komnunos and Junejo [18] proposes an encryption scheme which uses a cipher-text policy to anonymize attributes behind the implementation of brokering services and, therefore, protects the data against privacy attacks on cloud environments. The work does not consider topics as trust and security issues from a user perspective and its effects when defining data privacy policies.

The authors in [16] propose a Privacy-as-a-Service model, defined as a set of security protocols to provide a trusted environment that protects confidential data from unauthorized access in cloud infrastructures. The authors argue that cryptographic co-processors, used in their solution, demand high resource requirements, and this might be an expensive cost for the privacy gain they offer.

In [13], the authors presented a trustworthy system relying on an additive homomorphic encryption to ensure the privacy in smart metering infrastructure. The encryption scheme implements a modular addition operation by using shared keys and provides exchange

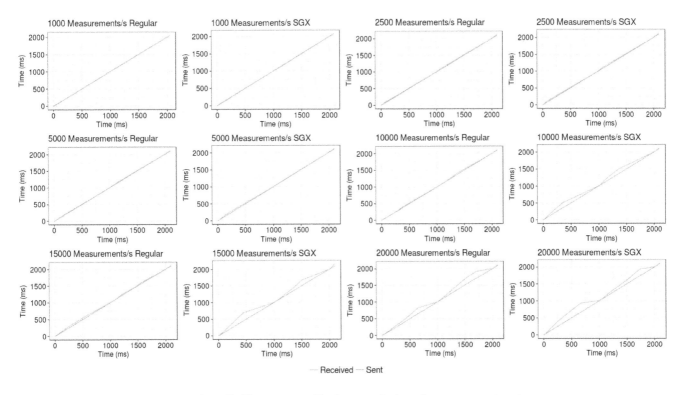

Figure 8: Detailed latency considering a variation of measurements rates.

random measurements among smart meters and utility suppliers. The protocols proposed could be archived using inexpensive smart cards. However, the aggregator must be previously attested to guarantee a trusted service.

Due to the high calculation cost of homomorphic encryption in data aggregation models, the solution in [27] proposes to perform data mining from secured data avoiding the need of users' secret key to access confidential aggregation of cloud users. The Privacy Preserving Data Mining (PPDM) technique satisfies the privacy of information stored in the cloud by the granularity level of the aggregation measurements in accordance with the level of secret key carried out of the service providers.

Another proposal [24] makes use of Intel SGX technology to provide a simple solution for privacy-preserving smart metering system. The authors have suggested a model designed by trusted smart meter devices exchanging consumer's measurements with the trusted aggregator, performed inside an SGX enclave, among a secure channel established during the attestation process.

6   CONCLUSIONS

In this paper, we have proposed a system that enables a data source that produces sensitive data to control the usage of this data by third parties. One application example is an Advanced Metering Infrastructure, where sources produce detailed metering that may reveal privacy-sensitive information such as consumer habits or, in worst cases, even detailed activities (e.g., TV preferences). In this example, the original data is consumed only by applications and services with higher levels of trust. Among these trusted services,

there could be anonymizers and aggregators that reduce the sensitivity of the data to make it consumable by less trusted services. In contrast to other approaches such as homomorphic encryption, our approach has a much lower overhead and can be more simply applied. We demonstrated its usage and feasibility through a set of experiments. As limitations, the approach depends on the usage of a specific hardware-supported extension, Intel SGX, but which is increasingly common in off-the-shelf machines. In addition, Intel also offers SGX virtualization by providing a modified KVM[13], capable of exposing SGX features of hosts to guest VMs, letting users have access to a preallocated EPC memory size. Virtualization support considerably reduces the obstacles of putting SGX support for cloud-based VMs. We have successfully configured this upstream KVM in OpenStack, the most-used open-source cloud management platform. Finally, our approach also does not protect against software bugs that could reveal or leak data.

ACKNOWLEDGMENTS

This research was partially funded by EU-BRA SecureCloud project (EC, MCTIC/RNP, and SERI, 3rd Coordinated Call, H2020-ICT-2015 Grant agreement no. 690111) and by CNPq, Brazil.

REFERENCES

[1] Ittai Anati, Shay Gueron, Simon Johnson, and Vincent Scarlata. 2013. Innovative technology for CPU based attestation and sealing. In *HASP '13: Proceedings of the 2nd International Workshop on Hardware and Architectural Support for Security and Privacy*, Vol. 13. ACM.

---

[13] https://github.com/01org/kvm-sgx/

[2] K. Carrie Armel, Abhay Gupta, Gireesh Shrimali, and Adrian Albert. 2013. Is disaggregation the holy grail of energy efficiency? The case of electricity. *Energy Policy* 52 (2013), 213 – 234. https://doi.org/10.1016/j.enpol.2012.08.062 Special Section: Transition Pathways to a Low Carbon Economy.

[3] Sergei Arnautov, Bohdan Trach, Franz Gregor, Thomas Knauth, Andre Martin, Christian Priebe, Joshua Lind, Divya Muthukumaran, Dan O'Keeffe, Mark L. Stillwell, David Goltzsche, David Eyers, Rüdiger Kapitza, Peter Pietzuch, and Christof Fetzer. 2016. SCONE: Secure Linux Containers with Intel SGX. In *Proceedings of the 12th USENIX Conference on Operating Systems Design and Implementation (OSDI'16)*. USENIX Association, Berkeley, CA, USA, 689–703. http://dl.acm.org/citation.cfm?id=3026877.3026930

[4] B. Asare-Bediako, W. L. Kling, and P. F. Ribeiro. 2012. Home energy management systems: Evolution, trends and frameworks. In *2012 47th International Universities Power Engineering Conference (UPEC)*. 1–5. https://doi.org/10.1109/UPEC.2012.6398441

[5] Manuel Barbosa, Bernardo Portela, Guillaume Scerri, and Bogdan Warinschi. 2016. Foundations of Hardware-Based Attested Computation and Application to SGX. In *2016 IEEE European Symposium on Security and Privacy (EuroS&P)*. IEEE, 245–260.

[6] Nipun Batra, Jack Kelly, Oliver Parson, Haimonti Dutta, William Knottenbelt, Alex Rogers, Amarjeet Singh, and Mani Srivastava. 2014. NILMTK: An Open Source Toolkit for Non-intrusive Load Monitoring. In *Proceedings of the 5th International Conference on Future Energy Systems (e-Energy '14)*. ACM, New York, NY, USA, 265–276. https://doi.org/10.1145/2602044.2602051

[7] J.M. Brook, S. Field, D. Shackleford, V. Hargrave, L. Jameson, and M. Roza. 2016. *The Treacherous 12: CSA's Cloud Computing Top Threats in 2016*. Technical Report. Cloud Security Alliance.

[8] N Busom, R Petrlic, F Sebé, C Sorge, and M Valls. 2016. Efficient smart metering based on homomorphic encryption. *Computer Communications* 82 (2016), 95–101.

[9] Shruti Chhabra and V. S. Dixit. 2015. Cloud Computing: State of the Art and Security Issues. *SIGSOFT Softw. Eng. Notes* 40, 2 (April 2015), 1–11. https://doi.org/10.1145/2735399.2735405

[10] Intel Corporation. 2015. Intel Software Guard Extensions. Cryptology ePrint Archive, Report 2016/086. (2015). https://software.intel.com/sites/default/.

[11] Victor Costan and Srinivas Devadas. 2016. Intel SGX Explained. Cryptology ePrint Archive, Report 2016/086. (2016). http://eprint.iacr.org/2016/086.

[12] Patrick Th. Eugster, Pascal A. Felber, Rachid Guerraoui, and Anne-Marie Kermarrec. 2003. The Many Faces of Publish/Subscribe. *ACM Comput. Surv.* 35, 2 (June 2003), 114–131. https://doi.org/10.1145/857076.857078

[13] Flavio D. Garcia and Bart Jacobs. 2011. Privacy-friendly Energy-metering via Homomorphic Encryption. In *Proceedings of the 6th International Conference on Security and Trust Management (STM'10)*. Springer-Verlag, Berlin, Heidelberg, 226–238. http://dl.acm.org/citation.cfm?id=2050149.2050164

[14] Ulrich Greveler, Peter Glösekötterz, Benjamin Justusy, and Dennis Loehr. 2012. Multimedia content identification through smart meter power usage profiles. In *Proceedings of the International Conference on Information and Knowledge Engineering (IKE)*. The Steering Committee of The World Congress in Computer Science, Computer Engineering and Applied Computing (WorldComp), 1.

[15] Matthew Hoekstra, Reshma Lal, Pradeep Pappachan, Vinay Phegade, and Juan Del Cuvillo. 2013. Using innovative instructions to create trustworthy software solutions.. In *HASP@ ISCA*. 11.

[16] Wassim Itani, Ayman Kayssi, and Ali Chehab. 2009. Privacy as a service: Privacy-aware data storage and processing in cloud computing architectures. In *8th IEEE International Symposium on Dependable, Autonomic and Secure Computing, DASC 2009*. 711–716. https://doi.org/10.1109/DASC.2009.139

[17] Xiaoqian Jiang, Shuang Wang, Zhanglong Ji, Lucila Ohno-Machado, and Li Xiong. 2012. A Randomized Response Model for Privacy-Preserving Data Dissemination. *2012 IEEE Second International Conference on Healthcare Informatics, Imaging and Systems Biology* 13, 6 (2012), 138–138. https://doi.org/10.1109/HISB.2012.63

[18] Nikos Komninos and Aisha Kanwal Junejo. 2015. Privacy Preserving Attribute Based Encryption for Multiple Cloud Collaborative Environment. In *Proceedings - 2015 IEEE/ACM 8th International Conference on Utility and Cloud Computing, UCC 2015*. 595–600. https://doi.org/10.1109/UCC.2015.104

[19] Frank McKeen, Ilya Alexandrovich, Alex Berenzon, Carlos V Rozas, Hisham Shafi, Vedvyas Shanbhogue, and Uday R Savagaonkar. 2013. Innovative instructions and software model for isolated execution.. In *HASP@ ISCA*. 10.

[20] Mohamed Nabeel, Ning Shang, and Elisa Bertino. 2012. Efficient Privacy Preserving Content Based Publish Subscribe Systems. In *Proceedings of the 17th ACM Symposium on Access Control Models and Technologies (SACMAT '12)*. ACM, New York, NY, USA, 133–144. https://doi.org/10.1145/2295136.2295164

[21] NIST. 2004. FIPS PUB 199: Standards for Security Categorization of Federal Information and Information Systems. *Fips* 199, February 2004 (2004), 13. https://doi.org/10.6028/NIST.FIPS.199

[22] Rafael Pires, Marcelo Pasin, Pascal Felber, and Christof Fetzer. 2016. Secure Content-Based Routing Using Intel Software Guard Extensions. In *Proceedings of the 17th International Middleware Conference (Middleware '16)*. ACM, New York, NY, USA, Article 10, 10 pages. https://doi.org/10.1145/2988336.2988346

[23] Felix Schuster, Manuel Costa, Cédric Fournet, Christos Gkantsidis, Marcus Peinado, Gloria Mainar-Ruiz, and Mark Russinovich. 2015. VC3: trustworthy data analytics in the cloud using SGX. In *2015 IEEE Symposium on Security and Privacy*. IEEE, 38–54.

[24] Leandro Ventura Silva, Rodolfo Marinho, Jose Luis Vivas, and Andrey Brito. 2017. Security and Privacy Preserving Data Aggregation in Cloud Computing. In *Proceedings of the Symposium on Applied Computing (SAC '17)*. ACM, New York, NY, USA, 1732–1738. https://doi.org/10.1145/3019612.3019795

[25] S. Subashini and V. Kavitha. 2011. Review: A Survey on Security Issues in Service Delivery Models of Cloud Computing. *J. Netw. Comput. Appl.* 34, 1 (Jan. 2011), 1–11. https://doi.org/10.1016/j.jnca.2010.07.006

[26] Jakub Szefer, Eric Keller, Ruby B. Lee, and Jennifer Rexford. 2011. Eliminating the Hypervisor Attack Surface for a More Secure Cloud. In *Proceedings of the 18th ACM Conference on Computer and Communications Security (CCS '11)*. ACM, New York, NY, USA, 401–412. https://doi.org/10.1145/2046707.2046754

[27] Mebae Ushdia, Kouichi Itoh, Yoshinori Katayama, Fumihiko Kozakura, and Hiroshi Tsuda. 2013. A Proposal of Privacy-Preserving Data Aggregation on the Cloud Computing. In *2013 16th International Conference on Network-Based Information Systems*. 141–148. https://doi.org/10.1109/NBiS.2013.24

[28] Jorge Werner, Carla Merkle Westphall, Rafael Weingärtner, Guilherme A. Geronimo, and Carlos B. Westphall. 2015. An approach to IdM with privacy in the cloud. In *Proceedings - 15th IEEE International Conference on Computer and Information Technology, CIT 2015, 14th IEEE International Conference on Ubiquitous Computing and Communications, IUCC 2015, 13th IEEE International Conference on Dependable, Autonomic and Secure Computing, DASC 2015 and 13th IEEE International Conference on Pervasive Intelligence and Computing, PICom 2015*. 168–175. https://doi.org/10.1109/CIT/IUCC/DASC/PICOM.2015.26

Reliable and Energy Efficient Resource Provisioning and Allocation in Cloud Computing

Yogesh Sharma
Western Sydney University
NSW, Australia
y.sharma@westernsydney.edu.au

Bahman Javadi
Western Sydney University
NSW, Australia
b.javadi@westernsydney.edu.au

Weisheng Si
Western Sydney University
NSW, Australia
w.si@westernsydney.edu.au

Daniel Sun
DATA61-CSIRO
Australia
daniel.sun@data61.csiro.au

ABSTRACT

Reliability and Energy-efficiency is one of the biggest trade-off challenges confronting cloud service providers. This paper provides a mathematical model of both reliability and energy consumption in cloud computing systems and analyses their interplay. This paper also proposes a formal method to calculate the finishing time of tasks running in a failure prone cloud computing environment using checkpointing and without checkpointing. To achieve the objective of maximizing the reliability and minimizing the energy-consumption of cloud computing systems, three resource provisioning and virtual machine (VM) allocation policies using the aforementioned mathematical models are proposed. These three policies are named Reliability Aware Best Fit Decreasing (RABFD), Energy Aware Best Fit Decreasing (EABFD), Reliability-Energy Aware Best Fit Decreasing (REABFD). A simulation based evaluation of the proposed policies has been done by using real failure traces and workload models. The results of our experiments demonstrated that by considering both reliability and energy factors during resource provisioning and VM allocation, the reliability and energy consumption of the system can be improved by 23% and 61%, respectively.

KEYWORDS

Cloud Computing; Failures; Reliability; Energy Consumption; Virtual Machines; Resource Provisioning; Bag of Tasks; Checkpointing

1 INTRODUCTION

Cloud computing has revolutionized the Information Technology sector by giving computing a perspective of service to users. Though the acceptance of cloud computing technology is increasing every day, it is still facing numerous challenges because of its complex and large-scale architecture. Reliability and Energy-efficiency are

two key challenges that need careful attention and investigation. In this study, reliability is considered as the probability with which an application/task will finish the execution before the occurrence of a failure. A failure in the services of a cloud costs significantly to both providers and customers. The report [12] from Ponemon institute in 2016 revealed that the average down-time cost of data centers due to outages is approximately $740,357 per year. According to the Information week, each year IT outages result in the revenue loss of more than $26.5 billion [19]. The energy requirement to operate the cloud infrastructure is also increasing in proportion to the operational costs. Approximately, 45% of the total operational expenses of IBM data centers goes in electricity bills. It has been estimated that the servers mounted in Microsoft's cloud based data-centers consumes around 2 terawatts-hours (TWh) of energy per year for which the company pays approximately $2.5 billion per year as electricity bills [1]. Apart from the operational costs, huge amount of energy consumption by cloud computing infrastructure causes huge amount of carbon and green house gases emission in the environment.

To maximize the reliability of the cloud computing services, all the cloud service vendors add back-up resources/hosts (hosts, nodes and resources are being used interchangeably in this work) and use replication as well as load balancing as fault tolerance mechanism. Adding extra resources increases energy consumption more steeply than the reliability. The key technique used to reduce the energy consumption is by running the resources on a low power scaling level or by turning off the under-utilized or idle resources such as back-up by migrating the running virtual machines (VM) from the under-utilized resources to other resources. Turning off the back-up resources will reduce the reliability of the system. For example, in the case of VM consolidation (key technique to reduce energy consumption in cloud computing systems), if a physical machine fails due to some hardware or software issues before the completion of tasks and there are no recovery/back-up resources, then all the VMs and their corresponding processes will have to start again. This will dramatically increase overheads such as energy consumption and resource utilization.

This creates a critical trade-off between the reliability and energy efficiency of the cloud computing systems. To make the cloud-computing systems reliable and energy-efficient, a mathematical framework is provided in this paper to show the interplay of these two factors. Following are the contributions of this work

(1) A mathematical model to calculate the reliability and energy consumption while executing the tasks by the VMs on cloud computing resources in the presence of failures.

(2) A formal method to calculate the finishing time of the tasks in the presence of failures running on cloud resources with and without checkpointing.

(3) Resource provisioning and VM allocation policies using the proposed models to optimize the reliability and energy-efficiency of the cloud computing systems.

The remainder of the paper is organized as follows: Section 2 gives a brief survey about the existing work on reliability and energy-efficiency of cloud computing systems jointly. Section 3 explains the system architecture used in this work followed by the workload model and deadline model. Section 4 presents the reliability model and application/task finishing time with the given reliability using checkpointing and without checkpointing. Section 5 includes the formulation of energy consumption while executing the tasks in the presence of failures. In section 6, resource provisioning and VM allocation policies using the proposed models are presented. Section 7 consists of the details about the system set-up, workload model, performance evaluation metrics and reports the results in graphical form. Section 8 concludes this work.

2 RELATED WORK

Most of the work in the literature either explored reliability or energy consumption of cloud computing systems. Very limited work has been done by combining these two variables. A survey of the state of art in reliability and energy efficiency mechanisms has been provided in our previous work [23]. This section discusses the recent works covering both reliability and energy efficiency.

It has been claimed that as the operating frequency of a system increases wrt to supply voltage, reliability of the system increases but energy efficiency decreases [28]. This makes the task scheduling a challenge to achieve these two contradictive goals at the same time. In response to the challenge three different algorithms such as SHRHEFT, SHRCPOP and SHREERM have been proposed by Longxin Zhang et al. [27]. Dynamic voltage scaling and shared recovery technique have been used to regulate the energy consumption and to ensure the reliability, respectively. After performing the experiments, it has been concluded that SHREERM algorithm surpasses the rest. With the same objectives, a genetic algorithm (BOGA) for task-scheduling to optimize the reliability and energy-consumption of high performance computing systems has been proposed by the same authors [26]. The performance of the proposed algorithm has been compared with other two algorithms such as modified MODE and MOHEFT and the superiority of the new algorithm has been shown over the other algorithms. All the approaches proposed in [27] [26] are focused specifically on high performance computing systems. It has also been assumed that at most one failure will occur during the life time of a task. In our work, this assumption has been rejected with the injection of multiple failures.

Xiwei Qiu et al. [21] provides a theoretical correlation model for the fine grained measurement of reliability, power consumption and performance of cloud computing systems. A frequency scaling based power model while considering maximum CPU utilization

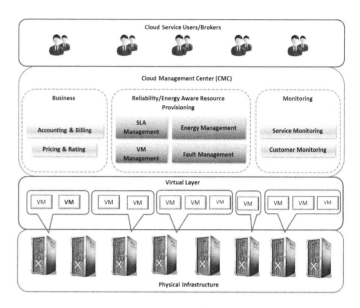

Figure 1: System Architecture

has been used where as we have formulated the power consumption based on variable utilization while operating CPU at maximum frequency. The proposed work has been analysed numerically except the reliability model which has been simulated. However, our evaluation of the proposed formulation has been done both analytically and by using simulation though only simulation based results have been reported.

Amir Varasteh et al. [24] have studied the interplay of energy consumption and reliability while performing the VM consolidation in cloud computing systems. A fine grained mathematical model has been provided to minimize the total data center cost while regulating the energy consumption and reliability. The proposed model has been analysed using matlab based simulation where as we have shown the interplay of both metrics using simulation based results using real life data. Authors have calculated the reliability of homogeneous systems as the function of system activity (on-off cycles) where as we have calculated the reliability under the occurrence of failures in a heterogeneous environment. Authors have used the random VM allocation to the physical machines to test their models. However, we have proposed three heuristics to allocate the VMs besides the random allocation.

3 SYSTEM ARCHITECTURE

The cloud computing environment considered in this work consists of a pool P of failure prone heterogeneous resources/nodes. From the resource pool, resources gets provisioned to run the heterogeneous VMs executing the tasks arriving at a specific rate. In Figure 1, the model has been divided into four different layers. The bottom layer consisting of the resources such as servers on top of which the VMs are mounted. The Virtual layer is responsible for the allocation of VMs according to the decisions made at the Cloud Management Center (CMC). The CMC is the heart of the architecture where all the reliability and energy aware resource provisioning and allocation policies are existing. The role of CMC is to gather the parameters from the energy managment and fault management modules and takes the decision about the VM allocation so that the reliability of the system will be maximized and energy consumption will be minimized. Users/Brokers are submitting their tasks to the CMC seeking execution before the deadline.

On the arrival of new tasks, the current status of the resources (gathered at monitoring module in CMC) and resource requirements of new tasks get evaluated at CMC. On the basis of the evaluation, optimized decisions about the resource provisioning and VM allocation takes place according to the proposed algorithms to regulate the reliability and energy-efficiency of the system. The number of VMs running on a provisioned node will not exceed the number of cores available on the node. One core will be allocated to each VM and VMs are not allowed to share the cores with each other (such configuration can be obtained in Xen [2] hypervisor). Memory of the host is being shared by the running VMs and to avoid the interference during run time, each VM has an exclusive share of the host memory.

3.1 Application Model

Bag-of-Task(BoT) applications, composed of bags or groups of independent and sequential compute intensive tasks arriving at a specific arrival rate (Table 2) have been used in this work. In BoT applications which can also be seen referred as Parameter Sweep Applications [8], there is no dependency and communication between the tasks. The most common examples of BoT applications are image manipulation applications (astronomy, image rendering, video survelliance), data mining applications, Monte Carlo simulations and intensive search applications. Each BoT consists of set of independent tasks, $T = \{t_i \mid 1 \le i \le n\}$. Every task t_i has a corresponding length, l_i. In this work, the length of a task has been refered to the number of instructions. For each task t_i a VM $vm_i \in VM$, where $VM = \{vm_i \mid 1 \le i \le n\}$ has been instantiated. To launch the desired number of VMs, a number of physical machines or nodes, $N = \{n_j \mid 1 \le i \le m\}$ gets provisioned according to the available CPU cores. Every task has a deadline d_i associated to it which has been calculated according to the model proposed in the following section.

3.2 Deadline Model

The tasks are non-preemptable and the execution of the application will be finished when the last task will complete the execution. Every task t_i has a corresponding deadline d_i, which has been calculated as

$$d_i = \begin{cases} s_i + (f.l_i), & \text{if } [s_i + (f.l_i)] < c_i \\ c_i, & \text{otherwise} \end{cases} \quad (1)$$

s_i, l_i and c_i are the starting time, task length and finishing time of a task t_i, respectively [15]. f is the stringency factor that defines the deadline strictness i.e. higher the value of f is, higher deadline relaxation the task has. All the proposed resource provisioning and allocation policies have been evaluated by using $f = 1.2$ i.e. normal deadline.

Rather than rejecting a task for a deadline miss (hard deadline), the soft deadline concept has been adopted which means it reduces

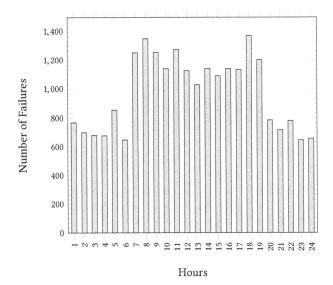

Figure 2: Failure count vs. daily hours

the value of the computation for the users [6]. More the execution of a task will be delayed, more the value will be reduced.

4 RELIABILITY MODEL

The proposed reliability model is based on the utilization of the system. Figure 2 shows the failure count per hour in LANL failure traces taken from Failure Trace Archieve [17], an online repository of failure traces gathered from various sites. It has been observed that during the working hours from 7 am to 7 pm, the number of failures are higher than the non-working hours. It can be interperated as a correlation between the occurrence of failures and system activity/utilization. During the working hours the utilization/activity of the systems is higher than the non-working hours which increases the occurrence of failures. The same conclusion has been drawn in [14] [22]. On the basis of the given conclusion, a linear failure rate (failure rate and hazard rate are being used interchangeably in this work) model directly proportional to the utilization has been proposed as follows

$$\lambda_{ij} = \lambda_{max_j} u_i^{\beta} \quad (2)$$

where, λ_{ij} is the failure rate of a VM vm_i running on a node n_j with utilization u_i and λ_{max_j} is the failure rate of node n_j at maximum utilization. In this work, it has been assumed that all the running VMs shares the maximum hazard rate similar to the physical node n_j which they are running on. β is a sensitivity factor which express the sensitivity of failure rate towards the utilizaiton. In this study, a strict linear relationship between the hazard rate and utilization of a system has been considered by taking β equal to 1. As failures in cloud computing systems are inevitable, every node n_j in the resource pool has a Mean Time between Failures ($MTBF_{max_j}$) at maximum utilization that has been calculated by the cloud coordinator at CMC empirically from the node history.

Hazard rate or Failure rate (λ_{max_j}) for a node n_j at maximum utilization will be calculated as

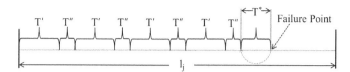

Figure 3: Recovery from Failure with Checkpointing

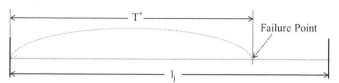

Figure 4: Recovery from Failure without Checkpointing

$$\lambda_{max_j} = \frac{1}{MTBF_{max_j}} \tag{3}$$

The failure rate has been assumed to be following poisson distribution [28][27] and remains constant for each utilization level. So the probability with which vm_i running on a node n_j with utilization u_i with hazard rate λ_{ij} will finish the execution of a task t_i of length l_i without the occurrence of a failure will be given as

$$R_{vm_{ij}} = \exp^{-\lambda_{ij} \times l_i} \tag{4}$$

To get the utilization of each VM, the length of corresponding tasks gets normalized wrt to the task of maximum length, l_{max}. In this work, VMs fail only when the node which they are running on fails. So the node and VMs have serial relationship such that when the node fails, all the associated VMs fail. The probability with which a node n_j will be able to finish the execution of all the m tasks being executed by m VMs before the occurrence of a failure has been calculated as

$$R_j = \prod_{i=1}^{m} (R_{vm_{ij}}) \tag{5}$$

However provisioned nodes fail independently [21]. Between the provisioned nodes, neither the serial relationship nor parallel relationship exists. So the reliability of the system has been calculated as the average of the reliabilitiy values possessed by all the provisioned nodes at a particular instance.

4.1 Fault Tolerance and Task Execution Model

In this work, two methods have been used to recover from a failure i.e. Checkpointing and Restart from the beginning. In the literature, checkpointing mechanism has been used intensively to provide fault-tolerance in cloud computing systems. Though the solutions provided by using checkpointing method are elegant, they are very costly in terms of overheads which make it some-times impractical. If a failure will not occur, checkpointing adds the overhead of 151 hours for a job of length 100 hours in a petaflop system [20]. However, if a failure occurs, re-execution of the failed task from the last checkpoint (Fig. 3) saves a good amount of re-execution period.

4.1.1 Finishing Time with Checkpointing. In the Figure 3, T' represents the checkpoint interval and T'' represents the checkpoint overhead such that time taken by the system to save the checkpoint of the running task on some stable storage. In this study, the value of T'' is equal to 20 seconds, which has been considered as the optimized minimum value in the previous studies [9]. We have assumed that the storage where all the checkpoints are getting stored is failure free. T^* represents the time required to re-execute

the part of the task that was lost because of the occurrence of a failure. To further reduce the checkpointing overhead, risk based checkpointing mechanism [18] has been used in this work. In risk based checkpointing, if the expected amount of lost work before the checkpoint is smaller than the cost of checkpoint T'' then skip the checkpoint.

To calculate the length of the lost part of the failed task t_i of length l_i that need to be re-executed on a node n_j, first it is required to calculate the interval of checkpointing T'_j for that node, which has been calculated as follows by using Young's formula [25]

$$T'_j = \sqrt{2 \times T'' \times MTBF_j} \tag{6}$$

$T^{\#}$ is the part of a task that had been executed before the occurrence of a failure. The number of checkpoint intervals that took place before the occurrence of a failure on a node n_j while executing the task t_i will be calculated as

$$N'_{ij} = \left\lfloor \frac{T^{\#}_{ij}}{T'_j} \right\rfloor \tag{7}$$

The length of the lost part of failed task t_i that need to be re-executed will be calculated as

$$T^*_{ij} = \left(\frac{T^{\#}_{ij}}{T'_i} - N'_{ij} \right) \times T'_i \tag{8}$$

Besides the checkpointing overheads and re-execution part of the failed task, time to return (TTR) from a failed state to running state also adds to the finishing time of a task. So, the finishing time of a task t_i of length l_i executing on node n_j after the occurrence of n failures and m checkpoints has been calculated as follows

$$T^{\$}_{ij} = \begin{cases} l_i + \sum_{k=0}^{n} T^*_{(ij)_k} + \left(T'' \times \sum_{q=0}^{m} N'_{(ij)_q} \right) + \sum_{k=0}^{n} TTR_{(ij)_k}, \\ \qquad\qquad\qquad\qquad\qquad\qquad \text{if } k, q > 0 \\ l_i \qquad\qquad\qquad\qquad\qquad\qquad \text{otherwise} \end{cases} \tag{9}$$

4.1.2 Finishing Time without Checkpointing. Due to the expensive implementation of checkpointing mechanism, restarting of the execution of a failed task or job from the beginning (Fig. 4) is more preferable in practice because of the less overheads. We are claiming the adoption of task restart mechanism on the basis of the discussions and surveys done at the Fujitsu Primergy high-performance, distributed-memory cluster named Raijin located at National Computing Infrastructure (NCI) facility in Australia[2]. As there are no checkpoints in this case, the lost part of the task that

[2]https://nci.org.au/systems-services/national-facility/peak-system/raijin/

need to be re-executed T^* is equal to the part of the task length that has been executed before the occurrence of a failure $T^\$$. So the finishing time of a task t_i of length l_i executing on node n_j after the occurrence of n failures has been calculated as follows

$$T_{ij}^\$ = \begin{cases} l_i + \sum_{k=0}^{n} T_{(ij)_k}^* + \sum_{k=0}^{n} TTR_{(ij)_k}, \text{if } k > 0 \\ l_i \qquad\qquad\qquad\qquad\qquad \text{otherwise} \end{cases} \quad (10)$$

For both of the above mentioned task recovery mechanisms, the total finishing time of all the t tasks running on a provisioned node n_j will be calculated as

$$T_j^\$ = \sum_{i=1}^{t} T_{ij}^\$ \quad (11)$$

Total finishing time of all the tasks running on n provisioned nodes in the presence of failures will be calculated as

$$T_{total}^\$ = \sum_{j=1}^{n} T_j^\$ \quad (12)$$

The change in the execution length of a BoT application consisting of t tasks because of the occurrence of failures will be given as the difference between the total finishing time and actual length of the application such that the total finishing time without failures

$$\Delta T^\$ = T_{total}^\$ - \sum_{i=1}^{t} l_i \quad (13)$$

5 ENERGY MODEL

Many devices such as CPU, storage, memory, network interfaces and other PCI devices contribute to the power consumption of the system. But in the literature, it has been argued that CPU is the biggest power consumer despite of the advancement in the hardware and software technology [4] [16]. Based on the literature, this work has been focused on the energy minimization by regulating the utilization of CPU while operating at maximum frequency. As assumed, nodes in the resource pool has different minimum (P_{min}) and maximum power (P_{max}) cosumptions. The power consumption by a VM vm_i with utilization u_i running on a node n_j will be calculated as

$$P_j(u_i) = (frac_j \times P_{max_j}) + ((1 - frac_j) \times P_{max_j} \times u_i) \quad (14)$$

$frac_j$ is the fraction of minimum, min_j and maximum, max_j power consumption for a node n_j [3]. The energy consumption is the amount of power consumed per unit time. In the presence of failures, the energy consumption is the sum of energy consumed while executing the task length and energy wastage because of the failure overheads. So the energy consumption by a VM, vm_i running on node n_j while executing a task of length l_i in the presence of failures will be calculated as

$$E_{vm_{ij}} = \left(P_j(u_i) \times l_i \right) + E_{waste_{ij}} \quad (15)$$

As shown in equations 9-10, the finishing time of a task changes because of the occurrence of failures. Along with the re-execution time, there are other factors that adds to the execution time of a task

such as down-time (TTR) i.e. time that system takes to restart the execution and other overheads. Only re-execution time of the task, checkpoint overheads and system down-time have been considered in this study to calculate the energy wastage. During the down-time, system is in non-working condition so it does not contribute to the energy wastage.

5.1 Energy wastage with checkpointing

For the checkpointing, the energy wastage will further split into the energy consumption while saving the checkpoints and energy consumption while re-executing the lost part of a task.

$$E_{waste_{ij}} = E_{checkpoint_{ij}} + E_{re-execute_{ij}} \quad (16)$$

The power consumption while saving the checkpoints on a disk consumes less power than power consumption during the execution of a task. In this study, $1.15 \times P_{min}$ has been taken as the power consumption while saving the checkpoints [10]. So the energy wastage while using the checkpointing has been calculated as

$$E_{checkpoint_{ij}} = \begin{cases} 1.15 \times P_{min_j} \times \left(T'' \times \sum_{q=0}^{m} N_{(ij)_q}' \right), \text{if } q > 0 \\ 0 \qquad\qquad\qquad\qquad\qquad\qquad\quad \text{otherwise} \end{cases} \quad (17)$$

The energy consumed while re-executing the lost part of the task t_i because of the occurrence of n failures has been calculated as

$$E_{re-execute_{ij}} = \begin{cases} P_j(u_i) \times \sum_{k=0}^{n} T_{(ij)_k}^*, \text{if } k > 0 \\ 0 \qquad\qquad\qquad\quad \text{otherwise} \end{cases} \quad (18)$$

5.2 Energy wastage without checkpointing

In the absence of checkpointing, the only energy that will be wasted is the energy consumption while performing the re-execution of the lost part of a task because of the occurrence of n failures

$$E_{waste_{ij}} = \begin{cases} P_j(u_i) \times \sum_{k=0}^{n} T_{(ij)_k}^*, \text{if } k > 0 \\ 0 \qquad\qquad\qquad\quad \text{otherwise} \end{cases} \quad (19)$$

So, the total energy consumption by n provisioned nodes allocated to m VMs while finishing all the tasks of BoT application in the presence of failures using checkpointing and without checkpointing will be calculated as

$$E_{total} = \sum_{i=1}^{n} \sum_{j=1}^{m} E_{vm_{ij}} \quad (20)$$

6 RESOURCE PROVISIONING AND VM ALLOCATION POLICIES

With the given BoT application consisting of a set of BoTs with n independent tasks in each and a pool of failure prone cloud resources, the challenge is how to provision the resources and allocate the VMs executing the tasks in order to maximize the reliability and minimize the energy consumption while keeping the turnaround time of every task less than corresponding deadline.

Table 1: Nomenclature used in algorithms and functions

Notation	Explanation
B	Set of Bag of Tasks
T	Set of Tasks in a Bag
t_i	i_{th} task
l_i	Length of i_{th} task
l_{max}	Length of a longest task in T
R	List of Resources/Nodes
R_{sorted}	Sorted list of Resources
V	Set of Virtual Machines (VMs)
V_{sorted}	Sorted list of VMs
r_j	j_{th} node
λ_j	Current Hazard Rate of j_{th} node
P_j	Current Power consumption of j_{th} node
$MTBF_j$	Current Mean Time Between Failure of j_{th} node
Ψ_j	Ratio of $MTBF_j$ and P_j
vm_i	i_{th} virtual machine
u_i	Utilization corresponding to i_{th} VM
RC_j	Remaining cores of j_{th} node
S_j	State of j_{th} node $i.e.$ failed or active
rel_{ij}	Reliability of i_{th} virtual machine on j_{th} node
pow_{ij}	Power consumption of i_{th} virtual machine on j_{th} node

The cloud co-ordinator periodically receives the BoTs at a fixed interval rate. As assumed, for each task in a BoT, one VM will be launched. So the number of VMs will be equal to the number of tasks that need to be executed. All the nodes at physical infrastructure layer (Fig. 1) have the hazard rate and power consumption at maximum utilization that has been recorded at CMC during previous executions. For simplicity, we have assumed that resource requirements of all the VMs will be fulfilled by the resources present in the cloud based data center. Depending on the objectives of the cloud provider three list based greedy heuristics such as Reliability Aware Best Fit Decreasing (RABFD), Energy Aware Best Fit Decreasing (EABFD) and Reliability-Energy Aware Best Fit Decreasing (REABFD) have been proposed to provision the resources and to allocate the VMs. As the base line policy, Opportunistic Load Balancing (OLB)[5] has been used.

Function 1 Reliability Aware Best Fit Decreasing (RABFD)

function RELIABILITYAWARE(R)
  // Calculate the current Hazard Rate of a resource by using equation 2
1: **for all** $j \in R$ **do**
2:   $\lambda_j \leftarrow r_j.calculateCurrentHazardRate()$
3: **end for**
4: **for all** $j \in R$ **do**
5:   $R_{sorted} \leftarrow \lambda_j.sortHazard\text{-}rateIncreasing()$
6: **end for**
7: **return** R_{sorted}
  end function

Algorithm 1 Resource Provisioning and VM Allocation

1: **Input: Set of Bag of Tasks, B; List of Resources, R and Policy**
2: **Output: Set of Provisioned Resources and Allocated VMs**
3: **if** $(Policy == RABFD)$ **then**
4:   $R_{sorted} \leftarrow$ RELIABILITYAWARE(R)
5: **else if** $(Policy == EABFD)$ **then**
6:   $R_{sorted} \leftarrow$ ENERGYAWARE(R)
7: **else if** $(Policy == REABFD)$ **then**
8:   $R_{sorted} \leftarrow$ RELIABILITYANDENERGYAWARE(R)
9: **else**
    //Default case is for OLB policy
10: **end if**
11: **for all** $b \in B$ **do**
12:   **for all** $i \in T$ **do**
13:     $vm_i = t_i.taskAssignment()$
14:     $V \leftarrow vm_i$
      // Calculating utilization of each VM
15:     $u_i = l_i/l_{max}$
16:     $U \leftarrow u_i$
17:   **end for**
    // Sorting VMs in decreasing order according to their utilization
18:   **for all** $i \in V$ **do**
19:     $V_{sorted} \leftarrow vm_i.sortUtilizationDecreasing()$
20:   **end for**
21:   **for all** $i \in V_{sorted}$ **do**
22:     $VM_{cores_i} \leftarrow vm_i.coresRequired()$
23:     **for all** $j \in R_{sorted}$ **do**
24:       **if** $((RC_j \geq VM_{cores_i})$ && $(S_j \neq failed))$ **then**
25:         $r_j \leftarrow vm_i.allocateHost()$
26:         $RC_j = RC_j - VM_{cores_i}$
        // Calculate VM reliability by using equation 4
27:         $rel_{ij} \leftarrow vm_i.calculateReliability()$
        // Estimate VM power consumption by using equa-equation 14
28:         $pow_{ij} \leftarrow vm_i.estimatePower()$
29:         **if** $(RC_j == 0)$ **then**
30:           $R_{sorted} = R_{sorted} - R_{sorted_j}$
31:         **end if**
32:         break
33:       **end if**
34:     **end for**
35:   **end for**
36: **end for**

6.1 Reliability Aware Best Fit Decreasing (RABFD)

In this policy (Function 1), all the VMs executing tasks of each incoming BoT will be sorted in decreasing order according to their utilization and all the resources will be sorted in increasing order according to their hazard-rate corresponding to the current utilization (equation 2). After sorting, the resource provisioning will be done and VM corresponding to each task will be instantiated (Algorithm 1). After the instantiation, the allocation of VMs will be done in such a way that the VM with maximum utilization will get allocated to a resource with minimum hazard-rate.

6.2 Energy Aware Best Fit Decreasing (EABFD)

This policy has been proposed in Function 2 to optimize the energy consumption by the VMs in the presence of failures. In this policy all the resources will be sorted in the increasing order according to their power consumption corresponding to the current utilization (equation 14), so that the VM with maximum utilization will be allocated to a node with minimum power consumption.

Function 2 Energy Aware Best Fit Decreasing (EABFD)

---

    function ENERGYAWARE(R)
    // *Calculate the current power consumption of a resource by using*
    equation 14
1: **for all** $j \in R$ **do**
2:    $P_j \leftarrow r_j$.calculateCurrentPowerConsumption()
3: **end for**
4: **for all** $j \in R$ **do**
5:    $R_{sorted} \leftarrow P_j$.sortPowerIncreasing()
6: **end for**
7: **return** R_{sorted}
    end function

6.3 Reliability-Energy Aware Best Fit Decreasing (REABFD)

The objective of this policy is to optimize the reliability and energy consumption both at the same time. In the given policy in Function 3, the ratio of $MTBF_j$ and power consumption, P_j corresponding to the current utilization for each node has been used to rank the resources. All the resources will be sorted in decreasing order according to the calculated ratio. A VM with maximum utilization gets allocated to a node with highest ratio value (Algorithm 1).

Function 3 Reliability and Energy Aware Best Fit Decreasing (REABFD)

---

    function RELIABILITYANDENERGYAWARE(R)
1: **for all** $j \in R$ **do**
2:    $MTBF_j \leftarrow r_j$.calculateCurrentMTBF()
3:    $P_j \leftarrow r_i$.calculateCurrentPowerConsumption()
4:    $\Psi_j \leftarrow (MTBF_j) / (P_j)$
5: **end for**
6: **for all** $j \in R$ **do**
7:    $R_{sorted} \leftarrow \Psi_j$.sortMTBFPowerRatioIncreasing()
8: **end for**
9: **return** R_{sorted}
    end function

6.4 Opportunistic Load Balancing(OLB)

This policy has been used as a baseline policy. In OLB, no criteria has been used to rank the resources and no preprocessing of VMs has been done based on their utilization as done in the previous policies. All the VMs executing tasks associated to incoming BoTs

gets allocated in random order as they are arriving to the next available node (Algorithm 1).

7 PERFORMANCE EVALUATION

In order to evaluate the architecture proposed in Figure 1 and to evaluate the proposed resource provisioning and VM allocation policies, we have extended a popular cloud computing simulator i.e. CloudSim [7] by adding failure injectors and fault tolerance mechanisms.

7.1 Datacenter Configuration

The hardware configuration of more than 2000 hosts of the datacenter has been taken from Los Alamos National Laboratory (LANL) data set of Failure Trace Archive (FTA)[17]. FTA is an online public repository providing failure traces gathered from 26 different computing sites. This work has used LANL traces specifically because of the precise details provided regarding the failure start time and end time, causes of failures and node configuration. Traces from LANL systems were collected between year June 1996 to November 2005 and covers data from 23 high performance computing systems consisting of 4750 nodes in total. The mean time between failures (MTBF) and mean time to return (MTTR) for each node at maximum utilization have been calculated by using the failure information provided in the traces. To calculate an accordant value of MTBF and MTTR, only the nodes with event count more than 3 in the traces have been considered in this work.

To calculate the power consumption, the values of minimum and maximum power consumptions corresponding to a node are taken from spec2008 benckmark[3]. To select the realistic datacenter nodes, we have matched the core count and memory capacity of the nodes with the values provided in the traces. This approach has been used by Peter Garraghan et al. [11] by using Google trace logs. On the basis of the match, we have selected Intel Platform SE7520AF2 Server Board, HP ProLiant DL380 G5, HP ProLiant DL758 G5, HP ProLiant DL560 Gen9 and Dell PowerEdge R830 as 2, 4, 32, 128 and 256 core nodes with 4GB, 16GB, 32GB, 64GB and 256GB memory, respectively.

7.2 Workload Model

To generate the BoTs workload, model proposed by Iosup et al. [13] has been used with parameters given in table 2. In the analysis it has been established that the arrival of jobs behaves differently in peak and off-peak times. To provision the enough number of nodes for the fair evaluation of proposed policies, the inter-arrival time has been modeled using peak time workload following Weibull distribution with scale and shape parameters equal to 4.25 and 7.86, respectively. Every incoming BoT consists of 2^x tasks where x follows Weibull distrubution with scale and shape parameters given in Table 2. The length or execution time of each task in a BoT has been modeled as normal distribution with mean and standard deviation (SD) values equal to 2.73 and 6.1, respectively. Every task has a corresponding deadline that has been calculated using equation 1 with stringency factor f = 1.2 i.e. normal deadline.

---

[3]https://www.spec.org/power_ssj2008/results/

Table 2: Workload Generation Parameters

Input Parameters	Distribution	Values
Inter-arrival time (BoT)	Weibull	Scale = 4.25, Shape = 7.86
Number of Tasks per BoT	Weibull	Scale = 1.76, Shape = 2.11
Average runtime per task	Normal	Mean = 2.73, SD = 6.1

Table 3: Simulation Configuration Parameters

Input Parameters	Values
Stringency Factor (f)	1.2
Sensitivity Factor (β)	1
Checkpoint Overhead (T_s)	20 secs

7.3 Performance Evaluation Metrics

To evaluate the performance of the proposed resource provisioning and VM allocation policies, the results of following metrics have been reported

(1) **Reliability**: The reliability with which the application has been executed on the provisioned resources.

(2) **Energy Consumption**: Energy consumption incurred by the provisioned resources while executing the application.

(3) **Energy Wastage**: The amount of energy wasted while re-executing the lost part of the task because of failures and related overheads.

(4) **Turnaround Time**: It is the time taken by each task of BoT application to finish.

(5) **Deadline-Turnaround Time Fraction**: It is the margin by which the turnaround time has been exceeded from the deadline.

(6) **Benefit Function**: It is the ratio of first two parameters, reliability and energy consumption.

All the reported results are the average of 50 simulations with Confidence Interval (CI) of 95%. All the simulations have been performed by using 1000 BoTs with total number of tasks ranges between 100000 to 120000.

7.4 Results and Discussions

Figure 5 presents the average reliability for each policy using checkpointing and without checkpointing. It can be seen that REABFD gives better reliability by approximately 5% from RABFD, 16% from OLB and 17% from EABFD with checkpointing. Also in the scenario of without checkpointing, REABFD gives better reliability by 6% from RABFD, 15% from OLB and 23% from EABFD. Figure also shows that policies with checkpointing gives better reliability by 5% to 9% than without checkpointing. This is due to the fact that after an event of a failure, the task length generally gets reduced in process of recovery from the last checkpoint (if any). For shorter task length, the system possess high reliability to execute the task without or before the occurrence of a failure. However, in the scenario without checkpointing, the task restarts from the beginning after an event of a failure. As the size of a resubmitted task remains same, reliability of a system also remains unchanged

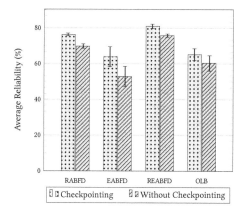

Figure 5: Average Reliability

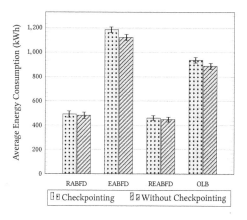

Figure 6: Average Energy Consumption

and relatively higher than checkpointing scenario. Moreover, in terms of reliability, REABFD without checkpointing has achieved almost similar reliability achieved by RABFD with checkpointing.

Figure 6 shows the average energy consumption incurred by all the policies with and without checkpointing. The energy consumption by REABFD is less in comparison to other policies with minimum difference of 7% from RABFD with and without checkpointing and maximum difference of 61% from EABFD with and without checkpointing. An interesting behaviour has been seen for EABFD policy as it consumes the maximum energy despite of the fact that it focuses on the provisioning of most energy efficient resources. From the given behaviour, it can be argued that the results are adverse. Rather than reducing the energy consumption, we ends up consuming more energy due to the energy losses incurred because of failure overheads (Fig. 7). In fact, it is better to use the random resource provisioning (OLB policy) than the energy aware resource provisioning in the presence of failures. In terms of energy wastage (Fig. 7), again REABFD outperforms all the policies with minimum improvement of approximately 8% and 11% over RABFD policy with and without checkpointing, respectively and maximum improvement of 67% and 70% over EABFD policy with and without

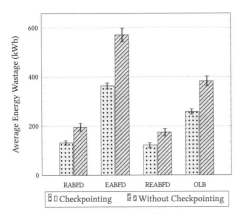

Figure 7: Average Energy Wastage

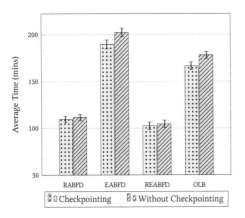

Figure 8: Average Turnaround Time

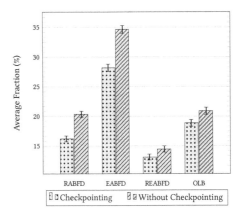

Figure 9: Average Deadline-Turnaround Time Fraction

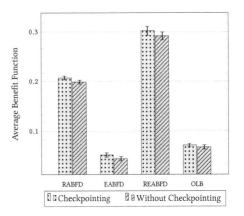

Figure 10: Average Benefit Function

checkpointing, respectively. Absence of any fault tolerance mechanism such as checkpointing further adds to these energy losses upto 36% because of the large re-execution overheads.

Figure 8 shows the average turnaround time, which is the time taken by each task of BoT application to finish. It can be seen that REABFD policy has the minimum turnaround time such that it took less time than what other policies took to finish the same application because of the less overheads incurred. REABFD policy has achieved better turnaround time by 7% from RABFD, 39% from OLB and 46% from EABFD for both checkpointing and without checkpointing scenarios. However, all the proposed policies have achieved better turnaround time while using checkpointing by 7% than without checkpointing because of less re-execution overheads occurred during the event of a failure. The achieved improvement in the turnaround time further justifies the improvements achieved in reliability and energy consumption for the REABFD policy.

Figure 9 shows, while executing the application by what percentage the makespan has been exceeded from the predefined deadline calculated by using equation 1. It can clearly be seen that for the secnarios without checkpointing, the makespan has been exceeded more upto 7% in comparison to the scenarios with checkpointing. This is because if a failure hits a scenario without checkpointing,

then the re-execution overhead is huge which is found to be approximately 36% higher in comparison to checkpointing, which makes the deadlines violated with greater margin than the checkpointing scenarios. Among all the proposed policies, REABFD again outperforms the other proposed policies by exceeding less by 3%, 6% and 15% with checkpointing and 6%, 7% and 20% without checkpointing in comparison to RABFD, OLB and EABFD, respectively.

To measure the effectiveness of all the proposed policies in terms of reliability and energy consumption at the same time, we have used the benefit function (Fig. 10), which is the ratio of reliability and energy consumption. It is infered that the policies considering reliability factor (RABFD and REABFD) while provisioning the resources has the better benefit function than the policy considering only energy-efficiency (EABFD) and policy considering neither reliability nor energy-efficiency (OLB). Among all the policies, REABFD performs better by improving the benefit function by 29% over RABFD, 82% over EABFD and 76% over OLB with checkpointing. However, in the secnario without checkpointing REABFD policy gives better value of benefit function by 34% over RABFD, 85% over EABFD and 78% over OLB.

8 CONCLUSION

In this paper, the problem of reliability and energy aware resource provisioning in cloud computing systems has been addressed. In solving this problem, a scalable and elastic cloud computing architecture has been proposed with three list based greedy heuristic algorithms such as Reliability Aware Best Fit Decreasing (RABFD), Energy Aware Best Fit Decreasing (EABFD) and Reliability-Energy Aware Best Fit Decreasing (REABFD). For fault tolerance, both re-execution from the beginning and checkpointing mechanism for task recovery have been considered. Our extensive experiments revealed that if the emphasis is given only to the energy optimization without consideration of reliability, then the results will be contrary to what we expect. Rather than reducing the energy consumption, we ends up consuming more energy due to the energy losses incurred because of failure overheads. Among the proposed policies, Reliability-Energy Aware Best Fit Decreasing (REABFD) policy outperforms all the other policies and reveals that if both reliability and energy efficiency factors of resources are considered at the same time then both factors can be improved to a larger extent than being regulated individually.

In future work, we will explore the use of machine learning methods to predict the occurrence of correlated failures. With the prediction results, VM consolidation mechanism will be adopted to further optimize the fault-tolerance and energy consumption of the cloud computing systems.

REFERENCES

[1] Sebastian Anthony. 2013. Microsoft now has one million servers–less than Google, but more than Amazon, says Ballmer. *ExtremeTech. ExtremeTech* 19 (2013).

[2] Paul Barham, Boris Dragovic, Keir Fraser, Steven Hand, Tim Harris, Alex Ho, Rolf Neugebauer, Ian Pratt, and Andrew Warfield. 2003. Xen and the art of virtualization. In *ACM SIGOPS operating systems review*, Vol. 37. ACM, 164–177.

[3] Anton Beloglazov, Jemal Abawajy, and Rajkumar Buyya. 2012. Energy-aware resource allocation heuristics for efficient management of data centers for cloud computing. *Future generation computer systems* 28, 5 (2012), 755–768.

[4] Anton Beloglazov, Rajkumar Buyya, Young Choon Lee, Albert Zomaya, et al. 2011. A taxonomy and survey of energy-efficient data centers and cloud computing systems. *Advances in computers* 82, 2 (2011), 47–111.

[5] Tracy D Braun, Howard Jay Siegel, Noah Beck, Ladislau L Bölöni, Muthucumaru Maheswaran, Albert I Reuther, James P Robertson, Mitchell D Theys, Bin Yao, Debra Hensgen, et al. 2001. A comparison of eleven static heuristics for mapping a class of independent tasks onto heterogeneous distributed computing systems. *Journal of Parallel and Distributed computing* 61, 6 (2001), 810–837.

[6] Rodrigo N Calheiros and Rajkumar Buyya. 2014. Energy-efficient scheduling of urgent bag-of-tasks applications in clouds through DVFS. In *Cloud Computing Technology and Science (CloudCom), 2014 IEEE 6th International Conference on.* IEEE, 342–349.

[7] Rodrigo N Calheiros, Rajiv Ranjan, Anton Beloglazov, César AF De Rose, and Rajkumar Buyya. 2011. CloudSim: a toolkit for modeling and simulation of cloud computing environments and evaluation of resource provisioning algorithms. *Software: Practice and experience* 41, 1 (2011), 23–50.

[8] Fabricio AB da Silva and Hermes Senger. 2011. Scalability limits of Bag-of-Tasks applications running on hierarchical platforms. *J. Parallel and Distrib. Comput.*

71, 6 (2011), 788–801.

[9] Nosayba El-Sayed and Bianca Schroeder. 2014. Checkpoint/restart in practice: When âĂŸsimple is betterâĂŹ. In *2014 IEEE International Conference on Cluster Computing (CLUSTER)*. IEEE, 84–92.

[10] Nosayba El-Sayed and Bianca Schroeder. 2014. To checkpoint or not to checkpoint: Understanding energy-performance-i/o tradeoffs in hpc checkpointing. In *2014 IEEE International Conference on Cluster Computing (CLUSTER)*. IEEE, 93–102.

[11] Peter Garraghan, Ismael Solis Moreno, Paul Townend, and Jie Xu. 2014. An Analysis of Failure-Related Energy Waste in a Large-Scale Cloud Environment. *IEEE Transactions on Emerging Topics in Computing* 2, 2 (2014), 166–180.

[12] Ponemon Institute. 2016. Cost of Data Center Outages. (2016), 1–21.

[13] Alexandru Iosup, Ozan Sonmez, Shanny Anoep, and Dick Epema. 2008. The performance of bags-of-tasks in large-scale distributed systems. In *Proceedings of the 17th international symposium on High performance distributed computing.* ACM, 97–108.

[14] Ravishankar K Iyer and David J Rossetti. 1986. A measurement-based model for workload dependence of CPU errors. *IEEE Trans. Comput.* 100, 6 (1986), 511–519.

[15] Bahman Javadi, Jemal Abawajy, and Rajkumar Buyya. 2012. Failure-aware resource provisioning for hybrid Cloud infrastructure. *Journal of parallel and distributed computing* 72, 10 (2012), 1318–1331.

[16] Tarandeep Kaur and Inderveer Chana. 2015. Energy efficiency techniques in cloud computing: A survey and taxonomy. *ACM Computing Surveys (CSUR)* 48, 2 (2015), 22.

[17] Derrick Kondo, Bahman Javadi, Alexandru Iosup, and Dick Epema. 2010. The failure trace archive: Enabling comparative analysis of failures in diverse distributed systems. In *10th International Conference on Cluster, Cloud and Grid Computing (CCGrid)*. IEEE/ACM, Melbourne, Victoria, Australia, 398–407.

[18] Adam J Oliner, Larry Rudolph, Ramendra K Sahoo, José E Moreira, and Manish Gupta. 2005. Probabilistic qos guarantees for supercomputing systems. In *Dependable Systems and Networks, 2005. DSN 2005. Proceedings. International Conference on.* IEEE, 634–643.

[19] Martin Perlin. 2012. Downtime, outages and failures-understanding their true costs. *Retrieved November* 25 (2012), 2012.

[20] Ian Philp. 2005. Software failures and the road to a petaflop machine. In *HPCRI: 1st Workshop on High Performance Computing Reliability Issues, in Proceedings of the 11th International Symposium on High Performance Computer Architecture (HPCA-11)*. San Francisco, California, USA, 125–128.

[21] Xiwei Qiu, Yuanshun Dai, Yanping Xiang, and Liudong Xing. 2016. A hierarchical correlation model for evaluating reliability, performance, and power consumption of a cloud service. *IEEE Transactions on Systems, Man, and Cybernetics: Systems* 46, 3 (2016), 401–412.

[22] Bianca Schroeder, Garth Gibson, et al. 2010. A large-scale study of failures in high-performance computing systems. *IEEE Transactions on Dependable and Secure Computing* 7, 4 (2010), 337–350.

[23] Yogesh Sharma, Bahman Javadi, Weisheng Si, and Daniel Sun. 2016. Reliability and energy efficiency in cloud computing systems: Survey and taxonomy. *Journal of Network and Computer Applications* 74 (2016), 66–85.

[24] Amir Varasteh, Farzad Tashtarian, and Maziar Goudarzi. 2017. On Reliability-Aware Server Consolidation in Cloud Datacenters. *arXiv preprint arXiv:1709.00411* (2017).

[25] John W Young. 1974. A first order approximation to the optimum checkpoint interval. *Commun. ACM* 17, 9 (1974), 530–531.

[26] Longxin Zhang, Kenli Li, Changyun Li, and Keqin Li. 2016. Bi-objective workflow scheduling of the energy consumption and reliability in heterogeneous computing systems. *Information Sciences* 379 (2016), 241–256.

[27] Longxin Zhang, Kenli Li, Keqin Li, and Yuming Xu. 2016. Joint optimization of energy efficiency and system reliability for precedence constrained tasks in heterogeneous systems. *International Journal of Electrical Power & Energy Systems* 78 (2016), 499–512.

[28] Dakai Zhu, Rami Melhem, and Daniel Mossé. 2004. The effects of energy management on reliability in real-time embedded systems. In *IEEE/ACM International Conference on Computer Aided Design (ICCAD-2004)*. IEEE, 35–40.

Exploiting Efficiency Opportunities Based on Workloads with Electron on Heterogeneous Clusters

Renan DelValle
SUNY at Binghamton
rdelval1@binghamton.edu

Pradyumna Kaushik
SUNY at Binghamton
pkaushi1@binghamton.edu

Abhishek Jain
SUNY at Binghamton
ajain13@binghamton.edu

Jessica Hartog
SUNY at Binghamton
jhartog1@binghamton.edu

Madhusudhan Govindaraju
SUNY at Binghamton
mgovinda@binghamton.edu

ABSTRACT

Resource Management tools for large-scale clusters and data centers typically schedule resources based on task requirements specified in terms of processor, memory, and disk space. As these systems scale, two non-traditional resources also emerge as limiting factors: power and energy. Maintaining a low power envelope is especially important during *Coincidence Peak*, a window of time where power may cost up to 200 times the base rate. Using Electron, our power-aware framework that leverages Apache Mesos as a resource broker, we quantify the impact of four scheduling policies on three workloads of varying power intensity. We also quantify the impact of two dynamic power capping strategies on power consumption, energy consumption, and makespan when used in combination with scheduling policies across workloads. Our experiments show that choosing the right combination of scheduling and power capping policies can lead to a 16% reduction of energy and a 37% reduction in the 99th percentile of power consumption while having a negligible impact on makespan and resource utilization.

KEYWORDS

Apche Mesos, Power, Energy, Efficiency, RAPL, Heterogeneous

1 INTRODUCTION

Resource management in large heterogeneous clusters is essential both to effectively use the available resources (such as processors, memory, and storage) and to reduce the cost in terms of the power envelope and energy usage. Apache Mesos [16] has emerged as the leader in the resource management space in the open source community. Mesos is akin to a distributed operating system, pooling together the available cores, system memory, and disk space for consumption by the applications on the cluster. Mesos' two-level scheduling scheme, along with its fair resource distribution policy, has shown to be successful for massive workload execution. Other efforts, such as Hadoop's YARN [30], work in a similar

manner. These cluster management tools have generated interest in the science and academic computing environments due to the recent availability of virtualized clouds for production use such as JetStream [29] and Chameleon [1]. However, Mesos and YARN do not have support for considering energy budgets and power envelope in their off-the-shelf packages.

Mesos, Hadoop's YARN, and other tools in this space, are designed to allow co-scheduling of workloads on worker nodes. As tasks are co-scheduled, the power they draw from the node is dependent on how efficiently co-scheduled tasks use hardware resources and how the peak power draws of tasks align. *Coincident Power* is the total power drawn from the cluster at any time. This value is dependent on the power consumed by all the tasks executing in the same instant. This includes the supporting software stack and hardware components. Ensuring that the cluster's desired power envelope is not breached requires workload shifting to ensure that the power peaks of various tasks do not align. Maintaining low power usage is especially important during the *Coincidence Peak*, a window of time where power may cost up to several times the base rate [23].

It is known that optimally co-scheduling applications to minimize peak power usage can be reduced to a multi-dimensional Bin-Packing problem and is NP-Hard [24]. Previously [13], we used Mesos and Aurora [7] to demonstrate how a policy driven approach, involving Bin-Packing workloads, can effectively reduce peak power consumption and energy usage. In our previous work [12], we introduced a pluggable power aware framework for Mesos, Electron. In this work, we deploy Electron with three different workloads, four different scheduling algorithms, and two different power capping strategies to quantify the effects that the different combinations of these three components have on power consumption, total energy consumption, and makespan.

Our workloads are composed of the DaCapo benchmarks [8], Phoronix benchmarks [6], and Scientific micro-benchmarks. The DaCapo benchmark suite is a set of open source, real-world applications that exercise the various resources within a compute node, while the Phoronix and scientific workloads are microbenchmarks. Our approach measures and monitors the power usage of CPU and Memory for each node using fine-grained power profiles provided by Intel's Running Average Power Limit (RAPL) [11] counters via the Linux Powercapping framework [5]. We use the power profiling data for a given benchmark and determine the approximate power usage.

We make the following contributions in this paper:

- We profile several different, well understood benchmarks and classify them using *k-means* clustering into low power consuming tasks and high power consuming tasks based on their power consumption.
- In contrast to the single type of workload used in our previous work [12], we use the benchmark classification to construct three kinds of workloads, each varying in power consumption. The different workloads are then used to quantify the power, energy, and makespan characteristics of the combinations of various scheduling policies and power capping strategies.
- We include two new scheduling policies and analyze their effect on power consumption, energy consumption, and makespan when used to schedule the different categories of workloads.
- We introduce a new power capping strategy to overcome certain limitations of the power capping strategies discussed in our previous work [12] and to further dampen large fluctuations in power consumption.
- We make recommendations based on our findings, on how different scheduling policies and power capping strategies should be used to satisfy Coincident Peak constraints and energy consumption requirements for a Mesos-based cluster.

2 MESOS

Apache Mesos is a fast evolving cluster manager capable of providing scalability to data center and cloud applications. Mesos currently powers several cloud infrastructures across the industry. Software such as Apple's Siri, Bloomberg's data analytics, and PayPal's Continuous Integration are built on top of Mesos [2].

Mesos combines resources such as CPU, memory, and storage into a shared pool. Resources from this pool are offered to applications that run on Mesos called *frameworks* [16]. Frameworks view the Mesos layer as a cluster-wide, highly-available, fault tolerant, and distributed operating system.

Mesos works as follows: (1) A daemon runs on each worker node, known as a Mesos Agent, discovers available resources from the worker and advertises them to the Mesos Master. (2) The Mesos Master makes these resources available to registered frameworks by sending course-grained *Resource Offers*. (3) A framework can choose to refuse an offer if it does not suit its needs or the framework can choose to use the offer to launch tasks.

3 ELECTRON

Electron [12] was built with both pluggable scheduling policies and pluggable power capping strategies. A high level view of Electron's architecture is shown in Figure 1. Electron is comprised of three main components: Task Queue, Scheduler, and Power Capper.
Task Queue: Maintains the tasks that are yet to be scheduled.
Scheduler: Checks whether the resource requirements for one or more tasks, in the Task Queue, can be satisfied by the resources available in the Mesos resource offers. If yes, those tasks are scheduled on the nodes corresponding to the consumed resource offer.
Power Capper: Responsible for power capping one or more nodes in the cluster through the use of RAPL [11]. The Power Capper

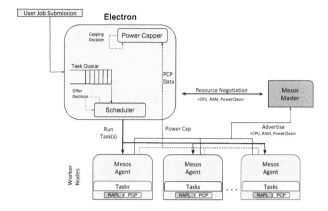

Figure 1: Architecture of Electron and Mesos. Electron's Scheduler component receives resource offers from Mesos and uses them to schedule tasks on worker nodes. The Power Capper component analyzes the power consumption of the worker nodes and decides whether or not to power cap one or more worker nodes.

monitors the power consumption of the nodes in the cluster which is retrieved through the use of Performance Co-Pilot [4]. A power capping policy that is plugged into Electron uses this information to make the decision to power cap or power uncap one or more nodes in the cluster.

3.1 Power Classes

We categorized the machines in our cluster into four power classes: A, B, C, and D based on their Thermal Design Power (TDP). Each node advertises its power class to the framework through the Mesos master. The specifications of the machines belonging to each power class are described in Section 4.1.

3.2 Consuming Mesos Offers

The core scheduling logic for a Mesos Framework's scheduler is defined based on how the framework consumes Mesos Offers. These offer selecting heuristics determine which jobs are co-located, and are therefore key in reducing *Coincident Peak* power. In this work we compare four such scheduling algorithms.

3.2.1 First-Fit (FF). For each offer the framework receives, it finds the first task in the job queue whose resource constraints are satisfied by the resources available in the offer. If a match is made between an offer and a task, the offer is consumed in order to schedule the matching task. Otherwise, it moves on to a new resource offer and the process of finding a suitable task is repeated.

3.2.2 Bin-Packing (BP). For each offer that is received by the framework, tasks are matched from a priority queue keyed by an approximation of the worst case power consumption using Median of Medians Max Power Usage (M^3PU) (described in Section 4.3). If a task's resource requirements match with the resources contained in a resource offer, the resources the task will use are subtracted from the available resources in this offer. If a task's resource requirements are not satisfied by the remaining resources, the next task in the queue is evaluated for fitness. We repeat this process until no task from the queue fits in the remaining resources. The offer is then consumed and the set of tasks evaluated to fit are scheduled to run.

The distribution of the workload when using Bin-Packing as the method of consuming Mesos offers for a Moderate Power Consuming Workload (described in Section 4.2) is shown in Figure 2a. Bin-Packing can lead to uneven distribution of tasks such that one class of machines handles roughly 44% of the work.

*3.2.3 **Max-Min (MM)**.* Although Bin-Packing reduces peak power consumption compared to a First-Fit policy, BP commonly leads to excessive co-location of high power consuming tasks, in turn increasing resource contention. This increase in resource contention can potentially result in stragglers and therefore have a significant impact on makespan. Max-Min is able to address this issue by picking a mixed set of tasks from the queue. Max-Min uses a double-ended queue *(deque)* sorted in non-decreasing M^3PU values, alternating between attempting to schedule tasks from the front and the back of the *deque*. If a task fits in the offer, the count of available resources is reduced and the process is continued until there are no more tasks that fit in an offer from the *deque*. Max-Min then moves on to the next offer.

The distribution of tasks when Max-Min is used as the scheduling policy for a Moderate Power Consuming Workload (described in Section 4.2) is shown in Figure 2b. Max-Min results in the resources contained in an offer to be consumed in quicker succession, thereby leading to a better distribution of the workload across the cluster. Compared to Figure 2a, the workload for Max-Min is better distributed among the power classes. However, *Max-Min* does not show a noticeable improvement in the distribution of high power consuming tasks when compared to *Bin-Packing*.

*3.2.4 **Max-GreedyMins (MGM)**.* Through experimentation we found that Max-Min has a significant impact on makespan when there is a higher proportion of low power consuming tasks. We created *Max-GreedyMins (MGM)* to counter MM's impact on makespan, and to further reduce peak power and energy consumption. MGM consumes offers by packing the low power consuming tasks at a faster rate than the high power consuming tasks. Like MM, unscheduled tasks are stored using a *deque* sorted in non-decreasing M^3PU. *MGM*, as shown in Algorithm 1, attempts to pack tasks into an offer by picking one task from the back of the *deque* followed by as many tasks as possible from the front of the *deque*, stopping when no more tasks can be fit into the offer. At this point, the policy moves on to the next Mesos offer and repeats the process.

The distribution of the workload when *MGM* is used as the scheduling policy for a Moderate Power Consuming Workload (described in Section 4.2) is shown in Figure 2c. When compared against *MM*, *MGM* distributes the workload across the cluster more evenly as it also spreads out high power consuming tasks amongst power classes. This improvement in the distribution of high power consuming tasks helps reduce starvation and thereby limits negative effects on makespan.

3.3 Power Capping Policies

*3.3.1 **Extrema**.* In our previous work, we presented a dynamic power capping strategy, Extrema [12], which is able to make trade-offs between makespan and power consumption. Extrema reacts

---

Algorithm 1 Max-GreedyMins

1: *sortedTasks* ← Tasks to schedule sorted in non-decreasing order by their corresponding M^3PU value.
2: *offer* ← Mesos offer.
3: **procedure** MAX-GREEDYMINS(*offer*, *sortedTasks*)
4:   **for** task in *sortedTasks*.Reverse() **do**
5:     **if** FIT(*offer*.UnusedResources(), task) **then**
         offer.schedule(task)
         sortedTasks.remove(task)
         break
6:     **end if**
7:   **end for**
8:   **for** task in *sortedTasks* **do**
9:     **for** instance in task.Instances() **do**
10:      **if** FIT(*offer*.UnusedResources(), task) **then**
           offer.schedule(task)
           sortedTasks.remove(task)
11:      **else**
           break
12:      **end if**
13:    **end for**
14: **end for**
15: **end procedure**

---

to power trends in the cluster and seeks to restrain the power consumption of the cluster to a power envelope defined by a high and low threshold. If the cluster's Average Historical Power (AHP) exceeds the high threshold, the node consuming the highest power is power capped to half its Thermal Design Power (TDP). TDP is the maximum power (turned to heat) that is expected to be dissipated, as listed by the chip manufacturer. On the other hand, if the cluster's AHP is lower than the low threshold, a node is uncapped. Nodes are fully uncapped in the reverse order in which they were capped. Extrema is successful in maintaining the power profile within a defined envelope, reducing power peaks while having a subdued impact on makespan.

*3.3.2 **Progressive Extrema**.* By observing the outcome of experiments using Extrema we have identified a few of its limitations:

(1) If every node in the cluster has already been capped but the AHP is still above the High threshold, Extrema is unable to perform any new action that may bring the AHP down.

(2) As Extrema caps nodes to 50% of their TDP and uncaps them to their full TDP, large differences in these values can result in nodes experiencing high power fluctuations.

(3) Extrema requires high and low thresholds to be manually predefined. It follows that prior knowledge of the workload greatly benefits the configuration of the high and low thresholds and by extension, the efficacy of Extrema.

While the last drawback still remains an open problem, we address the first two drawbacks through a modified version of Extrema named *Progressive Extrema*. Progressive Extrema, described in Algorithm 2, is similar to Extrema except for one key difference: power capping is applied in phases. Whereas picking a previously capped node as a victim in Extrema resulted in a *no-op*, in Progressive Extrema the same scenario results in a harsher capping value for the

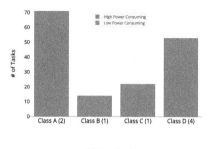

(a) Bin-Packing

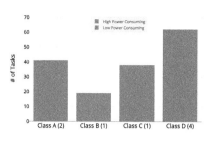

(b) Max-Min

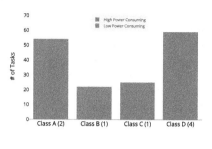

(c) Max-GreedyMins

Figure 2: Distribution of tasks by classification for a Moderate Power Consuming Workload. The number of nodes for each power class is shown in parentheses. Figure 2a shows Class A nodes processing more power intensive tasks than Class D nodes despite having half as many workers when using the Bin-Packing strategy. Figure 2b shows Class D bearing a larger burden than the rest of the classes with Max-Min while Figure 2c shows Class A and Class D completing about the same number of tasks with Class D processing more power intensive tasks.

victim. In the initial phase of Progressive Extrema's design, capping history is maintained for each node in an in-memory data structure. When a victim node is chosen for uncapping, the previous cap value in the node's history is used. Finally, Progressive Extrema also uses a *CapLimit* that defines the floor value beyond which a node should not be capped.

4 EXPERIMENTS

4.1 Setup

Our experiments were conducted on a research cluster which comprises the following components:

- 2 *Class A* nodes - Two 10 core, 20 thread Intel Xeon E5-2650 v3 @ 2.30GHz and 128 GB RAM

- 1 *Class B* node - One 8 core, 16 thread Intel Xeon E5-2640 v3 @ 2.60GHz and 128 GB RAM

- 1 *Class C* node - One 8 core, 16 thread Intel Xeon E5-2640 v3 @ 2.60GHz and 64 GB RAM

- 4 *Class D* nodes - Four 6 core, 12 thread Intel Xeon E5-2620 v3 @ 2.40GHz and 64 GB RAM

Each node runs a 64-bit Linux 4.4.0-64 kernel and shares an NFS server. Apache Mesos 1.1.0 is deployed as the cluster manager. The Electron framework is used as the sole Mesos framework to schedule workloads. Docker 1.13.1 is used as the container technology. Benchmarks are run inside Docker containers to ensure environment consistency across worker nodes. Performance Co-Pilot [4] is deployed across the cluster to collect metrics from all worker nodes. Metrics collected from worker nodes include energy measurements from RAPL[1] counters and various statistics about CPU and memory usage from each worker node's Linux kernel. No metrics are collected from our Master nodes as they do not run any workload and thus have limited impact on variable power and energy consumption.

Algorithm 2 Progressive Extrema Capping

1: **procedure** PROGEXTREMA($Threshold, InitCap, CapLimit$)
2:     $ClusterAvg \leftarrow Avg_{Running}(ClusterPower)$
3:     **if** ClusterAvg > Threshold.Hi **then**
4:         $Victims \leftarrow Sort_{non-inc}(AvgPowerNode[...])$
5:         $uncappedVictimFound \leftarrow false$
6:         **for** victim in Victims **do**
7:             **if** victim not in $CappedVictims$ **then**
8:                 Cap(victim, InitCap)
9:                 $CappedVictims[victim.Host] \leftarrow InitCap$
10:                 $uncappedVictimFound \leftarrow true$
11:             **end if**
12:         **end for**
13:         **if** uncappedVictimFound == false **then**
14:             **for** victim in $CappedVictims$ **do**
15:                 **if** victim.curCap > $CapLimit$ **then**
16:                     $newCap \leftarrow$ victim.curCap $\div$ 2
17:                     $Cap(victim, newCap)$
18:                     $CapVictims[victim.Host] \leftarrow newCap$
19:                 **end if**
20:             **end for**
21:         **end if**
22:     **end if**
23:     **if** ClusterAvg < Threshold.Low **then**
24:         $victim \leftarrow MaxCapped(CappedVictims)$
25:         $uncapValue \leftarrow CappedVictims[victim.Host] * 2$
26:         $Uncap(victim, uncapValue)$
27:         $CappedVictims[victim.Host] \leftarrow uncapValue$
28:         **if** victim.curCap == 100 **then**
29:             $delete(CappedVictims, victim.Host)$
30:         **end if**
31:     **end if**
32: **end procedure**

---

[1]RAPL only supports monitoring CPU and DRAM. Thus, any references to power and energy should be understood to mean energy consumed by CPU and DRAM.

Test suites	Description	Type
Audio Encoding★	Runtime measurement to encode WAV file to different audio formats.	CPU
Video Encoding†	Video encoding tests, processor tests and system performance testing.	CPU
Cryptography†	Cryptography tests such as OpenSSL and GnuPG.	CPU
Network Loopback★	Computer's networking performance testing.	Network
Avrora★	Multithreaded AVR microcontrollers simulator.	CPU
Batik★	Produces Scalable Vector Graphics images.	Memory
Eclipse★	Non-GUI jdt performance tests for the Eclipse IDE.	CPU
Jython★	Interprets the pybench Python benchmark.	CPU
Pmd†	Multithreaded Java source code analysis.	CPU
Tradebeans★	Daytrader benchmark run on GERONIMO with an in-memory H2 DB.	Memory
H2★	Executes transactions against a model of a banking application.	Memory
Xalan†	Multithreaded XML to HTML converter.	Mixed
Sunflow†	Renders a set of images using ray tracing.	CPU
miniFE[26]★	Finite element generation, assembly and solution for an unstructured grid problem.	CPU
DGEMM[27]†	Multi-threaded, dense-matrix multiplication.	CPU
STREAM[18]★	Calculates sustainable memory bandwidth and the computation rate for simple vector kernels.	Memory

Table 1: Workload benchmarks

The † symbol indicates a High Power Consuming benchmark while the ★ symbol indicates a Low Power Consuming benchmark as determined through profiling and k-means clustering.

4.2 Workloads

The benchmarks with which we created our Light, Moderate, and Heavy Power Consuming Workloads were derived from the DaCapo Benchmark suite [8], Phoronix Benchmark suite [6], MiniFE from Mantevo [26], and Stream and Dgemm from NERSC [3]. Benchmarks like HiBench[17] were not used as the current focus is only on benchmarks that are designed to run on a single node in the cluster.

Algorithm 3 Median Median Max Power Usage (M^3PU)

1: $R \leftarrow$ Number of individual runs.
2: $P \leftarrow$ Power.
3: $Peaks \leftarrow$ Power peaks per run.
4: $PC \leftarrow$ Power Classes.
5: **procedure** $M^3PU(Benchmarks[...], PC[...])$
6:     **for** bm in $Benchmarks$ **do**
7:         $MMPU \leftarrow List()$
8:         **for** pc in PC **do**
9:             $peaks \leftarrow bm.getPeaks(pc)$
10:             $mmpuPc \leftarrow$ BENCHMARK_MMPU$(peaks, pc)$
11:             $MMPU[...] \leftarrow mmpuPc$
12:         **end for**
13:         $M^3PU[bm] \leftarrow Median(MMPU[...])$
14:     **end for**
15: **end procedure**
16: **procedure** BENCHMARK_MMPU$(Peaks[R][P], PC)$
17:     $MaxPeaks \leftarrow List(R)$
18:     **for** i in 0 to R-1 **do**
19:         $MaxPeaks[i] \leftarrow$ MaxPeak$(Peaks[i])$
20:     **end for**
        return $Median(MaxPeaks) - StaticPower_{PC}$
21: **end procedure**

4.3 Median of Medians Max Power Usage

There are many ways of calculating a suitable global value to be used as an estimation of the power consumption for each benchmark. For this set of experiments we opted to use the Median of Medians of the Max Power Usage (M^3PU) value for each benchmark as an approximation of the power consumption in our workloads (described in Algorithm 3).

Since our cluster is heterogeneous, the estimated values varied between machines belonging to the four different power classes described in Section 4.1. For each benchmark, ten profiling runs were recorded on four nodes, one for each class. The max peak was found for each of the ten runs. Each power class then had ten max peaks from which the median was calculated. From the median we subtracted the median static power for each power class, generating a Median Max Power Usage (MMPU) of the benchmark for each power class. We used these values as an approximation of the worst case power consumption of the benchmark on any node in that power class. The four MMPU values were used as observations for our task classification described in Section 4.4.

In order to be able to build the data structures required for our scheduling policies we required a single value as a point of comparison for sorting. We opted to use the Median of the four MMPU values which represents a cluster-wide central tendency of power usage for each benchmark, resulting in a Median of Medians Max Power Usage (M^3PU) for each benchmark.

4.4 Task Classification

Using the well known *k-means* clustering algorithm with the four MMPU values of each benchmark as observations, we classified benchmarks into two categories: low power consuming and high power consuming. As a benchmark can be scheduled on any node in the cluster, the power consumption of the benchmark on different power classes needs to be considered. For this reason, the MMPU values for each power class were used as the observations instead of the global approximation M^3PU value. The classification of our benchmarks can be seen in Table 1. Using this classification we created three kinds of workloads: Light, Moderate, and Heavy. Each workload has a different ratio of low power consuming tasks to high power consuming tasks: Light (20:3), Moderate (10:6), and Heavy (5:12).

5 PERFORMANCE ANALYSIS

In this section, we analyze the performance of different strategies for consuming Mesos offers: *First-Fit (FF)*, *Bin-Packing (BP)*, *Max-Min (MM)*, and *Max-GreedyMins (MGM)*. We also study the effect of two power capping strategies, *Extrema* and *Progressive Extrema*, when used with each scheduling policy. To further discover strengths and weaknesses of a combination, we run three workloads: Light, Moderate, and Heavy. We quantify each combination of scheduling policy, power capping strategy, and class of workload based upon the following aspects: (1) ability to reduce peak power consumption, (2) ability to reduce energy consumption, and (3) impact on makespan.

5.1 Performance of Scheduling Policies

Tables 2, 3, and 4 compare the energy, makespan, and the 95th percentile in power consumption, for different scheduling policies for a Light, Moderate, and Heavy Power Consuming Workload respectively.

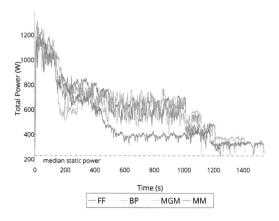

Figure 3: Power consumption of Light Power Consuming Workload when scheduled with different scheduling policies.

5.1.1 *Light Power Consuming Workload*. Figure 3 shows the power profiles of the execution of the Light Power Consuming Workload (LPCW) when using the previously mentioned scheduling policies.
Power: Both BP and MM experience improvements in the 95th percentile of power consumption when compared to FF and MGM, where BP slightly improves over MM by 6.1 Watts. The low power

	FF	BP	MM	MGM
Power (W)	1072.75	1033.1	1039.2	1094.8
Makespan (s)	1319	1417	1544	1122
Energy (kJ)	858	844.6	761.9	793

Table 2: Comparison of the effects of different scheduling policies for a Light Power Consuming Workload.

envelope for MM can be attributed to the fact that a larger number of high power consuming tasks complete execution earlier, leaving behind only low power consuming tasks running on the cluster.
Makespan: BP and MM experience a significant increase in makespan when compared to FF. The increase in makespan for BP can be attributed to excessive co-location of high power consuming tasks at a later execution stage, leading to an increase in resource contention for some nodes. Although MM address one of BP's shortcomings by scheduling high power consuming tasks earlier in the scheduling process, it suffers an increase in makespan as a result of delaying of the execution of many of the low power consuming tasks, leading to decreased throughput. From Table 2, we can see that MGM experiences a marked improvement in makespan when compared to FF, BP, and MM. MGM achieves this improvement by reducing the co-location of high power consuming tasks while concurrently consuming an increased amount of low power consuming tasks, thus being particularly beneficial for the ratio of low power consuming tasks to high power consuming tasks in the LPCW.
Energy: Although BP shows a slight improvement in energy consumption when compared to FF, the impact on makespan incurs a severe static power penalty. On the other hand, MM and MGM show a significant reduction in energy consumption when compared to BP and FF. Furthermore, MM experiences a 31.1 kJ reduction in energy consumption when compared to MGM. Although MM incurs a makespan penalty, it achieves this low energy consumption by maintaining a low power envelope. In contrast, MGM does not have a huge impact on the power peaks, but the significant reduction in makespan leads to an improvement in energy consumption as it avoids static power penalties.

	FF	BP	MM	MGM
Power (W)	1032.9	957	980	1049.4
Makespan (s)	1521	1602	1575	1450
Energy (kJ)	1183.8	1031	918.3	891.7

Table 3: Comparison of the effects of different scheduling policies for a Moderate Power Consuming Workload.

5.1.2 *Moderate Power Consuming Workload*. Figure 4 shows the power profiles of the execution of the Moderate Power Consuming Workload (MPCW) using the previously mentioned scheduling policies.
Power: Table 3 shows an improvement in the 95th percentile of power consumption for BP when compared to FF, MM, and MGM. However, MGM experiences a substantial reduction in the 90th percentile (not shown in the table) of power consumption, improving over FF, BP, and MM by 304 Watts, 88.8 Watts, and 39.8 Watts

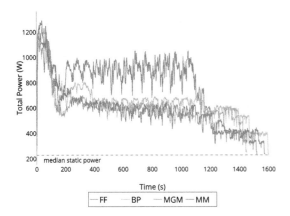

Figure 4: Power consumption of Moderate Power Consuming Workload when scheduled with different scheduling policies.

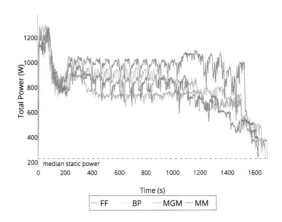

Figure 5: Power consumption of Heavy Power Consuming Workload when scheduled with different scheduling policies.

respectively. This discrepancy between 90th and 95th percentile in power consumption for MGM can be attributed to early execution of high power consuming tasks, leading to a high initial spike of power consumption. Throughout the rest of execution, MGM maintains a lower power profile in comparison to the other scheduling policies.

Makespan: BP suffers an increase in makespan when compared to FF, MM, and MGM, which can be attributed to BP co-locating several high power consuming tasks late in the task allocation process. This excessive co-location leads to an increase in contention for resources, thus increasing the completion times for these high power consuming tasks. MGM's reduction in makespan can be attributed to better distribution of high power consuming tasks across the worker nodes.

Energy: Although BP reduces the power envelope, the increase in makespan reduces the impact it has on the energy consumption due to the static power penalty. However, BP still consumes 152.8 kJ less than FF. On the other hand, MM and MGM are able to achieve a more heterogeneous mix of low power consuming and high power consuming tasks, thereby reducing energy consumption. As MGM results in a further increase in the distribution of high power consuming tasks across the cluster, it experiences a 26.6 kJ reduction in energy consumption when compared to MM.

	FF	BP	MM	MGM
Power (W)	1098.2	1006.5	1110.7	1028.2
Makespan (s)	1630	1683	1626	1697
Energy (kJ)	1546.4	1380.1	1259.1	1226.9

Table 4: Comparison of the effects of different scheduling policies for a Heavy Power Consuming Workload.

5.1.3 Heavy Power Consuming Workload. Figure 5 shows the power profiles of execution of the Heavy Power Consuming Workload (HPCW), using various scheduling policies.

Power: As the HPCW contains an increased number of high power consuming tasks, we can see a clear increase of power envelopes for all the policies. Table 4 shows that BP experiences a substantial

reduction in the 95th percentile of power consumption when compared to FF. Furthermore, BP is better than MM by 104.2 W in the 95th percentile of power consumption. Although MM improves the distribution of tasks across the cluster, it does not have a substantial impact in reducing the excessive co-location of high power consuming tasks for this power intensive workload. MGM, however, shows an improvement in the 95th percentile when compared to FF, BP, and MM, and this reduction can be attributed to a decrease in the co-location of high power consuming tasks, leading to a reduction in coincident peaks.

Makespan: Although MGM shows an improvement in power consumption, it delays the start time of execution of the high power consuming tasks. This increase in latency for power intensive tasks leads to an increase in makespan, as seen in the data shown in Table 4. In addition, as the workload gets more power intensive, MGM's detrimental impact on makespan might become more prominent. MGM shows a similar makespan to BP, posting just a 14 second difference, but the increase in makespan for BP can be attributed to resource contention of excessively co-located high power consuming tasks.

Energy: BP experiences a significant reduction in energy consumption when compared to FF, as seen in Table 4. Furthermore, MM and MGM experience a decrease in energy consumption when compared to BP. Although MM experiences a slight increase in energy consumption of around 32 kJ when compared to MGM, MM would be a more appropriate choice when scheduling a higher ratio of high power consuming tasks as MGM is more likely to have a negative impact on makespan as the ratio of high power consuming benchmarks to low power consuming benchmarks increases. Eventually, the increase in makespan would lead to the static power penalty nullifying energy decrease from maintaining a lower power envelope.

5.2 Power Capping Impact On Scheduling

In this section we quantify the impact of our set of Power Capping Strategies {Extrema, Progressive Extrema} across our set of different scheduling policies {FF, BP, MM, MGM}.

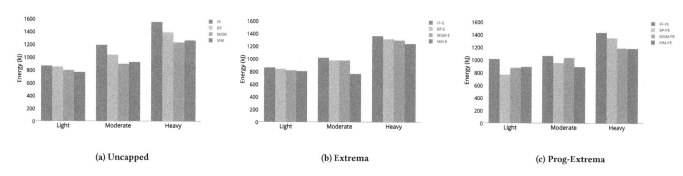

(a) Uncapped   (b) Extrema   (c) Prog-Extrema

Figure 6: Figure 6a shows the comparison of Cluster-wide Energy Consumption of different scheduling policies when used to schedule different classes of workloads (Light, Moderate and Heavy). Figures 6b & 6c compare Cluster-wide Energy Consumption of different scheduling policies in combination with the Extrema and the Progressive Extrema power capping policies for scheduling different classes of workloads.

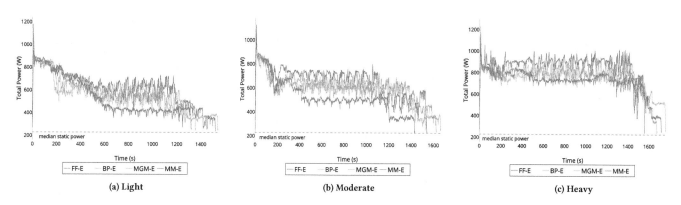

(a) Light   (b) Moderate   (c) Heavy

Figure 7: Cluster-wide Power Consumption for Extrema Capping for Light, Moderate and Heavy Power Consuming Workloads.

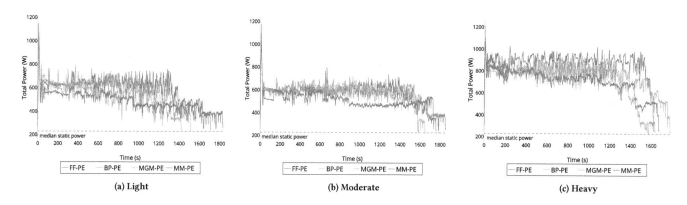

(a) Light   (b) Moderate   (c) Heavy

Figure 8: Cluster-wide Power Consumption for Progressive Extrema Capping for Light, Moderate and Heavy Power Consuming Workloads.

*5.2.1 **Extrema**.* Figure 7 shows the effect of using the Extrema power capping strategy when used alongside different scheduling policies for the Light, Moderate, and Heavy Power Consuming

Workloads (LPCW, MPCW, and HPCW respectively).
Power: Figure 7a shows the power profiles when Extrema is run

alongside the different scheduling policies for the LPCW. Compared to their uncapped runs FF, BP, MM, and MGM experience a reduction in the p95 of power consumption of 231 Watts, 190 Watts, 193 Watts, and 251 Watts, respectively, when running under the Extrema capping policy. For the MPCW, shown in Figure 7b, FF, BP, and MGM experience an improvement of 220 Watts, 74 Watts, and 7 Watts, respectively, in the 90th percentile of power consumption compared to the uncapped runs. On the other hand, MM with Extrema experiences an increase of 23 Watts in the 90th percentile of power consumption for the MPCW compared to its uncapped run. The effect of Extrema on MM is likely due to the size of tasks in the *deque* and the time Extrema needs to place power caps on each node. When all higher energy jobs remain in the *deque* after the lower energy jobs have been exhausted a higher percentage of nodes are capped and remain capped for a longer period of time. Further investigation into the exact circumstances that lead to a power increase in this instance is the subject of future work. Finally, when scheduling the HPCW the scheduling policies FF, BP, MM, and MGM show an improvement in the 90th percentile of power consumption (relative to their uncapped runs) of 118.5 Watts, 94.2 Watts, 116 Watts, and 35 Watts respectively.

Makespan: Extrema does not impact the makespan of FF as the workload is well distributed across the cluster. However, when Extrema is used alongside BP, the makespan is increased by 128 seconds, 67 seconds, and 76 seconds for LPCW, MPCW, and HPCW respectively. The makespan is not affected when Extrema is deployed on MM for the LPCW and MPCW. On the other hand, when Extrema and MM are used for the HPCW it experiences an increase in makespan of 94 seconds. This increase is due to RAPL lowering CPU clock speeds to stay within the power budget which has an adverse effect on the larger number of high power consuming tasks in contention for system resources. For the combination of Extrema and MGM there is an increase in makespan of 236 seconds for the LPCW and 179 seconds for the MPCW. This indicates that Extrema combined with MGM is not a good fit for systems that want to maintain a high Service Level Agreement (SLA) for processing LPCW and MPCW. There is no impact on the makespan when Extrema is combined with MGM for the HPCW as shown in Figure 7c as MGM is better at distributing the high power consuming tasks across the cluster compared to BP and MM.

Energy: In general, Extrema's reduction in peak power consumption is much more prominent than Extrema's increase in makespan. This leads to Extrema lowering the energy consumption for FF, BP, MM, and MGM for MPCW and HPCW. Figure 6b shows that when Extrema is used for the MPCW, the scheduling policies FF, BP, and MM experience a reduction in energy consumption of 171kJ, 53kJ, and 159kJ respectively when compared to their uncapped runs while MGM experiences an increase of 77 kJ in energy consumption compared to its uncapped run. When Extrema is used for the HPCW, our results show that compared to their uncapped runs FF, BP, and MM experience a reduction of 191kJ, 73 kJ, and 25 kJ respectively, while MGM experiences an increase of 24kJ. The increase in energy consumption for MGM for MPCW as well as HPCW can be attributed to the delayed start time for the high power consuming tasks, thus incurring a heavier static power penalty.

5.2.2 ***Progressive Extrema.*** The graphs in Figure 8 show the effect of using the Progressive Extrema power capping strategy alongside the scheduling policies described above for the Light (LPCW), Moderate (MCPW), and Heavy (HPCW) Power Consuming Workloads.

Power: Compared with the uncapped runs and against the Extrema capped runs Progressive Extrema reduces the initial power draw on a cluster. The initial power peaks are around 1200 Watts for the uncapped runs, around 830 Watts for the Extrema power capped runs, and have been reduced to around 600 Watts for the LPCW and MPCW as shown in Figures 8a and 8b. This reduction can be attributed to Progressive Extrema being able to more aggressively cap the already capped nodes and thereby quickly bringing down the power envelope closer to the predefined high and low thresholds. Analyzing the results shown in Figure 8, we observe that when compared to their corresponding uncapped runs, shown in Figures 3, 4, and 5, FF, BP, MM, and MGM experience a substantial reduction in the p95 of power consumption. FF experiences a p95 reduction in power consumption of 368, 374, and 141 Watts for LPCW, MPCW, and HPCW respectively. BP experiences a p95 reduction in power consumption of 405, 297, and 133 Watts for the LPCW, MPCW, and HPCW respectively. MM experiences a p95 reduction in power consumption of 457, 260, and 251 Watts for the LPCW, MPCW, and HPCW respectively. Finally, MGM experiences a p95 reduction in power consumption of 387, 401, and 155 Watts for the LPCW, MPCW, and HPCW respectively.

Makespan: Progressive Extrema has a negative impact on makespan as it is aggressive in power capping the nodes and therefore decreases CPU resources available to workloads. For the LPCW, FF, MM, and MGM experience an increase in makespan of 394, 293, and 396 seconds, respectively, when compared to their corresponding energy consumptions shown in Figure 6a. However, BP does not experience a significant impact on makespan for the LPCW when compared to its uncapped run. FF, BP, MM, and MGM experience an increase in makespan of 336, 53, 189, and 341 seconds, respectively for the MPCW when compared to their corresponding uncapped runs. BP and MM experience an increase in makespan of 102 and 52 seconds, respectively, for the HPCW. As FF and MGM distribute the high power consuming tasks more evenly, they do not experience an impact in makespan for the HPCW due to the decreased availability of CPU resources.

Energy: Progressive Extrema proves to be beneficial in significantly reducing the power envelopes and the power fluctuations across all runs. For the HPCW, Progressive Extrema reduces energy consumption for FF, BP, MGM, and MM by 120 kJ, 37 kJ, 45 kJ, and 83 kJ respectively, when compared to their uncapped runs. For the MPCW, all but MGM experience a reduction in energy consumption. FF, BP, and MM improve by 126 kJ, 85 kJ, and 33 kJ respectively. However, for the LPCW the significant impact on makespan leads to Progressive Extrema not having a substantial improvement in energy consumption when compared to uncapped runs with BP being the only exception where Progressive Extrema reduces the energy consumption of BP by 83 kJ.

6 RELATED WORK

Apart from the authors' initial work [12], we are not aware of any other work that discusses power and energy optimization for Mesos based clusters. There exist several complementary publications that focus on energy management via microarchitecture level optimizations, turning off or suspending nodes, and using Dynamic-Voltage and Frequency-Scaling (DVFS) schemes.

In [20, 22], the cluster is divided into hot and cold zones and a Covering Subset is determined that has at least one replica of each data block, and then nodes that can be suspended or shut down are chosen. Lang and Patel [21] identify when it is feasible to keep nodes off-line and boot them up once a job arrives. These approaches are not practical in Data Centers, which is where Apache Mesos is primarily used, as they negatively affect the responsiveness of the system for unexpected workloads [25].

Prior to the adoption of Mesos in the Apache community and the readily available nature of RAPL[11], Hartog et al. [14] leveraged the unified nature of MapReduce job scheduling to study scheduling of tasks in a cluster. To achieve this power consumption was constrained by scheduling using the constraint of keeping the CPU within a temperature range. In this work, we leverage the unified scheduler of Aurora on Mesos and RAPL metrics, in order to employ a similar algorithm which takes into account the power and energy consumption of the entire cluster. The goals here is also to maintain the power envelope within defined thresholds. Hartog et al. [15] also focus on fine grained task splitting in a MapReduce setup by using smaller subtasks to increase the opportunities to react to clusters with heterogeneous processing nodes, Similarly, we take into account the size of the tasks that we are trying to schedule and focus our scheduling based around task size.

Bodas et al. [9], developed a power-aware scheduler for SLURM that is based on monitoring the power usage and then using a uniform frequency mechanism to limit power. Just like our approach, they advocate for a policy-driven approach for high and low power consumers. Our work however, assumes that CPU frequency scaling mechanisms based on individual benchmarks are not practical for co-scheduled workloads in virtualized clusters.

Karakoyunlu et al. [19] developed a 2-approximation solution for minimizing energy consumption and balancing system load. Their schemes (Fixed Scheme, Dynamic Greedy Scheme, and Correlation-Based Scheme), are designed to link cloud storage needs to the cloud users. These policies can be adapted depending on the priorities set by the cloud storage system. Our work takes a similar approach but our policies are applied to affect the scheduling on Mesos clusters using CPU, memory, and power usage.

Sarood et al. [28], propose a software-based online resource management system and a scheme that uses an adaptive runtime system that can dynamically change the resource configuration of a running job. As a result resources allocated to currently executing jobs can be modified. While this work also allows power capping, it assumes job malleability such that resources can be dynamically changed for a running job. We assume that the resources allocated to a job cannot be changed as that is a tenet of Mesos's design.

In [10], Chandraseka et al. present the Power-check framework, which uses smart data-funneling mechanisms along with power capping to reduce the CPU utilization during the I/O phase of checkpointing applications. In comparison, we apply dynamic power-capping during all phases to maintain a power envelope.

7 CONCLUSION

There are trade-offs that must be made in order to operate a cluster under specific power and energy constraints. Some policies favor lowering the height of power peaks in the cluster, others favor a reduced makespan, while still others favor lower energy consumption. Although Max-Min and Max-GreedyMins outperform First-Fit and Bin-Packing in the metrics analyzed in this work, we acknowledge these scheduling policies may cause starvation for tasks in workloads that are between Light and Heavy Power Consuming. Guarding against task starvation is not addressed in this paper and will be the subject of future work. We have developed a few heuristics to enable Mesos-powered clusters to schedule with the aim of avoiding *Coincident Peak* power consumption, decreased power consumption, and decreased energy consumption while avoiding a large increase in makespan.

- Max-GreedyMins should be used when a workload requires high throughput and the scheduling time does not fall within the *Coincidence Peak*, regardless of the power intensity of the workload.
- When the workload consists of a higher proportion of high power consuming tasks, scheduling policies similar to Max-Min, are an appropriate choice. On the other hand, if the workload consists of a higher proportion of low power consuming tasks, then scheduling policies similar to Max-GreedyMins, are a more appropriate choice.
- To decrease power peaks and energy consumption, Extrema is best deployed as the power capping strategy to schedule Light and Moderate Power Consuming Workloads while Progressive Extrema is best suited for Heavy Power Consuming Workloads.

In our future work, we plan to develop a policy capable of switching between different scheduling policies and power capping strategies in order to adapt to a continuously changing workload.

REFERENCES

[1] 2014. Chameleon: A Large-scale, Reconfigurable Experimental Environment for Cloud Research. (2014). https://www.chameleoncloud.org
[2] 2015. Scaling Mesos at Apple, Bloomberg, Netflix and more - Mesosphere. (2015). https://mesosphere.com/blog/2015/08/25/scaling-mesos-at-apple-bloomberg-netflix-and-more/
[3] 2016. NeRSC Benchmark Distribution and Run Rules. (2016). http://www.nersc.gov/research-and-development/apex/apex-benchmarks/
[4] 2016. Performance Co-Pilot. (2016). http://www.pcp.io/
[5] 2016. Power Capping Framework. (2016). https://www.kernel.org/doc/Documentation/power/powercap/powercap.txt
[6] 2017. Phoronix Test Suite - Linux Testing and Benchmarking Platform, Automated Testing, Open-Source Benchmarking. (2017). http://www.phoronix-test-suite.com/
[7] Apache. 2017. Apache Aurora. (2017). http://aurora.apache.org/
[8] Stephen M. Blackburn, Samuel Z. Guyer, Martin Hirzel, Antony Hosking, Maria Jump, Han Lee, J. Eliot, B. Moss, Aashish Phansalkar, Darko Stefanović, Thomas VanDrunen, Robin Garner, Daniel von Dincklage, Ben Wiedermann, Chris Hoffmann, Asjad M. Khang, Kathryn S. McKinley, Rotem Bentzur, Amer Diwan, Daniel Feinberg, and Daniel Frampton. 2006. The DaCapo benchmarks. *ACM SIGPLAN Notices* 41, 10 (10 2006), 169.
[9] Deva Bodas, Justin Song, Murali Rajappa, and Andy Hoffman. 2014. Simple Power-Aware Scheduler to Limit Power Consumption by HPC System within a Budget. In *2014 Energy Efficient Supercomputing Workshop*. IEEE, 21–30.
[10] Raghunath Raja Chandrasekar, Akshay Venkatesh, Khaled Hamidouche, and Dhabaleswar K. Panda. 2015. Power-Check: An Energy-Efficient Checkpointing Framework for HPC Clusters. In *2015 15th IEEE/ACM International Symposium on Cluster, Cloud and Grid Computing*. IEEE, 261–270.

[11] Howard David, Eugene Gorbatov, Ulf R. Hanebutte, Rahul Khanaa, and Christian Le. 2010. RAPL. In *Proceedings of the 16th ACM/IEEE international symposium on Low power electronics and design - ISLPED '10*. ACM Press, New York, New York, USA, 189.

[12] Renan DelValle, Pradyumna Kaushik, Abhishek Jain, Jessica Hartog, and Madhusudhan Govindaraju. 2017. Electron: Towards Efficient Resource Management on Heterogeneous Clusters with Apache Mesos. In *2017 IEEE 10th International Conference on Cloud Computing (CLOUD)*. IEEE, 262–269. DOI: http://dx.doi.org/10.1109/CLOUD.2017.41

[13] Renan DelValle, Gourav Rattihalli, Angel Beltre, Madhusudhan Govindaraju, and Michael J. Lewis. 2016. Exploring the Design Space for Optimizations with Apache Aurora and Mesos. In *2016 IEEE 9th International Conference on Cloud Computing (CLOUD)*. IEEE, 537–544. DOI: http://dx.doi.org/10.1109/CLOUD.2016.0077

[14] Jessica Hartog, Elif Dede, and Madhusudhan Govindaraju. 2014. MapReduce framework energy adaptation via temperature awareness. *Cluster Computing* 17, 1 (3 2014), 111–127. DOI: http://dx.doi.org/10.1007/s10586-013-0270-y

[15] J. Hartog, R. Delvalle, M. Govindaraju, and M.J. Lewis. 2014. Configuring a MapReduce framework for performance-heterogeneous clusters. In *Proceedings - 2014 IEEE International Congress on Big Data, BigData Congress 2014*. DOI: http://dx.doi.org/10.1109/BigData.Congress.2014.26

[16] B Hindman, A Konwinski, and M Zaharia. 2011. Mesos: A Platform for Fine-Grained Resource Sharing in the Data Center. *NSDI* (2011).

[17] Shengsheng Huang, Jie Huang, Jinquan Dai, Tao Xie, and Bo Huang. 2010. The HiBench benchmark suite: Characterization of the MapReduce-based data analysis. In *2010 IEEE 26th International Conference on Data Engineering Workshops (ICDEW 2010)*. IEEE, 41–51.

[18] John D. McCalpin. 1995. Memory Bandwidth and Machine Balance in Current High Performance Computers. *IEEE Computer Society Technical Committee on Computer Architecture (TCCA) Newsletter* (1995), 19–25.

[19] Cengiz Karakoyunlu and John A. Chandy. 2016. Exploiting user metadata for energy-aware node allocation in a cloud storage system. *J. Comput. System Sci.* 82, 2 (3 2016), 282–309.

[20] Rini T. Kaushik and Milind Bhandarkar. 2010. GreenHDFS: towards an energy-conserving, storage-efficient, hybrid Hadoop compute cluster. (10 2010), 1–9.

[21] Willis Lang and Jignesh M. Patel. 2010. Energy management for MapReduce clusters. *Proceedings of the VLDB Endowment* 3, 1-2 (9 2010), 129–139.

[22] Jacob Leverich and Christos Kozyrakis. 2010. On the energy (in)efficiency of Hadoop clusters. *ACM SIGOPS Operating Systems Review* 44, 1 (3 2010), 61.

[23] Zhenhua Liu, Adam Wierman, Yuan Chen, Benjamin Razon, and Niangjun Chen. 2013. Data center demand response: Avoiding the coincident peak via workload shifting and local generation. *Performance Evaluation* 70, 10 (2013), 770–791.

[24] Silvano Martello, David Pisinger, and Daniele Vigo. 2000. The Three-Dimensional Bin Packing Problem. *Operations Research* 48, 2 (4 2000), 256–267.

[25] David Meisner, Christopher M. Sadler, Luiz Andr Barroso, Wolf-Dietrich Weber, and Thomas F. Wenisch. 2011. Power management of online data-intensive services. *ACM SIGARCH Computer Architecture News* 39, 3 (7 2011), 319.

[26] Michael A Heroux, Douglas W Doerfler, Paul S Crozier, James M Willenbring, H Carter Edwards, Alan Williams, Mahesh Rajan, Eric R Keiter, Heidi K Thornquist, and Robert W Numrich. 2009. *Improving performance via mini-applications*. Technical Report. Sandia National Laboratories.

[27] Sandia National Laboratories. 2016. DGEMM. (2016). http://www.nersc.gov/research-and-development/apex/apex-benchmarks/dgemm/

[28] Osman Sarood, Akhil Langer, Abhishek Gupta, and Laxmikant Kale. 2014. Maximizing Throughput of Overprovisioned HPC Data Centers Under a Strict Power Budget. In *SC14: International Conference for High Performance Computing, Networking, Storage and Analysis*. IEEE, 807–818.

[29] Craig A. Stewart, Daniel C. Stanzione, James Taylor, Edwin Skidmore, David Y. Hancock, Matthew Vaughn, Jeremy Fischer, Tim Cockerill, Lee Liming, Nirav Merchant, Therese Miller, and John Michael Lowe. 2016. Jetstream. In *Proceedings of the XSEDE16 on Diversity, Big Data, and Science at Scale - XSEDE16*. ACM Press, New York, New York, USA, 1–8.

[30] Vinod Kumar Vavilapalli, Siddharth Seth, Bikas Saha, Carlo Curino, Owen O'Malley, Sanjay Radia, Benjamin Reed, Eric Baldeschwieler, Arun C. Murthy, Chris Douglas, Sharad Agarwal, Mahadev Konar, Robert Evans, Thomas Graves, Jason Lowe, and Hitesh Shah. 2013. Apache Hadoop YARN. In *Proceedings of the 4th annual Symposium on Cloud Computing - SOCC '13*. ACM Press, New York, New York, USA, 1–16.

GPaaScaler: Green Energy Aware Platform Scaler for Interactive Cloud Application

MD Sabbir Hasan
INSA Rennes, INRIA, IRISA, UBL
Rennes, France
sabbir.hasan@inria.fr

Frederico Alvares
IMT Atlantique, INRIA, LS2N, UBL
Nantes, France
frederico.alvares@inria.fr

Thomas Ledoux
IMT Atlantique, INRIA, LS2N, UBL
Nantes, France
thomas.ledoux@inria.fr

ABSTRACT

Recently, smart usage of renewable energy has been a hot topic in the Cloud community. In this vein, we have recently proposed the creation of green energy awareness around *Interactive Cloud Applications*, but in static amount of underlying resources. This paper adds to previous ones as it considers elastic underlying infrastructure, that is, we propose a PaaS solution which efficiently utilize the elasticity nature at both infrastructure and application levels, by leveraging adaptation in facing to changing condition i.e., workload burst, performance degradation, quality of energy, etc. While applications are adapted by dynamically re-configuring their service level based on performance and/or green energy availability, the infrastructure takes care of addition/removal of resources based on application's resource demand. Both adaptive behaviors are implemented in separated modules and are coordinated in a sequential manner. We validate our approach by extensive experiments and results obtained over Grid'5000 test bed. Results show that, application can reduce significant amount of brown energy consumption by 35% and daily instance hour cost by 37% compared to a baseline approach when green energy aware adaptation is considered.

KEYWORDS

Interactive Cloud application; PaaS; Energy consumption; Autonomic computing; Green IT; Sustainable computing

1 INTRODUCTION

The fast growth of internet technology and proliferation of Cloud services have multiplied data centers number in recent years. In 2016, data centers around the world consumed 416.2 TWh of electricity, which is significantly higher than the UK's total consumption of about 300 TWh on the same year[1]. Although, numerous state-of-the-art energy efficient techniques have been adopted by industry and academia, a recent report suggests that energy usage in data centers is expected to increase by 4% until 2020, which will translate to higher carbon emission. Most of today's data centers consume grid tied brown energy, very few are partially powered by renewable energy. Therefore, energy efficient techniques alone is not going to reduce the carbon footprint since energy consumption will continue to grow. On the other hand, the ever increasing enthusiasm and consciousness of reducing energy consumption can lead towards smarter ways to consume energy in cloud data centers. While an efficient energy management technique in data center can reduce unnecessary use of brown energy and better utilize green energy without going to waste [8], [13], smarter ways of consuming energy in the presence/absence of renewable/green energy by an application can further reduce carbon footprint.

Traditionally, data centers host heterogeneous applications, such as *interactive* and *batch* applications/jobs. Goiri et al. [9], [10] first proposed a green energy adaptive framework for batch job oriented tasks *i.e.,* that facilitated the scheduling of these tasks to different times by respecting the deadline when green energy is available. On the contrary, interactive applications possess lesser flexibility, i.e., it should react with little to no latency, otherwise Quality of Service (QoS) can be seriously impacted. To cope up with these limitations, we have proposed a green energy adaptive solution to create green energy awareness inside the application that inherits the capability to smartly use the available green energy having *static* amount of underlying resources [14],[15].

But in a realistic cloud environment, resource requirement might exceed the currently provisioned resources. In contrast, when fewer resources are required, de-provisioning of resources can help to reduce unnecessary energy consumption. Therefore, the capability to detect when resources are required/dispensable and react to it so as to keep performance at a targeted level while energy consumption can be minimized is required. Taking application reconfiguration decision in isolation with resource scaling policies may lead to performance degradation and inconsistency to the system. Hence, coordination between two different types of elasticity (*i.e.,* application reconfiguration vs infrastructure (de)provisioning) is necessary.

---

[1]http://www.independent.co.uk/environment/global-warming-data-centres-to-consume-three-times-as-much-energy-in-next-decade-experts-warn-a6830086.html

Most of the work in the literature propose: (i) multiple autonomic loops in a coordinated manner to control cluster level resources (*i.e.*, one loop for controlling DVFS, another loop for deciding scaling actions)[21], [19]; (ii) per-application local manager which requests to a central autonomic manager to tune the number of cpu core, memory and to change the number of VM's [4], [3]; (iii) adaptive framework to coordinate between system level (DVFS) and application level (degrading quality) adaptation to improve performance and power efficiency [11].

It is clearly visible that - synergy between application and infrastructure based on green energy availability is missing despite having elasticity capability in both layers. We believe that, integrating the autonomic logics of the infrastructure with the one in the applications is a important research direction. Therefore, in response to the existing works, we propose a PaaS (Platform-as-a-Service) solution, named *GPaaScaler* that inherits the capability to adapt both at *application* and at *infrastructure* level in facing to changing condition *i.e.*, workload burst, performance degradation, quality of energy etc. We refer green energy to be better in quality, compared to brown energy. Application adaptation is realized by dynamically re-configuring application's mode/service level on the fly based on performance and/or green energy availability, whereas infrastructure adaptation takes care of addition/removal of resources based on application's resource demand. During application adaptation, any dynamic change at the software layer that impacts the energy profile can be considered as switching to higher or lower modes/service levels. To this point, we want to study the impact of application adaptation (based on the presence/absence of green energy) on infrastructure to have a global view of energy consumption incurred by the application. Furthermore, both adaptation technique is built in separate modules and coordinated in a sequential manner. For example, when application's performance decreases due to heavy load, the PaaS solution first triggers adaptation to application by downgrading the functionality according to signed SLA (Service Level Agreement) and invokes resource requests to infrastructure module. Followed by the invocation requests, infrastructure adaptation module analyzes and decides whether resources are going to be added or the request is to be ignored. We have tested our proposal at Grid'5000 test bed with a real life application, workload and energy profile to show that, when green energy aware adaptation is adopted, around 35% brown energy consumption can be reduced compared to a baseline approach. By reducing brown energy consumption, ratio of green energy to brown energy can be increased and subsequently carbon footprint can be appreciably reduced. The rest of the paper is organized as follows. Section 2 describes the GPaaScaler architecture. In Section 3, several Application controllers and a generic Infrastructure controller are designed to investigate their impacts on energy consumption and QoS properties and Section 4 validate approach through extensive experiments. Furthermore, in Section 5, we provide discussion based on results and observation. Section 6 describes the related works and we conclude our work in Section 7.

2 GPAASCALER ARCHITECTURE

This section presents our auto-scaler architecture named *GPaaScaler*, which continuously listens the instances of events *e.g.*, response time, green energy availability, working modes of application etc., pushed by SaaS(Software-as-a-Service) and IaaS(Infrastructure-as-a-Service) layers in a changing environment. Furthermore, it inherits the capability to actuate both at application and at infrastructure level. We use the most popular self-adaptive design framework: Monitor-Analyze-Plan- Execute-Knowledge (MAPE-K) loop [16] for our auto-scaler. Our contribution lies on the *analyze* and *plan* (A-P) block of this autonomic framework.

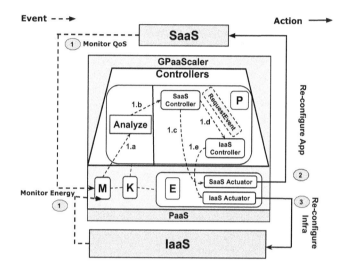

Figure 1: GPaaScaler architecture

Figure 1 presents the sequential control flow of the event in an ordered way (from 1.*a* to 1.*e*). Monitoring (M) block pushes listened events to *Analyze* block via (1.*a*) from SaaS layer (*i.e.*, response time, workload, application's working mode, etc.) and from IaaS layer (*i.e.*, quality of energy). Analyze (A) block is responsible for analyzing and decoupling events to extract the pertinent information and feed appropriate event to the event handler at the SaaS controller via 1.*b* flow. Once the events are received, Plan (P) block analyzes and matches to the predefined reactive or proactive rules and creates a configuration plan. The block pushes information through 1.*c* and 1.*e* to Execution (E) block, which consists of two types of actuator *i.e.*, SaaS and IaaS. These actuators act as an API to execute the action at application and at infrastructure layer respectively. Therefore, After the configuration plan, if needed, SaaS controller triggers action through SaaS actuator.

Most of the popular cloud applications provides some extra features (*e.g.*, several product recommendation in an e-commerce application), which enhances users quality of experience (QoE), but is not the core functionality of the service. These independent application components can be isolated to be activated/deactivated to provide different service levels to the end users. Different service levels can be also adopted to other Cloud applications, such as: (i) 2D/3D interactive applications over network (*e.g.*, architectural features where the rendering could be customized); (ii) On-line itineraries on maps with different details (*e.g.*, points of interest), etc. For the sake of generality, we propose three user experience levels. Mode High refers to high user experience while Mode Medium and Mode Low indicate to medium and low user experience respectively (see Figure 2). When current application behavior deviates from target system state in terms of SLA, the auto-scaler gracefully downgrades the user experience from higher mode to lower mode and vice-versa through proper actuator value. Once SaaS actuator triggers the adaptation plan, it passes request for addition/removal of resources event as $<< RequestEvent >>$ to IaaS controller if the former controller decides that application needs more/less resources, which is shown at Figure 1. Following the event, IaaS controller decides to take action via traditional infrastructure API (built in IaaS actuator) that is *scale-in* and *scale-out* or wait/discard the request issued by the SaaS controller. In addition, ①, ② and ③ depict the task flow of our auto-scaler. In summary, IaaS controller only gets activated if SaaS controller issues any $<< RequestEvent >>$. Since the public IaaS provider's does not expose their resource allocation policies to the upper layers *i.e.*, PaaS or SaaS, we consider infrastructure as a black box. Therefore, our proposed IaaS controller are unaware of resource allocation strategy, for instance, what types of VM is to be added/removed or location of VM's in specific servers etc.

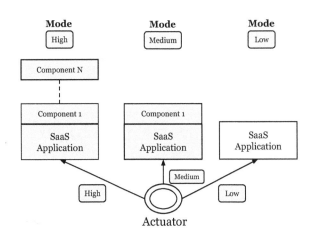

Figure 2: Applications mode under different service level

3 PROPOSED CONTROLLERS

This section describes several application controllers which have been extended to leverage the underlying elastic infrastructure and a generic infrastructure controller which can

be plugged with any application controller to control the elasticity capability of cloud infrastructure.

3.1 Application/SaaS controllers

We have designed and validated several single and mutiple metric application controllers which have the capability to re-configure SaaS application to keep it accessible and performant even at changing conditions at [13],[15]. In this article, we extend the Response time controller (performance aware) and Green Energy Controller (quality of resource aware) with increased capability to request of addition/removal of resources from the underlying elastic infrastructure.

Response Time controller (RT-C). Response time is an essential metric to guarantee cloud based application's performance. Our goal is to keep response time under certain threshold dynamically to maximize the availability of the service in unpredictable and variable workload condition. We closed the managed software system by a feedback loop, where in each control period, the output is forwarded as a Map of response time and workload arrival rate to compare with the target set-point. Afterwards, the information is forwarded to compute a function:

$$f(t) = 1 - \tilde{\lambda}(t) * \tilde{r}(t) \qquad (1)$$

where $\tilde{\lambda}(t) = \frac{\lambda(t-1)}{\lambda_{median}}$ and $\tilde{r}(t) = \frac{RT_{95}(t-1)}{RT_{setpoint}}$. Since, unpredictability and burstiness of user requests is common phenomena for Cloud application, we have considered workload arrival rate $\lambda(t)$ as a disturbance to the system. Ignoring the disturbance can lead to dramatic degradation of application performance. For capturing the change in the workload arrival rate, current workload arrival rate in the system is divided by median of previous arrival rates. A median filter is used with window size of four, that provides better estimation about variability of the workload arrival rate. Furthermore, the function $f(t)$ is computed at each t time to analyze how far the multiplication ratio of workload change and response time increment/decrement is from 1. The idea is to keep the function greater than 0 to stabilize the system to operate under target response time. If the function is positive and above a desired/predefined threshold, the controller keeps the highest user experience mode *i.e.*, mode 2. Since the controller is not aware of how much amount of underlying resources are used, it notifies the *vmRemove* event to the IaaS controller (see line 13, Algorithm 1). In case, the condition block falls to $f(t) \leq 0$, a $<< RequestEvent >>$ of *vmAdd* is notified to IaaS controller (see line 10, Algorithm 1).

Green Energy Controller (GE-C). While *RT-C* is built to avoid performance degradation by keeping response time to a target set point, is not aware of when green energy production is scarce or abundant to actuate application's mode. On the other hand, devising adaptation plan only based on green energy availability can dissatisfy reasonable QoS while workload arrival is higher. Therefore, we intend to build a controller which can make adaptive decision based on the

---

Algorithm 1: Response time controller (RT-C)

Input: $Thr_{rt}, \lambda = [0 \quad 0 \quad 0 \quad 0], setPoint, app$
Output: updated λ, $Curr_{mode}$ = Current application mode.

1 **if** *(handleEvent == responseTime)* **then**
2 $\quad \lambda(t-1) \leftarrow servedRequest$
3 $\quad enqueue(\lambda)$
4 $\quad f(t) \leftarrow 1 - (\lambda(t-1)/\lambda_{median}) * (RT_{95}/setPoint)$
5 $\quad$ **if** $(f(t) > 0) \wedge (function < Thr_{rt})$ **then**
6 $\quad\quad app.mode \leftarrow mode\ 1$
7 $\quad\quad RequestEvent \rightarrow vmAdd$ /* VM *Addition* request
$\quad\quad\quad$ event sent to IaaS controller along with RT_{95} and
$\quad\quad\quad$ workload-increment = $(\lambda(t-1)/\lambda_{median})$ */
8 $\quad$ **else if** $f(t) \leq 0$ **then**
9 $\quad\quad app.mode \leftarrow mode\ 0$
10 $\quad\quad RequestEvent \rightarrow vmAdd$ /* VM *Addition* request
$\quad\quad\quad$ event sent to IaaS controller along with RT_{95} and
$\quad\quad\quad$ workload-increment = $(\lambda(t-1)/\lambda_{median})$ */
11 $\quad$ **else**
12 $\quad\quad app.mode \leftarrow mode\ 2$
13 $\quad\quad RequestEvent \rightarrow vmRemove$ /* VM *Removal* request
$\quad\quad\quad$ event sent to IaaS controller along with RT_{95} and
$\quad\quad\quad$ workload-increment = $(\lambda(t-1)/\lambda_{median})$ */
14 $\quad dequeue(\lambda)$
15 $\quad Curr_{mode} = app.mode$
16 **return** λ, $Curr_{mode}$

---

better quality of energy *i.e.,* green energy and application's performance.

We distinguish between two control periods: long and short. Algorithm 2 presents two $<< handleEvent >>$ blocks, each associated with specific event *i.e.,* *greenEnergy* and *responseTime*. In *longer control period*, *greenEnergy* block decides application's mode based on green energy availability. Some sources of green energy are only available during certain times. For instance, solar energy is available during the day and the amount produced depends on the weather and the season [10]. Due to the intermittency, we have divided the total green energy production to three different regions *i.e.,* no green energy (at night), few (early morning and late afternoon) and adequate (mid-day). To distinguish between the regions we choose a static threshold Thr_{max}, above which the controller activates high user experience mode (mode 2). When green energy production falls between 0 and Thr_{max}, the controller chooses an actuator value that triggers the medium user experience mode (mode 1), and in case of current green energy amount is null, mode 0 is activated. In short, the controller activates higher or lower user experience mode based on the energy information pushed by infrastructure in longer control periods. In contrast, the *responseTime* block checks the response time periodically in *shorter control period* to identify overloaded condition in the system. If occurred, the controller downgrades the user experience to lower level. In summary, depending on the event, the specific block gets activated in Algorithm 2.

Afterwards, we try to investigate when performance indicator of an Application can trigger add/remove VM request. Since this controller have two feedback loops activating at two different control periods: long and short, and longer control period's decision depends only on the energy information,

hence we focus on the shorter control period loop which is based on response time event. The shorter control loop periodically checks if the targeted response time is violated by application by computing a function at line 15 at Algorithm 2. If the computed function becomes negative (f(t) $\leq$ 0) meaning, if the current response time is beyond or borderline to set point and/or the tendency of the workload is increasing, the controller downgrades the user experience by subtracting 1 from previous control period's decision value and notify a vmAdd event request to the infrastructure controller (see line 18, Algorithm 2). While the function is greater than 0, which suggests that the application is performing well by keeping current 95th percentile response time to the set point, application keeps the user experience as before but notify a vmRemove event request to the infrastructure controller (see line 21, Algorithm 2). In both cases, $<< RequestEvent >>$ notifies the specific event along with application's current 95th percentile response time and workload increment ratio to the IaaS controller.

Algorithm 2: Green Energy controller (GE-C)

Input: Thr_{max} = Threshold for green energy, $\lambda = [0 \quad 0 \quad 0 \quad 0]$,
$\quad\quad setPoint, Curr_{GE}$ = Current green energy production.
Output: updated λ, $Curr_{mode}$ = Current application mode.

1 /* *Initiates in longer control period* */
2 **if** *(handleEvent == greenEnergy)* **then**
3 $\quad$ **if** $Curr_{GE} == 0$ **then**
4 $\quad\quad app.mode \leftarrow mode\ 0$
5 $\quad$ **else if** $Curr_{GE} > Thr_{max}$ **then**
6 $\quad\quad app.mode \leftarrow mode\ 2$
7 $\quad$ **else**
8 $\quad\quad app.mode \leftarrow mode\ 1$
9 $\quad Curr_{mode} = app.mode$
10 **return** $Curr_{mode}$
11 /* *Initiates in shorter control period* */
12 **if** *(handleEvent == responseTime)* **then**
13 $\quad \lambda(t-1) \leftarrow servedRequest$
14 $\quad enqueue(\lambda)$
15 $\quad f(t) \leftarrow 1 - (\lambda(t-1)/\lambda_{median}) * (RT_{95}/setPoint)$
16 $\quad$ **if** $(f(t) \leq 0)$ *and* $(Curr_{mode} \neq 0)$ **then**
17 $\quad\quad app.mode \leftarrow Curr_{mode} - 1$
18 $\quad\quad RequestEvent \rightarrow vmAdd$ /* VM *Addition* request
$\quad\quad\quad$ event sent to IaaS controller along with RT_{95} and
$\quad\quad\quad$ workload-increment = $(\lambda(t-1)/\lambda_{median})$ */
19 $\quad$ **else if** $(f(t) > 0)$ **then**
20 $\quad\quad app.mode \leftarrow Curr_{mode}$
21 $\quad\quad RequestEvent \rightarrow vmRemove$ /* VM *Removal* request
$\quad\quad\quad$ event sent to IaaS controller along with RT_{95} and
$\quad\quad\quad$ workload-increment = $(\lambda(t-1)/\lambda_{median})$ */
22 $\quad$ **else**
23 $\quad\quad app.mode \leftarrow Curr_{mode}$
24 $\quad Curr_{mode} = app.mode$
25 $\quad dequeue(\lambda)$
26 **return** λ, $Curr_{mode}$

3.2 IaaS controller

While under-provisioning of resources can significantly hamper QoS properties by saturating application, over-provisioning of resources can increase energy consumption and other associated costs significantly. Therefore, the scaling decision, for instance, add resources (scale-out) or remove resources (scale-in) should be taken carefully to match with the applications resource demand. To meet *scale-out* condition, a reactive policy can be easily designed and implemented based on the monitored performance metrics or by listening to predefined appropriate events. A reactive policy is referred to a runtime decision based on current demand and system state - to add resources on the fly. On the contrary, reactive policies can not absorb the non-negligible resource/instance initiation time. In our case, when application starts to face high response time, both the SaaS controllers have the capability to downgrade the user experience level and to invoke an implicit event (vmAdd) request to IaaS controller. Therefore, the sequential operation can trigger the application to run at lower mode until the instance is launched and activated. Afterwards, the application reverts back to higher mode if it meets the condition after operation.

In contrast, when *scale-in* event (*i.e.*, fewer resources are required by application) is invoked by SaaS controllers, terminating instance based on reactive policy can have detrimental impact on the system [18]. For example, when application performs better by staying just below or borderline to set point, triggering *scale-in* action can make an application suffering from high response time to saturation. One way to overcome the problem is to VM resizing, that is to reduce the number of cpu cores on the fly by doing fine-grained analysis of resource requirements rather than terminating an entire instance, but popular hypervisors like KVM, VMware, Hyper-V does not allow removing cpu cores of guest VMs at runtime [20]. Additionally, instance termination can cause a sharp rise in response time reaching beyond the set point if workload's behavior or tendency is not taken into consideration. Therefore, devising a plan when to execute *scale-in* event is critical. On the other hand, if the consecutive scaling actions are carried out too quickly without being able to observe the impact of scaling action to the application, undesirable effects such as over and under-provisioning can occur which can leads to performance degradation and/or wastage of energy consumption.

Hence, the idea is to built a generic IaaS controller which is characteristically agnostic to SaaS controllers behavior. Whenever, an implicit event invocation (vmAdd, vmRemove) arrives to the controller, it activates the proper module by matching to the event. Since, two non-concurrent events can be invoked by SaaS controllers, our proposed IaaS controller contains two modules to handle each of them. We define a length of period called *coolingLength*, which is composed of instance activation time and the time it requires to impact on the application. Therefore, after triggering any scaling decision, this time period is updated to prevent any scaling decision to be made in between. Hence, when vmAdd event arrives to the controller, the *handleEvent == vmAdd* module matches the condition of not being at *coolingPeriod* with an and operator to maximum number of VM's a provider can be assigned to[2]. If it adheres the condition, *scale-out* decision is

---

[2]Amazon EC2 permits maximum 20 on-demand instances per user.

Algorithm 3: Infrastructure controller

Input: $[minVm, maxVm]$ = Minimum and maximum number of VM's.
$[RT_{95}, workload_{inc}]$ = Response time and workload increment sent by SaaS controller.
$[rt_{thr}, decWorkPerc]$ = Two tunable parameters.
Output: $vmNumber, coolingPeriod$

1 **if** *(handleEvent == vmAdd)* **then**
2   **if** $(currentTime \notin coolingPeriod) \wedge (vmNumber < maxVm)$ **then**
3      $triggerAction \rightarrow "scale - out"$ /* Passing API call through cloud infrastructure manager */
4      $vmNumber+ = 1$
5      $coolingPeriod+ = coolingLength$
6   **else**
7      $vmNumber = this.vmNumber$
8      $coolingPeriod = this.coolingPeriod$
9    $vmNumber = update(vmNumber)$
10    $coolingPeriod = update(coolingPeriod)$
11 **return** $vmNumber, coolingPeriod$

12 **if** *(handleEvent == vmRemove)* **then**
13   **if** $(currentTime \notin coolingPeriod) \wedge (rt_{thr} > RT_{95}) \wedge (vmNumber > minVm) \wedge ((workload_{inc} < decWorkPerc) \vee (Curr_{mode} = 0))$ **then**
14      $triggerAction \rightarrow "scale - in"$ /* Passing API call through cloud infrastructure manager */
15      $vmNumber- = 1$
16      $coolingPeriod+ = coolingLength$
17   **else**
18      $vmNumber = this.vmNumber$
19      $coolingPeriod = this.coolingPeriod$
20    $vmNumber = update(vmNumber)$
21    $coolingPeriod = update(coolingPeriod)$
22 **return** $vmNumber, coolingPeriod$

---

triggered via IaaS actuator and current number of VM and next *coolingPeriod* is updated (see line 3-5 of Algorithm 3). Otherwise, the module ignores the notification. On the other hand, when vmRemove event is invoked by SaaS controller, if the *handleEvent == vmRemove* module is not carefully designed, cloud application can face unstable phases *i.e.*, sharp rises of response time to saturate application. Therefore, only looking at *coolingPeriod* and minimum number of VM could be unwise and skeptical.

To overcome this situation, we introduce two key parameters which are tunable to identify when is the good time to release resources *i.e.*, perform scale-in action. The parameters are i) how far the current system's response time should be from set point? For example, x% less than target response time set point, which is denoted by rt_{thr} at Algorithm 3. ii) how much workload rate should decrease from the current trend? For instance, y% decrease in user requests than previous intervals, denoted by *decWorkPerc*. Hence, when *handleEvent == vmRemove* arrives to the IaaS controller, the module checks the cooling period, minimum number of VM, current response time condition with an AND operator. Additionally we put an OR operator between workload decrease parameter and current mode of the application. The rational behind that, in the absence of green energy, *GE-C* controller keeps the application at minimum level. Although, workload may be consistent or increasing, if this application controller invokes `vmRemove` event that matches to be outside of *coolingPeriod*, greater than minimum number of VM and reduced response time than the threshold, it will meet the *scale-in* condition and IaaS controller will trigger the action to release resources. On the other hand, *RT-C* will keep application at the highest mode when resources are slightly to abundantly over-provisioned. Thus, application being at *mode* = 0 and decreasing workload by y% percentage can not happen concurrently if response time is x% less than response time set point for this type of SaaS controller. Apart from *GE-C*, any SaaS controller which invokes `vmRemove` event and satisfies all the conditions mentioned above other than application mode being at lowest, will trigger *scale-in* action by IaaS controller.

4 EVALUATION

In this section, we present the evaluation results of proposed SaaS and IaaS controllers and their impact on cloud based application in terms of response time, energy consumption and cost. The goal is to advocate the benefits and limitations of each controller while experimenting with real cloud application and real workload traces.

4.1 Experimental setup

Infrastructure configuration. The experiments were conducted in Grid'5000 Lyon site, with 3 physical machines linked by a 10 Gbit/s Ethernet switch and connected to wattmeter. Each machine has two 2.3GHz Xeon processors (6 cores per CPU) and 16GB of RAM, running Linux 2.6. Openstack Liberty was used as platform, which requires one dedicated physical machine for the cloud controller management system. Consequently, the other physical machines were used as compute nodes to host VMs, which in turn, were pre-configured to run Ubuntu 12.04.

Application Configuration. We experimented with RUBiS application [1], an eBay like auction site, which is assumed to be a representative of popular e-commerce application and hence interactive web application. In Brownout [17], authors provided a user-to-user recommendation engine that is not core functionality of the service but can enhance user experience. Along with that, we implemented a fairly simple item-to-item recommendation, to offer another level of user experience, which is showed at Listing 1.

Listing 1: SQL statement for the recommender system.

```
1   SELECT
2       items1.id
3   FROM
4       items AS items1.id
5       JOIN comments AS c ON items1.id = c.item_id
6       JOIN items AS i2 ON items1.category = i2.category
7   WHERE
8       i2.id = :current_item_id AND
9       items1.nb_of_bids >= i2.item_id AND
10      items1.id != :current_item_id
11  ORDER BY rating DESC
12  LIMIT 10;
```

The simple recommendation engine can be summarized as "Retrieve 10 products from same seller and same product category which have higher or same user bid count with higher customer rating". Although both the recommendation engines lack the sophistication and worldly complexities, they do serve as a reasonable example of providing user experience that a cloud application can isolate from core functionality of the service to activate or deactivate at runtime. The recommendation is added to the item visualisation page and to enable it, we defined a function that reads a file, where actuator value is updated in each control period and execute the associated modes for each user request. For instance, Mode 1 activates the codes of recommendation one, mode 2 activates both recommendations and mode 0 provides no recommendation. Furthermore, the application is deployed with all its tiers *i.e.,* web and database server inside a VM using a LEMP stack[3]. Each application VM and Load-balancer (LB) VM were configured with 4 cores of CPU and 8GB of memory similar to Large flavor VM. Since, we used 2 compute servers, we could use maximum of 6 VMs and minimum at 2 VMs[4].

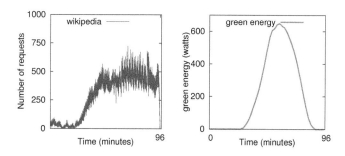

Figure 3: Workload trace

Platform and Workload. Our Proposed platform solution is hosted inside the cloud controller machine. It monitors the 95th percentile response time by aggregating the Nginx log of LB in each control period *i.e.,* 20 seconds, whereas green energy information is pushed by the infrastructure through an API in every 60 seconds. We have set rt_{thr}=80% and $decWorkPerc$=20% based on our observation at IaaS controller to evaluate our proposal. We took the real traffic pattern of wikipedia german page of one day [6] and scaled the data set to fit with our experiment, which is showed at Figure 3. To generate the workload, we used Gatling as load injector and chose an open system model, where user requests are issued without waiting for other users response from the system. Furthermore, we emulated read-only workload where each user arrives to the homepage, browse any item category from a vast catalog, click on a product to extract its information, view seller rating and his/her reputation related to the product. We traced the solar energy production that was added to the grid for one day (12th April,2016) from

---

[3]https://lemp.io/
[4]1 LB VM and 1 application VM

EDF, France[5] and scaled the values suited for our experiment. Furthermore, the duration of each experiment was 96min and each was run several times. We considered 96min as 24 hours, i.e., each 4min in our experiments correspond to 1 hour.

4.2 Consideration of delaying event

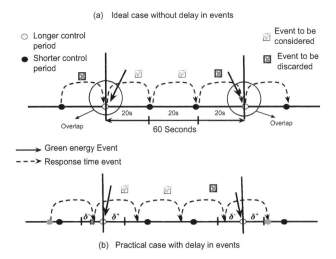

(a) Ideal case without delay in events

(b) Practical case with delay in events

Figure 4: Algorithm implementation in detail

From Section 3.1, we see that, *GE-C* controller has inner and outer loops ($<< handleEvent >>$ blocks) which are activated in different time-scales and push events to the controller to make decision. In our experiments, outer (longer control period) and inner (shorter control period) events arrived at 60 seconds and 20 seconds respectively to the controller, which is showed in Figure 4. Ideally, if both kinds of events arrive without any delay, two different events will overlap each other at some point. As our motivation is to maximize of green energy usage for *GE-C* controller, we always make primary decision based on the green energy event pushed by IaaS by ignoring the response time event which is activated as inner loop, if both the event arrives concurrently. Concretely, it suggests that, between two big decision events in 60 seconds, we consider only two inner loop events and take actions if it is necessary indicated in Figure 4(a).

But in case of delaying of any event, the scenario will not follow Figure 4(a). As discussed before, the primary decision always depends on green energy event. Even though we receive response time event, no action is taken unless the system's response time is high. Therefore, in case of delaying of response time event by micro to milliseconds, effects to the system remain almost unchangeable. In contrast, if the event delays by couple of seconds, for instance, inner loop event arrives just before or after the primary decision is made, it might affect the system dynamics to achieve the goal. To tackle the problem, we define a safety distance, denoted by

---

[5] http://www.rte-france.com/fr/eco2mix/eco2mix

δ^t to ensure that the controller does not take any action if response time event arrives in between "$PrimaryDecision - \delta^t$" and "$PrimaryDecision + \delta^t$". Figure 4(b) illustrates the phenomena by an example. For our case, we choose safety distance as, δ^t = Time frequency of inner loop / 2, which is equal to 10 seconds in our experiments.

4.3 Results

This section elaborately presents the results obtained during experiment at Grid'5000. We consider a baseline approach *i.e.*, non-adaptive controller (NA), which lacks the capability of application adaptation and rely only on infrastructure adaptation based on response time.

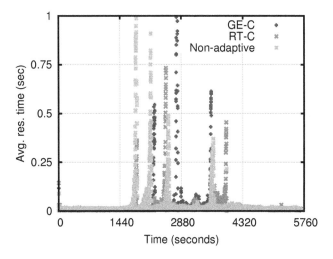

Figure 5: Response time incurred by application controllers

Response time. In Figure 5, we grouped response time by taking average over seconds. We kept response time set point as 1s. Since, our approach allows both level of adaptation depending on the changing environment, both RT-C and GE-C performed very closely by keeping 99th percentile response time around 274ms and 388ms. Figure 6 shows the distribution of response time for all the controllers. Although the baseline approach lacked application adaptation, it kept the 99th percentile response time around 500ms. On average, 3.7 million requests were injected during every experiment and only 7-20 requests failed for RT-C and 70-100 requests failed for GE-C. Therefore, both the controller ensure availability to five 9's (99.999%).

Energy Consumption. In our experiment, each 4 minutes were considered as an hour, thus we calculated the energy consumption of 24 hours, impacted by each controller, which is presented at Table 1 and 2. Each experiment was run several times and we found the energy consumption difference between each run was 1~2 watts. At first, we scaled down the wikipedia workload to test the application controllers with static infrastructure, that is, in any given time

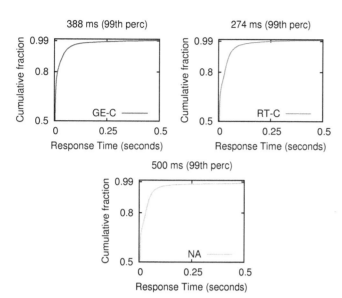

Figure 6: Response time incurred by application controllers in percentiles

application controllers were unable to use underlying elastic infrastructure. Table 1 summarizes that, GE-C can reduce brown energy consumption by 9.02% and 10.88% compared to NA and RT-C, while total energy consumption was reduced by 6.53% and 6.4% respectively. NA was supposed to consume more energy than RT-C since it lacks the capability to adapt application to lower level. Due to the heavy user requests at some periods, NA approach saturated RUBiS application which was unable to accept any requests which resulted lower availability and lower energy consumption. Although, GE-C controller consumed 1.2% more green energy than NA, the amount was 0.50% less than RT-C controller, (See Table 1)

Afterwards, we proceeded with usual settings with the experiment having infrastructure elasticity capability for all the application controllers. Table 2 shows that, GE-C can reduce significant amount of brown energy by 35.11% and 26.65% compared to NA approach and RT-C respectively. Interestingly, GE-C consumed less green energy (6.83% less than NA, 5.53% less than RT-C) than the other application controllers, although this application controller was designed to consume more green energy than its counterpart application controllers. The reason being that, GE-C activated higher application mode only in the presence of green energy, irrespective to the amount of user requests. Therefore, if the user requests are lower/higher while few green energy is available the controller activates medium service level mode (*i.e.,* mode 1 which activates 1 type of recommendation) and starts activating higher service level (*i.e.,* mode 2 which activates 2 different kinds of recommendation) when the amount of green energy increases. On the other hand, when green energy is scarce, application works at a low service level mode,

that is, user can access the system but no recommendation is provided. In this experiment, the user requests started growing when green energy were scarce. Therefore, NA and RT-C both activated more application VMs than GE-C to cope up with the workload, which can be seen at Figure 7. Moreover, Figure 7 shows that, GE-C followed green energy profile very closely while activating application VMs. It was possible due to fact that, we created green energy awareness to the application through *GPaaScaler*. GE-C and RT-C both used maximum of 4 VM's while NA approach used 5 VM's for same workload. The idea behind providing Table 1 and Table 2 is to show that, by exploiting elasticity capability at infrastructure level, application can reduce brown energy consumption even further.

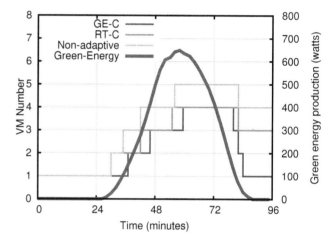

Figure 7: Number of VM usage during experiment

Cost analysis. Since, our proposed GPaaScaler architecture is agnostic to infrastructure provider and type, it can be plugged on top of public cloud infrastructure. Therefore, we wanted to validate how much each application controller would cost with same application and workload profile. Since, we used large flavor VM's, we fixed instance costs to 0.104$/hour. Moreover, we considered 4 minutes of duration to 1 hour in our experiment, we calculated the amount of instances and their duration throughout the experiment. We considered partial time spent in the experiment as full instance hour. Figure 8 shows the cost incurred by all the application controller. GE-C incurred 37.03% and 21.56% lesser cost than NA approach and RT-C.

5 DISCUSSION

After extensively analyzing both the controllers that we have designed, its evident that the GE-C can outperform RT-C and NA in terms of energy reduction and cost gains. In terms of performance, both the controller performs at the same level. We have investigated that, it takes approximately 5-6 seconds for the application to be stabilized with desired behavior after the application reconfiguration decision is triggered via

Table 1: Energy Consumption in Watts (Application adaptation)

Controller	Total Energy Consumption	Brown Energy Consumption	Green Energy Consumption
Non-Adaptive	3424.20	1934.66	1484.54
RT-C	3493.93	1975.18	1518.75
GE-C	3270.20	1760.09	1510.11
	(NA > 6.53%)(RT-C > 6.4%)	(NA > 9.02%) (RT-C > 10.88%)	(NA < 1.2%)(RT-C > 0.50%)

Table 2: Energy Consumption in Watts (Application and Infrastructure adaptation)

Controller	Total Energy Consumption	Brown Energy Consumption	Green Energy Consumption
Non-Adaptive	5912.49	2516.59	3395.9
RT-C	5574.78	2226.16	3348.62
GE-C	4796.17	1632.77	3163.4
	(NA > 18.88%)(RT-C > 13.96%)	(NA > 35.11%) (RT-C > 26.65%)	(NA > 6.83%)(RT-C > 5.53%)

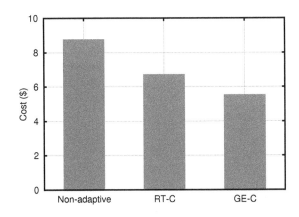

Figure 8: Cost analysis for VM usage

SaaS actuator. That suggests, if we fix the control time very small, the controller can take decisions before the system has been impacted by last control decision. Therefore, the safety time is required for a system to be evolved to a desired state. Furthermore, activating control loop more frequently can increase the overhead of the system by accumulating information from system logs. In case of infrastructure, stabilization occurred after 15-20 seconds. Although GE-C can provide lesser recommendations/optional components which can be "nice-to-have" component, SaaS providers can take advantage of this controller to propose new class of SLA to eco-friendly customers who are willing to involve in reducing energy consumption. Moreover, GE-C controller can help SaaS provider to reduce costs by using fewer instances/hours from Public Cloud. Additionally, IaaS provider will be benefited for hosting these applications, since the applications will be able to consume energy smartly. In the Result Section, Table 2 showed that, Green energy consumption for GE-C was slightly lower than the other controller. In contrast, GE-C reduced significant amount of Brown energy, thus the *Green-to-Brown* energy ratio can be increased, as

well as carbon footprint can be reduced. Although, with the change of workload and green energy profile, the values and numbers we have provided might change, but the tendency of the result will remain similar.

6   RELATED WORK

Green Energy aware Application adaptation. Goiri et al. [9] proposed *GreenSlot*, a parallel batch job scheduler for a datacenter powered by an on-site renewable plant. Based on the historical data and weather forecast, GreenSlot predicts the amount of solar energy that will likely to be available in the future and subject to its predictions, it schedules the workload by the order of least slack time first (LSTF), to maximize the green energy consumption while meeting the job's deadlines by creating resource reservations into the future. Later, their work evolved into data processing framework by proposing *GreenHadoop* [10]. The idea relies on deferring background computations *e.g.,* data and log analysis, long simulations etc. that can be delayed by a bounded amount of time in a data center to take advantage of green energy availability while minimizing brown electricity cost. The idea is to run fewer servers when brown energy is cheap, and even fewer (if at all necessary) when brown energy is expensive. In conclusion, their proposal leads to operating few hadoop clusters when green energy is scarce. Similar to this work, authors [12] proposed *GreenPar*, a scheduler for parallel high-performance applications to maximize using green energy in a partially powered data center and reduce brown energy consumption, while respecting performance aware SLA. When green energy is available, GreenPar increases the resource allocations to active jobs to reduce runtimes by speeding up the processes while slow down the jobs to a maximum runtime slowdown percentage that is defined in SLA during the scarcity of the green energy. However, all these works focused specifically around batch like applications where job arrives with a deadline, hence can be deferred and scheduled by following the green energy availability. On the other hand, we propose to create green energy awareness around the interactive kind of application to to be self adapted with the presence/absence of green energy. Recently, Klein et al. [17] introduced Brownout paradigm for dynamic adaptation in interactive application through control theory to withstand in unpredictable runtime variations. Content reconfiguration takes into account only the system response time so that to prevent system instability in sudden workload burstiness. While the novelty of the approach is well understood, how the controller should be designed to take the advantage of the presence of green energy and implemented in massively virtualized and distributed cloud environment to exploit the elastic nature of infrastructure, has not been addressed.

To this, in [22], the authors proposed *GreenWare*, a middleware system that maximize the usage of green energy in geo-distributed cloud scale data centers by dynamically dispatching workload requests by following renewable, subject to energy budget constraint. The middleware performs three steps: computes the hourly energy budget and historical behavior of workload, runs an optimization algorithm based on constrained optimization technique, lastly dispatches requests according to optimization plan. Similar to this, [7] proposed a flow optimization based framework for request-routing considering the trade-off between access latency, carbon footprint and electricity costs to upgrade the plan of choosing data center in specific intervals. Again these works focused more on load-balancing of user requests to different data centers to maximize the usage of green energy rather relying on application adaptation on the fly.

Platform adaptation. Shi et al. [19] proposed two control layer, one responsible for allocating resources to VM's depending on the performance, the other one as a power saving layer to dynamically save energy by tuning voltage and frequency (DVFS) while resource requirement is low. Both layers are designed as autonomic loops in a coordinated manner to control cluster level resources. Later, Hankendi et al. [11] proposed an adaptive framework that jointly utilizes system (DVFS) and application-level adaptation to improve efficiency of multi-core servers and reduction of power consumption. Application-level adaptation has been utilized to meet the performance and accuracy constraints, whereas to meet power constraints, system-level management was adopted. On the other hand, we propose to adopt sequential execution of adaptation technique both at application and infrastructure level that not only met performance but also reduced energy consumption at significant portion.

In contrast to prevoius works, authors at [5] presented an Energy Adaptive Software Controller (*EASC*) to make task and service oriented application adaptive to renewable energy availability. The work was part of by DC4Cities project [6], which aimed at gathering renewable energy related information from energy providers and energy constraint directives from Energy monitoring authority (in context of Smart city) through an interface. Following the information, the PaaS

[6]An European project on environmentally sustainable data centers for smart cities. Ended on 2016. http://www.dc4cities.eu

layer is responsible to adapt the application by satisfying energy related constraints to consume more green energy, therefore building more eco-efficient policies for data center. The authors proposed to forward the energy related information to PaaS level via an API, so that an optimization plan can be invoked which involves desired working modes of an application considering energy and SLA constraints. However, service oriented application *i.e.*, interactive application is defined as running web, database and mail servers and higher mode depicts multiple data center site is active with full capacity while lowest mode indicates running a single site with minimum capacity. Apart from that, Moreno et al. [2] proposed how different non-conflicting tactics (*e.g.*, remove one software component and add one server) can be triggered simultaneously so that system can transition from current to desired state. The challenge is to estimate how two types of tactics when applied together reacts to the system. For instance, removing software component can have immediate transition, whereas adding one server can make a delayed transition which is also associated with cost. Depending on the goal, the utility function can be maximized by choosing proper adaptation tactics. Again these works ignored how to adapt and define tactics to leverage green energy availability to either consume more green energy or less brown energy.

7 CONCLUSION

In this article, we proposed a green energy aware platform that creates awareness around interactive Cloud application and formulate strategy to understand when to trigger scaling decision based on reactive and pro-active scaling rules. Secondly, we use traditional API such as *scale-in* and *scale-out* to trigger decision based on the strategy we have devised. Later we validated our approach by extensive experiments and results obtained over Grid'5000 test bed. Results showed that, significant amount of brown energy and cost reduction is possible if application can be adapted based on green energy availability. For future work, we want to leverage micro-service architecture of an application to adapt itself in the presence of green energy. It would be interesting to deploy small and decoupled units of the application in a containerized approach (rather than VM) so that, each of the application component if required, can be scaled to guarantee better performance, self healing capabilities. Apart from that, resource can be assigned to specific components where it is required, thus over-provisioning of resource phenomena can be avoided resulting lesser energy consumption. Additionally, this investigation can leads to a decentralized autonomic behavior in modern application.

8 ACKNOWLEDGMENT

This work is supported by the EPOC project within the Labex CominLabs (http://www.epoc.cominlabs.ueb.eu/). Experiments presented in this paper were carried out using the Grid5000 testbed, supported by a scientific interest group hosted by INRIA and including CNRS, RENATER, and several Universities as well as other organizations (https://www.grid5000.fr).

REFERENCES

[1] 2009. RUBiS, Rice University Bidding System. (2009). http://rubis.ow2.org/ (Date last accessed July-2016).

[2] Gabriel A. Moreno, Javier Cámara, David Garlan, and Bradley R. Schmerl. 2016. Efficient Decision-Making under Uncertainty for Proactive Self-Adaptation. In *IEEE International Conference on Autonomic Computing, ICAC*. 147–156. https://doi.org/10.1109/ICAC.2016.59

[3] Stefania Costache, Samuel Kortas, Christine Morin, and Nikos Parlavantzas. 2017. Market-based autonomous resource and application management in private clouds. *Journal of Parallel and Distributed Computing* 100 (2017), 85–102. https://doi.org/10.1016/j.jpdc.2016.10.003

[4] Stefania Costache, Nikos Parlavantzas, Christine Morin, and Samuel Kortas. 2011. An Economic Approach for Application QoS Management in Clouds. In *Euro-Par 2011: Parallel Processing Workshops Bordeaux, France, August 29 - September 2, 2011*. 426–435. https://doi.org/10.1007/978-3-642-29740-3_48

[5] Corentin Dupont, Mehdi Sheikhalishahi, Michele Facca Federico, and Fabien Hermenier. 2015. An energy aware application controller for optimizing renewable energy consumption in Cloud computing data centres. In *8th IEEE/ACM Int. Conf. on Utility and Cloud Computing*. Limassol, Cyprus.

[6] Soodeh Farokhi, Pooyan Jamshidi, Drazen Lucanin, and Ivona Brandic. 2015. Performance-Based Vertical Memory Elasticity. In *IEEE Int. Conf. on Autonomic Computing*. 151–152. https://doi.org/10.1109/ICAC.2015.51

[7] Peter Xiang Gao, Andrew R. Curtis, Bernard Wong, and Srinivasan Keshav. 2012. It's not easy being green. In *Proceedings of the ACM SIGCOMM 2012 conference on Applications, technologies, architectures, and protocols for computer communication (SIGCOMM '12)*. ACM, 12. https://doi.org/10.1145/2342356.2342398

[8] Íñigo Goiri, William Katsak, Kien Le, Thu D. Nguyen, and Ricardo Bianchini. 2013. Parasol and GreenSwitch: Managing Datacenters Powered by Renewable Energy. ACM.

[9] Íñigo Goiri, Kien Le, Md. E. Haque, Ryan Beauchea, Thu D. Nguyen, Jordi Guitart, Jordi Torres, and Ricardo Bianchini. 2011. GreenSlot: Scheduling Energy Consumption in Green Datacenters. In *Proc. of Int. Conf. for High Performance Computing, Networking, Storage and Analysis*. ACM, Article 20, 11 pages.

[10] Íñigo Goiri, Kien Le, Thu D. Nguyen, Jordi Guitart, Jordi Torres, and Ricardo Bianchini. 2012. GreenHadoop: Leveraging Green Energy in Data-processing Frameworks. In *Proc. of the 7th ACM European Conf. on Comp. Syst.* ACM, 57–70.

[11] Can Hankendi, Ayse Kivilcim Coskun, and Henry Hoffmann. 2016. Adapt&Cap: Coordinating System- and Application-Level Adaptation for Power-Constrained Systems. *IEEE Design & Test* 33,

1 (2016), 68–76. https://doi.org/10.1109/MDAT.2015.2463275

[12] Md. E. Haque, Íñigo Goiri, Bianchini R., and Thu D. Nguyen. 2015. GreenPar: Scheduling Parallel High Performance Applications in Green Datacenters. In *Proceedings of the 29th ACM on International Conference on Supercomputing, ICS'15, Newport Beach/Irvine, CA, USA, June 08 - 11, 2015*. 217–227. https://doi.org/10.1145/2751205.2751221

[13] MD Sabbir Hasan, Yousri Kouki, Thomas Ledoux, and Jean-Louis Pazat. 2017. Exploiting Renewable sources : when Green SLA becomes a possible reality in Cloud computing. *IEEE Transactions on Cloud Computing* 5, 2 (April 2017), 1–1.

[14] Sabbir Hasan, Frederico Alvares, Thomas Ledoux, and Jean-Louis Pazat. 2016. Enabling Green Energy awareness in Interactive Cloud Application. In *Int. Conf. on Cloud Computing Technology and Science*. IEEE.

[15] Sabbir Hasan, Frederico Alvares, Thomas Ledoux, and Jean-Louis Pazat. 2017. Investigating Energy consumption and Performance trade-off for Interactive Cloud Application. *IEEE Transactions on Sustainable computing* 2, 2 (June 2017), 113–126.

[16] J. O. Kephart and D. M. Chess. 2003. The vision of autonomic computing. *Computer* 36, 1 (January 2003), 41–50. https://doi.org/10.1109/MC.2003.1160055

[17] Cristian Klein, Martina Maggio, Karl-Erik Årzén, and Francisco Hernández-Rodriguez. 2014. Brownout: Building More Robust Cloud Applications. In *Proc. of the 36th Int. Conf. on Software Engineering*. ACM. https://doi.org/10.1145/2568225.2568227

[18] Gabriele Mencagli, Marco Vanneschi, and Emanuele Vespa. 2014. A Cooperative Predictive Control Approach to Improve the Reconfiguration Stability of Adaptive Distributed Parallel Applications. *ACM Trans. Auton. Adapt. Syst.* 9, 1 (March 2014), 2:1–2:27. http://doi.acm.org/10.1145/2567929

[19] Xiaoyu Shi, Jin Dong, Seddik M. Djouadi, Yong Feng, Xiao Ma, and Yefu Wang. 2016. PAPMSC: Power-Aware Performance Management Approach for Virtualized Web Servers via Stochastic Control. *J. Grid Comput.* 14, 1 (2016), 171–191. https://doi.org/10.1007/s10723-015-9341-z

[20] Marian Turowski and Alexander Lenk. 2014. Vertical Scaling Capability of OpenStack - Survey of Guest Operating Systems, Hypervisors, and the Cloud Management Platform. In *Service-Oriented Computing - ICSOC 2014 Workshops - WESOA; SeMaPS, RMSOC, KASA, ISC, FOR-MOVES, CCSA and Satellite Events, Paris, France*. 351–362. https://doi.org/10.1007/978-3-319-22885-3_30

[21] Xiaorui Wang and Yefu Wang. 2011. Coordinating Power Control and Performance Management for Virtualized Server Clusters. *IEEE Trans. Parallel Distrib. Syst.* 22, 2 (2011), 245–259. https://doi.org/10.1109/TPDS.2010.91

[22] Yanwei Zhang, Yefu Wang, and Xiaorui Wang. 2011. GreenWare: Greening Cloud-Scale Data Centers to Maximize the Use of Renewable Energy.. In *ACM/IFIP/USENIX 12th International Middleware Conference (Lecture Notes in Computer Science)*. Springer, 143–164.

A Service-Oriented Co-Simulation: Holistic Data Center Modelling Using Thermal, Power and Computational Simulations

Stephen Clement
School of Computing
University of Leeds
Leeds, UK
s.j.clement@leeds.ac.uk

David McKee
School of Computing
University of Leeds
Leeds, UK
d.w.mckee@leeds.ac.uk

Jie Xu
School of Computing
University of Leeds
Leeds, UK
j.xu@leeds.ac.uk

ABSTRACT

Holistic modelling of a data center to include both thermodynamics and computational processes has the potential to revolutionize how data centers are designed and managed. Such a model is inherently multi-disciplinary, bringing together the computational elements studied by computer scientists; thermodynamics studied by mechanical engineers; and other aspects in the domain of electrical engineering. This paper proposes the use of the Internet of Simulation to allow engineers to build models of individual complex elements and deploy them as simulation services. These services can then be integrated as simulation system workflows. A proof of concept server simulation is presented, incorporating simulations of Central Processing Units (CPUs), heat sinks, and fans exposed using the Simulation as a Service (SIMaaS) paradigm. The integrated workflow of the server is then exposed as a service (WFaaS) to facilitate the building of an entire virtual data center. Unlike other data center simulations, this approach requires no direct characterisation of the hardware being simulated. Preliminary results are presented showing the effectiveness of the simulation technique and representative behaviour under various simulated cloud workloads. The benefits and future applications of this rapid prototyping approach extend to data center design and data center efficiency research.

CCS CONCEPTS

• **Computing methodologies** → **Modeling and simulation;** **Distributed simulation;** • **Computer systems organization** → **Cloud computing;** *Distributed architectures;* • **Hardware** → **Power and energy;**

KEYWORDS

Cloud; SOA; Services; Simulation; WFaaS; SIMaaS; IoS; Thermodynamics; Data-center

ACM Reference format:
Stephen Clement, David McKee, and Jie Xu. 2017. A Service-Oriented Co-Simulation: Holistic Data Center Modelling Using Thermal, Power and Computational Simulations. In *Proceedings of UCC '17: 10th International Conference on Utility and Cloud Computing, Austin, Texas USA, December 5–8, 2017 (UCC '17),* 9 pages.
https://doi.org/10.1145/3147213.3147219

1 INTRODUCTION

Data centers globally consume in the region of 3% of the world's electricity up from 1.3% in 2010 and 0.8% in 2005 [13, 21]. Fully understanding their workings in terms of computational processes, system architectures, cooling performance, as well as energy and power efficiencies is therefore of paramount importance as part of the digital economy [22]. However there has been no successful holistic simulation of a data center's computation and cooling. Such a simulation brings together the worlds of mechanical, electrical, and computational engineering. In this paper we present a proof of concept holistic model of server operation, encompassing computation through utilisation, power and thermal performance.

Previous authors have utilised complex simulation methods such as Computational Fluid Dynamics (CFD) simulations and trained models from empirical measurements [8]. However, this characterisation and modelling can be time consuming and requires access and measurement of specific exemplar hardware. Additionally the complexity of the models employed in these applications preclude rapid simulation of the computational, power and thermal performance. Instead we present an initial proof of concept showing that holistic server behaviour can be realistically characterised using readily available, public data from manufacturer datasheets and datasets. This data is used as parameters in the model allowing for rapid generation of simulations.

In this paper we adopt the Internet of Simulation (IoS) paradigm [18] using service orientation to construct such a multidisciplinary simulation of a server. The methods utilised in this paper could be used by the research community to develop energy aware data center systems or allow for rapid prototyping of virtual data centers. As a proof of concept simulations of CPUs, heat sinks, and fans are all exposed as services and integrated into a server system model which is then published as a workflow to be used in a virtual rack.

In the remainder of this paper section 2 presents some of the background for this work; section 3 details the models and methodology used with results presented in section 4. Conclusions and details of further work are discussed in Section 5.

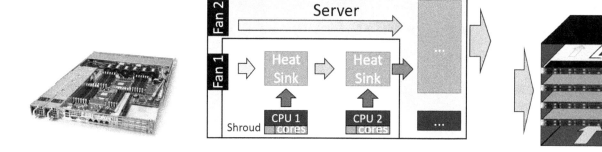

(a) Example Acer AR360 F2 server   (b) The abstract server architecture and air flow for the simulation   (c) The abstract rack architecture

Figure 1: The simulated system architecture of a rack with four servers and the corresponding airflows

2 BACKGROUND

Simulation of data centers is critical to understanding their global impact and providing a means to explore new approaches to improve their energy efficiency. For example globally data centers used 416 terrawatt hours of electricity in 2015 whilst the UK as a nation only consumed in the region of 300 terrawatt hours [21]. There has therefore been a push in recent years to provide *holistic models* of data centers power usage, however there remain significant limitations. One of the main limitations is the integration of the electrical and thermodynamic simulations with computational models of server utilisation. This integration and the resulting trade-offs that can be explored are critical to managing the costs associated with running a data center. It is therefore essential that improvements to energy efficiency also enable the utilisation of said data centers to be maximised as they are currently severely under-utilised, in some cases as low as 10% [10].

Currently, the efficiency of a data center is measured by the Power Usage Effectiveness (PUE) or Data Center Infrastructure Efficiency (DCiE) value. Both of these metrics compare the amount of energy used by the data center for computation against the total energy used by the data center [3]. Therefore while reducing total energy consumption of the data center is important, it is equally important to ensure that as much energy as possible is used for useful computation. Since cooling systems consume much of the non-IT equipment energy[17], understanding the relationships between data center operation and its heat generation can help to maximise efficiency. Therefore models that encompass computation, power consumption and heat generation can provide a tool to understand these relationships.

2.1 Modelling Power Consumption

Some of the existing simulations of data centers include power models but these are usually simple and generally focus on compute energy rather than the combination of compute and cooling. The CloudSim [4] provides a number of possible power models for servers, however these are based on a linear relationship between power consumption and CPU utilisation [16]. Other authors [2, 14] have presented power consumption models based on Virtual Machine (VM) utilisation and activity.

Ouraghan et al. [0] provide a model of power usage in data center servers aiming to bring together the domains of software, server

hardware, and cooling. The authors experimentally measured the power consumption by the server and fans under various workload utilisations. Subsequent work by Li et al. [15, 27] looked at simulating the cloud workload using CloudSim [4] and matched the resulting data with CFD results to estimate the server temperature for a given workload.

Additionally, there has been recent work in detailed simulation of processor power consumption. Walker et al.[24, 25] develop a thermally aware CPU power model which accounts for differences in power consumption due to the temperature of the processor. This model is achieved through experimental measurement and characterisation of an ARM CPUs.

These approaches are however not fully integrated and require the simulation designer to be an expert across all aspects of the system model. It is therefore vital that a new paradigm for simulating cyber-physical systems is developed allowing engineers and researchers to build highly detailed and complex models of individual components, such as heat sinks or software systems, and bring them together in an integrated System of Systems simulation.

2.2 Internet of Simulation

In order to facilitate an ecosystem of model sharing and simulation integration McKee et al. [18] propose the concept of Internet of Simulation (IoS). By using the infrastructure of Cloud computing massive-scale simulations can be run rapidly and at speed [9]. IoS therefore aims to facilitate the deployment of simulations as services (SIMaaS) which can then be integrated into other simulations as part of a more typical service-oriented workflow.

The workflows, which would be in essence system simulations, can then themselves be exposed as services (WFaaS). This provides a mechanism to iteratively build massively complex system models and simulations using the relevant expertise to accurately capture the nuances from each domain [5].

The remainder of this paper takes these IoS concepts and applies them to holistic server simulation.

3 MODELLING METHODOLOGY

An approximation of performance and power consumption of a server under static load can be made using available benchmarks [6] and manufacturer figures. However, this does not allow for the modelling of thermal performance and the load of any given server in a cloud data center depends on the utilisation of all VMs hosted on the machine. The future load of the server is also unknown as this is dependant on demand and the decisions of the scheduler.

Previous approaches to modelling the dynamic behaviour of servers or data centers require characterisation through experimentation on the specific hardware to be used or historical data collected from data centers with that same hardware. Both of these methods are resource intensive and do not allow characterisation without investment in hardware. Therefore we take a modelling approach that aims to characterise data center dynamics without experimental data collection by using readily available benchmark data, manufacturer's specifications and physics modelling. This lowers the cost of data center simulation and allows for research developing scalable, energy efficient data center technologies such as schedulers, cooling systems or new servers.

In order to capture these behaviours a dynamic model is required and each power consuming component is modelled independently and then co-simulated. In the case of this model we choose to model the processors, cooling components (fans and heatsinks) and residual components (power supply, motherboard, memory etc.). In this instance the server we are modelling does not include a GPU.

Based on the IoS paradigm each individual component of the system can be modelled independently. Each model therefore has defined interface expressing the inputs and outputs as well as all assumptions that are being made. For example the interface must capture the units of measurement as well as the metric prefix, such kilowatts. The individual models can then be exposed as services, using the SIMaaS paradigm, to be integrated. This integrated simulation (Workflow as a Service (WFaaS)) can be made available as a service to be used to test different data center configuration, experimental schedulers or novel cooling techniques.

The remainder of this section focusses on the construction of the individual models that are used to construct the simulation using iterative WFaaS design.

3.1 Abstract Server

An Acer AR360 F2 Server was chosen as a representative 1U server; its power ratings are available in the results of the SPECpower benchmark [6]. The server can be seen in Figure 1a and the abstract representation used in this paper's proof of concept is shown in Figure 1b. For the purposes of this paper the server is considered to utilise of two Intel Xeon E5-2660 CPUs as defined in the benchmark results [1]. Figure 1 shows the server has fans located at the front pushing air through the server towards the rear. On the one side are the CPUs located longitudinally with the warm air from CPU1 passing over CPU2 before leaving out the rear of the server, each CPU has a passive heat sink and is assumed to be shrouded. The output air from the second heat sink is mixed uniformly with the ambient air from fan 2 before passing out of the back of the server. This architecture allows us to characterise the remaining power consumption and heat generation of the server as a third heat sink, though this characterisation is not performed in this paper.

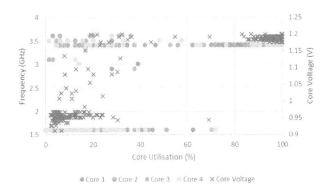

Figure 2: Dynamic voltage and frequency scaling against utilisation

3.2 CPU

In this server the single component responsible for most of the power consumption in a server is the CPU. The total power consumption of the CPU is a sum of dynamic and short-circuit power consumptions and losses due to leakage currents[23]:

$$P_{CPU} = P_{dyn} + P_{sc} + P_{leak}$$

Most of the power consumed by the CPU is then dissipated as heat which must be removed from the system via cooling.

Modern CPUs have multiple cores, with a multi-threaded workload each will have a different utilisation and therefore each will draw a different amount of power and dissipate a different amount of heat. The processor package includes a case which functions as a heat spreader. Thermal interface compound provides good thermal conductivity between the processor case and a cooler.

To characterise the power and cooling requirements of a given CPU manufacturers define a Thermal Design Power (TDP) in Watts. This describes the maximum power consumption of the processor and therefore the maximum heat power that the cooling system must be able to dissipate. These values are defined based on propriety workloads that are promised to be realistically complex. TDP does not represent the absolute maximum thermal output, it can be exceeded for short periods [12].

In a modern CPU there are a number of mechanisms that allow for more optimal power consumption and changes in performance. The primary method is Dynamic Voltage and Frequecy Scaling (DVFS) which allows the clock frequency of the processor and correspondingly the voltage to be adjusted to reduce power consumption or increase processor performance on demand [25]. Portions of the processor can also be disconnected from the clock signal to reduce switching power consumption, known as clock gating [26], or turned off completely (power gating) [11].

Data center workloads are often defined by a processor utilisation figure [7]. Figure 2 shows the changing frequency and voltage as the overall utilisation of the processor increases. This data was recorded from values reported by an Intel i5-2500K under a varying benchmark load. It is apparent that there is no strong correlation between the voltage and frequency states chosen by the processor and the reported utilisation or power consumption. As such it is difficult to directly model CPU performance state and power. Instead we use a function of overall utilisation to model CPU power consumption. Figure 3b shows power consumption under the same benchmark load collected from three separate Intel CPUs: i5-2500K, i5-4300U and Xeon E3-1270. While there are different core counts, TDPs and cache sizes, figure 3b shows that the power consumption relative to TDP is similar across all of our tests.

Therefore, since the TDP P_{TDP} of the chosen server's CPU is known we fit the bounded exponential function:

$$R_{TDP} = \frac{a - be^{-cu}}{100} \quad (1)$$

to our data in figure 3b and model power consumption as a factor of TDP R_{TDP} based on the overall CPU utilisation u (0% to 100%). Where a, b and c are fitting terms found to be 90, 80 and -0.03 respectively. Actual power consumption P_{CPU}(W) is then:

$$P_{CPU} = P_{TDP} * R_{TDP}$$

In this abstract server architecture we ignore the effects of thermal resistance in the interface compound and assume that heat is transferred directly into the heat sink.

To realistically model a modern CPU we must model multiple cores, this is especially important in cloud workloads where VMs with varying loads execute on different CPU cores. Since our models are based on overall utilisation we take the mean of all core utilisation to give an overall utilisation.

3.3 Heat Sink

In our abstract server model the CPU cooler is a passive heat sink, modelled as a heat exchanger using the NTU method as presented by Moffat [19]. Since this is an abstract model, we model the heat as completely uniform across the whole heat sink rather than modelling the heat transmission from the base to the fins. Additionally, we assume that that heat generated by the CPU is transmitted into the heat sink without losses. We only model the convective cooling as this is a much larger factor than radiative cooling since the heat sink is tightly enclosed in the 1U case so any energy lost from radiation will transfer to other components.

Using the NTU method, a normal heat exchanger with two fluids can be characterised by its effectiveness ϵ. This is a ratio of the actual heat transferred and the maximum possible heat transferral between the two fluids. Using the fluid with the lowest heat capacity C_{min} this is:

$$\epsilon = \frac{T_{cold\_out} - T_{cold\_in}}{T_{hot\_in} - T_{cold\_in}} \quad (2)$$

For a heat sink where there is no hot fluid, $C_{hot} = \infty$, and therefore the ratio is 0. It can be shown that in this special case the effectiveness ϵ if given by:

$$\epsilon = 1 - e^{-NTU} \quad (3)$$

where the number of transfer units NTU is a characterisation of the heat exchanger based on the heat exchanger geometry and the cooling fluid mass flow. This defined as:

$$NTU = \frac{UA}{C_{min}} = \frac{hA}{\dot{m}C_p} \quad (4)$$

where C_{min} is the smaller of the two fluid's heat capacities, in the case of a heat sink this is the air and is given by the product of the mass flow $\dot{m}$ and the specific heat capacity C_p of air. UA is product of the effective exchange area A and the overall heat transfer coefficient U of the cooler arrangement. Since we ignore the effects of the thermal compound and heat spreader we only need to characterise the heat sink transfer coefficient h measured in W/m^2 K. Which characterises the heat sink performance as a proportion of heat transfer to temperature difference. This parameter is often difficult to find and usually requires extensive measurement of the heat sink in operation. However, it is possible to characterise in our model based on a manufacturer's quoted TDP rating. For a given heat sink TDP $P_T DP$ the worst case is given by the maximum temperatures allowable by the CPU manufacturer in the server case T_{amb} and on the heat spreader T_{CMax}:

$$h = \frac{P_{TDP}}{A(T_{CMax} - T_{amb})} \quad (5)$$

Given this characterisation of h, NTU is:

$$NTU = \frac{P_{TDP}}{\dot{m}C_p(T_{CMax} - T_{amb})} \quad (6)$$

To calculate the energy transfer rate $\dot{Q}$ to the cooling air flow from the heat sink, we use:

$$\dot{Q} = \dot{m}C_p\epsilon(T_{Base} - T_{Inlet}) \quad (7)$$

The rate of change in temperature of the cooling air $\dot{\Delta T}$:

$$\Delta T = \frac{\dot{Q}}{\dot{m}C_p} \quad (8)$$

The change in temperature of the heat sink is calculated in a similar manner using the net energy transfer rate based on the input from the CPU and heat lost to the air.

3.4 Fan

Garraghan et al.[8] propose modelling the energy used by cooling equipment in addition to that used for computation. We utilise their presented model for fan power draw and model the generated air flow based on manufacturers specifications. Most fan data sheets specify a maximum volumetric flow G_{max} and speed N_{max}, these properties are linearly related. The volumetric flow G in m/s can be modelled based on fan speed N as:

$$G = \frac{NG_{max}}{N_{max}}$$

The mass flow $\dot{m}$ in kg/s of the cooling air from the fans is given by:

$$\dot{m} = \rho G$$

where ρ is the density of the air in kg/m^3. To avoid adding active controllers to the model, the speed of the fan is controlled using a logistic function based on CPU temperature. We set N_{min} to 7500RPM, the minimum speed measured by Garraghan [8].

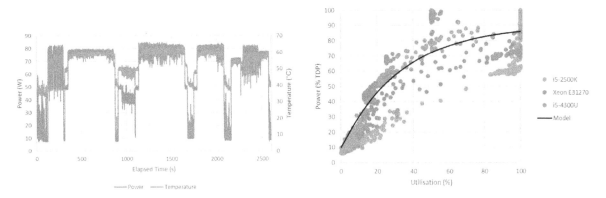

(a) Example benchmark of CPU temperature and power against time

(b) Measured power consumption relative to TDP against utilisation

Figure 3: CPU characterisation using experimental benchmarks

$$N_{scale} = \frac{1}{1 + 100e^{-0.125(T_{Base} - T_{Amb})}},$$
$$N = N_{min} + N_{scale}(N_{max} - N_{min})$$

Air density changes with respect to altitude (pressure) and temperature, however, as only a single rack is being simulated and we do not yet model the room cooling system, we hold the pressure constant at sea level and ambient temperature constant at 20 °C.

3.5 Residual Power Consumption

The components modelled so far are not the only sources of power consumption (or heat generation) within the server. The other computational components: motherboard, memory, chip set and drives all consume power. In addition, there are power losses in the power supply leading to higher power consumption. Unlike the CPU, these components do not self-report their power consumption. The actual power consumption is not easily derived without extensive measurement and benchmarking of the desired server. Instead we chose to compare the sum of the already modelled power consumptions against the recorded SPECPower results, see figure 4. We fit the polynomial:

$$P_{Res} = a + bu^c \tag{9}$$

to this data and use this function to model the residual power draw of the remaining system components. Where $a = 28$, $b = 127.5$ and $c = 3.2$.

3.6 Workflow

As a proof of concept towards simulating a data center we simulate multiple servers in a rack under a virtual cloud workload. The simulation is constructed by composing the component simulation services as a workflow, shown in figure 5. Presently, we only model the thermal effects of the CPUs and the airflow through the server. We do not model radiant heating between servers, this is analogous to having the servers well spread out in the rack.

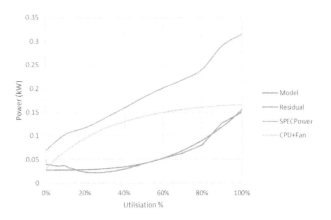

Figure 4: Modelled residual power consumption

The server assigns a workload to a VM, each operating on a single core so there is no over commitment. Each CPU has 4 cores so each server can host 8 VMs. The server controls fan speeds based on the temperature of CPU1. The integrated server is then exposed as a simulation using the WFaaS concept further combined into a rack containing 4 servers.

4 EVALUATION

For an evaluation of this proof of concept simulation, we simulate the rack operating in a constant ambient air temperature. There will be no external cooling accounted for and no recirculation of air once it leaves the server. A number of theoretical workloads will be presented to the servers and the resulting power draw and temperature changes of the CPU's will be modelled. The models were implemented as individual simulation services in SEED [9], a distributed discrete time-step simulator, for this evaluation. For this proof of concept, we will evaluate whether the static behaviour of the server matches that in the benchmark and whether the dynamic

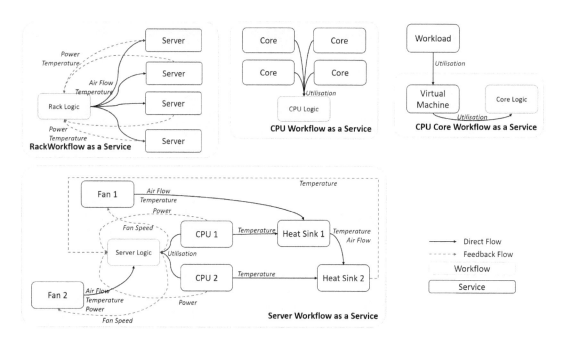

Figure 5: Component and system simulations as services

behaviour of the system at CPU, server and rack levels reasonably reflects that seen in real systems.

4.1 Workload Modelling

In the context of Cloud computing Fehling et al. [7] identified five core workload patterns:

(1) **Static** workloads where the resource utilisation over time is constant. This can be extended to consider the workload as static within a variance and can therefore be guaranteed to not exceed a given threshold.

(2) **Continuously Changing** workload is where the utilisation is either continuously growing or else continuously shrinking.

(3) **Periodic** where the resource utilisation peaks at reoccurring time intervals.

(4) **Unpredictable** refers to a random utilisation and can be considered as a generalisation of periodic workloads.

(5) **Once-in-a-lifetime** workload refers to general workload that is predictable disturbed by a peak utilisation which only occurs once. This is a particular case of the periodic workload pattern where the time-frame is particularly long.

To test the simulation the continuously changing ramped, and periodic type workloads are used. Additionally, features of the static, unpredictable and once-in-a-lifetime workloads are combined into a single step utilisation parametrised by a constant load, duration and start time. Where a single utilisation pattern is required at the server level, identical workloads are simulated on each of the 8 VMs hosted on the machine resulting in this load being applied at the server level. For rack level simulation each VM is given a different workload, either a periodic or a step load with random parameters of phase.

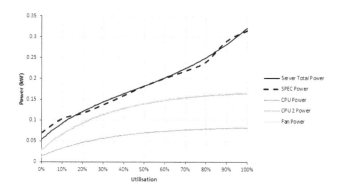

Figure 6: Modelled cumulative power consumption compared to results of SPECPower Benchmark for this server

4.2 Individual Server Behaviour

A single server instance was tested in isolation with a uniform VM utilisation across all cores to ensure that the server behaviour is realistic and matches existing data. To capture the behaviour at varying utilisations a ramped load from 0% to 100% utilisation is used. We also tested the server using step loads to verify the modelled thermal behaviour.

Figure 6 shows the cumulative modelled power consumption of the server at differing total utilisations. The total power consumption in the model shows a large degree of agreement with the measured results of the SPECPower benchmark [6] with an R-Squared value of 0.99. The CPU power model is easily identified as it is defined based on mean utilisation, additionally we can see that the overall effect of the fans on power consumption is very small. So although Garrahgan et al. [8] note that the cooling equipment

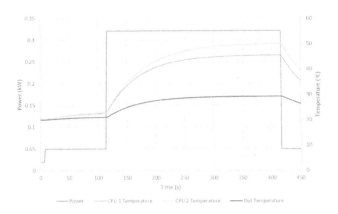

Figure 7: Thermal response of step load

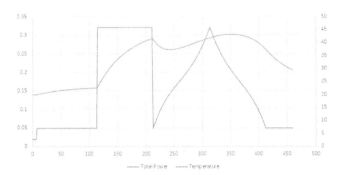

Figure 8: Single server behaviour under varying loads

is not constant and therefore should be, we note that the overall effect is small.

The thermal behaviour of the server is shown in figure 7. To most clearly show the temperature modelling of the system a step load of 100% utilisation is applied to the CPUs for a short period and the temperature of each heatsink is recorded. The servers start *cold* at an ambient room temperature of 20°C. The figure shows the expected heating and cooling curves for temperature, a large degree of heat begins as soon as the load is initiated. Once the load is reduced, the temperature immediately falls following the expected cooling curve. This matches the observed behaviour in the benchmark, figure 3a, though slower as the heatsinks have more mass than the CPU packages. The linear arrangement of the CPU means that the cooling air flow reaching the second CPU's heat sink is warmer and therefore less effective than the first CPU. This is clearly shown in the graph, the temperature of CPU 2 is 5°C higher than CPU 1. We also model the final air temperature exiting the server which has been heated by heat sink 1 and heat sink 2. The temperatures reached by the system are reasonable given the specifications of the CPU and the characteristics of the cooler with neither CPU exceeding its stated maximum case temperature.

The final characterisation of the single server involves a step workload followed by a linearly increasing and then decreasing workload. The power and temperature modelled by the server for this workload is shown in figure 8. The shape of the workload can be inferred from the power consumption. Here we see that the thermal behaviour of the system lags behind the power consumption and utilisation as there is additional energy in the system which cannot be expelled before reaching the peak of the ramped load. This is expected, realistic behaviour.

4.3 Cloud Workload Behaviour

Since the server has been developed using IoS we can readily compose multiple server simulations together into a rack by adding a component which distributes workloads across the servers. To simulate a cloud workload on the server a VM is assigned to each core of the modelled CPUs. Each VM has a different workload applied to it. One half of the VMs are given periodic workloads with

variations in the phase of the period and the other half are given step workloads with a random start time and duration.

Figure 9 shows the cloud workload applied to one of the servers. The grey lines indicate the workload of each VM and the grey shaded area indicates the average workload of the server. From figure 9 the dynamic behaviour of the system is evident in the power and temperature plots. We can see that the each element in the system behaves differently under this varying load which could not be modelled without separating the components into discrete simulations

Figure 10 shows the behaviour of the four servers operating in parallel. The workloads are largely in phase so the power and temperature effects on the servers are also largely similar. The difference in overall utilisation of servers ranges between 10-20% but despite this difference, there are no large variances in the power or temperature.

4.4 Strengths and Limitations

The evaluation shows that the dynamic behaviour of the servers is reasonably realistic and will be physically accurate since much of the underlying model is physics based. A major strength of this approach is the lack of any required experimentation or historical data for the server being modelled. The only experimental measurements that were required characterised a range of CPU's which allows us to approximate any CPU behaviour based on manufacturers specifications. Additionally, the methodology adopted means that the simulation can be easily reconfigure to simulate a new server or a different rack configuration. The distributed simulator used allows for potential speed up in execution with more machines. Even on a single machine with an Intel i5 processor and 16GB of RAM execution speeds were only approximately 14x real-time.

This work is an initial proof of concept and therefore there are some limitations and many opportunities for future work. Firstly, the assumptions and methodologies demonstrated in this paper must be validated against experimental measurements of an operating server. This would allow a more thorough characterisation of CPU thermal performance and power consumption with respect to utilisation. It would also allow us to more accurately model the individual server elements power draw and characterise the motherboard and power supplies as another heat exchanger with a known heat transfer coefficient. This would allow a more accurate modelling of final air temperature exiting the rear of the server.

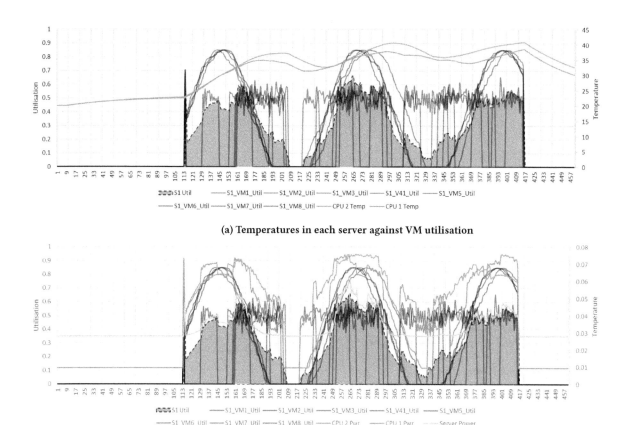

(a) Temperatures in each server against VM utilisation

(b) Server power consumption against VM utilisation

Figure 9: Server rack power consumption and temperatures under a simulated cloud workload

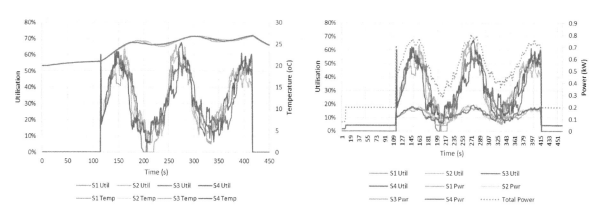

(a) Temperatures in each server against VM utilisation

(b) Server power consumption against VM utilisation

Figure 10: Server rack power consumption and temperatures under a simulated cloud workload

In addition to a complete validation of model, other elements can be added due to the extensible nature of the simulation workflow. Given a characterisation of their performance, it would be possible to add additional components into the server such as power supplies or DIMM memory. A more detailed thermal simulation could also be achieved by modelling the thermal resistance of the thermal interface compound between the CPU and heat sink, as well as the heat spread through the heat sink.

5 CONCLUSION

In this paper we have presented a medium fidelity model of a cloud server where we modelled the relationships between the execution and thermodynamic behaviour of the server. The parameters used in this modelled are based on publicly available datasets and manufacturer data sheets or fitted against data from three different computers, therefore this model is easily changed to simulate a different server than the one chosen here. The behaviour of the modelled server was demonstrated under different cloud workloads, with the resulting temperature and power consumptions being reasonably realistic given the lack of experimental measurements available

We followed an IoS approach to construct this simulation and therefore adding more servers or other elements is easily achieved. Each of the sub-components of the workflow shown in Figure 5 are independent and therefore can be changed to add more detail without affecting other components. Additionally, by combining multiple workflows it is possible to scale this simulation to simulate multiple servers and the cooling systems such as in a much larger data center.

Given the server is represented as a WFaaS we can combine multiple servers together with models of air conditioning units and model the total thermal performance and power consumption of a virtual data center. For this purpose the benefits of our approach are the rapid speed in which different cooling solutions could be tested without physical prototypes. With a more detailed execution model, the macro effects of software behaviours on power consumption and cooling can investigated, for example the choice of scheduler or the cost of the long tail problem. The modular nature of the simulation due to IoS means that any of these changes are implemented as new services and easily incorporated into the new simulation workflow.

Extending the IoS techniques to their limit will allow the construction of entire virtual systems, from data centers through to cities [20]. This will facilitate a huge opening of research opportunities, studying digital systems at a scale that has never been seen before.

ACKNOWLEDGMENTS

This work forms part of the University of Leeds centre for city simulation: VirtuoCity and has been supported by various grants including UK-EPSRC grant EP/K014226/1 and the China National Key Research and Development Program (No. 2016YFB1000101 and 20016YFB1000103)

REFERENCES

[1] Acer Incorporated. 2013. Acer Incopated Acer AR360 F2. (2013). https://www.spec.org/power
[2] A. E. Husain Bohra and V. Chaudhary. 2010. VMeter: Power modelling for virtualized clouds. In *2010 IEEE International Symposium on Parallel Distributed Processing, Workshops and Phd Forum (IPDPSW)*. 1–8.
[3] Gemma A. Brady, Nikil Kapur, Jonathan L. Summers, and Harvey M. Thompson. 2013. A case study and critical assessment in calculating power usage effectiveness for a data centre. *Energy Conversion and Management* 76 (2013), 155 – 161.
[4] Rodrigo N Calheiros, Rajiv Ranjan, Anton Beloglazov, César A. F. De Rose, and Rajkumar Buyya. 2011. CloudSim: a toolkit for modeling and simulation of cloud computing environments and evaluation of resource provisioning algorithms. *Softw. Pract. Exp.* 41, 1 (jan 2011), 23–50.
[5] SJ Clement, DW Mckee, and Jie Xu. 2017. Service-Oriented Reference Architecture for Smart Cities. In *IEEE International Symposium on Service-Oriented System Engineering*. IEEE.
[6] Standard Performance Evaluation Corporation. 2008. SPEC Power Benchmark. (2008). https://www.spec.org/power_ssj2008/results/
[7] Christoph Fehling, Frank Leymann, Ralph Retter, Walter Schupeck, and Peter Arbitter. 2014. *Cloud Computing Patterns*. Springer Vienna, Vienna.
[8] Peter Garraghan, Yaser Al-Anii, Jon Summers, Harvey Thompson, Nik Kapur, and Karim Djemame. 2016. A unified model for holistic power usage in cloud datacenter servers. In *Proceedings of the 9th International Conference on Utility and Cloud Computing - UCC '16*. ACM Press.
[9] Peter Garraghan, David McKee, Xue Ouyang, David Webster, and Jie Xu. 2016. SEED: A Scalable Approach for Cyber-Physical System Simulation. *IEEE Transactions on Services Computing* 9, 2 (mar 2016), 199–212.
[10] Albert Greenberg, James Hamilton, David A Maltz, and Parveen Patel. 2008. The cost of a cloud: research problems in data center networks. *ACM SIGCOMM computer communication review* 39, 1 (2008), 68–73.
[11] Zhigang Hu, Alper Buyuktosunoglu, Viji Srinivasan, Victor Zyuban, Hans Jacobson, and Pradip Bose. 2004. Microarchitectural techniques for power gating of execution units. In *Proceedings of the 2004 international symposium on Low power electronics and design*. ACM, 32–37.
[12] Intel Corporation. 2015. *Intel Xeon Processor E5-1600/2600/4600 v3 Product Families: Thermal Mechanical Specification and Desgin Guide*. http://www.intel.com/content/www/us/en/processors/xeon/xeon-e5-v3-thermal-guide.html
[13] Jonathan Koomey. 2011. Growth in data center electricity use 2005 to 2010. *A report by Analytical Press, completed at the request of The New York Times* 9 (2011).
[14] Bhavani Krishnan, Hrishikesh Amur, Ada Gavrilovska, and Karsten Schwan. 2011. VM Power Metering: Feasibility and Challenges. *SIGMETRICS Perform. Eval. Rev.* 38, 3 (Jan. 2011), 56–60.
[15] Xiang Li, Peter Garraghan, Xiaohong JIANG, Zhaohui Wu, and Jie Xu. 2017. Holistic Virtual Machine Scheduling in Cloud Datacenters towards Minimizing Total Energy. *IEEE Transactions on Parallel and Distributed Systems* (2017), 1–1.
[16] W. Long, L. Yuqing, and X. Qingxin. 2013. Using CloudSim to Model and Simulate Cloud Computing Environment. In *2013 Ninth International Conference on Computational Intelligence and Security*. 323–328.
[17] Tao Lu, Xiaoshu Lü, Matias Remes, and Martti Viljanen. 2011. Investigation of air management and energy performance in a data center in Finland: Case study. *Energy and Buildings* 43, 12 (2011), 3360 – 3372.
[18] DW Mckee, SJ Clement, X Ouyang, J Xu, R Romano, and J Davies. 2017. The Internet of Simulation, a Specialisation of the Internet of Things with Simulation and Workflow as a Service (SIM/WFaaS). In *2017 IEEE Symposium on Service-Oriented System Engineering (SOSE)*. IEEE.
[19] Robert J. Moffat. 2007. Modeling Air-Cooled Heat Sinks as Heat Exchangers. In *Twenty-Third Annual IEEE Semiconductor Thermal Measurement and Management Symposium*. IEEE.
[20] Richard Romano, Natasha Merat, Erik Thomasson, David Hogg, David McKee, and Jie Xu. 2017. Institute for Transport Studies: VirtuoCITY. (2017). https://www.its.leeds.ac.uk/research/featured-projects/virtuocity/
[21] Tom Bawden. 2016. Global warming: Data centres to consume three times as much energy in next decade, experts warn | The Independent. (2016). http://www.independent.co.uk/environment/global-warming-data-centres-to-consume-three-times-as-much-energy-\in-next-decade-experts-warn-a6830086.html
[22] Paul Townend, Jie Xu, Jon Summers, Daniel Ruprecht, and Harvey Thompson. 2016. Holistic data centres: Next generation data and thermal energy infrastructures. In *2016 IEEE 35th Int. Perform. Comput. Commun. Conf.* IEEE, 1–2.
[23] Karel De Vogeleer, Gerard Memmi, Pierre Jouvelot, and Fabien Coelho. 2014. The Energy/Frequency Convexity Rule: Modeling and Experimental Validation on Mobile Devices. In *Parallel Processing and Applied Mathematics*. Springer Berlin Heidelberg, 793–803.
[24] M. J. Walker, S. Diestelhorst, A. Hansson, D. Balsamo, G. V. Merrett, and B. M. Al-Hashimi. 2016. Thermally-aware composite run-time CPU power models. In *2016 26th International Workshop on Power and Timing Modeling, Optimization and Simulation (PATMOS)*. 17–24.
[25] M. J. Walker, S. Diestelhorst, A. Hansson, A. K. Das, S. Yang, B. M. Al-Hashimi, and G. V. Merrett. 2017. Accurate and Stable Run-Time Power Modeling for Mobile and Embedded CPUs. *IEEE Transactions on Computer-Aided Design of Integrated Circuits and Systems* 36, 1 (Jan 2017), 106–119.
[26] Qing Wu, Massound Pedram, and Xunwei Wu. 2000. Clock-gating and its application to low power design of sequential circuits. *IEEE Transactions on Circuits and Systems I: Fundamental Theory and Applications* 47, 3 (2000), 415–420.
[27] Zhaohui Wu, Xiang Li, Peter Garraghan, Xiaohong Jiang, Kejiang Ye, and Albert Y. Zomaya. 2016. Virtual Machine Level Temperature Profiling and Prediction in Cloud Datacenters. In *2016 IEEE 36th International Conference on Distributed Computing Systems (ICDCS)*. IEEE.

Low Latency Stream Processing: Apache Heron with InfiniBand & Intel Omni-Path

Supun Kamburugamuve
School of Informatics, Computing, and Engineering
Indiana University
Bloomington, IN 47408
skamburu@indiana.edu

Karthik Ramasamy
Streaml.io
Palo Alto, CA
karthik@streaml.io

Martin Swany
School of Informatics, Computing, and Engineering
Indiana University
Bloomington, IN 47408
swany@indiana.edu

Geoffrey Fox
School of Informatics, Computing, and Engineering
Indiana University
Bloomington, IN 47408
gcf@indiana.edu

ABSTRACT

Worldwide data production is increasing both in volume and velocity, and with this acceleration, data needs to be processed in streaming settings as opposed to the traditional store and process model. Distributed streaming frameworks are designed to process such data in real time with reasonable time constraints. Apache Heron is a production-ready large-scale distributed stream processing framework. The network is of utmost importance to scale streaming applications to large numbers of nodes with a reasonable latency. High performance computing (HPC) clusters feature interconnects that can perform at higher levels than traditional Ethernet. In this paper the authors present their findings on integrating Apache Heron distributed stream processing system with two high performance interconnects; InfiniBand and Intel Omni-Path and show that they can be utilized to improve performance of distributed streaming applications.

CCS CONCEPTS

•**Networks** →**Network performance analysis; Data center networks;** •**Computer systems organization** →**Data flow architectures;** Cloud computing;

KEYWORDS

Streaming data, InfiniBand, Omni-Path, Apache Heron

1 INTRODUCTION

With ever increasing data production by users and machines alike, the amount of data that needs to be processed has increased dramatically. This must be achieved both in real time and as batches to satisfy different use cases. Additionally, with the adoption of devices into Internet of Things setups, the amount of real time data are exploding, and must be processed with reasonable time constraints. In distributed stream analytics, the large data streams are partitioned and processed in distributed sets of machines to keep up with the high volume data rates. By definition of large-scale streaming data processing, networks are a crucial component in transmitting messages between the processing units for achieving efficient data processing.

There are many hardware environments in which big data systems can be deployed including High performance computing (HPC) clusters. HPC clusters are designed to perform large computations with advanced processors, memory, IO systems and high performance interconnects. High performance interconnects in HPC clusters feature microsecond latencies and large bandwidths. Thanks to recent advancements in hardware, some of these high performance networks have become cheaper to set up than their Ethernet counterparts. With multi-core and many-core systems having large numbers of CPUs in a single node, the demand for high performance networking is increasing as well.

Advanced hardware features such as high performance interconnects are not fully utilized in the big data computing frameworks, mostly because they are accessible to low level programming languages and most big data systems are written on Java platform. In recent years we have seen efforts to utilize high performance interconnects into big data frameworks such as Spark [24] and Hadoop [22]. Big data frameworks such as Spark and Hadoop focus on large batch data processing and hence their communication requirements are different compared to streaming systems which are more latency sensitive.

There are many distributed streaming frameworks available today for processing large amounts of streaming data in real time. Such systems are largely designed and optimized for commodity hardware and clouds. Apache Storm [29] was one of the popular early systems developed for processing streaming data. Apache Heron [1] [19] is similar to Storm with a new architecture for streaming data processing. It features a hybrid design with some of the performance-critical parts written in C++ and others written in Java. This architecture allows the integration of high performance enhancements directly rather than going through native wrappers

UCC'17, December 5–8, 2017, Austin, Texas, USA
© 2017 ACM. ISBN 978-1-4503-5149-2/17/12...$15.00
DOI: http://dx.doi.org/10.1145/3147213.3147232

---

[1] http://incubator.apache.org/projects/heron.html

such as Java Native Interface(JNI). When these systems are deployed on clusters that include high performance interconnects, they need to use an TCP interface to high performance interconnect which doesn't perform as well as a native implementation.

To utilize these hardware features, we have integrated InfiniBand and Intel Omni-Path interconnects to Apache Heron to accelerate its communications. InfiniBand [4] is an open standard protocol for high performance interconnects that is widely used in today's high performance clusters. Omni-Path [6] is a proprietary interconnect developed by Intel and is available with the latest Knights Landing architecture-based (KNL) [27] many-core processors. With this implementation, we have observed significantly lower latencies and improved throughput in Heron. The main contribution in this work is to showcase the benefits of using high performance interconnects for distributed stream processing. There are many differences in hardware available for communications with different bandwidths, latencies and processing models. Ethernet has comparable hardware available to some of the high performance interconnects; it is not our goal to show that one particular technology is superior to others, as different environments may have alternate sets of these technologies.

The remainder of the paper is organized as follows. Section 2 presents the background information on InfiniBand and Omni-Path. Section 3 describes the Heron architecture in detail and section 4 the implementation details. Next the experiments conducted are described in sections 5 and results are presented and discussed in section 6. Section 7 presents related work. The paper concludes with a look at future work.

2 BACKGROUND

2.1 InfiniBand

InfiniBand is one of the most widely used high performance fabrics. It provides a variety of capabilities including message channel semantics, remote memory access and remote atomic memory operations, supporting both connection-oriented and connectionless endpoints. InfiniBand is programmed using the Verbs API, which is available in all major platforms. The current hardware is capable of achieving up to 100Gbps speeds with microsecond latencies. InfiniBand does not require the OS Kernel intervention to transfer packets from user space to the hardware. Unlike in TCP, its protocol aspects are handled by the hardware. These features mean less CPU time spent on the network compared to TCP for transferring the same amount of data. Because the OS Kernel is bypassed by the communications, the memory for transferring data has to be registered in the hardware.

2.2 Intel Omni-Path

Omni-Path is a high performance fabric developed by Intel. Omni-Path fabric is relatively new compared to InfiniBand and there are fundamental differences between the two. Omni-Path does not offload the protocol handling to network hardware and it doesn't have the connection oriented channels as in InfiniBand. Unlike in InfiniBand the Omni-Path network chip can be built into the latest Intel Knights Landing (KNL) processors. Omni-Path supports tagged messaging with a 96 bit tag in each message. A Tag can carry any type of data and this information can be used at the application to distinguish between different messages. Omni-Path is designed and optimized for small high frequency messaging.

2.3 Channel & Memory Semantics

High performance interconnects generally supports two modes of operations called channel and memory semantics [13]. With channel semantics queues are used for communication. In memory semantics a process can read from or write directly to the memory of a remote machine. In channel mode, two queue pairs for transmission and receive operations are used. To transfer a message, a descriptor is posted to the transfer queue, which includes the address of the memory buffer to transfer. For receiving a message, a descriptor needs to be submitted along with a pre-allocated receive buffer. The user program queries the completion queue associated with a transmission or a receiving queue to determine the success or failure of a work request. Once a message arrives, the hardware puts the message into the posted receive buffer and the user program can determine this event through the completion queue. Note that this mode requires the receiving buffers to be pre-posted before the transmission can happen successfully.

With memory semantics, Remote Direct Memory Access(RDMA) operations are used. Two processes preparing to communicate register memory and share the details with each other. Read and write operations are used instead of send and receive operations. These are one-sided and do not need any software intervention from the other side. If a process wishes to write to remote memory, it can post a write operation with the local addresses of the data. The completion of the write operation can be detected using the completion queue associated. The receiving side is not notified about the write operation and has to use out-of-band mechanisms to figure out the write. The same is true for remote reads as well. RDMA is more suitable for large message transfers while channel mode is suitable for small messages. In general RDMA has $1 - 2\mu s$ latency advantage over channel semantics for InfiniBand and this is not significant for our work.

2.4 Openfabrics API

Openfabrics [2] provides a library called libfabric [12] that hides the details of common high performance fabric APIs behind a uniform API. Because of the advantage of such an API, we chose to use libfabric as our programming library for implementing the high performance communications for Heron. Libfabric is a thin wrapper API and it supports different providers including Verbs, Aries interconnect from Cray through GNI, Intel Omni-Path, and Sockets.

2.5 TCP & High performance Interconnects

TCP is one of the most successful protocols developed. It provides a simple yet powerful API for transferring data reliably across the Internet using unreliable links and protocols underneath. One of the biggest advantages of TCP is its wide adoption and simplicity to use. Virtually every computer has access to a TCP-capable adapter and the API is well supported across different platforms. TCP provides a streaming API for messaging where the fabric does not maintain message boundaries. The messages are written as a stream of bytes to the TCP and the application has to define mechanisms such as

---

[2] https://www.openfabrics.org/

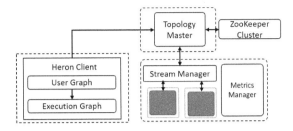

Figure 1: High level architecture of Heron. Each outer box shows a resource container allocated by a resource scheduler like Mesos or Slurm. The arrows show the communication links between different components.

placing markers in between messages to indicate the boundaries. On the other hand, InfiniBand and Omni-Path both support message boundaries.

High performance interconnects have drivers that make them available through the TCP protocol stack. The biggest advantage of such implementation is that an existing application written using the TCP stack can use high performance interconnect without any modifications to the code. It is worth noting that the native use of the interconnect through its API always yields better performance than using it through TCP/IP stack. A typical TCP application allocates memory in user space and the TCP stack needs to copy data between user space and Kernel space. Also each TCP invocation involves a system call which does a context switch of the application. Recent advancements like Netmap [26] and DPDK [11] removes these costs and increases the maximum number of packets that can be processed per second. Also it is possible to achieve direct packet copy from user space to hardware. High performance fabrics usually do not go through OS kernel for network operations and the hardware is capable of copying data directly to user space buffers. InfiniBand offloads the protocol processing aspects to hardware while Omni-Path still involves the CPU for protocol processing.

3 APACHE HERON

Heron is a distributed stream processing framework developed at Twitter and now available as an open source project in Apache Incubator [3]. Heron is similar to Apache Storm in its API with many differences in underlying engine architecture. It retains the same Storm API, allowing applications written in Storm to be deployed with no or minimal code changes.

3.1 Heron Data Model

A stream is an unbounded sequence of high level objects named events or messages. The streaming computation in Heron is referred to as a Topology. A topology is a graph of nodes and edges. The nodes represent the processing units executing the user defined code and the edges between the nodes indicate how the data (or stream) flows between them. There are two types of nodes: spouts and bolts. Spouts are the sources of streams. For example, a Kafka [18] spout can read from a Kafka queue and emit it as a

stream. Bolts consume messages from their input stream(s), apply its processing logic and emit new messages in their outgoing streams.

Heron has the concept of a user defined graph and an execution graph. The user defined graph specifies how the processing units are connected together in terms of message distributions. On the other hand, the execution graph is the layout of this graph in actual nodes with network connections and computing resources allocated to the topology to execute. Nodes in the execution graph can have multiple parallel instances (or tasks) running to scale the computations. The user defined graph and the execution graph are referred to as logical plan and physical plan respectively.

3.2 Heron Architecture

The components of the Heron architecture are shown in Fig. 1. Each Heron topology is a standalone long-running job that never terminates due to the unbounded nature of streams. Each topology is self contained and executes in a distributed sandbox environment in isolation without any interference from other topologies. A Heron topology consists of multiple containers allocated by the scheduler. These can be Linux containers, physical nodes or sandboxes created by the scheduler. The first container, referred to as the master, always runs the Topology Master that manages the topology. Each of the subsequent containers have the following processes: a set of processes executing the spout/bolt tasks of the topology called Heron instances, a process called a stream manager that manages the data routing and the connections to the outside containers, and a metrics manager to collect information about the instances running in that container.

Each Heron instance executes a single task of the topology. The instances are connected to the stream manager running inside the container through TCP loop-back connection. It is worth noting that Heron instances always connect to other instances through the stream manager and they do not communicate with each other directly even if they are on the same container. The stream manager acts as a bridge between Heron instances. It forwards the messages to the correct instances by consulting the routing tables it maintains. A message between two instances in different containers goes through two stream managers. Containers can have many Heron instances running in them and they all communicate through the stream manager. Because of this design, it is important to have highly efficient data transfers at the stream manager to support the communication requirements of the instances.

Heron is designed from the ground up to be extensible, and important parts of the core engine are written in C++ rather than Java, the default language of choice for Big Data frameworks. The rationale for the use of C++ is to leverage the advanced features offered by the OS and hardware. Heron instances and schedulers are written in Java while stream manager and topology master are written in C++.

3.2.1 Acknowledgements. Heron uses an acknowledgement mechanism to provide at least once message processing semantics that ensures the message is always processed in the presence of process/machine failures. In order to achieve at least once, the stream manager tracks the tuple tree generated while a message progresses through the topology. When a bolt emits a message, it anchors the

---

[3]https://github.com/twitter/heron

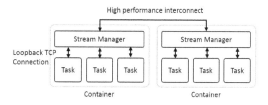

Figure 2: Heron high performance interconnects are between the stream managers

new message to the parent message and this information is sent to originating stream manager (in the same container) as a separate message. When every new message finishes its processing, a separate message is again sent to the originating stream manager. Upon receiving such control messages for every emit in the message tree, the stream manager marks the message as fully processed.

3.2.2 Processing pipeline. Heron has a concept called max messages pending with spouts. When a spout emits messages to a topology, this number dictates the amount of in-flight messages that are not fully processed yet. The spout is called to emit messages only when the current in-flight message count is less than the max spout pending messages.

3.3 Heron Stream Manager

Stream manager is responsible for routing messages between instances inside a container and across containers. It employs a single thread that use event-driven programming using non-blocking socket API. A stream manager receives messages from instances running in the same container and other stream managers. These messages are Google protocol buffer [30] serialized messages packed into binary form and transmitted through the wire. If a stream manager receives a message from a spout, it keeps track of the details of the message until all the acknowledgements are received from the message tree. Stream manager features a in-memory, store and forward architecture for forwarding messages and can batch multiple messages into single message for efficient transfers. Because messages are temporarily stored, there is a draining function that drains the store at a user defined rate.

4 IMPLEMENTATION

Even though high performance interconnects are widely used by HPC applications and frameworks, they are not often utilized in big data systems. Furthermore, experiences in using these interconnects in big data systems are lacking in the public domain. In this implementation, InfiniBand and Omni-Path interfaces with Heron through its stream manager, as shown in Fig. 2. InfiniBand or Omni-Path message channels are created between each stream manager in the topology. These then carry the data messages going between the stream managers. The control messages that are sent between stream manager and topology master still use the TCP connections. They are not frequent and do not affect the performance of the data flow. The TCP loop-back connections from the instances to the stream manager are not altered in this implementation as loop back connection is much more efficient than the

network. Both InfiniBand and Omni-Path implementations use channel semantics for communication. A separate thread is used for polling the completion queues associated with the channels. A credit based flow control mechanism is used for each channel along with a configurable buffer pool.

4.1 Bootstrapping

InfiniBand and Omni-Path require information about the communication parties to be sent out-of-band through other mechanisms like TCP. InfiniBand uses the RDMA(Remote direct memory access) Connection manager to transfer the required information and establish the connections. RDMA connection manager provides a socket-like API for connection management, which is exposed to the user in a similar fashion through Libfabric API. The connection manager also uses the IP over InfiniBand network adapter to discover and transfer the bootstrap information. Omni-Path has a built-in TCP server for discovering the endpoints. Because Omni-Path does not involve connection management, only the destination address is needed for communications. This information can be sent using an out-of-band TCP connection.

4.2 Buffer management

Each side of the communication uses buffer pools with equal size buffers to communicate. Two such pools are used for sending and receiving data for each channel. For receiving operations, all the buffers are posted at the beginning to the fabric. For transmitting messages, the buffers are filled with messages and posted to the fabric for transmission. After the transmission is complete the buffer is added back to the pool. The message receive and transmission completions are discovered using the completion queues. Individual buffer sizes are kept relatively large to accommodate the largest messages expected. If the buffer size is not enough for a single message, the message is divided in to pieces and put into multiple buffers. Every network message carries the length of the total message and this information can be used to assemble the pieces.

The stream manager de-serializes the protocol buffer message in order to determine the routing for the message and handling the acknowledgements. The TCP implementation first copies the incoming data into a buffer and then use this buffer to build the protocol buffer structures. This implementation can directly use the buffer allocated for receiving to build the protocol message.

4.3 Flow control at communication level

Neither InfiniBand nor Omni-Path implement flow control between the communication parties, and it is up to the application developer to implement the much higher level functions [33]. This implementation uses a standard credit-based approach for flow control. The credit available for sender to communicate is equal to the number of buffers posted into the fabric by the receiver. Credit information is passed to the other side as part of data transmissions, or by using separate messages in case there are no data transmissions to send it. Each data message carries the current credit of the communication party as a 4-byte integer value. The credit messages do not take into account the credit available to avoid deadlocks, otherwise there may be situations where there is no credit available to send credit messages.

4.4 Interconnects

Infiniband implementation uses connection-oriented endpoints with channel semantics to transfer the messages. The messages are transferred reliably by the fabric and the message ordering is guaranteed. The completions are also in order of the work request submissions.

Intel Omni-Path does not support connection-oriented message transfers employed in the Infiniband implementation. The application uses reliable datagram message transfer with tag-based messaging. Communication channels between stream managers are overlaid on a single receive queue and a single send queue. Messages coming from different stream managers are distinguished based on the tag information they carry. The tag used in the implementation is a 64-bit integer which carries the source stream manager ID and the destination stream manager ID. Even though all the stream managers connecting to a single stream manager are sharing a single queue, they carry their own flow control by assigning a fixed amount of buffers to each channel. Unlike in Inifiniband, the work request completions are not in any order of their submission to the work queue. Because of this, the application keeps track of the submitted buffers and their completion order explicitly.

IP over Fabric or IP over InfiniBand(IPoIB) is a mechanism to allow a regular TCP application to access the underlying high performance interconnects through the TCP Socket API. For using IPoIB heron stream manager TCP sockets are bound to the IPoIB network interface explicitly without changing the existing TCP processing logic.

5 EXPERIMENTS

An Intel Haswell HPC cluster was used for the InfiniBand experiments. The CPUs are Intel Xeon E5-2670 running at 2.30GHz. Each node has 24 cores (2 sockets x 12 cores each) with 128GB of main memory, 56Gbps InfiniBand interconnect and 1Gbps dedicated Ethernet connection to other nodes. Intel Knights Landing(KNL) cluster was used for Omni-Path tests. Each node in KNL cluster has 72 cores (Intel Xeon Phi CPU 7250F, 1.40GHz) and is connected to a 100Gbps Omni-Path fabric and 1Gbps Ethernet connection. There are many variations of Ethernet, InfiniBand and Omni-Path performing at different message rates and latencies. We conducted the experiments in the best available resources to us.

We conducted several micro-benchmarks to measure the latency and throughput of the system. In these experiments the primary focus was given to communications and no computation was conducted in the bolts. The tasks in each experiment were configured with 4GB of memory. A single Heron stream manager was run in each node. We measured the IP over Fabric (IPoIB) latency to showcase the latency possible in case no direct implementation of InfiniBand or Omni-Path.

5.1 Experiment Topologies

To measure the behavior of the system, two topologies shown in Fig. 4 and Fig. 3 is used. Topology A in Fig. 3 is a deep topology with multiple bolts arranged in a chain. The parallelism of the topology determines the number of parallel task for bolts and spout in the topology. Each adjacent component pair is connected by a

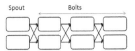

Figure 3: Topology A: Deep topology with a spout and multiple bolts arranged in a chain. The spout and bolt run multiple parallel instances.

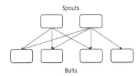

Figure 4: Topology B: Shallow topology with a spout and bolt connected in a shuffle grouping. The spout and bolts run multiple parallel instances.

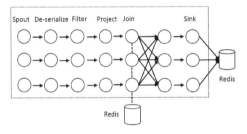

Figure 5: Yahoo Streaming benchmark with 7 stages. The join bolts and sink bolts communicate with a Redis server.

shuffle grouping. Topology B in Fig. 4 is a two-component topology with a spout and a bolt. Spouts and bolts are arranged in a shuffle grouping so that the spouts load balance the messages among the bolts.

In both topologies the spouts generated messages at the highest sustainable speed with acknowledgements. The acknowledgements acted as a flow control mechanism for the topology. The latency is measured as the time it takes for a tuple to go through the topology and its corresponding acknowledgement to reach the spout. Since tuples generate more tuples when they go through the topology, it takes multiple acknowledgements to complete a tuple. In topology A, it needs control tuples equal to the number of Bolts in the chain to complete a single tuple. For example if the length of the topology is 8, it takes 7 control tuples to complete the original tuple. Tests were run with 10 in flight messages through the topology.

5.2 Yahoo streaming benchmark

For evaluating the behavior with a more practical streaming application, we used a benchmark developed at Yahoo![4] to test streaming frameworks. We modified the original streaming benchmark to support Heron and added additional features to support our case. The modified benchmark is available open source in Github [5]. It focuses

---

[4]https://yahooeng.tumblr.com/post/135321837876/benchmarking-streaming-computation-engines-at

[5]https://github.com/iotcloud/streaming-benchmarks.git

on an advertisement application where ad events are processed using a streaming topology as shown in Fig. 10. We changed the original benchmark to use a self-message-generating spout instead of reading messages through Kakfa [18]. This was done to remove any bottlenecks and variations imposed by Kafka.

The benchmark employs a multiple stage topology with different processing units. The data is generated as a JSON object and sent through the processing units, which do de-serialization, filter, projection and join operations on each tuple. At the joining stage, it uses a Redis [8] database to query data about the tuples. Additionally, the last bolt saves information to the Redis database. At the filter step about 66% of the tuples are dropped. We use an acking enabled topology and measured the latency as the time it takes for a tuple to go through the topology and its ack to return back to the spout. For our tests we used 16 nodes with 8 parallelism at each step, totaling 56 tasks. Each spout was sending 100,000 messages per second, which gave 800,000 messages per second in total. Note that this topology accesses the Redis database system for 33% messages it receives.

6 RESULTS & DISCUSSION

Fig. 6 shows the latency of the Topology A with varying message sizes and parallelism for IB, TCP and IPoIB. InfiniBand performed the best while Ethernet showed the highest latency. Fig. 7 shows the latency of the Topology B with varying message sizes and parallelism as in Fig. 6. For small messages, we see both IPoIB and Ethernet performing at a similar level while InfiniBand was performing better. When increasing the parallelism, the latency increased as expected and InfiniBand showed a smaller increase than IPoIB and Ethernet. As expected Topology B showed less improvements compared to Topology A. For most practical applications, the minimum latency possible will be within the results observed in these two topologies as these represent the minimum possible topology and a deep topology for most practical applications.

Fig. 8 shows the latency results of Omni-Path implementation with Topology A, in the KNL cluster for large and small messages. IPoFabric is the IP driver for Omni-Path. The KNL machine has less powerful CPU cores and hence the latency was higher compared to InfiniBand in the tests. Fig 10 shows the latency distribution of the Topology A with 100 and 10 inflight messages with 128k message size for TCP and IB. The graphs show that the network latencies are according to a normal distribution with high latencies at the 99th percentile. Fig. 11 shows the latency distribution seen by the Yahoo stream benchmark with InfiniBand fabric. For all three networking modes, we have seen high spikes at the 99th percentile. This was primarily due to Java garbage collections at the tasks which is unavoidable in JVM-based streaming applications. The store and forward functionality of the stream manager contributes to the distribution of latencies as a single message can be delayed up to 1ms randomly at stream manager.

Fig. 9 present the message rates observed with Topology B. The experiment was conducted with 32 parallel bolt instances and varying numbers of spout instances and message sizes. The graph shows that InfiniBand had the best throughput, while IPoIB achieved second-best and Ethernet came in last. Fig. 9 c) and d) show the throughput for 128K and 128 bytes messages with varying number

of spouts. When the number of parallel spouts increases, the IPoIB and Ethernet maxed out at 16 parallel spouts for 128k messages, while InfiniBand kept on increasing. Fig. 12 shows the total time required to serialize protocol buffers and time it took to complete the same number of messages with TCP and IB implementations. It is evident that IB implementation overhead is much less compared to TCP.

The results showed good overall results for InfiniBand and Omni-Path compared to the TCP and IPoIB communication modes. The throughput of the system is bounded by the CPU usage of stream managers. For TCP connections, the CPU is used for message processing as well as the network protocol. InfiniBand, on the other hand, uses the CPU only for message processing at the stream manager, yielding better performance.

The results showed much higher difference between TCP and InfiniBand for large message sizes. For small messages the bandwidth utilization is much lower than large messages. This is primarily due to the fact that CPU is needed to process every message. For larger messages, because of the low number of messages transferred per second, the CPU usage is low for that aspect. For smaller messages, because of the large number of messages per second, the CPU usage is much higher. Because of this, for small messages, the stream managers saturate the CPU without saturating the communication channel. For practical applications that require large throughput, Heron can bundle small messages into a large message in-order to avoid some of the processing overheads and transfer overheads. This makes it essentially a large message for the stream manager and large message results can be observed with elevated latencies for individual messages. We used 10 buffers with 1 megabyte allocated to each for sending and receiving messages. Protocol buffers are optimized for small messages and it is unlikely to get more than 1 megabyte messages for streaming applications targeting Heron.

The KNL system used for testing Omni-Path has a large number of processes with less CPU frequencies compared to Haswell cluster. In order to fully utilize such a system, multiple threads need to be used. For our implementation we did not explore such features specific to KNL and tried to first optimize for the Omni-Path interconnect. The results show that Omni-Path performed considerably better than the other two options. In this work the authors did not try to pick between Omni-Path or InfiniBand as a better interconnect as they are tested in two completely different systems under varying circumstances. The objective of the work is to show the potential benefits of using interconnects to accelerate stream processing.

7 RELATED WORK

In large part, HPC and Big Data systems have evolved independently over the years. Despite this, there are common requirements that raise similar issues in both type of systems. Some of these issues are solved in HPC and some in Big Data frameworks. As such, there have been efforts to converge both HPC and Big Data technologies to create better systems that can work in different environments efficiently. SPIDAL [9] and HiBD are two such efforts to enhance the Big Data frameworks with ideas and tools from HPC. This work is part of an ongoing effort by the authors to improve stream engine performance using HPC techniques. Previously we

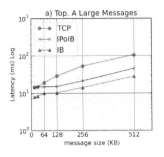
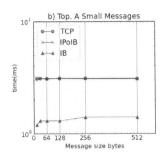
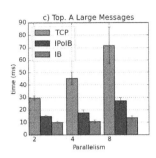
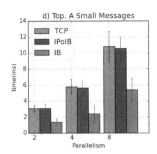

Figure 6: Latency of the Topology A with 1 spout and 7 bolt instances arranged in a chain with varying parallelism and message sizes. a) and b) are with 2 parallelism and c) and d) are with 128k and 128bytes messages. The results are on Haswell cluster with IB.

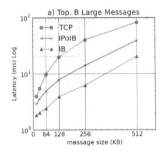
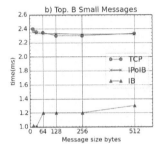
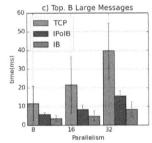
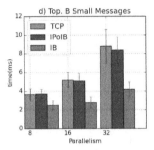

Figure 7: Latency of the Topology B with 32 parallel bolt instances and varying number of spouts and message sizes. a) and b) are with 16 spouts and c) and d) are with 128k and 128bytes messages. The results are on Haswell cluster with IB.

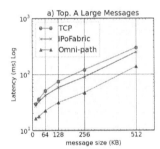
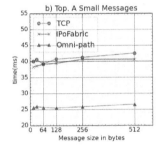
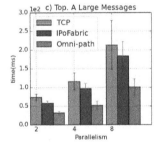
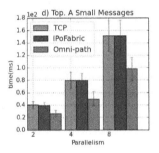

Figure 8: Latency of the Topology A with 1 spout and 7 bolt instances arranged in a chain with varying parallelism and message sizes. a) and b) are with 2 parallelism and c) and d) are with 128k and 128bytes messages. The results are on KNL cluster.

showed [15] how to leverage shared memory and collective communication algorithms to increase the performance of Apache Storm. Also the authors have looked at various available network protocols for Big Data applications [28].

There are many distributed stream engines available today including Apache Spark Streaming [32], Apache Flink [7], Apache Apex [1] and Google Cloud Data flow [3]. All these systems follow the data flow model with comparable features to each other. Stream bench [21] is a benchmark developed to evaluate the performance of these systems in detail. These systems are primarily optimized for commodity hardware and clouds. There has been much research

done around Apache Storm and Apache Heron to improve its capabilities. [10] described architectural and design improvements to Heron that improved its performance much further.

In recent years there have been multiple efforts to integrate high performance interconnects with machine learning and big data frameworks. InfiniBand has been integrated into Spark [24] where the focus is on the Spark batch processing aspects rather than the streaming aspects. Spark is not considered a native stream processing engine and only implements streaming as an extension to its batch engine, making its latency inadequate for low latency applications. Recently InfiniBand has been integrated into Hadoop [22], along with HDFS [13] as well. Hadoop, HDFS and

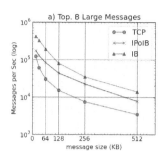
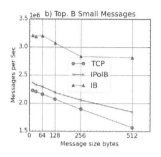
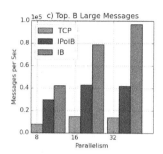
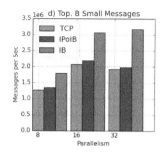

Figure 9: Throughput of the Topology B with 32 bolt instances and varying message sizes and spout instances. The message size varies from 16K to 512K bytes. The spouts are changed from 8 to 32.

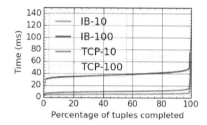

Figure 10: Percent of messages completed within a given latency for the Topology A with in-flight messages at 100 and 10 with 128K messages and 8 parallelism

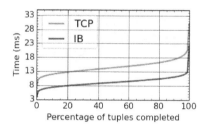

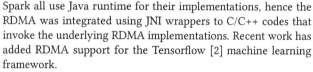

Figure 11: Percent of messages completed within a given latency for the Yahoo! streaming benchmark with InfiniBand network. The experiment was conducted in Haswell cluster with 8 nodes and each stage of topology have 8 parallel tasks.

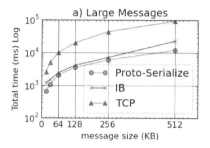

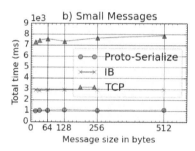

Figure 12: The total time to finish the messages vs the total time to serialize the messages using protobuf and Kryo. Top. B with 8 parallelism for bolts and spouts used. Times are for 20000 large messages and 200000 small messages. The experiment is conducted on Haswell cluster.

Spark all use Java runtime for their implementations, hence the RDMA was integrated using JNI wrappers to C/C++ codes that invoke the underlying RDMA implementations. Recent work has added RDMA support for the Tensorflow [2] machine learning framework.

High performance interconnects have been widely used by the HPC community, and most MPI(Message passing Interface) implementations have support for a large number of interconnects that are available today. Some early work that describes in detail about RDMA for MPI can be found in [20]. There has even been some work to build Hadoop-like systems using the existing MPI capabilities [23]. Photon [16] is a higher level RDMA library that

can be used as a replacement to libfabric. RoCE [5] and iWARP [25] are protocols designed to use RDMA over Ethernet to increase the maximum packets per second processed at a node while decreasing latency. Heron doesn't take into account the network when scheduling tasks into available nodes and it would be interesting to consider network latencies as described in [14, 17] for task scheduling.

8 CONCLUSIONS & FUTURE WORK

Unlike other Big Data systems which are purely JVM-based, Heron has a hybrid architecture where it uses both low level and high level languages appropriately. This architecture allows the addition of high performance enhancement such as InfiniBand natively rather than going through additional layers of JNI as done in high performance Spark and Hadoop. With InfiniBand and Omni-Path integration to Heron, we have seen good performance gains both in latency and throughput. With InfiniBand integration we have seen the communication overhead is moving closer to object serialization cost. The architecture and the implementations can be improved further to reduce the latency and increase the throughput of the system. Even though the authors use Apache Heron in this paper, it is possible to implement high performance interconnects to other stream processing engines such as Apache Flink [7], Apache Spark [31] and Apache Apex [1] using JNI wrappers.

Past research has shown that the remote memory access operations of InfiniBand are more efficient than using channel semantics for transferring large messages. A hybrid approach can be adopted to transfer messages using both channel semantics and memory semantics. It is evident that the CPU is a bottleneck at the stream managers to achieve better performance. The protocol buffer processing along with message serialization are the dominant CPU consumers. A more efficient binary protocol that does not require protocol buffer processing at the stream manager can avoid these overheads. Instances to stream manager communication can be improved with a shared memory approach to avoid the TCP stack. With such approach the InfiniBand can be improved to directly use the shared memory for the buffers without relying on data copying.

Because of the single-process single-threaded approach used by Heron processes, many core systems such as Knights Landing cannot get optimum performance out of Heron. Having a hybrid architecture where multiple threads are used for both communication and computation utilizing the hardware threads of the many core systems can increase the performance of Heron in such environments. Since we are using a fabric abstraction to program InfiniBand and Omni-Path with Libfabric, the same code can be used with other potential high performance interconnects, though it has to be evaluated in such environments to identify possible changes. We would like to continue this work to include more high level streaming operations such as streaming joins, reductions on top of high performance interconnects.

ACKNOWLEDGMENT

This work was partially supported by NSF CIF21 DIBBS 1443054 and NSF RaPyDLI 1415459. We thank Intel for their support of the Haswell system, and extend our gratitude to the FutureSystems team for their support with the infrastructure. We would like to thank Heron team for their support of this work.

REFERENCES

[1] 2017. Apache Apex: Enterprise-grade unified stream and batch processing engine. (2017). https://apex.apache.org/
[2] Martın Abadi, Ashish Agarwal, Paul Barham, Eugene Brevdo, Zhifeng Chen, Craig Citro, Greg S Corrado, Andy Davis, Jeffrey Dean, Matthieu Devin, and others. 2016. Tensorflow: Large-scale machine learning on heterogeneous distributed systems. *arXiv preprint arXiv:1603.04467* (2016).
[3] Tyler Akidau, Robert Bradshaw, Craig Chambers, Slava Chernyak, Rafael J Fernández-Moctezuma, Reuven Lax, Sam McVeety, Daniel Mills, Frances Perry, Eric Schmidt, and others. 2015. The dataflow model: a practical approach to balancing correctness, latency, and cost in massive-scale, unbounded, out-of-order data processing. *Proceedings of the VLDB Endowment* 8, 12 (2015), 1792–1803.
[4] InfiniBand Trade Association and others. 2000. *InfiniBand Architecture Specification: Release 1.0.* InfiniBand Trade Association.
[5] Motti Beck and Michael Kagan. 2011. Performance Evaluation of the RDMA over Ethernet (RoCE) Standard in Enterprise Data Centers Infrastructure. In

[6] Mark S Birrittella, Mark Debbage, Ram Huggahalli, James Kunz, Tom Lovett, Todd Rimmer, Keith D Underwood, and Robert C Zak. 2015. Intel® Omni-path Architecture: Enabling Scalable, High Performance Fabrics. In *High-Performance Interconnects (HOTI), 2015 IEEE 23rd Annual Symposium on.* IEEE, 1–9.
[7] Paris Carbone, Stephan Ewen, Seif Haridi, Asterios Katsifodimos, Volker Markl, and Kostas Tzoumas. 2015. Apache flink: Stream and batch processing in a single engine. *Data Engineering* (2015), 28.
[8] Josiah L Carlson. 2013. *Redis in Action.* Manning Publications Co.
[9] Geoffrey Fox, Judy Qiu, Shantenu Jha, Saliya Ekanayake, and Supun Kamburugamuve. 2015. Big data, simulations and hpc convergence. In *Workshop on Big Data Benchmarks.* Springer, 3–17.
[10] Maosong Fu, Ashvin Agrawal, Avrilia Floratou, Graham Bill, Andrew Jorgensen, Mark Li, Neng Lu, Karthik Ramasamy, Sriram Rao, and Cong Wang. 2017. Twitter Heron: Towards Extensible Streaming Engines. *2017 IEEE International Conference on Data Engineering* (Apr 2017). http://icde2017.sdsc.edu/industry-track
[11] S. Gallenmller, P. Emmerich, F. Wohlfart, D. Raumer, and G. Carle. 2015. Comparison of frameworks for high-performance packet IO. In *2015 ACM/IEEE Symposium on Architectures for Networking and Communications Systems (ANCS).* 29–38. DOI:http://dx.doi.org/10.1109/ANCS.2015.7110118
[12] P. Grun, S. Hefty, S. Sur, D. Goodell, R. D. Russell, H. Pritchard, and J. M. Squyres. 2015. A Brief Introduction to the OpenFabrics Interfaces - A New Network API for Maximizing High Performance Application Efficiency. In *2015 IEEE 23rd Annual Symposium on High-Performance Interconnects.* 34–39. DOI:http://dx.doi.org/10.1109/HOTI.2015.19
[13] Nusrat S Islam, MW Rahman, Jithin Jose, Raghunath Rajachandrasekar, Hao Wang, Hari Subramoni, Chet Murthy, and Dhabaleswar K Panda. 2012. High performance RDMA-based design of HDFS over InfiniBand. In *Proceedings of the International Conference on High Performance Computing, Networking, Storage and Analysis.* IEEE Computer Society Press, 35.
[14] Virajith Jalaparti, Peter Bodik, Ishai Menache, Sriram Rao, Konstantin Makarychev, and Matthew Caesar. 2015. Network-Aware Scheduling for Data-Parallel Jobs: Plan When You Can. In *Proceedings of the 2015 ACM Conference on Special Interest Group on Data Communication (SIGCOMM '15).* ACM, New York, NY, USA, 407–420. DOI:http://dx.doi.org/10.1145/2785956.2787488
[15] Supun Kamburugamuve, Saliya Ekanayake, Milinda Pathirage, and Geoffrey Fox. 2016. Towards High Performance Processing of Streaming Data in Large Data Centers. In *HPBDC 2016 IEEE International Workshop on High-Performance Big Data Computing in conjunction with The 30th IEEE International Parallel and Distributed Processing Symposium (IPDPS 2016), Chicago, Illinois USA.*
[16] Ezra Kissel and Martin Swany. 2016. Photon: Remote memory access middleware for high-performance runtime systems. In *Parallel and Distributed Processing Symposium Workshops, 2016 IEEE International.* IEEE, 1736–1743.
[17] Adrian Klein, Fuyuki Ishikawa, and Shinichi Honiden. 2012. Towards Network-aware Service Composition in the Cloud. In *Proceedings of the 21st International Conference on World Wide Web (WWW '12).* ACM, New York, NY, USA, 959–968. DOI:http://dx.doi.org/10.1145/2187836.2187965
[18] Jay Kreps, Neha Narkhede, Jun Rao, and others. 2011. Kafka: A distributed messaging system for log processing. In *Proceedings of the NetDB.* 1–7.
[19] Sanjeev Kulkarni, Nikunj Bhagat, Maosong Fu, Vikas Kedigehalli, Christopher Kellogg, Sailesh Mittal, Jignesh M Patel, Karthik Ramasamy, and Siddarth Taneja. 2015. Twitter heron: Stream processing at scale. In *Proceedings of the 2015 ACM SIGMOD International Conference on Management of Data.* ACM, 239–250.
[20] Jiuxing Liu, Jiesheng Wu, Sushmitha P Kini, Pete Wyckoff, and Dhabaleswar K Panda. 2003. High performance RDMA-based MPI implementation over Infini-Band. In *Proceedings of the 17th annual international conference on Supercomputing.* ACM, 295–304.
[21] Ruirui Lu, Gang Wu, Bin Xie, and Jingtong Hu. 2014. Stream bench: Towards benchmarking modern distributed stream computing frameworks. In *Utility and Cloud Computing (UCC), 2014 IEEE/ACM 7th International Conference on.* IEEE, 69–78.
[22] Xiaoyi Lu, Nusrat S Islam, Md Wasi-Ur-Rahman, Jithin Jose, Hari Subramoni, Hao Wang, and Dhabaleswar K Panda. 2013. High-performance design of Hadoop RPC with RDMA over InfiniBand. In *2013 42nd International Conference on Parallel Processing.* IEEE, 641–650.
[23] Xiaoyi Lu, Fan Liang, Bing Wang, Li Zha, and Zhiwei Xu. 2014. DataMPI: extending MPI to hadoop-like big data computing. In *Parallel and Distributed Processing Symposium, 2014 IEEE 28th International.* IEEE, 829–838.
[24] Xiaoyi Lu, Md Wasi Ur Rahman, Nusrat Islam, Dipti Shankar, and Dhabaleswar K Panda. 2014. Accelerating spark with RDMA for big data processing: Early experiences. In *High-performance interconnects (HOTI), 2014 IEEE 22nd annual symposium on.* IEEE, 9–16.
[25] M. J. Rashti and A. Afsahi. 2007. 10-Gigabit iWARP Ethernet: Comparative Performance Analysis with InfiniBand and Myrinet-10G. In *2007 IEEE International Parallel and Distributed Processing Symposium.* 1–8. DOI:http://dx.doi.org/10.1109/IPDPS.2007.370480

[26] Luigi Rizzo. 2012. Netmap: a novel framework for fast packet I/O. In *21st USENIX Security Symposium (USENIX Security 12)*. 101–112.

[27] A. Sodani. 2015. Knights landing (KNL): 2nd Generation Intel xAE; Xeon Phi processor. In *2015 IEEE Hot Chips 27 Symposium (HCS)*. 1–24. DOI:http://dx.doi.org/10.1109/HOTCHIPS.2015.7477467

[28] Brian Tierney, Ezra Kissel, Martin Swany, and Eric Pouyoul. 2012. Efficient data transfer protocols for big data. In *E-Science (e-Science), 2012 IEEE 8th International Conference on*. IEEE, 1–9.

[29] Ankit Toshniwal, Siddarth Taneja, Amit Shukla, Karthik Ramasamy, Jignesh M Patel, Sanjeev Kulkarni, Jason Jackson, Krishna Gade, Maosong Fu, Jake Donham, and others. 2014. Storm@ twitter. In *Proceedings of the 2014 ACM SIGMOD international conference on Management of data*. ACM, 147–156.

[30] Kenton Varda. 2008. Protocol buffers: Googlefis data interchange format. *Google Open Source Blog, Available at least as early as Jul* (2008).

[31] Matei Zaharia, Mosharaf Chowdhury, Tathagata Das, Ankur Dave, Justin Ma, Murphy McCauley, Michael J Franklin, Scott Shenker, and Ion Stoica. 2012. Resilient distributed datasets: A fault-tolerant abstraction for in-memory cluster computing. In *Proceedings of the 9th USENIX conference on Networked Systems Design and Implementation*. USENIX Association, 2–2.

[32] Matei Zaharia, Tathagata Das, Haoyuan Li, Scott Shenker, and Ion Stoica. 2012. Discretized streams: an efficient and fault-tolerant model for stream processing on large clusters. In *Presented as part of the*.

[33] Yibo Zhu, Haggai Eran, Daniel Firestone, Chuanxiong Guo, Marina Lipshteyn, Yehonatan Liron, Jitendra Padhye, Shachar Raindel, Mohamad Haj Yahia, and Ming Zhang. 2015. Congestion Control for Large-Scale RDMA Deployments. In *Proceedings of the 2015 ACM Conference on Special Interest Group on Data Communication (SIGCOMM '15)*. ACM, New York, NY, USA, 523–536. DOI:http://dx.doi.org/10.1145/2785956.2787484

Scalable and Adaptive Software Defined Network Management for Cloud-hosted Group Communication Applications

Prithviraj Patil*
The MathWorks Inc
Natick, Massachusetts, USA
prithviraj6116@gmail.com

Akram Hakiri
Univ de Carthage, ISSAT
Mateur, Bizerte, Tunisia
akram.hakiri@gmail.com

Shashank Shekhar and
Aniruddha Gokhale
Dept of EECS, Vanderbilt University
Nashville, Tennessee, USA
{shashank.shekhar,a.gokhale}@
vanderbilt.edu

ABSTRACT

Group communications form the primary communication pattern for many cloud-hosted applications and cloud infrastructure management services, such as system health monitoring, multimedia distribution, collaborative applications and distributed databases. Although IP multicast has been used to support group communication semantics in diverse Internet-based distributed applications, its deployment in cloud Data Center Networks (DCNs) has been limited due to its higher resource consumption, scalability, and stability issues, which in turn degrades the utility of the cloud. Software Defined Networking (SDN) has enabled the re-engineering of multicast capabilities to overcome these limitations. To that end, this paper presents an autonomous, dynamic and flexible middleware solution called SDN-based Multicast (SDMC), which provides both network load-aware and switch memory-efficient group communication semantics in DCNs. Thus, SDMC improves DCN resource utilization while allowing applications to remain agnostic to the underlying group communication semantics by efficiently toggling between unicast and multicast in accordance with changing network bandwidth and switch memory usage. Empirical studies comparing SDMC with traditional IP multicast shows up to 60% better latency performance for different DCNs topologies, and up to 50% better performance in the switch memory utilization for multicast groups exceeding size 30.

CCS CONCEPTS

• **Networks** → **Network resources allocation**; **Cloud computing**; **Data center networks**; • **Computer systems organization** → *Cloud computing*; *Fault-tolerant network topologies*;

KEYWORDS

Cloud Computing; Adaptive Multicast; Software Defined Network; OpenFlow; Data Center Networks.

---

*Work conducted as part of doctoral studies at Vanderbilt University.

---

1 INTRODUCTION

Many cloud infrastructure management tasks as well as cloud-hosted applications require group communication semantics in cloud Data Center Networks (DCNs) [3]. For example, DCNs must offer diverse elasticity techniques to provide commodity and tenant-based services for scaling up or down of computing, storage and network resources, e.g., Amazon Elastic Compute Cloud (Amazon EC2) and services like Twitter and Facebook, which use multicast-centric architectures. Additionally, several fault management strategies, such as passive and active replication, failover, state synchronization of cluster servers and quorum management in active replication require group communications to tolerate and mitigate faults [37].

Group communication is also used to enforce security solutions in DCNs, such as prevention, detection and removal of malware and viruses, as well as in performing bulk software installment, update, and upgrade [28]. For example, software management tools for cloud infrastructure like Chef send the same commands to multiple (i.e., 100s of) virtual machines during software installation and update. Likewise, access control policies in DCNs use group communication to manage users, groups, passwords, and user privileges [30].

Two key considerations dictate the performance of group communications in DCNs. First, the router/switch's available network capacity (i.e., available bandwidth) is required to estimate the bandwidth available for data traffic and control messages that can be forwarded along their multiple ports concurrently [32]. Hence, the ability to instrument the router's (or switch's) network capacity is crucial to estimating the network load in terms of the overall bandwidth that a router/switch is able to support. Second, since the memory of the routers/switches (including their queuing buffers) holds packets and connection state information of the traffic transiting across the network devices, it is important to maintain the router/switch memory utilization under a given threshold to avoid buffer overflows [12].

Group communication semantics for contemporary DCN-hosted applications are often realized using multicast, e.g., IP multicast (IPMC), which is a commonly used group communication protocol in the Internet to support multi-point communication requirements so as to conserve bandwidth and reduce the load on servers [23]. IPMC, however, incurs substantial security, performance and scalability degradation in DCNs, e.g., IPMC can be exploited for distributed Denial-of-Service attack [1]. Moreover, existing multicast routing algorithms, such as Protocol-Independent Multicast (PIM) (e.g., PIM Sparse Mode (PIM-SM) and PIM Dense Mode (PIM-DM)) and Multicast Open Shortest Path First (MOSPF), require substantial manual deployment and management efforts by the cloud operators [19]. Furthermore, the Internet Group Management Protocol (IGMP) [7], which is used by IPMC for dynamic membership registration, sends multiple messages to all the routers to notify the occurrence of group events, which requires significant CPU resources, and substantial memory resources to hold the table size for IP multicast [26].

A further downside with IPMC concerns its limited state space in commodity routers which impedes router functionality since they must maintain routing states and perform a costly and wasteful per-group translation [31]. Hence, packet filtering becomes ineffective in large multicast groups and in turn the overwhelmed receivers will begin dropping packets. Although several improvements, such as Hierarchy-Aware multicast [25], multi-path routing [18], and Bloom filter-based group management [15], address these issues, they cannot be readily adopted in DCNs due to their complexity, security issues, and the manual efforts required in managing them.

Being cognizant of the switch memory utilization as well as the network load to avoid drastic problems is a critical requirement for any group-based communication semantics in DCNs. Complicating this requirement is the fact that DCNs often comprise a very large number of distributed network equipment, which makes it harder to instrument, coordinate and maintain a consistent and global view of the system without developing additional and complex solutions. It is in this context that emerging approaches in the form of Network Function Virtualization (NFV) or network softwarization and Software-Defined Networking (SDN) [13] hold promise [27]. NFV, for instance, aims to virtualize a set of network functions by moving network function into software packages, meaning that building a service chain no longer requires acquiring hardware. Complementing NFV is SDN which separates the control plane from the data or forwarding plane. NFV can enable multicast routing on SDN by constructing a traffic forwarding topology, deploying the required multicast functions and steering traffic through the constructed multicast trees [35]. Recent efforts [5, 9] have used SDN for efficient bandwidth management during the creation of multicast trees by using topology information in DCNs. Despite this promise, current approaches cannot autonomously adapt to the network load and router (or SDN switch) memory utilization, which is critical to the scalability of group communications, and also for monitoring and evaluating network performance in DCNs.

To leverage the benefits of NFV/SDN while addressing unresolved challenges and limitations in recent SDN-based multicast efforts, we propose an autonomic Cloud resource management architecture called SDN-based Multicast (SDMC) to achieve utility in clouds by supporting dynamic and flexible, network load-aware and switch memory-efficient group communications in DCNs. SDMC is not a new multicast protocol; rather it is a SDN-enabled distributed middleware framework for improving utility in DCNs that provides dynamic resource management by intelligently and dynamically switching different group communications flows between unicast and multicast thereby balancing between network bandwidth and switch memory utilization. SDMC is fully decoupled from any specific multicast protocol, such as IPMC. Moreover, the middleware aspect enables a large number of DCN-based group communication applications and services to avail of our adaptive resource management solution.

The key contributions of these paper are:

- We describe the architectural innovations and algorithms in SDMC that provide an autonomous, adaptive and flexible network link and switch memory load-aware multicast approach for data center networks.
- We present details of our distributed SDMC middleware, which is manifested in the form of (i) a suite of SDN network applications hosted on a SDN controller and OpenFlow-enabled switches [24], and (ii) a SDN middleware layer on the network hosts where applications reside.
- We evaluate the effectiveness of our approach in different data center network topologies along a number of metrics, such as load variations and switch-memory utilization.

The rest of the paper is organized as follows: Section 2 describes the design and implementation details of SDMC. Section 3 provides an empirical evaluation of SDMC. Section 4 discusses related work and compares them to SDMC. Finally, Section 5 presents concluding remarks alluding to lessons learned and future work.

2 DESIGN AND IMPLEMENTATION OF SDMC

This section delves into the details of SDMC. We first present three key contributions in SDMC required to support application-agnostic dynamic and adaptive resource management, and then present the architectural details that enable us to realize utility in the cloud. Subsequently we present the algorithms that use the framework to perform an adaptive, network link and switch memory load-aware multicast for data center networks.

2.1 Contribution 1: Two-level SDMC-ID Structure

A key requirement for SDMC is to support application-agnostic adaptive behavior and promote the reuse of multicast routing trees. To that end, SDMC defines a new multicast identifier space called SDMC-ID.[1] The SDMC-ID space is divided into two regions: application-level (or external, i.e., ID_e) and network-level (or internal, i.e., ID_i). Applications using SDMC interact using only the external SDMC-IDs while the network data path deals only with internal SDMC-IDs. To keep applications agnostic of internal IDs, SDMC supports a translation layer in the form of a middleware on each host (see Section 2.4). This two-level SDMC-ID structure allows SDMC to use the same multicast routing tree (with the same internal SDMC-ID) with overlapping receivers belonging to two different external SDMC IDs.

SDMC maintains the mapping between the two types of IDs by encoding the participants' external multicast channel IDs and the node-specific internal IDs, and storing it in each immediate SDN router/switch without requiring packet header modification. As shown in Figure 1, traditional multicast uses the same multicast ID for all the communication needs. In contrast, SDMC uses the external SDMC multicast ID for communication between application endpoints (i.e., sender and receiver) and network endpoints (i.e., switches or controller). For the communication between the controller and switches, SDMC uses the corresponding internal

---

[1]We use SDMC-ID to denote both the identifier space for SDN-enabled multicast as well as the actual external or internal IDs assigned to a flow. Its semantics should be evident from the context.

multicast ID. Hence, the communication over lines 1, 2 and 3 uses external (or application-level) multicast ID while the communication over lines 4 and 5 uses internal (or network-level) multicast ID.

(a) Traditional Multicast Topology

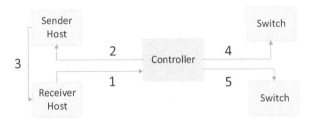

(b) Architecture of the SDN-enabled Multicast Approach

Figure 1: Comparison between the SDN-enabled Multicast and Traditional IP Multicast

2.2 Contribution 2: Lazy Initialization Strategy

Our second contribution lies in the initialization process for the SDMC senders/receivers and the SDMC routing tree creation, which uses a lazy approach to reduce the initial latency that is otherwise incurred by the receivers in traditional multicast and also to allow flexibility in adapting dynamically to the network load and switch memory. SDMC exhibits this lazy approach in its operation while switching to multicast communication from the default unicast. Specifically, the immediate SDN router/switch does not rely on multicast routing information right away; rather it can be stateless for forwarding since it uses existing unicast routing information.

This lazy approach manifests itself in three different situations. First, when a new receiver requests to listen on an external SDMC-ID, it is not immediately added to the SDMC-ID as a multicast receiver but rather as a unicast destination for all the existing senders of that SDMC-ID, if any. Second, the SDMC multicast routing tree for a new receiver is created in the controller but is not installed (e.g., in the form of OpenFlow rules [4]) in the switches right away. Third, when a receiver (or sender) leaves the SDMC-ID group, the multicast tree is not updated immediately. All these decisions (i.e., when to add a receiver as a multicast destination; when to install the multicast routing tree in switches; and when to update the multicast routing tree after a receiver leaves) are taken by SDMC holistically based on all other SDMC sender/receiver statuses and depending on the network load and switch-memory utilizations (see the algorithms in Section 2.5).

Figure 2 shows the lazy initialization of a sender. It shows the setup when two receivers subscribe to this sender. Even though the

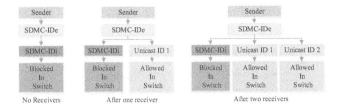

Figure 2: Initial SDMC Sender Setup showing External and Internal SDMC-IDs

sender has a multicast ID attached to it, receivers are added as a unicast destination to reduce the start-up latency. This enables the receiver to receive packets immediately since there is no need to create any multicast routing tree in the switches. The corresponding behavior on the receiver side appears in Figure 3. As seen from these figures, both the sender and receiver use only the external SDMC-ID, i.e., ID_e in Figures 2 and 3, which is mapped either to an internal SDMC-ID (multicast), i.e. ID_i in Figures 2 and 3 or a unicast, transparently to the application layer.

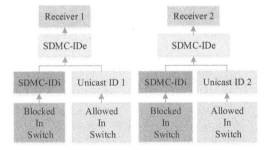

Figure 3: Initial SDMC Receiver Setup

2.3 Contribution 3: Network Link and Switch Memory Monitoring

To make dynamic resource management decisions, SDMC must periodically keep track of the utilizations of network links and switches. SDN switches use counters for tracking the number of packets that are sent through a given link and record link forwarding success and failure. This is used to track the bandwidth utilization and detect if certain packets are consuming more bandwidth than anticipated. Using these counters, the controller can make a decision about the link utilization. To that end, SDMC provides a special capability in the SDN controller via a network management application (see Section 2.4). SDMC then populates the network link utilization information against the SDMC-IDs which are using that link for unicast for a given receiver. The network topology corresponding to this scenario is shown in Figure 4.

SDMC also keeps track of the memory utilization of the network switches with the help of the controller. Since the controller installs rules in the switches, it knows exactly how many Open-Flow rules exist on each of the switches. Each switch comes with a maximum number of OpenFlow rules that it can accommodate. So we measure the switch-memory utilization as the number of

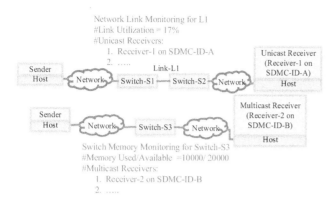

Figure 4: Network Link and Switch Memory Monitoring

actual OpenFlow rules installed in the switch against the maximum number of OpenFlow rules allowed.

2.4 Putting it Together: SDMC Architecture and Middleware Design

To support the key capabilities of SDMC outlined above, SDMC is realized as a distributed SDN-based middleware framework shown in Figure 5, which comprises the following: the core intelligence of SDMC is made available as a suite of SDN applications (called SDN NetApps in SDN parlance) that execute inside a (logically) centralized controller as shown in the figure; and as a SDN middleware layer available on each host where the senders and receivers use the APIs provided by SDMC. SDMC uses the traditional OpenFlow channel for communication between the controller and SDN routers, where these routers are connected to host machines (physical or virtual). The use of SDN principles allows SDMC to be flexible and dynamic. The remainder of this section explains each component.

SDMC SDN controller: The DCN is managed by a (logically) centralized SDN controller, which is placed on a dedicated machine(s) with dedicated out-of-band connections to all the OpenFlow-enabled routers. The SDMC-specific SDN NetApps hosted on the controller provide the core intelligence of SDMC as follows:

- *Topology Discovery:* This NetApp provides autonomous discovery of joining and leaving routers and hosts. It uses the link layer discovery protocol (LLDP) to assist the controller in identifying the joining or leaving multicast group participants.
- *Topology Management:* This NetApp creates a graph topology of all nodes connected to the controller. By manipulating the connected graph, the controller can activate or de-activate the connected routers, hosts and the links connecting them.
- *Monitoring:* This NetApp provides real-time reports on various network parameters, such as bandwidth utilization, latency, packet error rates, resource utilization, etc to the controller.
- *Routing:* This NetApp implements the multicast intelligence (explained in Section 2.5.3) to build the dynamic multicast routing tree at run-time.

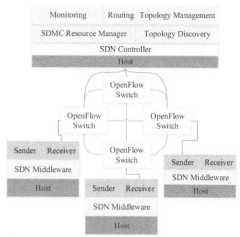

Yellow is SDMC contributions

Figure 5: SDMC Architecture

- *Resource Manager:* This NetApp manages the SDMC ID space and the mapping between the external and internal IDs (explained in Sections 2.5.1 and 2.5.2), and determines and enforces the resource management decisions (explained in Section 2.5.4).

OpenFlow-enabled switches: In a typical DCN, a number of OpenFlow-enabled switches are connected to form a network with topologies like mesh, tree or jellyfish. Each switch contains an OpenFlow client to connect to the SDN controller. The OpenFlow client conforms to the OpenFlow protocol by providing capabilities to add, remove, update, and delete packets inside the network devices. The OpenFlow logic is designed in terms of flow processing controlled by a group of flow tables. Flow tables are composed of a set of entries to process packets whose headers match predefined patterns in the header field. The OpenFlow protocol specifies the formats of the messages exchanged between controllers and remote switches through a secure channel so that commands and packets can be exchanged securely. The mapping of the data plane into forwarding tables provides a simple abstraction to describe the common requirements of network equipment to store, process, and forward packets hop-by-hop. Thus, the abstraction provided by the OpenFlow protocol enables the use of open and standardized interfaces that can be used to program network devices in a vendor-agnostic manner.

Host machines and SDMC middleware: Multicast functionalities, which deal with overlay multicast, are implemented using SDMC's SDN middleware that runs in each of the host machines. The SDN middleware controls the communication using a host manager service to translate endpoints listening on multicast IDs into multiple unicast IDs, and switch endpoints from unicast to multicast and vice-versa transparently to the applications. Those endpoints can decide whether senders or receivers are able to send or listen only on SDMC IDs or not.

Host manager: The host manager NetApp (not shown) keeps track of all machines connected to the network. This application is used by SDMC to communicate with the SDMC middleware on the host machines. This application is required since we build a hybrid multicast protocol by combining application-level multicast (or overlay multicast) and native network-level-multicast.

SDMC participants: The SDMC participants (senders and receivers) run on top of the SDMC middleware on the hosts.

2.5 SDMC Behavior and its Dynamic Resource Management Algorithms

We now describe the runtime operation of SDMC and explain its dynamic resource management algorithms. We illustrate these operations in the form of sequence of activities executed by SDMC in response to various events like sender and receiver join, and sender and receiver leave.

2.5.1 Algorithm for Sender Join. When a participant (sender) wants to send data on an application-level SDMC-ID, M^e, the following sequence of steps described in lines 4–10 of Algorithm 1 are carried out.

Algorithm 1: Joining Multicast Group

Data: M^e, M^i, U_{r1}, U_{r2}
Result: sender or receiver joined SDMC

1 senderJoinRequest(M^e);
2 receiverJoinRequest(M^e, U_{r1});
3 **while** *Listening* **do**
4   **if** *sender* **then**
5   **if** *firstsender* **then**
6   create new M^i for M^e; installOFTransRule($M^e \rightarrow M^i$) in this sender
      and in all the existing receivers;
7   **else**
8   retrieve M^i for M^e; installOFTransRule($M^e \rightarrow M^i$) in this sender;
9   **end**
10   installOFTransRule($M^e \rightarrow U_{r1}, U_{r2}, \ldots$) in all the senders;
11   **else**
12   addUnicastDestToSenders(U_{r1});
13   nonBlocking_AddToMulticastTree(U_{r1});
14   waitForTriggerToToggleToMulticast(U_{r1});
15   **end**
16 **end**

- The sender uses its SDN middleware to forward the request to the SDMC Routing NetApp. The latter assigns an appropriate internal SDMC-ID M^i to correspond to the requested application-level SDMC ID, M^e. The SDMC Routing NetApp at the controller side installs an OpenFlow rule in the edge switch of the sender to block all the traffic with destination ID M^i.

- Thereafter, if this sender is the first sender for M^e, then the SDN middleware on the sender node (and for all the existing receivers) installs a translation rule for $M^e \leftrightarrow M^i$ in the host middleware so that (1) when sender sends packets on external SDMC-ID M^e, it gets translated to internal SDMC ID M^i and also (2) when any receiver receives the packet with SDMC-ID M^i, it gets translated to application-level external SDMC-ID M^e.

- Additionally, the SDN middleware of the joining sender installs the translation rule $M^e \rightarrow (M^i, U_{r1}, U_{r2})$, to convert M^e into destinations of the existing unicast receivers, i.e. U_{r1} and U_{r2}. This step is performed only if at least one receiver is listening on M^e as a unicast destination. This allows the sender to start sending packets using unicast immediately instead of incurring the delay in traditional multicast.

2.5.2 Algorithm for Receiver Join. Similar to the joining of a sender, when a joining receiver wants to listen on an application-level SDMC-ID M^e, it requests its SDN middleware to retrieve the internal network-level SDMC-ID M^i from the SDMC SDN NetApp. Then, the SDN middleware installs two translation rules $M^e \leftrightarrow M^i$ and $M^e \leftrightarrow U_r$ (where U_r is the unicast ID of this receiver), while giving preference to the $M^e \leftrightarrow U_r$ rule over $M^e \leftrightarrow M^i$ so that the first rule gets matched. This forces the receiver to listen on the unicast ID instead of multicast ID to begin with. This is part of the lazy initialization of SDMC receivers.

Lines 11–15 of Algorithm 1 illustrate the joining operation for a SDMC receiver. The following sequence of steps are followed:

- When a new receiver (r1) sends a request to listen on M^e, the receiver is not immediately added to M^e as a multicast destination. Instead it is added as a unicast destination (as U_{r1}) for all the existing senders of M^e.

- Next, SDMC concurrently creates a multicast routing tree for a new receiver as explained in Section 2.5.3. Even though every existing sender of M^e has a multicast ID (in the form of M^i) attached to it, new receivers are added as unicast destinations for reducing the startup latency. This allows the joining receiver to receive packets immediately.

- The receiver is transparently switched to multicast only if the network link utilization crosses a threshold limit, as explained in Section 2.5.4.

As part of these steps, the SDMC SDN NetApp searches for all the senders of M^i and adds the unicast destination of U_r in their SDN middleware translation rules. Then, it requests the unicast routing paths for this receiver to every sender of M^i from the Routing module at the SDN controller. Based on these routing paths, it then updates the controller's routing table by adding a sender-receiver pair against each appropriate network link and switch.

2.5.3 Multicast Tree Calculation. In the current IP multicast, the number of multicast forwarding states is proportional to the number of multicast groups where the number of multicast groups grow proportionally to the number of forwarding states. Additionally, the number of control messages required to maintain the forwarding states will grow in the same manner. This scalability issue has to be solved before multicast can be deployed over the Internet. To address this issue, SDMC allows optimally aggregating multicast groups so that the controller can aggregate local groups into virtual meta-groups to perform routing tree aggregation and addressing.

To that end, the SDMC Routing NetApp in the SDN controller implements Algorithm 2 to compute the multicast tree. Based on inputs from the topology discovery NetApp, it keeps track of all links in the network and adds them to the link list (L), and creates a list of nodes (N) joining those links as shown in lines 1 to 6. Moreover, since there could be multiple multicast groups in the DCN, SDMC finds the address of the group from the list of all available multicast groups and returns a list of routers in the same group, i.e., the multicast tree (lines 7–9). Subsequently, SDMC calculates the shortest path in the multicast tree and installs the OpenFlow rules for that multicast tree (lines 10 and 11).

Since the DCN environment can carry multiple concurrent multicast sessions, SDMC allows accommodating all the multicast groups while allowing the optimization of the network resource among

---

Algorithm 2: Minimum Steiner Multicast Tree and Route Calculation

Data: M^e, N
Result: Minimum Steiner Multicast Tree
1 **foreach** M^e *in N* **do**
2   **if** M^e ! *visited* **then**
3   visited.add(M^e);
4   tree.append(M^e);
5   **end**
6 **end**
7 **for** $i \leftarrow tree[0]$ *to len(tree)* **do**
8   multicastTree= Steiner(tree,M^i, M^e);
9 **end**
10 installMulticastRules(multicastTree,M^i, M^e);
11 **return** *multicastTree*;

---

multiple co-existing multicast trees. As shown in line 8 in Algorithm 2, SDMC allows multicast tree packing based on the least cost tree (Steiner tree) to perform adaptive resource management. In random graphs, such as distributed routers in the Internet, the Steiner tree is known to be NP-Complete. Nonetheless, the routers and switches in DCNs are organized as structured graphs so that it is possible to build optimal or near-optimal routing trees using a Steiner tree.

Furthermore, as SDMC can dynamically perform the multicast-to-unicast translation, a source group can send an aggregation packet to the edge switch using the unicast ID, typically IP unicast address, so that the controller installs the required OpenFlow rule to perform multicast group registration. This strategy offers bandwidth efficiency for a large number of OpenFlow rules because the translation happens likely close to the receiver. This way, SDMC drastically reduces the required network states and concentrates them in a single switch at the network edge close to the receiver. Furthermore, the application remains agnostic to the rest of the network topology changes because transparent to the application, SDMC makes trade-offs to retain the benefits of group communication by dynamically switching between unicast and multicast, and effectively limiting the explosion of the network states during the communication.

2.5.4 Adaptive Resource Management. SDMC keeps track of network links and their utilization with the help of the SDMC Monitoring NetApp. Then, it populates the link utilization information against the SDMC-IDs which are using that link for the unicast for a receiver. Additionally, SDMC also keeps track of the memory utilization of the network switches with the help of the controller. SDMC reduces switch memory utilization by dynamically switching some multicast receivers to unicast destinations. This is due to the removal from the switch of OpenFlow rules used for multicast routing of those toggled receivers. Similarly, SDMC also reduces link utilization by switching some unicast receivers to multicast destinations, which reduces packet duplication and hence decreases network link utilization. In this way, SDMC trades off link and switch memory utilization keeping both of them below the threshold limits. In current work we do not consider both metrics at once. Moreover, SDMC also does not handle the case when both metrics are high, nor does it handle oscillations in adaptations.

Based on insights from [2], we maintain the threshold limits under 70% of the resource utilization to avoid possible SLA violation while decreasing the energy consumption as soon as possible. To trigger the dynamic adaptations, SDMC registers listener events in the SDMC Monitoring NetApp to get notifications about link and switch memory threshold violations. Algorithm 3 describes the procedure for this dynamic and adaptive resource management.

Algorithm 3: Adapting to network link and switch memory utilization

Data: switch(s1), Link(l1), receiver(r1, U_{r1}), SDMC(M^i)
Result: Receiver toggled between multicast and unicast & resource utilization kept under threshold
1 **if** *ThresholdViolationDetect(switch s1)* **then**
2   addUnicastDestToSender(U_{r1});
3   discardDuplicates(r1);
4   listenOnUnicast(r1);
5   removeFromMulticast(U_{r1},M^i);
6   stopListenOnMulticast(r1,M^i);
7 **end**
8 **if** *ThresholdViolationDetect(link l1)* **then**
9   addToMulticast(U_{r1},M^i);
10   discardDuplicates(r1);
11   listenOnMulticast(r1,M^i);
12   RemoveUnicastDestFromSender(U_{r1});
13   stopListenOnUnicast(r1);
14 **end**

SDMC continually monitors link and switch memory utilization. As shown in Lines 1–6 of Algorithm 3, when a switch memory reaches the threshold limit, first, SDMC updates the translation rule in the SDN middleware of all the senders by adding in its mapping the unicast address of $r1$, i.e., $M^e \leftrightarrow (M^i, U_{r2})$ would become $M^e \leftrightarrow (M^i, U_{r1}, U_{r2})$. Then, SDMC instructs the receiver to listen on its own unicast ID (U_{r1}) along with multicast ID M^i. At this point the SDN middleware of $r1$ starts receiving duplicate packets: one each from unicast and multicast destinations. SDMC, however, instructs the SDN middleware of $r1$ to discard any duplicate packets. Hence, the application-level receiver ($r1$) receives only a single copy of each packet. Now, since $r1$ does not need multicast destination support, SDMC can safely remove OpenFlow entries in the router that were installed before to reach $r1$. This step reduces the switch memory utilization. At this point, $r1$'s SDN middleware again starts to receive only a single copy of each packet but through unicast destination. Now, SDMC instructs $r1$ to stop listening on multicast ID M_i altogether. In this way, $r1$ is toggled from multicast to unicast to reduce the switch memory utilization.

In the same way, when a link utilization crosses threshold limit, SDMC reduces link utilization (Lines 8–13 in Algorithm 3) as follows. First, SDMC updates the multicast routing tree for multicast ID of $r1$ (M^i) inside the SDN routers by adding flow entries that allow $r1$ to be reached by all the senders of M^i. Then, SDMC instructs the receiver to listen on multicast ID M^i along with its own unicast ID (U_{r1}). At this point, the SDN middleware of $r1$ starts receiving duplicate packets: one each from unicast and multicast destination. SDMC, however, instructs the middleware of $r1$ to discard the duplicate packets. Hence, the application level receiver ($r1$) receives only a single copy of each packet. Then, SDMC updates the translation rule in the SDN middleware of all the senders by removing in its mapping the unicast address of the $r1$, e.g., $M^e \leftrightarrow (M^i, U_{r1}, U_{r2})$ would become $M^e \leftrightarrow (M^i, U_{r2})$. This step reduces the network link utilization as each sender now sends one less copy of each packet. At this point, $r1$'s SDN middleware again starts to receive only a single copy of each packet but through the multicast destination. Now, SDMC instructs $r1$ to stop listening on unicast ID U_{r1} altogether. In this way, $r1$ is switched from unicast to multicast to reduce the network link utilization.

3 EXPERIMENTAL EVALUATION

We evaluated SDMC using an emulated DCN testbed comprising Mininet [14] as the network emulator with OpenFlow virtual switches used for creating different DCN topologies. We implemented SDMC using the Python-based POX SDN controller. For senders and receivers, we developed a representative publish-subscribe application which runs as a SDMC participant (sender or receiver) and is hosted on 200 virtual hosts. We also created up to 500 multicast groups for these participants. We arranged these 200 virtual hosts in four different topologies, viz., Jelly-fish, Tree, Fat-tree and Random, which are the most used network topologies in DCNs. We argue that these topologies have diverse dissemination paths that highlight the advantages of SDMC. We evaluate SDMC in terms of initial setup latency, network overhead, switch-memory utilization, and packet loss and compare it against traditional IP multicast.[2]

3.1 Average Initialization Setup Time

Multicast service mode needs an initialization setup time to enable receivers to join the group and perform their membership. The initial setup time is measured as the time for processing a receiver's joining-request by the controller. It does not concern actually sending or receiving packets. So the time between some receiver A contacting the controller that it wants to join and the controller replying back with a message of "membership successful" is the initial setup time. In IPMC this time involves updating all sender-to-receiver mcast trees but in SDMC it only involves updating the sender switches. Thus, SDMC's receiver-initiated group membership allows better management of the leaf nodes.

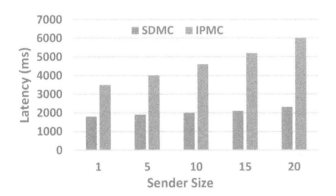

Figure 6: Setup Latency Induced by Increasing Multicast Senders

Figure 6 shows the receiver-initiated setup time in terms of number of senders in the group. For this experiment, the sender would send packets with max UDP size (65K) at some constant rate. The

[2]SDMC is decoupled from IPMC. Moreover, comparing SDMC performance with other multicast protocols is part of future work.

transmission rate was same for all the senders (1 Mbps), which was set by the mininet virtual switches and communication was through UDP channel. The figure shows that SDMC incurs less setup latency than IPMC. In particular, in all cases the average initialization latency incurred is at least 50% less than IP multicast. This is due to the fact that SDMC defers creating the routing tree in the controller to a later time. Since the controller has global knowledge of all the joining/leaving nodes, it programs the switches by injecting OpenFlow rules, which allows receivers to join the multicast tree at a later time. This approach is different from traditional IP multicast, which involves IGMP snooping to filter the unwanted multicast packets. These results validate our claims about better latency performance compared to traditional IP multicast.

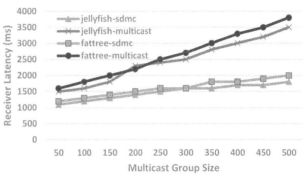

(a) JellyFish and FatTree Topologies

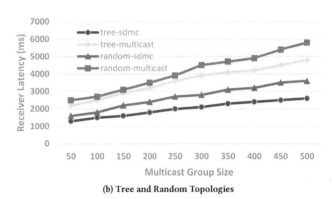

(b) Tree and Random Topologies

Figure 7: Initial Receiver Latency for SDMC and IP Multicast

Additionally, we measured the initialization setup time for different network topologies in DCNs. Figure 7 shows the setup delay for the most common data center network topologies, viz. jellyfish, tree, flat-tree, and random topologies. It shows that SDMC incurs less setup time compared to traditional multicast in all the four DCN topologies. Again, the evaluation results confirm the efficiency of our SDN-enabled multicast compared to traditional IP multicast.

3.2 Adaptiveness to Network Load

To evaluate the awareness and adaptation capabilities of SDMC to router capacity, we performed network load measurements in four of the data center network topologies, i.e., jellyfish, mesh, tree, and random topologies. Figure 8 shows the network load for SDMC and IP multicast. SDMC efficiently switches between unicast and multicast based on network load as described in Algorithm 3. When network load is less, SDMC uses unicast while it switches to multicast when network load increases.

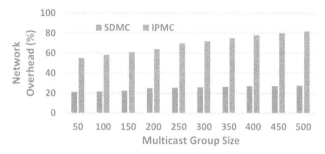

Figure 8: Network Overhead for SDMC and IP Multicast

As seen from Figure 8, SDMC adapts to network load by toggling between unicast and multicast. In particular, SDMC incurs up to 25% network overhead when increasing the number of multicast groups up to 500. Conversely, IP multicast incurs up to 80% of network overhead.

3.3 Adaptiveness to Switch-Memory Utilization

Figure 9 shows the switch memory utilization for IPMC and SDMC to evaluate the effectiveness of our approach in avoiding the switch buffer overflow. SDMC requires 50% less memory utilization as measured in terms of the number of OpenFlow rules that are stored in switch buffers compared to IPMC once the number of multicast groups exceeds size 30. This is due mainly to the fact that OpenFlow rules are injected by the SDN controller only when missing packets or unrecognized packets transit through the switch. Thereafter, the switch will send a request to the controller to install new rules.

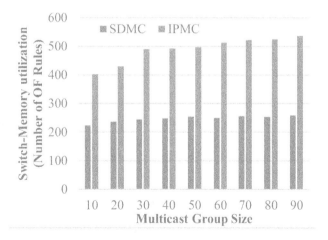

Figure 9: Switch-Memory Utilization for SDMC and IP Multicast

Moreover, as described in Algorithm 3, when the switch memory utilization crosses a threshold limit, i.e. 70% of the available resources as described in Section 2.5.4, SDMC toggles to unicast. This

helps to reduce load on switch memory buffers resulting in less switch buffer overflows. This approach is different from traditional multicast, which performs stateful packet forwarding, because it needs to maintain the same state across all the transit switches. Our results, show that our approach succeeds in improving switch memory utilization compared to IP multicast.

3.4 Evaluating the Packet Loss

We evaluated the packet loss and studied its impact in affecting the network's application behavior. Packet loss can occur when the traffic transmitted to the receivers across a particular link exceeds the capacity of that link. Additionally, another source of packet loss is that short-lived bursts of traffic may occur and deteriorate the network performance for a short time. By characterizing the link utilization through the packet loss we can better investigate the bottlenecks, if any, of our SDN-enabled multicast approach. Note that SDMC ensures that the sender does not send duplicate packets. Hence, during dynamic adaptation, the receiver will not receive any duplicates but can received packets out of order, which we assume will be handled by the application layer since the underlying protocol we use is UDP.

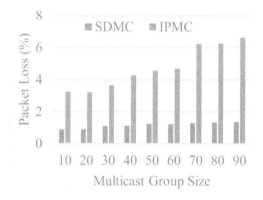

Figure 10: Packet Loss for SDMC and IP Multicast

Figure 10 illustrates the packet loss for the IP multicast and compare it to our approach in SDMC. This figure shows that our approach presents a less than 2% of packet loss, which is better than the traditional multicast that experiences more than 6% of packet loss, when the number of multicast groups exceeds size 70. These results demonstrate that our SDN-enabled multicast performs better data transmission compared to IP multicast.

4 RELATED WORK

This section describes related work on resource management solutions for group communications in data center networks and compares it to the SDMC solution.

4.1 Scalable Multicast Routing in DCNs

Due to the many different challenges incurred in deploying group communications in DCNs, scalable multicast routing has been an important topic of research. In [16], Bloom filter-based group management was introduced to compress multicast routing entries by removing computations of distributed routes from multicast routers. Similarly, BUFFALO [33] distributes IP forwarding tables on each router interface and requires one Bloom filter on each router interface. A similar idea was discussed in [6] to encode the multicast tree information into in-packet Bloom filters. Despite the advantages of Bloom filter-based multicast in reducing flow entries, such approaches require installing Bloom filters in each switch port to perform the compression actions. Moreover, in typical high-density Ethernet port routers installed in DCNs, it is difficult to maintain efficient memory utilization since dealing with false positives in the lookup incur additional router overhead.

The Hierarchy-Aware multicast framework [25] relies on Distributed Hash Tables (DHTs) to create multicast forwarding trees for dynamic membership management in overlay DCNs. Nonetheless, DHT-like tree creation pays less attention to the links at the bottom of the tree, which results in suboptimal routing when top-down data forwarding is performed. Dual-structure Multicast (DuSM) [5] classifies multicast groups based on their flow granularity. First, large (i.e., elephant) flows are detected and classified in the same multicast trees to which higher bandwidth is allocated. Then, multicast-to-unicast translation rules are performed for all the other short (i.e., mice) flows. Although such an approach allows control over traffic congestion in DCNs, it is difficult to adopt it in latency-sensitive applications associated with bursty mice traffic, which represent most of the traffic transiting the DCNs.

Recent efforts [17, 18] introduced Reliable Data Center Multicast (RDCM) by exploiting the multi-path diversity available in highly connected DCNs. RDCM creates backup overlays for every multicast routing tree, and switches among them as per network load fluctuations. Similarly, a unified unicast-multicast framework was introduced in the Code-Oriented eXplicit multicast (COXcast) project [10], where a unicast path is created to the underlying routers and then multicast trees are created by encoding the output port bitmap of nodes on the path between the source and destination. Our approach is similar to RDCM and DuSM in that SDMC achieves fault tolerant and network-efficient communication by bypassing initial multicast tree creation and switching to unicast instead. Similar to COXcast that uses both a common identifier and a node-specific key to route packets to multiple receivers, SDMC introduces two-level identifiers to interact with multiple end hosts and routers, respectively.

Unlike these approaches, SDMC moves the multicast management logic from routers to a centralized SDN controller, which holds all the intelligence required to manage multicast groups. The SDN controller leverages high-density links in DCNs to provide a global view of the entire network and installs multicast flow entries in the routers.

4.2 SDN-enabled Multicast in DCNs

Prior research on multicast issues in SDN-enabled group communications exist. For instance, [26] extends IP multicast using OpenFlow for dynamic group management rather than employing the traditional IGMP protocol [7]. The authors introduce a VXLAN [21] controller to perform Ethernet-over-IP encapsulation over a logical "tunnel." Similarly, in [8], the authors introduce IP-over-Labeled Optical Burst Switching (LOBS) network to encapsulate multicast

messages over a Layer 2 tunneling protocol. OpenFlow is used to build and delete multicast trees using a unified SDN control plane.

CastFlow [22] moves IP multicast management to a centralized SDN controller, and IP multicast trees are calculated using OpenFlow. The controller implements the IGMP messaging layer to handle joining/leaving messages when they are received by the first router. Inspired by CastFlow, Software-Defined Multicast (SDM) [29] was introduced to manage live streaming traffic in the ISP's networks. It combines IP multicast functionality with unicast data delivery using OpenFlow to achieve efficient traffic delivery. SMARTFlow [20] uses an OpenFlow controller to calculate multicast trees based on the Spanning Tree algorithm and encapsulates multicast messages in smart grids over Ethernet MAC addresses. The authors in [11] present Scalar-pair Vectors Routing and Forwarding (SVRF), which encodes multicast group addresses into scalar-pair vectors to identify outgoing ports for delivery of unicast and multicast packets.

Using a remote SDN controller to perform multicast management was also introduced in OpenFlow Multicast (OFM) [34]. OFM maintains a multicast rule database to store all flow entries for all routers managed by the controller. OFM holds a state database to store multicast group members and their state information. However, in practice it is hard to forecast all possible flow entries that can match against future arriving multicast group members. The Avalanche Routing Algorithm (AvRA) [9] was introduced to minimize the size of the routing tree. It enables efficient bandwidth management by using a centralized SDN controller to gather topology information in DCNs that do not have traditional IP multicast. Likewise, the authors in [36] propose building multicast trees for video conferencing by using a SDN controller, where source-based multicast trees are constructed for end-to-end packet delivery.

Our approach in SDMC allows managing multicast communications in overlay data center networks using OpenFlow. Compared to CastFlow, SDMC eliminates periodic join/leave messages generated by IGMP. Rather, by using the topology discovery module, the controller keeps track of all joining and leaving nodes in real-time thereby addressing the hardware resource problem. Furthermore, compared to Avalanche, which achieves data rates up to 12% better than IP multicast, in applications deployed in the Portland Fat Tree topology, SDMC demonstrates a more general framework that can address different topologies like tree, random, mesh, and jellyfish. For instance, SDMC's jellyfish topology, which supports more servers than an equal-cost Avalanche fat-tree topology, achieves often up to 60% better average latency. Moreover, Avalanche gets up to 35% reduction, compared to IP multicast, in the number of links that are less than 5% utilized, once the number of multicast groups exceeds 1,000. In contrast, the performance of SDMC is up to 50% better, compared to IP multicast, in the switch memory utilization, once the number of multicast groups exceeds just 50. Additionally, SDMC provides a monitoring module for traffic monitoring and merging trees to detect the switch between unicast and multicast.

5 CONCLUSIONS

This paper presented the design, implementation and evaluation of a SDN-enabled multicast solution called SDMC for autonomous, adaptive and flexible network load-aware and switch memory-efficient group communications in data center networks. SDMC, which is provided as a middleware suite, uses a combination of unicast and software-defined multicast, and dynamically switches between them while ensuring that end applications remain agnostic to the adaptation yet provide superior performance over either only unicast or multicast cases, which ultimately improves the utility of the clouds. Experimental evaluation of our solution shows that SDMC performs up to 50% better compared to IP multicast alone in terms of network load-awareness, and switch-memory utilization efficiency, and up to 60% better for latency performance. SDMC is available in open source at **https://github.com/prithviraj6116/sdmc**.

Presently, SDMC makes adaptation decisions considering only one criteria at a time, i.e., utilization of network link or switch memory, and does not handle potential oscillations in the adaptation. Our future work will focus on handling them together with weights assigned to each depending on the needs of the group communication traffic. We will also support distributed SDMC controllers using blockchains, which supports novel consensus algorithms to improve controller coordination, consistency, and reliability for holding persistent data sharing and enabling selective privacy.

ACKNOWLEDGMENTS

This work was funded partially by the Fulbright Visiting Scholars Program and NSF CNS US Ignite 1531079. Any opinions, findings, and conclusions or recommendations expressed in this material are those of the author(s) and do not necessarily reflect the views of NSF, DGA, CNES or the Fulbright program.

REFERENCES

[1] Dmitry Basin, Ken Birman, Idit Keidar, and Ymir Vigfusson. 2010. Sources of Instability in Data Center Multicast. In *Proceedings of the 4th International Workshop on Large Scale Distributed Systems and Middleware (LADIS '10)*. 32–37.
[2] Anton Beloglazov, Jemal Abawajy, and Rajkumar Buyya. 2012. Energy-aware resource allocation heuristics for efficient management of data centers for Cloud computing. *Future Generation Computer Systems* 28, 5 (2012), 755 – 768.
[3] M. Chen, H. Jin, Y. Wen, and V. C. M. Leung. 2013. Enabling technologies for future data center networking: a primer. *IEEE Network* 27, 4 (2013), 8–15.
[4] OpenFlow Consortium et al. [n. d.]. OpenFlow Switch specification v1. 0. ([n. d.]).
[5] W. Cui and C. Qian. 2015. Scalable and Load-Balanced Data Center Multicast. In *2015 IEEE Global Communications Conference (GLOBECOM)*. 1–6.
[6] Z. Guo and Y. Yang. 2015. Exploring Server Redundancy in Nonblocking Multicast Data Center Networks. *IEEE Trans. Comput.* 64, 7 (2015), 1912–1926.
[7] Hugh Holbrook, Storigen Systems, and Brian Haberman. 2015. Using Internet Group Management Protocol Version 3 (IGMPv3) and Multicast Listener Discovery Protocol Version 2 (MLDv2) for Source-Specific Multicast. RFC 4604. (1 Oct. 2015).
[8] Linfeng Hong, Dongxu Zhang, Hongxiang Guo, Xiaobin Hong, and Jian Wu. 2013. OpenFlow-based multicast in IP-over-LOBS networks: A proof-of-concept demonstration. In *2012 17th Opto-Electronics and Communications Conference*.
[9] A. Iyer, P. Kumar, and V. Mann. 2014. Avalanche: Data center Multicast using software defined networking. In *2014 Sixth International Conference on Communication Systems and Networks (COMSNETS)*. 1–8.
[10] W. K. Jia. 2014. A Scalable Multicast Source Routing Architecture for Data Center Networks. *IEEE Journal on Selected Areas in Communications* 32, 1 (January 2014), 116–123.
[11] W. K. Jia and L. C. Wang. 2013. A Unified Unicast and Multicast Routing and Forwarding Algorithm for Software-Defined Datacenter Networks. *IEEE Journal on Selected Areas in Communications* 31, 12 (2013), 2646–2657.
[12] M. A. Khoshkholghi, M. N. Derahman, A. Abdullah, S. Subramaniam, and M. Othman. 2017. Energy-Efficient Algorithms for Dynamic Virtual Machine Consolidation in Cloud Data Centers. *IEEE Access* 5 (2017), 10709–10722.
[13] D. Kreutz, F.M.V. Ramos, P. Esteves Verissimo, C. Esteve Rothenberg, S. Azodolmolky, and S. Uhlig. 2015. Software-Defined Networking: A Comprehensive Survey. *Proc. IEEE* 103, 1 (2015), 14–76.
[14] Bob Lantz, Brandon Heller, and Nick McKeown. 2010. A network in a laptop: rapid prototyping for software-defined networks. In *Proceedings of the 9th ACM SIGCOMM Workshop on Hot Topics in Networks*. ACM, 19.

[15] Dan Li, Henggang Cui, Yan Hu, Yong Xia, and Xin Wang. 2011. Scalable data center multicast using multi-class bloom filter. In *Network Protocols (ICNP), 2011 19th IEEE International Conference on*. IEEE, 266–275.
[16] D. Li, Y. Li, J. Wu, S. Su, and J. Yu. 2012. ESM: Efficient and Scalable Data Center Multicast Routing. *IEEE/ACM Transactions on Networking* 20, 3 (June 2012), 944–955.
[17] D. Li, M. Xu, Y. Liu, X. Xie, Y. Cui, J. Wang, and G. Chen. 2014. Reliable Multicast in Data Center Networks. *IEEE Trans. Comput.* 63, 8 (Aug 2014), 2011–2024.
[18] Dan Li, Mingwei Xu, Ming-chen Zhao, Chuanxiong Guo, Yongguang Zhang, and Min-you Wu. 2011. RDCM: Reliable data center multicast. In *INFOCOM, 2011 Proceedings IEEE*. IEEE, 56–60.
[19] Xiaozhou Li and Michael J. Freedman. 2013. Scaling IP Multicast on Datacenter Topologies. In *Proceedings of the Ninth ACM Conference on Emerging Networking Experiments and Technologies (CoNEXT '13)*. 61–72.
[20] Yona Lopes, Natalia C. Fernandes, Carlos A. M. Bastos, and Débora C. Muchaluat-Saade. 2015. SMARTFlow: A Solution for Autonomic Management and Control of Communication Networks for Smart Grids. In *Proceedings of the 30th Annual ACM Symposium on Applied Computing*.
[21] Mallik Mahalingam, T. Sridhar, Mike Bursell, Lawrence Kreeger, Chris Wright, Kenneth Duda, Puneet Agarwal, and Dinesh Dutt. 2015. Virtual eXtensible Local Area Network (VXLAN): A Framework for Overlaying Virtualized Layer 2 Networks over Layer 3 Networks. RFC 7348. (14 Oct. 2015).
[22] Cesar AC Marcondes, Tiago PC Santos, Arthur P Godoy, Caio C Viel, and Cesar AC Teixeira. 2012. CastFlow: Clean-slate multicast approach using in-advance path processing in programmable networks. In *Computers and Communications (ISCC), 2012 IEEE Symposium on*. IEEE, 000094–000101.
[23] Mike McBride. 2013. *Multicast in the Data Center Overview*. Internet-Draft draft-ietf-mboned-dc-deploy-01. Internet Engineering Task Force. https://datatracker.ietf.org/doc/html/draft-ietf-mboned-dc-deploy-01 Work in Progress.
[24] Nick McKeown, Tom Anderson, Hari Balakrishnan, Guru Parulkar, Larry Peterson, Jennifer Rexford, Scott Shenker, and Jonathan Turner. 2008. OpenFlow: enabling innovation in campus networks. *ACM SIGCOMM Computer Communication Review* 38, 2 (2008), 69–74.
[25] K. Nagaraj, H. Khandelwal, C. Killian, and R. R. Kompella. 2012. Hierarchy-aware distributed overlays in data centers using DC2. In *2012 Fourth International Conference on Communication Systems and Networks (COMSNETS 2012)*. 1–10.
[26] Yukihiro Nakagawa, Kazuki Hyoudou, and Takeshi Shimizu. 2012. A Management Method of IP Multicast in Overlay Networks Using Openflow. In *Proceedings of the First Workshop on Hot Topics in Software Defined Networks*.
[27] P. Pan and T. Nadeau. 2013. *Software-Defined Network (SDN) Problem Statement and Use Cases for Data Center Applications*. Technical Report 00.
[28] N.B. Roy and D. Das. 2015. Application of MultiCast Tree concept to cloud security with optimization algorithm for node search technique. In *Electrical, Electronics, Signals, Communication and Optimization (EESCO), 2015 International Conference on*. 1–6.
[29] Julius Rückert, Jeremias Blendin, and David Hausheer. 2015. Software-Defined Multicast for Over-the-Top and Overlay-based Live Streaming in ISP Networks. *Journal of Network and Systems Management* 23, 2 (2015), 280–308.
[30] K. Sriprasadh, Saicharansrinivasan, O. Pandithurai, and A. Saravanan. 2013. A novel method to secure cloud computing through multicast key management. In *Information Communication and Embedded Systems (ICICES), 2013 International Conference on*. 305–311.
[31] Ymir Vigfusson, Hussam Abu-Libdeh, Mahesh Balakrishnan, Ken Birman, Robert Burgess, Gregory Chockler, Haoyuan Li, and Yoav Tock. 2010. Dr. Multicast: Rx for Data Center Communication Scalability. In *Proceedings of the 5th European Conference on Computer Systems (EuroSys '10)*. 349–362.
[32] Han Wang, Ki Suh Lee, Erluo Li, Chiun Lin Lim, Ao Tang, and Hakim Weatherspoon. 2014. Timing is Everything: Accurate, Minimum Overhead, Available Bandwidth Estimation in High-speed Wired Networks. In *Proceedings of the 2014 Conference on Internet Measurement Conference (IMC '14)*. 407–420.
[33] Minlan Yu, Alex Fabrikant, and Jennifer Rexford. 2009. BUFFALO: Bloom Filter Forwarding Architecture for Large Organizations. In *Proceedings of the 5th International Conference on Emerging Networking Experiments and Technologies (CoNEXT '09)*. 313–324.
[34] Yang Yu, Qin Zhen, Li Xin, and Chen Shanzhi. 2012. OFM: A Novel Multicast Mechanism Based on OpenFlow. *Advances in Information Sciences & Service Sciences* 4, 9 (2012).
[35] S. Q. Zhang, Q. Zhang, H. Bannazadeh, and A. Leon-Garcia. 2015. Routing Algorithms for Network Function Virtualization Enabled Multicast Topology on SDN. *IEEE Transactions on Network and Service Management* 12, 4 (2015), 580–594.
[36] M. Zhao, B. Jia, M. Wu, H. Yu, and Y. Xu. 2014. Software defined network-enabled multicast for multi-party video conferencing systems. In *2014 IEEE International Conference on Communications (ICC)*. 1729–1735.
[37] Wenbing Zhao, P.M. Melliar-Smith, and L.E. Moser. 2010. Fault Tolerance Middleware for Cloud Computing. In *Cloud Computing (CLOUD), 2010 IEEE 3rd International Conference on*. 67–74.

Proactive Re-replication Strategy in HDFS based Cloud Data Center

Thanda Shwe
Computer Science and Electrical Engineering
Graduate School of Science and Technology
Kumamoto University
2-39-1 Kurokami, Chuo-ku
Kumamoto 860-8555, Japan
thandashwe@gmail.com

Masayoshi Aritsugi
Big Data Science and Technology
Faculty of Advanced Science and Technology
Kumamoto University
2-39-1 Kurokami, Chuo-ku
Kumamoto 860-8555, Japan
aritsugi@cs.kumamoto-u.ac.jp

ABSTRACT

Cloud storage systems use data replication for fault tolerance, data availability and load balancing. In the presence of node failures, data blocks on the failed nodes are re-replicated to other remaining nodes in the system randomly, thus leading to workload imbalance. Balancing all the server workloads namely, re-replication workload and current running user's application workload during the re-replication phase has not been adequately addressed. With a reactive approach, re-replication can be scheduled based on current resource utilization but by the time replication kicks off, actual resource usage may have changed as resources are continuously in use. In this paper, we propose a proactive re-replication strategy that uses predicted CPU utilization, predicted disk utilization, and popularity of the replicas to perform re-replication effectively while ensuring all the server workloads are balanced. We consider both reliability of a data block and performance status of nodes in making decision for re-replication. Simulation results from synthetic workload data demonstrate that all the servers' utilization is balanced and our approach improves performance in terms of re-replication throughput and re-replication time compared to baseline Hadoop Distributed File System (HDFS). Our proactive approach maintains the balance of resource utilization and avoids the occurrence of servers' overload condition during re-replication.

CCS CONCEPTS

• Information systems → Information storage systems; Storage replication; Storage recovery strategies; *Information storage systems*; *Storage architectures*; *Cloud based storage*;

KEYWORDS

Fault tolerance; HDFS; prediction; replication

1 INTRODUCTION

Cloud storage systems such as Google File System (GFS)[12] and Hadoop Distributed File System (HDFS) [21] play a fundamental role in cloud computing architecture to store, process and manage a large amount of data. As they are accommodated on commodity servers that are frequently failed, a traditional way of data replication, i.e., replicating the data three times within the same cluster, is currently being used for fault tolerance, availability, data locality and load balancing purposes. Among the cloud storage systems, HDFS is the most widely used and is open source. By default, HDFS replicates their data on random nodes in different racks with replication factor of three[21].

When a node failure occurs, source and destination data nodes for re-replication are selected in a random manner which can lead to workload imbalance in some of the nodes[26]. In addition, performing re-replication without considering the current running workload can decrease the performance of current running user's application workload in the system. Moreover, the work in [12] demonstrated that it took about 23 minutes to restore the data blocks on the failed node when a single node was failed in a 227 nodes cluster. With concurrent failure of two data nodes, 266 data blocks have only one remaining replica. Although re-replication was triggered with the highest priority for those 266 data blocks, it took 2 minutes to restore the second replica. If another type of data loss incident occurs before the second replica could be restored, data block will be completely lost. Although this must be very rare, re-replication strategy should be considered for any kind of failures.

In view of this, effective re-replication strategy is needed to distribute the data on a failed node to other nodes. It will balance re-replication workload among the nodes based on current workload of the system. The strategy must also need to consider both reliability and performance perspectives.

Other studies [14, 15] demonstrated that random re-replication suffered load imbalance, creating a high load on a small number of nodes and proposed replica reconstruction schemes that mainly focused on balancing the replication jobs among the nodes in the single rack cluster and extended their work for the multi-rack cluster. They considered balancing the re-replication workload but they did not address to balance both re-replication workload and current running workload in the system. The work in [8] introduced the Copyset replication technique under independent failures and correlated failures, showing that the technique could reduce the probability of data loss. Their approach targeted to evaluate the durability of the system but how to restore the lost blocks effectively was not studied. Our previous work in [22] took into consideration both performance and reliability perspectives and schedules re-replication depending on the utilization of resources by current running jobs. This approach had a reactive nature and re-replication was scheduled using current resource utilization. Although source and destination nodes were selected based on resource utilization of current running workload, i.e.,we select low utilization nodes to allocate replicas and schedule to perform re-replication but by the time re-replication kicks off, actual resource usage may change since the resource usage of each node changes frequently in accordance with time. To perform re-replication in proactive aspects effectively, in [23] we investigated feasibility of using prediction methods, namely linear regression and local regression to estimate short time future resource utilization. We observed the prediction accuracy and execution time of two prediction methods and found that prediction with local regression was closer to actual value than linear regression and the execution time difference between the two methods was not significant. Based on this feasibility study of using prediction methods for proactive re-replication, we aim to fill the gap mentioned above.

The main contributions of this work can be summarized as follows:

(a) We propose a proactive re-replication strategy to make the decisions of which data blocks to re-replicate urgently and where to place the data blocks with the goal of balancing both re-replication workload and current user's application workload of the system.

(b) We apply local regression to predict resource utilization to avoid probability of overload condition during re-replication phase.

(c) We develop a priority based replication that walks a fine line between aggressive replication that incurs impact on foreground process and lazy replication that reduces data durability.

(d) We consider from both physical side, i.e., resource utilization status of datanodes, and cyber side, i.e., popularity of data blocks, to perform re-replication.

(e) We extend CloudSim to simulate HDFS environment especially for metadata management and failure handling in case of datanode failure.

This paper proposes a proactive re-replication strategy based on predicted CPU and disk utilization while ensuring all the servers' utilization is balanced. The CPU and disk utilization is estimated by local regression method. We use the historical data values received from each node through heartbeat message to predict CPU and disk utilization and use these utilization information to perform re-replication effectively. A priority grouping scheme is applied to balance the reliability and performance perspectives. The proposed strategy leverage the insight that the average utilization of server in the cluster is under 50 %[2] and the vast of time that the server spent is under 10 % utilization [19] that makes it attractive to pick more data blocks to be replicated in a short time frame. The proposed strategy balances the servers' utilization during re-replication phase. It also increases the re-replication throughput, re-replication time and reduces the probability of overloaded condition.

This paper is organized as follows. Section 2 presents related work. Section 3 describes the proactive re-replication approach based on local regression. Section 4 discusses the evaluation and simulation results of the proposed system and Section 5 describes the conclusion and future work.

2 RELATED WORK

Although there are a large number of researches on replication strategy in cloud data storage systems, little attention has been paid to re-replication. Only two recent works dealt with the specific cases of re-replication in HDFS system.

Higai et al. [14] proposed two replica reconstruction schemes, an optimization scheme and a heuristic scheme that aimed to balance the workloads of replication processes during the re-replication phase. In their proposed schemes, the nodes were arranged in a virtual ring structure and data blocks were transferred based on this one-directional ring structure to minimize the difference of the amount of data transfer of each node. It was demonstrated through several experiments that replica reconstruction throughput of the proposed schemes had significant improvement over the default scheme. However, their work mainly intended to maintain the replica reconstruction workload balance among the nodes and did not address the impact and status of current running jobs in the system.

They extended their work for multiple racks cluster [15]. In their proposed scheme, data transfer in a rack was performed based on the one-directional ring structure and inter-rack data transfer was carried out in a round robin manner. The source and destination data nodes were selected to balance the load of each data node with respect to data transfer during re-replication. Although re-replication jobs were scheduled by controlling the number of streams between racks and giving priority for the blocks based on consideration of the loads of networks and fault tolerance, number of streams (dfs.namenode. replication. max-streams) could not be changed dynamically depending on the intra-rack and inter-rack number of blocks that were needed to be replicated. In addition, although their work focused on balancing the load of re-replication jobs, the impact on the foreground process was rarely considered. Our approach differs from the previous two techniques in a way that our strategy allocates the data blocks with the goal of balancing re-replication workload among the nodes based on current workload of the system. In addition, we make priority groups based on popularity of the particular data block and number of remaining replicas in the system while balancing the reliability and performance of the system.

In terms of proactive replication, a few studies have been published. The works in [1, 4, 16] focused to predict the future file demand and increase replication factor mainly for data availability and performance issues. Bui et al. [4] proposed adaptive replication management system to provide data availability by enhancing the data locality metric, thus resulting in performance improvement of Hadoop system. They applied supervised machine learning approach to predict potential access of files, adjust the replication factor and allocate the replicas. Ananthanarayanan et al.[1] proposed Scarlett that used historical file usage statistics to predict the popularity of the replicas and adjust the replication factor within storage budget, not to create too many replicas that waste both storage and network bandwidth. Kousiouris et al. [16] studied multiple time step ahead prediction of files based on fourier series analysis and used prediction result to determine replication factor that balanced the increasement in availability and disk usage. Another type of proactive replication is to create replicas periodically at the fixed low rate based on the failure prediction of the nodes [11, 24]. Duminuco et al.[11]proposed to predict the failure behavior using a model that consisted of network of queues and adjusted the repair rate of data blocks based on changes in the statistical properties of failures, thus maximizing the smoothness of the bandwidth needed for the repairs. Sit et al.[24] studied a proactive approach that created additional replicas periodically at a fixed low rate under bandwidth budget specified by the operator. But these works are mostly found in peer to peer environment. Our approach is proactive in the sense that reactive re-replication approach lacks the ability to foresee the possible resource utilization of the nodes and schedule to allocate the large number of replicas on the current low utilization nodes. However, selected node is not a low utilization node any more at the time of actual re-replication because the resource usage of each node changes frequently in accordance with time.

Wu et al.[27] proposed Intelligent Data Outsourcing(IDO) that proactively identified the popular data and migrated them to a different set of RAID in advance by predicting occurrence of background tasks such as RAID reconstruction, RAID re-synchronize, disk scrubbing, and RAID reshape. Their research work showed that user tasks could be executed effectively and background tasks could be accelerated, thus improving the reliability and performance of the system. Based on inspiration of their previous work, they proposed PP(Popularity-based Proactive Data Recovery)[28]for data recovery process in the context of HDFS RAID environment. In their work, popular data were identified and maintained in the normal operation state and in case of node failure, they were recovered firstly in order to serve the user requests quickly without waiting time. They proved that data recovery time and execution time could be reduced. The main concepts of these two studies were identification of popular data and migration or recovery of data proactively but balancing the server utilization while performing data recovery and migration was not addressed.

Cidon et al.[8] studied the probability of data loss when 1% of the nodes were concurrently failed and demonstrated that random replication scheme almost guaranteed to lose data. They presented that Copyset replication significantly reduced the frequency of data loss events. They also proposed tiered replication [7] by dividing the cluster into primary and backup tiers and observed the probability of data loss under independent and correlated node failures by allocating the first two replicas on the primary tier and the third replica on the backup tier. Their approach targeted to evaluate the durability of the system but the aspect of restoring the lost blocks effectively was not studied.

3 PROACTIVE RE-REPLICATION STRATEGY

3.1 HDFS Revisted

HDFS is a distributed file system that is designed for storing and processing of very large files, running on clusters of commodity hardware where component failures are common. A node in the

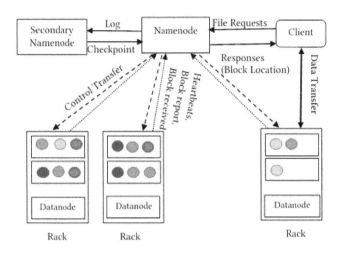

Figure 1: HDFS Architecture.

HDFS cluster consists of both computing units and directly attached storage disks. An HDFS cluster has two types of node operating in a master-worker pattern: a namenode (master) and a number of datanodes (workers)[26]. Figure 1 shows the architecture of HDFS.

The namenode coordinates with datanodes for storing, retrieving and managing of files. It also maintains metadata for all the files in the system, such as files and blocks namespaces, file to blocks mapping, location of the blocks and keeps them on its main memory for fast random access. The namenode does not keep the persistent record of the location of data blocks but collects the blocks location from data nodes at system startup and updates information through heartbeat message. Files and blocks namespaces and files to blocks mapping are logged in secondary namenode in order to restore namenode state in case of failure but locations of the blocks are not logged and the locations are sent from datanode periodically through heartbeat message. Although metadata operation is performed by namenode, data transfer does not flow through namenode[26].

Datanodes are responsible to store and retrieve blocks as files of their local file system and communicate to the namenode periodically. They send heartbeat message at every three seconds to indicate that they are alive and to inform the namenode about their load and free space. Datanodes report list of blocks that they are managing at every hour by default and also send the newly received block when they receives a new block.

HDFS divides the data file into sequence of blocks with default block size of 64MB or the client can define size of the data block (64MB or 128 MB) for each file; all blocks in a file except the last block are the same size. As HDFS clusters are built on less reliable commodity hardware, replicating data blocks can provide fault tolerance. In addition, another reason for replicating data blocks is data locality that can access to the data block with better proximity to the node where computation is performed, thus can reduce the network cost across racks and the default replication factor in HDFS is three. The default replication factor can be changed for the whole system or for a single data file. In a cluster, small number of nodes are grouped together and installed in a rack using one network switch. There may be several number of racks depending on the size of cluster or data center. HDFS's rack aware replica placement policy allocates the primary replica on one node in the local rack. The second replica is placed on a node in a different remote rack. The third replica is placed on a different node in the same remote rack. The goal of rack aware replica placement policy is to improve data reliability, availability and network bandwidth utilization[26].

Since HDFS is built on commodity hardware, one of the main goals of HDFS is to detect failure and automatic recovery of data blocks. The namenode checks the status of nodes at periodic interval through heartbeat message. When the namenode detects a node failure, lost replicas are restored to other live nodes according to their defined replication factor. HDFS configuration parameters, such as dfs.namenode.replication.work.multiplier.per.iteration and dfs.namenode.replication.max-streams can be adjusted depending on how much we want to speed up the re-replication process.

3.2 Proposed Strategy Overview

In this section, we propose a proactive re-replication strategy based on local regression. The re-replication scheduling is performed by namenode by the following two components. The datanodes measure and send the CPU and disk utilization information to the namenode through heartbeat message at periodic interval. The overview of system architecture is shown in Fig. 2.

(a) Prediction Module: This module has two sub-components: the monitor and the predictor. The monitor gathers and stores CPU and disk utilization from all the datanodes through heartbeat message. It provides collected past utilization data to the predictor. The predictor is responsible for estimating CPU utilization and disk utilization for the next interval based on the usage history. It uses local regression based resource utilization prediction technique to forecast the future CPU and disk utilization for each node. This prediction module will be presented in Section 3.3.

(b) Replica Management Module: Data blocks on the failed node are grouped with priority according to the number of replicas remaining and popularity of the replica in order to schedule re-replication that walks a fine line between aggressive re-replication and delay re-replication. Replicas' priority grouping methodology will be explained in Section 3.4. Replication scheduler decides how many replicas will be allocated to which node by using prediction results of utilization information and set the re-replication schedule according to the priority group. The detailed re-replication strategy will be discussed in Section 3.5.

3.3 CPU and Disk Utilization Prediction based on Local Regression

The appropriate nodes for re-replication are selected based on the system resource utilization information. If we collect resource utilization information rightly after a node failure occurs, it may take time to collect resource utilization information of all the nodes in the system. Although we select the appropriate node for re-replication, at the time of actual re-replication, that node is not a low utilization node any more at the time of actual re-replication

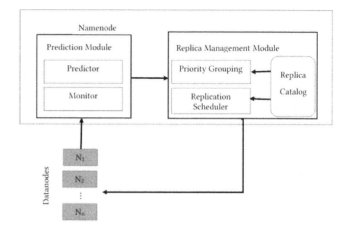

Figure 2: Overview of proactive replication strategy.

because the resource usage of each node changes frequently in accordance with time. Thus, if we can predict resource utilization for short time, re-replication scheduling decision could be enhanced with predictive aspect.

We considered linear regression[20] and local regression[9] to predict resource utilization based on historical resource usage information. This information can be obtained from the heartbeat message. Based on our initial evaluation of choosing the suitable prediction methods for resource usage estimation as in [23], we observed that the prediction with local regression was closer to actual value than linear regression. Although the average execution time of linear regression was slightly faster than local regression method, the execution time difference between the two methods was not significant. Thus, we used local regression to predict CPU and disk utilization.

Each node measures and sends the current CPU and disk utilization to the namenode through heartbeat message. When the namenode detects the node failure in the system, it uses current CPU and disk utilization along with historical values to predict future resource utilization based on local regression. Local regression divides utilization data into localized subsets and assigns neighborhood weight value using the tricube weight function. Having information about the current resource utilization and the future resource utilization can help the replication scheduler to make more informed decisions that will balance the server utilization during the re-replication phase and can avoid the occurrence of overload condition.

3.4 Replicas' Priority Grouping

To perform re-replication, statically, we can adjust HDFS configuration parameters depending on how much we want to speed up the re-replication process. However, if the system is busy with foreground jobs, aggressive re-replication can decrease their performance. On the other hand, delay scheduling of re-replication may have high probability of data loss.

In addition, we consider to avoid creating load imbalance as much as possible on the remaining live servers in the presence of failures which may have severe performance impact. To see

Table 1: Replicas' Priority Grouping

Group Name	Data Popularity	No.of.Replicas Left
G1	√	1
G2	×	1
G3	√	2
G4	×	2

the point clearly, a scenario is considered where data block-B is stored in nodes N1, N2, and N3 with HDFS default replication policy. Assume that, data block-B is popular and will be accessed by 300 clients simultaneously and access to block-B can be sent to the primary data or second or third replicas for load balancing or the nearest replica may be chosen to avoid the overhead of remote data access. Nodes N1, N2 and N3 serve 100 requests each. In the presence of node-N1 failure, all the requests that have to be served by N1 will be directed to nodes N2 and N3. Nodes N2 and N3 will be overloaded if we cannot restore the lost copy of the data block-B as quickly as possible. Thus, quick restoration of popular block is important and we consider this issue in our re-replication strategy. Moreover, research works[27, 28] proved that recovering popular data first could reduce recovery time and execution time so that future access to popular data could be served effectively.

Based on the assumption that the popular files in the past will be accessed more than the others in the future due to temporal locality, a popular file is determined by analyzing the number of accesses to the data file from users. We adopt the approach in [25] to define the threshold value to decide whether a data block is popular or not. The average number of accesses $\overline{NOA}$ is used as the threshold. $\overline{NOA}$ can be calculated as $\overline{NOA} = \frac{1}{|H|} \sum_{h \in H} NOA(h)$, where $|H|$ is the number of records in H that is the access history table, and each record h in H indicates the number of accesses $NOA(h)$ for data block h.

In view of this, our proposed system takes into consideration both reliability of data and performance degradation of the foreground jobs and proposes to schedule re-replication based on different priority groups. Priority is defined based on the number of current replicas available in the system and popularity of the replicas. As in Table 1, the data blocks that need to be re-replicated are grouped into four priority groups: Group 1 is for blocks which are popular and only one replica remains in the system. Group 2 is for blocks which are unpopular and one replica remains in the system. Then Group 3 is for blocks which are popular and two replicas remain in the system. And the last group, Group 4 is for blocks which are unpopular and two replicas remain in the system.

3.5 Re-replication Heuristics Scheme

Algorithm 1 describes the pseudo code of our proactive re-replication strategy.Firstly, we record the lost data blocks in failed node as replicaList and record the list of datanodes with its predicted CPU and disk utilization as nodeList. Then, we divide the replicas that need to be re-replicated into four priority groups based on popularity of the replicas and number of remaining replicas as we discussed in Section 3.4. For the blocks in each priority group, equal number of blocks are set in each node as initial value by dividing the number

of blocks in particular priority group by the number of nodes in the system. Then, migrating value for each node is calculated by using predicted CPU utilization, predicted disk utilization and the number of blocks assigned to that node. The weight value used in calculating migrating value is relative importance value of CPU and disk utilization. Then maximum and minimum migrating values are found among the nodes and the difference between maximum migrating value and minimum migrating value are calculated. The number of blocks that will be assigned to each node is adjusted by the iteration based on the difference in migrating value. This process continues until the difference in migrating value is less than 1 that means that the number of blocks can not be adjusted any more based on the migrating values of the nodes. At the end of this iteration, the number of blocks that will be assigned to each node is achieved for one priority group and then schedule re-replication with number of blocks assigned to each node. This process[line:3-17] is repeated for the remaining priority groups.

Algorithm 1: Proactive Re-replication Strategy

Require: replicaList: data blocks that are stored in failed node
Require: nodeList: datanodes with its predicted CPU and disk utilization

1 Divide replicaList into four priority groups;
2 **for** *each priority group in replicas' priority group* **do**
3   **for** *replica in each priority group* **do**
4   Assign equal number of replicas in each node
5   **end**
6   **while** $Diff < 1$ **do**
7   **for** *each node in nodeList* **do**
8   Calculate MigratingValue;
            /* *MigratingValue = weightValue * predictedCPU + weightValue * predictedDisk + numberofassignedblocks* */
9   **end**
10   Find max and min MigratingValues;
11     $Diff = max.MigratingValue - min.MigratingValue$;
12   **if** $Diff > 1$ **then**
13   Add one replica to node of min.MigratingValue;
14   Remove one replica from node of max.MigratingValue;
15   **end**
16   **end**
17   Schedule re-replication with number of blocks assigned to each node;
18 **end**

3.6 Discussion

As the proposed system takes into account that the cyber feature of data blocks, the namenode needs to maintain the access history of every data block in order to determine whether the data block is popular or not. In addition, the namenode has to store the resource utilization information to predict the future resource utilization. Thus, the extra space for managing these meta-data is needed for the proposed system. We also argue that we predict the CPU and disk utilization of every node in the system, then we use these predicted utilization information in order to select the appropriate nodes for re-replication. Thus, accuracy of prediction can have influence on the system. As the proposed system utilized the fact that the average utilization of servers in the cluster is under 50%[2, 19], it is capable of higher throughput and quick re-replication. We recognize that if the cluster is fully utilized, it may have impact on the performance of current running jobs in the system. We plan to consider this issue in the future work.

4 EVALUATION

4.1 Simulation Setup

We used CloudSim [5] as the simulation environment to evaluate our proposed system. CloudSim is a discrete event simulator that supports modeling and simulation of cloud system components such as data centers, hosts, CPU components, RAM, storage, VMs, and provisioning policies as well as power aware simulation and internal network topology. Due to its extensibility, it can be easily customized and modified by extending the class, with a few changes to the core component of the CloudSim.

Although CloudSim provides fundamental components to simulate cloud data storage, such as hard drives, SAN storage and files, it has limitations for disk I/O processing. CloudSimEx [13] extends modeling disk I/O processing alongside with CPU processing for jobs and integrates the modules for disk I/O processing in the CloudSim simulator. We have extended some native class of CloudSimEx to simulate our proposed strategy.

Moreover, in order to simulate the HDFS environment, such as metadata management on the namenode and heartbeat mechanism for failure node detection, we have extended a module for proactive re-replication in CloudSim simulator. The work in [10] designed a simulator to simulate the HDFS environment as close as possible to the original system. Both CloudSim and that simulator are event based and language of implementation is java. Thus, we extracted some of the functions from that simulator and integrated into CloudSim with little adaption. The list of main classes implemented for replica management is as follows:

(a) Heartbeat: This entity represents the heartbeat mechanism in the HDFS that sends the signal to the namenode in a periodic time interval to inform the node status and resource utilization information. This class needs to be initialized like any other CloudSim entities before starting the simulation.

(b) Replication Scheduler: This entity accesses the replica catalog and performs re-replication when there is a node failure. In the actual system, maintaining metadata and handling of replication scheduling is performed by the namenode. Replication scheduler is a separate entity and is not deployed within a node.

(c) Replica Catalog: This is made for storing the current location of blocks that are stored in different data nodes. It also maintains access history of the data blocks that will be used to determine the popularity of the blocks.

(d) Fault Injector: This entity is responsible for inserting failure at random time. It will generate an event and inject fault

Table 2: Simulation Parameters

Parameter	Value
Total Data	75000*64MB
Nodes/rack	8
No.of.Racks	5
Replication Factor	3
Disk/Ram/CPU Capacity	CPU=2660
	(MIPS= HP ProLiant ML110 G5 server)
	RAM=4G
	Disk=1T
Network	1Gbps

into the system to simulate a failure. The host selection process is performed randomly at every time when a fault is inserted.

In order to achieve a realistic simulated environment, the detailed simulation configurations were set as shown in Table 2. We run the simulation for 24-hour period. A cluster with 40 data nodes that are assigned in five different racks was created in the simulation environment. For simplicity and ease of evaluation, at the beginning of the simulation, blocks were equally distributed on nodes in the cluster. It is assumed that one data block is the replication element and it also represents one data file.

We used the web application workload [18] that represents resource demand of web application in the context of cloud environments. In this work, as distributions and parameters that represent the workload patterns are presented, we used the information to model resource utilization of a single session that makes up the workload. We applied poisson distribution for session arrival based on arrival pattern of a small web site that is described in [13]. In addition, in order to model realistic simulations, Zipf distribution was used to mimic the file access pattern[3]. We applied exponential distribution to determine failure's insertion time to the system. Recent researches [6] measured the failure percentage of the cluster and showed the failure percentage was about 0.5% to 1 % and we therefore simulated 1% of node failures in the system. In all experiments, we compared our proactive re-replication strategy with baseline HDFS. Thus, firstly, we implemented the default baseline HDFS re-replication policy in order to simulate in CloudSim environment with the following configuration parameters:

(a) Default replication factor and rack aware policy.

(b) The selection of nodes to re-replicate was chosen randomly.

(c) The configuration parameter to control speed of re-replication, dfs.namenode.replication.work.multiplier.per.iteration, was set to its default value, 2. It means that the number of blocks that will be re-replicated at every scheduling interval is 2* number of nodes in the system.

4.2 Results

To observe the impact of our proactive re-replication strategy, we have measured the CPU and disk utilization of each node in the system for both our proposed strategy and baseline HDFS. Our approach provides load balance during the re-replication stage.

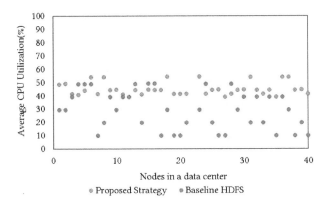

Figure 3: Average CPU utilization during re-replication stage.

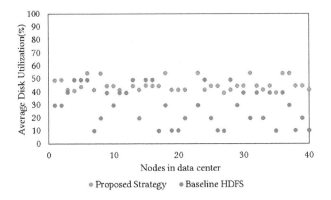

Figure 4: Average Disk utilization during re-replication stage.

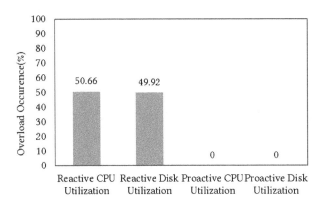

Figure 5: Occurrence of overload condition.

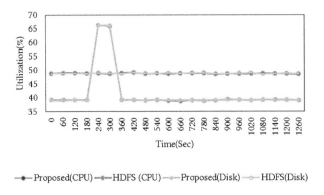

Figure 6: Workload during re-replication.

Figs. 3 and 4 show the CPU and disk utilization of each node in the cluster, respectively. We observe that although proposed strategy utilized higher percentage of resource than baseline HDFS, it can balance the CPU and disk utilization of all nodes in the cluster during the re-replication stage. Re-replication with baseline HDFS occurs high CPU and disk utilization in some of the nodes and some other nodes are underutilized.

Fig. 5 shows probability for the occurrence of overload condition of nodes. The goal of this evaluation is to demonstrate the effect of using proactive re-replication. Our evaluation does not evaluate over utilization or underutilization of a node through the whole simulation time because we just consider the re-replication stage. Since the resource usage of each node changes frequently in accordance with time, we investigate how the proactive re-replication avoids the occurrence of overload condition at the time of actual re-replication. When a node has higher utilization at the time of actual re-replication than at the time of scheduling, we count it as overload condition. We get the probability by dividing the number of overload conditions by the total number of repaired blocks. We compare proactive re-replication to reactive re-replication which

is not predicted CPU and disk utilization and used previous utilization information for re-replication scheduling. Fig.5 shows that proactive approach can reduce the occurrence of CPU and disk over utilization to 0.

To find out how the re-replication impacts the system, we chose a random node and examined the resource utilization during the re-replication phase as shown in Fig.6. The proposed strategy performed re-replication between the time frame 0 and 540 while the baseline HDFS performed between the time frame 0 and 1260. During the re-replication phase, proposed strategy consumed higher percentage of resource than baseline HDFS in the short time frame. This is because we utilized the fact that the utilization of each node in cluster is between 10%-50% [2] and schedule more data blocks to re-replicate in the short time frame thus results in increasing the MTTR and re-replication throughput, leads to consequently increases the reliability and performance of the system. But if the utilization of the servers in the system is too high, it may have impact on the performance of current running jobs in the system.

We investigate the number of blocks that are received by each node in the cluster during the re-replication phase for both re-replication strategies. The re-replication with baseline HDFS allocate large number of blocks on some small number of nodes that could lead to load imbalance in the system. As we can see in Fig.7,

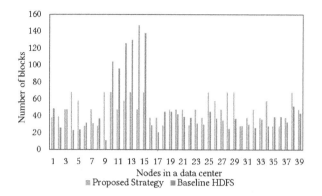

Figure 7: Number of blocks received by each node.

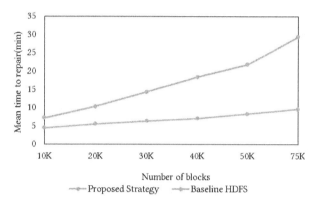

Figure 8: MTTR for different number of blocks.

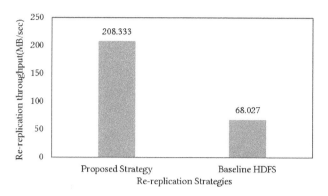

Figure 9: Re-replication throughput.

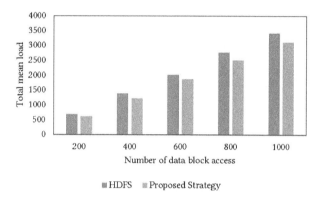

Figure 10: Mean load with varying number of block accesses.

our proposed strategy can balance the total number of blocks received by each node and it also took into consideration the resource utilization of current running jobs in the system.

In Fig. 8, we examine the mean time to repair with varying the number of blocks. In this figure, to find out the effect of mean time to repair with increasing the number of blocks, we set the number of blocks to 10K, 20K, 30K, 40K, 50K and 75K. Regardless of the number of blocks, our proposed strategy reduces more mean time to repair than baseline HDFS.

Fig.9 represents the comparison of re-replication throughput of our proposed scheme with the baseline HDFS. In our proactive re-replication strategy, we try to balance the re-replication jobs with consideration of current running jobs in the system and apply the priority grouping scheme to balance between aggressive re-replication and delay re-replication. According to this, our proposed strategy achieves higher re-replication throughput with less performance impact on the foreground jobs.

In order to observe the effectiveness of priority grouping scheme, we define mean load of data block as an evaluation metric and its computation is based on the work in [17], where load of file was defined by combining two file characteristics, namely access rate and service time as a joint metric. The metric in our evaluation is defined as mean load which will be shared by the number of

replicas for each data block as follows:

$$mean\ load = \frac{access\ rate * service\ time}{no.of\ .replicas}$$

where service time is the combination of seek time, rotational delay and transfer time,and access rate is the rate of requests to the data block. We assume that service time of the block access is fixed as all the blocks are same size and all disks have same performance characteristics.

In this experiment, we assigned varying number of block accesses to 200, 400, 600, 800 and 1000 before both the proposed scheme and baseline HDFS finish restoring replicas. These blocks were accessed at random time and block access rate follow Zipf distribution. In our work, we simply set the service time to access 64 MB block to 15 ms because transfer rate and disk performance parameters vary among disks. We run the simulation for ten times and take the average. It should be noted that lower value of mean load means block access load can be shared on more replicas which increases the concurrent access to the data block. In Fig.10, we can see that our proposed strategy has lower value of mean load than baseline HDFS because our proposed strategy gives priority to restore popular blocks as fast as possible. Thus, block access load can be shared on three replicas while block access load on baseline HDFS will be shared on two replicas before re-replication finish.

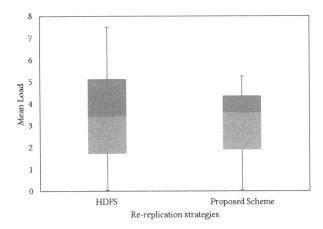

Figure 11: Mean load distribution.

Fig.11 shows the distribution range for mean load. We took the mean load data with 1000 block access for ten times of simulation. Thus, the number of mean load data to draw the box plot is 10000. In this figure, we can see that the median value for both re-replication strategies are approximately around 3.5. The mean value for proposed scheme is 3.11 and 3.48 for baseline HDFS.The third quartile for proposed strategy is 4.35 and 5.13 for HDFS. As 75% of mean load distribution of proposed strategy falls under 4.35 and the maximum value for HDFS is also higher than proposed strategy, our proposed strategy demonstrates that block access load for popular replicas can be shared on more replicas, thus consequently improving concurrent access to the data block and can increase performance of the system.

5 CONCLUSION

We presented the proactive re-replication strategy that exploited local regression to predict future CPU and disk utilization. This approach was proactive in the sense that re-replication was performed on the predicted resource utilization as resource usage of the nodes changed frequently with time. We applied replicas' priority grouping to balance the reliability and performance perspectives. Using such techniques, CPU and disk utilization during the re-replication stage was balanced and the probability of occurrence of over load condition was prevented. Consequently, the proposed strategy achieved servers' utilization balance, high re-replication throughput and mean time to repair than baseline HDFS.

We plan to extend our strategy by exploring several research directions. First, we will investigate the possibilities of adjusting to schedule re-replication based on average utilization of the whole cluster and its changes from time to time in order to reduce impacts to user application jobs under high utilization condition. Second,we will consider other workloads including data analytic workload which have high CPU and disk utilization to explore the range of applicability of proposed strategy. Third, we will consider incorporating our proposed strategy into current existing re-replication mechanism of HDFS and evaluating the effectiveness of the strategy on real test bed. Fourth, in order to predict CPU and disk utilization for complex workload patterns with high prediction accuracy, we will investigate applying prediction methods that can give high prediction accuracy and their overhead on the system. Finally, we will consider thermal balancing of the servers during re-replication stage to save energy consumption of the cluster.

REFERENCES

[1] G. Ananthanarayanan, S. Agarwal, S. Kandula, A. Greenberg, I. Stoica, D. Harlan, and E. Harris. 2011. Scarlett: Coping with skewed content popularity in MapReduce clusters. In *Proceedings of the Sixth Conference on Computer systems.* https://doi.org/10.1145/1966445.1966472

[2] L.A. Barroso and U. Holzle. 2007. The case for energy-propotional computing. *Computer* 40, 12 (2007). https://doi.org/10.1109/MC.2007.443

[3] L. Breslau, P. Cao, L. Fan, G. Phillips, and S. Shenker. 1999. Web caching and zipf-like distributions: evidence and implications. In *Proceedings of the 18th Annual Joint Conference of the IEEE Computer and Communications Societies.* https://doi.org/10.1109/INFCOM.1999.749260

[4] D.-M. Bui, S. Hussain, E.-N. Huh, and S. Lee. 2016. Adaptive replication management in HDFS based on supervised learning. *IEEE Transcations on Knowledge and Data Engineering* 28, 6 (2016). https://doi.org/10.1109/TKDE.2016.2523510

[5] R.N. Calheiros, R. Ranjan, A. Beloglazov, C.A.F.D. Rose, and R. Buyya. 2011. CloudSim: A toolkit for modeling and simulation of cloud computing environments and evaluation of resource provisioning algorithms. *Software-Practice and Experience* 41, 1 (2011). https://doi.org/10.1002/spe.995

[6] R.J. Chansler. 2012. Data availability and durability with the Hadoop distributed file system. *The USENIX Magazine* 37 (2012).

[7] A. Cidon, R. Escriva, S. Katti, M. Rosenblum, and E.G. Sirer. 2015. Tiered replication: a cost-effective alternative to full cluster geo-replication. In *Proceedings of the 2015 Usenix Annual Technical Conference.*

[8] A. Cidon, S.M. Rumble, R. Stutsman, S. Katti, J. Ousterhout, and M. Rosenblum. 2013. Copysets:reducing the frequency of data loss in cloud storage. In *Proceedings of the 2013 USENIX Annual Technical Conference.* 37–48.

[9] W.S. Cleveland. 1979. Robust locally weighted regression and smoothing scatter plots. *J. Amer. Statist. Assoc.* 74, 368 (1979). https://doi.org/10.1080/01621459.1979.10481038

[10] C. Debians, P.A.-T. Togores, and F. Karakusoglu. 2012. HDFS Replication Simulator. (2012). Retrieved December 1, 2016 from https://github.com/peteratt/HDFS-Replication-Simulator

[11] A. Duminuco, E. Biersack, and T. En-Najjary. 2007. Proactive replication in distributed storage systems using machine availability estimation. In *Proceedings of the International Conference on Emerging Networking Experiments and Technologies.* https://doi.org/10.1145/1364654.1364689

[12] S. Ghemawat, H. Gobioff, and S.-T. Leung. 2003. The Google file system. In *Proceedings of the 19th ACM Symposim on Operating Systems Principles.* https://doi.org/10.1145/945445.945450

[13] N. Grozev and R. Buyya. 2015. Performance modelling and simulation of three-tier applications in cloud and multi-cloud environments. *Comput. J.* 58, 1 (2015). https://doi.org/10.1093/comjnl/bxt107

[14] A. Higai, A. Takefusa, H. Nakada, and M. Oguchi. 2014. A study of effective replica reconstruction schemes at node deletion for HDFS. In *Proceedings of the 14th IEEE/ACM International Symposium on Cluster, Cloud and Grid Computing.* https://doi.org/10.1109/CCGrid.2014.31

[15] A. Higai, A. Takefusa, H. Nakada, and M. Oguchi. 2014. A study of replica reconstruction schemes for multi-rack HDFS clusters. In *Proceedings of the IEEE/ACM 7th International Conference on Utility and Cloud Computing.* https://doi.org/10.1109/UCC.2014.28

[16] G. Kousiouris, G. Vafiadis, and T. Varvarigou. 2013. Enabling proactive data management in virtualized Hadoop clusters based on predicted data activity patterns. In *Proceedings of the Eighth International Conference on P2P, Parallel, Grid, Cloud and Internet Computing.* https://doi.org/10.1109/3PGCIC.2013.8

[17] L.-W. Lee, P. Scheuermann, and R. Vingralek. 2000. File Assignment in parallel I/O systems with minimal variance of service time. *IEEE Trans. Comput.* 49, 2 (2000). https://doi.org/10.1109/12.833109

[18] D. Magalhaes, R.N. Calheiros, R. Buyya, and D.G.Gomes. 2015. Workload modeling for resource usage analysis and simulation in cloud computing. *Journal of Computers and Electrical Engineering* 47, C (2015). https://doi.org/10.1016/j.compeleceng.2015.08.016

[19] D. Meisner, B.T. Gold, and T.F. Wenisch. 2009. PowerNap: eliminating server idle power. In *Proceedings of the 14th International Conference on Architectural Support for Programming Languages and Operating Systems.* https://doi.org/10.1145/1508244.1508269

[20] G.A.F. Seber and A.J. Lee. 2003. *Linear Regression Analysis* (2nd. ed.). John Wiley and Sons.,Inc. https://doi.org/10.1002/9780471722199

[21] K. Shvachko, H. Kuang, S. Radia, and R. Chansler. 2010. The Hadoop distributed file system. In *Proceedings of the IEEE 26th Symposium on Mass Storage Systems and Technologies.* https://doi.org/10.1109/MSST.2010.5496972

[22] T. Shwe and M. Aritsugi. 2016. A re-replication approach in HDFS based cloud data center. In *Proceedings of the AUN/SEED-NET Regional Conference on Computer and Information Engineering.*

[23] T. Shwe and M. Aritsugi. [n.d]. A data re-replication scheme and its improvement toward proactive approach. ([n.d]). submitted for publication.

[24] E. Sit, A. Haeberlen, F. Dabek, B.G. Chun, H. Weatherspoon, R. Morris, M.F. Kaashoek, and J. Kubiatowicz. 2006. Proactive replication for data durability. In *Proceedings of the Fifth International Workshop on Peer-to-Peer Systems.*

[25] M. Tang, B.-S. Lee, X. Tang, and C.-K. Yeo. 2006. The impact of data replication on job scheduling performance in the data grid. *Future Generation Computer Systems* 22, 3 (2006). https://doi.org/10.1016/j.future.2005.08.004

[26] T. White. 2012. *Hadoop: The Definitive Guide* (3rd. ed.). O' Reilly Media, Inc.

[27] S. Wu, H. Jiang, and B. Mao. 2015. Proactive data migration for improved storage availability in large-scale data centers. *IEEE Trans. Comput.* 64, 9 (2015). https://doi.org/10.1109/TC.2014.2366734

[28] S. Wu, W. Zhu, B. Mao, and K.Li. 2017. PP: Popularity-based Proactive Data Recovery for HDFS RAID Systems. *Future Generation Computer Systems* (2017). https://doi.org/10.1016/j.future.2017.03.032

RT-SANE : Real Time Security Aware Scheduling on the Network Edge

Anil Singh
Department of Computer Science &
Engineering, Indian Institute of
Technology
Ropar, India
anil.singh@iitrpr.ac.in

Nitin Auluck
Department of Computer Science &
Engineering, Indian Institute of
Technology
Ropar, India
nitin@iitrpr.ac.in

Omer Rana
School of Computer Science &
Informatics, Cardiff University
Cardiff, UK
ranaof@cardiff.ac.uk

Andrew Jones
School of Computer Science &
Informatics, Cardiff University
Cardiff, UK
jonesacf@cardiff.ac.uk

Surya Nepal
Distributed Systems Security Group,
CSIRO
Sydney, Australia
surya.nepal@data61.csiro.au

ABSTRACT

Edge computing extends a *traditional* cloud data centre model often by using a microdata centre (*mdc*) at the network edge for computation and storage. As these edge devices are in proximity to users, this results in improved application response times and reduces load on the cloud data center (*cdc*). In this paper, we propose a security and deadline aware scheduling algorithm called *RT-SANE* (Real-Time Security Aware scheduling on the Network Edge). Applications with stringent privacy requirements are scheduled on an *mdc* closer to the user, whereas others can be scheduled on a *cdc* or a remote *mdc*. We also discuss how application performance and network latency influence the choice of an *mdc* or *cdc*. The intuition is that due to a lower communication latency between the user & the *mdc*, more applications are able to meet their deadlines when run on the *mdc*. Conversely, applications with loose deadlines may be executed on a *cdc*. In order to facilitate this, we also propose a distributed orchestration architecture and protocol that is both performance & security aware. Simulation results show that *RT-SANE* offers superior real-time performance compared to a number of other scheduling policies in an Edge computing environment, while meeting application privacy requirements.

CCS CONCEPTS

• **Networks** → **Cloud computing**; • **Software and its engineering** → **Real-time schedulability**; • **Information systems** → *Network attached storage*; • **Security and privacy** → *Distributed systems security*; • **Human-centered computing** → *Ubiquitous and mobile computing theory, concepts and paradigms*;

UCC'17, December 5–8, 2017, Austin, Texas, USA
© 2017 Association for Computing Machinery.
ACM ISBN 978-1-4503-5149-2/17/12...$15.00
https://doi.org/10.1145/3147213.3147216

KEYWORDS

Internet of Things; IoT; Fog Computing; Edge Computing; Cloud Computing; Cloudlets; Micro Data Centers; Cloud Data Center; Distributed Orchestration; Real-Time; Security.

1 INTRODUCTION

Applications utilizing Internet of Things (IoT) devices are increasingly generating large volumes of data, that needs to be processed within a particular deadline [16]. Although numbers vary (across Gartner, Cisco and other market forecasts), it is estimated that by 2020, there will be multi-billion devices connected to the Internet [25]. In order to effectively analyze the vast quantities of data generated by these devices, it becomes imperative to build scalable, distributed systems that can respond to this data management and analysis challenge. Smart phones these days have better hardware specifications than desktops of not too long ago. Such devices have enabled the processing of data intensive applications closer to the data generation sources. The data offloaded by these devices may be processed at a remote data center [15], which is also the dominant mode of operation at present. However, there may be considerable network delay between the devices and the remote data center, implying that by the time the data reaches the data center it may be difficult to reach their Quality of Service (QoS) targets [1] – especially in the case of real-time applications [18]. In such applications, data analysis must be completed within a pre-specified deadline to meet user requirements. Examples of such systems include real time gaming, streaming of audio/ video content over the Internet, command and control systems within built environments or in intelligent transport, etc.

To overcome latency associated with migrating data across a network for processing, it makes sense to leverage the infrastructure at the edge of the network [3] to perform partial computation. Such infrastructure may include routers, switches, gateways, and integrated access devices used for offloading some of the computation originally meant for the data center. This Edge computing model has been described in [15, 17]. Typically, applications access the cloud through access points, which allow the data to travel across the network to the data center. A key insight here is that such access points may be extended to provide computing and storage services at the network edge, via cloudlets/micro data centers (*mdcs*). Devices such as smart phones can communicate with micro data centers, which in turn communicate with the cloud data center (*cdc*). The *mdcs* may also communicate with each other to share application (execution) state, for example, to share the state of applications that are preempted from their local *mdc*, due to mobility, and are resumed on another *mdc* in their new coverage area.

In this paper, we propose *RT-SANE*, a security aware, real-time scheduling algorithm to support integration of an *mdc* and *cdc*, to balance performance and data privacy/security constraints of applications. The algorithm is security-aware, in the sense that private applications are executed only on the local/private *mdc* of a user. Semi-private applications may be executed on the local/private *cdc*. Public applications may be sent to a remote *mdc* or *cdc* for execution. Subject to meeting security constraints, *RT-SANE* schedules applications with tight deadlines on a local or remote *mdc*. Applications with loose deadlines may be sent to either the local or remote *cdc*.

An application where such an algorithm may be useful is "Ambient Assisted Living". Consider the case of elderly people having weak eyesight living alone in their homes. They could use a device like Google Glass to recognize people who come to visit them. A small database of images of known people could be stored at the local *mdc* of the person. This would make the image matching algorithm run with minimal latency, as an image match request does not need to be transmitted to a *cdc* for processing. Moreover, the database of known people is private to the user and does not need to be stored at the *cdc*. Storing images on the *mdc* may also have privacy limitations, based on organizations from which visitors originate. There is therefore a need to consider a more balanced approach for hosting such data between an *mdc* and a *cdc*.

The rest of this paper is organized as follows. Section II comprises a brief survey of related work. A distributed orchestration architecture and protocol is described in section III. The model and problem formulation is discussed in section IV. The *RT-SANE* algorithm is described in section V, with simulation results in Section VI. Finally, section VII concludes the paper.

2 RELATED WORK

Performing all computations at a cloud data center has shortcomings, as it places a heavy load on the cloud infrastructure. This can cause response time delays to user applications. This delay may be acceptable for applications such as web browsing, for others such as interactive gaming, this delay could be unacceptable. This is where edge computing devices could play a role. If some of the computation could be performed close to the user(s) at the network edge, the response times could greatly improve. Edge computing could also be used in environments with limited resilience (or a high failure rate), such as in a disaster recovery scenario [21]. In these applications, overcoming failures in communication networks and reduced response times are of paramount importance. Users in a "smart home", for example, may not be comfortable in sending their sensitive data to a cloud for computation. However, they may accept use of resources at the edge of the network, that may be

under their control/ownership. However, there is a need for application scheduling schemes on the network edge that are security aware. Edge computing seems to be a viable alternative due to its promise of providing lower response times and better security.

An overview of edge computing is provided in [20], where authors also present several case studies that can benefit from edge computing. Some of these applications are video analysis, smart homes, smart cities, augmented reality, visual entertainment games, connected health, among others. Two scheduling algorithms for edge networks have been proposed [23, 24]. The common thread in both these works is that the authors attempt to exploit the edge of the network to perform computation. In [24], the authors propose an ILP (Integer Linear Programming) based algorithm to solve the scheduling problem. The proposed *iFogStor* system provides close to optimal results, although at a high cost, making the outcome difficult to scale to large problem sizes. In the same paper, a heuristic version of the algorithm, called *iFogStorZ*, approximates the result at an economical cost. However both [23, 24] do not take application deadlines into account.

There has been some work on mobility aware task allocation for cloud computing [12, 13]. In [12], the authors carry out a survey of scheduling algorithms in cloud computing. Furthermore, they propose an allocation algorithm that is mobility aware. In [13], the authors propose a heuristic algorithm that tries to balance the trade-off between the application makespan and the monetary cost of cloud resources. However, in both [12] & [13], real-time tasks with deadlines have not been considered.

Real-time scheduling has received significant attention in the past [9–11]. A number of algorithms have been proposed for various kinds of architectures (both uni- and multi-processor systems). However, there is limited work on real-time scheduling in edge networks [14]. To the best of our knowledge, no single algorithm for edge networks has been proposed that is security aware, and that considers real-time tasks with deadlines. We have tried to fill this void in this work.

3 DISTRIBUTED ORCHESTRATION ARCHITECTURE & PROTOCOL

3.1 Distributed Orchestration Architecture

A centralized orchestration has a number of shortcomings. First, it has a single point of failure and is less resilient to attacks, such as a Denial of Service attack. Second, it is inherently unsuitable for edge computing due to the extra latency introduced by the need to do frequent communication with the centralized orchestrator that is deployed in the cloud. To address this challenge, we introduce a fully-decentralized distributed orchestration mechanism using the underlying principal of a collaborative multi-agent system. In our model, each computing device in the network has an orchestration agent. For each job, the orchestration agent creates job specific agent instances at different nodes and they collaboratively work towards achieving the goal (i.e., completing the user job at a minimum cost within a given deadline, without violating a specified security requirement).

A conceptual architecture of our distributed orchestration mechanism for edge computing is shown in figure 1. In the figure, a user

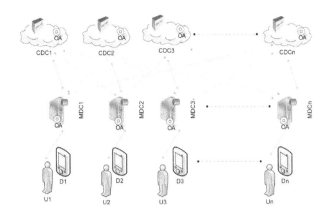

Figure 1: Distributed Orchestration Architecture (DOA) for Edge Computing

has a mobile device (D_x), which can sense data, build a computational job, receive results from job execution, and act on the results (visualization or actuation). The user job is submitted to an *mdc* capable of storing data and executing jobs with low latency. For simplicity, we assume that each user device is connected to one *mdc* (local *mdc*). Similarly, each *mdc* is connected to at least one *cdc*. We assume that a device D_x has trust in its local/home *mdc*. The home *cdc* is classified as semi-trusted, i.e., it can execute the job as requested, but cannot guarantee the privacy of data and jobs. Other non-local/remote *mdcs* and *cdcs* are untrusted.

3.2 Best Effort Orchestration Protocol

Next, we describe an orchestration protocol by considering three different cases: (a) a job executes at its local *mdc*, (b) a job executes at its local *cdc*, and (a) a job executes at a remote *mdc*. Figure 2 shows a sequence diagram for these three different cases, illustrating a best effort orchestration protocol.

In the first case, device (D_1) submits a job to its local *mdc* (mdc_1), which is able to meet all the specified requirements of cost, deadline and security. The job is executed at the local *mdc* and the result sent back to the device. As a local *mdc* is trusted, this case represents a scenario of job execution with the highest level of security. In the second case, the job submitted by D_1 cannot be executed on the local *mdc*. This could be due to the *mdc* being busy performing another job, and the job to be executed cannot meet the deadline if it waits until the completion of all scheduled jobs. In such cases, the local *OA* interacts with a *cdc* (cdc_1) to create a proxy agent, which takes over the responsibility of job completion. The result is returned to D_1 via mdc_1. This case represents a scenario where a job can execute on a semi-trusted resource and is able to meet the two other requirements (i.e., cost and deadline). In the third case, the job cannot be completed by the local *cdc* (cdc_1). This means the home *cdc* has to find other *cdcs* or *mdcs* that can complete the job. In our example, cdc_1 first contacts cdc_2, but it cannot meet the latency requirement. This means the job has to be computed closer to the device to meet latency requirements. Next, cdc_2 finds another *mdc* closer to D_1 that can meet these latency requirements. It instantiates a new proxy agent at the remote *mdc* (mdc_3) and passes the job to it. It terminates the local *OA* instance as it is

no longer needed. Now, mdc_3 completes the job and returns the results directly to mdc_1, which then passes it to D_1. All proxy agent instances for a specific job are terminated once the job is completed.

4 SYSTEM MODEL & PROBLEM FORMULATION

Table 1: Table of Key Notations

C	Set of Cloud Data Centers
c_l, c_f	Local & remote cloud data centers
M	Set of micro-data centers
m_l, m_f	Local & remote micro data centers
J	Set of all jobs/applications
U	Set of users
u_i	Particular user $u_i \in U$
D	Set of Devices
D_i	Particular device $D_i \in D$
j_i	Specific job/task/application $\in J$
T_j	Set of tags assigned to jobs
T_r	Set of tags assigned to resources
t_{j1}, t_{j2}, t_{j3}	Tag for private, semi-private, public jobs
t_{r1}, t_{r2}, t_{r3}	Tag for trusted, semi-trusted, untrusted resource
$cp(m)$	capacity of *mdc* m
$cp(c)$	capacity of *cdc* c
$ted(j_i)$	Total execution cost of job j_i
$et(j_i)$	Execution cost of an interaction of j_i
$st(j_i)$	Start time of job j_i
$ct(j_i)$	Completion time of job j_i
$d(j_i)$	Deadline for task j_i
$cd(u_i, j_i, m_l)$	Communication delay for j_i between m_l and u_i
$cd(u_i, j_i, c_l)$	Communication latency for j_i between u_i and c_l
DC	Deployment cost
UT_{m_l}, UT_{m_f}	Utilization for m_l & m_f
UT_{c_l}, UT_{c_f}	Utilization for c_l & c_f

The key notations used in the system model are shown in table I. The architecture of our system consists of a set of x cloud data centers, $C = \{c_1, c_2, c_3, ..., c_x\}$. A cloud data center c is of two types: local (c_l) or remote (c_f). Each cloud data centre is connected to a set of z micro-data centers, $M = \{m_1, m_2, m_3, ..., m_z\}$. A micro-data centre *mdc* can be of two types: local (m_l) or remote (m_f). Each *mdc* has processing capacity, denoted by $cp(m)$, given in Millions of Instructions per Second (MIPS) – a MIPS rating has been used to ensure that it aligns with the use of iFogSim used here. Other alternative metrics to capture the computing capacity of a *cdc* or *mdc* may also be used. We assume that all the *mdcs* have the same processing capability, i.e., they are homogeneous. The implication of this is that each job takes the same time to execute on each *mdc*. This assumption is made to explain the model and the problem; however, the model and problem are valid beyond this assumption. There is a communication link from each $c \in C$ to each $m \in M$. Each link has a bandwidth of bw.

Let U be the set of all users, such that $U = \{u_1, u_2, u_3, ..., u_n\}$. Let D be set of all devices, such that $D = \{D_1, D_2, D_3, ..., D_n\}$.

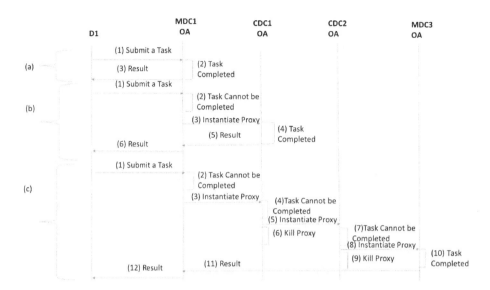

Figure 2: Sequence diagram illustrating the Orchestration Protocol

Each user u_i has an associated device D_i. Each user also has a set of jobs/applications that need to be executed on the cdc or mdc. Let J be the set of all such jobs, such that, $J = \{j_1, j_2, j_3, \dots j_y\}$. Each job j_i is represented as a tuple: $< et(j_i), d(j_i), t(j_i) >$. Here, $et(j_i)$ is the execution time of the job, $d(j_i)$ is the deadline of the job, & $t(j_i)$ is the security tag assigned to the job. Since jobs have real-time processing requirements, they need to be executed before their deadline. In this work, we assume that the jobs are non-preemptive, which implies that once a job has started execution, it may not be interrupted to execute another job. Both preemptive and non-preemptive scheduling algorithms have their pros and cons, which are beyond the scope of this paper.

Table 2: Mapping based on Security Tags

	t_{r1}	t_{r2}	t_{r3}
t_{j1}	Y	N	N
t_{j2}	Y	Y	N
t_{j3}	Y	Y	Y

Each job $j_i \in J$, has one of three security tags attached to it. The set of security tags assigned to a job is given by $T_j = \{t_{j1}, t_{j2}, t_{j3}\}$. Tag t_{j1} is attached to jobs that are "private", implying that the owner of the job wants it to be executed on on his/her local mdc. Tag t_{j2} is attached to jobs that are "semi-private", implying that they may be executed on the user's local cdc. Finally, tag t_{j3} is attached to jobs that are "public", meaning they may be executed on any resource, including other $cdcs$ & $mdcs$.

Similarly, execution resources also have security tags assigned to them. The set of security tags assigned to resources is given by $T_r = \{t_{r1}, t_{r2}, t_{r3}\}$. Tag t_{r1} is attached to resources that are "highly trusted", which is the user's own mdc. Resources that are "semi-trusted", for example, the local cdc are assigned a tag of t_{r2}. Finally, tag t_{r3} is attached to resources that are "untrusted", such as $mdcs$

& $cdcs$ which are outside the user's home network. Table II shows the possible mappings of jobs to resources. A 'Y'denotes a valid mapping, and a 'N'denotes a mapping that is not valid.

Provided the security constraints given in table II are met, given J, the jobs with "loose deadlines" are executed on the cdc, and the jobs with "tight" deadlines are sent to the mdc for execution. We discuss the proposed algorithm in greater detail in section V. Out of J, let us say that J' jobs are sent to the $mdcs$ for execution, where $J' \leq J$. Trivially, $J - J'$ jobs are executed on the cdc. The total execution duration of a job $j_i \in J$, is given by $ted(j_i)$. This corresponds to the time for which the user will interact with the application. For example, this could be the total amount of time that a user is playing an on-line multi-player game. An interactive application, such as the one just mentioned, consists of multiple interactions between the system and the user. Let the execution time of such a single interaction on be $et(j_i)$.

The start time of j_i is denoted by $st(j_i)$. Since we consider independent jobs, all jobs can start at time 0. The completion time of j_i is denoted by $ct(j_i)$. Formally, $ct(j_i) = st(j_i) + et(j_i)$. The communication latency between job j_i of user u_i and its local mdc, m_l is denoted by $cd(u_i, j_i, m_l)$. We assume that bw is the bandwidth of the communication link between the user and a local mdc. The size of the data transmitted by the user is given by $s(j_i)$. The time to initialize the communication link is denoted by t. Also, the cost of transferring the state of the job is $sc(u_i, j_i, m_l)$. The communication cost between a user u_i, a job j_i & an m_l can now be modeled as:

$$cd(u_i, j_i, m_l) = t + sc(u_i, j_i, m_l) + \frac{s(j_i)}{bw} \qquad (1)$$

The jobs assigned to the local mdc, m_l need to finish before their deadline, i.e.:

$$st(j_i) + et(j_i) + cd(u_i, j_i, m_l) \leq d(j_i) \qquad (2)$$

Based on the security tags, jobs may be sent to c_l for execution. The communication delay between a job j_i, of user u_i and c_l is denoted by $cd(u_i, j_i, c_l)$. This latency may be modeled as follows:

$$cd(u_i, j_i, c_l) = t + sc(u_i, j_i, c_l) + \frac{s(j_i)}{bw} \qquad (3)$$

Here, job j_i is executed on its local cloud data center c_l and must finish before the deadline. In other words:

$$st(j_i) + et(j_i) + cd(u_i, j_i, c_l) \le d(j_i) \qquad (4)$$

Adding a job j_i to an mdc should not result in the deadline of the currently executing/scheduled jobs to be missed. Let $J(m_l)$ be the set of all jobs that are currently running on a m_l. Let $et(j)$ be the execution time of $j \in J(m_l)$. A new job p may be chosen for execution on m_l, if and only if the following condition holds:

$$\forall j \in J(m_l), \forall m_l \in M, st(j) + et(j) + cd(u_i, j, m_l) \le d(j_i) \qquad (5)$$

Given that n is the number of jobs, let n' be the number of jobs that meet their assigned deadlines, where $n' \le n$. We define Success Ratio (SR) as the *ratio of the number of jobs that meet their deadlines to the total number of jobs considered*. Hence, $SR = \frac{n'}{n}$. SR is an important criteria, as it influences the accuracy of running a particular application on a distributed infrastructure.

Next, we model the cost of deployment, i.e. the cost to execute jobs on m_l and c_l. This cost is represented by $DC(m_l)$ & $DC(c_l)$ respectively. $DC(m_l)$ has several components, such as the communication delay between the jobs and the mdc. This is represented by $cd(u_i, j_i, m_l)$. Another component is the cost to power on the mdc server, if it is not already running. This is given by $in(m_l)$. In case the server is on, this cost is ignored. The third component is the time that the server has to be operational for executing the jobs. This is represented as $t(m_l)$. The deployment cost for each $m_l \in M$ is given by:

$$DC(m_l) = in(m_l) + \sum cd(u_i, j_i, m_l) + t(m_l) \qquad (6)$$

Let $J(m_l)$ be the set of jobs dispatched to $m_l \in M$. Let $et(j_i, m_l)$ be the execution cost of one particular job $j_i \in J(m_l)$ assigned to m_l, where $t(m_l)$ can be represented as:

$$\sum et(j_i, m_l), \forall j_i \in J(m_l) \qquad (7)$$

The deployment costs of all $m_l \in M$ can be specified as:

$$DC(M_L) = \sum DC(m_l) \qquad (8)$$

Likewise, the deployment cost for a local cloud data center $c_l \in C$ can be expressed as:

$$DC(c_l) = in(c_l) + \sum cd(u_i, j_i, c_l) + t(c_l) \qquad (9)$$

$t(c_l)$ can be represented as:

$$\sum et(j_i, c_l), \forall j_i \in J(c_l) \qquad (10)$$

The deployment costs of all $c_l \in C$ can be written as:

$$DC(C_L) = \sum DC(c_l) \qquad (11)$$

Finally, the total cost of deployment on all local $cdcs$ & $mdcs$ is given by:

$$DC = DC(M_L) + DC(C_L) \qquad (12)$$

Next, we model the utilizations of the m_l and c_l. For a particular user u_i, the utilization of an mdc, $m_l \in M$ can be expressed as:

$$UT_{m_l}(u_i) = \frac{\sum et(j_i, m_l)}{cp(m_l)}, \forall j_i \in J(m_l) \qquad (13)$$

Similarly, the utilization of a cdc, $c_l \in C$ can be expressed as:

$$UT_{c_l}(u_i) = \frac{\sum et(j_i, c_l)}{cp(c_l)}, \forall j_i \in J(c_l) \qquad (14)$$

Here, $J(c_l)$ is the set of all jobs assigned to cdc, c_l.

For a particular user u_i, the total utilization of the local mdc and cdc of a specific user u_i can be expressed as:

$$UTL(u_i) = UT_{m_l}(u_i) + UT_{c_l}(u_i)$$

The total system utilization, for all users, can now be represented as:

$$UTL(system) = \sum_{i=1}^{n} UTL(u_i)$$

Note that a similar formulation will hold for remote $mdcs$ & $cdcs$.

The optimisation problem that we solve in this work can be formulated as follows:

Maximize SR, i.e. maximize $\frac{n'}{n}$ & $UTL(System)$, while minimizing $DC, \forall m \in M, \forall c \in C$, subject to the security tag based jobs $\rightarrow$ resources mapping shown in table II. This mapping ensures that the privacy concerns of users are taken into account. Maximizing SR implies maximizing the number of jobs for which the following constraints hold:

$$st(j_i) + et(j_i) + cd(u_i, j_i, m) \le d(j_i)$$
$$st(j_i) + et(j_i) + cd(u_i, j_i, c) \le d(j_i)$$
$$\forall j_i \in J, \forall m \in M, \forall c \in C, \forall u_i \in U$$

5 PROPOSED ALGORITHM *RT-SANE*

In this section, we discuss the proposed algorithm *RT-SANE* (Real-Time Security Aware Scheduling on the Network Edge). As explained in the last section, there are three categories of security tags assigned to jobs – t_{j1} for private jobs, t_{j2} for semi-private jobs, & t_{j3} for public jobs. Likewise, there are three security tags assigned to resources – t_{r1} for highly trusted resources, t_{r2} for semi-trusted resources, & t_{r3} for untrusted resources. For a particular user $u_i \in U$, we assume that their local mdc, m_l is trusted, their local cdc, c_l is semi-trusted, & all other $mdcs$ and $cdcs$ are untrusted. The set of jobs that need to be executed - J, is separated into two different scheduling queues. Queue Q_1 contains only trusted jobs, whereas queue Q_2 contains semi-trusted & un-trusted jobs. We now define *four schedulability conditions*.

- **MDC deadline condition (C_1)**: $st(j_i) + et(j_i) + cd(u_i, j_i, m) \le d(j_i)$, this condition is met.
- **CDC deadline condition (C_2)**: $st(j_i) + et(j_i) + cd(u_i, j_i, c) \le d(j_i)$, this condition is met.

- **MDC spare capacity condition (C_3):** $\forall j_i, \forall m$, if $et(j_i) \leq (cp(m) - \sum et(j_i, m))$, this condition is met.
- **CDC spare capacity condition (C_4):** $\forall j_i, \forall c$, if $et(j_i) \leq (cp(c) - \sum(et(j_i, c)))$, this condition is met.

Here, m could be a local or remote mdc. Similarly, c is a local or remote cdc. The rationale for conditions C_1 & C_2 is that the algorithm executes jobs on resources only if the deadlines are met. The rationale for conditions C_3 & C_4 is that it makes sense to execute jobs on the resources, only if the resources have sufficient spare capacity available.

The algorithm *RT-SANE* works as follows. First, the quantities st, ct, cd are calculated for all $j_i \in J$. All the jobs to be scheduled are added to a scheduling queue Q. All jobs in Q are sorted in increasing order of deadlines, so that the job at the head of the queue has the smallest deadline. If multiple jobs have the same deadline, their execution order may be picked randomly. Next, for all private jobs, the scheduler tries to execute them on their local mdc m_l, provided the job will finish before the deadline, and provided the local mdc has sufficient spare capacity available (conditions C_1 & C_3 are met). If either or both conditions are not met, the job needs to wait and be re-submitted later. In this case, the distributed orchestrator can preempt the execution of the job. For all semi-private and public jobs, the scheduler first tries to execute them on the local mdc or on the local cdc. If this is not possible, due to the local cdc and mdc being overloaded, the job is executed on a remote mdc or cdc. If the deadline condition for the remote mdc is met, and the remote mdc has sufficient spare capacity available, the job is executed on the remote mdc. Otherwise, the job is executed on the remote cdc. In order to be scheduled on either an mdc or a cdc, the four conditions described above have to be met for all $mdcs$ & $cdcs$.

Algorithm 1 RT-SANE

1: **procedure** RT-SANE
2:     *Calculate st, ct, cd, $\forall j_i \in J$.*
3:     *Populate Q with tags t_{j_1}, t_{j_2} & t_{j_3} jobs.*
4:     *Arrange Q in increasing order of deadlines.*
5:     *$\forall j_i$ with tag t_{j_1}:*
6:     **if** (C_1 is met on m_l) && (C_3 is met on m_l) **then**
7:         *schedule j_i on its local mdc m_l.*
8:     **else**
9:         *re-submit job later.*
10:     *$\forall j_i$ with tags t_{j_2} or t_{j_3}:*
11:     **if** (C_1 is met on m_l) && (C_3 is met on m_l) **then**
12:         *schedule j_i on its local mdc m_l.*
13:     **if** (C_2 is met on c_l) && (C_4 is met on c_l) **then**
14:         *schedule j_i on its local cdc c_l.*
15:     **if** (C_1 is met on m_f) && (C_3 is met on m_f) **then**
16:         *schedule j_i on a remote mdc m_f.*
17:     **if** (C_2 is met on c_f) && (C_4 is met on c_f) **then**
18:         *schedule j_i on a remote cdc c_f.*
19:     *Calculate DC, UT, $\forall c, m \in C, M$.*

---

6 SIMULATION RESULTS & DISCUSSION

The goal of the simulations reported in this section is to evaluate the performance of the proposed algorithm *RT-SANE* using a sample scenario, as described in Figure 1. The proposed algorithm is based on the Distributed Orchestration Architecture & Protocol discussed earlier in section III. The Distributed Orchestration Protocol has three cases: (a) a job is executed on the local mdc, (b) a job is executed on the local cdc, (c) a job is executed on the remote cdc or mdc. In terms of the security requirements, the local mdc is trusted, the local cdc is semi-trusted, and the remote $cdcs$ & $mdcs$ are untrusted.

6.1 Simulation Setup & Parameters

For the simulation, a scenario based on Figure 1 has been set up. There are 6 users $u_1, ..., u_6$. Each user u_i is running job j_i on device $D_i, \forall i = 1 - 6$. The job execution cost is varied uniformly from 500 – 5500 MIPS/job (this expresses the computational requirement of each job to be scheduled via *RT-SANE*). Users and their jobs are submitted to $mdcs$ which can communicate to $cdcs$. Each user u_i has a local mdc, a local cdc, & remote $mdcs$ & $cdcs$. The number of $mdcs$ has been fixed at two. The processing capacity of the $mdcs$ has been fixed at 1000 MIPS and of the $cdcs$ has been fixed at 44800 MIPS.

Each mdc & cdc has a distributed Orchestration Agent (OA) running on it. Each OA creates job specific agent instances that collaboratively work together to fulfill the performance and security requirements of the jobs.

The simulations were run on iFogSim [6], which enables us to simulate different characteristics of an mdc and cdc. iFogSim is particularly relevant for this work as it focuses on the evaluation of resource management policies across fog and cloud environments. iFogSim is centered on the use of a Sense-Process-Actuate model, which makes it relevant for a number of different types of edge devices. All iFogSim simulations have been run on a machine with an Intel Xeon 2.40 GHz Processor and 12GB of RAM. In iFogSim, a class named *MultipleApps* has been created. This represents 6 different independent jobs, each having 1 module. The *MIPS* capacity requirements and job deadlines have been declared in this class. The capacity of $mdcs$ and $cdcs$, the communication delay cd, and the assignment of modules have also been specified in this class. The function *updateAllocatedMips* (in FogDevice class) is responsible for allocating *MIPS* load for different modules. This has been modified to take into account the deadlines and *FCFS* scheduling methods, in addition to the time shared method already included in iFogSim distribution. The job priority queue stores the modules in non-decreasing order of their deadlines (head-tail) or in *FCFS* order. A function has been created in the same class to check whether a module has finished its execution or not. If it has, then it is removed from the priority queue, so that remaining jobs will get all the available *MIPS* of the $mdcs$ & the $cdcs$.

The following parameters have been used in the simulations:

(1) Success Ratio (SR) = $\frac{n'}{n} \times 100$ (as described previously – i.e. percentage of completed tasks vs. those submitted).
(2) Throughput: number of jobs that are able to finish execution in a specified time interval.

(3) *MIPS* Load: This is the *MIPS* requirement of all the jobs. The *MIPS* value of each job was uniformly selected from the range (500 - 5500). The average of the *MIPS* values for all jobs was then calculated. This value was then multiplied by a factor of 1 to 6 to get a range of *MIPS* loads.

(4) Deadline Factor (*DF*): This is the range over which the deadlines of the jobs have been varied. A low value indicates tight deadlines overall in the system & vice versa. A lower bound for the job deadline $d(j_i)$ was calculated, equal to $ect(j_i)$. From this, the average deadline value of the system was calculated. This value was then multiplied by a factor of 1 to 6 to get a range of deadline factor values.

(5) Delay Factor (*DLF*): This is the range for the communication delay between the users, the *mdc* and the *cdc*s. A low value indicates less overall communication delays and vice versa. Initial delay values were 2 milliseconds from user to *mdc* and 100 milliseconds from user to *cdc*. These have then been increased by 10 milliseconds repeatedly to get the *DLF* values.

6.2 Results & Discussion

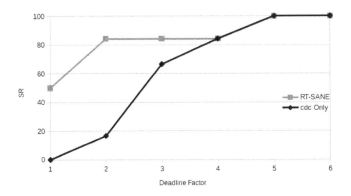

Figure 3: Effect of *DF* on *SR*

6.2.1 Effect of including Edge capability on Performance: The goal of this set of simulations is to show that using *mdc*s as an additional resource for scheduling jobs, besides the cloud, results in a higher Success Ratio. In the first simulation of this section, we compare the effect of increasing the Deadline Factor (*DF*) on the Success Ratio (*SR*) for two algorithms: *RT-SANE* & *cdc – only*. In the *cdc – only* algorithm, all jobs are directly sent to the cloud data center for execution. The overhead of doing this is that all jobs need to undergo significant communication delays. The *OA*s in *RT-SANE*, on the other hand, try to schedule the jobs on the local *mdc* first (case (a)). The number of *mdc*s was fixed at 2. The communication delay between users & the *mdc*s was fixed at 2 milliseconds, & the communication delay between users & the *cdc* was fixed at 100 milliseconds. The Deadline Factor was calculated as described earlier in section VI(a). The results of this simulation are shown in Figure 3. As illustrated, increasing the *DF* value leads to an increase in the *SR* value. This may be explained as follows. Increasing the *DF* value leads to the "loosening up" of the deadlines,

i.e. their values become larger. Hence, the jobs are able to meet their deadlines, even after incurring the large communication delays to the cloud. We also observe that for lower *DF* values, the proposed algorithm *RT-SANE* offers a better *SR* than the *cdc – only* algorithm. This is because the *OA* first schedules jobs on the *mdc*s, which have a much smaller communication latency than the cloud. Hence, a larger number of jobs are able to meet their deadlines. After a particular *DF* value, both algorithms offer similar performance, as by now, the deadlines have become so "loose", that one may also schedule jobs only on the cloud, without missing the deadlines.

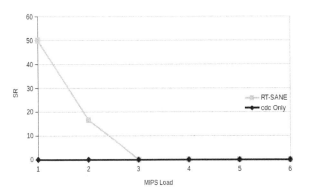

Figure 4: Effect of *MIPS* Load on *SR*

In the second simulation of this section, we study the effect of increasing the *MIPS* load on the *SR*. Again, the number of jobs was fixed at 6, & the number of *mdc*s was fixed at 2. The *MIPS* value of each job was uniformly selected from the range (500 - 5500). The *MIPS* load was calculated as described in section VI(a). The results of this simulation are shown in Figure 4. For low values of *MIPS* load, *RT-SANE* offers high *SR* values. This is because the task specific agents are able to schedule a large number of jobs at the local *mdc* (case (a)). We observe that increasing the *MIPS* load reduces the *SR*, because we are effectively increasing the computation load being placed on the *mdc*s and *cdc*s. As this load increases, initially, the local *mdc*s reach their capacity, so the *OA* needs to create proxy agents to schedule the jobs on the local *cdc*s (case(b)). As the *MIPS* load further increases, the local *cdc* also becomes overloaded, and the *OA* creates proxy agents to execute jobs on remote *cdc*s and *mdc*s (case(c)). In the *cdc – only* scheduling algorithm, none of the jobs are able to meet their deadline, even for lower *MIPS* load values. We attribute this to the tight deadlines that have been assigned to the jobs. If the deadlines are "looser", some jobs may meet their deadlines, even if they are scheduled on the cloud. We observe from this simulation, that for tight deadlines, the proposed algorithm *RT-SANE* offers a much better performance than the *cdc – only* algorithm, especially for lower *MIPS* load values. For high *MIPS* load values, both algorithms show similar performance, as the computation load is much greater than the processing capacity, & this leads to all deadlines being missed, irrespective of the algorithm.

In the third simulation of this section, we study the effect of the Delay Factor (*DLF*) on the *SR*. The communication delay between users & the *mdc*s was fixed at 2 milliseconds, & the communication delay between users & the *cdc* was fixed at 100 milliseconds. From

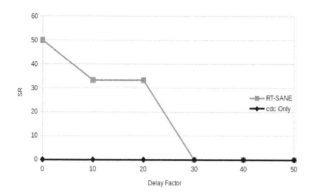

Figure 5: Effect of *DLF* on *SR*

these initial values, the *DLF* was calculated as described in section VI(a). The results of this simulation are shown in Figure 5. We observe that increasing the *DLF* leads to a decrease in the *SR*. This can be explained as follows. As we are adding more delay to the network, more jobs reach their execution destination (*mdcs* & *cdcs*) later. Hence, they end up missing their deadlines. Essentially, as we increase the *DLF*, the number of jobs for whom case (a) is satisfied becomes less. Hence, jobs need to be sent to the *cdc*, & this delay causes the jobs to miss their deadlines. We also observe that *RT-SANE* offers a better performance than the *cdc – only* option, in terms of a higher *SR*. This is because, *RT-SANE* effectively utilizes the *mdcs* for the execution of jobs, in addition to the *cdc*. Beyond a particular *DLF* value, both algorithms offer similar performance, as by now, the delays are so high that even the presence of *mdcs* does not help in meeting job deadlines. For lower *DLF* values, however, *RT-SANE* offers a much better performance.

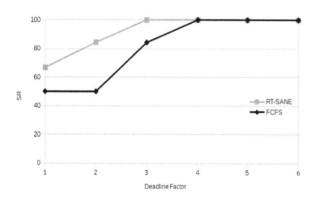

Figure 6: Effect of *DF* on *SR*(Deadline Heuristics)

6.2.2 Effect of Deadline Heuristics on Performance: The goal of this part of the simulation is to show that while scheduling jobs on the network edge (*mdcs*), using an effective heuristic results in better performance, in terms of a higher Success Ratio. In the first simulation, we observe the effect of varying the Deadline Factor *DF* on the performance for both *RT-SANE* & First Come First Serve (*FCFS*) heuristics. The number of jobs was fixed at 6,

and the number of *mdcs* was fixed at 2. The communication delay between users and the *mdcs* was fixed at 2 milliseconds, & the communication delay between users and the *cdc* was fixed at 100 milliseconds. The *DF* was calculated as shown in section VI(a). The results of this simulation are shown in Figure 6. We observe that increasing the Deadline Factor (*DF*) leads to an increase in the *SR*. This is because as the *DF* is increasing, deadlines are becoming looser, and the scheduling algorithms are able to ensure that a larger number of jobs can finish before their deadline. We also observe that for lower *DF* values, *RT-SANE* offers higher *SR* values than *FCFS*. This is because it applies the earliest deadline first heuristic, i.e. jobs with earlier deadlines are being executed earlier. Hence, they have a greater chance of finishing before their deadline, versus the case in which jobs are strictly executed first come first serve. Beyond a particular *DF* values, both algorithms show the same *SR* values. By now, the deadlines are so loose that the order of execution of the jobs has no impact. From this simulation, we observe that for lower *DF* values, *RT-SANE* offers a higher *SR*, as it uses an intelligent heuristic for scheduling jobs.

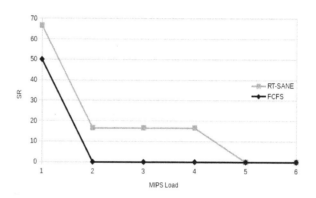

Figure 7: Effect of *MIPS* Load on *SR* (Deadline Heuristics)

In the second simulation, we study the effect of *MIPS* load on *SR*, for both *RT-SANE* & *FCFS*. The *MIPS* value of each job was uniformly selected from the range (500 - 5500). The *MIPS* load was calculated as shown in section VI(a). The results of this simulation are shown in Figure 7. We observe that as we increase the *MIPS* load, the *SR* values decreases. For lower *MIPS* load values, the job specific agents are able to execute the jobs on the local *mdc*, so the *SR* values are high. For higher *MIPS* load values, the *OA* needs to create proxy agents to execute the jobs on the local *cdc*, or on the remote *cdcs* & *mdcs*, so the *SR* values are low. However, the performance of *RT-SANE* is observed to be better than that of *FCFS*, as it is intelligently executing the earlier deadline jobs first, whereas, in *FCFS*, the jobs are scheduled in the order that they arrive. Hence, we observe that for lower MIPS load values, it makes sense to execute jobs using *RT-SANE*, as it offers a higher *SR*. For higher *MIPS* load values, the computation load placed on the system is far greater than the capacity, so the choice of heuristic becomes immaterial.

Next, we study the effect of increasing the Delay Factor *DLF* on *SR*. The communication delay between users & the *mdcs* was fixed at 2 milliseconds, & the communication delay between users

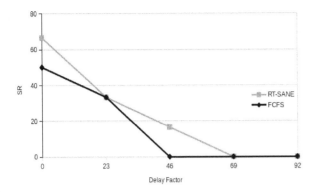

Figure 8: Effect of *DLF* on *SR* (Deadline Heuristics)

& the *cdc* was fixed at 100 milliseconds. From these initial values, the *DLF* was calculated as described in section VI(a). The results for this simulation are shown in Figure 8. Increasing *DLF* reduces the *SR*, as an increasing *DLF* leads to more delay being induced in the network, which results in jobs reaching the *mdcs* later. As *DLF* increases, the number of jobs for which case (b) holds increases, as the local *mdc* is overloaded. Eventually, the number of jobs for which case (c) holds increases, as the local *cdc* is overloaded. This result in more jobs missing their deadlines. However, *RT-SANE* demonstrates a better performance than *FCFS*, as it picks jobs with earlier deadlines to execute first. Hence, a larger number of tasks are able to finish before their deadline.

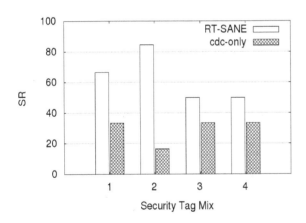

Figure 9: Effect of Security Tag Mix Cases on *SR*

6.2.3 Effect of Security on Performance: The goal of this simulation was to study the effect of security tag assignment on the system performance. Several "security tag mixes" were considered, as shown in table III. As an example, in *case*₁, 1/3rd of the jobs were private, 1/3rd of the jobs were semi-private, & 1/3rd of the jobs were public. We considered 4 different cases, with different mixes for private, semi-private, & public jobs for each case. Note that all private, semi-private, & public jobs are assigned security tags of t_{j1}, t_{j2}, & t_{j3} respectively. The number of jobs was fixed at 6, & the

number of *mdcs* was fixed at 2. The communication delay between users & the *mdcs* was fixed at 2 milliseconds, & the communication delay between users & the *cdc* was fixed at 100 milliseconds. The results for this simulation are shown in Figure 9. In general, *RT-SANE* offers a better *SR* than the *cdc − only* approach, partly because of the earliest deadline heuristic employed in *RT-SANE*, that ensures that a larger number of jobs meet their deadlines, & partly because of the fact that the private jobs cannot be executed on the cloud in the *cdc − only* approach. When we go from case 1 to case 2, we observe that the *SR* for *RT-SANE* goes up. This is because, the number of semi-private & public jobs has been reduced. So, a lesser number of jobs are going to the cloud for execution. However, the *SR* value for *cdc − only* reduces. This is because the number of private jobs has now gone up, & such jobs cannot be executed on the *cdc*. We observe from this simulation that the proposed algorithm *RT-SANE* effectively handles the security constraints of jobs, while offering a good *SR*, something which the *cdc − only* algorithm is unable to do.

Table 3: Various "Security Tag Mixes" Considered

	Frac. (t_{j1})	Frac. (t_{j2})	Frac. (t_{j3})
Case₁	1/3	1/3	1/3
Case₂	2/3	1/6	1/6
Case₃	1/6	1/6	2/3
Case₄	1/6	2/3	1/6

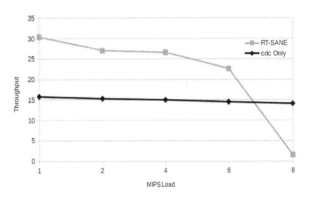

Figure 10: Effect of *MIPS* Load on Throughput

6.2.4 Effect of MIPS Load on Throughput: In the last simulation, we consider the effect of *MIPS* Load on another system metric – throughput. In this case, we assume that the deadlines are very "loose", so the main goal is to maximize the system throughput. A value of 10 milliseconds has been taken as the unit time. The number of jobs was fixed at 6, and the number of *mdcs* was fixed at 2. The communication delay between users & the *mdcs* was fixed at 2 milliseconds, & the communication delay between users and the *cdc* was fixed at 100 milliseconds. The *MIPS* load for jobs was calculated as described in section VI(a). The results for this simulation are shown in Figure 10. We observe that *RT-SANE* offers better throughput values than the *cdc − only* approach. This is due to the presence of *mdc*s, which are additional resources that can be allocated to the jobs (case(a)). This results in a larger number of jobs finishing per unit time. We also observe that interestingly, as the *MIPS* load increases, although the throughput values for *cdc − only* are lower, the degradation is graceful. This is because the *cdc* has a much larger capacity than the *mdc*s. Hence, it can handle an increase in the *MIPS* load. The *mdc*s, on the other hand, due to their limited capacity, cannot handle the *MIPS* load increase that well. However, since the user to *mdc* delay is low, they play a part in *RT-SANE* by offering better system throughput. We observe that the proposed algorithm *RT-SANE* offers a higher throughput than the *cdc − only* algorithm, especially for low *MIPS* load values.

7 CONCLUSIONS

One of the bottlenecks of processing data on the cloud is the large communication latency to user devices. This latency may be detrimental to real-time applications with stringent deadlines. This is exactly where edge devices can make an impact. As compared to sending all applications to the cloud for execution, scheduling applications with tight deadlines on edge devices can offer better performance, in terms of a higher Success Ratio, and support security concerns associated with moving data to a cloud data centre. The proposed algorithm, *RT-SANE*, is both security & performance aware. Private jobs are sent only to the local *mdc* for execution. Semi-private jobs may be executed at the local *cdc*, and public jobs may be executed on remote *mdc*s or *cdc*s. Subject to specific security constraints, jobs with tight deadlines are scheduled on the *mdc*s. Only if the *mdc*s are overloaded, are the jobs sent to the *cdc* for execution. In order to facilitate this, we have also proposed a Distributed Orchestrator based architecture and protocol. Simulation results (carried out using iFogSim) demonstrate that the proposed algorithm offers superior performance in terms of a higher Success Ratio, by taking into account the multi-tier nature of the Edge/Cloud architecture, while also meeting the security needs of the applications.

As part of future work, we plan to incorporate more complex precedence constrained (workflows) in our job model. Additionally, we are also interested in considering the case of "heterogeneous" *mdc*s & *cdc*s.

ACKNOWLEDGMENT

The work reported in this paper was partially enabled by the European Union's Horizon 2020 research and innovation programme under grant agreement No 643963 (SWITCH Project).

REFERENCES

[1] Fog Computing and the Internet of Things: Extend the Cloud to Where the Things Are, Cisco White Paper, 2015.
[2] A. V. Daesterjerdi and R. Buyya, Fog Computing: Helping the Internet of things to realize their potential, IEEE Computer, vol. 49, no. 8, pp. 112-116, 2016.
[3] L. F. Bittencourt, O. Rana, and I. Petri, Cloud Computing at the Edges, Springer International Publishing, 2016, pp. 3-12.
[4] F. Bonomi, R. Milito, P. Natarajan, and J. Zhu, Fog Computing: A platform for Internet of things and analytics, Springer International Publishing, 2014, pp. 169-196.
[5] B. Jennings and R. Stadler, Resource management in clouds: survey and research challenges, Journal of Network and Systems Management, vol. 23, no. 3, 2015, pp. 567-619.
[6] H. Gupta, A. V. Dastjerdi, S. K. Ghosh, and R. Buyya, iFogSim: A toolkit for modeling and simulation of resource management techniques in Internet of things, edge and fog computing environments, CORR abs, vol. 1606.02007, 2016. [Online]. Available: http://arxi.org/abs/1606.02007.
[7] L. F. Bittencourt, E. R. M. Madeira, and N. L. S. Da Fonseca, Scheduling in hybrid clouds, IEEE Communications Magazine, vol. 50, no. 9, 2012, pp. 42-47.
[8] J. D. Montes, M. Abdelbaky, M. Zhou, and M. Parashar, Cometcloud: Enabling software-defined federations for end-to-end application work-flowsâĂİ, IEEE Internet Computing, vol. 19, no. 1, 2015, pp. 69-73.
[9] C. L. Liu and J. W. Layland, Scheduling algorithms for multiprogramming in a hard real-time environment, Journal of the ACM, vol. 20, no. 1, 1973, pp. 46-61.
[10] Z. Guo and S. Baruah, A neurodynamic approach for real-time scheduling via maximizing piecewise linear utility, IEEE Transactions on Neural Networks and Learning Systems, vol. 27, no. 2, 2016, pp. 238-248.
[11] J. Singh, S. Betha, B. Mangipudi, N. Auluck, Contention aware energy efficient scheduling on heterogeneous multiprocessorsâĂİ, IEEE Transactions on Parallel and Distributed Systems, vol. 26, no. 5, 2014, pp. 1251-1264.
[12] B. A. Hridita, M. Irfan & M. S. Islam, Mobility aware task allocation for mobile cloud computing, International Journal of Computer Applications, Vol. 137, No. 9, 2016 pp. 35-41.
[13] X. D. Pham & E. N. Huh, Towards task scheduling in a cloud fog computing system. The 18th Asia-Pacific Network Operations and Management Symposium, APNOMS, Kanazawa, Japan, October 5-7, 2106, pp. 1-4.
[14] M. Shojafar, N. Cordeschi and E. Baccarelli, âĂİEnergy-efficient adaptive resource management for real-time vehicular cloud servicesâĂİ, IEEE Transactions on Cloud Computing, preprint, April 6, 2016, pp. 1-14.
[15] L. F. Bittencourt, M. M. Lopes, I. Petri and O. Rana, Towards virtual machine migration in fog computing, The 10th International conference on P2P, Parallel, Grid, Cloud and Internet Computing (3PGCIC), November 4-6, 2015, Krakow, Poland, pp. 1-8.
[16] F. Xia, L. T. Yang, L. Wang and A. Vinel, Internet of Things, Editorial, International Journal of Communication Systems, Vol. 25, 2012, pp. 1101-1102.
[17] A. V. Dastjerdi, H. Gupta, R. N. Calheiros, S. K. Ghosh and R. Buyya, Fog computing: principles, architectures, and applications, Internet of Things: Principles and Paradigms, R. Buyya and A. Dastjerdi (eds), Morgan Kaufmann, ISBN: 978-0-12-805395-9, Burlington, Massachusetts, USA, May 2016.
[18] J. W. S. Liu, âĂİReal-Time SystemsâĂİ, Prentice Hall, April 2000, 592 pages.
[19] S. Sharif, P. Watson, J. Taheri, S. Nepal, and A. Zomaya, Privacy-aware scheduling SaaS in high performance computing environments, IEEE Transactions on Parallel & Distributed Systems, vol. 28, no. 4, April 2017, pp. 1176-1188.
[20] W. Shu, J. Cao, Q. Zhang, Y. Li, and L. Xu, Edge computing: vision and challenges, IEEE Internet of Things Journal, vol. 3, no. 5, October, 2016, pp. 637-646.
[21] M. Satyanarayanan, G. Lewis, E. J. Morris, S. Simanta, J. Boleng, K. Ha, The role of cloudlets in hostile environments, IEEE Pervasive Computing, October, 2013, pp. 40-49.
[22] M. Satyanarayanan, Augmenting cognition, IEEE Pervasive Computing, April, 2004, pp. 4-5.
[23] S. Shekhar, A. D. Chhokra, A. Bhattacharjee, G. Aupy, and A. Gokhale, INDICES: Exploiting edge resources for performance aware cloud hosted services, First IEEE/ACM International Conference on Fog & Edge Computing, Madrid, Spain, May 14, 2017, pp. 75-80.
[24] M. I. Naas, P. R. P. Orange, J. Boukhobza, L. Lemarchand, iFogStor: an IoT data placement strategy for fog infrastructure, First IEEE/ACM International Conference on Fog & Edge Computing, Madrid, Spain, May 14, 2017, pp. 97-104.
[25] D. Evans, The Internet of Things, how the next evolution of the Internet is changing everything, Cisco White Paper, April 2011.

Locality-Aware Load Sharing in Mobile Cloud Computing

Albert Jonathan
University of Minnesota
Minneapolis, MN
albert@cs.umn.edu

Abhishek Chandra
University of Minnesota
Minneapolis, MN
chandra@cs.umn.edu

Jon Weissman
University of Minnesota
Minneapolis, MN
jon@cs.umn.edu

ABSTRACT

The past few years have seen a growing number of mobile and sensor applications that rely on Cloud support. The role of the Cloud is to allow these resource-limited devices to offload and execute some of their compute-intensive tasks in the Cloud for energy saving and/or faster processing. However, such offloading to the Cloud may result in high network overhead which is not suitable for many mobile/sensor applications that require low latency. So, people have looked at an alternative Cloud design whose resources are located at the edge of the Internet, called Edge Cloud. Although the use of Edge Cloud can mitigate the offloading overhead, the computational power and network bandwidth of Edge Cloud's resources are typically much more limited compared to the centralized Cloud and hence are more sensitive to workload variation (e.g., due to CPU or I/O contention). In this paper, we propose a locality-aware load sharing technique that allows edge resources to share their workload in order to maintain the low latency requirement of Mobile-Cloud applications. Specifically, we study how to determine which edge nodes should be used to share the workload with and how much of the workload should be shared to each node. Our experiments show that our locality-aware load sharing technique is able to maintain low average end-to-end latency of mobile applications with low latency variation, while achieving good utilization of resources in the presence of a dynamic workload.

KEYWORDS

Mobile Cloud Computing, Edge Cloud, Load Sharing

1 INTRODUCTION

The past few years have seen a growing number of devices that are connected to the Internet. The type of devices varies from statically installed public sensors such as smart traffic light systems and weather forecasting sensors to privately owned mobile devices [1] such as smart phones, smart watches, wearable health sensors, etc. [1, 3, 36, 39]. This rapid growth is predicted to continue increasing as Cisco estimates that there will be approximately 50 billion devices that are connected to the Internet by 2020 [10].

---

[1]In this paper, we refer to any type of resource-limited devices as mobile devices

UCC '17, December 5–8, 2017, Austin, TX, USA
© 2017 Association for Computing Machinery
ACM ISBN 978-1-4503-5149-2/17/12...$15.00
https://doi.org/10.1145/3147213.3147228

Today's mobile devices are still facing challenges due to their limited resources such as CPUs, storage, and battery power. Yet, these resources will be unable to satisfy most of today's mobile applications that require low latency to the users while they constantly produce or consume data [9, 21, 30]. Recent research has looked at the opportunity of integrating Cloud Computing platforms that provide much more powerful computation and/or storage resources to assist many mobile applications. Furthermore, people have looked at an alternative Cloud design consisting of resources that are located at the edge of the Internet, called *Edge Clouds* [4, 18, 31, 35, 40, 43]. The main benefit of using an Edge Cloud is to mitigate the overhead of computational offloading since they are closer to the users [2], thus reducing the processing time and/or saving energy consumption on the devices.

Although there have been a number of works that provide various computational offloading techniques in the context of mobile-edge computing [2, 8, 12], there are few works that have looked at *which* edge nodes the computational should be offloaded to. The problem of node selection for computational offloading is interesting for a couple reasons: First, the type of edge resources are typically highly heterogeneous in terms of both their computational power and latency to end-users. The resources vary from edge servers provided by Internet service providers (ISPs) to network access points and they provide varying network latency and bandwidth. Second, the dynamic nature of workload makes the node selection problem more challenging since resources in Edge Cloud are typically much more limited compared to the centralized Cloud's resources. Although the mobility aspect of end-users may add additional dynamic to the workload, we argue that the user's mobility is much less time sensitive compared to the changes in workload. For example, trending topic spreads much faster compared to human's mobility.

In this paper, we propose a locality-aware load sharing technique in the context of Mobile-Edge Computing (MEC). Specifically, we study the problem of *which* nodes should be selected for load sharing and *how much* workload should be shared to each of the nodes while considering the heterogeneity aspect of the edge nodes' resources. Our goal is to maintain the low latency requirement of common mobile applications that are continuously producing and consuming data in the case of runtime dynamics that may cause a contention in a node's network resources.

Our system constitutes different layers of Cloud resources ranging from distant resource-rich Cloud servers to edge resources with less computational resources that are closer to the end-users. It provides a location-based edge node discovery mechanism that allows users to find the closest available nodes. The edge nodes in our system are aware of the availability of their *neighboring nodes*. A

---

[2]The closeness is measured in term of network latency rather than actual physical distance.

node is considered as a *neighbor* to another node if they are located close to each other. This neighborhood information is maintained by each node and is used for workload sharing in the case of high workload. To prevent sharing workload with a neighbor that has already had high workload, each node periodically shares its load information to all of its neighbors. This neighbor-awareness is useful to guarantee low overhead in sharing a workload. This locality-aware load sharing mechanism allows load sharing with little overhead and thus is able to maintain the low latency requirement of mobile applications in the case of workload dynamics.

We evaluate our system and techniques using a real geo-distributed Edge Cloud platform deployed on PlanetLab [7] testbed. Our experiments are based on a sample of real Twitter trace from December 2015 which consists of approximately 4 million tweets/day. We show that our locality-aware load sharing technique is able to better satisfy the application's latency goal even when there is an increase in the workload. We also show that our load sharing technique results in up to 1.5X and 3X lower latency for 95th percentile latency compared to an Edge Cloud system that does not consider load sharing and the centralized Cloud platform respectively.

2 BACKGROUND

Heterogeneous Edge Resources. Nodes in an Edge Cloud are located at the edge of the Internet and hence are closer to the end-users. They generally provide less computaional power but lower latency to the end-users compared to the Data Center's nodes. Edge nodes are also typically more heterogeneous in terms of their computational hardwares as well as network connectivity: cloudlets, servers provided by ISPs, home servers, to access points that use Wi-Fi, bluetooth, etc. To handle this heterogeneity, some works have proposes a common interface and mechanism for mobile devices by providing a virtualization layer that encapsulates a mobile-application execution inside virtualized machines (VMs) or containers [19, 26, 31]. This mechanism allows variety of applications from possibly different devices to run concurrently in isolation.

Computational Offloading in Mobile-Edge Computing. In the context of Mobile-Edge Computing (MEC), the main purpose of the Cloud is to support mobile devices by allowing them to offload their data processing to the Cloud's nodes for better performance and/or saving energy consumption [8, 24, 25, 27]. For example, a compute-intensive object/image analysis on a mobile device can be processed on one of the Cloud's nodes that is equipped with GPUs, leaving only the final image rendering to be processed on the mobile device itself. Throughout the paper, we assume that the decision on which parts of application programs that should be offloaded to the Cloud have already been made externally.

Low Latency Requirement of Mobile Applications. Many emerging mobile applications are latency sensitive since they are interactive applications [1, 6, 9]. For example, interactive collaborative mobile games require continuous image processing and augmented reality applications on wearable devices require very low latency for better user experiences [15, 25, 42]. Many applications also require data aggregation from mobile devices. For example, a real time event detection in a social network application that detects

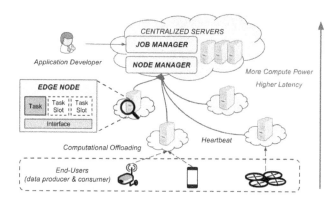

Figure 1: Edge Cloud System Model

earthquake needs to aggregate a vast number of microblogs that are originated from a specific area and detect the trend. These applications require low latency while continuously producing and consuming data. In a MEC environment, workload may change frequently due to the nature of hotspots. Nevertheless, the Cloud should satisfy each application's desired goal regardless of the runtime dynamics.

Location Property of Mobile Applications. Geographic or location information has become an important factor for many mobile/sensor applications. There are many applications that use and rely on the users' locations in providing their services. For example, numerous recent augmented reality games rely on their users' locations. Another example includes map-based applications and environmental monitoring that use sensor-equipped mobile devices [22, 25, 33]. These applications share a common property of continuous data production/consumption and they need the support from Clouds' resources for processing their data efficiently. Furthermore, some of them rely on information aggregation from other nearby users' activities such as real-time traffic detection that needs to aggregate information from nearby drivers to detect whether a certain road is congested and multi-player mobile games that need to detect the availability of other players for matchmaking.

3 EDGE CLOUD MODEL & IMPLEMENTATION

In this section, we discuss the Edge Cloud system that we consider throughout this paper. Figure 1 shows the system model. It consists of 1) a set of components that are hosted in a centralized reliable server: *Node Manager* and *Job Manager*; and 2) a set of edge nodes that are distributed across geographic locations [18].

3.1 System Components

• **End-Users and Applications.** The end-users are any type of resource-limited devices that rely on an Edge Cloud's supports by offloading their computational to the Cloud's nodes. In this paper, we mainly focus on a class of applications that requires low latency while continuously producing and consuming data. We consider a *task* as an instance of an application that is running on a node and a task may consume one or more inputs from possibly different input providers/end-users.

• **Edge Nodes.** The edge nodes are computational resources that are geographically distributed. They provide a common interface that allows end-users to offload their data to be processed on the nodes.

• **Node Manager.** The Node Manager is responsible for monitoring the availability of all nodes in the system. It uses a *heartbeat* mechanism to detect node failures. Nodes that do not respond to the heartbeat message in a timely manner will be considered unavailable. Each node information that is monitored by the Node Manager is periodically shared to the *Job Manager*.

• **Job Manager.** The Job Manager provides an interface for application developers [3] to submit their applications to the system. It is responsible for scheduling, deploying, and managing all tasks that are running on the nodes.

3.2 Implementation

Computational Offloading. All tasks that are running on our edge nodes are encapsulated inside a virtualized layer and thus are independent of the applications. This computational offloading mechanism is done using the following steps: 1) The end-user sends its data to one or more edge nodes through the nodes' interface layer (this is done in the background). This interface is implemented using a generic socket layer and so is independent of the type of the applications. We assume that the application program itself that is running on the node has already been deployed to the nodes. In a real deployment, this decision depends on each application's area of interests such as the environment or location. For example, in a city traffic monitoring, the program should only be pushed to the nodes that are located in that city. We consider this deployment issue to be orthogonal to our work. 2) The edge node processes the data as an input to a task that is running on a *task slot*, which is an abstraction of computational resources on which a task can be deployed. So, the number of task slots of a particular node corresponds to the number of tasks that can be run concurrently on the node. We use the number of CPUs as a metric to determine the number of slots of a particular node. 3) Once the processing is complete, the node sends the result back to the users. Inactive tasks that are deployed on the node can be terminated using a *least-recently-used* policy.

Node Monitoring. To monitor the availability of each node, the Node Manager periodically sends a heartbeat message to every node. Each node includes some additional information to its heartbeat response: 1) The node's location, which can also be estimated using a geo-location service, 2) The number of available task slots, and 3) The current load information of every task that is currently running on the node. The location information of a node is used to determine *which* node an end-user should be associated with to minimize the connectivity overhead between them (will be discussed later Section 5). The location information is also used as a metric to determine the neighborhood information that is used for locality-aware load sharing (will be discussed in Section 6). The

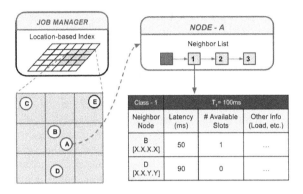

Figure 2: Neighbor Index Structure

number of available task slots and the load factor are used to determine the resource availability of the nodes and its current load respectively. The Node Manager periodically gathers all of this information and forward it to the Job Manager which will use this information for task management and scheduling.

Locating an Edge Node. When an end-user tries to discover an edge node for offloading her computation, she will need to query the availability of the nodes in the system. When the Job Manager receives this query, it will return a set of possible edge nodes where the user can connect to. Once the user receives this response, she can connect to any of the nodes without going to the Job Manager again and any subsequent requests can be directly sent to the nodes. The decision on *which* nodes the Job Manager should return will be discussed in Section 5.

4 LOCALITY-AWARENESS

Having discussed the system model, we will now define the locality-awareness property that we have implemented in our system. This locality-awareness is used to intelligently associate end-users to one of the edge nodes in the system (Section 5) and to handle runtime dynamics through load sharing (Section 6).

4.1 Node Neighborhood

The Job Manager periodically gets an update about the nodes' availability along with their resource information from the Node Manager. It stores this information in a global location-based index structure (shown in Figure 2). The main purpose of this index structure is to quickly find and map a node to one of the index's cells based on the node's location. This index is also used to cluster nodes based on their locations to determine the neighborhood of nodes. Nodes that are located close to each other will be mapped to the same index cell. Nodes that lie within the same index cell or in adjacent cells to a node will be considered as its neighbors, since intuitively they are close to each other.

Although an actual geographic distance between two end-points may not guarantee a low latency between them in a wide-area setting, large values of geographic distance between two end-points have a strong tendency of having circuitous routing as studied by previous works [28, 32]. Furthermore, a node's IP-address can be

---

[3]An application developer is not part of the runtime entities. Its only task is to deploy an application to the system (e.g., traffic monitor organization, social network analyzer, etc.).

used to estimate its location in the network and the linearized distances between two end-points have been shown to have a strong correlation to end-to-end delay.

The size of the index cell also determines the size of the neighborhood and it should be configurable depending on how close a node should be considered a neighbor. If the size of the cell was set too big, e.g., $1000x1000km^2$, this would not give a meaningful filtering result since nodes that are very far from each other would still be considered as neighbors. On the other extreme, limiting the size of each cell too small, e.g., $100x100m^2$ would filter too many nodes that in reality have low inter-node latency. We evaluate the effect of the cell size later in the experimental section. The location-based index can also be implemented using a different index structure that provides a more sophisticated partitioning scheme that partition the location in a gradual manner such as an R-tree.

4.2 Neighbor-Aware Edge Nodes

The neighboring information that is maintained by the Job Manager is shared to all the nodes. Thus, each node in the system is aware of the availability of its neighbors. Whenever a node joins (leaves) the system, the Job Manager will add (remove) the node information from its index structure and propagate this update to all nodes within the neighborhood. When an edge node initially joins the system, it will use the neighboring information and measure the estimated network latency to each of its neighbors. Once the node gets the estimated latency to its neighbors, the node will use this information to further filter and classify its neighbors by constructing a hierarchical data structure. This hierarchical data structure defines the priority of the neighbors (shown in Figure 2). Each level i in the hierarchy consists of all neighbor nodes whose latency to the node, L, is within a latency threshold: $(i - 1)T < L \leq iT$ where $i \geq 1$ and $i = 1$ is the top most level. This latency threshold T is set as a system parameter depending on the sensitivity required to the latency. For example, a neighbor node will be classified as a top-class neighbor if the latency between them is less than $T = 100ms$. On the other hand a neighbor node that has significantly high latency $L > 500ms$ can be ignored even if it is located in an adjacent cell.

This neighboring hierarchy is constructed and maintained by each node, meaning that any particular node may be classified to different levels by different nodes. For example, a node A may be classified as a top-level neighbor by node B since they are close to each other, but is considered as a third-level neighbor by node C since they are far away from each other. Nodes within the same class can be considered to have similar latency. The main reason of classifying nodes into different classes rather than simply sorting the nodes based on their latency is that it is less susceptible to latency variance. Thus, every node in the system is aware of the availability of its neighboring nodes and the latency to its neighbors.

To maintain an accurate and up-to-date latency between nodes, a node will have to frequently monitor the latency to all of its neighbors and update any of the latency information that has a large change. Although this fine grained monitoring will result in a high accuracy, in a large-scale environment, this may incur a high monitoring overhead. Furthermore, if the nodes in the system are

relatively static (regardless of the mobility of the end users), the network latency between nodes should be relatively stable. We rely on an estimation to determine the latency between nodes. Initially, each node will try to get an estimate of the network latency to each of its neighbors by sending multiple sizes of data to get an estimate latency for each data size. We assume that each individual data that is sent between nodes can be mapped to the latency prediction mapping. We believe this assumption is reasonable since each individual offloading request/data for most mobile applications is typically small (e.g., image update, sensor reading, etc.) [3, 13, 15] and thus its latency can be predicted within a small error margin. Although the size of each individual update is small, the challenge comes from the rate which may constrain the network availability of each node.

The location-based index that is maintained by the Job Manager determines the initial range of neighboring nodes that need to be monitored by each node. This may have a drawback of having false positive and false negative nodes during the pruning step which correspond to ignoring nodes that are located outside the neighboring bounding box with low inter-node latency and including nodes within the bounding box that have high inter-node latency respectively. However, this early pruning gives the benefit of removing the majority of high latency nodes which is highly beneficial in a real Mobile-Edge Computing environment consisting of a large scale of edge nodes.

Our Edge Cloud design pushes most of the decision making to the edges rather than relying on the global decision made by the Job Manager. This is made possible since each edge node itself has a complete knowledge of its neighbors. For example, in the case of workload burst, an edge node may determine which of its neighbors can be used to share its workload based on the latency information between them which can be used as a projection of latency that determines the computational hand-off overhead. Although the localized decision may be sub-optimal compared to a global decision, it gives us the benefit of allowing decisions to be made quicker and preventing potential bottlenecks in the centralized server.

5 EDGE NODE DISCOVERY

In this section, we discuss the node discovery mechanism to find any edge nodes that are located close to end-users. Most Mobile-Edge Computing applications rely on discovering nodes within the end-user's network coverage area. This means that an end-user can only discover edge nodes that are within the user's area or within the same network range (connected by local area network or within access points that are only a few hops away). This is a common approach for discovering nearby nodes especially for most sensor/IoT devices that use a broadcast discovery mechanism to find nearby edge nodes. Although this mechanism guarantees that the nodes that are found have little overhead to the users, this mechanism greatly limits the range of possible edge nodes that the users can utilize, leading to several disadvantages. First, when there are no available nodes within a close network range, nodes that are a few hops away with available resources may not be discovered at all, and hence the users are unable to utilize the nodes. Second, an edge node that is within the discovery range may have a high processing load or high network I/O loads (e.g., due to a hotspot). Thus, offloading to an already-overloaded node may even degrade the overall performance to the users. Hence, a user should be exposed to more node selection options.

Our edge node discovery mechanism relies on the global node availability provided by the Job Manager. It allows end-users to find a wide range of edge nodes even if there are no available nodes within the users' network range. Note that our technique does not eliminate the node discovery mechanism that allow end-users to find nodes that are located within a close network range. Instead, it can be used as an additional mechanism if the previous mechanism could not find any nearby edge nodes. The Job Manager uses user's location information to find any nodes that are located close to her by using the location-based index discussed in the previous section. Although the list of nodes that are returned by the Job Manager may include some nodes that do not have very low latency to the user, the list guarantees the closest available nodes in the system.

Once a user has been associated with a specific node, the node will share its neighboring node information to the user. This mechanism is used to handle potential failures of the associated node. When the associated node fails, its users can quickly find other nearby nodes from the node's neighboring list. In this case, the latency to a neighboring node is used as a projection to the latency between the user to the neighbor node. This results in a short distance from the neighbor node to the user since the distance between the failed node and its neighbors is small. If there was no available node in the neighboring list, the user would have to query the Job Manager again following the same steps as for initial node discovery mechanism.

6 LOCALITY-AWARE LOAD SHARING

As the number of resource-limited devices that are connected to the Internet increases rapidly along with the number of compute-intensive applications running on these devices, more and more applications would rely on Cloud's support for processing their data. This may cause a dynamic and skewed workload distribution which results in a particular set of edge nodes being heavily used and potentially becoming a bottleneck while leaving other nodes idle. If the system is unable to detect such a behavior, the use of the Edge Cloud for computational offloading may worsen the overall performance compared to leaving the computation on the devices themselves even with some of them have limited computing power. Although edge nodes have relatively more powerful computational capability compared to most mobile/sensor devices, these nodes typically have much more limited resources (e.g., CPU power, memory capacity, etc.) and network bandwidth compared to Data Center's nodes. So, these nodes are more prone to becoming overloaded compared to nodes in a centralized Cloud. Without the capability of sharing or balancing their workload, the use of edge nodes can potentially hurt the application desired goals. Thus, there is a need for Edge Cloud systems to handle such workload dynamics to maintain the low end-to-end latency requirement of mobile applications.

A common technique to handle workload dynamics in distributed systems is to dynamically share some of the workload to other nodes that are relatively idle. The load sharing in the context of

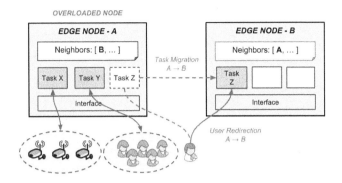

Figure 3: Load Sharing Mechanism

Mobile-Edge Computing (MEC) can be performed in two steps: 1) By handing-off some of the tasks to other nodes that are lightly loaded, and 2) By redirecting some of the end-users to other nodes if the high load is caused by a large volume of end-users connecting to a hotspot node [11, 14, 34, 37]. The latter case may require a task to be handed-off first from the overloaded node to the new nodes before redirecting its users to the new nodes (shown in Figure ??). The mechanism for seamlessly migrating a task from one node to another has been intensively studied in the context of handling user's mobility in MEC environment [12, 14, 34]. Similar mechanism can be used to handle task migration. However, the load sharing problem is still left with the question on *when* to share the workload and *which* nodes the workload should be shared with.

One possible metric to determine whether a node is overloaded is by monitoring if there is a slowdown of any of its tasks. This metric, however, only detects whether a node is overloaded and cannot be used to determine whether the node should share its workload since the latter requires a knowledge of the load information of other nodes as well. The problem of load sharing in MEC becomes more challenging since the edge nodes are highly distributed and may be connected by heterogeneous WAN with limited network bandwidth, unlike the intra-Data Center network. So, the system should carefully consider *which* nodes (if any) the workload should be shared with. A poor decision in selecting nodes for load sharing may worsen the overall performance to the end-users. For example, it may not be desirable to offload a task to another node that has already been heavily loaded or had its network congested, or to a node that incur too much network latency because it is far away from the user. This may result in an increase in the overall end-to-end latency caused by resource contention as in the former case, and high task migration or latency overhead in the latter case.

We propose a locality-aware load sharing technique with the goal of achieving applications latency goals in the case of dynamic workload. We achieve this goal by selectively choosing nodes where an overloaded node should share its workload with in order to prevent the possible issues that are discussed above. Our technique considers the nodes' resource availability, their current load, as well as the overhead of migrating the task and redirecting the users. All of this information can be obtain from the neighboring information that is maintained by each node.

To determine whether a node needs to share its workload, we rely on a per-application's desired-latency goal L_{app}. The goal of

Input : neighbor-list $N = \langle N_0, ... N_z \rangle$, latency-goal L_{app}
Output: $n \in N$
for *index level* $i : 0 \rightarrow z$ **do**
　if $iT < L_{app}$ **then**
　　for $n \in N_i$ **do**
　　　if *n not busy and has slot* **then**
　　　　return n;
　　　end
　　end
　else
　　cannot find node, return;
　end
end

Algorithm 1: Node Selection for Load Sharing

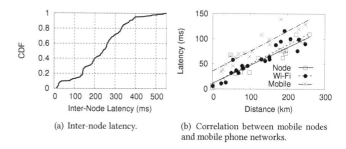

(a) Inter-node latency.　　　(b) Correlation between mobile nodes and mobile phone networks.

Figure 4: Edge Node Deployment

the system is to keep the end-to-end latency below the application's goal. To achieve this, each node needs to monitor the end-to-end latency information of each of its tasks which includes the time needed to process the offloaded data as well as the time taken to send the data between the user and the node. Each node periodically monitors the average latency $\bar{L}$ of a given task within the last time window t (e.g., $t = 30 seconds$). If $\bar{L} < L_{app}$, the node does not need to share its workload. Otherwise, the node will start to locate one of its neighbors to share its workload with. To determine *which* node to share the workload with, it traverses its neighboring hierarchy starting from the top level as shown in Algorithm 1 and finds any nodes that have an available task slot and are not overloaded. Neighbor nodes that are located within the same level will be considered to have similar latency to the node and thus the node may rely on other factors such as their computation power, current loads, etc.

Whenever a node decides to share its workload, we limit the number of additional neighbor node to share by 1 every t. If $\bar{L} > L_{app}$ even after the node has shared its workload, the node will locate an additional neighboring node to further reduce its workload. Thus, the amount of sharing increases gradually every t. The value of t itself provides a trade-off between the responsiveness to workload change and the waste of computation resources respectively. We implement such policy to prevent a node from hoarding its neighbors' resources in a short time period, resulting in an exhaustion of resources for other tasks and unpredictability of loads. Gradually acquiring resources will also prevent interference of already running tasks on the neighboring node due to a sudden increase in the number of additional shared tasks. This approach also performs well in practice since workload changes usually increase/decrease in a gradual manner within a few seconds.

Once a neighboring node is selected, the node needs to determine the amount of workload that should be shared with its neighbor based on the workload characteristic over the last t window. To determine this, the node will find the ratio of its workload to share to its neighbors by solving the following equation:

$$Min(Max((r_{self} * \bar{L}), ..., (r_i * \bar{L}_i))), where \sum r = 1 \quad (1)$$

where r_{self} and r_i are the ratios of the workload to be run on the original node and neighbor node i respectively. L and L_i are the

estimated latency of accessing the original node and the neighboring node which is obtained from the neighboring information. We estimate the latency between end-user to the neighboring node using a projection of the inter-node latency. The Max property in the function is used since the completion time is typically determined by the completion time of processing the last record. The optimization problem is then to minimize the overall time.

These load sharing ratios for each node will be used for workload in the next t interval. If $\bar{L}$ falls below λL_{app}, the node will gradually reduce the number of neighbors it used to share the workload with. The reason of adding a λ factor is to prevent a fluctuation in latency. For example, if we set $\lambda = 1$ and $\bar{L} = 290ms < L_{app} = 300ms$ after the node shares 40% of its workload to another node and decides that it will stop sharing the workload since $\bar{L} < L_{app}$, this may increases $\bar{L}$ again in the next t window. In this case, the latency of the application will fluctuate for every t interval. We set $\lambda = 0.8$ in our deployment since it works well with the dynamism of the workload we consider.

7 EXPERIMENTAL EVALUATION

7.1 Experimental Setup and Methodology

Edge Cloud System Setup. We evaluated our Edge Cloud system using 20 physical PlanetLab [7] nodes (with up to 3 virtual nodes in each location) that are geographically distributed across the U.S. (ranging from U.S. West to U.S. East). We did not consider nodes that are located in the same physical machine as neighbors to each other since doing so will completely eliminate the latency to the neighboring nodes which is unrealistic in a real deployment. Both the Job Manager and the Node Manager were deployed on a reliable centralized server located in Minnesota. This centralized server did not participate in any task processing and it was not a bottleneck in our deployment since its only purpose was for node monitoring and task scheduling. Figure 4(a) shows the inter-node latency in our deployment. We can see that sending data to a distant node may incur up to 40X higher latency compared to sending the data to a nearby node. This shows the importance of node selection policy for workload sharing.

We simulated the end-users using a daemon program running on 10 different PlanetLab nodes and 10 other PlanetLab nodes as the workload generator where some of them are actually the same nodes. These nodes are not part of the edge nodes that are contributing as compute nodes. We call these simulated users as *mobile nodes*. We validated our methodology of simulating the mobile

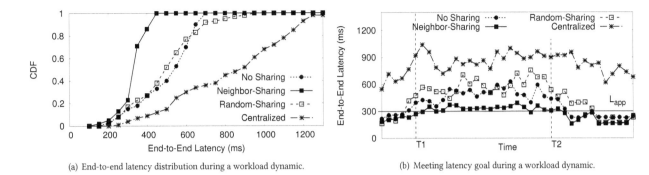

(a) End-to-end latency distribution during a workload dynamic.　　　　(b) Meeting latency goal during a workload dynamic.

Figure 5: Benefit of Locality-Aware Load Sharing

users using mobile nodes (Figure 4(b)). We compared the latency of accessing the edge nodes using mobile nodes with the latency of accessing edge nodes using mobile phones with Wi-Fi and mobile network (*Node*, *Wi-Fi*, and *Mobile* respectively). We see that they have a strong correlation.

The location-based index of the Job Manager is implemented using a grid index with 144 cells (unless explicitly specified) which partitions the geographic U.S. map into equal size of cells based on the coordinates. Nodes that lie within the same cell or one of the adjacent cells are considered as neighbors. For the neighboring list that is maintained by each node, we set the threshold of each level i to $T_i = i * 100ms$ with a maximum of 3 levels. Thus, neighboring nodes that are $> 300ms$ away will not be considered for workload sharing. We also set the evaluation time window t to 10 seconds. So, each node will evaluate whether to share its workload based on the workload characteristic in the past $t = 10$ seconds.

Workload Trace and Applications. We used a real three-day Twitter sample trace as our workload that contains approximately 4 million tweets per day. This trace was obtained from December 2015 and it includes dynamic workload over time from real mobile users. We sped up the tweet rate by 24X since the trace only shows a fraction of the real Twitter workload. This is done to better see the effect of overloaded nodes in a real deployment. The tweet data sources are partitioned and deployed to the nodes based on each tweet's location coordinates. So, the skewness of workload and the location of hotspots are naturally included in the workload.

We use a location-based top-k popular topic as our application that is executed on the edge nodes. This application aggregates all the tweets within a specific region and returns the top k words. The data processing on the edge nodes itself incurs only a small fraction of the end-to-end latency which is the time taken from the time the end-user sends the data to the edge node to the time the user obtains the result. We observe that the major fraction of the end-to-end latency is incurred by the wide-area network latency for offloading the data. This is reasonable for many Mobile-Cloud applications since most of the task processing can typically be processed with low processing time.

System Comparison. We compare our neighbor-aware load sharing technique (*Neighbor Sharing*) with 1) The use of an Edge Cloud that does not consider load sharing (*No Sharing*), 2) The use of an Edge Cloud that use load sharing with random node selection to

determine which nodes a workload should be shared with (*Random Sharing*), and 3) The use of a centralized Cloud (*Centralized*) as our baselines. All of the Edge Cloud usages were deployed using the same node deployment while in the centralized case, we deployed more nodes/resources in a single location to simulate a higher computational power available in a centralized Cloud.

In the case of Random-sharing, an overloaded node would randomly choose any available nodes ignoring the latency overhead between them that is used as a projection to the end-user and the current workload of the other nodes. On the other hand, the overloaded nodes in the Neighbor-sharing would only consider sharing their workload to nodes that are located close to the overloaded nodes and the nodes are only selected if they are not overloaded. The nodes in the centralized Cloud itself are deployed using PlanetLab nodes. Furthermore, for the centralized result, we deployed the Centralized server in different number of locations for each iteration: U.S. West, U.S. Mid-West, and U.S. East.

7.2 Benefit of Locality-aware Load Sharing

In the following set of experiments we evaluate our locality-aware load sharing technique in the case of dynamic workload. We set the application's latency goal L_{app} to 300 ms and gradually scale up/down the workload by up to 14X. Figure 5 shows the performance impact caused by the workload dynamic. We make a few observations from the result. First, we can see that the use of Edge Cloud significantly outperforms the use of centralized Cloud in all of the cases as shown in Figure 5(a) which shows the latency CDF of all approaches. We also observe that the increase in workload did not have significant slow down in the computation time performed on the node itself. Rather, the latency incurred by the data offloading to an edge node is the dominant factor due to the contention of the limited wide-area network bandwidth. Thus, although the centralized Cloud deployment has more processing power (lower computation time), it still suffers from the high overhead between the mobile nodes to the centralized nodes.

Secondly, we observe that the node selection decision for load sharing is critical. We can see from Figure 5(a) that the Random-sharing performs worse compared to the Neighbor-sharing. The reason is that in the Random-sharing approach, an overloaded node might select one of its neighbors that are far away to the users or neighbors that have already had high load. Comparing the No-sharing and the Random-sharing approaches, we can also see that

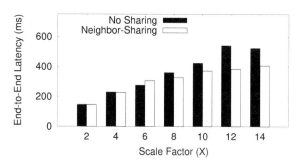

Figure 6: Increase in Latency Over Scaled Workload

the latter performs better than the former approach below the 75th percentile but has a longer tail later in the distribution. This shows that randomly selecting nodes to share a workload may result in selecting nodes with very high overhead and may suffer at a higher percentile.

Thirdly, our neighbor-aware load sharing is able to maintain a close gap to the application-specified latency goal that was set to 300 ms in this case. Figure 5(b) shows a snapshot of the trace during a dynamic workload where the workload increased from T_1 to T_2 and decreased afterward. Before T_1, all Edge Cloud approaches performed comparably. However, as the workload increased ($T_1 < T < T_2$), some of the edge nodes became overloaded and started to result in a higher end-to-end latency. Approaches that consider load sharing (Random-sharing and Neighbor-sharing) started to look for other nodes for sharing their workload.

We can see that the Neighbor-sharing is able to maintain a close gap to the application latency goal (within 20% increase in latency). If there were no neighboring nodes that could provide low overhead, the overloaded node would handle the tasks by itself. However, if there were any nearby nodes with low network latency overhead, it would start sharing the workload to one of the neighboring nodes. When the workload decreased at T_2 and the end-to-end latency dropped below the threshold, all policies that used load sharing mechanism started to decrease the number of shares and eventually stopped sharing their workload. These results show that the use of Edge Cloud is not sufficient to satisfy application's latency goal especially in the case of dynamic workload.

We also observe the scalability of our locality-aware load sharing approach by scaling up the load with different scale factors. Figure 6 shows the impact to end-to-end latency due to an increase in the workload. We can see that even with the Neighbor-sharing approach, the latency may still increase beyond the end-to-end latency-desired goal. The main reason to this is that some of the edge nodes in our deployment did not have any neighbors where they can share their workload with. Thus, they caused a slowdown to the overall time. However, it increases in a much more graceful way compared to the No-sharing approach. We also see that the number of tasks that satisfied the latency goal is much higher than the No-sharing approach.

7.3 Impact of Neighbor Distance

In this experiment we study the effect of setting the minimum distance between nodes which we call as *neighbor distance* as a parameter to determine whether a node should be considered as a

neighbor. At one extreme, the neighbor distance may cover the entire area which make every node consider all other nodes as its neighbors. In this case, nodes that are very far away may still be selected for workload sharing since they are considered as its neighbor. This is effectively similar to the random node selection approach with an additional consideration of not selecting busy nodes. At the other extreme, the index cell size may be limited to have a very small coverage which makes a node only consider another node as its neighbor if they are very close to each other.

Figure 7 shows the impact of varying the number of grid cells to the end-to-end latency. The larger the number of the grid cells is, the smaller the neighbor distance is and vise versa. We can see that the performance improved as we increased the number of cells but later decreased as the number of cells was set too high (number of cells = 256). The reason behind the improvement in the early increasing number of cells is because the neighboring list only included nodes that were actually close to each other. However, as we limited the cell size too small, more and more nodes were not able to find any neighbors and hence were unable to share their workload. This pattern will converge as the number of neighbor nodes for each node reaches 0.

Figure 7(b) explains this phenomenon. With cell size equals to 1, all of the nodes were considered as neighbors to every node even if some of them are very far away (one in U.S. West and the other one is in U.S. East). As the number of cells increases (the neighbor distance/cell size decreases), less number of nodes were considered as neighbors but these neighbor nodes were actually close to the node itself.

7.4 Handling Node Failure

In this experiment we show the benefit of neighbor-awareness in the case where the node that has been associated with an end-user fails. When the node fails, the end-user can quickly re-associate herself to one of the node's neighbors without requesting for a new node from the centralized server. This mechanism is made possible since this neighbor node information is shared to the user.

In this experiment, we did not add any other variations to the workload. Figure 8 shows the impact of adding failure to nodes in our system. We randomly terminated any of edge nodes that were supporting any end-users starting from time T_1. We can see that by having a knowledge of the availability of the alternative nodes, the end-user can quickly re-associate herself to one of the failed node's neighbors. There is a small increase in the latency due to the timeout mechanism that was used to detect node failure and re-association time to the new node. On the other hand, if there was no information of the availability of the neighboring nodes, the end-user would have to connect to the centralized server. In either case, when the failed node returns at time T_2, the user could be redirected back to the recovered node or kept being supported by the covering node depending on whether the current end-to-end latency met the application-desired latency goal. If the latency has already met the latency goal, there is no reason for re-associating back to the recovered node. We also plot the latency of the centralized Cloud to show that the use of Edge Cloud still outperform the centralized Cloud even in the case of node failure. This shows

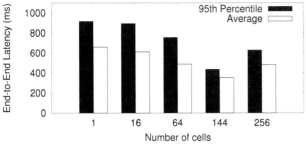

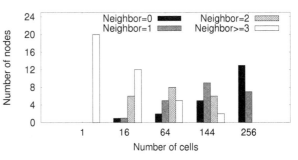

(a) Effect of different cell sizes to the overall end-to-end latency.   (b) Neighboring node distribution over different cell sizes

Figure 7: Effect of Different Cell Sizes to the Performance

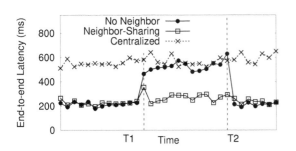

Figure 8: Maintaining Low Latency During Node Failure

that using an Edge Cloud platform is more suitable for the Mobile-Cloud Computing applications that we consider compared to the use of centralized Cloud even if the Edge Cloud is more susceptible to failures.

8 RELATED WORK

There are a number of projects that have looked at the opportunity of utilizing Cloud resources to support mobile/sensor devices. Most of them focus on the oportunity of reducing the processing time or saving energy consumption or both. [2, 8, 16, 27, 31, 40]. Others [13, 17, 20, 41] have also looked at mobile data management and utilizing Cloud's storage services for managing mobile users' data by using Cloud's resources as caches or consistency management. Although many of these works are relevant, most of these systems do not consider the runtime dynamics which are common in Mobile-Edge Computing environment. Our work is different from most of the existing works in that we focus on handling runtime dynamics where some of the edge nodes may become a bottleneck due to changes in workload. Furthermore, we study the problem of selecting *which* nodes should be selected for load sharing and *how much* of the workload should be shared if a node decides to share its workload. Existing mechanism for computational offloading and policies that determine which parts of the computation should be offloaded can be applied to our work.

Load balancing is a common technique that has been extensively studied in the area of distributed systems, Cloud Computing, network routing, and peer-to-peer systems [5, 23, 29, 38]. Most of the existing techniques rely on the tasks scheduling decision that determines where to schedule new tasks on the system to balance

the workload. Our work, however, is different from them in that we focus on the Mobile-Edge Computing environment where the nodes are interconnected by wide-area network. In our context, the load sharing is done using a user redirection and task migration rather than tasks scheduling. Furthermore, our main goal is not to get a balance workload in the system. Instead, we try to achieve each application's desired latency goals during workload dynamics.

9 CONCLUSION AND FUTURE WORK

In this paper, we study the problem of load sharing to handle runtime dynamics in a Mobile-Edge Computing (MEC) environment. Our motivation is based on the dynamic property of the workload in MEC along with the low latency requirement for many of today's mobile/IoT applications. The Edge Cloud platform that has been proposed to provide computational offloading support for mobile applications faces additional challenges in handling workload dynamics since the nodes in Edge Clouds are typically connected by WAN with high network latency and limited bandwidth. We propose a locality-aware load sharing technique that allows edge nodes to share their workload to other nodes to meet the low latency requirement of the mobile applications in the case of workload increases. Our load sharing technique allows nodes to 1) Intelligently determines whether to share their workload to other nodes, 2) Selectively chooses which nodes the workload should be shared with, and 3) Determines how much of the workload should be shared. Our experimental results based on a real Twitter's trace show that our locality-aware load sharing technique is able to keep the overall latency of mobile applications close to the applications' desired goals as well as better utilize resources even in the case of dynamic workload.

In the future, we would like to consider the overhead of task migration between nodes in addition to the data transfer overhead and incorporate the cost to the load sharing decision. Furthermore, we would also like to consider different classes of mobile applications whose execution time itself may be the dominant part of the computational offloading overhead. In this case, the system should consider this variety of applications and may make the load sharing decision differently. Lastly, we would also like to integrate the energy consumption consideration on the mobile devices and allows the device itself to intelligently determine whether to use a Cloud's resources during a high workload condition.

10 ACKNOWLEDGMENT

The authors would like to acknowledge grant NSF CSR-1162405 and CNS-1619254 that supported this research.

REFERENCES

[1] Suman Banerjee and Dapeng Oliver Wu. 2013. Final report from the NSF Workshop on Future Directions in Wireless Networking. (2013).

[2] Marco V Barbera, Sokol Kosta, Alessandro Mei, and Julinda Stefa. 2013. To offload or not to offload? the bandwidth and energy costs of mobile cloud computing. In *INFOCOM, 2013 Proceedings IEEE*. IEEE, 1285–1293.

[3] David Barrett. 2013. One surveillance camera for every 11 people in Britain, says CCTV survey. *The Telegraph* 10 (2013).

[4] Flavio Bonomi, Rodolfo Milito, Jiang Zhu, and Sateesh Addepalli. 2012. Fog computing and its role in the internet of things. In *Proceedings of the first edition of the MCC workshop on Mobile cloud computing*. ACM, 13–16.

[5] Valeria Cardellini, Michele Colajanni, and Philip S Yu. 1999. Dynamic load balancing on web-server systems. *IEEE Internet computing* 3, 3 (1999), 28–39.

[6] Kyungmin Lee David Chu, Eduardo Cuervo, Johannes Kopf, Sergey Grizan, Alec Wolman, and Jason Flinn. [n. d.]. Outatime: Using Speculation to Enable Low-Latency Continuous Interaction for Cloud Gaming. ([n. d.]).

[7] Brent Chun, David Culler, Timothy Roscoe, Andy Bavier, Larry Peterson, Mike Wawrzoniak, and Mic Bowman. 2003. Planetlab: an overlay testbed for broad-coverage services. *ACM SIGCOMM Computer Communication Review* 33, 3 (2003), 3–12.

[8] Eduardo Cuervo, Aruna Balasubramanian, Dae-ki Cho, Alec Wolman, Stefan Saroiu, Ranveer Chandra, and Paramvir Bahl. 2010. MAUI: making smartphones last longer with code offload. In *Proceedings of the 8th international conference on Mobile systems, applications, and services*. ACM, 49–62.

[9] Stephen R Ellis, Katerina Mania, Bernard D Adelstein, and Michael I Hill. 2004. Generalizeability of latency detection in a variety of virtual environments. In *Proceedings of the Human Factors and Ergonomics Society Annual Meeting*, Vol. 48. SAGE Publications Sage CA: Los Angeles, CA, 2632–2636.

[10] Dave Evans. 2011. The internet of things: How the next evolution of the internet is changing everything. *CISCO white paper* 1 (2011), 1–11.

[11] Chaima Ghribi, Makhlouf Hadji, and Djamal Zeghlache. 2013. Energy efficient vm scheduling for cloud data centers: Exact allocation and migration algorithms. In *Cluster, Cloud and Grid Computing (CCGrid), 2013 13th IEEE/ACM International Symposium on*. IEEE, 671–678.

[12] Mark S Gordon, Davoud Anoushe Jamshidi, Scott A Mahlke, Zhuoqing Morley Mao, and Xu Chen. 2012. COMET: Code Offload by Migrating Execution Transparently.. In *OSDI*, Vol. 12. 93–106.

[13] Trinabh Gupta, Rayman Preet Singh, Amar Phanishayee, Jaeyeon Jung, and Ratul Mahajan. 2014. Bolt: Data Management for Connected Homes.. In *NSDI*. 243–256.

[14] Kiryong Ha, Yoshihisa Abe, Zhuo Chen, Wenlu Hu, Brandon Amos, Padmanabhan Pillai, and Mahadev Satyanarayanan. 2015. *Adaptive vm handoff across cloudlets*. Technical Report. Technical Report CMU-CS-15-113, CMU School of Computer Science.

[15] Kiryong Ha, Zhuo Chen, Wenlu Hu, Wolfgang Richter, Padmanabhan Pillai, and Mahadev Satyanarayanan. 2014. Towards wearable cognitive assistance. In *Proceedings of the 12th annual international conference on Mobile systems, applications, and services*. ACM, 68–81.

[16] Karim Habak, Mostafa Ammar, Khaled A Harras, and Ellen Zegura. 2015. Femto clouds: Leveraging mobile devices to provide cloud service at the edge. In *Cloud Computing (CLOUD), 2015 IEEE 8th International Conference on*. IEEE, 9–16.

[17] Wassim Itani, Ayman Kayssi, and Ali Chehab. 2010. Energy-efficient incremental integrity for securing storage in mobile cloud computing. In *Energy Aware Computing (ICEAC), 2010 International Conference on*. IEEE, 1–2.

[18] Albert Jonathan, Mathew Ryden, Kwangsung Oh, Abhishek Chandra, and Jon Weissman. 2017. Nebula: Distributed Edge Cloud for Data Intensive Computing. *IEEE Transactions on Parallel and Distributed Systems* (2017).

[19] Sudarsun Kannan, Ada Gavrilovska, and Karsten Schwan. 2011. Cloud4Home–Enhancing Data Services with@ Home Clouds. In *Distributed Computing Systems (ICDCS), 2011 31st International Conference on*. IEEE, 539–548.

[20] Johannes Kolb, William Myott, Thao Nguyen, Aniruddha Chandra, and Jon Weissman. 2014. Exploiting User Interest in Data-Driven Cloud-Based Mobile Optimization. In *Mobile Cloud Computing, Services, and Engineering (Mobile-Cloud), 2014 2nd IEEE International Conference on*. IEEE, 228–235.

[21] Kyungmin Lee, David Chu, Eduardo Cuervo, Johannes Kopf, Alec Wolman, Yury Degtyarev, Sergey Grizan, and Jason Flinn. 2015. Outatime: Using speculation to enable low-latency continuous interaction for mobile cloud gaming. *GetMobile: Mobile Computing and Communications* 19, 3 (2015), 14–17.

[22] Min-Joong Lee and Chin-Wan Chung. 2011. A user similarity calculation based on the location for social network services. In *Database Systems for Advanced Applications*. Springer, 38–52.

[23] Lei Lei, Zhangdui Zhong, Kan Zheng, Jiadi Chen, and Hanlin Meng. 2013. Challenges on wireless heterogeneous networks for mobile cloud computing. *IEEE Wireless Communications* 20, 3 (2013), 34–44.

[24] Dawei Li, Theodoros Salonidis, Nirmit V Desai, and Mooi Choo Chuah. 2016. DeepCham: Collaborative Edge-Mediated Adaptive Deep Learning for Mobile Object Recognition. In *Edge Computing (SEC), IEEE/ACM Symposium on*. IEEE, 64–76.

[25] Christian Licoppe and Yoriko Inada. 2006. Emergent uses of a multiplayer location-aware mobile game: The interactional consequences of mediated encounters. *Mobilities* 1, 1 (2006), 39–61.

[26] Peng Liu, Dale Willis, and Suman Banerjee. 2016. ParaDrop: Enabling Lightweight Multi-tenancy at the NetworkâĂŹs Extreme Edge. In *Edge Computing (SEC), IEEE/ACM Symposium on*. IEEE, 1–13.

[27] Emiliano Miluzzo, Ramón Cáceres, and Yih-Farn Chen. 2012. Vision: mClouds-computing on clouds of mobile devices. In *Proceedings of the third ACM workshop on Mobile cloud computing and services*. ACM, 9–14.

[28] Venkata N Padmanabhan and Lakshminarayanan Subramanian. 2001. An investigation of geographic mapping techniques for Internet hosts. In *ACM SIGCOMM Computer Communication Review*, Vol. 31. ACM, 173–185.

[29] Ananth Rao, Karthik Lakshminarayanan, Sonesh Surana, Richard Karp, and Ion Stoica. 2003. Load balancing in structured P2P systems. *Peer-to-Peer Systems II* (2003), 68–79.

[30] Mahadev Satyanarayanan. 1996. Fundamental challenges in mobile computing. In *Proceedings of the fifteenth annual ACM symposium on Principles of distributed computing*. ACM, 1–7.

[31] Mahadev Satyanarayanan, Paramvir Bahl, Ramón Caceres, and Nigel Davies. 2009. The case for vm-based cloudlets in mobile computing. *Pervasive Computing, IEEE* 8, 4 (2009), 14–23.

[32] Lakshminarayanan Subramanian, Venkata N Padmanabhan, and Randy H Katz. 2002. Geographic Properties of Internet Routing.. In *USENIX Annual Technical Conference, General Track*. 243–259.

[33] Pratap Tokekar, Deepak Bhadauria, Andrew Studenski, and Volkan Isler. 2010. A robotic system for monitoring carp in Minnesota lakes. *Journal of Field Robotics* 27, 6 (2010), 779–789.

[34] Franco Travostino, Paul Daspit, Leon Gommans, Chetan Jog, Cees De Laat, Joe Mambretti, Inder Monga, Bas Van Oudenaarde, Satish Raghunath, and Phil Yonghui Wang. 2006. Seamless live migration of virtual machines over the MAN/WAN. *Future Generation Computer Systems* 22, 8 (2006), 901–907.

[35] Luis M Vaquero and Luis Rodero-Merino. 2014. Finding your way in the fog: Towards a comprehensive definition of fog computing. *ACM SIGCOMM Computer Communication Review* 44, 5 (2014), 27–32.

[36] George Vellidis, Michael Tucker, Calvin Perry, Craig Kvien, and C Bednarz. 2008. A real-time wireless smart sensor array for scheduling irrigation. *Computers and electronics in agriculture* 61, 1 (2008), 44–50.

[37] Shiqiang Wang, Rahul Urgaonkar, Murtaza Zafer, Ting He, Kevin Chan, and Kin K Leung. 2015. Dynamic service migration in mobile edge-clouds. In *IFIP Networking Conference (IFIP Networking), 2015*. IEEE, 1–9.

[38] Xianglin Wei, Jianhua Fan, Ziyi Lu, and Ke Ding. 2013. Application scheduling in mobile cloud computing with load balancing. *Journal of Applied Mathematics* 2013 (2013).

[39] W Wen. 2008. A dynamic and automatic traffic light control expert system for solving the road congestion problem. *Expert Systems with Applications* 34, 4 (2008), 2370–2381.

[40] Ben Zhang, Nitesh Mor, John Kolb, Douglas S Chan, Ken Lutz, Eric Allman, John Wawrzynek, Edward Lee, and John Kubiatowicz. 2015. The cloud is not enough: saving iot from the cloud. In *7th USENIX Workshop on Hot Topics in Cloud Computing (HotCloud 15)*.

[41] Irene Zhang, Niel Lebeck, Pedro Fonseca, Brandon Holt, Raymond Cheng, Ariadna Norberg, Arvind Krishnamurthy, and Henry M Levy. 2016. Diamond: Automating Data Management and Storage for Wide-Area, Reactive Applications.. In *OSDI*. 723–738.

[42] Tan Zhang, Aakanksha Chowdhery, Paramvir Victor Bahl, Kyle Jamieson, and Suman Banerjee. 2015. The design and implementation of a wireless video surveillance system. In *Proceedings of the 21st Annual International Conference on Mobile Computing and Networking*. ACM, 426–438.

[43] Jiang Zhu, Douglas S Chan, Mythili Suryanarayana Prabhu, Prem Natarajan, Hao Hu, and Flavio Bonomi. 2013. Improving web sites performance using edge servers in fog computing architecture. In *Service Oriented System Engineering (SOSE), 2013 IEEE 7th International Symposium on*. IEEE, 320–323.

Is Singularity-based Container Technology Ready for Running MPI Applications on HPC Clouds? *

Jie Zhang
The Ohio State University
Columbus, Ohio
zhanjie@cse.ohio-state.edu

Xiaoyi Lu
The Ohio State University
Columbus, Ohio
luxi@cse.ohio-state.edu

Dhabaleswar K. Panda
The Ohio State University
Columbus, Ohio
panda@cse.ohio-state.edu

ABSTRACT

The Message Passing Interface (MPI) standard has become the de facto programming model for parallel computing with the last 25-year continuous community effort. With the development of building efficient HPC clouds, more and more MPI-based HPC applications start running on cloud-based environments. Singularity is one of the most attractive container technologies to build HPC clouds due to the claimed reproducible environments across the HPC centers. However, our investigations in the literature show that there is a lack of a systematical study on evaluating the performance of Singularity with various benchmarks and applications on different types of HPC platforms. Without these studies, it remains difficult to tell the community whether Singularity-based container technology is ready or not for running MPI applications on HPC clouds to gain desired performance. To fill this gap in the literature, as a third-party, we first propose a four-dimension evaluation methodology to cover various aspects and based on that, we conduct extensive studies on evaluating the performance of Singularity on modern processors, and high-performance interconnects. Performance results prove that Singularity-based container technology can achieve near-native performance for both Intel Xeon and Intel Xeon Knights Landing (KNL) platforms with different memory access modes (i.e., cache, flat). Singularity also shows very little overhead for running MPI-based HPC applications on both Omni-Path and Infini-Band networks. With the verification of our results, we believe that Singularity can be used for building next-generation HPC clouds with near-native performance as well as desired cloud features such as easy management and deployment.

KEYWORDS

Container, Singularity, Intel KNL, Intel Omni-Path, MPI, HPC Clouds

*This research is supported in part by National Science Foundation grants #CNS-1419123, #IIS-1447804, and #CNS-1513120.

1 INTRODUCTION

Thanks to the continuous community effort since 25 years ago, the Message Passing Interface (MPI) standard has been becoming the de facto programming model for parallel computing, compared with other models such as Partitioned Global Address Space (PGAS) [8, 14, 15, 17, 20]. At the point of celebrating 25 years of MPI, if we look back at history, we can see that most of MPI-based HPC applications were run on native environments for achieving high performance, which is always the first goal of designing efficient MPI runtimes and applications.

With the latest technology developments, the community is trying to bring cloud-based techniques, concepts, and associated benefits into the HPC world, which forms an active research area – building efficient HPC clouds [10–13, 16, 25, 30]. On this front, container-based virtualization technologies (such as Docker [6], Singularity [16]) have been seen as the most promising ways for building HPC clouds due to their claimed low overhead compared to hypervisor-based virtualization (such as KVM, Xen). However, based on our earlier experiences with Docker [9, 31], we find that if we run MPI applications inside default Docker instances without changing Docker configurations and MPI runtime designs, Docker shows a significant amount of overhead compared to the native environment. This result violates our earlier intuition that Docker-like container technologies should have similar performance as native environments.

Due to the overhead and other disadvantages of Docker for HPC [16], in these days, Singularity has become one of the most attractive container technologies in the HPC field. Singularity community has claimed that the primary design goals of Singularity is to provide the reproducible environments across the HPC centers and to deliver the near-native performance for HPC applications. With our earlier experiences with Docker, we cautiously take the performance of Singularity into account. Through an extensive survey among the related literatures, however we find that there is a lack of a systematical study on evaluating the performance of Singularity with various benchmarks and applications on different modern HPC platforms, including different processor architectures (e.g., Xeon, Xeon Phi [26]), different types of interconnects (e.g., Omni-Path [3], InfiniBand), etc. Without these studies, it is difficult to find out that – *"Is Singularity-based container technology ready for running MPI applications on HPC clouds with different kinds of cutting-edge hardware technologies?"*

1.1 Contributions

To fill this gap in the literature, as a third-party, we first propose a four-dimension evaluation methodology to cover various aspects and based on that, we conduct an extensive study on evaluating the performance of Singularity on modern processors, and high-performance interconnects. Performance results prove that Singularity-based container technology can achieve near-native performance for both Intel Xeon and Intel Xeon Knights Landing platforms with different memory access modes (i.e., cache mode, flat mode). Singularity also shows very little overhead (less than 8%) for running MPI point-to-point and collective benchmarks and HPC applications on both Omni-Path and InfiniBand networks. To the best of our knowledge, this is the first paper that systematically evaluates the performance of running MPI-based applications on Singularity with modern processor architectures and high-performance networks and share our results with the community. To summarize, this paper makes the following key contributions:

- Presents a four-dimension (i.e., processor architectures, network types, memory modes, virtualization overhead) based evaluation methodology to cover various aspects of characterizing Singularity performance
- Conducts extensive performance evaluation experiments on cutting-edge hardware technologies, such as Intel Xeon, KNL, Omni-Path, and InfiniBand, which are the most important drivers for modern HPC platforms
- Provides detailed performance reports and analysis of running MPI benchmarks and applications with Singularity on different platforms

We validate the effectiveness and efficiency of Singularity as an important technology player in this field. Through our studies, we believe that Singularity can be used for building next-generation HPC clouds with near-native performance as well as desired cloud features such as easy management and deployment.

The rest of the paper is organized as follows. In Section 2, we describe the background knowledge related to this work. Evaluation methodology of this paper is elaborated in Section 3. Section 4 presents the evaluation results. Section 5 discusses the related work. Finally, we summarize conclusion in Section 6.

2 BACKGROUND

2.1 Container-based Virtualization

Virtualization provides the abstractions of multiple virtual resources by utilizing an intermediate software layer on top of the underlying system. There are several virtualization techniques. Hypervisor-based virtualization is one of the most popular techniques. Figure 1 shows a hypervisor-based virtualization, in its most common form, consists of a hypervisor, also called the virtual machine monitor (VMM), on top of a host operating system that provides a full abstraction of VM. In this example, each VM executes completely isolated from the others and has its own operating system.

Container-based virtualization is a lightweight alternative to the hypervisor-based virtualization. As shown in Figure 1, the host kernel allows the execution of several isolated user space instances to run a different software stack (system libraries, services, applications). Container-based virtualization provides self-contained execution environments, effectively isolating applications that rely on the same kernel in the Linux operating system, but it does not introduce a layer of virtual hardware. There are two core mature Linux technologies to build containers, namely namespaces and cgroups. First, namespace isolation can be used to isolate a group of processes at various levels: networking, filesystem, process identifiers (PIDs), host name and domain name (UTS), inter-process communication (IPC) and users. Namespaces provide processes with a virtual view of their operating environments. Second, cgroups (control groups) can be used to limit and isolate the use of resources like CPU, memory, disk I/O, and network, from of a collection of processes.

Docker [6] is a popular open-source platform for building and running containers and offers several important features, including portable deployment across machines, versioning, reuse of container image and a searchable public registry for images. In addition, users could use docker to share certain namespaces with either the host or other containers. For example, sharing the host's process (PID) namespace allows the processes within the containers to see all of the processes on the system. In addition, sharing IPC namespace can accelerate inter-process communication with shared memory segments, semaphores, and message queues. However, the MPI library still needs modification to take advantage of these flexibilities.

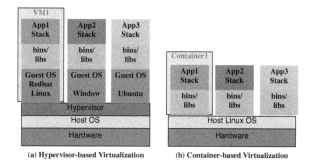

(a) Hypervisor-based Virtualization   (b) Container-based Virtualization

Figure 1: Hypervisor- and Container-based Virtualization

2.2 Singularity

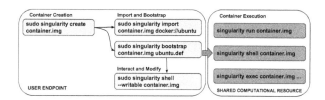

Figure 2: Singularity usage workflows

Singularity [16] enables users to have full control of their environment. This means that a non-privileged user can "swap out" the operating system on the host for one they control. So if the host system is running RHEL6 but your application runs in Ubuntu, you can create an Ubuntu image, install your applications into that image, copy the image to another host, and run your application on that host in its native Ubuntu environment. As shown in Figure 2, the standard Singularity usage workflow involves a working endpoint (left) where the user has root, and a container can be created, modified and updated, and then transferred to a shared computational resource (right) to be executed at scale. Moreover, Singularity also allows the users to leverage the resources of whatever host you are on. This includes HPC interconnects, resource managers, file systems, GPUs and/or accelerators, etc. Singularity does this by enabling several key facets: 1. Encapsulation of the environment; 2. Containers are image based; 3. No user contextual changes or root escalation allowed; 4. No root owned daemon processes. Singularity uses the filesystem (mount), PID and user namespaces.

2.3 Intel KNL Architecture

Intel Knights Landing (KNL) is the successor to Knights Corner (KNC) many-core architecture that is a self-booting processor which packs up to six Teraflops of computing throughput. KNL comes equipped with 68-72 cores located on 34-36 active tiles. Each tile has a single 1-megabyte L2 cache that is shared between the two cores and each core further supports four threads by hyperthreading. A 2D-mesh interconnect is used for on-die communication by the cores, memory and I/O controllers, and other agents.

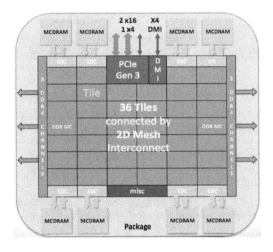

Figure 3: Intel KNL Overview [26]

2.4 Intel KNL Memory Modes

KNL comprises of six DDR4 channels and eight Multi-Channel DRAM (MCDRAM) channels. The MCDRAM memory can yield an aggregate bandwidth of 450 GB/s in contrast with DDR4 memory which can yield 90 GB/s, hence aptly referred

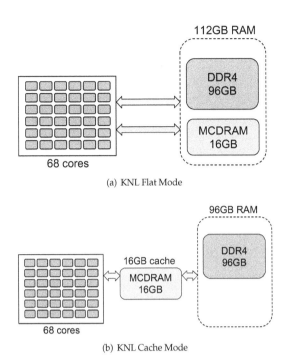

(a) KNL Flat Mode

(b) KNL Cache Mode

Figure 4: KNL Memory Modes [27]

to as High Bandwidth Memory (HBM). The processor's memory mode determines whether the fast HBM operates as RAM, as direct-mapped L3 cache, or as a mixture of the two. From a software perspective, the two common ways of directing allocations on the HBM is through the use Linux NUMA utilities or through the memkind library [21]. Through these utilities, programs can direct perform memory allocations on either the DRAM or HBM in the flat and hybrid modes of operation.

2.4.1 Cache Mode. This mode is shown in Figure 4(b). The fast HBM is configured as an L3 cache. The operating system transparently uses the HBM to move data from main memory. In this mode, the user has access to 96GB of RAM, all of it traditional DDR4.

2.4.2 Flat Mode. This mode is shown in Figure 4(a). DDR4 and HBM act as two distinct Non-Uniform Memory Access (NUMA) nodes. Therefore, it is possible to specify the type of memory (DDR4 or HBM) when allocating memory. In this mode, the user has access to 112GB of RAM: 96GB of traditional DDR and 16GB of fast HBM. By default, memory allocations occur in DDR4.

2.4.3 Hybrid Mode. In this mode, the MCDRAM is configured so that a portion acts as L3 cache and the rest as RAM (a second NUMA node supplementing DDR4).

2.5 Cluster Modes

The details for KNL are proprietary, but the key idea is that each tile tracks an assigned range of memory addresses. It does so on behalf of all cores on the chip, maintaining a data structure (tag directory) that tells it which cores are using data from its assigned addresses. Coherence requires both tile-to-tile and tile-to-memory communication. Cores that read or modify data must communicate with the tiles that manage the memory associated with that data. Similarly, when cores need data from main memory, the tile(s) that manage the associated addresses will communicate with the memory controllers on behalf of those cores. The KNL achieves this in different cluster modes. Each cluster mode, specified in the BIOS as a boot-time option, represents a tradeoff between simplicity and control. There are three major cluster modes with a few minor variations:

2.5.1 All-to-All Mode. All-to-all is the most flexible and most general mode, intended to work on all possible hardware and memory configurations of the KNL. But this mode also may have higher latencies than other cluster modes because the processor does not attempt to optimize coherency-related communication paths.

2.5.2 Quadrant Mode. This mode attempts to localize communication without requiring explicit memory management by the users. It achieves this by grouping tiles into four logical/virtual (not physical) quadrants, then requiring each tile to manage HBM addresses only in its own quadrant (and DDR addresses in its own half of the chip). This reduces the average number of "hops" that tile-to-memory requests require compared to All-to-All mode, which can reduce latency and congestion on the mesh.

2.5.3 Sub-NUMA Clustering Mode. This mode, abbreviated SNC, divides the chip into two/four NUMA nodes so that it acts like a two/four-socket processor. SNC aims to optimize coherency-related on-chip communication by confining this communication to a single NUMA node when it is possible to do so. This requires explicit manual memory management by the programmer/user (in particular, allocating memory within the NUMA node that will use that memory) to achieve any performance benefit.

2.6 Intel Omni-Path Architecture (Intel OPA)

The Intel OPA is designed to enable a broad class of computations requiring scalable, tightly coupled CPU, memory, and storage resources. Integration between devices in the Intel OPA family and Intel CPUs enable improvements in system level packaging and network efficiency. When coupled with the new user-focused open standard APIs developed by the OpenFabrics Alliance (OFA) Open Fabrics Initiative (OFI), host fabric interfaces (HFIs) and switches in the Intel OPA family are optimized to provide low latency, high bandwidth, and high message rate. Intel OPA provides important innovations to enable a multigeneration, scalable fabric, including link layer reliability, extended fabric addressing, and optimizations for high core count CPUs. Datacenter needs are also a core focus for Intel OPA, which includes: link level traffic flow optimization to minimize datacenter jitter for high priority packets, robust partitioning support, quality of service support, and a centralized fabric management system [3].

3 EVALUATION METHODOLOGY

We follow a four-dimensional approach to conducting the performance evaluation, as shown in Figure 5. The four dimensions are virtualization solution, modern processor architecture, memory access mode, and interconnect technology, respectively.

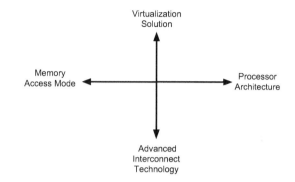

Figure 5: Evaluation Dimensions

Virtualization Solution In this dimension, we utilize Singularity as a representative container based solution. The native performance is also provided to evaluate the related overhead. This will show us the performance of different virtualization solutions and their respective overheads.

Processor Architecture Intel Xeon Haswell and Intel Knight Landing architectures are adopted to evaluate the performance of Singularity-based solution. Intel Xeon Haswell is a representative of traditional multi-core architecture, which is the prevalent architecture in the HPC domain [2], while Intel Knight Landing represents the many-core architecture, as we introduced in Section 2.3.

Memory Access Mode Intel Xeon Haswell is a multi-core architecture. All the cores on it are grouped into two different NUMA nodes, which makes the access distance to memory varying for the cores on different NUMA nodes. As mentioned in Section 2.4, Intel KNL comprises of two types of memory channels, DDR4 and MCDRAM channels. Subsequence, the memory mode can be configured in different ways, which also will impact the performance of the Singularity-based solution.

Advanced Interconnect Technology We use InfiniBand and Intel-OmniPath in this dimension. We evaluate the performance of the Singularity-based solution on InfiniBand and Intel-OmniPath interconnects, respectively. The evaluation on this dimension helps us learn the performance characterization of the Singularity-based solution on these different advanced interconnects.

We use different MPI level micro-benchmarks and applications to conduct the evaluation. We start the performance studies with two MPI point-to-point operations (Latency and Bandwidth), followed by four collective operations (Broadcast, Allgather, Allreduce, and Alltoall). Finally, two representative HPC applications, as shown in Table 1 are selected to integrally evaluate the performance under native and Singularity environment. By following the above methodology, we present a comprehensive performance characterization of Singularity for HPC on multi-/many-core clusters.

4 PERFORMANCE EVALUATION

In this section, we describe the experimental setup, provide the results of our experiments, and give an in-depth analysis of these results.

4.1 Experimental Setup

Chameleon Cloud We use 32 bare metal InfiniBand nodes on this testbed, where each has 24 cores delivered in dual socket Intel Xeon E5-2670 v3 Haswell processors with 128 GB main memory and equipped with Mellanox ConnectX-3 FDR (56 Gbps) HCAs with PCI Express Gen3 interfaces. We use CentOS Linux release 7.1.1503 (Core) with kernel 3.10.0-229.el7.x86_64 as the host OS and MLNX_OFED_LINUX-3.4-2.0.0 as the HCA driver.

Local cluster (Nowlab): We use four KNL nodes in this testbed. Each node is equipped with Intel Xeon Xeon Phi(TM) CPU 7250 (1.40GHz), 96GB host memory, and 16GB MCDRAM, and Omni-Path HFI Silicon 100 Series fabric controller. The operating system used is CentOS 7.3.1611 (Core), with kernel version 3.10.0-514.16.1.el7.x86_64. OFED-3.18-3 is used as the driver of the Omni-Path fabric controller.

Singularity 2.3 is used to conduct all the Singularity related experiments. All applications and libraries used in this study are compiled with gcc 4.8.3 compiler. All MPI communication performance experiments use MVAPICH2-2.3a and OSU micro-benchmarks v5.3. Experimental results are averaged across five runs to ensure a fair comparison.

4.2 MPI Point-to-Point Communication Performance

Figure 6 shows the performance of MPI point-to-point communication on Haswell architecture. Since each node has two CPU sockets, we measure the intra-node point-to-point communication performance in terms of intra-socket and inter-socket for Singularity and native, which are presented in Figure 6(a) and Figure 6(c). We observe that the intra-socket case has better performance than the inter-socket case, with respect to the latency and bandwidth aspects. For instance, the native latency of intra-socket case is merely 3.36μs at 16 Kbytes message size, while it is 5.18μs for the inter-socket case. Similarly, the bandwidth of intra-socket and inter-socket cases at 16Kbytes message size achieve 9.8GB/s and 5.3GB/s, respectively. It is because the memory access across the different NUMA node has to go over the QPI link, which is much slower than accessing local memory within the same NUMA node. We also notice that the performance difference is gradually decreased, as the message size increases. Figure 6(b) and Figure 6(d) show the inter-node point-to-point communication performance in terms of latency and bandwidth. Given that 56 Gbps Mellanox ConnectX-3 FDR HCA is used in this testbed, the peak bandwidth can be achieved up to around 6.4GB/s. On the aspect of virtualization solution, we can clearly observe that there is minor overhead for Singularity solution, compared with

native performance. The evaluation results indicate that the overhead is less than 7%.

Figure 7 shows the point-to-point communication performance on KNL architecture with Cache memory mode. Please note that we separate the message sizes into two ranges, which are 1B-16KB and 32KB-4MB respectively to clearly present the performance trends. Since there is only one NUMA node on KNL architecture, we do not consider intra/inter-socket anymore here. This architecture of only one NUMA node also avoids the performance bottleneck from QPI link as exists in Haswell architecture. The MPI point-to-point latency performance is presented in Figure 7(a) and Figure 7(b). The evaluation results indicate that the latency performance on KNL with cache memory is worse than the performance on Haswell architecture. For example, the intra-node and inter-node latency at four bytes message size are 1.13μs and 2.68μs, respectively, while they are 0.2μs and 1.08μs on Haswell architecture. The reason mainly comes from three aspects. One is because the CPU frequency on KNL is much lower than the one on Haswell. The second reason is that KNL has relatively complex cluster mode due to its nature of many-core processor. The communication between the core and the corresponding memory controller takes the extra time, which increases the overall latency. In addition, maintaining the cache coherency across a large number of cores on KNL architecture is more costly compared with that of the multi-core processor. Another interesting thing we observe in Figure 7(b) and Figure 7(d) is that the inter-node latency is better than the intra-node latency after around 512 Kbytes. It is because the Omni-Path interconnect has better performance than that of the shared memory-based transfer for the large message size, especially considering the complex and costly memory access and cache coherency operations within one node. Moreover, since each KNL node is equipped with one Omni-Path fabric controller (100Gbps), we can see the peak bandwidth can be achieved up to around 9.2GB/s. The evaluation results also indicate that the Singularity-based virtualization solution merely incurs less than 8% overhead, which is similar to what we observed in Figure 6.

We then measure the point-to-point communication performance with Flat memory mode on KNL, which is shown in Figure 8. As discussed in Section 2.4, we are able to explicitly specify the type of memory (DDR or MCDRAM) when allocating the memory. We thus conduct the experiments with DDR and MCDRAM, respectively. The evaluation results show that there is no significant difference between the performance with DDR and the one with MCDRAM. Similar to the observation we have in Cache mode, the inter-node latency is also lower than the intra-node latency after around 1 Mbytes, The peak bandwidth is also able to reach 9.2GB/s, and Singularity-based virtualization can deliver near-native performance as well. Compared with the Cache mode performance earlier, We can also observe that the intra-node bandwidth with Cache mode in Figure 7(c) is slight worse than that with Flat mode in Figure 8(c). The cache misses on MCDRAM are the primary factor in the performance difference between addressable memory MCDRAM and cache MCDRAM, so using the Cache

Table 1: Benchmarks and representative HPC Applications for Evaluation

Application	Description
Graph500	Graph500 [28] is one of the representative benchmarks of Data intensive supercomputer applications. It exhibits highly irregular communication pattern.
NAS	NAS [1] contains a set of benchmarks which are derived from the computing kernels, which is common on Computational Fluid Dynamics (CFD) applications. These represent the class of regular iterative HPC applications.

mode could get close to or even match the performance with the Flat mode. However, there is still some inherent overhead associated with using MCDRAM as the cache.

4.3 MPI Collective Communication Performance

In this section, we conduct the communication performance evaluation with four commonly used MPI collective operations, which are MPI_Bcast, MPI_Allghaer, MPI_Allreduce, and MPI_Alltoall. Figure 9 shows the evaluation results with 512 Processes across 32 nodes with Haswell architecture, while Figure 10 and Figure 11 present the corresponding results with 128 Processes across two KNL nodes with cache and flat memory modes, respectively. Overall, Singularity-based virtualization solution is still able to deliver the near-native performance with less than 8% overheads on all the four operations. In addition, when the message size exceeds around 256 Kbytes, we can clearly see the benefits for all the four collective operations with MCDRAM in flat memory mode. The benefits can be up to 38%, 56%, 67%, and 16% for MPI_Bcast, MPI_Allghaer, MPI_Allreduce, and MPI_Alltoall, respectively. As the message size increases, the data can not fit in L2 cache anymore. Compared with DDR, MCDRAM is able to more efficiently deliver the data through its 'Multi-Channel' architecture to processes that are involved in the collective operations. On the other hand, Singularity-based virtualization solution consistently reflects this performance characteristic on the native environment.

4.4 Application Performance

In this section, we evaluate the application performance with NAS and Graph500, respectively. The application performance with 512 MPI processes on Haswell is presented in Figure 12. The performance with 128 MPI processes on KNL with cache and flat modes are shown in Figure 13 and Figure 14, respectively. Six different benchmarks included in NAS test suite are presented as labels on the x-axis of Figure 12(a), 13(a), and 14(a). Most of them are computation-intensive, the communication only takes a small portion of the total execution time. That is the reason that there is no clear performance difference between DDR and MCDRAM in the Flat mode in Figure 14(a). The FT performance gets improved with MCDRAM since it involves a large number of alltoall operations. Graph500 is a data-analytics workload, which heavily utilizes point to point communication (MPI_Isend and MPI_Irecv) with 4 Kbytes message size for BFS search of the random vertices. The x-axis represents the different problem size by the SCALE-edgefactor pairs. SCALE is the logarithm base two of the number of vertices, while edgefactor indicates the ratio of the graph's edge count to its vertex count. For instance, (24,16) represents a

graph with 16M (2^{24}) vertices and 256M ($16*2^{24}$) edges. As what we observe earlier in Figure 8, MCDRAM and DDR have similar performance for Graph500 in the Flat mode here. The evaluation results for all the three cases in Figure 12- 14 show that, compared with the native performance, Singularity-based container technology only introduces less than 7% overhead, which stems from the inherent cost of the containerization. Therefore, it reveals a promising way for efficiently running MPI applications on HPC clouds.

5 RELATED WORK

As an interesting alternative to the hypervisor-based solutions, container technology has been popularized during the last several years as a lightweight virtualization solution. More and more studies focus on evaluating the performance of different hypervisor-based and container-based solutions for HPC. Wes Felter et al. [7] explores the performance of traditional virtual machine deployments (KVM) and contrasts them with the use of Docker. They use a suite of workloads that stress CPU, memory, storage, and networking resources. Their results show that containers result in equal or better performance than VMs in almost all cases. In addition, they found that both VMs and containers require tuning to support I/O-intensive applications [7]. Xavier et al. [29] conduct an in-depth performance evaluation of container-based virtualization (Linux VServer, OpenVZ, and LXC) and hypervisor-based virtualization (Xen) for HPC in terms of computing, memory, disk, network, application overhead, and isolation. In the work of Cristian et al. [24], the authors evaluate the performance of Linux-based container solutions using the NAS parallel benchmarks, in the various ways of container deployment. The evaluation shows the limits of using containers, the type of application that suffer the most and until which level of oversubscription containers can deal with without impacting considerably the application performance. Yuyu et al. [32] compare the virtualization (KVM) and containerization (Docker) techniques for HPC in terms of features and performance using up to 64 nodes on Chameleon testbed with 10GigE networks.

Recently, several HPC-focused implementations of Linux containers are emerging. Shifter [25] is one of these efforts from NERSC to make the user-defined stack available to HPC users. Shifter offers a standard, repeatable image building workflow through Docker. The user can submit the image to an unprivileged but trusted image gateway, which injects configuration and binaries, converts it to an ext4 filesystem image, and copies this image to a parallel filesystem visible from compute nodes. This insulates the network filesystem from image metadata traffic. Shifter is the first HPC-targeted solution for the user-defined stack with a good workflow and direct resource access. However, it relies on trusted and privileged operations, its

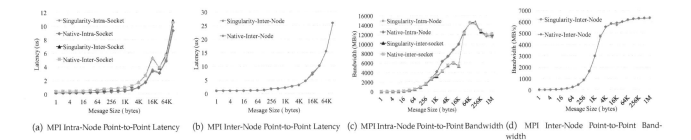

(a) MPI Intra-Node Point-to-Point Latency   (b) MPI Inter-Node Point-to-Point Latency   (c) MPI Intra-Node Point-to-Point Bandwidth (d) MPI Inter-Node Point-to-Point Bandwidth

Figure 6: MPI Point-to-Point Communication Performance on Haswell

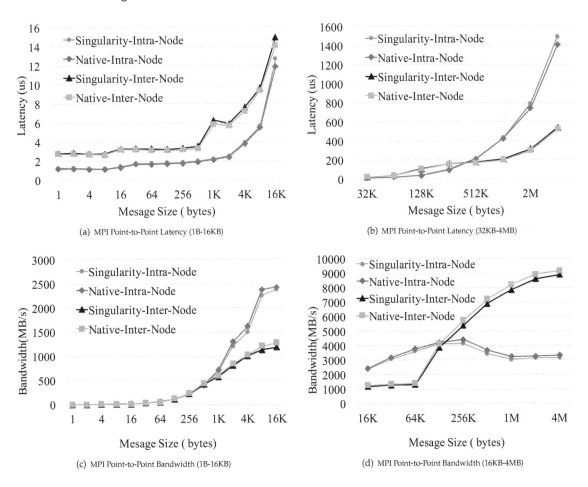

(a) MPI Point-to-Point Latency (1B-16KB)   (b) MPI Point-to-Point Latency (32KB-4MB)

(c) MPI Point-to-Point Bandwidth (1B-16KB)   (d) MPI Point-to-Point Bandwidth (16KB-4MB)

Figure 7: MPI Point-to-Point Communication Performance on KNL with Cache Mode

resource manager integration increases complexity, and it requires servers and daemons for the image gateway.

Charliecloud [22] uses the user and mount namespaces to run Docker containers with no privileged operations or daemons on center resources to provide the user-defined services in a usable manner while minimizing the risks: security, support burden, missing functionality, and performance. Nevertheless, there are several prominent issues with it, such as

compatibility, dependency, and user-driven features. The software makes use of kernel namespaces that are not deemed stable by multiple prominent distributions of Linux (e.g. no versions of Red Hat Enterprise Linux or compatibles support it), and may not be included in these distributions for the foreseeable future [16]. In addition, the workflow begins with Docker. While Docker is becoming a standard technology in the industry, it would be desirable to not bind with it for baseline operation. Although it has less than 500 lines of code, this

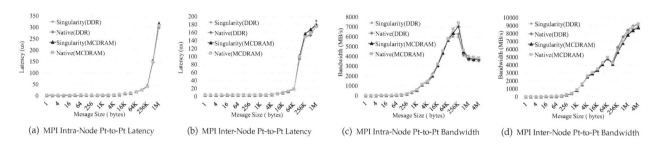

Figure 8: MPI Point-to-Point Communication Performance on KNL with Flat Mode

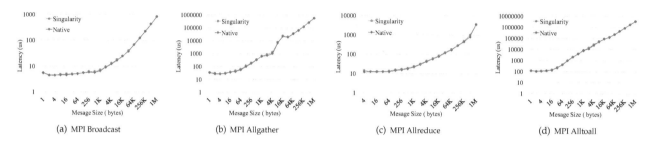

Figure 9: MPI Collective Communication Performance with 512-Process on Haswell

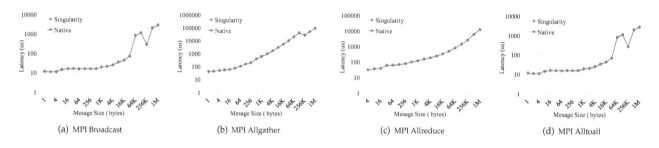

Figure 10: MPI Collective Communication Performance with 128-Process on KNL with Cache Mode

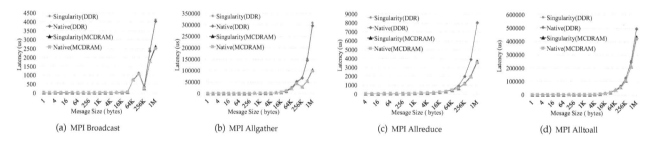

Figure 11: MPI Collective Communication Performance with 128-Process on KNL with Flat Mode

is an indication of having a lack of user-driven features, like native GPU support in Singularity.

rkt [23] is an open source Go project backed by CoreOS, Inc. rkt avoids the need for trusted daemons and optionally uses the user namespace, but it is still a large project with much functionality not focused for HPC. It can run Docker images and also provides a competing image specification language.

However, the performance evaluation for singularity is missing on multi-/many-core clusters, which is a key component in HPC field. Therefore, we conduct a comprehensive performance evaluation using point-to-point, collective microbenchmarks and several representative HPC applications on multi-/many-core clusters.

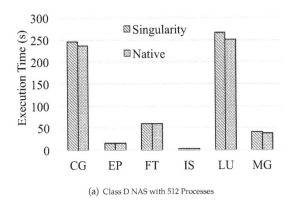

(a) Class D NAS with 512 Processes

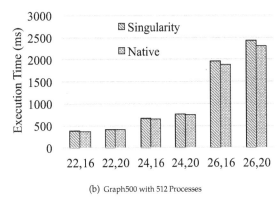

(b) Graph500 with 512 Processes

Figure 12: Application Performance with 512-Process on Haswell

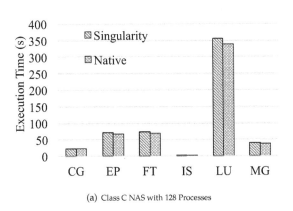

(a) Class C NAS with 128 Processes

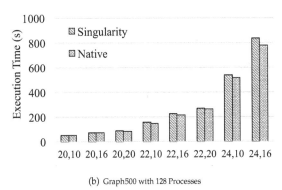

(b) Graph500 with 128 Processes

Figure 13: Application Performance with 128-Process on KNL with Cache Mode

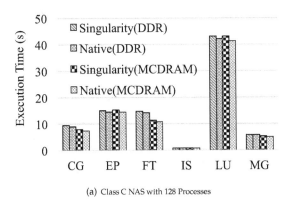

(a) Class C NAS with 128 Processes

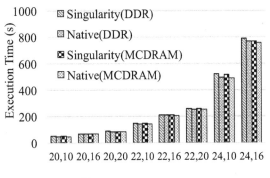

(b) Graph500 with 128 Processes

Figure 14: Application Performance with 128-Process on KNL with Flat Mode

6 CONCLUSION AND FUTURE WORK

Singularity has become an attractive and popular container technologies to build HPC clouds, however, there is a lack of a systematical study on the performance of Singularity in the HPC clouds. In this paper, we first propose a four-dimension evaluation methodology, which includes modern processor architecture, high performance interconnects, memory mode, and virtualization overhead. Based on that, we conduct the comprehensive studies to evaluate the performance of Singularity. The performance results demonstrate that Singularity-based container technology can achieve near-native performance for both Intel Xeon and Intel Xeon Knights Landing (KNL) platforms with different memory access modes. It also shows that Singularity has very little overhead for running MPI-based HPC applications on both Omni-Path and Infini-Band networks. Therefore, we believe that Singularity provides a promising way to build the next-generation HPC clouds with near-native performance as well as desired cloud features such as easy management and deployment.

Large-scale data analytics is another popular topic on HPC cloud environment [4, 5]. In the future, we plan to extend the evaluation with large-scale data analytics workloads. In addition, one-sided programming model [18, 19] has been shown to benefit applications with irregular communication patterns. we also plan to extend the evaluation for one-sided programming model with Singularity-based container technology.

REFERENCES

[1] NAS Parallel Benchmarks. http://www.nas.nasa.gov/Resources/Software/npb.html.

[2] W. Bao, C. Hong, S. Chunduri, S. Krishnamoorthy, L.-N. Pouchet, F. Rastello, and P. Sadayappan. Static and Dynamic Frequency Scaling on Multicore CPUs. *ACM Trans. Archit. Code Optim.*, 13(4), Dec. 2016.

[3] M. S. Birrittella, M. Debbage, R. Huggahalli, J. Kunz, T. Lovett, T. Rimmer, K. D. Underwood, and R. C. Zak. Intel Omni-path Architecture: Enabling Scalable, High Performance Fabrics. In *2015 IEEE 23rd Annual Symposium on High-Performance Interconnects*, Aug 2015.

[4] L. Cheng, S. Kotoulas, T. E. Ward, and G. Theodoropoulos. Robust and Skew-resistant Parallel Joins in Shared-Nothing Systems. In *Proceedings of the 23rd ACM International Conference on Conference on Information and Knowledge Management*, CIKM '14, pages 1399–1408, 2014.

[5] L. Cheng, I. Tachmazidis, S. Kotoulas, and G. Antoniou. Design and Evaluation of Small-large Outer Joins in Cloud Computing Environments. *Journal of Parallel and Distributed Computing*, 110, 03 2017.

[6] Docker. https://www.docker.com/.

[7] W. Felter, A. Ferreira, R. Rajamony, and J. Rubio. An Updated Performance Comparison of Virtual Machines and Linux Containers. Technical Report RC25482 (AUS1407-001), 2014.

[8] J. Jose and J. Zhang and A. Venkatesh and S. Potluri and D. K. Panda. A Comprehensive Performance Evaluation of OpenSHMEM Libraries on InfiniBand Clusters. In *Proceedings of the First Workshop on OpenSHMEM and Related Technologies. Experiences, Implementations, and Tools - Volume 8356*, OpenSHMEM 2014, Annapolis, MD, USA, 2014.

[9] J. Zhang and X. Lu and D. K. Panda. High Performance MPI Library for Container-based HPC Cloud on InfiniBand Clusters . In *The 45th International Conference on Parallel Processing (ICPP '16)*, Philadelphia, USA, August 2016.

[10] J. Zhang and X. Lu and D. K. Panda. High-Performance Virtual Machine Migration Framework for MPI Applications on SR-IOV enabled InfiniBand Clusters. In *2017 IEEE International Parallel and Distributed Processing Symposium (IPDPS)*, Orlando, USA, May 2017.

[11] J. Zhang and X. Lu and D. K. Panda. Designing Locality and NUMA Aware MPI Runtime for Nested Virtualization based HPC Cloud with SR-IOV Enabled InfiniBand . In *13th ACM SIGPLAN/SIGOPS International Conference on Virtual Execution Environments (VEE '17)*, Xi'an, China, April 2017.

[12] J. Zhang, X. Lu, J. Jose, M. Li, R. Shi, D. K. Panda. High Performance MPI Library over SR-IOV Enabled InfiniBand Clusters. In *Proceedings of International Conference on High Performance Computing (HiPC)*, Goa, India, December 17-20 2014.

[13] J. Zhang, X. Lu, J. Jose, R. Shi, D. K. Panda. Can Inter-VM Shmem Benefit MPI Applications on SR-IOV based Virtualized InfiniBand Clusters? In *Proceedings of 20th International Conference Euro-Par 2014 Parallel Processing*, Porto, Portugal, August 25-29 2014.

[14] J. Jose, K. Hamidouche, X. Lu, S. Potluri, J. Zhang, K. Tomko, and D. K. Panda. High Performance OpenSHMEM for Xeon Phi Clusters: Extensions, Runtime Designs and Application Co-design. In *2014 IEEE International Conference on Cluster Computing (CLUSTER)*, pages 10–18, Sept 2014.

[15] J. Jose, K. Hamidouche, J. Zhang, A. Venkatesh, and D. K. Panda. Optimizing Collective Communication in UPC. In *2014 IEEE International Parallel Distributed Processing Symposium Workshops*, pages 361–370, May 2014.

[16] G. M. Kurtzer, V. Sochat, and M. W. Bauer. Singularity: Scientific Containers for Mobility of Compute. *PLOS ONE*, 12:1–20, 05 2017.

[17] M. Li, K. Hamidouche, X. Lu, J. Zhang, J. Lin, and D. K. Panda. High Performance OpenSHMEM Strided Communication Support with Infini-Band UMR. In *2015 IEEE 22nd International Conference on High Performance Computing (HiPC)*, pages 244–253, Dec 2015.

[18] M. Li, K. Hamidouche, X. Lu, H. Subramoni, J. Zhang, and D. K. Panda. Designing MPI Library with On-demand Paging (ODP) of Infiniband: Challenges and Benefits. In *Proceedings of the International Conference for High Performance Computing, Networking, Storage and Analysis*, SC '16, pages 37:1–37:11, Piscataway, NJ, USA, 2016.

[19] M. Li, X. Lu, K. Hamidouche, J. Zhang, and D. K. Panda. Mizan-RMA: Accelerating Mizan Graph Processing Framework with MPI RMA. In *2016 IEEE 23rd International Conference on High Performance Computing (HiPC)*, pages 42–51, Dec 2016.

[20] J. Lin, K. Hamidouche, J. Zhang, X. Lu, A. Vishnu, and D. K. Panda. Accelerating k-NN Algorithm with Hybrid MPI and OpenSHMEM . In *OpenSHMEM 2015 for PGAS Programming in the Exascale Era* , Baltimore Region, MD, USA, August 2015.

[21] Memkind. http://memkind.github.io/memkind/.

[22] R. Priedhorsky and T. Randles. Charliecloud: Unprivileged Containers for User-Defined Software Stacks in HPC. Technical Report LA-UR 16-22370v4, 2007.

[23] rkt. https://coreos.com/rkt.

[24] C. Ruiz, E. Jeanvoine, and L. Nussbaum. Performance Evaluation of Containers for HPC. In *10th Workshop on Virtualization in High-Performance Cloud Computing (VHPC)*, Vienna, Austria, Aug 2015.

[25] Shifter. https://github.com/NERSC/shifter.

[26] A. Sodani. Knights landing (KNL): 2nd Generation Intel®Xeon Phi processor. In *2015 IEEE Hot Chips 27 Symposium (HCS)*, pages 1–24, Aug 2015.

[27] TACC Stampede Cluster. www.xsede.org/resources/overview.

[28] The Graph500. http://www.graph500.org.

[29] M. Xavier, M. Neves, F. Rossi, T. Ferreto, T. Lange, and C. De Rose. Performance Evaluation of Container-Based Virtualization for High Performance Computing Environments. In *Parallel, Distributed and Network-Based Processing (PDP), 2013 21st Euromicro International Conference on*, pages 233–240, Belfast, Northern Ireland, Feb 2013. doi: 10.1109/PDP.2013.41.

[30] J. Zhang, X. Lu, M. Arnold, and D. Panda. MVAPICH2 over OpenStack with SR-IOV: An Efficient Approach to Build HPC Clouds. In *Cluster, Cloud and Grid Computing (CCGrid), 2015 15th IEEE/ACM International Symposium on*, pages 71–80, May 2015.

[31] J. Zhang, X. Lu, and D. K. Panda. Performance Characterization of Hypervisor-and Container-Based Virtualization for HPC on SR-IOV Enabled InfiniBand Clusters. In *2016 IEEE International Parallel and Distributed Processing Symposium Workshops (IPDPSW)*, pages 1777–1784, May 2016.

[32] Y. Zhou, B. Subramaniam, K. Keahey, and J. Lange. Comparison of Virtualization and Containerization Techniques for High Performance Computing. In *Proceedings of the 2015 ACM/IEEE conference on Supercomputing*, Austin, USA, Nov 2015.

A Crop Water Stress Monitoring System Utilising a Hybrid e-Infrastructure

Gaojie Sun*
School of Engineering
The University of Melbourne
Melbourne, Australia
chrissun.sea@gmail.com

Hongzhen Xie†
School of Engineering
The University of Melbourne
Melbourne, Australia
hongzhenx@student.unimelb.edu.au

Richard O. Sinnott
Computing and Information Systems
The University of Melbourne
Melbourne, Australia
rsinnott@unimelb.edu.au

ABSTRACT

There are many challenges involved in irrigation systems in agricultural environments. Many approaches simply support crop watering as a simple standardised solution - watering the fields uniformly. However, depending on the topology of the ground and the crop species that exists, considerable improvements can be achieved that can greatly impact on the overall crop yield. Too little watering or too much watering in the wrong areas can impact the overall output. With the rapid growth in unmanned aerial vehicles (UAVs) and drones, image capture technology is now readily available. If the water-stressed areas could be identified, irrigation systems could offer targeted irrigation to only those crops in need. To support this, a crop water stress monitoring system has been designed utilising the thermal images of the crops. The analysis of such data can be computationally demanding when large crop fields are considered, hence the system has been designed to use multi-core high performance computing and Cloud-based systems. This paper outlines the requirements and design of the crop water stress monitoring system and how it provides an efficient and effective analysis of crop water stress index. The paper also benchmarks the algorithms across the hybrid infrastructure.

KEYWORDS

Irrigation, water stress, crop water stress index, parallelisation

1 INTRODUCTION

Intelligent irrigation of agricultural crops is critical. Agriculture is one of the largest consumers of water. Therefore, efficient and effective irrigation can not only increase crop production but also support water conservation [18]. In many areas of Australia, the driest inhabited continent, annual water demand of crops is often much higher than annual precipitation. Considering the water efficiency of the irrigation system, a more water-efficient approach is highly

---

*Sun and Xie contributed equally to this work.
†Sun and Xie contributed equally to this work.

UCC'17, December 5–8, 2017, Austin, TX, USA.
© 2017 Association for Computing Machinery.
ACM ISBN 978-1-4503-5149-2/17/12...$15.00
https://doi.org/10.1145/3147213.3147222

desirable. In most situations, different areas of crops have different water stress conditions with different levels of water requirements. Water efficiency can be improved by precisely irrigating water-stressed crops and reducing the irrigation for these areas with low water requirements without sacrificing the overall yield.

For estimation of crop water stress conditions, the crop's canopy temperature is a key indicator of water requirements [19]. To be more specific, when crops are water-stressed, in order to reduce the loss of the moisture, the stomas of the leaves close to prevent transpiration [11]. This interrupts the energy dissipation and leads to a rise in leaf temperature [14]. As such, when the water stress of a crop increases, its transpiration will decrease and the temperature will rise. Thus it is possible to create a crop water stress index (CWSI), which indicates the underlying water stress conditions, merely by monitoring the crop's canopy temperature. There are now many devices (UAVs and drones) that are equipped with thermal imaging capabilities, however, the associated data can be voluminous and the processing demands can be significant. Identifying slight temperature changes in hectares of crops of multi-terabytes of data can result in large-scale computational processing demands. The primary end users of advanced agricultural irrigation systems (farmers) are not typically savvy in large-scale data processing systems. The focus of this paper is to develop a scalable infrastructure that supports the variable data processing demands in identifying water-stressed crops. This has direct implications for many key agricultural areas of Australia (and elsewhere), e.g. wine-growing, fruit-growing as well as more traditional grain-growing farming enterprises.

One major challenge is the collection of the crop's canopy temperature. It is important to put forward a highly available and economical method for common crop growers. The traditional methods of measuring the canopy temperature need access to and use of large amounts of climatic data [6], and as such they are time-consuming and labour intensive. They often involve many field technicians traversing fields with handheld thermometers to collect the data or using visual observation [9]. For gardeners, this may be sufficient but for large scale crop growers, this will not be adequate.

Moreover, this method usually cannot ensure a high degree of accuracy due to the fact that the data may be obtained from a subset of the farming area, and the localised environmental conditions may change especially for farms with varying ground topologies. To overcome this problem, an automated system has been designed to collect the canopy temperature data. This system uses data captured from drones equipped with a thermal imaging camera to take images of the entire crop area within minutes [8]. Depending on the size of the fields, however, the data can run to many terabytes.

After acquiring the drone-based thermal images, the data needs to be used to create a crop water stress index [1]. Software (MatLab) has been written to support this, however this was targeted to run on a single laptop and would not scale to the kinds of data that farmers really need support for or with the kind of resolution that would identify specific areas of crops in water need. However since the image analysis program is computationally intensive especially for large fields or when multiple users use the analysis system, scalability is essential. To tackle this, the MatLab algorithms were deployed on targeted HPC systems at the University of Melbourne and ported to Cloud-based platforms across Australia. End users are offered a simple web interface for interacting with these resources. This paper focuses on the large-scale infrastructure required for building the thermal image analysis system used to identify the water stress status of crops and to locate water-stressed crops. The paper also covers benchmarking of the system on hybrid infrastructures.

The rest of this paper is structured as follows. Section II covers the background and related work. Section III presents the image analysis algorithm design. Section IV presents an overview of the architecture of the system. Section V gives a case study of the system. Section VI focuses on a comparison of the performance of the hybrid e-Infrastructure. Finally, section VII draws conclusions on the work as a whole and identifies areas of future work.

2 RELATED WORK

It is indicated in [21] that water stress can greatly influence plant height and the overall weight. Under water stress conditions, plants will reduce their size and quality, losing their market value through yield reduction. Thus, irrigation of crops is an important element in providing sufficient crop yields. This is especially needed when there is insufficient or excess rainfall.

Many different irrigation scheduling methods have been used worldwide [15]. These are based on weather data, the visible changes in plant characteristics, the appearance of the soil, or soil moisture monitoring which uses tensiometer devices to measure the moisture level of the soil. However, for large farms, considerable resources (money) is required to put so many devices in farms to enhance the accuracy of measuring water stress levels.

Another way to tackle this is by using thermal remote sensing which converts the invisible radiation patterns of leaves into visible images and subsequently using this information to determine particular thermal properties and features of crops [17]. These thermal images are usually caught by drones, a type of low-cost autonomous aerial vehicles that brings more business potential in near future. The main prototype is using this inexpensive vehicle to fly pre-programmed missions and taking thermal images of particular areas [10]. The analysis of thermal images has crossed over various areas. For example, a new method was proposed in [2] to estimate fruit yield during the growing season by analyzing temperature gradient between fruits and their background. Thermal images have also been proved to be useful tools to detect disease of plants with the help of analysis of the maximum temperature

difference within a leaf or a canopy [4][5][13]. However, the scaling of the solutions has hitherto not been achieved for large-scale agricultural enterprises.

It is known that once plants are under water stress conditions, their stomata begin to close and cease to transpire, which can cause the plant to "heat up" and the canopy temperature to rise [17]. Based on this theory, an algorithm was developed to assess crop water stress and irrigation scheduling information, using an optical image taken from the plant canopy which was aligned with the underlying infra-red (IR) image [3]. This was then used to extract the leaf area using Gaussian mixture distribution extraction techniques to get the distribution of the temperature of the leaves. Thus the crop water stress index can be obtained based on the leaf temperature distribution.

A major challenge is scaling these algorithms up to large-scale agricultural farms (where they are really needed). Several applications have already been implemented to process agricultural data on HPC and Cloud. A method introduced in [12] uses Cloud infrastructures to provide advice and recommendations regarding the analysis of data on the Cloud with the consideration of performance in particular. A web-based system described in [20] supports the processing of geospatial tasks on the Cloud by providing high-performance service-oriented computing capabilities. [16] explores rapid processing methods and strategies for remote sensing images, and makes comparisons with other computing paradigms.

We recognise that a range of infrastructures are now available and any solution must accommodate such heterogeneity of solutions. To address this, in this work, we develop a hybrid solution that leverages both HPC and Cloud-based facilities. Specifically, we utilise the high performance computing system SPARTAN at the University of Melbourne (https://dashboard.hpc.unimelb.edu.au). This provides a 4000-core server cluster with high-speed (10Gb) interconnection between all compute nodes. This system also offers a MatLab (https://au.mathworks.com) environment for researchers at the University of Melbourne.

In addition, we utilise the National eResearch Collaboration Tools and Resources Project Research Cloud (NeCTAR - https://nectar.org.au). NeCTAR is a federally funded project that offers an OpenStack-based Cloud infrastructure that is free to all academic researchers across Australia. NeCTAR offers 30,000 physical servers accessible through multiple availability zones across Australia. This is complemented by large-scale data storage solutions offered (again free!) to Australian academics as part of the Research Data Services (RDS - www.rds.edu.au) program. As part of the RDS program, the University of Melbourne currently makes available over 5 Petabytes of data storage to researchers. NeCTAR itself provides an Infrastructure-as-a-Service platform where instances of virtual machines can be created either through the NeCTAR dashboard (accessible through the Internet2 Shibboleth-based Australian Access Federation (AAF - www.aaf.edu.au)) or through associated tooling, e.g. use of libraries such as Boto (https://pypi.python.org/pypi/boto) for instance creation and management and Ansible (https://pypi.python.org/pypi/ansible) for deployment and configuration of software systems. Boto provides a client library for the OpenStack Nova compute component. These solutions allow for automatic deployment and configuration of virtual machines in a highly flexible and scalable manner. For this work, eight virtual machines (VMs) (each with 8GB RAM and 50 GB volumes) were utilised. Due to the licensing restrictions of Mat-Lab, it was not possible to run the existing MatLab algorithms on NeCTAR, hence they had to be ported to another solution: Octave (https://www.gnu.org/software/octave/). Octave is a free software solution featuring a high-level programming language used for numerical computations.

Compared to other existing applications on Cloud or HPC, the hybrid processing system combines two processing platforms and provides an algorithm to schedule tasks to allow flexible use and optimal performance in use of these platforms. The solution offers a simple, but well-defined user management component tailored to users. The platform enables users to run their jobs to obtain an optimal performance through a targeted algorithm that schedules tasks based on the status of processing platforms and the size of the job.

Another challenge to be tackled was how to parallelise the algorithms to speed up the processing time of large thermal image data. The parallelisation approach and the use of MPI are described in the following sections.

3 IMAGE ANALYSIS ALGORITHM DESIGN

3.1 Problems in Analysis Program

The critical procedure for estimating the water stress condition is to calculate the crop water stress index (CWSI) from the thermal image. The CWSI can be quantified in a generic form [7], as below:

$$CWSI = \frac{T_c - T_w}{T_d - T_w}$$

In this formula, T_d and T_w represent the temperatures of dry (non-transpiring) and wet (fully-transpiring) leaves respectively. T_c is related to the actual temperature of the leaves. It can be inferred from the pixel-by-pixel temperature data stored in a thermal image. T_d and T_w can be estimated from the leaf temperature distribution. Therefore, the key issue of calculating CWSI is to build a temperature distribution model of the crop to estimate the T_d and T_w. Once the T_d and T_w are determined, the CWSI can be calculated.

The analysis program is based on the assumption that the temperature distribution of crops belonging to one species and a given soil type follows a mixture of two Gaussian distributions [13]. As shown in Figure 1, since the temperature of crops is lower than that of the soil, one of the two distributions (the smaller mean value) represents the temperature distribution of the crops, and the other (with relative higher mean value) is the soil temperature distribution.

If the whole temperature data stored in the thermal image is used to fit the Gaussian Mixture Model (GMM), then the cross section of the two distributions is unavoidable. This is manifested as a kind of noise for a given pixel since it combines crop or soil thermal readings. Ideally, it is desirable to obtain the temperature distribution model for crops separately from the soil distribution. Therefore, the noise part in the GMM should be reduced or eliminated. In fact, the noise comes from edge temperature between the crops and soil in the thermal image. As such, before building the GMM, the edge should be detected and reduced from the thermal image. Then, as shown in Figure 2, the GMM built with the remaining temperature

data can be clearly divided into the crop temperature distribution model and the soil temperature distribution model respectively.

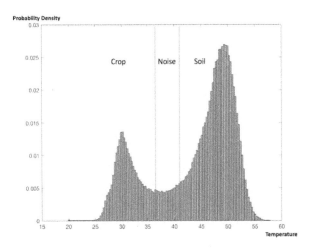

Figure 1: Gaussian Mixture Model With Noise

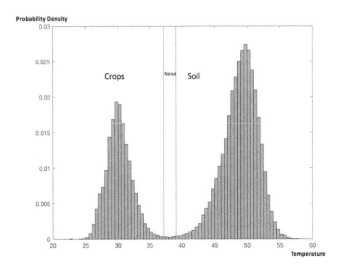

Figure 2: Gaussian Mixture Model With Reduction Noise

3.2 Image Processing Algorithm

The image analysis program (shown in Figure 3) is responsible for converting the thermal image to the crop water stress index map. The original laptop-based program was implemented in MatLab. It supported the following sequence of steps:

Step 1. Edge detection: The program first takes the thermal image, which contains the temperature data, as input. It then detects the edge of the image and outputs a binary matrix in which edge pixel values are set to 0 and the others are set to 1.

Step 2. Edge Elimination: Because the edge pixel value in the

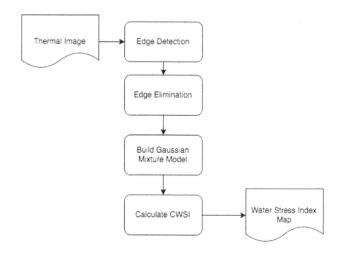

Figure 3: Algorithm Flow Chart

binary matrix is 0, it can be treated as a mask to eliminate the edge information from the original thermal image. In this step, the edge data will be removed by multiplying two matrices, namely the original temperature matrix of the thermal image and the binary matrix obtained from step 1.

Step 3. Building the GMM: After eliminating the noise data and the edge temperature data, the remaining temperature data in the thermal image can be used to build the Gaussian Mixture Models. If the image contains multiple crop species, multiple GMMs can be built for each species in the image in order to improve the accuracy of the model, since different species have different temperature distributions.

Step 4. Calculating CWSI: Once step 3 is completed (as shown in Figure 4), the crop's temperature distribution model can be obtained from the Gaussian Mixture Model by selecting the distribution with the lower mean value from the mixture model. The T_d and T_w can then be determined based on the assumption that 95% of the crops are in the normal condition, which means that the temperature for the non-transpiring leaf is the highest temperature value among the 95% of crops and the temperature for the fully-transpiring leaf is the lowest temperature value amongst them. From this and according to the formula described in section III, the CWSI for the whole image can be estimated. Finally, the crop water stress index can be established.

3.3 Image Processing Parallelisation

When the analysis program processes large images, the analysis time will dramatically increase due to the substantial increase in the number of matrix operations. This is exacerbated when multiple users submit a great number of images to the system. Therefore the analysis program utilises large scale heterogeneous computational resources including both HPC and Cloud infrastructures. The key idea is that each processor (core) is responsible for processing a subfield of a given thermal image.

Step 1 and 2: (Figure 5(a)) For the Edge detection and elimination steps, the input image will be cut into different sub-images,

based on the current resource availability. Each processor will take one sub-image and subsequently detect the edges and then eliminate the identified edges from those images.

Step 3: (Figure 5(b)) Creation of the Gaussian Mixture Model cannot generally be parallelised in MatLab and Octave because the construction of a GMM needs to use the whole temperature data to fit the model. However, there is one exception to this: when the image contains many crop species. In this case, multiple GMMs need to be built for each of these species and these can subsequently be built in parallel on different processors. The utilisation of the processor in this step is low since all processors are not needed to build the GMM.

Step 4: (Figure 5(c)) In this step, each processor will process one subfield of the input image. In particular, if the sub-image contains many crop species, the processor should use the corresponding GMM to calculate the CWSI of the sub-image.

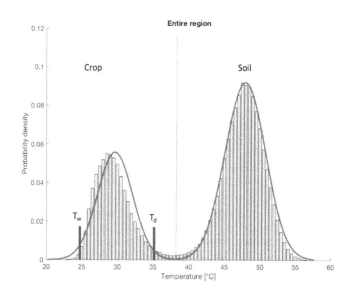

Figure 4: Utilisation of the GMM

4 SYSTEM ARCHITECTURE

A simplified view of the system is shown in Figure 6. The platform has been designed for users who have already collected the thermal images of the crops (by UAVs or drones). They upload their data (images) to the system to analyse the crop water stress index. The system allows multiple users to upload numerous data sets and submit multiple jobs at the same time and subsequently utilise the HPC (SPARTAN) and Cloud (NeCTAR) systems

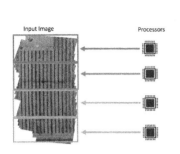

(a) Parallelisation of Edge Detection

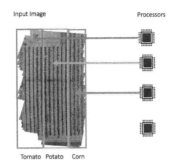

(b) Parallelisation in Building the GMM

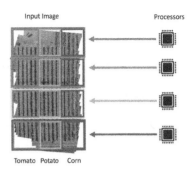

(c) Parallelisation in Calculating the CWSI

Figure 5: CWSI Parallelisation Algorithm

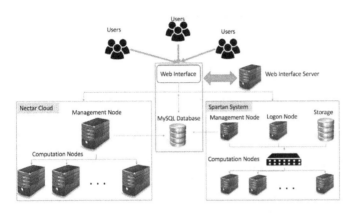

Figure 6: Analysis Program System Architecture

The analysis program is accessible via a web interface. The web interface provides users with a user-friendly means to submit their thermal images and manage the submitted jobs. The web interface supports an authentication mechanism to restrict access to appropriate researchers (or farmers). When the user submits their jobs, they can check the status of the jobs running on the Cloud and/or SPARTAN systems. The decision where to run the jobs depends on the available computational resources. Users also can choose the computation system they wish to use to analyse their images. The system supports various job management capabilities. Firstly, it provides a service for checking the status of jobs. If the job is still processing, the overall status and each processorâĂŹs status can be updated in real time. If the job is finished, the result, the crop water stress index, can be viewed online. Second, the user can also delete the job through the web interface. If the job is still running, this operation will cancel the processing of this job and free the computational resources. If the job is complete, it will delete the result stored in the system. Finally, the web interface also provides a data download service.

A MySQL database has been adopted as the core data management software in the analysis system. It is installed on a server node along with the web interface. It is mainly responsible for storing the status of the job, the status of each processor, the user's information, links to the submitted thermal images and the crop water stress

index maps. These data are generated from the web interface to the two management nodes of the NeCTAR Cloud and SPARTAN systems. They can also be queried and visualised through the web interface.

For the NeCTAR Cloud, there are a number of nodes that have been allocated specifically for this project. One node is treated as the management node and the others are treated as computational (data processing) nodes. The management node is used to receive jobs from the web interface and to subsequently schedule these jobs. In addition, it manages the computational resources and monitors and logs their status information, including the status of the job and the load on each computational resource. When the user submits their job, they can choose the number of the cores they need to use for the computation. Once the job is successfully submitted, the management node will prepare a set of computation nodes to analyse the image. These nodes that are responsible for one job, can exchange execution information through Message Passing Interface (MPI) capabilities developed to support the multicore parallelisation.

In terms of the SPARTAN system, this is similar to the NeCTAR Cloud. It contains a management node, a login node and a large number of computational nodes. It also contains a database to support the management of the SPARTAN system. The login node provides the authentication service that ensures that authorised users are able to use the SPARTAN system. The SPARTAN management node has the same functionality as the management node for the NeCTAR Research Cloud.

4.1 NeCTAR Research Cloud Computation Platform

For the implementation on the NeCTAR Research Cloud, the key components not only contain the implementation of the parallelised image processing program but also a job scheduler that is responsible for scheduling jobs and allocating computational resources. The implementation itself leverages the open source Octave, Message Passing Interface (MPI) libraries and support for resource management (Simple Linux Utility for Resource Management (SLURM - https://slurm.schedmd.com/overview.html)).

It was necessary to provide job management software to manage jobs due to the limited computational resources available. When multiple jobs are submitted to the system, if the computation resources are inadequate for the total requirement of the submitted jobs, these jobs should be executed in a certain order, e.g. the submitted order. We utilise the SLURM scheduler, which is an open source and highly scalable cluster management and job scheduling system. For this purpose, SLURM has a centralised manager to monitor and schedule jobs. In addition, each computational node has a daemon used to receive jobs, execute jobs, return their status and wait for more jobs.

For the implementation of the parallelised analysis program, MPI is used to provide single program multiple data (SPMD) programming capabilities. It supports the use of multicores across different HPC nodes (servers) to parallelise the whole data processing activity. Each node has one copy of the analysis program that is managed by the SLURM daemon. When a job is submitted to the cloud system, the management node will reserve a set of computation nodes according to the requirements of computation resources of the job. Moreover, the daemons on the computation nodes will take the thermal image of the job as the input and each core will be responsible for the analysis of the subfields in the input image.

4.2 SPARTAN Platform

On SPARTAN, the implementation language used is MatLab. Mat-Lab provides a Parallel Computing Toolbox used for supporting parallelisation of a job and solving computational and data-intensive problems using multicore processors. SPMD is one of the solutions provided by Toolbox to speed up processing time, using a pool of MatLab workers to process the body of each statement in parallel. Each worker in the pool contains a unique value of a variable *labindex*. Different workers communicate or transfer data by *labSend* and *labReceive*. Values returned are converted to composite objects on the MatLab client, which contains references to the values stored on the remote MatLab workers. The original image is evenly divided into several parts, and then each worker processes part of the data based on its *labindex*. The resource management solution of SPARTAN is also based on SLURM.

4.3 Batch Processing

For NeCTAR, when a user submits a job, a set of virtual machines (VMs) will be created according to the requirement for the computation resources and necessary softwares (Octave and SLURM) will be installed on these VMs to process the job. In order to reduce the time for installing softwares on virtual machines, scripted solutions such as Ansible are used. The execution time in using the Cloud platform includes two parts: creation and configuration of the VMs and the actual data processing of the image data on the Cloud.

The SPARTAN HPC facility is a shared computing system at the University of Melbourne. When a user submits a job, it may take some time to wait for the computation resources to be available - so called queueing time. A range of queues have been set up on SPARTAN to deal with serial jobs, fast jobs or parallel jobs that typically have a longer execution time and demand more computational resources. In the system design the resources on SPARTAN are set at a maximum of 8 cores for any one job, whilst for NeCTAR

it an upper limit of 32 cores for a given job can be specified. These were selected on the resources available on the HPC and Cloud systems. It is noted that NeCTAR offers a diverse range of VMs from m1.small: 1 core, 4GB RAM machines with 30GB secondary disk up to m1.xxlarge: 16 cores, 64GB RAM machines with 480GB secondary storage.

When a user submits a batch of jobs without specifying the platform, the web interface will determine where to schedule the jobs in order to reduce the overall processing time. In general, when the job is small, it is faster to process it on SPARTAN, since the queueing time on the *fast* queue is much less (typically around 10s) than the time for creating VMs on NeCTAR (typically 180s). Furthermore, the efficiency of MatLab is much higher than that of Octave. However, when the job is large, it is typically more desirable to process it entirely on NeCTAR, since it can utilise more cores across different nodes to speed up the overall processing time. The simplified job scheduling algorithm is shown below:

Data: Submitted Jobs
Result: Scheduling Jobs to reduce the processing time
Initialization: Put jobs into Queue Q;
while *Q is not empty* **do**
  $j \leftarrow Dequeue(Q)$;
  if $size(j) \leq 500MB$ **then**
    schedule j to SPARTAN with [4-8] cores;
  else
    schedule j to NeCTAR with 32 cores;
  end
end

Algorithm 1: Simplified Job Scheduling Algorithm

---

5 CASE STUDY

To understand how this system can be used to analyse water stress across a range of scenarios - in the sense that image is not simply processed in a fixed platform but users can choose the platform, the processing mode and have different data sizes - we present how the platform provides the status of available resources for users so that they can choose the processing modes based on the current system status.

To begin with, users need to log in to their account based on their assigned username and password. If they do not yet have an account, they can choose to register one. Once they have logged in to the system, they can check the status of the two processing platforms and the status of their own tasks. Figure 7 shows the typical status of the available resources in the two platforms (NeCTAR and SPARTAN) including the total number of cores and the available number of cores. The number of submitted jobs will also be listed, e.g. how many tasks this user has submitted, how many jobs are still processing and how many have successfully completed. Based on the status of the processing platforms, users can decide which platform they wish to use to analyse their crop data as well as how many resources they wish to use. In addition to the thermal image data, a CSV file containing the boundary information of the area covered in the image should be uploaded as well as the thresholds for the minimum temperature and maximum temperature. Figure

Figure 7: Overview of System Status

8 illustrates how a user can process their images on NeCTAR. For NeCTAR users, the number of nodes (VMs) and the number of cores (vCPUs) need to be provided, whilst for SPARTAN users, only the number of cores is required. It is common knowledge that with more cores being used, the processing time will speed up, however, in the case of NeCTAR delays may be caused by the time to create instances of the VM used for data processing, whilst for SPARTAN, delays may be caused by the queueing and overall load on the (shared) system.

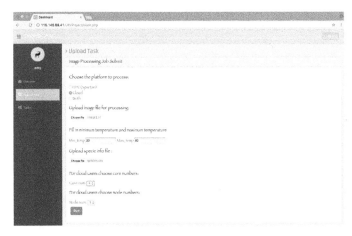

Figure 8: NeCTAR And SPARTAN User Interface

Once a task has been successfully submitted, the status of resources and user's task summary will be updated. A task management part is also used to help users manage their uploaded tasks, e.g. view processor status and task status, delete tasks, view and download results. Figure 9 shows the management interface of a typical job. For each submitted job, there are three types of processing status for a given job: queuing, processing or completed. Users can choose to suspend or cancel a job. Once the job has been completed, users can see the result or choose to download the result to their own computer.

Figure 9: Job Management Part

One key part of the system is that users can check the status of each processor, indicating the stage that each processor has reached. Figure 10 shows that, whilst there are 12 processors in total only 1 processor is currently building the GMM model of this image and the others are just waiting. The status of each processor is updated in real time.

Figure 10: Processor Status

Figure 11(a) illustrates one sample of a thermal image. Figure 11(b,c) shows the analysed result of this image. It is noticeable that some areas in this image are red which means that these areas are water-stressed, while those blue areas indicate that areas are in a normal condition.

6 PERFORMANCE COMPARISON

In this section, the execution time in use of the two different platforms is considered using three different sizes images. The sizes of data used in these three test samples are listed in Table 1. This includes the size of the image file and the associated matrix size. For each sample, we calculate the processing time on the two platforms with different numbers of cores and then make comparisons. In particular, the queueing time on SPARTAN and the time for creating VMs on NeCTAR are considered as well. We set the maximum

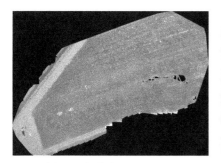

(a) Standard Thermal Image
(b) Processed CWSI for Standard Thermal Image
(c) Higher Resolution CWSI for Subsection of Field

Figure 11: Image Analysis Examples

core number for one job on SPARTAN to 8, while on NeCTAR, each VM has 4 cores and 8 instances were used in these experiments (hence jobs can use 32 cores). It is important that the system has been designed to scale however and further resources can be allocated/used.

Table 1: Size Information of Sample

Sample	File Size(MB)	Matrix Size
sample1	34.4	4190*5597
sample2	453.6	20255*11194
sample3	1392.64	24306*27985

The first sample used an input image of 34.4MB, with a matrix of 4190*5597. Figure 12 shows the performance of the first sample. As the number of cores increases, the processing time (naturally!) reduces. Without considering the queueing time on SPARTAN or the time for creating VMs on NeCTAR, before any parallelisation has been made, the job takes approximately 140s (SPARTAN) and 270s (NeCTAR) to get the analysis results using a single core. However, when using 32 cores on NeCTAR and 8 Cores on SPARTAN, it takes almost 50s on both platforms. It is noted that the analysis time of the job includes the time for creating VMs on NeCTAR and this is far more time-consuming.

The second sample used was much larger with a thermal image of 453.6MB and a matrix of 20255*11194. Figure 13 gives the execution time of sample 2. The performance of sample 2 shows a similar trend as sample 1. The more cores utilised, the less time required for the analysis. It takes approximately 3,320s (NeCTAR) and 2,150s (SPARTAN) respectively using one core to complete the data processing. In addition, when using 32 cores on NeCTAR, NeCTAR is slightly faster than SPARTAN without considering the time for creating VMs. In this case, however, the time for creating VMs is less time-consuming compared to the overall analysis time.

The final sample used is a thermal image of 1392.64 MB with a matrix of 24306*27985. Figure 14 shows that for this sample, the fastest execution time on the two platforms is almost 813s (NeCTAR) and 1,429s (SPARTAN) respectively without considering the queueing time and the time for creating VMs. In this situation, when using the maximum number of cores, NeCTAR is much faster than SPARTAN. In this case, the time for creating VMs has very

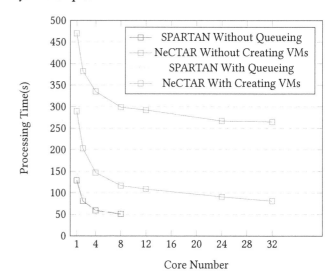

Figure 12: Performance of Sample 1

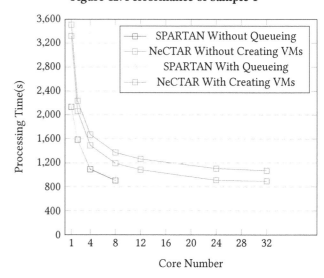

Figure 13: Performance of Sample 2

limited influence on the total analysis time.   From these results, it is easy to see that the total processing time on SPARTAN is faster

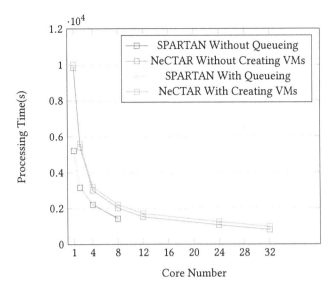

Figure 14: Performance of Sample 3

than that on the NeCTAR Research Cloud when the image data sizes are small since the time for creating VMs on NeCTAR is dominant. However, when the data increases in size since NeCTAR can provide more cores than SPARTAN, the degree of parallelism of NeCTAR is much higher than that of SPARTAN and the analysis time of NeCTAR eventually makes it worthwhile moving to the Cloud. In general, when using the same number of cores, the processing time on SPARTAN is always less than that of NeCTAR. This is also impacted by the language (Octave) used to implement the processing algorithm on the Cloud and the commercial software (MatLab) used on SPARTAN with itâĂŹs improved optimisation for matrix calculations.

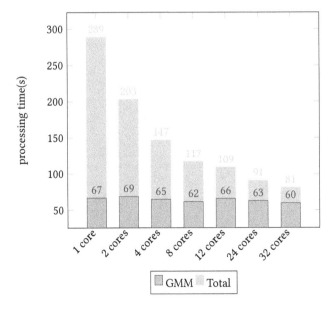

Figure 15: Processing time of different part

It is worth noting that there are two main bottlenecks in the system that exists. One is the time for communication between different nodes or different cores. The other is in creating the Gaussian Mixture Model which cannot be parallelised. Figure 15 uses one sample as an example showing the time of this processing part in isolation. It is noticeable that even if the number of cores increases to 32, it still takes about 1 minute to build the model of the whole image. This is because there is no parallelisation in the GMM part. Thus, during the processing of this part of the algorithm, only one processor is needed while the others are waiting for next stage.

7 CONCLUSIONS AND FUTURE WORK

In this paper, we have introduced an infrastructure to support agricultural image water stress analysis. To scale the offering to support large agricultural farms dealing with highly disaggregated data sets, the system needs access to large scale infrastructure - both data and computation. As described, the thermal images themselves are processed in three steps. First, edge detection processes are run over the whole image. Then for each crop species in the image, a Gaussian Mixture Model is built based on specific areas of the image. Finally, a water stress index is calculated according to the mean value from the Gaussian model.

The whole processing algorithm has been parallelised to improve the performance in processing time across two heterogeneous platforms (NeCTAR and SPARTAN). We have benchmarked the algorithms on heterogeneous e-Infrastructure across these HPC and Could platforms. As more cores are used, the processing time is reduced. However, we identify bottlenecks that prevent significant enhancements offered by parallelisation. Firstly the time consumption between different nodes and cores and secondly in building the Gaussian Mixture Model. One possible solution to tackle this is by re-sampling which allows building the Gaussian Mixture Model of one particular species, i.e. only part of the image are required for building the model instead of the whole image.

This work also developed a web interface for users who want to analyse their thermal images to obtain water stress levels over larger areas. This interface helps users access remote processing platforms and monitor available resources as well as manage their own tasks (submitting, deleting and tracking the status of jobs), as well as checking the status of processors and jobs to make suitable resource selection choices.

There are a lot of improvements that can be made to enhance the performance of the whole system. First, the GMM part could be sped up by re-sampling. Second, more analysis over thermal imagery could be made, not only for water stress, but also for disease detection, greenhouse monitoring amongst other applications. The web interface could also be made more interactive, providing a more user-friendly interface. Factoring in data transport times is a further area of exploration of increasing importance in use of the Cloud for big data processing jobs.

A final work that is also being considered is in integrating the system to support real-time data collection. Thus as the farmers collect data with drones the data could be processed in real-time and targeted thermal imagery of those areas that have water stress issues can be identified in more detail.

ACKNOWLEDGMENTS

The authors would like to thank the NeCTAR and Research Data Services (RDS - www.rds.edu.au) projects for the resources that have been made (freely!) available to support this work. Thanks are also given to the HPC administrators at the University of Melbourne for their continued support. Final thanks are also given to the scientific collaborators involved in this work - most notable Dr Dongryeol Ryu and Dr Suyoung Park.

REFERENCES

[1] Malveaux C., Hall S.G., and Price R. 2014. Using Drones in Agriculture: Unmanned Aerial Systems for Agricultural Remote Sensing Applications. *American Society of Agricultural and Biological Engineers* 141911016 (July 2014). https://doi.org/10.13031/aim.20141911016

[2] Stajnko D., Lakota M., and Hocevar M. 2004. Estimation of number and diameter of apple fruits in an orchard during the growing season by thermal imaging. *Computers and Electronics in Agriculture* 42 (January 2004), 31–42. https://doi.org/10.1016/S0168-1699(03)00086-3

[3] Martin E. 2005. Methods of Determining When to Irrigate. *Cooperative Extension. College of Agriculture and Life Sciences, The University of Arizona, Tucson* (June 2005), 91–98. https://doi.org/10.1093/jxb/erj170

[4] Oerke E.-C., Lindenthal M., Frohling P., and Steiner U. 2005. Digital Infrared Thermography for the Assessment of Leaf Pathogens. *The 5th European Conference on Precision Agriculture* (June 2005), 91–98. https://doi.org/10.3920/978-90-8686-549-9

[5] Oerke E.-C., Steiner U., Dehne H.-W., and Lindenthal M. 2006. Thermal Imaging of Cucumber Leaves Affected by Downy Mildew and Environmental Conditions. *Experimental Botany* 57 (May 2006), 2121–2132. https://doi.org/10.1093/jxb/erj170

[6] Meinke H. and Stone R.C. 1997. On tactical crop management using seasonal climate forecasts and simulation modelling: a case study for wheat. *Scientia Agricola* 54 (June 1997), 121–129. https://doi.org/10.1590/S0103-90161997000300014

[7] Jones H.G., Stoll M., Santos T., Sousa C.D., Chaves M.M., and Grant O.M. 2002. Use of infrared thermography for monitoring stomatal closure in the field: application to grapevine. *Journal of Experimental Botany* 53 (March 2002), 2249–2260. https://doi.org/10.1016/j.future.2013.05.002

[8] Berni J.A., Zarco-Tejada P.J., Suarez L., and Fereres E. 2009. Thermal and narrow-band multispectral remote sensing for vegetation monitoring from an unmanned aerial vehicle. *IEEE Transactions on Geoscience and Remote Sensing* 47 (February 2009), 722–738. https://doi.org/10.1109/TGRS.2008.2010457

[9] Ray D. Jackson. 1983. Assessing moisture stress in wheat with hand-held radiometers. *International Society for Optics and Photonics* 0356 (June 1983), 121–129. https://doi.org/10.1117/12.934042

[10] Lian Pin Koh and Serge A. Wich. 2012. Dawn of Drone Ecology: Low-Cost Autonomous Aerial Vehicles for Conservation. *Tropical Conservation Science* 5(2) (June 2012), 121–132. https://doi.org/10.1177/194008291200500202

[11] Guilioni L., Jones H.G., Leinonen I., and Lhomme J.P. 2008. On the relationships between stomatal resistance and leaf temperatures in thermography. *Agricultural and Forest Meteorology* 148, 11 (July 2008), 1908–1912. https://doi.org/10.1371/journal.pone.0066016

[12] Hori M., Kawashima E., and Yamazaki T. 2010. Application of cloud computing to agriculture and prospects in other fields. *Fujitsu Scientific Technical Journal* 46 (October 2010), 446–454. https://doi.org/10.1109/IJCSS.2011.40

[13] Lindenthal M., Steiner U., Dehne H.-W., and Oerke E.-C. 2005. Effect of Downy Mildew Development on Trans- piration of Cucumber Leaves Visualized by Digital Infrared Thermography. *Phytopathology* 95 (March 2005), 233–240. https://doi.org/10.1094/PHYTO-95-0233

[14] Gontia N.K. and Tiwari K.N. 2008. Development of crop water stress index of wheat crop for scheduling irrigation using infrared thermometry. *Agricultural water management* 95, 10 (July 2008), 1908–1912. https://doi.org/10.1016/j.agwat.2008.04.017

[15] The State of Victoria. 1996. Agriculture Victoria. (June 1996). Retrieved June, 15th 2017 from http://agriculture.vic.gov.au/agriculture/farm-management/soil-and-water/irrigation/about-irrigation

[16] Wang P., Wang J., Chen Y., and Ni G. 2013. Rapid processing of remote sensing images based on cloud computing. *Future Generation Computer Systems* 29 (March 2013), 1963–1968. https://doi.org/10.1016/j.future.2013.05.002

[17] Pinter Jr P.J., Hatfield J.L., Schepers J.S., Barnes E.M., Moran M.S., Daughtry C.S., and Upchurch D.R. 2003. Remote sensing for crop management. *Photogrammetric Engineering and Remote Sensing* 69 (June 2003), 647–664. https://doi.org/10.14358/PERS.69.6.647

[18] Mo X., Liu S., Lin Z., Xu Y., Xiang Y., and McVicar T.R. 2005. Prediction of crop yield, water consumption and water use efficiency with a SVAT-crop growth model using remotely sensed data on the North China Plain. *Ecological Modelling* 183, 2 (April 2005), 301–322. https://doi.org/10.1016/j.ecolmodel.2004.07.032

[19] Wang X., Yang W., Wheaton A., Cooley N., and Moran B. 2010. Automated canopy temperature estimation via infrared thermography: A first step towards automated plant water stress monitoring. *Computers and Electronics in Agriculture* 73, 1 (July 2010), 74–83. https://doi.org/10.1016/j.compag.2010.04.007

[20] Chen Z., Chen N., Yang C., and Di L. 2012. Cloud computing enabled web processing service for earth observation data processing. *IEEE journal of selected topics in applied earth observations and remote sensing* 5 (July 2012), 1637–1649. https://doi.org/10.1109/JSTARS.2012.2205372

[21] Baher Z.F., Mirza M., Ghorbanli M., and Bagher R.M. 2002. The influence of water stress on plant height, herbal and essential oil yield and composition in Satureja hortensis L. *Flavour and Fragrance Journal* 17 (July 2002), 275âÄŞ277. https://doi.org/10.1002/ffj.1097

Integrating Continuous Security Assessments in Microservices and Cloud Native Applications

Kennedy A. Torkura, Muhammad I.H. Sukmana, Christoph Meinel

Hasso-Plattner-Institute, University of Potsdam,

Potsdam,Germany

Email: firstname.lastname@hpi.de

ABSTRACT

Cloud Native Applications (CNA) consists of multiple collaborating microservice instances working together towards common goals. These microservices leverage the underlying cloud infrastructure to enable several properties such as scalability and resiliency. CNA are complex distributed applications, vulnerable to several security issues affecting microservices and traditional cloud-based applications. For example, each microservice instance could be developed with different technologies e.g. programming languages and databases. This diversity of technologies increases the chances for security vulnerabilities in microservices. Moreover, the fast-paced development cycles of CNA increases the probability of insufficient security tests in the development pipelines, and consequent deployment of vulnerable microservices. Furthermore, cloud native environments are ephemeral, microservices are dynamically launched and de-registered, this factor creates a *discoverability* challenge for traditional security assessment techniques. Hence, security assessments in such environments require new approaches which are specifically adapted and integrated to CNA. In fact, such techniques are to be *cloud native* i.e. well integrated into the cloud's fabric. In this paper, we tackle the above-mentioned challenges through the introduction of a novel *Security Control* concept - the *Security Gateway*. To support the Security Gateway concept, two other concepts are proposed: *dynamic document store* and *security health endpoints*. We have implemented these concepts using cloud-native design patterns and integrated them into the CNA workflow. Our experimental evaluations validate the efficiency of our proposals, the time overhead due to the security gateway is minimal and the vulnerability detection rate surpasses that of traditional security assessment approaches. Our proposal can therefore be employed to secure CNA and microservice-based implementations.

CCS CONCEPTS

• **Security and privacy** → **Vulnerability management**; *Web protocol security*; **Vulnerability management**; **Software and application security**; **Web application security**; *Vulnerability scanners*; *Network security*; *Web protocol security*; • **Computer systems**

organization → *Cloud computing*; **Distributed architectures**; **Cloud computing**; *n-tier architectures*;

KEYWORDS

Security Assessment, Microservices, Vulnerability Detection, Cloud Native Applications, Vulnerability Assessment, Application Security

1 INTRODUCTION

CNA are currently hyped owing to the benefits they offer such as increased productivity, massive scalability and reduced costs. In reality, CNA combine microservices and cloud design patterns since monolithic applications acquire *cloud-native* features when developed using microservices and cloud native design patterns such as *resiliencey, isolated-states* and *loose-couplenesss* [14].This approach to cloud application development is core to the success of companies like e.g Netflix [22]. These benefits however introduce security issues similar to those prevalent in microservices e.g. microservices communicate over networks which may be insecure and exposed to security attacks like Man in the Middle (MiTM) attacks and session hijacking. Similarly, given microservices communications are multi-faceted, the number of *entry* and *exit points* increases, invariably enlarging CNA *attack surfaces* [17]. Furthermore, microservices could be developed with different technologies e.g. programming languages, frameworks or databases [20]. This technological diversity complicates vulnerability detection since each technology has to be identified and inspected for vulnerabilities.

An approach for reducing CNA attack surfaces consists in employing continuous security assessment [12]. Continuous security assessments are used for vulnerability detection in applications and networks. Detected vulnerabilities are thereafter patched, essentially reducing the chances for security attacks. Traditionally, security assessments are configured for statically deployed applications and network hosts. However, in CNA deployments microservices are dynamically orchestrated owing to factors such as scaling requirements and complexities in cloud systems which cause failures [22]. Therefore, traditional security assessment techniques are challenged with *discoverability* problems i.e. the capacity to constantly locate deployed microservices. Furthermore, traditional security assessment techniques fail to explore REST web services, which are the core of microservice implementations [26]. However, the exploration phase is a prerequisite for vulnerability detection in web services and web applications. This exploration difficulty emerges since web services are not implemented with well defined interfaces like web applications. [1]

Permission to make digital or hard copies of all or part of this work for personal or classroom use is granted without fee provided that copies are not made or distributed for profit or commercial advantage and that copies bear this notice and the full citation on the first page. Copyrights for components of this work owned by others than ACM must be honored. Abstracting with credit is permitted. To copy otherwise, or republish, to post on servers or to redistribute to lists, requires prior specific permission and/or a fee. Request permissions from permissions@acm.org.

UCC'17, December 5–8, 2017, Austin,TX, USA

© 2017 Association for Computing Machinery.

ACM ISBN 978-1-4503-5149-2/17/12...$15.00

https://doi.org/10.1145/3147213.3147229

---

[1] https://www.owasp.org/index.php/REST_Assessment_Cheat_Sheet

Contribution In this paper, we introduce a methodology for integrating continuous security assessment in microservices and CNA. Our methodology, is realized by an innovative concept, the notion of a *Security Gateway*. The security gateway serves as a security control for enforcing security policies. Note that we use the term *security gateway* here in the context of security assessments, which is different from how the term is used in other contexts e.g. application firewalls [21] and network routers [18]. In order to support the security gateway concept, we propose two additional concepts: *dynamic document store* and *security health endpoints*. The dynamic document store helps the security gateway to overcome the challenge of detecting vulnerabilities in microservices. Security scanners are unable to crawl web services, as a pre-requisite for vulnerability detection. Microservices are affected by this challenge since they are often implemented as REST web services. The dynamic document stores overcome this challenge by generating and retaining OpenAPI [2](formerly Swagger) documents for every microservice. The scanner thereafter leverages these documents for vulnerability detection. The security health endpoint effectively affords security observability by easily providing security health information for every deployed microservice instance.

In the next section, we discuss related works, followed by a background of this paper, an overview of CNA, security challenges in CNA deployments and a problem statement description. In Section 3, we describe the design and system model of our prototype. The implementation details of our framework are presented in Section 5. In Section 6, we evaluate our work and highlight our next steps in Section 7. Section 8 concludes the paper.

2 RELATED WORK

Our work differs from most existing work in the context of CNA since we focus on the security of microservices deployed in production cloud-native environments. Most existing works on microservices security focus on security mechanisms such as encryption, authentication and authorization. While these security mechanisms improve security, the challenge of vulnerability detection and security assessments remains untackled. In [7] the challenges of deploying microservices to cloud platforms were highlighted including the security issues, however the authors offered no practical solutions to the raised issues. Thanh et al. [25] introduced an approach that allows developers and CSPs integrate security and privacy requirements across application lifecycles. Their focus was on security practices in development pipelines, we are more concerned with security measures for CNA deployed to production environments. However, their proposals could be combined with ours to enable a holistic security approach in CNA i.e. vulnerability detection coordination through application lifecycles. Savchenko et al. [20] introduced a methodology for validating microservice cloud applications. There are two shortcomings in this work, first it is not clear if the proposed framework is evaluated and tested, secondly the work is limited to development environments and focuses on non-security tests e.g. unit tests and integration tests.

In this section, we discuss the general concepts underlying CNA and related security challenges. We use Spring PetClinic [3] as an example, to illustrate our points . Spring PetClinic is an open-source Java application commonly used for research and demonstration purposes. Several versions have been developed to demonstrate different design patterns or concepts, here we use the microservices version aimed at demonstrating microservices and CNA. Note that CNA are still evolving, hence similar applications could have different service decomposition and interaction models, yet the concepts and security challenges are generally similar.

2.1 Cloud-Native Applications - An Overview

CNA combine two major application design concepts: microservices and cloud application design [14]. Microservices concepts decompose monolithic applications into smaller, independent, narrowly focused components i.e. *microservices*. Microservices communicate amongst themselves using lightweight communication protocols such as REST and Thrift[4]. On the other hand, Cloud Application Architectures (CAA) describe the general structure of cloud applications and specific application components e.g. user interfaces, processing, and data handling [8]. CAA specifies several cloud application design patterns such as *loose-coupling*, *circuit-breaker* and *gate-keeper*. Applications developed using CAA and Microservice Architectures (MSA) become *cloud native* i.e. optimized to fully exploit the benefits of cloud environments [14]. Examples of real CNA deployments include Netflix, Uber and Heroku cloud.

CNA differ from traditional, monolithic cloud applications particularly from a design and deployment perspective. Traditional application are deployed using techniques optimized for virtualized datacenters [15]. For example, in the traditional deployment model, the monolithic version of the Spring PetClinic application [5] will be deployed to the cloud by bundling the entire application stack e.g. the three-tier web application into a WAR file, which will be subsequently deployed in a cloud Virtual Machine (VM) as illustrated in Figure 1. Hence, all processes for visiting the PetClinic will run in a single process (i.e. the Visits service in Figure 1) .

There are several drawbacks to this approach, we highlight three here. Firstly, scaling the application is rigid and inflexible. Every component of the application has unique scaling requirements e.g. the creation of new customers by the Customers service is not as frequent as processing visitors, handled by the Visits service. Yet, in order to scale the monolithic application, the entire application has to be replicated, this is costly in terms of resources and time. Secondly, monolithic applications reduce innovation e.g. the ability to leverage appropriate methods for the right tasks. Monolithic applications are usually developed with one programming language/frameworks and database, hence an attempt to change the internal structure or introduce new features could mean complete re-build or huge re-factoring efforts. Lastly, managing the application becomes more difficult as it grows in size and complexity. The distribution of tasks among DevOps teams gets more difficult, which results to slow development and deployment [22].

These challenges are addressed by CNA, for example, scaling is cheaper and flexible, involving only the specific microservice affected by load pressure rather than the entire application. This is possible since an application is decomposed into several small,

---

[2]https://github.com/OAI/OpenAPI-Specification
[3]https://github.com/spring-petclinic/spring-petclinic-microservices

[4]https://thrift.apache.org/
[5]https://github.com/spring-projects/spring-petclinic

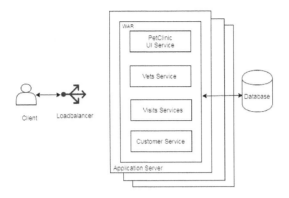

Figure 1: Monolithic Spring PetClinic

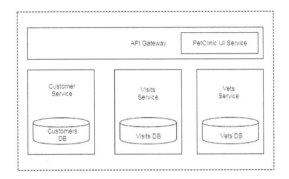

Figure 2: Evolved Architecture of PetClinic with CNA Support Functions

focused and autonomous units which are loosely coupled. So, for the microservice-implemented Spring PetClinic application (see Figure 2) each microservice is built, scaled, managed, deployed independently. Also, different technologies stacks can be employed for each microservice based on which one effectively achieves the tasks [15].

3 BACKGROUND AND PROBLEM

3.1 Security Challenges in Cloud-Native Applications

Several security issue are introduced when applications are migrated to cloud native environments. We discuss some of these security challenges next.

3.1.1 Distributed Communication. CNA use distributed communications methods to communicate amongst participating microservices. These communications methods are lightweight e.g. REST, Thrift and are relayed over the network, typical of distributed systems. Consequently, microservice communications are vulnerable to network attacks such as MiTM attack and session/token hijacking. A successful attack against these communication processes could negatively impact on microservices cooperation and orchestration as well as compromise the security of the application [7].

3.1.2 Ephemeral Nature of Resources. Microservices are dynamically deployed resulting to constantly changing parameters such as ip addresses, port numbers and service endpoints. This dynamism places an overhead for security tasks e.g. security assessments which are traditionally configured for static network resources, hosts and applications. These security processes are challenged with methods for discovering microservice endpoints, identifying when microservice instances are scaled, and differentiating versioned microservice instances. This discoverability challenge is similar to that of virtualized environments, but occurs at the application layer hence virtualization-based solutions do solve this specific challenge.

3.1.3 Trust Amongst Inter-Communicating Microservices. All inter-communicating service instances are assumed to operate within a common security trust domain hence certain security precautions are lowered. However, this could introduce security issues for example an attacker who gains control over a microservice could propagate an attack against other microservices [7].

3.1.4 REST-related Challenges. REST is a favoured design pattern for implementing CNA. REST exposes resources using endpoints easily accessible to several applications such as mobile clients and IoT devices. Nevertheless, unlike with web applications, automated security assessments for RESTful applications is challenging[4]. Security scanners detect vulnerabilities in web applications by iteratively fetching and crawling through web-page links i.e. to discover entry and exit points. This is possible since web applications have well defined interfaces. Following the *crawling phase*, security scanners send random requests and analyse responses for security vulnerabilities. On the other hand, web services do not have well defined interfaces as web applications. It is therefore challenging for automated tools to discover entry and exit points. Moreover, the responses produced by REST*ful* applications could be dynamically generated at request time unlike web applications whose responses are predictable.

3.1.5 Cloud-Specifc Vulnerabilities. CNA are deployed in cloud environments, hence become vulnerable to the peculiar security issues affecting the cloud i.e. cloud-specific vulnerabilities [9]. The *Cloud Security Shared Responsibility Model* [3] explicity proposed an approach for resolving these cloud-specific vulnerabilities. For example, on Infrastructure as a Service (IaaS) platforms, application owners (cloud users) are responsible for securing rented VMs or containers, configuring firewalls and security groups e.t.c. Implicitly, CNA deployments are requirred to employ this model for securing deployed microservices.

3.1.6 Challenges Owing to Diversity of Development Approaches. Microservices are built with different business capabilities by different development teams, which may use different technologies i.e. different programming languages and frameworks [20]. The motivation for this approach is to use the best tool for specific problems. While this feature aids in productivity, it complicates security. For example, the example Spring PetClinic application consists of four microservices, three developed in Java and the last one developed in JavaScript. Applying vulnerability detection techniques in this application requires employment of different configuration for each microservice based on the development language. This is imperative given the uniqueness of vulnerabilities per technology. Furthermore, developers integrate several open source components while developing, according to OWASP [27], these components could be laden with vulnerabilities.

3.2 Problem Definition

3.2.1 Challenges to Continuous Security Assessments and Vulnerability Management. Continuous security assessments are useful for identifying vulnerabilities in applications and networks. Identification of vulnerabilities and timely patching reduces attack surfaces and thwarts malicious attacks. While security assessments in traditional applications target statically deployed applications and systems, CNA deployments are ephemeral. Microservices are dynamically launched and de-registered, owing to scaling requirements and complexities in distributed systems. Hence, a *discoverability* challenge emerges for traditional security assessment techniques i.e. the capacity to constantly locate deployed microservices. Furthermore, the diversity of technologies in microservices increases the chances for security vulnerabilities. Also, the prevalence of fast-paced development cycles in microservice-based architectures (to meet *time-to-market*) hinders comprehensive security tests in development pipelines. Consequently, vulnerable microservices could be pushed to production environments. Novel security assessments techniques specifically adapted and integrated to cloud native environments are therefore required to tackle these security challenges.

3.2.2 Limitations of Prior Research. Prior research efforts are focused at security measures such as authentication and authorization in microservices e.g. using token based-authorization like JSON Web Token (JWT)[6]. Other works consider effective monitoring approaches such as integrating network security monitoring with cloud Software Defined Networks (SDN). Some works investigate on injecting security in microservices Continuous Integration (CI) or Continuous Development (CD) pipelines. Though these security approaches are valuable, they do not tackle the challenge of vulnerability detection and security assessments as highlighted in the previous subsection. The ability to evaluate the security state of microservices could aid in identifying compromised microservices and reducing the attack surfaces. Moreover, security evaluations are key regulatory and compliance requirements especially for cloud applications [1]. For example, the Centre for Internet Security recommends implementation of continuous vulnerability assessments to identify and mitigate vulnerabilities.[7] To the best of our knowledge, there are no research efforts focused in this direction. Traditional security assessment methods do not handle the challenge of effectively conducting security assessments in CNA. We aim at helping security teams implement robust vulnerability management and mediation systems that are native to the cloud i.e. suited for CNA.

4 DESIGN AND SYSTEM MODEL

In order to ensure continuous security assessment in CNA, several requirements are to be met. These requirements are discussed in

---

[6]https://jwt.io/
[7]https://www.cisecurity.org/controls/continuous-vulnerability-assessment-and-remediation/

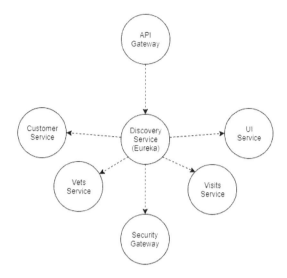

Figure 3: Security Gateway Deployed in CNA

the next subsection. Following, we highlight on how we satisfy these requirements through the construction of a *security gateway*, *adaptive security store* and *security health metrics endpoint*. We conclude this section with a discussion on methods for external security tests.

4.1 Requirements for Security Assessments in CNA

We identified five requirements to be met for continuous security assessments in microservices-based implementations and CNA. Firstly, the security assessment solution must be have the capacity of discovering all registered microservice instances in an application. This requirement has several security benefits such as inserting security control for enforcing security policies e.g. baseline security assessment. Which leads to the second requirement, support for security policies. Security policies are useful for security automation and control. Fine grained security policies provide for security efficiency. Accordingly, the solution should support a wide range of security policies and also enforce these policies. Thirdly, the solution must be *tamper-proof* i.e. isolated from possible attacks. It should not be discoverable by other microservices except the core services e.g. *service registry and discovery* and *API Gateway*. We apply the concept *security VMs* [24] to achieve this. Security VMs are isolated from application VMs using cloud networks i.e. SDN. Fourthly, the solution must effectively resolve the technologies used in developing microservice instances. Given that each microservice can be developed with a different technology, employing generic security testing policies might not be as effective as policies that specifically tackle the development technology. For example, a Java application should be tested with a policy that specifies Java vulnerabilities. Hence the solution should be able to automatically identify the development technology and test it accordingly. We satisfy this requirement by implementing the *dynamic document stores*, details are at Section 4.4.

4.2 Security Gateway

Security Enforcement Points (SEP) are commonly used to enforce security policies at run-time. For example in [2], Almorsy et al leveraged SEP to enforce security policies by intercepting and validating requests sent against critical components. We apply the concept of SEP, however in a different manner through the construct - the *Security Gateway*. The security gateway, though similar to the microservices *gateway pattern* [8] differs operationally. The security gateway is the centre for satisfying the requirements earlier discussed in Section 4.1. While the API-Gateway pattern is concerned with efficient routing of incoming and outgoing traffic, the security gateway (see Figure 3) serves as a SEP for the policies described in Section 6.3. Our definition also differs from the use of the term *security gateways* in the context of application firewalls [21] and network routers [18]. Our definition is applicable in the context of security assessments, and is extensible for enforcement of security policies for other security approaches e.g. security monitoring. There are two modes for operating the security gateway:

- Strict Mode: The secure mode implements a strict policy enforcement strategy. Microservice instances are not registered with the service discovery server if they do not satisfy the security policy being implemented. This mode could be very useful when security measures are to be strictly observed e.g. in the aftermath of a serious vulnerability like *ShellShock* [9], when a zero-tolerance approach for security vulnerabilities ia applied.
- Permissive Mode: In the permissive mode, the policy could specify a set of rules which could be combined to determine the action to be taken. e.g. a security metric could be specified an the minimum baseline.

4.3 Support for Security Policies

Automatic identification of security vulnerabilities improves the security posture of CNA, however another desirable feature is the ability to actively enforce certain actions based on security issues discovered such as vulnerabilities. An approach for enforcing such actions is by adopting security policies. Security policies are bast practices for implementing security in enterprises [23]. These policies aid in keeping production environments healthy by defining risk levels and appropriate actions when policies are breached. Several security policy languages have been proposed and implemented for evaluating and enforcing enterprise security policies. Most of the existing policy languages are specifically for web applications and SOAP-based webservices e.g. WS-SecurityPolicy [5]. There are currently no policy languages for RESTful web service security. This is a challenge for security enforcement in CNA. In this work, we propose the use of security policies for vulnerability detection and security assessment. The Security Gateway serves as a SEP by enforcing our proposed policies. We propose the following policies:

- Global Policy - These are policies that are applied to all the microservices in an application e.g. baseline security policies which are applicable to every microservice being pushed from the development pipeline to production environments.

- Microservice-Specific Policy - Ideally, every microservice would have a specific policy used for continuous security assessment. These policies are defined based on the implementation details of each microservice. This approach aims at improving efficiency of security testing by targeting specific microservice implementation technologies. For example, assuming the Visits service of the Spring PetClinic application was developed with Ruby programming language. A security policy specifying vulnerabilities announced at the Ruby security advisories [10] or OWASP Ruby Cheatsheet [11] would be used for testing the service.
- VM and Container Policy - This policy caters for the security issues that might exist in at the infrastructure level in a cloud native environment. CNA are usually deployed in VMs and containers that could be insecure. This challenge is prevalent with container-based deployments given that over 30 percent of official images in docker hub contain high priority vulnerabilities [10]. This policy could act as a security control for automating security testing of such images and containers to detect vulnerabilities. Similarly, routine assessments may be configured for continuous security assessments of VMs and containers.

4.4 Dynamic Documentation for Security Assessments

The challenges of using security scanners for conducting security tests against REST*ful* resources were previosulsy highlighted in Section 3. An approach for overcoming this challenge consists in leveraging web service description documents [4]. Web service description documents are machine readable documents containing information e.g. operations of web services. These documents have been used extensively in Service-Oriented Architectures (SOA) to provide functions of web services to clients and other application e.g. for third party application integration and consumption of service by external entities. Examples of such documents include Web Services Description Language (WSDL) [12], Web Application Description Language (WADL)[13], OpenAPI [14] and RAML [15]. Security tools e.g. security scanners can consume these documents and extract information requisite for security testing. Since there is no standardized documentation convention for REST architectures, we use OpenAPI (formerly called Swagger). OpenAPI documents are typically formatted in JSON, which is preferred over XML-based documents given the later are complex [13]. We propose the provision of OpenAPI documents for every microservice instance in an application. Each microservice can be designed to automatically generate an OpenAPI document on-demand. The documents can thereafter be retained in external repositories in accordance with *externalized configuration* cloud native design pattern[16]. Hence, microservice OpenAPI documents can be retained outside the codebase, in *dynamic document store* together with configuration files

---

[8]http://microservices.io/patterns/apigateway.html
[9]https://nvd.nist.gov/vuln/detail/CVE-2014-6271
[10]https://www.ruby-lang.org/en/security/
[11]https://www.owasp.org/index.php/Ruby_on_Rails_Cheatsheet
[12]https://www.w3.org/TR/wsdl
[13]https://www.w3.org/Submission/wadl/
[14]https://github.com/OAI/OpenAPI-Specification
[15]https://raml.org/
[16]http://microservices.io/patterns/

which are kept in *config servers*. This approach aids in flexibility as several applications could utilize the configuration concurrently, and the configuration files can be retained in versions e.g. deployed in git repositories. Similarly, the security policies earlier described in Section 6.3 can be also retained in the dynamic document store. The store can be protected with token-based authentication e.g. JWT or other automated authentication methods.

4.5 Security Health Endpoint

Health Endpoint Monitoring Pattern provides for periodic health checks against applications via heartbeat checks [11]. These heartbeat checks are necessary to quickly identify failures e.g. performance related failures. This approach to situational awareness fulfils the *observability* tenet of microservices.[17] Yet, the above described approaches do not include information on the security state of the microservice instances, which is also important for efficient, real-time security monitoring. The distributed nature of microservices further complicates security monitoring, hence an approach for easily acquiring the security status of a microservice instances is beneficial. However, there are currently no methods for easily accessing the security health of microservices instances asides log aggregation, which requires parsing and analysis for actionable intelligence to be derived. Hence, in this work, we introduce the concept of *Security Health Endpoint*. Asides the initial pre-registration assessment tests, we automate scheduled security scans to continuously detect vulnerabilities. The results of these scans are easily accessible by authenticated administrators at specified endpoints similar to accessing health checks. For example, the security health metric for the visits service (Figure 2) can be accessed using the url *http://localhost:8090/security-health* whereas the health checks are accessed at *http://localhost:8090/health*. These security health information show the most recent security assessment result with the most important aspects such as name of vulnerabilities, solution, vulnerability metrics such as CVEs and CWEs. These information can be directly consumed by other deployed security applications and used for security tasks such as automated configuration of Firewall-as-a-Service (FWaaS) rules and integration of vulnerability information into Intrusion Detection Systems (IDS) and Security Information and Events Management (SIEM) [19].

4.6 External Security Assessments

In CNA deployments where security assessments are to be conducted by external services e.g Security-as-a-Service (SecaaS) offerings, the API gateway may be configured to grant access to such services after due authentication/authorization. The external service could be given access to the *dynamic security store* earlier introduced in Section 4.4, where the OpenAPI documents are retained. Also, given OpenAPI provides for custom document definition, more than one variant of these documents may be retained e.g. for internal and external assessments or even kept in versions by leveraging git repositories as dynamic document stores. [18]

---

[17]http://microservices.io/
[18]https://12factor.net/config

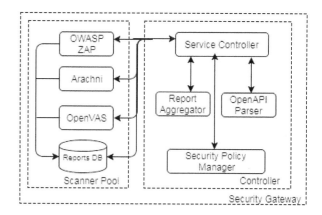

Figure 4: Security Gateway Architecture

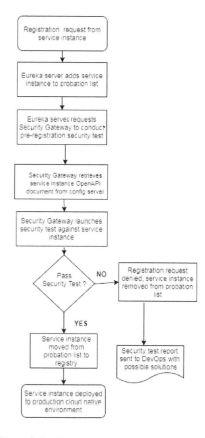

Figure 5: Workflow of the Pre-registration Security Assessment

5 IMPLEMENTATION

This section provides implementation details of our prototype. For cloud environment, we used *OpenStack Newton*. We describe the implementation of the security gateway, security health endpoint, pre-registration security assessments and microservices vulnerability tracking.

5.1 Implementing the Security Gateway

The core of our implementation is a pluggable the Security Gateway (see Figure 4), which directly interacts with the Service Registry and Discovery Service (Eureka server) for policy enforcement and vulnerability assessment. It was necessary to alter the default service instance registration behaviour of the Eureka server. There are several frameworks for implementing the Service Registry and Discovery in CNA including Netflix Eureka[19], Apache Zookeeper [20] and Hashicorp Consul [21]. We opted for Netflix Eureka considering its wide adoption and "battle-tested" performance and since it is already included in the Spring Cloud framework which we already used for most part of our implementation. Netflix Eureka implements *client-side service discovery pattern*, clients are responsible for locating other service instances by contacting service registries. We adapt Spring Cloud's implementation of Netflix Eureka server [22] to route every initial registration request to the Security Gateway. Several challenges are encountered owing to this modification. Firstly, the default asynchronous heartbeat of 30 seconds, was increased to 90 seconds between the Eureka server and client was increased. The heartbeat is used by Eureka server to evaluate the state of registered clients, i.e. if UP of DOWN. A microservice instance is automatically de-registered after 3 failed heartbeat checks(default heartbeat period is 30 seconds). Since the duration of security scanning operations could be lengthy, we extended the heartbeat duration to 90 seconds for registration requests. During the period, requesting microservice instances are initially added to a *probation list* pending the completion of the *pre-registration security assessment*. The Eureka server triggers the security gateway to commence the preregistration assessment, with three inputs : the OpenAPI document location, application name, and application homepage url. These information is directly retrieved from the information supplied by the microservice instance in the registration request. Access to the production environment is granted to the requesting instance based on the result and the operation mode of the security gateway (earlier discussed in Section 4.2) pre-registration assessment.

5.2 Pre-Registration Security Assessment

Figure 5 is a flowchart that illustrates the pre-registration security assessment. This assessment can be easily adapted to enforce an enterprise's security policy for example service instances might only be registered if the security policy is fulfilled. Security policies could be useful in checking for specific vulnerabilities. For example, Listing 1 is a baseline security policy for testing service instances for *SQL Injection, XSS and CSRF* vulnerabilities. This is especially useful in the aftermath of the disclosure of a high-risk vulnerability e.g. a policy could be configured to test if a service instance has the Shell-Shock vulnerability. The *scan policy manager* (Figure 4) translates the policy to the specific format for the configured vulnerability scanners. Each scan can be carried out by several security scanners, in-sequence after which the results are automatically compared and de-duplicated for repetitions. This approach reduces the chances of false positives, a major challenge of vulnerability scanners. The

---

Listing 1: Security Health Endpoint Output for Visits Microservice

```
{
"policy_name":"Global Policy",
"policy_type" : "Baseline Security Policy",
"attack_strength" : "medium",
"max_permissible_risk" : "high",
"scope" : {
    "depth_limit" : 5
},
"checks" : ["sql_injection","xss","csrf"],
"plugins" : {"discovery checks":"mild",
"cross_site_scripting":"medium",
"cross_site_request_forgery":"medium",
"sql_injection":"medium"},
"no_fingerprinting" : false,
"authorized_by" : "CAVAS_admin"
}
```

scan scheduler can be easily configured to test service instances and instance hosts e.g. VMs or containers at a specified time using a specific scan policy.

5.3 Security Health Endpoints

The Health Endpoint Monitoring Pattern [11] is commonly implemented in microservices to expose health metrics per service instance at specific paths such as *GET localhost:9966/health*. As earlier discussed in Section 5.3, we propose the inclusion of security health endpoints in CNA. To afford this feature, we implement *security health endpoint resources* in each Spring PetClinic microservice. These resources are capable of retrieving the current security assessment result from the security gateway by sending GET requests. For example on receipt of a GET request against the Visits service (*GET localhost:9966/security-health*, the Visits service sends a request to the Security Gateway to retrieve the most recent security testing report, which is subsequently returned to the requester in json format (Listing 2).[23]

5.4 Microservices Vulnerability Tracking

The ability to track vulnerability across the life-cycle of microservices is a necessary feature for applications deployed in production environments. A core benefit of this feature is the ability to understand the security state of an application by mapping vulnerability life-cycles with software life cycles. This knowledge is useful when making decisions e.g about the design of future applications or for version and feature improvements. We discussed the concept of *Security Health Metrics* in Section 5.3. Though these metrics are available at instance endpoints, they do not provide detailed information on the security history necessary for vulnerability tracking e.g. security test results of service instances. However, these metrics are useful for understanding distributed applications (in accordance with the *observability* pattern) hence the visualization of several microservices components e.g. Eureka dashboard for Eureka server,

---

Table 1: Summary of Test Environment

Environment Variable	Value
Server Operating System	Ubuntu 14.04 Trusty Tahr
Cloud Environment	OpenStack Newton
RAM	32GB
HardDrive Capacity	500GB

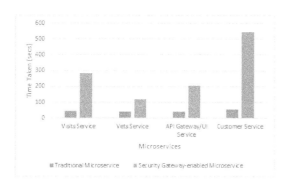

Figure 6: Time Overhead due to Security Gateway Pre-registration Security Test

Hystrix dashboard for Hystrix circuit breaker [24]. There are no integrated solutions for viewing security health and security status history for service instances. In order to provide this functionality, we integrated a vulnerability management system using *DefectDojo* [25]. DefectDojo is an open-source OWASP project for vulnerability management, it offers features available on commercial systems such as application vulnerability tracking, unified custom report generation and vulnerability metrics aggregation. DefectDojo provides an API through which we send security testing results for every microservice. This result can be subsequently visualized and organised for security analysis like analysing the security progress of a microservice, analysing security vulnerabilities, patching tasks e.t.c. Moreover, this implementation can be also used in a Security Operation Center.

6 EVALUATION

We evaluate our prototype with the Spring PetClinic application earlier introduced in Section 3. The aim of our evaluation is threefold, first we aim at measuring the overhead incurred by the *discovery and service registry service (Eureka Server)* in handling registration requests due to the *Security Gateway*. Secondly, we want to evaluate the performance of security tests using *dynamic document stores* vis-a-vis traditional security assessment methods i.e. for discovering the entry points of each target microservice being accessed. Thirdly, we demonstrate with a case study the effectiveness of our prototype in enforcing security policies. Table 1 is the configuration of our OpenStack cloud test environment.

---

[24]https://github.com/Netflix/Hystrix/wiki/How-it-Works
[25]https://github.com/OWASP/django-DefectDojo

Listing 2: Security Health Endpoint Output for Visits Microservice

```
{
"sourceid": "1",
"method": "GET",
"evidence": "The query time is controllable
using parameter value [' | case randomblob
(100000) when not null then \"\" ...
"pluginId": "40024",
"cweid": "89",
"confidence": "Medium",
"wascid": "19",
"description": "SQL injection may be possible",
"messageId": "55902",
"url": "http://localhost:9966/security-health",
"reference": "https://www.owasp.org/index.php/
Top_10_2010-A1 \nhttps://www.owasp.org/index.php/
SQL_Injection_Prevention_Cheat_Sheet",
"solution": "Do not trust client side input, even
if there is client side validation in place. In
general, type check all data on the server side.
\nIf the application uses JDBC, use PreparedStatement
or CallableStatement.
"alert": "SQL Injection - SQLite",
"param": "query",
"attack": "' | case randomblob(100000) when not
null then \"\" else \"\" end | '",
"name": "SQL Injection - SQLite",
"risk": "High",
"id": "111"
}
```

6.1 Security Gateway Time Overhead

Two versions of the Eureka server are used : *Version A* - default Eureka Server and *Version B* - Security Gateway enabled Eureka Server i.e adapted to cater for the requirements of the security gateway. We use the Spring PetClinic as the test application. First, the supporting microservices are deployed i.e. Eureka server, configuration service and API gateway. These microservices are not evaluated since they are standard static components. Thereafter, we deployed our security gateway and then launched the other service instances one after the other, while measuring the time taken from start to registration. For the tests, we use a baseline security policy for testing which checks for SQL injection, HTTP Parameter pollution and CSRF vulnerabilities. Figure 6 is the graph representing the time-overhead, we observe the customer service has an overhead of 490 seconds being the service with the largest code-base, while the Vets service has an overhead of 79 seconds. The customer service has a larger attack surface therefore more calls are made to identify entry points resulting to longer security testing duration. Despite the time taken in testing the microservices, some vulnerabilities have been discovered that could expose the application if taken to the production environment. Moreover, the time taken for security testing is negligible and would not hinder speedy development. The testing duration can be can be drastically reduced if security testing

Table 2: Comparison of Vulnerability Detection Using Dynamic Document Store

With/Without	Number of Vulnerabilities Detected
Using Dynamic Document Store	20
Not Using Dynamic Document Store	6

is integrated in the development pipeline. The security gateway can be extended to handle security tests in development, in this case, the security policies will be adapted to focus on detecting previously un-tested vulnerabilities.

6.2 Vulnerability Detection with Dynamic Document Store

We evaluated the efficiency of our dynamic document store i.e. using OpenAPI versus direct testing with security scanners. For this test, we configured a *global security policy* scheduled the Security Gateway to run a test against the Spring PetClinic application. The first test used the dynamic document store, while the second test ran without it. Table 2 shows that 20 vulnerabilities are detected when using the dynamic document store. Without the dynamic document store, 6 vulnerabilities were discovered. Since we were testing, with insecure mode of the security policy, the service instances were allowed to go into production. However, if the *secure mode policy* was activated, the service instance with security issues would be prevented from going into production i.e. not registered with Eureka server. In such cases, the responsible developer will be informed to fix the discovered vulnerabilities. A report detailing the security issues with possible solutions will be sent to the developer.

6.3 Enforcement of Security Policies

In order to demonstrate the efficiency of the security gateway in enforcing security policies, we push another microservice called the *PetsFans microservice* to production. The PetsFans microservice is to cater for a fictitious *PetFans foundation*. We use the baseline security policy in Listing 1 to ensure that new service instances with vulnerability risk ratings up to *high* are not registered. We then launch the PetsFan microservice, the security gateway is thereafter called by the Eureka server to test PetsFan microservice using the new security policy. The test reveals that the microservice has 69 vulnerabilities including 5 XSS vulnerabilities with a risk ranking *high*, see an example of a discovered high risk vulnerabilities in Figure 7. Accordingly, PetsFan microservice is not permitted into the production environment, rather a report of the security test is sent to the DevOps describing the security issues found and possible solutions. For space limitations, details of the results and vulnerabilities discovered are not included in this paper.

7 FUTURE WORK

We like to explore the integration of our concept into development pipelines, as an optimization effort to reduce the duration of pre-registration tests and strategize security testing for different versions of a microservice. Vulnerability Correlation [16] provides

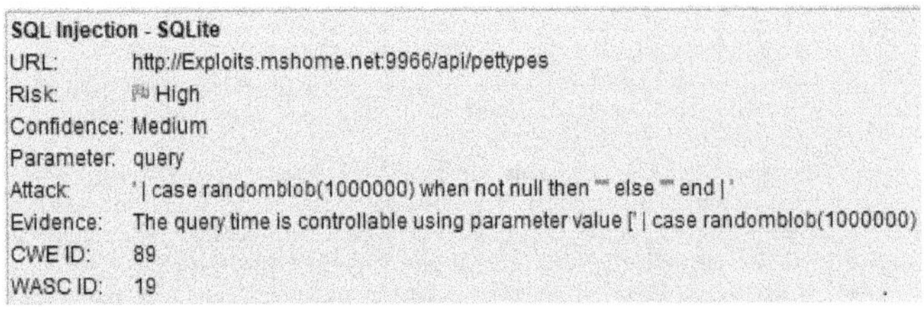

Figure 7: Example of High Risk SQL Injection Vulnerability discovered during Pre-Registration Assessment of PetsFan Microservice Using a Global Security Policy

opportunities for investigating relationships between vulnerabilities affecting applications and networks. This concept could be applied to vulnerability management in CNA to better understand the relationships between vulnerabilities in intercommunicating microservices, hence its integration in our proposal is an interesting effort. Furthermore, inclusion of of state-aware security testing techniques [6] in the *security gateway* could optimize performance.

8 CONCLUSION

CNA are designed to maximally explore the benefits of the cloud by applying microservices and cloud-focused design patterns. However these patterns introduce security issues such as enlarged attack surfaces, trustworthiness-based attacks and MiTM attacks owing to network-based communication. Similarly, microservices could be implemented with diverse technologies which may include vulnerability laden open-source frameworks. In this paper, we tackle these security challenges by integrating automated vulnerability detection techniques in microservices. We introduce the concept of *security gateway*, which serves as an efficient *security enforcement point* for enforcing security policies e.g the *global security policies* ensure microservices pushed into production do not have specific vulnerabilities expressed in the security policy. We adapt the Netflix discovery and registry service (*Eureka server*) to function in a more secure way, in-collaboration with the security gateway. We also introduce the concept of *dynamic document stores* to overcome the challenges faced by security scanners in detecting web services vulnerabilities. In order to have security *observability* or *situational awareness* of microservices, we propose the concept of *security health endpoints*, which functions similar to the health endpoint, but provides security information useful for various security tasks e.g. automated rule configurations for FWaaS and IDS. In order to demonstrate the effectiveness of our prototype, we conduct experimental evaluations. Our prototype effectively detects several vulnerabilities and the time-overhead for the pre-registration security assessments are negligible. Also, the vulnerability detection rate surpasses traditional vulnerability detection techniques.

REFERENCES

[1] Cloud Security Alliance. 2011. Domain 4: Complaince and Audit Management. (2011). https://cloudsecurityalliance.org/wp-content/uploads/2011/09/Domain-4.doc
[2] Mohamed Almorsy, John Grundy, and Amani S Ibrahim. 2014. Adaptable, model-driven security engineering for SaaS cloud-based applications. *Automated software engineering* 21, 2 (2014), 187–224.

[3] Mohamed Almorsy, John Grundy, and Ingo Müller. 2016. An analysis of the cloud computing security problem. *arXiv preprint arXiv:1609.01107* (2016).

[4] Nuno Antunes and Marco Vieira. 2016. Designing vulnerability testing tools for web services: approach, components, and tools. *International Journal of Information Security* (2016), 1-23.

[5] Giovanni Della-Libera, Martin Gudgin, Phillip Hallam-Baker, Maryann Hondo, Hans Granqvist, Chris Kaler, Hiroshi Maruyama, Michael McIntosh, Anthony Nadalin, Nataraj Nagaratnam, et al. 2002. Web services security policy language (WS-SecurityPolicy). *Public Draft Specification (Juli 2005)* (2002).

[6] Adam Doupé, Ludovico Cavedon, Christopher Kruegel, and Giovanni Vigna. 2012. Enemy of the State: A State-Aware Black-Box Web Vulnerability Scanner.. In *USENIX Security Symposium*, Vol. 14.

[7] Christian Esposito, Aniello Castiglione, and Kim-Kwang Raymond Choo. 2016. Challenges in Delivering Software in the Cloud as Microservices. *IEEE Cloud Computing* 3, 5 (2016), 10-14.

[8] Christoph Fehling, Frank Leymann, Ralph Retter, Walter Schupeck, and Peter Arbitter. 2014. *Cloud Computing Patterns: Fundamentals to Design, Build, and Manage Cloud Applications.* Springer. https://doi.org/10.1007/978-3-7091-1568-8

[9] Bernd Grobauer, Tobias Walloschek, and Elmar Stocker. 2011. Understanding cloud computing vulnerabilities. *IEEE Security & Privacy* 9, 2 (2011), 50-57.

[10] Jayanth Gummaraju, Tarun Desikan, and Yoshio Turner. 2015. *Over 30% of official images in docker hub contain high priority security vulnerabilities.* Technical Report. Technical report, BanyanOps.

[11] A. Homer, J. Sharp, L. Brader, M. Narumoto, and T. Swanson. 2014. *Cloud Design Patterns.* Microsoft Press.

[12] SANS Institute. 2016. Reducing Attack Surface: SANS Second Survey on Continuous Monitoring Programs. (2016). https://www.sans.org/reading-room/whitepapers/analyst/reducing-attack-surface-sans%E2%80%99-second-survey-continuous-monitoring-programs-37417

[13] Jacek Kopecký, Karthik Gomadam, and Tomas Vitvar. 2008. hrests: An html microformat for describing restful web services. In *Web Intelligence and Intelligent Agent Technology, 2008. WI-IAT'08. IEEE/WIC/ACM International Conference on*, Vol. 1. IEEE, 619-625.

[14] Nane Kratzke and René Peinl. 2016. ClouNS-a Cloud-Native Application Reference Model for Enterprise Architects. In *Enterprise Distributed Object Computing Workshop (EDOCW), 2016 IEEE 20th International*. IEEE, 1-10.

[15] Frank Leymann, Uwe Breitenbücher, Sebastian Wagner, and Johannes Wettinger. 2016. Native Cloud Applications: Why Monolithic Virtualization Is Not Their Foundation. In *International Conference on Cloud Computing and Services Science.* Springer, 16-40.

[16] Xuejiao Liu, Debao Xiao, Nian Ma, and Jie Yu. 2009. *A Scalable, Vulnerability Modeling and Correlating Method for Network Security.* Springer Berlin Heidelberg, Berlin, Heidelberg, 217-227. https://doi.org/10.1007/978-3-642-10485-5_16

[17] Pratyusa K Manadhata, Yuecel Karabulut, and Jeannette M Wing. 2009. Report: Measuring the Attack Surfaces of Enterprise Software. *ESSoS* 9 (2009), 91-100.

[18] Rolf Oppliger. 1998. Security at the Internet layer. *Computer* 31, 9 (1998), 43-47.

[19] Sebastian Roschke, Feng Cheng, Robert Schuppenies, and Christoph Meinel. 2009. Towards Unifying Vulnerability Information for Attack Graph Construction.. In *ISC.* Springer, 218-233.

[20] Dmitry I Savchenko, Gleb I Radchenko, and Ossi Taipale. 2015. Microservices validation: Mjolnirr platform case study. In *Information and Communication Technology, Electronics and Microelectronics (MIPRO), 2015 38th International Convention on*. IEEE, 235-240.

[21] David Scott and Richard Sharp. 2002. Abstracting application-level web security. In *Proceedings of the 11th international conference on World Wide Web*. ACM, 396-407.

[22] Matt Stine. 2015. *Migrating to Cloud-Native Application Architectures.* O'Reilly Media, Inc.1005 Gravenstein Highway North, Sebastopol, CA 95472.

[23] Subashini Subashini and Veeraruna Kavitha. 2011. A survey on security issues in service delivery models of cloud computing. *Journal of network and computer applications* 34, 1 (2011), 1-11.

[24] Yuqiong Sun, Susanta Nanda, and Trent Jaeger. 2015. Security-as-a-service for microservices-based cloud applications. In *Cloud Computing Technology and Science (CloudCom), 2015 IEEE 7th International Conference on*. IEEE, 50-57.

[25] Tran Quang Thanh, Stefan Covaci, Thomas Magedanz, Panagiotis Gouvas, and Anastasios Zafeiropoulos. 2016. Embedding security and privacy into the development and operation of cloud applications and services. In *Telecommunications Network Strategy and Planning Symposium (Networks), 2016 17th International.* IEEE, 31-36.

[26] Marco Vieira, Nuno Antunes, and Henrique Madeira. 2009. Using web security scanners to detect vulnerabilities in web services. In *Dependable Systems & Networks, 2009. DSN'09. IEEE/IFIP International Conference on*. IEEE, 566-571.

[27] Dave Wichers. 2013. Owasp top-10 2013. *OWASP Foundation, February* (2013).

Machine Learning GPU Power Measurement on Chameleon Cloud

Extended Abstract

Joon-Yee Chuah
Texas Advanced Computing Center
Austin, Texas
jchuah@tacc.utexas.edu

ABSTRACT

Machine Learning (ML) is becoming critical for many industrial and scientific endeavors, and has a growing presence in High Performance Computing (HPC) environments. Neural network training requires long execution times for large data sets, and libraries like TensorFlow implement GPU acceleration to reduce the total runtime for each calculation. This tutorial demonstrates how to 1) use Chameleon Cloud to perform comparative studies of ML training performance across different hardware configurations; and 2) run and monitor power utilization of TensorFlow on NVIDIA GPUs.

CCS CONCEPTS

• **Computing methodologies** → **Graphics processors**; *Machine learning*; • **Hardware** → **Power estimation and optimization**;

KEYWORDS

ACM proceedings; machine learning; GPU; power

1 INTRODUCTION

The increase in deep learning applications has created a high demand for GPU optimization of training tasks to quickly process large data sets. Training is frequently performed using cloud resources such as Microsoft Azure and Google Cloud Platform. While many service users are billed by training runtime, infrastructure providers must evaluate hardware for system design with respect to power consumption. The ability to measure power consumption and utilization of a GPU that is executing a deep learning training algorithm allows researchers to optimize both codes and hardware selection.

2 TUTORIAL DETAILS

2.1 Experimentation on Chameleon Cloud

Determining optimal performance per watt for Machine Learning requires comparative studies across a variety of hardware. Baremetal access in a cloud environment enables these types of studies. Chameleon Cloud, an NSF funded test bed system with NVIDIA M40, K80 and P100 GPUs on PCIE and NVLink, is the perfect platform for this task.

2.2 Tutorial Summary

This tutorial will begin with an overview of ML concepts that can be used to design an experiment. Hands-on tutorial exercises will include launching a pre-configured TensorFlow instance on a Chameleon Cloud single-tenant bare-metal node, executing a convolutional neural network training task that performs CIFAR-10 image classification, and sampling and plotting power data available through the NVIDIA Management Layer on a Jupyter Notebook, a common tool in Machine Learning. Subsequent exercises will teach participants how to request additional metrics from the NVIDIA Management Layer, alter deep learning training parameters, and measure additional training tasks.

2.3 Audience

The intended audience of this tutorial are researchers interested in measuring performance and power utilization on GPUs, as well as researchers interested specifically in machine learning performance. In addition, individuals interested in learning to use bare metal cloud systems to evaluate hardware for system design will benefit from this hands-on tutorial. The prerequisites for the audience include a basic knowledge of Python, the ability to log in remotely to an ssh system with a provided private key, and a beginning familiarity of ML. To participate in exercises, attendees are expected to bring a laptop with an ssh client and web browser. Training accounts for Chameleon Cloud will be provided.

ACKNOWLEDGMENTS

Results presented in this tutorial were obtained using the Chameleon testbed supported by the National Science Foundationnder the proposal *Collaboartive Research: Chameleon: A Large-Scale Reconfigurable Experimental Environt for Cloud Research* (Award No. 1743354)

Cloud-Based Interactive Video Streaming Service

Mohsen Amini Salehi

HPCC lab., School of Computing and Informatics,
University of Louisiana at Lafayette
Lafayette, Louisiana, USA
amini@louisiana.edu

ABSTRACT

A wide range of applications, from e-learning to natural disaster management are reliant on video streaming. Video streaming will construct more than 80% of the whole Internet traffic by 2019. Currently, video stream providers offer little or no interactive services on their streamed videos. Stream viewers, however, demand a wide variety of interactive services (*e.g.*, dynamic video summarization or dynamic transcoding) on the streams. Taking into account the long tail access pattern to video streams, it is not feasible to preprocess all possible interactions for all video streams. Also, Processing them is also not feasible on energy- and compute-limited viewers' thin-clients. The proposed research provides a cloud-based video streaming engine that enables interactive video streaming. Interactive Video Streaming Engine (IVSE) is generic and video stream providers can customize it by defining their own interactive services, depending on their applications and their viewers' desires. The engine enacts the defined interactive services through on-demand processing of the video streams on potentially heterogeneous cloud services, in a cost-efficient manner, and with respect to stream viewers' QoS demands.

KEYWORDS

Cloud Computing, Video Streaming, Resource Allocation, Real-time Processing

1 INTRODUCTION

Thanks to the high speed Internet, basic video streaming has become an ordinary service nowadays. However, what is offered currently is far from the higher level services that enable stream viewers to *interact* with the video streams. *Interactive video streaming* is defined as processing of a video stream upon viewersâĂŹ requests for that video. For instance, a viewer may request to watch a video stream with a particular resolution [4]. Another example, is a viewer who requests to view a summary of a video stream.

Current interactive video streaming services are very limited and often require preprocessing of the video streams. However, given the diversity of services offered in an ideal interactive video streaming and the long tail access pattern to the video streams [9], offering interactive video streaming based on lazy (*i.e.,* on-demand)

UCC'17, , December 5–8, 2017, Austin, TX, USA.
© 2017 Copyright held by the owner/author(s).
ACM ISBN 978-1-4503-5149-2/17/12.
https://doi.org/10.1145/3147213.3149451

processing of the video streams is required. Such computationally-intensive processing should be achieved in a real-time manner and guarantee specific QoS demands of the viewers.

Cloud services have provided an ideal platform for video streaming providers to satisfy the computational demands needed for interactive video streaming [4]. However, the common problem in utilizing cloud services [7, 8] for interactive video streaming is: *how to provide a robust interactive video streaming service through guaranteeing QoS desires of the viewers, while incurring the minimum cost for the cloud services?* Accordingly, the objective of this research is to present challenges, structures, and methods required to enable interactive video streaming that guarantee QoS in a cost-efficient manner. In particular, we present a framework for interactive video streaming called *Interactive Video Streaming Engine* (IVSE) that deals with the challenges of cloud-based interactive video streaming services and provides methods to address these challenges.

The reason that video streaming tasks need independent study is that they have unique characteristics. Video streaming tasks have individual deadlines that can be a hard deadline (in live streams [2]) or a soft deadline (in Video On Demand (VOD) [4]). Recent studies (*e.g.,* [6]) show that viewers often watch the beginning of video streams, as such, the quality of delivering the startup of video streams is of paramount importance. Accordingly, video streams have unique QoS demands that are defined as: minimizing missing tasks' individual deadlines and minimizing the startup delay of the streams.

Depending on the type of video stream content, their processing times (*i.e.,* execution time) vary on different types of processing services (*i.e.,* Virtual Machines) offered by cloud providers. Hence, to schedule video streaming tasks, we potentially deal with mapping tasks to heterogeneous cluster of Virtual Machines (VMs). In such a heterogeneous computing environment, predicting the execution time of of video streaming tasks is necessary to efficiently map tasks to VMs. Execution time prediction is viable thorough historic execution information for VOD streams, however, this is not the case in live streams, where video streaming tasks are generated and processed for the first time [1]. Processing performance of cloud VMs may vary over time or even VM failure can occur. In this case, all video streams assigned to those VMs cannot proceed with streaming. Hence, execution of video streams are required and failed tasks have to be rescheduled with a high priority to enable smooth video streaming. The access rate to video streams in a repository is not uniform. In fact, access patterns to video streams exhibits a long-tail pattern [9]. As such, caching methods are required to identify *hot* video streams and appropriately cache (store) them using different cloud storage services.

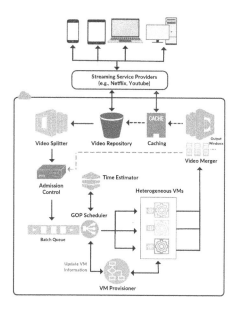

Figure 1: Cloud-based Interactive Video Streaming Engine (IVSE)

1.1 Interactive Video Streaming Engine (IVSE)

IVSE facilitates cost-efficient and QoS-aware interactive live or VOD streaming using cloud services for different type of subscribers. IVSE is extensible, meaning that the video stream provider is able to introduce new interactive services on video streams and the core architecture can accommodate the services while respecting the QoS and cost constraints of the video stream provider.

An overview of IVSE is presented in Figure 1. Upon receiving a streaming request, Video Splitter partitions the video into several Group of Pictures (*GOPs*) [3] that can be processed independently. Each GOP is treated as a task with an individual deadline which is the presentation time of the first frame in that GOP. The Admission Control component prioritizes dispatching of the GOPs to the scheduling queue. The VM Provisioner component allocates heterogeneous VM(s) from cloud to execute GOPs. Each VM is assigned a local queue to preload GOPs' data before execution. VM Provisioner component monitors the performance of VMs and adaptively configures the heterogeneity of the VM cluster based on the workload. Time Estimator provides predictive information on the affinity of GOP tasks with various VM types. The Scheduler component uses the estimation information for efficient allocation of tasks to VMs. Video Merger rebuilds the processed stream using an output window for each stream. In the event that a GOP is delayed (*e.g.*, due to failure), Video Merger asks the Admission Control to resubmit the GOP urgently. The Caching component decides if a part of, or the whole processed stream should be stored.

In summary, this this research project describes innovations in interactive video streaming particularly in the following areas:

- Robust, cost-efficient, and self-configurable VM provisioning policy: We explain novel methods to provision a dynamic VM cluster that conforms its heterogeneity according to the arriving requests (see [4] for further details).
- Heterogeneity and QoS aware scheduling method. It efficiently schedules streaming tasks on available heterogeneous

VMs with the goal of minimizing both missing tasks' deadlines and their startup delays (see [4] for further details).
- Execution time prediction for video streaming tasks: We elaborate on the influential factors of the video streaming tasks execution times. In addition, we explain the way to model affinity exists between heterogeneous VMs and tasks while considering their cost difference (see [10] for further details).
- A priority-aware admission control method: That prioritizes submission of streaming tasks to minimize the startup delay. The method can also consider the viewer subscription priority, and network speed at the viewers' end.
- Cost-efficient caching methods: We will elaborate on the trade-off between computation versus storage for video streams. We also provide a formal way to measure the hotness of video streams and provide methods that perform caching based on the hotness measure (see [5] for further details).

2 CONCLUSIONS

Video streaming is one of the prominent services of the current and future Internet. Viewers increasingly request for more interactions on the streamed videos. In this research, we provide an Interactive Video Streaming Engine (IVSE) that leverages cloud computing in an efficient way to provide flexible interactivity for the streamed videos. IVSE can be easily extended with new video processing services and can support live and on-demand streaming.

REFERENCES
[1] Matin Hosseini, Mohsen Amini Salehi, and Raju Gottumukkala. 2017. Enabling Interactive Video Stream Prioritization for Public Safety Monitoring through Effective Batch Scheduling. In *Accepted in the 19th IEEE International Conference on High Performance Computing and Communications* (Bankok).
[2] Xiangbo Li, Mohsen Amini Salehi, and Magdy Bayoumi. 2016. VLSC: Video Live Streaming Using Cloud Services. In *Proceedings of 5th IEEE International Conferences on Big Data and Cloud Computing*. 595–600.
[3] Xiangbo Li, Mohsen Amini Salehi, and Magdy Bayoumi. Oct. 2015. Cloud-Based Video Streaming for Energy- and Compute-Limit Thin Clients. In *the Stream2015 Workshop at Indiana University*.
[4] Xiangbo Li, Mohsen Amini Salehi, Magdy Bayoumi, and Rajkumar Buyya. 2016. CVSS: A Cost-Efficient and QoS-Aware Video Streaming Using Cloud Services. In *Proceedings of the 16th IEEE/ACM International Conference on Cluster Cloud and Grid Computing (CCGrid '16)*.
[5] Darwich Mahmoud, Beyazit Ega, Salehi Mohsen Amini, and Bayoumi Magdy. 2017. Cost Efficient Repository Management for Cloud-Based On-Demand Video Streaming. In *In proceedings of 5th IEEE Internationa Conference on Mobile Cloud Computing, Services, and Engineering (MobileCloud)*. 1–6.
[6] Lucas CO Miranda, Rodrygo LT Santos, and Alberto HF Laender. 2013. Characterizing video access patterns in mainstream media portals. In *Proceedings of the 22nd International Conference on World Wide Web*. 1085–1092.
[7] Murali K. Pusala, Mohsen Amini Salehi, Jayasimha R. Katukuri, Ying Xie, and Vijay Raghavan. 2016. *Massive Data Analysis: Tasks, Tools, Applications, and Challenges*. Springer India, New Delhi, 11–40.
[8] Mohsen Salehi and Rajkumar Buyya. 2010. Adapting Market-Oriented Scheduling Policies for Cloud Computing. In *Algorithms and Architectures for Parallel Processing*. ICA3PP '10, Vol. 6081. 351–362.
[9] Navin Sharma, Dilip Kumar Krishnappa, David Irwin, Michael Zink, and Prashant Shenoy. 2013. Greencache: Augmenting off-the-grid cellular towers with multimedia caches. In *Proceedings of the 4th ACM Multimedia Systems Conference*. 271–280.
[10] Li Xiangbo, Joshi Yamini, Darwich Mahmoud, Landreneau Brade, Amini Salehi Mohsen, and Bayoumi Magdy. 2017. Performance Analysis and Modeling of Video Transcoding Using Heterogeneous Cloud Services. In *IEEE Transactions on Parallel and Distributed Systems*. 1–12.

Practical Tooling for Serverless Computing

Josef Spillner
Zurich University of Applied Sciences
School of Engineering, Service Prototyping Lab (blog.zhaw.ch/icclab/)
Winterthur, Switzerland
josef.spillner@zhaw.ch

ABSTRACT

Cloud applications are increasingly built from a mixture of runtime technologies. Hosted functions and service-oriented web hooks are among the most recent ones which are natively supported by cloud platforms. They are collectively referred to as serverless computing by application engineers due to the transparent on-demand instance activation and microbilling without the need to provision infrastructure explicitly. This half-day tutorial explains the use cases for serverless computing and the drivers and existing software solutions behind the programming and deployment model also known as Function-as-a-Service in the overall cloud computing stack. Furthermore, it presents practical open source tools for deriving functions from legacy code and for the management and execution of functions in private and public clouds.

CCS CONCEPTS

• **Networks** → **Cloud computing**; • **Software and its engineering** → *Automatic programming*; *Software as a service orchestration system*;

KEYWORDS

serverless; microservices; FaaS; hosted functions; tutorial

ACM Reference format:
Josef Spillner. 2017. Practical Tooling for Serverless Computing. In *Proceedings of UCC'17: 10th International Conference on Utility and Cloud Computing, Austin, Texas, USA, December 5–8, 2017 (UCC'17)*, 2 pages.
https://doi.org/10.1145/3147213.3149452

1 EMERGENCE OF SERVERLESS COMPUTING

Across the cloud computing industry, there is a large trend to move up the stack. Infrastructure management has become a commodity while in parallel, developer-facing platforms have become numerous and widespread. The ability to deploy applications directly from source without intermediate packaging as virtual machine images or container images increases the rapid service creation and reduces issues related to the configuration of the development environment. Apart from pushing monolithic code trees, the fine-grained deployment of individual functions in Function-as-a-Service (FaaS) environments is becoming more common, in particular for cloud

automation, cloud-device coupling, and infrequently used web services [5]. FaaS brings utility computing closer to reality due to real on-demand enablement and microbilling of service invocations without having to pay for idle periods. It also drives the decomposition of applications into microservices, leading to more cloud-native applications. Businesses around the world have thus started to embrace FaaS through the paradigm of seemingly serverless computing.

Academics have started to describe and analyse FaaS through surveys and experiments [1, 9, 10] as well as economic analysis [3, 8, 15] and dedicated workshops (for instance WoSC'17 [4]). Still, not much is known about which tools to use for producing, deploying and running functions. This tutorial consolidates and enhances knowledge about such tools in order to achieve two goals: first, foster more experimental research on the topic; and second, enrich rapid transfer into education with hands-on competences. Fig. 1 puts the relevant tool categories into perspective concerning stacks and roles in the larger cloud computing ecosystem with its XaaS service models. FaaS refines the PaaS layer with a higher degree of abstraction to convey the desired serverless experience to application engineers. In the following paragraphs, the tool categories will be explained along with prototypical research implementations.

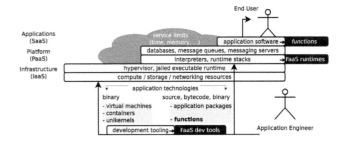

Figure 1: Function development and execution tools in the cloud computing ecosystem.

2 SERVERLESS FOUNDATIONS

From a software engineering perspective, functions in the cloud resemble functions or methods in modelling and programming languages. Functions are engineered in almost arbitrary languages following conventions for function parameters, return values and stateless execution semantics. The engineering is an activity of programming or meta-programming through transformation or transpilation of legacy code, followed by an implementation-dependent build process. Parameters are passed explicitly per request or implicitly through environment variables and other read-only data spaces. Function implementations are thus tangible microservices in the form of source code, byte code or executables, including containers.

Based on this definition, the foundations then encompass all concepts, terminologies, emerging reference architectures and development and usage patterns for the lifecycle of services implemented as functions. Recent research sheds some light on the challenges associated with this service model. For instance, in contrast to virtual machines it is not possible to provision resource-differentiated function instance types in commercial services [14].

3 TOOLING FOR SERVERLESS CONTEXTS

Two categories of tools can be distinguished: function development, including deployment, testing and debugging, and execution.

3.1 Development Tools

Development tools determine how well and efficiently functions can be created and offered as microservices on the market. Often, the development process requires provider-specific SDKs and APIs, although higher-level programming libraries and cross-provider abstraction frameworks like PyWren and the Serverless Framework exist [2, 7]. A recent trend is the semi-automated decomposition of legacy code into functions through a process called FaaSification. In practice, not all functions can or should be exported this way. Through annotations on the programming level, developers can selectively specify and configure the transformations. The configuration includes the location of the target environment and the execution characteristics. Tool implementations exist for Java and Python, for instance Podilizer, Termite and Lambada [12, 13]. In case functions are to be called from other functions, the function locality needs to be configured as well. The mechanics of such calls involve again provider-specific SDKs, e.g. Boto for Python, and appropriate permissions.

3.2 Execution Tools

Functions are executed in private or public cloud services. Commercial public services mostly depend on proprietary implementations, including Azure Functions, AWS Lambda and Google Cloud Functions. Open source runtime environments such as OpenWhisk, Fission, OpenFaaS or IronFunctions enable private deployments, but are also increasingly used in public clouds such as Bluemix. Furthermore, there are attempts to replicate the runtime characteristics of the proprietary services in open source tools such as Docker-LambCI. Despite being open source, most of the runtimes require an effort-intensive setup and operation. Academic approaches include OpenLambda [6] and Snafu [11], the Swiss Army Knife of Serverless Computing which integrates on demand with other runtimes and thus allows for controlled experiments.

Apart from the runtime, the execution depends on how a function is triggered (e.g. through a network protocol or a timer) and how requests are routed to the runtime. Often, API gateways are instrumental in achieving the necessary degree of automation. Given the stateless nature of functions, stateful services such as blob stores or databases need to be coupled which may introduce additional delays and cost.

3.3 Limitations and Challenges

While many practical tools will become available in the next year or two, resolving many of the initial issues associated with FaaS, the research potential remains high. Researchers need to identify possibilities as well as documented and undocumented limitations through analytical work given specialised tools. Within some years, hybrid orchestrations of microservices with containers and functions are going to become common, yet there are no languages available to express the compositions. Container orchestration (e.g. Docker Compose) and function orchestration (e.g. Step Functions) are still separate also in terms of tools, as well as in terms of ecosystems (e.g. Docker Hub). Another challenge are Deep FaaSification processes which streamline the conversion of legacy code into functions by incorporating a semantic code analysis. Improved debugging, profiling and autotuning of functions is also required. First commercial tools such as X-Ray and Stackdriver exist to introspect function execution, but no research work is known on such tools and their effectiveness remains unknown.

REFERENCES

[1] Ioana Baldini, Paul C. Castro, Kerry Chang, Perry Cheng, Stephen J. Fink, Vatche Ishakian, Nick Mitchell, Vinod Muthusamy, Rodric M. Rabbah, Aleksander Slominski, and Philippe Suter. 2017. Serverless Computing: Current Trends and Open Problems. CoRR abs/1706.03178 (2017). http://arxiv.org/abs/1706.03178
[2] Austen Collins, Eslam Hefnawy, and Philipp Müns. 2017. Serverless - The Serverless Application Framework. online: serverless.com. (2017).
[3] Adam Eivy. 2017. Be Wary of the Economics of "Serverless" Cloud Computing. IEEE Cloud Computing 4, 2 (2017), 6–12. https://doi.org/10.1109/MCC.2017.32
[4] Geoffrey C. Fox, Vatche Ishakian, Vinod Muthusamy, and Aleksander Slominski. 2017. Status of Serverless Computing and Function-as-a-Service(FaaS) in Industry and Research. CoRR abs/1708.08028 (2017). http://arxiv.org/abs/1708.08028
[5] Alex Glikson, Stefan Nastic, and Schahram Dustdar. 2017. Deviceless edge computing: extending serverless computing to the edge of the network. In Proceedings of the 10th ACM International Systems and Storage Conference, SYSTOR 2017, Haifa, Israel, May 22-24, 2017. 28:1. https://doi.org/10.1145/3078468.3078497
[6] Scott Hendrickson, Stephen Sturdevant, Tyler Harter, Venkateshwaran Venkataramani, Andrea C. Arpaci-Dusseau, and Remzi H. Arpaci-Dusseau. 2016. Serverless Computation with OpenLambda. In 8th USENIX Workshop on Hot Topics in Cloud Computing (HotCloud). Denver, Colorado, USA.
[7] Eric Jonas, Shivaram Venkataraman, Ion Stoica, and Benjamin Recht. 2017. Occupy the Cloud: Distributed Computing for the 99%. CoRR abs/1702.04024 (2017). http://arxiv.org/abs/1702.04024
[8] Philipp Leitner, Jürgen Cito, and Emanuel Stöckli. 2016. Modelling and managing deployment costs of microservice-based cloud applications. In Proceedings of the 9th International Conference on Utility and Cloud Computing, UCC 2016, Shanghai, China, December 6-9, 2016. 165–174. https://doi.org/10.1145/2996890.2996901
[9] Maciej Malawski. 2016. Towards Serverless Execution of Scientific Workflows - HyperFlow Case Study. In Proceedings of the 11th Workshop on Workflows in Support of Large-Scale Science co-located with The International Conference for High Performance Computing, Networking, Storage and Analysis (SC 2016), Salt Lake City, Utah, USA, November 14, 2016. 25–33. http://ceur-ws.org/Vol-1800/paper4.pdf
[10] Josef Spillner. 2017. Exploiting the Cloud Control Plane for Fun and Profit. arχiv:1701.05945. (January 2017).
[11] Josef Spillner. 2017. Snafu: Function-as-a-Service (FaaS) Runtime Design and Implementation. arχiv:1703.07562. (March 2017).
[12] Josef Spillner. 2017. Transformation of Python Applications into Function-as-a-Service Deployments. arχiv:1705.08169. (May 2017).
[13] Josef Spillner and Serhii Dorodko. 2017. Java Code Analysis and Transformation into AWS Lambda Functions. arχiv:1702.05510. (February 2017).
[14] Josef Spillner, Cristian Mateos, and David A. Monge. 2017. FaaSter, Better, Cheaper: The Prospect of Serverless Scientific Computing and HPC. In 4th Latin American Conference on High Performance Computing (CARLA). To appear.
[15] Mario Villamizar, Oscar Garces, Lina Ochoa, Harold Castro, Lorena Salamanca, Mauricio Verano, Rubby Casallas, Santiago Gil, Carlos Valencia, Angee Zambrano, and Mery Lang. 2017. Cost comparison of running web applications in the cloud using monolithic, microservice, and AWS Lambda architectures. Service Oriented Computing and Applications 11, 2 (2017), 233–247. https://doi.org/10.1007/s11761-017-0208-y

Understanding Performance Interference Benchmarking and Application Profiling Techniques for Cloud-hosted Latency-Sensitive Applications

Shashank Shekhar
Dept of EECS, Vanderbilt University
Nashville, Tennessee, USA
shashank.shekhar@vanderbilt.edu

Yogesh Barve
Dept of EECS, Vanderbilt University
Nashville, Tennessee, USA
yogesh.d.barve@vanderbilt.edu

Aniruddha Gokhale
Dept of EECS, Vanderbilt University
Nashville, Tennessee, USA
a.gokhale@vanderbilt.edu

ABSTRACT

Modern data centers are composed of heterogeneous servers with different architectures, processor counts, number of cores and speed. They also exhibit variability in memory speed and size, storage type and size and network connectivity. In addition, the servers are multi-tenant, often hosting latency sensitive applications in addition to the traditional batch processing applications. To provide bounded and predictable latencies, it is necessary for the cloud providers to understand the performance interplay among the co-hosted applications. To that end, we present our integrated and extensible framework called INDICES for users to conduct a variety of performance benchmarking experiments on multi-tenant servers. The framework also performs centralized data collection for a range of resource usage and application performance statistics in order to model the performance interference and estimate the execution times for the cloud hosted applications.

CCS CONCEPTS

• **Computer systems organization** → **Cloud computing**; • **Computing methodologies** → *Distributed algorithms*;

KEYWORDS

Cloud Computing; Performancing Monitoring; Cloud Benchmark; Performance Interference; Resource Management

1 INTRODUCTION

Cloud infrastructure providers must have an up to date understanding of the usage of their cloud resources so that they can effectively manage their cloud platforms while supporting multi-tenancy. At the same time, timely and scalable access to various resource usage statistics is critical to service providers, who host their services in the cloud. This is required in order to ensure that their applications provide the required quality of service to their customers through elastic and on demand auto-scaling while minimizing service-hosting costs. Thus, these providers must understand how their services will perform under a variety of multi-tenancy scenarios and workload patterns. Conducting such benchmarking

experiments and obtaining the desired resource statistics to pinpoint the sources of problems, such as the level of performance interference, is a hard problem.

Statistics collection in the cloud is a hard problem for a variety of reasons including multi-tenancy, heterogeneity in hardware and operating systems, and availability of hardware-specific, low-level statistics collection tools all of which make it extremely complex for providers to use existing capabilities and extend them as hardware changes and the statistics collection needs change. These challenges are further amplified as cloud platforms increasingly span fog and edge resources. Thus, a framework that is extensible and provides a higher level of abstraction to make it easy to use is needed.

Although, data collection tools such as collectd [5] and benchmarking frameworks such as CloudSuite [4], PARSEC [1] and YCSB [2] are designed to benchmark cloud applications and collect metrics, they do not focus on modeling performance interference on multi-tenant heterogeneous servers. On the other hand, a benchmark like iBench [3] tries to quantify the data-center performance interference, but they provide only some of the building blocks, thereby making the users responsible to develop and integrate the capabilities and deal with the complexities of low level details.

To overcome these challenges, this tutorial presents a framework called INDICES (INtelligent Deployment for ubIquitous Cloud and Edge Services) [6], which builds on collectd and provides an integrated and extensible framework for users to conduct a variety of performance benchmarking experiments and collect a range of resource usage and application performance statistics. Thus, INDICES enables the performance modeling of cloud-hosted applications on heterogeneous multi-tenant servers.

The rest of the paper is organized as follows: Section 2 presents the framework description; Section 3 describes the tutorial organization; and finally Section 4 presents concluding remarks.

2 FRAMEWORK DESCRIPTION

The INDICES framework consists of multiple components. The primary component is the data collection framework, which is built using the collectd [5] monitoring tool which has a plugin-based extensible architecture. We developed plugins to collect micro-architectural metrics, which are necessary for accurate performance interference modeling. In addition, the framework also collects virtual machine (VM) or Docker container-specific metrics. The standalone metric collection framework was integrated with InfluxDB time-series database such that centralized data collection can be performed and aggregated. Figure 1 depicts the data collection architecture.

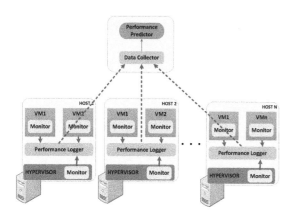

Figure 1: INDICES Data Collection Architecture

The other key component of the framework is the benchmarking component. This consists of a number of latency-sensitive client-server target applications. In addition, there are other workload applications that are used to cause performance interference on the target applications. The final component is the performance modeling component. Using the collected metrics, it helps in developing the application sensitivity and pressure as described in our prior work [6].

3 TUTORIAL ORGANIZATION

The tutorial has been divided into two sections. First we introduce the INDICES framework and explain the design details. This session includes the following:

- Motivation of the subject by highlighting the importance of resource monitoring in distributed and cloud systems alluding to the complexities in monitoring of system performance.
- Highlighting the causes of application performance interference and its relevance in the cloud, fog and edge computing realm.
- Introduction to the design of the INDICES framework and its underlying technologies.
- Short demo of INDICES used in application performance benchmarking.

In the second half, the audience will perform hands-on activities that include:

- INDICES Benchmarking-I: Configuration & Setup
- INDICES Benchmarking-II. Execution and deployment of the framework for benchmarking and monitoring of a target application under various collocated benchmarking applications (e.g: PARSEC, STREAM)
- Discussions about the results.

Using INDICES framework, one can quickly observe performance characteristics of applications deployed under various computing environments with heterogeneous resources. Moreover, using the INDICES framework one can test the target applications'

performance interference avoidance strategies which are inherent factors resulting in poor application performance in multi-tenant distributed systems. By using a concrete example from the PARSEC-based benchmarking tool to observe performance interference effects in distributed systems, the audience will discover the ease of use, detailed system metrics logging and visualization benefits from using the INDICES framework in a practical and research problem.

Upon completing this tutorial, attendees will be able to:

- Recognize the inherent and accidental complexities involved in designing and developing applications for distributed systems.
- Gain knowledge as to how the INDICES framework can help alleviate application interference issues by better designing applications to be tolerant to such system behavior.
- Acquire hands-on knowledge on how to use the INDICES framework for benchmarking and monitoring application performance interference and other system characteristics.

4 CONCLUSIONS

This paper described an extensible benchmarking, and metrics collection and analysis framework called INDICES, which is useful in determining performance interference in cloud data centers and fog/edge environments alike. In turn these metrics can serve to make effective dynamic resource management decisions in the cloud. The source code for the INDICES framework is available at: https://github.com/doc-vu/indices.

ACKNOWLEDGMENTS

This work was funded by NSF CNS US Ignite 1531079. Any opinions, findings, and conclusions or recommendations expressed in this material are those of the author(s) and do not necessarily reflect the views of NSF.

REFERENCES

[1] Christian Bienia, Sanjeev Kumar, Jaswinder Pal Singh, and Kai Li. 2008. The PARSEC benchmark suite: characterization and architectural implications. In *17th international conference on Parallel architectures and compilation techniques*. ACM, 72–81.
[2] Brian F Cooper, Adam Silberstein, Erwin Tam, Raghu Ramakrishnan, and Russell Sears. 2010. Benchmarking cloud serving systems with YCSB. In *Proceedings of the 1st ACM symposium on Cloud computing*. ACM, 143–154.
[3] Christina Delimitrou and Christos Kozyrakis. 2013. ibench: Quantifying interference for datacenter applications. In *Workload Characterization (IISWC), 2013 IEEE International Symposium on*. IEEE, 23–33.
[4] Michael Ferdman, Almutaz Adileh, Yusuf Onur Koçberber, Stavros Volos, Mohammad Alisafaee, Djordje Jevdjic, Cansu Kaynak, Adrian Daniel Popescu, Anastasia Ailamaki, and Babak Falsafi. 2012. Clearing the clouds: a study of emerging scale-out workloads on modern hardware. In *Proceedings of the 17th International Conference on Architectural Support for Programming Languages and Operating Systems, ASPLOS 2012, London, UK, March 3-7, 2012*. 37–48. https://doi.org/10.1145/2150976.2150982
[5] Florian Forster. 2017. Collectd - The System Statistics Collection Daemon. http://collectd.org. (2017).
[6] Shashank Shekhar, Ajay Chhokra, Anirban Bhattacharjee, Guillaume Aupy, and Aniruddha Gokhale. 2017. INDICES: Exploiting Edge Resources for Performance-Aware Cloud-Hosted Services. In *2017 IEEE 1st International Conference on Fog and Edge Computing (ICFEC)*. Madrid, Spain, 75–80. https://doi.org/10.1109/ICFEC.2017.16

HPC Meets Cloud: Building Efficient Clouds for HPC, Big Data, and Deep Learning Middleware and Applications*

Dhabaleswar K. Panda
The Ohio State University
Columbus, Ohio
panda@cse.ohio-state.edu

Xiaoyi Lu
The Ohio State University
Columbus, Ohio
luxi@cse.ohio-state.edu

ABSTRACT

Significant growth has been witnessed during the last few years in HPC clusters with multi-/many-core processors, accelerators, and high-performance interconnects (such as InfiniBand, Omni-Path, iWARP, and RoCE). To alleviate the cost burden, sharing HPC cluster resources to end users through virtualization for both scientific computing and Big Data processing is becoming more and more attractive. In this tutorial, we first provide an overview of popular virtualization system software on HPC cloud environments, such as hypervisors (e.g., KVM), containers (e.g., Docker, Singularity), OpenStack, Slurm, etc. Then we provide an overview of high-performance interconnects and communication mechanisms on HPC clouds, such as InfiniBand, RDMA, SR-IOV, IVShmem, etc. We further discuss the opportunities and technical challenges of designing high-performance MPI runtime over these environments. Next, we introduce our proposed novel approaches to enhance MPI library design over SR-IOV enabled InfiniBand clusters with both virtual machines and containers. We also discuss how to integrate these designs into popular cloud management systems like OpenStack and HPC cluster resource managers like Slurm. Not only for HPC middleware and applications, we will demonstrate how high-performance solutions can be designed to run Big Data and Deep Learning workloads (like Hadoop, Spark, TensorFlow, CNTK, Caffe) in HPC cloud environments.

CCS CONCEPTS

• **General and reference** → **Design**; • **Computer systems organization** → **Architectures**; **Parallel architectures**; **Cloud computing**;

KEYWORDS

HPC Clouds, Virtual Machine, Container, InfiniBand, MPI, Big Data, Deep Learning

---
*This research is supported in part by National Science Foundation grants #CNS-1419123, #IIS-1447804, and #CNS-1513120.

1 INTRODUCTION

The deployment of HPC systems is delivering unprecedented performance to scientific computing, data analytics, and emerging deep learning applications. However, the costs of such high-end clusters have remained prohibitive for a large number of institutions and users. One method to alleviate the cost bottleneck is to utilize the Cloud Computing model, which offers Infrastructure as a Service (IaaS) through leveraging various virtualizaiton technologies. IaaS reduces personnel costs through high degrees of automation and enables a better overall utilization when compared to dedicated clusters. Although virtualization technology has the potential to dramatically reduce the cost of compute cycles, several fundamental challenges need to be addressed for designing virtualized clusters that can deliver the performance of dedicated high-end computing clusters. In order to help make HPC technologies available to more scientists and researchers, our proposed tutorial focuses on how to design efficient HPC clouds with high-performance networking technologies.

A big hurdle of using virtualization technology is the unsatisfactory virtualized I/O performance delivered by underlying virtualized environments [4]. The main reason of the poor I/O performance with virtualization designs is that they do not provide an efficient mechanism to share the PCI bus which connects the CPU to the network card due to lack of hardware support. Recently, a new networking virtualization capability, Single Root I/O Virtualization (SR-IOV) [4] is introduced for high-performance interconnects such as InfiniBand and high-speed Ethernet. It specifies native I/O Virtualization (IOV) capabilities and enables us to provision the internal PCI bus interfaces between multiple virtual machines. SR-IOV opens up new opportunities for designers to achieve near native performance for I/O devices on VMs, by virtue of bypassing the hypervisor and host operating system. However, it is to be noted that there are still critical challenges that need to be carefully addressed to enable the adoption of SR-IOV in HPC clouds.

In this tutorial, we first provide an overview of popular virtualization system software on HPC cloud environments, such as hypervisors, containers, OpenStack, Slurm, etc. Then we provide an overview of high-performance interconnects and communication mechanisms on HPC clouds, such as InfiniBand, RDMA, SR-IOV, IVShmem, etc. We further discuss the opportunities and technical challenges of designing high-performance MPI runtime over these environments. Next, we introduce our proposed novel approaches to enhance MPI library design over SR-IOV enabled InfiniBand clusters with both virtual machines and containers [2, 7, 9]. A high-performance virtual machine migration framework [8] over SR-IOV enabled InfiniBand clusters will be discussed in the tutorial. We also discuss how to integrate these designs into popular cloud management systems like OpenStack [5] and HPC cluster resource managers like Slurm [6]. Not only for HPC middleware and applications, we will demonstrate how high-performance solutions can be designed to run Big Data [1, 3] and Deep Learning workloads (like Hadoop, Spark, TensorFlow, CNTK, Caffe) in HPC cloud environments.

2 TUTORIAL OUTLINE

The tutorial is organized along the following topics with a detailed time budget (half-day):

(1) Introduction to Cloud Computing and Virtualization Technologies (10 mins)
(2) Architecture Overview of Cloud System Software (15 mins)
 - Hypervisor-based Virtualization
 - Container-based Virtualization
 - OpenStack and Other Cloud Resource Managers
 - Slurm and SPANK
(3) Overview of Modern Interconnects, Protocols, and Storage Architectures for HPC Clouds (25 mins)
 - InfiniBand, 10/40/100 GigE, iWARP, RoCE, Omni-Path technologies
 - High-Performance Communication Mechanisms on HPC Clouds (e.g., RDMA, PCI Passthrough, SR-IOV, IVShmem, CMA, etc.)
 - SSD/NVM-based storage and Cloud Storage Systems (e.g., OpenStack Swift)
(4) Architecture Overview of HPC, Big Data, and Deep Learning Middleware (20 mins)
 - Message Passing Interface (MPI)
 - MapReduce, YARN, HDFS, Spark, HBase
 - Caffe, TensorFlow, BigDL
(5) Opportunities and Challenges of Building HPC Clouds on Modern Networking and Storage Architectures (20 mins)
(6) Overview of Benchmarks and Applications using MPI, Hadoop, Spark, gRPC/TensorFlow, Caffe, BigDL (20 mins)
(7) Designing High-Performance MVAPICH2 MPI Library on HPC Clouds and In-Depth Performance Evaluation (20 mins)
 - VM-aware MVAPICH2 on InfiniBand Clusters
 - Live-Migration Support in MVAPICH2 for SR-IOV enabled InfiniBand
 - Container-aware MVAPICH2 on InfiniBand Clusters
 - MVAPICH2 on Nested Cloud Environments
(8) Designing High-Performance Big Data Libraries on HPC Clouds and In-Depth Performance Evaluation (20 mins)
 - RDMA-based Designs for Hadoop Components
 - Locality-aware Design for RDMA-Hadoop

 - RDMA-based Swift Cloud Storage System for Big Data Workloads
(9) Designing High-Performance Deep Learning Libraries on HPC Clouds and In-Depth Performance Evaluation (15 mins)
 - RDMA-based Designs for Deep Learning over Big Data Stacks (e.g., CaffeOnSpark, TensorFlowOnSpark, BigDL)
 - In-Depth Characterization on Performance, Accuracy, Scalability, and Resource Utilization
(10) Integrated Designs with OpenStack and Slurm (10 mins)
 - Extending OpenStack and Slurm for Managing SR-IOV and IVShmem
 - OpenStack Heat-based Complex Appliances for MPI and Hadoop
 - A Demo with Heat Appliances
(11) Conclusion (5 mins)

REFERENCES

[1] S. Gugnani, X. Lu, and D. K. Panda. Designing Virtualization-Aware and Automatic Topology Detection Schemes for Accelerating Hadoop on SR-IOV-Enabled Clouds. In *Proceedings of the 8th IEEE International Conference on Cloud Computing Technology and Science (CloudCom)*, pages 152–159, Luxembourg, December 2016.
[2] J. Zhang, X. Lu, J. Jose, M. Li, R. Shi, D. K. Panda. High Performance MPI Library over SR-IOV Enabled InfiniBand Clusters. In *Proceedings of International Conference on High Performance Computing (HiPC)*, Goa, India, December 17-20 2014.
[3] X. Lu, D. Shankar, S. Gugnani, H. Subramoni, and D. K. Panda. Impact of HPC Cloud Networking Technologies on Accelerating Hadoop RPC and HBase. In *Proceedings of the 8th IEEE International Conference on Cloud Computing Technology and Science (CloudCom)*, pages 152–159, Luxembourg, December 2016.
[4] X. Lu, J. Zhang, and D. K. Panda. Building Efficient HPC Cloud with SR-IOV Enabled InfiniBand: The MVAPICH2 Approach. In *Book - Research Advances in Cloud Computing*. Springer International Publishing, 2017.
[5] J. Zhang, X. Lu, M. Arnold, and D. Panda. MVAPICH2 over OpenStack with SR-IOV: An Efficient Approach to Build HPC Clouds. In *15th IEEE/ACM International Symposium on Cluster, Cloud and Grid Computing (CCGrid)*, pages 71–80, May 2015.
[6] J. Zhang, X. Lu, S. Chakraborty, and D. K. Panda. Slurm-V: Extending Slurm for Building Efficient HPC Cloud with SR-IOV and IVShmem. In *Proceedings of the 22Nd International Conference on Euro-Par 2016: Parallel Processing - Volume 9833*, pages 349–362, New York, NY, USA, 2016. Springer-Verlag New York, Inc.
[7] J. Zhang, X. Lu, and D. K. Panda. High Performance MPI Library for Container-based HPC Cloud on InfiniBand Clusters . In *The 45th International Conference on Parallel Processing (ICPP '16)*, Philadelphia, USA, August 2016.
[8] J. Zhang, X. Lu, and D. K. Panda. High-Performance Virtual Machine Migration Framework for MPI Applications on SR-IOV enabled InfiniBand Clusters. In *2017 IEEE International Parallel and Distributed Processing Symposium (IPDPS)*, Orlando, USA, May 2017.
[9] J. Zhang, X. Lu, and D. K. Panda. Designing Locality and NUMA Aware MPI Runtime for Nested Virtualization based HPC Cloud with SR-IOV Enabled InfiniBand . In *13th ACM SIGPLAN/SIGOPS International Conference on Virtual Execution Environments (VEE '17)*, Xi'an, China, April 2017.

Exploring the Potential of FreeBSD Virtualization in Containerized Environments

Francesc-Xavier Puig, J. J. Villalobos, Ivan Rodero*, Manish Parashar

Rutgers Discovery Informatics Institute (RDI²), Rutgers University, Piscataway, New Jersey

*irodero@rutgers.edu

ABSTRACT

Enterprise and Cloud environments are rapidly evolving with the use of lightweight virtualization mechanisms such as containers. Containerization allow users to deploy applications in any environment faster and more efficiently than using virtual machines. However, most of the work in this area focused on Linux-based containerization such as Docker and LXC and other mature solutions such as FreeBSD Jails have not been adopted by production-ready environments. In this work we explore the use of FreeBSD virtualization and provide a comparative study with respect to Linux containerization using Apache Spark. Preliminary results show that, while Linux containers provide better performance, FreeBSD solutions provide more stable and consistent results.

1   INTRODUCTION

Containerization, also called container-based virtualization, is being widely adopted in industry, academia, scientific communities and Cloud environments [3]. For example, Google took its container technology to the next level and adopted Ubuntu to run Docker containers, among others. In addition to solving long standing software development portability issues and increasing performance compared to virtual machines, containers are also able to live-migrate in multi-cloud deployments and there are many mature systems available for deployment automation, scaling and management of containerized applications such as Mesos, Kubernetes, Marathon, Amazon's EC2 Container Service and IBM Bluemix. Linux and FreeBSD, two Unix-like operative systems, are living in very different realities today. Linux, without any doubt, is the most widespread Unix-like operating system in all areas, whether business or academia environments, and has been supported by many companies. Nevertheless, FreeBSD [2] has not found its place in the market and it is only used in some specific environments despite proved to be more stable and even faster than Linux in some scenarios. Although FreeBSD adapted featuring of engine versions and support of mature, stable and secure virtualization mechanisms such as Jails, with the emergence of Clouds and Big Data, Linux has been positioned ahead and most of the production-ready containerized solutions are based on Linux. Furthermore, most of the existing

related literature focuses on Linux-based containerization technologies such as Docker and LXC [1] as a viable mechanism to improve productivity, resource consolidation and workload scheduling.

This effort aims at characterizing the execution of production workloads on both Linux and FreeBSD operating systems. We specifically use Apache Spark workloads as a driving use case. Other factors taken into account for the exploration of the system design space are the use of operating system virtualization (through LXC containers in Linux and Jails in FreeBSD) and the programming language used on top of Apache Spark (i.e., Python and Scala). A better understanding of virtualization mechanisms is critical as most of the current and ongoing systems exploit virtualization to improve resource utilization; however, the potential overheads/tradeoffs need to be quantified and incorporated into the system models.

2   EVALUATION METHODOLOGY

In the proposed architecture, the physical nodes host the virtual nodes and are primarily responsible for managing the storage export services for these nodes. The physical nodes are the only ones with direct access to physical resources and make up GlusterFS or HDFS volumes. These volumes are exposed to the virtual nodes through its own physical host. Two different types of nodes are considered: (1) Master: nodes are interconnected via Apache Zookeeper to implement a highly available (HA) cluster – in the evaluation described below the HA cluster has 3 master nodes, and (2) Slaves/Workers: nodes are connected to the Master to form the Apache Spark cluster – the number of these nodes varies and it is important that it can scale up easily. The empirical experimental evaluation was conducted in an environment composed of physical servers with 12-core Xeon processors. The workloads used in this effort include Spark PI, PageRank and a set of benchmarks that are part of SparkPerf, which is facilitated by the Spark community. The different workloads are based on typical functions designed for Big Data applications. This work considered the following set of benchmark applications from SparkPerf (TestRunner) : scheduling-throughput, aggregate-by-key, aggregate-by-key-int, aggregate-by-key-naïve, sort-by-key, sort-by-key-int, count, and count-with-filter. The selected benchmark applications have been configured for optimal performance and have been evaluated using versions written in Scala and Pyton programming languages, which adds another dimension to the comparison.

3   PRELIMINARY RESULTS

The results obtained from the experimental evaluation in the environment described above show that the executions in Linux are slightly faster than in FreeBSD. They also demonstrate that container-based virtualization is a viable option as it does not greatly impact performance on these executions. Figure 1 provides

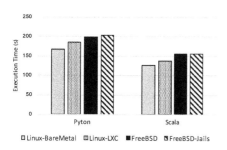

Figure 1: Execution of Aggregate By Key on Linux/LXC and FreeBSD/Jails using Python and Scala

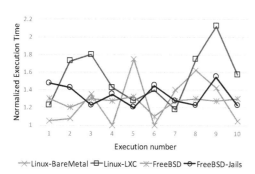

Figure 2: Normalized execution time (to minimum value) of ten executions of Spark PI with different configurations

the results for the aggregate-by-key benchmark, which is representative as the results for the other benchmarks follow a similar trend. The execution behavior is very similar for bare metal and virtualized environments for both Linux (LXC) and FreeBSD (Jails). As expected, the results show that Scala implementations run faster than Python implementations and Scala is more stable than Python, which is consistent for the different environments.

Figure 2 shows the results obtained with Spark Pi, which uses a Monte Carlo method. This method estimates the value of Pi by performing an aggressive parallelization. The goal of this evaluation is studying the variability of the results with moderate network and file system I/O utilization. The figure shows the results for a total of 10 executions per cluster and configuration. The executions were initiated via launcher (cluster mode) and a script was used to run a new instance every 10 seconds until the end of the executions. The results show that the outcomes using Linux are quite irregular (i.e., high variability in execution time) with both bare metal and LXC container-based configurations. Conversely, FreeBSD is more regular with average execution time values similar to Linux. This behavior is exacerbated with a larger amount of processor cores, i.e., the variability with Linux is higher with a larger core count.

Figure 3 shows the results obtained with PageRank, which is an algorithm to assign a numerical weight to the relevance of the elements of an indexed set. One use case of this algorithm is Google's search engine results page. The evaluation was conducted with two different input data sets, the first one of only 72MB size and the second one of 1.1GB size. The executions were initiated via

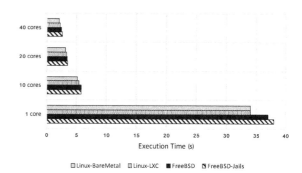

Figure 3: Execution time of PageRank with different number of compute cores and configurations

launcher (cluster mode). The results show that executions on Linux are faster than those on FreeBSD. The figure also shows that the difference between Linux and FreeBSD is consistent as the number of cores increases. This is also consistent with the results shown in Figure 1 (i.e., more I/O-bound workload).

4 CONCLUSION AND FUTURE WORK

In this paper, we explored the potential of FreeBSD virtualization (i.e., Jails) with respect to Linux-based solutions. We deployed a proof-of-concept architecture on both Linux and FreeBSD and compared the execution time of Spark workloads in these two environments. Preliminary results show that, while Linux containers provide better performance, FreeBSD solutions provide more stable results. It supports that FreeBSD virtualization can be a good candidate for relevant containerized systems (e.g., when execution time variability is not tolerable). This motivates us to explore FreeBSD usage modes in both Cloud-oriented infrastructures but also for next generation HPC deployments (e.g., high performance big data analytics). Our ongoing work includes a more comprehensive characterization of containerization technologies, exploring other tradeoffs such as those related to energy/power and resource utilization, and characterizing different big data processing frameworks (e.g., streaming solutions) with different operating system and containerization choices. This is especially interesting in order to understand appropriate design choices and policies that can optimize energy consumption and manage power budgets.

ACKNOWLEDGMENTS

This research is supported in part by NSF via grants numbers ACI 1464317, ACI 1339036 and ACI 1441376. This research was conducted as part of the Rutgers Discovery Informatics Institute (RDI²).

REFERENCES

[1] Emiliano Casalicchio and Vanessa Perciballi. 2017. Measuring Docker Performance: What a Mess!!!. In *Proceedings of the 8th ACM/SPEC on International Conference on Performance Engineering Companion (ICPE '17 Companion)*. ACM, New York, NY, USA, 11–16. https://doi.org/10.1145/3053600.3053605
[2] G. McKusick, M.and Neville-Neil and R. Watson. 2014. *The Design and Implementation of the FreeBSD Operating System, Second Edition*. Vol. 42. Pearson Education.
[3] S. J. Vaughan-nichols. 2006. New Approach to Virtualization Is a Lightweight. *Computer* 39, 11 (Nov 2006), 12–14. https://doi.org/10.1109/MC.2006.393

GO-MaDE: Goal Oriented Mashup Development Editor to Provide Extended End User Support for Developing Service Mashups

Sumaira Sultan Minhas[Ω, ¶], Pedro Sampaio [Ω], Nikolay Mehandjiev [Ω]

[Ω]Alliance Manchester Business School, University of Manchester, UK

[¶]Fatima Jinnah Women University, Rawalpindi, Pakistan

sumaira.minhas@gmail.com, {p.sampaio, n.mehandjiev} @manchester.ac.uk

ABSTRACT

In order to provide end users with suitable support to develop distributed situational applications for themselves, this poster provides the tool architecture for a meta-design platform – GO-MaDE (Goal Oriented MAshup Development Editor) to help end users design for themselves. The tool employs a new development style for Mashups and is designed to generate mashup specifications by allowing end users to specify their expectations in a goal-oriented style. Go-MaDE over-arches two different research areas: Goal based methods and service compositions/mashup technology. Specifically, it can be regarded as one of the pioneering works of service based compositions in the context of mashup technology and can be placed in a broader area of Goal-oriented service engineering.

KEYWORDS

Service Mashups; Goals; Mashup Design Tool; End Users.

1. INTRODUCTION

In the wake of the unprecedented growth of internet and enabling technologies, the idea of end-user development (EUD) has given rise to a new breed of applications: web/service mashups. To support mashup development, different tools, techniques and methods have been developed [1][2][3]. One of the main challenges facing mashup development is the technical barrier of mashup platforms that most of the users do not seem to overcome due to their non-IT background [4][5]. These technical needs of the mashup platforms comprise the programming needs, use of computer-based concepts and terminologies, lack of visual models, lack of understanding of end-users' mental models and lack of proper, up-to-date documentation.

The recent trend of composing services in a Lego-like fashion has given rise to a number of tools that enables End Users (EU) to combine different web components and come up with a solution to serve the need at hand. However, these efforts have focused mainly on the description and handling of the composition activity and little attention has been paid to the dynamics of request formulation by the end-users. The research in focus here and the proposed tool (GO-MaDE) under discussion in the following paragraphs is a concentrated effort to address this gap.

For our approach, we have redefined the mashup development process (Figure 1) to introduce the phases of conception and translation to incorporate the concept of end-users' expectations and requirements and identify it separately from the actual composition of services [6]. The experiments conducted in this regard also support our hypothesis that incorporating end users' expectations explicitly during mashup development is not only recommended but can also be used as a means of overcoming reported mashup development challenges [6].

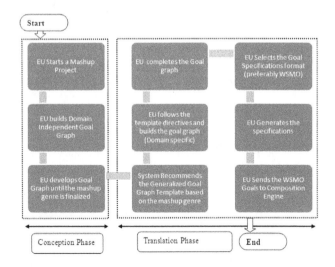

Figure 1. Flow of Activities in Proposed Mashup Development Process

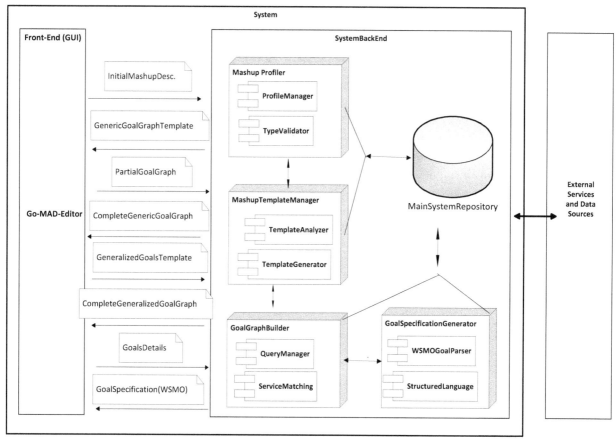

Figure 2. Overview of GO-MaDE Architecture

2. GO-MaDE Architecture

The GO-MaDE has four main logical components (fig. 2) besides the GUI and data layers: a mashup profiler, a Mashup Template Manager, a Goal Graph Builder, and a Goal Specifications Generator. The Mashup Profiler communicates with the EU to record basic information about the EU's target mashups at the time of initiation of a new mashup project through system dialogues. It is also responsible for gathering the information about the new mashup project to confirm the type of mashup which is to be used in later steps. The next component is the Template Manger which analyses the basic mashup profile generated by the mashup Profiler and uses that information to suggest and generate a customized goal graph template which is later used to develop goal graph with the help of next component, the Goal Graph Builder. The Goal Graph Builder uses the help of two of its sub-components: Query Manager and Service Matching to reformulate the queries for each goal graph and help the user develop his goal graph that is a model of the EU's requirements and design of his/her target mashup project. The last component Goal Specification Generator takes input of the complete goal graph and generates mashup goal specifications that represent a complete set of EU requirements and design including the concrete services and data sources along with the required manipulations and processing.

3. CONCLUSIONS

As a tool that provides extended support for mashup development, GO-MaDE employs goal templates and meta-design principles. It demonstrates the practical applicability of goal-based methods in the context of end user mashups and provides researchers with a new direction in mashup development tools that does not only concentrate on the composition phase but involves the end users in the design phase as well.

REFERENCES

[1] Caruccio, L., Deufemia, V. and Polese, G. 2016. A Wizard Based EUDWeb Development Process. Empowering Organizations. Springer. 173–185.
[2] Mehandjiev, N., Namoune, A., Wajid, U., Macaulay, L. and Sutcliffe, A. 2010. End user service composition: Perceptions and requirements. Web Services (ECOWS), 2010 IEEE 8th European Conference on (2010), 139–146.
[3] Minhas, S.S., Sampaio, P. and Mehandjiev, N. 24. A Framework for the Evaluation of Mashup Tools. Services Computing (SCC), 2012 IEEE Ninth International Conference on. (24), 431–438. DOI:https://doi.org/10.1109/SCC.2012.19.
[4] Namoun, A., Nestler, T. and De Angeli, A. 2010. Conceptual and usability issues in the composable web of software services. Springer.
[5] Namoun, A., Wajid, U. and Mehandjiev, N. 2010. Service Composition for Everyone: A Study of Risks and Benefits. Service-Oriented Computing. ICSOC/ServiceWave 2009 Workshops. A. Dan, F. Gittler, and F. Toumani, eds. Springer Berlin Heidelberg. 550–559.
[6] Minhas, S.S., Sampaio, P. and Mehandjiev, N. 2016. Proposing a new process model for mashup development by applying meta-design principles and goals for managing end user expectations. Multi-Topic Conference (INMIC), 2016 19th International (2016), 1–5.

Benchmarking Automated Hardware Management Technologies for Modern Data Centers and Cloud Environments

Elham Hojati
Department of Computer Science at
Texas Tech University
elham.hojati@ttu.edu

Yong Chen
Department of Computer Science at
Texas Tech University
yong.chen@ttu.edu

Alan Sill
High Performance Computing Center
at Texas Tech University
alan.sill@ttu.edu

ABSTRACT

Traditional management standards are often insufficient to manage modern data centers at large scale, which motivates the community to propose and develop new management standards. The most popular traditional standard for monitoring and controlling the health and functionality of a system at hardware layer is Intelligent Platform Management Interface (IPMI). Redfish is a new hardware-based management technology designed as the next-generation management standard. The goal of this study is to investigate hardware management technologies and to find out if they are powerful enough to meet demands of modern data centers. Particularly, we focused on Redfish and IPMI, and we benchmarked and compared them from four different aspects: latency, scalability, reliability, and security. Our result shows that there is a trade-off between improving the performance of a system and increasing the security and the reliability of that. Our results show that Redfish is more secure and more reliable, but the performance of IPMI tends to be better.

KEYWORDS

Redfish, IPMI, cloud environments, data centers, benchmarking

ACM Reference Format:
Elham Hojati, Yong Chen, and Alan Sill. 2017. Benchmarking Automated Hardware Management Technologies for Modern Data Centers and Cloud Environments . In *UCC '17: 10th International Conference on Utility and Cloud Computing*. ACM, Austin, TX, USA, 2 pages. https://doi.org/10.1145/3147213.3149212

1 INTRODUCTION

In this research study, we focus on two hardware management technologies for data centers, IPMI (Intelligent Platform Management Interface) [1] and Redfish [2]. We compare them from four different aspects: latency, scalability, reliability, and security. Our result shows that there is a trade-off between improving the performance of a system and increasing the security and the reliability of that. Redfish is more secure, but the performance of IPMI is usually better than Redfish.

2 METHODOLOGY

This research mainly focuses on benchmarking and comparing two different hardware management tools for data centers, Redfishtool [3] and IPMItool [4]. We run Redfishtool in two different modes: Redfish in the raw mode; and Redfish in full tree traversal mode, we call it Redish in short. In the tree traversal mode, Redfish command traverses URIs until it finds asked information. But in the raw mode, it goes exactly through the specified URI, not all of them. [3].

2.1 Benchmarking Environment

This research was performed using the QUANAH cluster hosted at the High Performance Computing Center of Texas Tech University. The cluster was installed from the scratch with 64-bit version CentOS 7.2.1511 with kernel version 3.10. QUANAH cluster contains 224 Redfish enabled compute nodes from Dell Inc. The general specifications of the hardware of each node include: Intel Xeon CPU E5410 with 36 cores, 192GB RAM, and networks including 1Gbps Ethernet and 100Gbps Intel Omnipath. All required packages for running IPMItool and Redfishtool were installed on the controller node of the cluster, named Charlie.

2.2 Benchmarking Methodology

To benchmark the latency, we selected a list of management and monitoring actions, and for each action in the list, we provided the appropriate commands in IPMItool and Redfishtool (by considering which action in Redfishtool is equivalent to the action in IPMItool). For each tool, we developed a bash script that checks the latency of the action for each of the nodes of the cluster using that tool. By running the scripts, the latency of each action was evaluated and compared.

The list of actions selected to benchmark latency contains: Temperature Checking, Fan Speed Checking, Sensor Data Record (SDR) Checking, Chassis Status Checking, System Event Log (SEL) Checking , Field Replaceable Unit (FRU) Checking , and User Account Checking. To benchmark the scalability, we varied the size of the cluster under test, and observed the impact of the changes on the performance of running hardware monitoring commands on the cluster. To compare reliability and security, we considered network protocols used for transferring and securing information in Redfish and IPMI technology.

3 TESTS AND RESULTS

In the latency test, we primarily focus on benchmarking the latency of Redfish and IPMI by running various commands to query information of a node in the cluster. This process uses a black box approach for benchmarking and comparing these two technologies. Figure 1 reports one of these results: the latency of retrieving

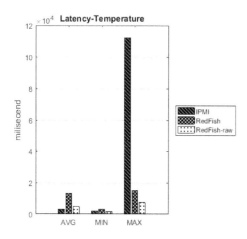

Figure 1: Latency comparison of querying temperature using IPMI, Redfish, and Redfish-raw

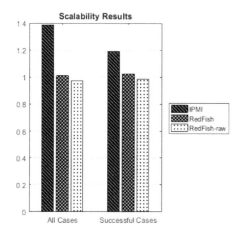

Figure 2: Scalability comparison of querying temperature using IPMI, Redfish, and Redfish-raw

temperature data using IPMI, Redfish (Redfish in full tree traversal mode), and Redfish-raw. Those results show that the performance of IPMI is generally better than Redfish based on the latency of the response. Figure 2 plots the scalability in querying temperature data using IPMI, Redfish, and Redfish-raw. The best scalability was achieved for the Redfish in the raw mode. from reliability aspect, IPMI uses UDP protocol for communication which is not a reliable protocol. But Redfish uses TCP protocol as its transport layer protocol, which is a reliable protocol with error checking and error recovery. Therefore, the reliability of Redfish is better than IPMI. Furthermore, Redfish uses HTTPS and TLS protocol to achieve security in its connections, which is stronger than RMCP+ used by IPMI to make its connections secure. Therefore the security of Redfish is better than IPMI.

Table 1: Overall Result

Tool	Latency	Scalability	Reliability	Security
IPMI	√√	√	×	×
Redfish	×	√√	√	√
Redfish-raw	√	√√√	√	√

Table 1 shows an overall comparison based on our benchmarking results. The traditional standard, IPMI, has better performance (considering the latency of running management and monitoring commands) than Redfish. Redfish is more reliable and more secure than IPMI. Redfish also has better simplicity of usage from our evaluations and experiences. The scalability result shows that Redfish in the raw mode has the best scalability, which is often critical for large-scale data centers nowadays.

4 CONCLUSION

Data centers and cloud environments are complex and dynamic. There is a strong desire for benchmarking and evaluating technologies and standards for dynamic cloud environments and data centers compared to traditional static systems. In this research, we focused on one of the most important traditional management standards, IPMI, and the new standard, Redfish. The goal of this research is to benchmark these hardware management technologies based on four different properties, latency, scalability, reliability, and security. We intended to develop quantitative comparison of these technologies and standards for modern scalable clouds and data centers.

This current research has also identified that the latency of Redfish can be further improved by issuing commands at once in a scatter/gather fashion. Moreover, the performance of a particular individual command will not matter significantly if many of them can be issued simultaneously and collectively. Even a large number of commands can be issued within a small amount of time. It would be difficult to perform such collective optimizations with IPMI as it uses a UDP transportation protocol and can have possible message losses. On the other hand, Redfish adopts a TCP transportation protocol and such collective optimizations are possible. We plan to further study these optimization strategies in the near future.

ACKNOWLEDGMENTS

This research is supported by the Cloud and Autonomic Computing site and High Performance Computing Center at Texas Tech University and the collaboration with Dell Inc.

REFERENCES

[1] 2013. *IPMI -Intelligent Platform Management Interface Specification Second Generation v2.0.* Document Revision 1.1. Intel Hewlett-Packard NEC Dell.
[2] 2016. *Redfish Scalable Platforms Management API Specification Document.* Technical Report.
[3] DMTF. 2017. Redfishtool. (2017). https://github.com/DMTF/Redfishtool
[4] BSD License. 2017. IPMItool. (2017). https://sourceforge.net/projects/ipmitool/

Analysis of the Effects and Factors of Implementing Cloud Business Intelligence in Banking Systems

MohammadBagher Sayedi
Business Management Department at
Islamic Azad University, Arak Branch
sayedi@fksahar.ir

Peyman Ghafari
Business Management Department at
Islamic Azad University, Arak Branch
p-ghafari@iau-arak.ac.ir

Elham Hojati
Computer Science Department at
Texas Tech University
elham.hojati@ttu.edu

ABSTRACT

Nowadays, the new big challenge in banking systems is dealing with large amount of sensitive data. Cloud Business Intelligence is a new technology to handle big data storing, sharing, and computing. Business Intelligence is a management concept which discuses about data processing, and extracting business information from raw business data. It helps to improve business management and make optimized business decisions that leads to improve the performance and financial benefits of the organization. The other important technology for big data computing is the concept of cloud computing, a notion in information technology area. Cloud computing is a model which provides a general access to the shared resources and services, such as infrastructure, platform, and software. Cloud Business Intelligence refers to the combination of the mentioned technologies. This notion provides Business Intelligence as a service over a cloud environment. The goal of this research is exploring effects and factors of using cloud business intelligence in banking systems. This study addresses the benefits, problems, and challenges of using cloud business intelligence in the banking systems, and examines the impact of using this technology on the reliability and credibility of banking systems. The purpose of this study is helping banking systems to move from using traditional models towards applying cloud ones, increase reliability, availability, and transactions speed, reduce the cost of banks, and in other words, moving towards modern banking systems. The results help us to select the best type of cloud business intelligence for a specific organization based on the characteristics of that.

KEYWORDS

Cloud Environment , Business Intelligence, Cloud Business Intelligence, Banking Systems

ACM Reference Format:
MohammadBagher Sayedi, Peyman Ghafari, and Elham Hojati. 2017. Analysis of the Effects and Factors of Implementing Cloud Business Intelligence in Banking Systems. In *UCC '17: 10th International Conference on Utility and Cloud Computing*. ACM, Austin, TX , USA, 2 pages. https://doi.org/10.1145/3147213.3149213

1 INTRODUCTION

In this research we focus on the concept of cloud business intelligence [3]. This concept is a combination of two technologies, business intelligence (BI) [3] and cloud computing [4]. Based on the definition of NIST, Cloud computing is an on-demand ubiquitous model for getting access to a collection of computing resources such as software, infrastructure, and platform via network [4]. Business Intelligence is a management concept which explains the process of delivering useful information to make the best business decisions in an appropriate amount of time [3]. Cloud business intelligence tries to provide Business Intelligence as a service via a cloud environment. Some of the advantages of using cloud BI are: reducing the costs of buying software, and infrastructure, scalability, and improving the ability of sharing resources and services. Also, using cloud BI has some challenges, such as security, transferring a large amount of data, efficiency, integration, and reliability. Furthermore, in large sized organizations, the costs of using public cloud services is a challenge, and using a private cloud is a better solution. The main contributions of our research are:

(1) We provide a survey of using Cloud BI in different types of organizations, and various models of that.
(2) We provide a model to show effects of using Cloud BI in banking systems. We consider advantages, disadvantages and possible challenges of applying this technology. We are going to verify our model using qualitative surveys, and questionnaire methods.
(3) We investigate factors of using cloud BI in banking systems. We are going to verify our assumptions using qualitative surveys, questionnaire methods, and data mining.
(4) We are going to define a metric that each banking system could decide which cloud BI model is the best model for it, based on its characteristics.

2 RELATED WORK

Several researches have been done about implementing and applying cloud business intelligence in organizations with various types and different sizes. Table 1 has collected some of them more related to the banking systems. The first research [2] has introduced a maturity model of business intelligence in medium and small-sized organizations. It uses a pilot test in a medium-sized organization, and an empirical investigation using a survey to verify the model and the maturity of that. The second research [1] describes a new business model by performing banking transactions, which are a type of business intelligence actions, over clouds. This paper has analyzed challenges, cons, and pros of performing banking transactions over clouds using a survey method.

Table 1: a collection of researches related to applying cloud business intelligence in organizations

Paper	Year	Research method	Results
Maturity Model for BI [2]	2013	pilot test/survey	introduce,verify a maturity model for BI in Small and Medium Enterprises.
Cloud Transaction Banking [1]	2014	survey	analyze challenges, cons, and pros of banking transactions over clouds.
BI in Organizations [5]	2015	interview	analyze the possibility of using BI in organizations, new BI models.
BI in Banking [7]	2015	text mining	study the main problems of banking (2002-2013), and BI as their solution.
Toward Better Use of BI [6]	2016	qualitative surveys	study BI concept and the use of that in twenty different organizations.

The Third research [5] has explored applying business intelligence in organizations and the possibility of that, in different organizations. It provides several BI models for organizations as well. Based on this paper, using BI has some benefits such as making better decisions, improving performance, and business process in organizations. But the results show there are some challenges in using BI, for small and local organizations. The next research [7] has studied main problems of banking systems, between 2002 nd 2013, and Business intelligence as their solution. It applies text mining and latent Dirichlet allocation techniques to gather information. The last research [6] has studied Business intelligence, and the benefits of that. It has applied a qualitative surveys over twenty different organizations to explore the possibility of better use of Business intelligence in organizations. Our research tries to focus on Banking systems and investigating factors, and effects of using cloud business intelligence in those enterprises.

3 METHODOLOGY

We want to explore the factors that influence the possibility of using Cloud BI, from the computing experts view, and the effects of using this technology form the customer view. We are going to investigate how this technology affects the reputation of a banking system. We want to investigate that by analyzing several factors of customer satisfactions. The results helps us to select the best type of cloud business intelligence for a specific organization, based on the characteristics of that.

At first, we consider some of the characteristics that may affect the possibility of using a cloud business technology. the selected characteristics are: 1- Type of banking system (weather they are public or private), 2- the level of financial support of the system, and 3- the scope of the system (or the size of that). We are going to find how these characters effects the possibility of using cloud business intelligence, and also which type of cloud business intelligence model is more suitable for the specific banking system. The second step of the project is exploring the effects of using cloud business intelligence on the customer satisfaction, bank reputation, and system costs, by considering all the advantages and disadvantages of that. We are going to use qualitative surveys, questionnaire methods, and data mining to analyze the use of cloud business intelligence technology. Figure 1 shows our research model. In this picture, rectangular shapes show factors that affect the possibility

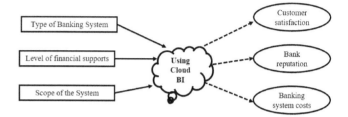

Figure 1: Our Research model, Rectangles show factors, and Ovals demonstrate effects of using cloud BI

of using a cloud business intelligence model, and elliptic parts demonstrate effects of using cloud business intelligence.

4 CONCLUSION

Banking system is a type of system which deals with a big amount of sensitive data. It needs to use new technologies for better performance, more effective decisions, and better system management. Cloud business intelligence is one of the newest techniques, with some cons, and pros. We are going to explore the factors that influences the possibility of using Cloud BI. Based on the results, we can decide which type of cloud business intelligence model is better for a specific banking system. The goal of this research is to help banking systems to move from traditional technologies towards a modern banking system.

REFERENCES

[1] Carlo R. W. de Meijer and Alastair Brown. 2014. Transaction banking in the cloud: Towards a new business model. *Journal of Payments Strategy & Systems* 8, 2 (2014), 206–223.
[2] Semma El Alami Faycal Fedouaki, Chafik Okar. 2013. A maturity model for Business Intelligence System project in Small and Medium-sized Enterprises: an empirical investigation. *IJCSI International Journal of Computer Science Issues* 10, 1 (2013).
[3] Kazeli H. 2014. Cloud Business Intelligence. *In: Abramowicz W., Kokkinaki A. (eds) Business Information Systems Workshops. BIS 2014. Lecture Notes in Business Information Processing* 183 (2014), 307–317.
[4] P. Mell and T. Grance . 2011. The NIST Definition of Cloud Computing. *National Institute of Standards and Technology* (2011).
[5] Celina M. Olszak. 2015. Business Intelligence and Analytics in Organizations. *Springer International Publishing Switzerland* (2015), 89–109.
[6] Celina M Olszak. 2016. Toward Better Understanding and Use of Business intelligence in organizations. *Information System Management* 33, 2 (2016), 105âĂŞ123.
[7] Paulo Rita SÃ•rgio Moro, Paulo Cortez b. 2015. Business intelligence in banking: A literature analysis from 0002 to 0013 using text mining and latent Dirichlet allocations. *Expert Systems with Applications, Elsevier Ltd* 42 (2015), 1314âĂŞ1324.

An Actor-Based Framework for Edge Computing

Austin Aske
School of Engineering and Computer Science
Washington State University Vancouver
Vancouver, WA 98686, USA
austin.aske@wsu.edu

Xinghui Zhao
School of Engineering and Computer Science
Washington State University Vancouver
Vancouver, WA 98686, USA
x.zhao@wsu.edu

ABSTRACT

The Actor model provides inherent parallelism, along with other convenient features to build large-scale distributed systems. In this paper, we present ActorEdge, an Actor based distributed framework for edge computing. ActorEdge provides straitforward integration with existing technologies, while enabling application developers to dynamically utilize computational resources on the edge of the clouds. ActorEdge has proven to outperform cloud computing options by providing superior quality of service, measuring a 10x lower latency, 30% less jitter, and greater bandwidth. Using this framework, programmers can easily develop and deploy their applications on a heterogeneous system, including cloud servers/data centers, edge servers, and mobile devices.

CCS CONCEPTS

•Computing methodologies → Distributed computing methodologies;

KEYWORDS

Actors, Edge Computing, Mobile Clouds, Cloud Computing

1 INTRODUCTION

Edge computing is gaining interest and popularity in part due to the growing number of connected devices, latency sensitive applications, and Internet of Things (IoT) [4]. Cloud computing is widely used to offload complex computations that are not suitable for resource constrained mobile devices. Current cloud computing infrastructure has limitations i.e. bandwidth, security, and latency, which is driving edge computing research and development. In recent years, many edge computing frameworks have been proposed which simplify the utilization of cloudlet VM's with OpenStack++ [2], or access points services with ParaDrop [3]. However, most of these systems approach edge as a localized version of cloud computing or web services, which do not efficiently utilize the resources on the edge. In this paper, we propose an edge computing framework, ActorEdge, providing micro services at the edge of the network for bandwidth and latency sensitive applications though an actor based paradigm [1].

UCC '17, December 5–8, 2017, Austin, TX, USA.

© 2017 Copyright held by the owner/author(s). 978-1-4503-5149-2/17/12.
DOI: https://doi.org/10.1145/3147213.3149214

2 ACTOREDGE

ActorEdge is implemented in Objective C, making it compatible with MacOS and iOS devices. Objective C was chosen for two main reasons: 1) it allows for very dynamic run-time operations, and 2) it is compatible with Apple operating systems, which are mostly excluded from current offloading edge computing frameworks. ActorEdge is an actor-based system, and it utilizes a hierarchical architecture, shown in Figure 1. Due to limited space, all details about ActorEdge cannot be described, but we highlight three main design decisions: actor system implementations, communication protocol, and resource discovery.

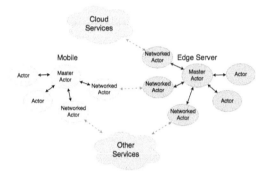

Figure 1: System Architecture of ActorEdge

Actor System - The Actor model of concurrency provides a convenient way to build large-scale distributed systems, because of the inherent parallelism it offers. As a result, the Actor model has been widely used in a variety of distributed applications, especially for cloud-based applications. Most recently, the Actor model has also been widely used in many cloud-based applications, such as Facebook and Twitter, among others [1]. In the Actor model, autonomous concurrently executing objects called actors, communicate with each other using buffered, asynchronous, point-to-point messages. An actor encapsulates a state, a number of methods (which can change the state of the actor), and a thread of control. Actors are distributed over time and space. Each actor has a globally unique mail address, and it maintains a queue of unprocessed messages it has received. ActorEdge uses the Actor model as the underlying computational framework. As illustrated in Figure 1, at the top level of every ActorEdge system, there exist a master actor. The MasterActor is a singleton class which keeps track of all the actors on each device, and it is the entry point for creating and killing actors. The next major component to ActorEdge is the Actor class. This class encapsulates logic of computation, and it is the basic building block of the system. Each Actor has its own

NSOperationQueue, which acts as the mailbox in the theoretical model of Actors. Actors also have isolated state which is held by a NSDictionary functioning as a key-value store. Extending the ACActor class is the ACNetworkedActor class which adds a TCP/IP connection and a set of additional keys to address the connection.

Communication Protocol - To allow for straitforward integration with web technologies, ActorEdge uses JSON formatted messages over TCP/IP connections. Using JSON messages allows for many web services to be adopted to work with the protocol. In the situation when a programmer needs to have HTTP, UDP, or any other protocol ActorEdge's base Actor class can easily be extended to convert to and from an arbitrary protocol using the NSInvocation API's. There is future work to be done in unifying communications into an abstract protocol allowing further customization and building HTTP compliant networked actors.

Resource Discovery - As mobile devices travel between local networks, it is critical for them to easily discover edge resources, for this ActorEdge supports Apple's zero configuration service protocol called Bonjour(DNS-SD). Using Bonjour edge or mobile devices can advertise services to the local DNS server allowing for dynamic discovery of edge services. This approach is advantageous because it allows distributed management of resources and minimizing the dependence on centralized cloud services.

3 EXPERIMENTAL RESULTS

To evaluate ActorEdge, a series of experiments have been conducted to measure the framework and network topology for latency, jitter, and bandwidth. Each of the metrics are designed to display the advantages and usability of ActorEdge in future applications. The tests are designed to illustrate the advantages of edge computing conceptually, and the need for an agile solution for mobile devices.

Hardware - The test utilized three classes of hardware; cloud server, edge server, and mobile devices. The cloud server consisted of two different Amazon EC2 instances, one being a t2.micro single 2.5 GHz vCPU server with 1 GB of memory, two being a c4.2xlarge server with 8 2.9 GHz vCPUs and 15 GB memory. Meanwhile, the edge was facilitated by a 2.5 GHz i7 MacBook Pro with 16 GB of memory. The final hardware class used was an iPhone 6 and an iPhone 7+ for the mobile components.

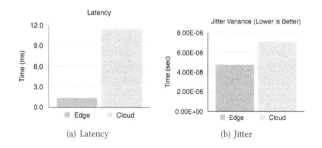

(a) Latency   (b) Jitter

Figure 2: EC2 Instance vs. Edge Server

Latency - Latency testing was performed by measuring the round trip time of a minimal ACMessage between a mobile device, edge server, and cloud server. Figure 2(a) shows that the edge outperforms the cloud with 10x lower latency. This performance

increase can be primarily be attributed to the proximity of the edge services and the minimal hops required to access the edge services.

Jitter - Jitter is an important metric for evaluating the ActorEdge's usability in real time applications which involve streaming data, such as augmented reality and virtual reality. This test was carried out by having the server send ACMessages to a mobile device at a consistent interval of 10 milliseconds. Measuring the relative time between messages upon arrival we can analyze the period and drift in timing, or jitter. Figure 2(b) shows that the variance in the time intervals between messages is approximately 30% less using the edge server vs cloud. The improvement in jitter can be explained by having only 2 hops between edge service and mobile device, resulting in less network interference causing inconsistencies in the network.

Bandwidth - Bandwidth was measured between a mobile device (iPhone 7+) to another mobile device, edge server, and cloud server using an open-source software iperf. On each system iperf was started and listening for TCP/IP connections. Next, using an iPhone 7+ running iperf each system was tested using the bandwidth test. As can be seen from Figure 2 the bandwidth performance is significantly better on the edge and mobile devices.

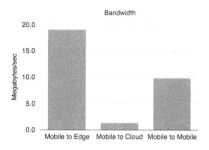

Figure 3: Bandwidth Test

4 CONCLUSION

ActorEdge framework allows for easy integration with existing technologies while benefiting from a simplified Actor based concurrency model. Additionally, ActorEdge has proven to outperform cloud computing options by providing superior quality of service. ActorEdge demonstrated a 10 times lower latency, 30% less jitter, and greater bandwidth. ActorEdge was also found to perform well for real-time and augmented reality applications that are latency sensitive. For future work, we are developing a dynamic resource provision layer for ActorEdge, and exploring different applications for evaluating this framework.

REFERENCES

[1] G. Agha. 2014. Actors Programming for the Mobile Cloud. In *2014 IEEE 13th International Symposium on Parallel and Distributed Computing*. 3–9.
[2] Kiryong Ha and Mahadev Satyanarayanan. 2015. Openstack++ for cloudlet deployment. *School of Computer Science Carnegie Mellon University Pittsburgh* (2015).
[3] Peng Liu, Dale Willis, and Suman Banerjee. 2016. ParaDrop: Enabling Lightweight Multi-tenancy at the Networkfis Extreme Edge. In *Edge Computing (SEC), IEEE/ACM Symposium on*. IEEE, 1–13.
[4] Blesson Varghese, Nan Wang, Sakil Barbhuiya, Peter Kilpatrick, and Dimitrios S Nikolopoulos. 2016. Challenges and Opportunities in Edge Computing. In *Smart Cloud (SmartCloud), IEEE International Conference on*. IEEE, 20–26.

Cloud-based Hint Application of Relevant Meeting Materials Using OCR and ASR Text Information

Jiawei Yong
System Research & Development Center
Ricoh Institute of ICT
Ricoh Company, LTD, Japan
kai.yuu@nts.ricoh.co.jp

Katsumi Kanasaki
System Research & Development Center
Ricoh Institute of ICT
Ricoh Company, LTD, Japan
katsumi.kanasaki@nts.ricoh.co.jp

Ryoh Furutani
Interaction Design Office
Corporate Design Center
Ricoh Company, LTD, Japan
ryoh.furutani@nts.ricoh.co.jp

Kiyohiko Shinomiya
System Research & Development Center
Ricoh Institute of ICT
Ricoh Company, LTD, Japan
kshino@nts.ricoh.co.jp

Toshiyuki Furuta
System Research & Development Center
Ricoh Institute of ICT
Ricoh Company, LTD, Japan
furutat@nts.ricoh.co.jp

Shohichi Naitoh
System Research & Development Center
Ricoh Institute of ICT
Ricoh Company, LTD, Japan
shohichi.naitoh@nts.ricoh.co.jp

ABSTRACT

In the meeting being held , sometimes we need to confirm a lot of past relevant meeting materials. However, as the number of meetings has become larger, the retrieval of relevant meeting materials has become much more difficult. What's more, the retrieval action should not interrupt the meeting process unless on participant's own intention. Therefore, during the meeting, an efficient hint method for essential meeting materials without interrupting meeting process is urgently needed. In this paper, we provide a cloud- based application for real-time meeting materials hint in the meeting being held.

KEYWORDS

OCR, ASR, Meeting Materials, Cloud-based Application

1 INTRODUCTION

With the rapid development of information technology, the scales and category of information are growing larger and wider. As a consequence, it is extremely difficult for common users to retrieve relevant information in a short time. What's worse, when we hold meeting to draw a conclusion about concerned issues, it becomes much harder to retrieve desired information due to the consistency and timeliness of meeting. Therefore, according to the different meeting objectives, our issues become the followings: Firstly, how to utilize proactive information delivery in specific meeting scene for outputting high-related materials without participants' preparation. Secondly, how to hint to participants for precise high-related meeting materials by user interface without interrupting the meeting process.

UCC '17, December 5–8, 2017, Austin, TX, USA
© 2017 Copyright held by the owner/author(s).
ACM ISBN 978-1-4503-5149-2/17/12. . . $15.00
https://doi.org/10.1145/3147213.3149215

For 1st issue, since we intend to generate retrieval query without participants' preparation, we shall make flexible use of multimedia data of meeting. The research on lecture video indexing and search [4] applying standard OCR software for gathering textual metadata achieves good results in lecture video retrieval. As to the 2nd issue, an essential UI design is needed to exhibit high-related meeting materials on a fit time and place without interrupting the meeting process. The researches [3], have introduced common interruptions especially in office and what UI can support to coordinate interruption. The whole workflow for hinting to participants for related materials is depicted in Figure 1.

2 RETRIEVAL STRATEGY FOR MATERIALS OUTPUT

Since we use Elasticsearch as our retrieval engine, we shall maximize the advantages of its algorithms [1] to realize our related materials retrieval function conveniently. What's more, as we have depicted in Figure 1, there is another mode for web retrieval besides

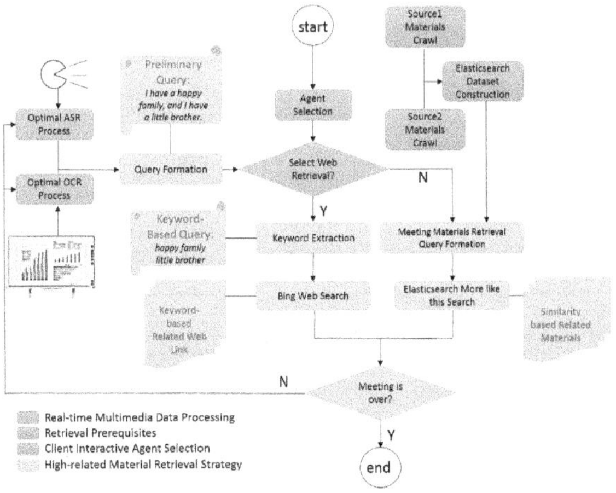

Figure 1: The whole retrieval strategy workflow.

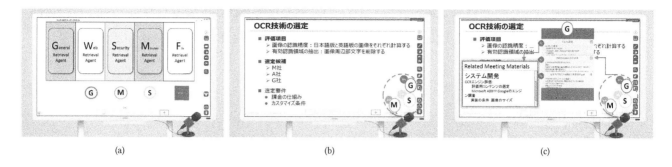

Figure 2: (a) Selecting the retrieval agents before meeting (b) Scoring the relevancy during the meeting, (c) Showing the details of materials for participants

meeting material retrieval in our application. Although we are able to gather sufficient recognition text information by ASR and OCR during meeting being held, it is vital to note that how to form input query [2] automatically as retrieval prerequisites urgently needs to be solved. In order to form the retrieval query, here we use the sum of ASR and OCR recognition transcript as our preliminary query. The reason for that is to mitigate the bad effects of misrecognition in respective transcript.

If users select the web material retrieval mode with respect to user's intention, a further simplification treatment should be executed on query since there are too much useless words in gathered recognition text information especially in OCR. Therefore, we provide the extraction rules of keyword in user's preliminary query during Japanese meeting as below:

- If the part of speech (pos) of Japanese word kj in preliminary query q is proper noun except people's name, we regard kj as a Japanese keyword.
- As to English word in preliminary query, assume that there won't be too many English words during Japanese daily meeting, any English word ke that appears is considered as a keyword.

To realize the selection rules of keyword above, we can easily obtain the pos of each Japanese word by Elasticsearch. For instance, by means of Kuromoji tokenizer, Japanese words can be classified by pos to extract proper nouns. English word can be extracted since English letters can be easily recognized.

We can realize different retrieval functions based on different formations of queries defined above. Since sometimes we are looking forward to retreiving information in some specific aspects or just reflecting progress on real-time topics, participants shall either use emphasis retrieval query (asr+ocr+keyword) by registering keywords in advance before the meeting, or directly use passive retrieval query (asr+ocr) during the meeting.

3 UI DESIGN FOR HINT APPLICATION

Since our materials retrieval could be realized by the above workflow, how to show high-related meeting materials without interruption becomes the urgent problem. We consider to exhibit the retrieval results onto the presentation display in order to achieve information sharing among all participants. However, if the display is mixed up with results and presentation contents, the normal presentation can be suffered from bad visual effects. Therefore a good timing to hint participants is when system actually find out the most relevant documents. If participants would look over the retrieval details, they could take further action at the cost of suspending the meeting. Here according to the participants' different retrieval intentions, we plan to provide several agents on behalf of different search datasets and directions.

In order to avoid interruption during the meeting, we shall provide a powerful evidence to hint participants that it is maybe a right time to check results because of the found materials' high-relevancy. Therefore, we determine to show related meeting materials' relevancy score to motivate participants. If it is necessary to cast a glance at the retrieval results, the brief information including the snippet shall be visible. Furthermore, if they would like to look over the details of meeting materials, the details' link could be accessed by browser. Our interactive UI design is shown in Figure 2.

4 CONCLUSION AND FUTURE WORK

In this paper, we have introduced our cloud-based IWB hint application under consideration in appropriate way of retrieval output, besides the interactive UI design. In accordance with the requirements of Amazon Elasticsearch service, our past meeting materials have been extracted under our data structure as input, and we have also presented a retrieval strategy for output. For fear that the retrieval results might be interruption, a user-friendly UI has been designed to guarantee the right-time hint.

As the future work, more experiments and evaluations shall be conducted in order to illustrate the usability of our application. Assume that if we gather enough feedback and records of materials selection, the approach of learning to rank for further improving retrieval accuracy becomes practicable.

REFERENCES

[1] Trey Grainger, Timothy Potter, and Yonik Seeley. 2014. Solr in action. *Cherry Hill: Manning* (2014).
[2] In-Ho Kang and GilChang Kim. 2003. Query type classification for web document retrieval. In *Proceedings of the 26th annual international ACM SIGIR conference on Research and development in informaion retrieval*. ACM.
[3] Daniel C. McFarlane and Kara A. Latorella. 2001. The scope and importance of human interruption in human-computer interaction design. *Human-Computer Interaction* 17, 1 (2001), 1–61.
[4] Tayfun Tuna, Jaspal Subhlok, and Lecia Barker. 2012. Development and evaluation of indexed captioned searchable videos for stem coursework. In *Proceedings of the 43rd ACM technical symposium on Computer Science Education*. ACM.

DISCO — Distributed Computing as a Service

Balazs Meszaros
ZHAW School of Engineering
Obere Kirchgasse 2
8401, Winterthur, Switzerland
mesz@zhaw.ch

Dr. Piyush Harsh
ZHAW School of Engineering
Obere Kirchgasse 2
8401, Winterthur, Switzerland
harh@zhaw.ch

Prof.-Dr. Thomas Michael
Bohnert
ZHAW School of Engineering
Obere Kirchgasse 2
8401, Winterthur, Switzerland
bohe@zhaw.ch

ABSTRACT

The setup of distributed computing clusters and the installation of data analysis frameworks can be cumbersome and requires a great deal of knowledge in a plenitude of fields. We have developed DISCO, a service which is alleviating the data scientist from these hurdles. This paper shows up the competitiveness of DISCO with an existing solution.

1 INTRODUCTION

Over the past decade, Big Data has gained much traction in the world of computer science. Many companies and institutes are deciding to store data, whether on-site or in the cloud. This data is analysed at some point so that information can be extracted, being it for research, marketing reasons or other purposes.

Because of this paradigm shift towards Big Data, new problems are arising regarding storage and processing. Nowadays, commodity computers can be used to perform the storage and the analysis of this data. Especially with connecting multiple computers to a distributed computing cluster, a new level of complexity is reached.

The Hadoop [2] ecosystem merges distributed data retention and distributed data processing in a single framework which can be easily extended to serve new fields. What still remains is the complexity of a system consisting of a large number of individual computers, such as network complexities or the client configuration. A fully automated deployment can happen on a virtual cluster, which does not always impede the performance. [7]

Another benefit of a virtual system is the possibility of only creating it for a particular analytic task or re-creating it easily instead of fixing it if problems arise. That can result in financial and time savings.

Our objective is to implement a system which combines these benefits and automatically creates a distributed computing cluster as a service, including Hadoop or any other distributed computing framework installed on it, solely based on a few key metrics provided by the end user. In this paper, we are proposing a system called DISCO that is achieving this with a powerful, easily extensible architecture.

In section Comparison, DISCO is compared to the cloud deployment system Apache Ambari, [1] which can setup Hadoop and its

UCC'17, December 5–8, 2017, Austin, Texas, USA
© 2017 Copyright held by the owner/author(s). ACM ISBN 978-1-4503-5149-2/17/12.
DOI: http://dx.doi.org/10.1145/3147213.3149216

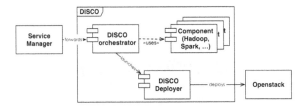

Figure 1: DISCO Architecture.

associated frameworks on an already existing distributed computing cluster.

2 SOLUTION

A solution for deploying virtual distributed computing clusters in an automated way is implemented by the framework DISCO. [5] The main objective of this project is to have an orchestration framework which guides distributed computing clusters through all phases of their lifecycle while maintaining a user-friendly interface towards the data scientist without impeding the configurability.

DISCO is built on the concept of components which can be included into the final cluster. Figure 1 shows the core of DISCO. The Service Manager is the orchestrating engine of the DISCO framework which keeps track of the state of each virtual cluster. The DISCO orchestrator compiles a heat orchestration template [3] from the given data out of the individual components. The components represent individual distributed computing frameworks to be installed on the cluster automatically. The DISCO deployer receives the final heat template and forwards it to the cloud management framework OpenStack. [6]

DISCO implements every state of a regular cloud orchestrator and executes the state changes upon internal or external request.

Upon receiving an HTTP POST request with the required parameters, DISCO is starting the planning phase. That entails the creation of a blueprint for the virtual cluster to be deployed including the frameworks which are to be installed.

After planning is completed, DISCO is switching internally to the deployment process and therefore sending the blueprint to the cloud management framework. A unique ID is returned to DISCO which is stored locally. The running phase is not an explicit phase within DISCO; it merely refers to the cluster being setup and executed by the cloud management framework.

This state enables the end user to choose one of three different actions. In the retrieval phase (started with a HTTP GET request), information about the cluster is fetched from the cloud management framework and returned to the end user. If the cluster is to be

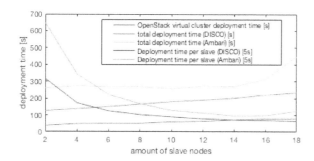

Figure 2: Cluster Deployment Time.

updated such as suspended or resumed (upon HTTP POST request in run state), DISCO switches to the update state. After completing either of these two actions, DISCO is switching back to the running state.

The third phase switch (initialised by an HTTP DELETE request) is starting the deletion of the virtual cluster. This request is forwarded to the cloud management framework. After disposal is complete, the cluster details are erased from within DISCO.

3   COMPARISON: DISCO & AMBARI

In the course of our works, DISCO was directly compared to Ambari. The results of the two deployment time measurements are shown in figure 2.

The three generally ascending lines depict OpenStack's cluster deployment time, and DISCO's as well as Ambari's total deployment time respectively.

In case of the DISCO system deployment, the cluster and the framework deployment time added up resulted in a total of 2.1m for 2 slave nodes to 3.9m for 18 slave nodes respectively. The net deployment time per slave node however decreased from 65.5s per node for a two-slave cluster to 13s per node for an 18 slave cluster. For Ambari, the deployment times were generally higher than for DISCO. In the test scenario for 2 slave nodes, the total deployment time was more than twice as long as for DISCO. (259.5s vs. 127s) This imbalance became smaller with the addition of new slave nodes until it reached its minimum in the case of 14 slave nodes. Beyond that point, the ratio of Ambari deployment times vs. DISCO deployment times was increasing again.

The higher deployment time of Ambari can be attributed to its utilisation of integration testing after deployment. Integration testing for DISCO is not necessary as the entire environment is purely virtual, as opposed to Ambari which can also deploy Hadoop on a physical cluster.

The deployment time per slave node is in both cases decreasing with the addition of new slave nodes due to a high parallelism, always orchestrated from the master node over SSH.

These findings show that the deployment time of a DISCO cluster linearly grows with cluster size. Due to a high overhead in small clusters, the per-slave deployment time is constantly sinking. Also, the increase in total deployment time should approach a logarithmic function when the amount of slave nodes is increasing as the sequential overhead of the setup process becomes negligible compared to the parallel part.

With DISCO's dependency handling of the individual components, it was possible to write a cluster-tailored software deployment process which also takes into account the local hardware specifics. In the case of Hadoop, this was achieved with the recommendations of [4]. The dependency handling generally alleviates the component developer from installing more than what is not implemented yet in a different component. In the course of our test series, we could verify the feasibility of such a system with Hadoop.

These findings show a high versatility of DISCO coupled with a short deployment time. Especially individual researchers and research groups working together on experiments can make easy use of DISCO by creating virtual computing clusters on demand and deleting them as soon as the required analysis has been performed. The high extensibility of DISCO components makes it specially comfortable to use DISCO with newly created analysis software which is not integrated into other competing deployment workflows or which needs a higher level of testing.

4   CONCLUSION AND FUTURE WORK

DISCO, a framework for the automatic deployment of a distributed computing cluster with a ready-to-operate distributed computing framework installed was realised. During its implementation, special attention was paid to other implementations' shortcomings and strengths to optimise DISCO. It is easily extendable with new distributed computing frameworks and achieves the deployment and configuration in a fast and transparent way.

We compared DISCO's performance with Apache Ambari. We analysed their deployment differences and mentioned the key target groups who can profit most from DISCO's features.

The next steps in this project will be integrating other distributed computing frameworks and a recommendation engine for easily selecting the optimal choice based on the targeted use case of the individual scientist.

REFERENCES
[1] Ambari 2017. Apache Ambari. (2017). Retrieved June 22, 2017 from http://ambari. apache.org/
[2] Hadoop 2014. Apache Hadoop. (2014). Retrieved July 14, 2017 from http://hadoop. apache.org/
[3] Heat 2014. Heat. (2014). Retrieved June 22, 2017 from http://ambari.apache.org/
[4] Hortonworks Inc. 2015. *Hortonworks Data Platform*. Hortonworks Inc. https://docs.hortonworks.com/HDPDocuments/HDP2/HDP-2.3.4/bk_ installing_manually_book/bk_installing_manually_book.pdf.
[5] Balazs Meszaros. 2016. DISCO Github website. (2016). Retrieved February 7, 2017 from https://wiki.openstack.org/wiki/Heat
[6] Openstack 2017. Openstack. (2017). Retrieved July 10, 2017 from https://www. openstack.org/
[7] Jianwu Wang, Prakashan Korambath, and Ilkay Altintas. 2011. A Physical and Virtual Compute Cluster Resource Load Balancing Approach to Data-Parallel Scientific Workflow Scheduling. In *2011 IEEE World Congress on Services (SERVICES)*. IEEE, San Diego Supercomput. Center, UCSD, San Diego, CA, USA. https://doi.org/10.1109/SERVICES.2011.50

ACKNOWLEDGMENTS

The authors would like to thank the SwissUniversities SCALE-UP project for facilitating this research with its grant 151-011.

IoT Implementation for Cancer Care and Business Analytics/Cloud Services in Healthcare Systems

Adeniyi Onasanya
Department of Computer Science
University of Regina
onasanya@uregina.ca

Maher Elshakankiri
Department of Computer Science
University of Regina
Maher.Elshakankiri@uregina.ca

1 INTRODUCTION

The advances in the Internet of Things (IoT) technology have significantly impacted our way of life, which has been seen in a variety of application domains, including healthcare. Most of the papers reviewed touched on some of the services in healthcare, there is practically little or no literature on the application or implementation of IoT in cancer care services. This has prompted the need to (re)assess the provision and positioning of healthcare services to harness the benefits associated with the use of IoT technology.

This research proposes the implementation of an IoT based healthcare system focusing on two services, namely, cancer care and business analytics/cloud services. This combination proffers solution and framework for analyzing health data gathered from IoT through various sensor networks and other smart devices to help healthcare providers to turn a stream of data into actionable insights and evidence-based healthcare decision-making to improve and enhance cancer treatment.

2 NETWORK METHODOLOGY & ANALYSIS

In supporting the proposed IoT based healthcare system, the use of sensors and actuators cannot be overemphasized because they are seen as an important component of the IoT technology [1, 3]. Body wireless sensor networks (BWSN) have now a broad range of applications: e.g. remote monitoring of physiological data, tracking and monitoring doctors and patients [2], and drug administration, and therefore they are becoming a prevalent solution in remote healthcare monitoring and chronic disease detecting.

The wireless devices are strategically attached to or implanted within human body to monitor patient under surveillance, in order to collect objective measures or data. Once deployed, the sensor nodes form an autonomous wireless ad hoc network, which will be embedded in the main network for the service. In the use of WSNs, some characteristics, such as routing protocols from one source to another have to be addressed. This can be achieved through appropriate routing strategies that are capable of managing the trade-off between optimality and efficiency to ensure computation and communication capabilities [3].

3 SOLUTIONS FOR HEALTHCARE SERVICES

3.1 Cancer Care Services

The IoT technology can be applied in cancer care treatment by seamless and secure integration of wireless technologies for medical procedures, including chemotherapy treatments, monitoring, alerting, and following-up. Cancer treatments can be enhanced by attaching WSNs to patients such that the health practitioners can be alerted of any changes, complications, adverse drug effects and allergies, missed medications, haemoglobin level sensing and monitoring, drug allergic detection, drug interaction monitoring, etc. The wireless sensors detect automated alerts and blocks for incorrect prescriptions, and also automatically monitor and manage the creatinine value as used in the computation of Glomerular Filtration Rate (GFR) used in dosing for certain chemotherapy treatment.

It is also practicable to monitor cancer patients remotely by caregivers and families through WSNs. The cancer care services incorporate clinical devices that provide assistance to cancer patients in the event of any problems or complications through process or procedure automation, remote monitoring, communication alerts, and analysis based on IoT technologies. As related to the radiation oncology treatment, the linear accelerators (linacs) for radiation therapy can also be monitored by IoT connected devices. Fig. 1 illustrates the network design of the proposed cancer care services.

The Health Level-7 (HL7) connectivity is equipped with HL7 interface based on semantics and XML technology for data definition and message exchanging, sharing and reusing within and between lab centres, hospitals, and health regions, which interoperates two or more systems for information exchange and use. The Digital Imaging and Communications in Medicine (DICOM) connectivity, on the other hand, facilitates connection between the radiology centres to help expedite diagnosis and treatment, thereby linking networks together for diagnostic image transmission. The cancer care services through electronic medical record and embedded systems, such as Laboratory Interface System (LIS), Pathology Interface System (PIS) and Radiology Interface System (RIS), serve as access points for the health providers to access patient information relating to lab results, malignancy or abnormal (pathology) results, and radiology results. The RIS interfaces with the DICOM connectivity for the transfer or exchange of diagnostic imaging results from radiology centres while the LIS and PIS interface with the HL7 connectivity for the transfer or exchange of lab and pathology results from the lab services. All these systems along with the pharmacy, medical oncology, and radiation oncology servers allow access to comprehensive patient chart information from any device, either at the clinic(s) or via remote VPN access from outside the clinic(s).

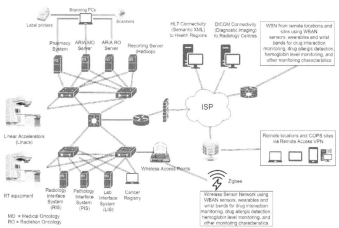

Figure 1: Cancer Care Services Network Architecture

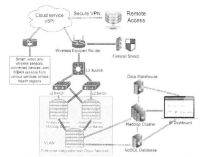

Figure 2: Business Analytics/Cloud Services Architecture

3.2 Business Analytics and Cloud Services

Through the business analytics and cloud services, patient health data are streamed from various sources and then deployed into the cloud so that the ever-increasing data can be managed and shared across the health care systems, services and sites. This, in fact, has put challenges for data to be analyzed, interpreted, aggregated, manipulated, clustered, and collaborated and made available for analytics, reporting and decision-making processes such as predictive, prescriptive, descriptive, and precision medicine using appropriate analytical tools and algorithms such as Bayesian networks, machine learning, deep learning, etc as applicable for medical and research related decisions and purposes. The solution is intended to engage data analytics in order to gain insights from all patient data that will be coming from various services in order to analyze the quality of care and risk, disease and epidemic pattern, patient/facility monitoring and optimization, etc. It will allow healthcare providers to turn stream of data into actionable insights and evidence-based healthcare decision-making about the health conditions of patients, and will also help the health providers and clinical experts to stay on top of the latest trends and breakthroughs in clinical and health care using appropriate analytics tools. The cloud approach is beneficial as it facilitates communications and data exchanges across the services and healthcare sites to the data center and reporting solution situated at the data center location. The details of the network architecture for the business analytics and cloud services are as depicted in Fig. 2. In processing and solving many types of workloads associated with massive amounts of data involved, the Hadoop Cluster or framework is considered to ensure transformations between source systems and data warehouses due to its wide range of benefits [4].

3.3 Operational Challenges and Security Issues

Certainty, there are some operational challenges and security issues that may impact the implementation of IoT-based healthcare system. These include but not limited to: government policies, rules, and regulation for compatible interfaces, network resources, protocols across various devices and equipment and platforms, interoperability issues, device diversity, vulnerability of security and devices, security breach, interests of various stakeholders of various health organizations and authorities, ownership of data collected and stored, data consent and utilization, just to mention a few. Other considerations can be inherent from those wireless devices and sensors that can impact the performance. These are: loss of signals and connectivity; strength and security of the communication channels; power capacity of the connected devices; frequency of charging sensors; wireless technologies that support low energy, etc.

It becomes extremely important to address and manage those issues and challenges based on the following approaches: ensure due diligence with all stakeholders, vendors and government representatives to ensure compliance and adherence to all sorts of policies and legislation; ensure user privacy, authentication and security are strictly adhered to; ensure reliability of network communication; ensure network that is able to accommodate different sensors and connected devices; ensure the use of low power consumption for the sensors such that the frequency of charging them is minimal; and ensure provisions for adaptability, adjustability, scalability, manageability, and supportability of the network for additional devices and services for future growth.

4 CONCLUSIONS AND FUTURE WORK

In conclusion, the proposed research work provides an implementation of the IoT based healthcare system with reference to cancer care and business analytics/cloud services for enhanced electronic health initiative, treatment, diagnosis, caring and monitoring of cancer patients. In the network design, a mesh topology is proposed such that every node in the network has a connection to each of the other nodes. There is a variety of services offered and delivered in healthcare related environment, but we have only covered the cancer care and business analytics/cloud services in this research. We anticipate integrating and considering more services in our future work in the same research domain that will ensure a more robust healthcare delivery.

ACKNOWLEDGMENTS

The work has been partially supported by the University of Regina, Department of Computer Science, Graduate Student Travel Award.

REFERENCES

[1] A Wireless Sensor Networks Bibliography. Autonomous Networks Research Group. http://ceng.usc.edu/~anrg/SensorNetBib.html#0103. Retrieved on May 25, (2017).
[2] Riazul Islam, S. M., Kwak, D., Kabir, H., Hossain, M., Kwak, K.S.: The IoT for Health Care: A Comprehensive Survey. IEEE Access, 3, 678 – 708, (2015).
[3] Sohraby, K., Minoli, D., Znati, T.: Wireless Sensor Networks: technology, protocols, and applications, John Wiley & Sons, Inc., Hoboken, New Jersey (2007).
[4] Stackowiak, R., Licht, A., Mantha, V., Nagode, L.: Big Data and The IoT. Enterprise Information Architecture for A New Age. Apress Ontario, (2015).

Utility-Driven Deployment Decision Making

Radhika Loomba
Intel Labs Europe
Leixlip, Ireland
radhika.loomba@intel.com

Thijs Metsch
Intel Labs Europe
Leixlip, Ireland
thijs.metsch@intel.com

Leonard Feehan
Intel Labs Europe
Leixlip, Ireland
leonard.feehan@intel.com

Joe Butler
Intel Labs Europe
Leixlip, Ireland
joe.m.butler@intel.com

ABSTRACT

This paper presents the formulation of two utility functions, for the resource provider and the service customer respectively, to enable the orchestrator to consider business goals/incentives when making comparisons between deployments. The use of cost elements in these utilities further supports a precise exposure of the value proposition of differentiated or heterogeneous infrastructure, which is greatly beneficial to resource providers.

CCS CONCEPTS

• **Applied computing** → **Data centers**; • **Software and its engineering** → **Distributed systems organizing principles**;

KEYWORDS

cloud orchestration; multi attribute utility theory; resource management; deployment decision making;

1 INTRODUCTION

Leveraging cloud computing service-models, resource providers deploy and maintain multiple workloads across globally distributed heterogeneous data centers. Although virtualization provides a great deal of flexibility, their challenge is to properly provision resources and reduce operational expenses, whilst honouring the individual SLA (Service Level Agreement) negotiated with the customer, wherein QoS (Quality of Service) requirements, including performance metrics are specified. This applies to several scenarios such as initial placement, re-balancing (e.g. VM migration) and capacity planning.

Widely studied as the problem of optimally mapping available resources with service needs, approximation algorithms, stochastic bin-packing methods and multiple other heuristics have been presented by researchers for efficient deployment. However, current commercial and open-source orchestration solutions schedule either pessimistically to avoid conflicts and workload-pattern-induced performance issues or too optimistically to avail improved

TCO (total cost of ownership) opportunities. Additionally, the limited consideration of objectives and parameters during analysis, along with the absence of comparison techniques between possible solutions, hinders insight driven decisions.

This work presents the use of Multi-Attribute Utility Theory (MAUT) [1] to quantify potential deployment solutions, defined by two multiplicative utility functions, one for the resource provider and one for the service customer. In contrast to the work by John Wilkes [3], the two utilities are quantified during the deployment and capacity planning phase supporting insight-driven decision making. This provides a novel platform to compare and contrast deployment solutions, mitigating the abstraction issue in the cloud: supporting the precise exposure of value proposition of differentiated or heterogeneous infrastructure that are of particular benefit to the resource providers.

2 ALGORITHM DESIGN

A multi-layered, graph model of the physical and logical layers [2], topology and updated information of the services and resources represents the distributed infrastructure or 'landscape'. The service request is composed of multiple service components and a mapping indicates allocation of resources required by the request, to the

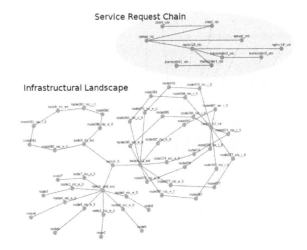

Figure 1: Representation of a deployment of the service request on the infrastructure landscape, with omitted storage resource entities and neighbourhood workloads for clarity.

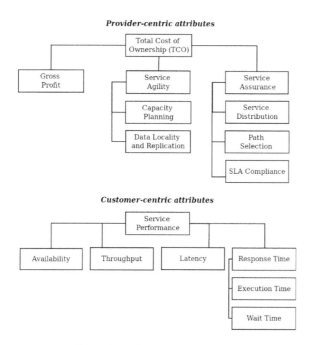

Provider-centric attributes

Customer-centric attributes

Figure 2: Attribute classification of a set of attributes $\mathcal{A}$ = $\mathcal{A}_s \cup \mathcal{A}_c$, with provider-centric attribute $a_s \in \mathcal{A}_s$ where $|\mathcal{A}_s| \geq 2$ and customer-centric attribute $a_c \in \mathcal{A}_c$ where $|\mathcal{A}_c| \geq 2$.

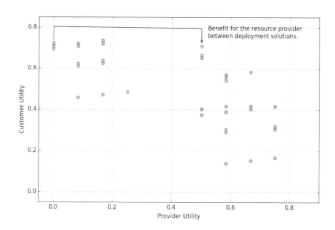

Figure 3: 2D Representation of deployment solutions by their provider utilities and customer utilities for a placement groups.

nodes of the (heterogeneous) landscape, based on node types (e.g. vCPU mapped to CPU or vNIC to a port of a NIC). Such a mapping has been represented in Fig. 1.

Several distinct yet complementary objectives of the resource provider and service customer are modelled in our formulation as provider-centric attributes where $|\mathcal{A}_s| \geq 2$ and customer-centric attributes $a_c \in \mathcal{A}_c$ where $|\mathcal{A}_c| \geq 2$, as shown in Fig. 2. The Multi-Attribute Utility Theory (MAUT) combines the individual non-independent 'reward' of the attributes in a multiplicative function, providing a novel analytical platform to consistently rank solutions. It uses decomposed assessment of the utilities for each attribute to define $\mathcal{U}_S$ which stands for the resource provider utility and $\mathcal{U}_C$ which stands for the service customer utility, as represented in Eq. 1. Here, each attribute is given a weight to indicate its importance or priority represented by α_{a_s} or α_{a_c}, whilst dependence on other attributes is represented by β_{a_s} or β_{a_c}. These values evolve with each service request and incorporate the trade-offs or relational operations between the attributes considered, thereby supporting a more constructive study.

$$\forall a_s \in \mathcal{A}_s, \forall a_c \in \mathcal{A}_c :$$
$$\mathcal{U}_S = \prod_{|\mathcal{A}_s|} (\alpha_{a_s} \cdot U(a_s) + \beta_{a_s})$$
$$\mathcal{U}_C = \prod_{|\mathcal{A}_c|} (\alpha_{a_c} \cdot U(a_c) + \beta_{a_c}) \qquad (1)$$
$$\sum \alpha_{a_s} = 1$$
$$\sum \alpha_{a_c} = 1$$

Thus, the two utilities are modelled to capture the benefits and shortcomings of each resource-request mapping based on the individual choice of attributes (by the resource provider and the service customer). This has the added benefit of providing intelligence to the orchestrator to enable reasoning over the benefits of one deployment over another, while mitigating the abstraction issue in the cloud. Additionally, this further supports a trade-off between provider and customer objectives, as priority weights can be allocated to the utility scores.

3 RESULTS AND CONCLUSION

A Python-based simulation is used to calculate the utilities for possible deployment solutions. A 2-D representation of these solutions, as presented in Fig. 3, highlights the opportunity for optimizing provider utility whilst providing the same customer utility. This is of great benefit to the resource provider, as operational expenses can be decreased whilst maintaining customer satisfaction and high levels of performance.

Our approach of using utility theory to quantify potential deployment solutions, based on multiple resource provider and service customer oriented attributes, thus enables the orchestrator to optimally deliver value from differentiating platform features and reason between these deployment solutions considering business objectives.

ACKNOWLEDGMENTS

The authors would like to thank the members of the Cloud Services Lab, Intel Labs Europe for their contributions. An initial part of the research work was also funded by the European H2020 projects, CloudLightning (Grant Number: 643946) and Superfluidity (Grant Number: 671566).

REFERENCES

[1] James S. Dyer. 2005. *MAUT– Multi Attribute Utility Theory*. Vol. 78. Springer, New York, NY, 265–292. https://doi.org/10.1007/0-387-23081-5_7
[2] Thijs Metsch, Olumuyiwa Ibidunmoye, Victor Bayon-Molino, Joe Butler, Francisco Hernández-Rodriguez, and Erik Elmroth. 2015. Apex Lake: A Framework for Enabling Smart Orchestration. In *Proceedings of the Industrial Track of the 16th International Middleware Conference (Middleware Industry '15)*. ACM, New York, NY, USA, 1:1–1:7. https://doi.org/10.1145/2830013.2830016
[3] John Wilkes. 2009. *Utility Functions, Prices, and Negotiation*. John Wiley & Sons, Inc. 67–88 pages. https://doi.org/10.1002/9780470455432.ch4

Towards Digital Twins Cloud Platform:

Microservices and Computational Workflows to Rule a Smart Factory

Kirill Borodulin
borodulinkv@susu.ru
South Ural State University
Chelyabinsk, Russia

Gleb Radchenko
gleb.radchenko@susu.ru
South Ural State University
Chelyabinsk, Russia

Aleksandr Shestakov
alshestakov@susu.ru
South Ural State University
Chelyabinsk, Russia

Leonid Sokolinsky
leonid.sokolinsky@susu.ru
South Ural State University
Chelyabinsk, Russia

Andrey Tchernykh
chernykh@cicese.mx
CICESE Research Center
Ensenada, Mexico

Radu Prodan
radu@dps.uibk.ac.au
University of Innsbruck
Innsbruck, Austria
Institute of Information Technology
University of Klagenfurt
Klagenfurt, Austria

ABSTRACT

The concept of "Industry 4.0" considers smart factories as data-driven and knowledge enabled enterprise intelligence. In such kind of factory, manufacturing processes and final products are accompanied by virtual models – Digital Twins. To support Digital Twins concept, a simulation model for each process or system should be implemented as independent computational service. The only way to implement an orchestration of a set of independent services and provide scalability for simulation is to use a cloud computing platform as a provider of the computing infrastructure. In this paper, we describe a Digital Twin-as-a-Service (DTaaS) model for simulation and prediction of industrial processes using Digital Twins.

CCS CONCEPTS

• **Information systems → Web services;** • **Computer systems organization → Cloud computing;**

KEYWORDS

cloud computing, container-as-a-service, Digital Twin, smart manufacturing, software-as-a-service, platform-as-a-service, digital twin-as-a-service, workflow, microservice, Industry 4.0

1 INTRODUCTION

The smart manufacturing concept is now one of the main development trends in the industry. One of the key approaches to this concept is a "Digital Twin" concept. *The Digital Twin (DT)* supports virtual models of real equipment, industrial process, and final products. The Digital Twin provides methods of analysis of data from diverse types of sensors installed on the objects for tuning and actualization of their virtual state. The DT applies different

UCC 17, December 5–8, 2017, Austin, TX, USA
© 2017 Copyright held by the owner/author(s).
ACM ISBN 978-1-4503-5149-2/17/12.
https://doi.org/10.1145/3147213.3149234

mathematical models for simulation of the processes of interest that are implemented using statistical methods, data mining, and finite element method, etc.

To develop a DT of an industrial process or equipment, we can present it as a computational workflow composed of a set of computational services that represent models for process stages and their interaction [3]. Each of these computing methods defines specific requirements for the necessary computational resources. One of the possible solutions that provide high flexibility on the one hand, and high computing performance on the other hand, is to use containerization technology [1]. Thus, it is needed to provide a cloud system that uses "Container-as-a-Service" model, that would support the Digital Twin execution. In this paper, we describe a model of the Digital Twins Cloud Platform for simulation of industrial processes in the form of workflows.

2 THE DIGITAL TWIN

The Digital Twin is a hierarchical system of mathematical models, computational methods and software services, which provides near real-time synchronization between the state of the real-world process or system and its virtual copy. We can highlight a Distributed Virtual Test-Bed (DiVTB) [4] technology that provides a simulation of industrial process and systems based on data provided by end-user, as one of the predecessors of the Digital Twin concept. Up to now, the difficulty of near real-time data harvesting from the objects of interest has been the main obstacle to the broad application of the DT technology. Using this data and analysis methods, we can design the Digital Twins of smart factory's industrial processes and sophisticated end-products. The following characteristics of the DT can be highlighted:

- *Real-time reflection.* A DT is a reflection of a physical object (equipment, process or system) that keeps ultra-high synchronization and fidelity with the real-world [2].
- *Hierarchy.* A DT of an industrial process can contain DTs of the process stages, which, in turn, contain DTs of the equipment enforcing these stages.
- *Self-evolution.* Since a DT provides a reflection of the object or process, it should perform undergoing continuous model

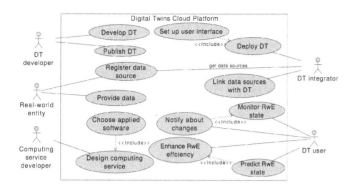

Figure 1: Digital Twins Cloud Platform use-cases

improvement through comparing the simulation process with physical object or process, concurrently.

- *Flexibiliy.* The DT uses diverse types of models to simulate a real object's current state. The comprehensive and well-timed state reflection can be obtained only by usage of models with the accuracy, necessary and sufficient for satisfying the "real-time reflection" requirement.

3 THE CONCEPT OF THE DIGITAL TWIN CLOUD PLATFROM

To provide the DT execution, we design a Digital Twins Cloud Platform, which provides a dynamic allocation of computing resources and provides an API to present the DTs as a microservices. Thus, DTs Cloud Platform provides a "Digital Twin-as-a-Service" (DTaaS) cloud model. The DTaaS model presents the DT as a set of cloud services to store and to analyse the data gathered from sensors, simulation of the real-world objects, and their visualization of the virtual representation.

The DTs Cloud Platform provides the following levels of abstraction:

(1) *The level of the Digital Twin user.* On this level, the user can get an access to the available DTs in the form of cloud applications based on the "Software-as-a-Service" model.

(2) *The level of the Digital Twin developer.* At this level, the cloud platform provides resources for the development of DTs based on a "Platform-as-a-Service" model. A DT is described as a computational workflow, the nodes of which correspond to the Computing Services and other DTs, while links correspond to the data flow between nodes.

(3) *The level of the Computing Service developer.* At this level, the cloud platform provides an API for Computing Service development based on a "Backend-as-a-Service" model. A Computing Service is represented as a microservice responsible for specific data processing operation or execution of a specific set of computational methods.

(4) *The level of the cloud infrastructure provider.* At this level, instances of Computing Services are mapped to the cloud computing resources provided by the cloud platform based on "Container-as-a-Service" model.

We can define the following main actors, who interact with the DTs Cloud Platform (see Fig. 1).

(1) *Digital Twin user* utilize DTs to get the necessary information about real-world entities, such as their status, notification about real-world entity state changes, prediction of their behavior and parameters under certain conditions, recommendations of the enchantment of real-world entity efficiency, etc.

(2) *Digital Twin integrator* is responsible for the deployment of DTs on industrial objects through a connection of real-world entities with their virtual representation, setting up and provision of DT user interfaces.

(3) *Digital Twin developer* uses Computing Services of the DTs Cloud Platform to develop a DT and publishes it into a DT Marketplace.

(4) *Computing service developer* designs Computing Services that implement models of real-world entities using in-house developed components, along with available applied software packages and frameworks.

(5) *Real-world entity* is a real-world process, system, or equipment fitted with sensors. These sensors gather and send the data to the DTs Cloud Platform for storage and analysis. Also, data can be received from derivative data sources, like SCADA, MES, etc., and typed manually.

As a direction of further research, we plan to design an architecture of cloud platform, that supports execution of Digital Twins and to provide resource management methods of the cloud system through "Container-as-a-Service" (CaaS) model.

ACKNOWLEDGMENTS

The reported paper is supported by the RFBR research project No.: 15-29-07959, by Act 211 Government of the Russian Federation contract 02.A03.21.0011 and research project No.: 5077019, by Austrian Research Promotion Agency

REFERENCES

[1] Carl Boettiger. 2015. An introduction to Docker for reproducible research. *ACM SIGOPS Operating Systems Review* 49, 1 (2015), 71–79. https://doi.org/10.1145/2723872.2723882 arXiv:1410.0846

[2] Edward Glaessgen and David Stargel. 2012. The Digital Twin Paradigm for Future NASA and U.S. Air Force Vehicles. In *53rd Structures, Structural Dynamics and Materials Conference - Special Session: Digital Twin.* https://doi.org/10.2514/6.2012-1818

[3] Prakashan Korambath, Jianwu Wang, Ankur Kumar, Jim Davis, Robert Graybill, Brian Schott, and Michael Baldea. 2016. A smart manufacturing use case: Furnace temperature balancing in steam methane reforming process via kepler workflows. *Procedia Computer Science* 80 (2016), 680–689. https://doi.org/10.1016/j.procs.2016.05.357

[4] Gleb Radchenko and Elena Hudyakova. 2012. A service-oriented approach of integration of computer-aided engineering systems in distributed computing environments. In *UNICORE Summit 2012, Proceedings*, Vol. 15. 57–66. http://www.scopus.com/inward/record.url?eid=2-s2.0-84877685818

Author Index